THE JOURNAL
of
PHARMACOLOGY
and
EXPERIMENTAL THERAPEUTICS

founded by John J. Abel

VOLUME 124

SEPTEMBER - DECEMBER 1958

Official Publication
of the American Society for Pharmacology and
Experimental Therapeutics Incorporated

BALTIMORE, MARYLAND

REGISTER OF ARTICLES

124:1 Sept 58

8050 The synthesis and estimation of N-C^{14}-methyl labeled levorphanol and its biological disposition in the monkey, dog and rat. L. A. Woods, L. B. Mellett, K. S. Andersen.------------------ 1
8051 The fate of papaverine in man and other mammals. J. Axelrod, R. Shofer, J. K. Inscoe, W. M. King, A. Sjoerdsma.-------------- 9
8052 Studies on the biological disposition of streptovaricin (dalacin), a new antibiotic. D. P. Wallach, J. G. Wagner.----- 16
8053 Comparison of the vascular actions of 1, 1-dimethyl-4-phenyl-piperazinium and tetramethylammonium. M. M. Winbury.---------- 25
8054 Action of cigarette smoke on cardiovascular hemodynamics and oxygen utilization in the dog. G. A. Kien, N. Lasker, T. R. Sherrod.--- 35
8055 Factors influencing contraction in glycerinated myocardial fibers. F. N. Briggs.------------------------------------- 43
8056 Temperature and resting potential of diaphragm muscle in a CO_2-bicarbonate medium. R. Creese, N. W. Scholes, D. B. Taylor.--- 47
8057 Antiarrhythmics. Quinidine-like activity of some ataraxic agents. R. B. Arora.--- 53
8058 Some cardiovascular effects of norethandrolone (nilevar), testosterone and progesterone. C. G. Van Arman, V. A. Drill.------- 59
8059 A study of the peripheral and central actions of dibromopyruvic acid. W. R. Martin, D. H. Abdulian, K. R. Unna, H. Busch.----- 64
8060 The anti-tremorine effect of some drugs as determined by Haffner's method of testing analgesia in mice. G. Chen.----------- 73
8061 Chlorpromazine II: The effects of chlorpromazine on evoked potentials in the midbrain reticular formation. E. W. J. DeMaar, W. R. Martin, K. R. Unna.---------------------------------- 77
8062 _In vitro_ anaphylactic and nonanaphylactic responses of organs of immunized guinea pigs. S. Katsh.---------------------------- 86
8063 A minimum error table for parallel line biological assays. M. C. Sheps, K. H. Hendrie.--------------------------------------- 94
8064 Pharmacodynamic aspects of allyl alcohol toxicity. J. K. Kodama, C. H. Hine.-- 97

124:2 Oct 58

8065 Protein binding of radioactive digitoxin. J. L. Spratt, G. T. Okita.--- 109
8066 Subcellular localization of radioactive digitoxin. J. L. Spratt, G. T. Okita.-- 115
8067 Reflexes from the intestinal mesentery elicited by veratridine, acetylcholine and nicotine. W. K. Riker.-------------------- 120
8068 Concerning the mechanisms of the cardiovascular actions of hexahydro-1-azepinepropionamidoxime (SU-4029). R. A. Maxwell, A. J. Plummer, A. I. Daniel, F. Schneider, H. Povalski.---------- 127
8069 The effect of atropine upon mammalian striated muscle. C. tum-Suden.-- 135
8070 The effect of atropine upon skeletal muscle in the goat with myotonia congenita. C. tum-Suden, R. M. Stoufer.------------- 142
8071 The anticonvulsant actions of methazolamide (a carbonic anhydrase inhibitor) and diphenylhydantoin. W. D. Gray, C. E. Rauh, A. C. Osterberg, L. M. Lipchuck.----------------------- 149

8072 Effects of anticonvulsant drugs on recovery time from tonic-clonic seizures in mice and rats. D. H. Tedeschi, E. A. Swinyard.-- 161
8073 Some effects of analgesic and analgesic-antagonist drugs on intestinal motility. G. W. Gray.------------------------------ 165
8074 The effect of estrogens on uterine blood flow in the rat. S. M. Kalman.--- 179
8075 Heart lesions in mice caused by treatment with bishydroxy-coumarin (dicumarol). F. I. Dessau, S. Klein, L. Lipchuck, J. O'Grady, J. Tsalikis.------------------------------------- 182

124:3 Nov 58

8076 The relationship between iproniazid metabolism and the duration of its effect on monoamine oxidase. S. Hess, H. Weissbach, B. G. Redfield, S. Udenfriend.------------------------------ 189
8077 The influence of various factors on the enzymatic conversion of organic thiophosphates to anticholinesterase agents. S. D. Murphy, K. P. DuBois.------------------------------------- 194
8078 The high energy phosphate content of cardiac muscle under various experimental conditions which alter contractile strength. R. F. Furchgott, T. de Gubareff.---------------------------- 203
8079 Adrenergic blocking action of tetrazotized diorthoanisidine. E. J. Cafruny, E. F. Domino, L. Beck.--------------------------- 219
8080 Adrenergic blockade of the mammalian heart by a dichloro analogue of isoproterenol. N. C. Moran, M. E. Perkins.----------- 223
8081 The effects of sympathomimetic drugs on renal vessels. D. M. Aviado, Jr., A. L. Wnuck, E. J. de Beer.--------------------- 238
8082 Studies on veratrum alkaloids. XXVII. The negative chronotropic action of veratramine and reserpine in the heart depleted of catechol amines. I. R. Innes, O. Krayer.-------------------- 245
8083 Concentration of free and conjugated morphine in brain and other tissues of tolerant and nontolerant rabbits. R. Siminoff, P. R. Saunders.-- 252
8084 Acute pharmacological studies of some new morphine derivatives. R. Okun, H. W. Elliott.--------------------------------------- 255
8085 Analgesic potency of normorphine in patients with postoperative pain. L. Lasagna, T. J. De Kornfeld.------------------------- 260
8086 Effects of single doses and chronic administration of ethanol and experimental seizures in mice. D. G. McQuarrie, E. Fingl.- 264

124:4 Dec 58

8087 Biochemical alterations of liver function by the halogenated hydrocarbons. I. In vitro and in vivo changes and their modification by ethylenediamine tetraacetate. D. N. Calvert, T. M. Brody.--- 273
8088 Degradation of mescaline by amine oxidases. E. A. Zeller, J. Barsky, E. R. Berman, M. S. Cherkas, J. R. Fouts.------------- 282
8089 The comparative distribution of C^{14}-labeled 2-dimethylamino-ethanol and choline in the mouse. D. P. Groth, J. A. Bain, C. C. Pfeiffer.--- 290

8090 Metabolic fate of levo-3-hydroxy-N-allylmorphinan (levallorphan). G. J. Mannering, L. S. Schanker.------------------------------ 296
8091 Urinary 17-ketosteroid excretion during a cycle of addiction to morphine. A. J. Eisenman, H. F. Fraser, J. Sloan, H. Isbell.-- 305
8092 Enhancement of sodium salicylate absorption by mephenesin. J. J. Carr, G. J. Mouratoff, R. C. Batterman.----------------- 312
8093 Diuretic effects of formoguanamine and other s-triazines. C. M. Kagawa, C. G. Van Arman.------------------------------------- 318
8094 The action of rauwolfia alkaloids on the heart rate and on the functional refractory period of atrio-ventricular transmission in the heart-lung preparation of the dog. I. R. Innes, O. Krayer, D. R. Waud.-- 324
8095 The dual nature of the action of succinylcholine on respiration in cross-circulated dogs. M. H. Harmel, B. D. King, F. F. Kao.-- 333
8096 Threshold dose and time course of norepinephrine depletion of the mammalian heart by reserpine. D. R. Waud, S. R. Kottegoda, O. Krayer.--- 340
8097 Comparative pharmacology of chlorpheniramine (chlor-trimeton) and its optical isomers. F. E. Roth, W. M. Govier.------------ 347
8098 Analysis of the relationship between drug-induced convulsions and mortality in rats. B. Blum, S. Zacks.-------------------- 350

NOTICE

to Subscribers and Readers

Attention is directed to the current method (ACC) of using entry numbers opposite the unit terms and names comprising the Subject and Author sections of the Journal index. These entry numbers coincide with the appropriate accession numbers listed serially at the left of the titles in the Register of Articles.
Their purpose is to condense and unify the three parts of the index, and to expedite its use.

For details of the ACC indexing system please see: This Journal, "Index Notices", Vol. 122:2, Jan., and Vol. 122: N1-2, April, 1958.

THE SYNTHESIS AND ESTIMATION OF N-C^{14}-METHYL LABELED LEVORPHANOL AND ITS BIOLOGICAL DISPOSITION IN THE MONKEY, DOG AND RAT[1]

L. A. WOODS, L. B. MELLETT AND KATHRYN S. ANDERSEN

Department of Pharmacology, University of Michigan Medical School, Ann Arbor

Received for publication April 24, 1958

Much valuable information on the biologic disposition of the potent analgesic agents has been obtained with colorimetric methods of drug estimation. However, it has become increasingly apparent that more sensitive techniques are necessary to give essential data on selective distribution of the narcotic drugs in brain tissue and on plasma levels and excretion in the non-tolerant human subject. The use of radioactive-labeled analgesics, *i.e.*, morphine (Elliott *et al.*, 1954; Achor and Geiling, 1956), codeine (Adler *et al.*, 1955), meperidine (Plotnikoff *et al.*, 1952), and methadone (Elliott *et al.*, 1949), has seemed most promising for such studies. Accordingly, methods of extraction were developed in this laboratory for the routine analysis of multiple samples of C^{14}-labeled levorphanol which provided specificity of estimation and insured minimum self-absorption of radioactivity by the actual material being counted.

Levorphanol (Levo-Dromoran, *levo*-3-hydroxy-M-methylmorphinan) was selected as the agent for study since the N-C^{14}-methyl labeled derivative could be synthesized simply and in good yield from *levo*-3-hydroxymorphinan and C^{14}-formaldehyde. Furthermore, this narcotic agent is similar to morphine in chemical structure and spectrum of pharmacologic action. Levorphanol is a more potent analgesic agent than morphine (Randall and Lehmann, 1950; Benson *et al.*, 1953) and exhibits an addiction liability of high order in human subjects (Isbell and Fraser, 1953) and monkeys (Deneau and Seevers, unpublished observations).

The synthesis of N-C^{14}-methyl labeled levorphanol, its estimation in biological materials and the results of studies on biologic disposition in the dog, rat and monkey are described in this report.

METHODS. *Synthesis of N-C^{14}-methyl labeled levorphanol.* The N-C^{14}-methyl labeled levorphanol was prepared from *levo*-3-hydroxymorphinan and C^{14}-formaldehyde by modification of the macro procedure provided by Dr. Aeschlimann, Hoffmann-LaRoche, Inc. The original compounds and basic procedures have been described previously by Schnider and Grüssner (1949, 1951) and Schnider and Hellerbach (1950). C^{14}-paraformaldehyde was obtained commercially and converted to C^{14}-formaldehyde immediately before use. Paraformaldehyde *per se* was inactive as an N-methylating agent and the use of commercially available C^{14}-formaldehyde was unsatisfactory in the procedure as described. The N-methylation was performed on amounts of 0.37 to 0.78 *mM* of the *levo*-3-hydroxymorphinan with a 20 per cent excess of the C^{14}-paraformaldehyde.

C^{14}-formaldehyde was generated by mixing 30.0 mgm. (1.0 *mM*) of C^{14}-paraformaldehyde (approximately 1 millicurie/*mM*), 0.4 ml. of 1.0 *N* sulfuric acid, and 1.2 ml. of distilled water and heating the mixture for one hour in a 12-ml. pear-shaped flask immersed in an oil bath heated at 130 ± 2°C. The C^{14}-formaldehyde gas was passed from the generator flask through a bent glass tube leading to within 0.5 cm. of the surface of a solution of 190 mgm. (0.78 *mM*) of *levo*-3-hydroxymorphinan in 11.7 ml. of absolute methanol contained in a glass reduction flask of a micro-atmospheric pressure hydrogenator. After the formaldehyde had been evolved from the paraformaldehyde and trapped in the glass reduction vessel, the reaction mixture was maintained at 50 ± 5° C. for 45 to 55 minutes and then hydrogenated over Raney nickel catalyst prepared according to Vogel (1948). Although the reduction was probably complete in a shorter interval, the mixture was shaken with the catalyst under hydrogen for about 2½ hours. The catalyst was removed immediately by centrifugation and washed with methanol. The washings were added to the supernatant fluid and the combined solutions were evaporated to dryness at reduced temperature and pressure

[1] Preliminary reports of these studies appear in Fed. Proc., **16:** 322, 348, 1957.

under nitrogen. The white residue was dissolved with warming in 0.94 ml. of tert.-butyl alcohol. A small amount of insoluble material was removed by centrifugation. Different runs were combined at this point to yield a uniform product. Crystallization was induced by seeding and the powdery addition product was washed with cold tert.-butyl alcohol before drying *in vacuo*. The yield of the butyl alcohol complex in several combined runs was 79.4 per cent calculated from the *levo*-3-hydroxymorphinan.

The tert.-butyl alcohol complex (369 mgm., 1.12 *mM*) and *d*-tartaric acid (168 mgm., 1.12 *mM*) were dissolved with warming in 3.26 ml. of distilled water. The solution was slowly cooled to room temperature, seeded and allowed to remain undisturbed for 24 hours. The crystals of N-C^{14}-methyl levorphanol *d*-tartrate were removed by centrifugation, washed with a minimal amount of cold water and dried *in vacuo*. The product melted at 114.5 to 116.5°C. (uncorr.); the melting point reported for this compound was 113 to 115°C. (Schnider and Grüssner, 1951). The yield for the conversion from the butyl alcohol complex to the tartrate was 418 mgm. (0.94 *mM*, 84.6 per cent, and an over-all yield beginning with *levo*-3-hydroxymorphinan of 67.2 per cent, most of the loss being mechanical. The product was shown to have identical R_f values with authentic nonlabeled levorphanol on chromatograms developed with various mixtures of n-butanol, acetic acid and water. Radioactivity was demonstrated only in one spot which was the labeled levorphanol.

Estimation in biological materials. A sample of 4.0 ml.[2] of diluted plasma, urine or fecal extract is mixed with 1.0 ml. of a 0.1 per cent (as free base) aqueous solution of nonlabeled levorphanol tartrate (carrier), 4.0 ml. of 1.4 *M* aqueous Na_2HPO_4, and 10.0 ml. of ethylene dichloride[3] ($EtCl_2$) in a 35-ml. centrifuge tube[4]. The mixture is shaken 30 minutes with an International shaker machine at 280 to 300 oscillations per minute using special bottle holders described previously (Woods *et al.*, 1951) and centrifuged[5]. The aqueous layer (upper) is removed by aspiration with a water pump. The $EtCl_2$ extract is shaken by hand for 30 seconds with 4 ml. of 0.25 *M* Na_2HPO_4. The mixture is centrifuged and the aqueous layer removed as above. An aliquot of 8 ml. (or less if difficulty is encountered in separating the layers) of the $EtCl_2$ extract is transferred, using a 10-ml. graduated pipette, to a 35-ml. centrifuge tube containing 5 ml. of 0.5 *N* HCl. The mixture is shaken mechanically for 10 minutes, centrifuged and the $EtCl_2$ layer (bottom) removed carefully by aspiration with a clean glass tube (with narrow tip) for each sample. An aliquot of 4.5 ml.[6] of the acid extract is transferred to a 35-ml. centrifuge tube and 1 ml. of 10 per cent NaOH[6], 4 ml. of 1.4 *M* Na_2HPO_4, and 10 ml. of $EtCl_2$ added, successively. The mixture is shaken mechanically for 30 minutes, centrifuged and the aqueous layer (upper) removed. The $EtCl_2$ extract is washed with 4 ml. of 0.25 *M* Na_2HPO_4 which is removed by aspiration. With the aid of a graduated 10.0-ml. blow-out pipette, an 8.0-ml. aliquot of the $EtCl_2$ extract is transferred to the barrel of a 10-ml. syringe arranged as follows: On the tip of the syringe is placed a 1¼ inch no. 25 stainless steel needle, in the lumen of which has been introduced no. 25 stylet wire[7] of sufficient length to extend several mm. into the barrel of the syringe as well as beyond the tip of the needle. The position of the syringe is adjusted so that the stylet wire contacts the center of a 1¼ inch cupped aluminum planchet which in turn has been placed on a Fisher Slide Warmer set at 38°C. The $EtCl_2$ evaporates as it slowly runs onto the center of the planchet. About 7 to 12 hours is required but usually the evaporation is performed in a hood over night. A rack (capacity of 24) with spring metal clips is used to hold the syringe barrels over the slide warmer. A cover over all but the rear of the apparatus prevents dust from accumulating on the sample pans. After the syringe is empty the inner surface of the barrel is washed with 1 ml. of $EtCl_2$ which is allowed to drip through the needle onto the planchet. The solid levorphan base is converted into the hydrochloride by the addition of 4 drops of a 50 per cent methanol-ethanol mixture containing 1 ml. of conc. HCl per 100 ml. of solvent mixture. The drops are added carefully to dissolve the base and to make a thin layer, but to avoid the spreading of the drug to the rim of the planchet. The alcoholic HCl is added while the planchet is on the Fisher Slide Warmer or on a warm "hot plate." After the spreading of the

[2] This volume contained no more than 2 ml. of undiluted plasma or urine or 1 gm. of tissue.

[3] Purified as described by Woods *et al.* (1951).

[4] Pyrex glass-stoppered centrifuge tubes with a tapered bottom were used routinely.

[5] Plasma occasionally gave emulsions. The aqueous layer (upper) was removed by aspiration and the emulsified $EtCl_2$ agitated with a glass rod and then centrifuged again to obtain a clear extract in $EtCl_2$.

[6] The HCl and NaOH solutions must be titrated against each other so that when the acid aliquot is mixed with the base a pH of 7 to 9 results. If such is not true the concentration of one solution must be adjusted. If an aliquot of acid smaller than indicated is used, then less base must be employed.

[7] The authors express appreciation to Miss Katherine I. John of the Becton-Dickinson Co., Rutherford, N. J., for providing us with this stylet wire.

sample, the planchet is allowed to remain 15 to 30 minutes on the Fisher Slide Warmer or "hot plate" and then desiccated 12 hours over $CaCl_2$ before being counted in a gas-flow counter. The radioactivity on each planchet is counted for a sufficient period to provide a standard error of $\pm$ 2 per cent or less.

All samples were analyzed in duplicate and the drug on each sample pan was re-spread by the addition of 4 to 8 drops of the 50 per cent methanol-ethanol using the technique noted above and counted a second time. The highest count for each sample was averaged with its duplicate determination. Further spreading either did not change or reduced the count. Known concentrations of 5 to 1000 millimicrogm. of radioactive levorphanol (from the same source as that used to inject animals in subsequent experiments) were carried through the procedure as described above. A straight line relationship resulted when the resulting counts per minute (CPM) were plotted against the concentration. Subsequently, unknown samples were carried through the procedure as described and the CPM determined. The concentration was calculated from the graph prepared previously. A duplicate of a known low to moderate concentration of labeled levorphanol was analyzed parallel with each group of unknowns to serve as a continuous check of the technique.

The total drug, radioactive plus nonlabeled levorphanol, *i.e.*, one mgm., in aqueous solution carried through the above procedure and assayed with ultraviolet absorption gave results with a standard deviation of no more than $\pm$1 per cent. The variation in CPM for known concentrations of radioactive levorphanol was considerably greater, being approximately the same as the recovery of labeled drug added to plasma and urine as noted below. Such results suggest that the major variable in this technique is in the spreading of the drug on the planchet and subsequent counting. It has been impossible to ascertain the reasons for this variability.

The minimum amount of radioactive levorphanol (specific activity of about 1 millicurie/*mM*) which could be detected reliably in original urine or plasma was 2.5 millimicrogm./ml. The recovery of 2.5 to 5.0 millimicrogm./ml. of added C^{14}-labeled levorphanol from plasma, feces or urine was 105 $\pm$ 15 per cent, and for 10 to 1000 millimicrogm./ml. was 100 $\pm$ 6 per cent.

Total levorphanol, free plus conjugated, was determined by autoclaving the whole plasma, urine or fecal extract with 1/10 volume of conc. HCl for 30 minutes at 20 lb. pressure. The acid was carefully neutralized to pH 7 to 9 with a small volume of NaOH of suitable concentration before the samples were analyzed as described above.

The entire fecal sample for a given period was homogenized with an appropriate volume of 0.5 *N* HCl using a Waring blendor. A 25-ml. aliquot of the fecal homogenate was diluted to 50 ml. with 20 per cent TCA and the mixture centrifuged. The supernatant solution was removed, neutralized carefully with NaOH and 4-ml. aliquots removed for analysis.

Studies on the distribution of authentic and apparent radioactive levorphanol between $EtCl_2$ and buffers of varying pH indicate that the method of estimation described above is highly specific. The results are presented in table 1.

Plasma levels and excretion in the dog and monkey. Female animals were employed in these experiments. Urine and plasma samples were obtained using techniques described previously for the dog (Cochin *et al.*, 1954) and monkey (Mellett and Woods, 1956). Accordingly, the urine samples were obtained with a catheter for the first 9 hours and cage-collected thereafter except for catheterization at 24 hours. The latter samples were combined with the cage-collected samples of the 9 to 24 hour period. The animals were placed in a metabolism cage with stainless steel sides and bottom when samples were not

TABLE 1

The distribution of authentic and apparent levorphanol between ethylene dichloride and buffers of varying pH*

Ten ml. of the ethylene dichloride extract† containing the levorphanol (C^{14}-labeled and carrier) and 5 ml. of 0.25 *M* phosphate buffers were shaken mechanically for 30 minutes to insure equilibrium.

pH‡ of Buffer	Per Cent Extraction§	
	Authentic drug	Apparent* drug
6.8	79.6	79.8
7.1	65.0	65.3
7.4	49.3	51.7
7.7	36.3	34.8
8.0	23.9	21.3

* From autoclaved monkey urine.

† This is the extract which would be evaporated on the planchet in the method as described in this paper.

‡ The pH of each buffer was adjusted to the indicated value with a line operated Beckman pH meter.

§ Each figure represents the average of triplicate determinations.

being withdrawn. Fecal and urine samples were obtained through 72 hours. The dose of levorphanol was 0.2 or 2.0 mgm./kgm.[8] injected subcutaneously.

Simultaneous determination of urinary excretion and $C^{14}O_2$ elimination. An autoclave of about 2 ft. diameter was adapted for these experiments. Inside the chamber was placed a stainless steel liner covering about the bottom ⅓ of the autoclave and provided with a wire mesh false bottom. The latter allowed the urine to drip through the mesh, being retained by the bottom of the liner. At the end of 24 hours the animals were removed from the chamber and the dogs or monkeys catheterized. This urine sample, if any, was combined with the sample obtained from the bottom of the liner which was washed with an adequate amount of 0.1 *N* HCl.

The $C^{14}O_2$ was collected as follows: Compressed air was passed at a rate of 8 to 12 liters per minute,[9] first through a gas absorption bottle with a sintered glass plate containing 200 ml. of 30 per cent NaOH (changed every 6 hours) and then through a long glass tube (4.2 cm. diameter) containing soda lime and Drierite. The air was subsequently passed through a copper coil immersed in a pail of ice water [10] and then into the autoclave behind a baffle. Accordingly, the air entering the chamber was CO_2-free, dry and cool. The exit air from the chamber was passed through a tube containing Drierite and then into an absorption tower with a sintered glass plate containing 200 ml. of 2 *N* NaOH. This NaOH was changed hourly and analyzed for $C^{14}O_2$. Preliminary experiments showed that 93 per cent of the CO_2 was absorbed in one absorption tower so all samples were corrected to the 100 per cent value. An aliquot of 20 ml. of the NaOH solution containing the $Na_2C^{14}O_3$ was pipetted into a 50-ml. centrifuge tube to which was then added 6.0 ml. of 5 *M* NH_4Cl and 10 ml. of 1.5 *M* $BaCl_2$, in that order. The mixture was allowed to stand for 10 minutes and completeness of precipitation was tested by the dropwise addition of the $BaCl_2$ solution. The precipitate was transferred quantitatively to a weighed sintered glass crucible with the aid of three 10-ml. portions of distilled water. The crucible containing the $BaCO_3$ was dried overnight at 105° C. and weighed. The dry precipitate was transferred to a thick walled homogenizing tube and 10 ml. of 95 percent ethanol were added and the mixture homogenized for several minutes with a tight fitting plastic pestle until a fine suspension resulted. Two-ml. aliquots of the resulting homogenate were transferred to each of three weighed stainless steel planchets and the material allowed to dry at room temperature. The planchets were re-weighed and the radioactivity was determined in a gas-flow counter. Corrections were made for self-absorption, aliquots and sample size according to the methods of Calvin *et al.* (1949).

One dog, one monkey, or 8 to 10 rats (one-half male, one-half female) in two suitable cages, were placed in the chamber. The radioactive levorphanol was injected subcutaneously in a dose of 2 mgm./kgm.

Results. I. *Plasma levels and excretion of free and conjugated levorphanol in dogs and monkeys.* The results of typical experiments on plasma levels in the dog and monkey after the subcutaneous injection of 2 mgm./kgm. of levorphanol are shown in figure 1. Absorption of the drug by this route is very prompt. The maximum concentrations of free levorphanol were observed at about 30 minutes after administration and of conjugated levorphanol about 60 to 90 minutes after injection. Ten hours after administration the concentration of free levorphanol in the plasma of both the dog and monkey ranged from 5 to 10 millimicrogm./ml. but in 24 hours was less than 2.5 millimicrogm./ml. Conjugated levorphanol was detectable in the plasma of most animals 24 hours after the injection of the drug. The biologic half-life of free levorphanol, based on plasma levels in both the dog and monkey after a dose of 2 mgm./kgm., was approximately 75 to 90 minutes, and that for conjugated levorphanol about three hours. The apparent biologic half-life reported by Shore *et al.* (1955) for levorphanol in the dog was less than one hour. These investigators injected the drug intraperitoneally which might account for the slight difference as compared with the results described above. A pattern of plasma levels was observed in the dog after the subcutaneous injection of 0.2 mgm./kgm. of levorphanol (figure 2) similar to that observed after 2 mgm./kgm. of drug. With the former dose of drug the dogs showed definite pharmacologic effects including analgesia and sedation.

The data on the excretion of free and conjugated levorphanol in the dog and the monkey are summarized in table 2. The monkey excreted in the urine 2 to 3 per cent of the administered levorphanol as free drug and 23 to 48 per cent as

[8] In all instances the dose was calculated in terms of free base but the drug was injected as an aqueous solution of the tartrate salt.

[9] Measured with a Fisher Flowrator.

[10] It was necessary to cool the air to maintain the chamber and animals at 25 to 28°C.

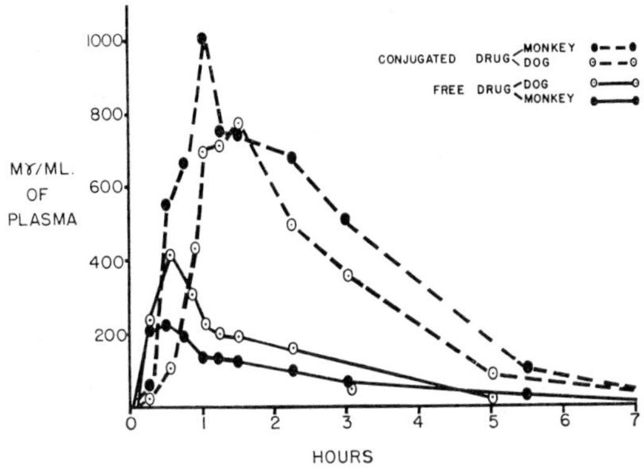

FIG. 1. Plasma levels of free and conjugated levorphanol in the dog and monkey after subcutaneous injection of 2 mgm./kgm. of the N-C^{14}-methyl labeled drug.

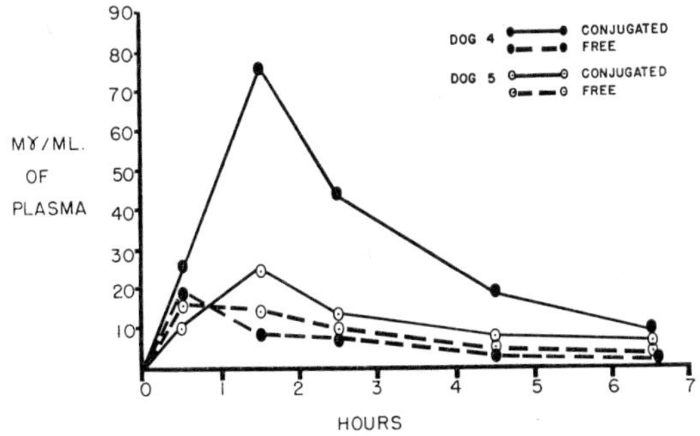

FIG. 2. Plasma levels of free and conjugated levorphanol in two dogs after the subcutaneous injection of 0.2 mgm./kgm. of the N-C^{14}-methyl labeled drug.

conjugated drug. In the dog the percentage of free levorphanol in the urine is somewhat higher, being 3 to 8 per cent of the dose, and the conjugated about 27 to 47 per cent of the administered drug. The rate of urinary elimination of levorphanol (free and conjugated) was very rapid. During the first 5 hours after injection, about 50 per cent of the total levorphanol to be excreted was found in the urine of the dog, and 75 to 80 per cent in the monkey. Levorphanol (primarily conjugated) was detectable in the urine of the dog or the monkey 72 hours after the administration of 2 mgm./kgm. of drug. Neither free nor conjugated levorphanol was present in significant amounts in the feces of the dog or monkey.

II. *Elimination of $C^{14}O_2$ and urinary levorphanol in rats, dogs and monkeys.* In each experiment, the elimination of $C^{14}O_2$ was determined hourly for 24 hours and the total 24-hour output of urine was obtained. The urine was analyzed for total radioactivity and total levorphanol (free and conjugated). The results of these experiments are presented in table 3. The monkey, and especially the rat, showed appreciably more radioactivity in the urine than total extractable levorphanol. The urine obtained from the dogs used in these experiments contained an amount of radioactivity which was approximately equal to the total levorphanol (free and conjugated).

There was a marked species difference in the quantity of $C^{14}O_2$ elimination, very little occurring in the dog, a small but significant amount occurring in the rat, and a very appreciable amount resulting in the monkey. The latter species excreted nearly one-fourth of the administered radioactivity as $C^{14}O_2$. In the monkey approximately 80 to 90 per cent of the administered levorphanol can be accounted for as $C^{14}O_2$ and urinary radioactivity (mostly levorphanol). Only 50 per cent of the administered levorphanol can be recovered as $C^{14}O_2$ and urinary radioactivity (including levorphanol) in the rat and dog.

The maximum rate of elimination of $C^{14}O_2$ in the monkey was observed in the 3-hour sample

TABLE 2

Urinary and fecal excretion† of free and conjugated C^{14}-labeled levorphanol in the dog and monkey after the subcutaneous injection of the drug*

Species	Dose	Per Cent Recovery of Administered Drug			
		Urinary			Fecal
		Free	Conjugated	Total	Total
	mgm./kgm.				
Monkey					
384	2.0	2.4	48	50	0.7
378	2.0	2.8	23	26	0.1
Dog					
1‡	2.0	5.2, 5.1	27, 40	32, 45	0.1, —
2	2.0	7.5	31	39	0.01
3	2.0	4.8	41	47	—
4	0.2	2.7	47	50	—
5	0.2	3.3	35	38	—

* Urine was collected via catheters for the first 9 to 10 hours and at the 24-hour collection. All other samples were cage collected.

† Samples were obtained through 72 hours.

‡ Experiments were performed on this dog with an intervening period of 10 months.

TABLE 3

Urinary total levorphanol and total radioactivity and exhaled $C^{14}O_2$ in the monkey, dog and rat for the first 24 hours after the subcutaneous injection of 2 mgm./kgm. of levorphanol*

	Per Cent of Administered Drug					
	Monkey		Dog		Rat	
	384	378	1	2	Group I (7 Animals)	Group II (9 Animals)
Urine						
Total levorphanol†	47	24	49	25	25	23
Total radioactivity‡	73	54	60	28	54	47
$C^{14}O_2$	17	24	1.5	1.0	5.3	4.3
Total radioactivity (urine and $C^{14}O_2$)	90	78	62	29	59	51

* The urine was cage-collected as described in the text. The dogs and monkeys were catheterized at the end of the 24-hour period and the urine so obtained was combined with the cage-collected sample.

† It was obvious from the determinations of "free" levorphanol that in most experiments much of the conjugated drug had been hydrolyzed to the free form because of the method of cage-collection. Accordingly, only total levorphanol is given here.

‡ This was determined by evaporating 1 ml. of a minimum of 1:50 dilution of the urine sample and spread as well as possible with the 50 per cent methanol-ethanol mixture. Each sample was run in triplicate and repeated several times. The results are probably no more reliable than ±15 per cent.

which was about one hour later than maximum urinary excretion of total levorphanol. Two-thirds of the total $C^{14}O_2$ to be eliminated was excreted during the first 6 hours after administration. Small but significant amounts of $C^{14}O_2$ were still being excreted in this species at the end of 24 hours.

Discussion. The method for the estimation of C^{14}-labeled levorphanol described in this communication is sufficiently sensitive to permit the use of small doses of drug in laboratory animals and human studies and requires small samples of the biological materials for analysis. If a drug with a higher specific activity than 1 millicurie/*mM* were used, a proportionately greater sensitivity would be attained. The extraction procedures provide specificity for the estimation of C^{14}-labeled levorphanol and reduce the problem of dilution with nonlabeled carbon and subsequent self-absorption. These are points to be emphasized for the use of radioactive tracer techniques in studies on physiological disposition of drugs. Since doses of 0.2 mgm./kgm. of levorphanol gave satisfactory data on plasma levels and urinary excretion in the dog, there is every reason to believe the procedures noted above will make it possible to obtain information on plasma levels of potent analgesics in nontolerant human subjects.

The plasma concentrations of free levorphanol parallel, approximately, the intensity of depression of the central nervous system in both the dog and monkey. These observations give support to the suggestion that levorphanol penetrates quite promptly into the central nervous system once the drug is absorbed into plasma.

There is disagreement as to whether levorphanol is excreted to any significant extent as the free drug in the urine of the dog. Fisher and Long (1953) have indicated that 7 to 15 per cent of levorphanol is excreted as the free form in the urine of dogs given 5 mgm./kgm. of the tartrate salt intramuscularly. On the other hand, Shore *et al.* (1955) reported negligible amounts of free levorphanol in urine of dogs receiving 5 mgm./kgm. of the drug by intraperitoneal injection. Our 6 experiments were performed on 5 dogs injected subcutaneously, the early urine samples being obtained by catheter, and a significant quantity of free levorphanol was found in the urine of all animals. The early urine samples, during the first two hours, showed the highest concentrations. Differences between our results and those of Shore *et al.* (1955) must be explained by the difference in the sensitivity of the methods, the dose and/or the route of administration. It has been our experience that conjugated levorphanol is quite labile in urine. In the experiments where the urine was collected in a large stainless steel pan in the chambers utilized for the study of $C^{14}O_2$ elimination, almost all of the levorphanol was as the free form. Since the same animals had been studied previously with the technique of catheter collection of urine it was obvious that hydrolysis of the conjugate had occurred. The dilute acid used to wash out the stainless steel pans may have hydrolyzed the conjugate or perhaps fecal contamination may have provided enough enzymatic activity to perform the hydrolysis. When the urine samples were collected by catheter in both monkeys and dogs the values for the determination of free levorphanol were very consistent. All urine samples were treated with toluene to prevent bacterial contamination and refrigerated immediately after collection. Many of these urine samples were checked 3 or 4 times for as long intervals as 3 to 4 weeks after collection and the concentration of free levorphanol did not change in the catheterized specimens. However, urine samples which were cage-collected occasionally did change quite markedly, there being a loss of conjugated levorphanol and an increase in free levorphanol.

The elimination of $C^{14}O_2$ *in vivo* by the several animal species following the administration of N-C^{14}-methyl labeled levorphanol confirms the report of the N-demethylation of levorphanol as demonstrated *in vitro* by Axelrod (1956). The low values for the elimination of $C^{14}O_2$ in the dog indicate that N-demethylation of levorphanol in this species is of very little importance as a route of drug alteration. This observation is in agreement with the studies of Shore *et al.* (1955) who were unable to demonstrate any "nor-levorphanol" in dog urine. However, it is quite apparent that the rat and especially the monkey are capable of metabolizing the levorphanol in this manner. The monkey and the dog have been reported to metabolize codeine differently (Woods *et al.*, 1956), the monkey, but not the dog, showing significant O-demethylation.

The evidence which has been presented in this communication indicates that the fecal elimination of free or conjugated levorphanol is minimal in the dog or monkey. Nevertheless, it is entirely possible that metabolites of levorphanol other than the conjugate may be eliminated in feces.

SUMMARY

The synthesis of N-C^{14}-methyl labeled levorphanol is reported. A method is described for the estimation of N-C^{14}-methyl labeled levorphanol in biological material which is sensitive to a level of 2.5 millimicrogm./ml. of plasma or urine (if 2-ml. samples are analyzed) when the drug has a specific activity of about 1 millicurie/*mM*. The procedure has been shown to be specific for levorphanol and to give adequate recoveries.

Plasma levels of free and conjugated levorphanol have been obtained for the dog and monkey after the subcutaneous injection of 0.2 and 2.0 mgm./kgm. of drug. In both species the biologic half-life of free levorphanol in the plasma was about 75 to 90 minutes, whereas the biologic half-life of conjugated levorphanol was about 3 hours.

About 2.5 per cent of the levorphanol administered to the monkey appeared in urine as free levorphanol and 35 per cent as conjugated levorphanol. In the dog, the percentage of free levorphanol in urine was somewhat higher, averaging 4.4 per cent, the conjugated levorphanol amounting to 42 per cent. Less than 0.1 per cent of the administered dose is excreted in the feces of either species.

The dog excretes a very small percentage of the radioactivity of the administered levorphanol as $C^{14}O_2$, although the rat eliminates about 5 per cent and the monkey about 20 per cent. The total radioactivity in monkey urine, and especially in rat urine, exceeds the total levorphanol (free plus conjugated).

ACKNOWLEDGMENTS. The authors are indebted to Mrs. Laura Dawson, Mrs. Jeanette McLaughlin, Miss Beverly Waterman and Salah El-Dareer for invaluable technical assistance, and to Dr. J. A. Aeschlimann of Hoffmann-La-Roche, Nutley, N. J., for the supply of *levo*-3-hydroxymorphinan and the details of its N-methylation with formaldehyde. Acknowledgment is given for support in part by Michigan Memorial Phoenix Grants #101 and #116 and the United States Public Health Service Grant #B-625.

REFERENCES

AXELROD, J.: THIS JOURNAL, **117**: 322, 1956.

ACHOR, L. B., AND GEILING, E. M. K.: THIS JOURNAL, **117**: 16, 1956.

ADLER, T. K., FUJIMOTO, J. F., WAY, E. L., AND BAKER, E. M.: THIS JOURNAL, **114**: 251, 1955.

BENSON, W. M., STEFKO, P. L., AND RANDALL, L. O.: THIS JOURNAL, **109**: 189, 1953.

CALVIN, M., HEIDELBERGER, C., REID, J. C., TOLBERT, B. M., AND YANKWICH, P. E.: Isotopic carbon, techniques in its measurement and chemical manipulation, Appendix VI, John Wiley & Sons, Inc., New York, 1949.

COCHIN, J., HAGGART, J., WOODS, L. A., AND SEEVERS, M. H.: THIS JOURNAL, **111**: 74, 1954.

ELLIOTT, H. W., CHANG, F. N-H., ABDOU, I., AND ANDERSON, H. H.: THIS JOURNAL, **95**: 494, 1949.

ELLIOTT, H. W., TOLBERT, B. M., ADLER, T. K., AND ANDERSON, H. H.: Proc. Soc. Exper. Biol. & Med., **85**: 77, 1954.

FISHER, A. L., AND LONG, J. P.: THIS JOURNAL, **107**: 241, 1953.

ISBELL, H., AND FRASER, H. F.: THIS JOURNAL, **107**: 524, 1953.

MELLET, L. B., AND WOODS, L. A.: THIS JOURNAL, **116**: 77, 1956.

Plotnikoff, N. P., Elliott, H. W., and Way, E. L.: This Journal, **104:** 377, 1952.

Randall, L. O., and Lehmann, G.: This Journal, **99:** 163, 1950.

Schnider, O., and Grüssner, A.: Helv. chim. acta, **32:** 821, 1949.

Schnider, O., and Grüssner, A.: Helv. chim. acta, **34:** 2211, 1951.

Schnider, O., and Hellerbach, J.: Helv. chim. acta, **33:** 1437, 1950.

Shore, P. A., Axelrod, J., Hoghen, C. A. M., and Brodie, B. B.: This Journal, **113:** 192, 1955.

Vogel, A. I.: A textbook of practical organic chemistry including qualitative organic analysis, p. 807. Longmans, Green and Co., New York, 1948.

Woods, L. A., Cochin, J., Fornefeld, E. J., McMahon, F. G., and Seevers, M. H.: This Journal, **101:** 188, 1951.

Woods, L. A., Muehlenbeck, H. E., and Mellett, L. B.: This Journal, **117:** 117, 1956.

8051

THE FATE OF PAPAVERINE IN MAN AND OTHER MAMMALS[1]

JULIUS AXELROD, ROBERT SHOFER, JOSEPH K. INSCOE, WILLIAM M. KING AND ALBERT SJOERDSMA

National Institute of Mental Health and National Heart Institute, National Institutes of Health, Public Health Service, U. S. Department of Health, Education and Welfare, Bethesda, Maryland

Received for publication May 7, 1958

Papaverine has been used extensively as a pharmacological agent for many years, yet little attention has been given to the fate of this drug in the animal body. Previous investigations have shown that only negligible amounts of papaverine were excreted unchanged in the urine (Zahn, 1915; Levy, 1945; Elek and Bergman, 1953). Elek and Bergman (1953) also observed the excretion of considerable amounts of an unidentified metabolite of papaverine.

The development of a specific and sensitive method for the estimation of papaverine in biologic media made possible an extensive study of the fate of this drug in man and other mammalian species. This communication describes investigations on the physiological disposition, metabolic fate and enzymatic transformation of papaverine, 1-(3′,4′-dimethoxybenzyl)-6, 7-dimethoxyisoquinoline (figure 1).

METHODS AND MATERIALS. *Estimation of papaverine and its metabolites.* Papaverine is isolated from biological material at an alkaline pH (pH 8.0 or higher) by extraction into n-heptane. The drug is then returned to 0.1 *N* HCl and assayed spectrophotometrically at 251 mμ and 266 mμ. Reading the optical density at two wave lengths serves to eliminate the effects of interfering substances present in biological material.

Procedure for plasma. Pipette 1 to 5 ml. of plasma (containing 0.5 to 5 microgm. of papaverine), 5 ml. water and 0.1 ml. of 10 *N* NaOH into a 60 ml. glass-stoppered bottle. Add 25 ml. of n-heptane containing 2 per cent isoamyl alcohol[2] and shake for 15 minutes. Centrifuge the bottle and transfer 20 ml. of the organic phase to a 40 ml. glass-stoppered, tapered centrifuge tube containing 1 ml. of 0.1 *N* HCl. Shake for 10 minutes and carefully remove the heptane phase by aspiration. Transfer an aliquot of the acid extract to a microcuvette and read the optical density at 251 mμ and 266 mμ in a Beckman spectrophotometer adapted for the measurement of small volumes. The papaverine concentration in the solution equals $(U_A - U_B/S_A - S_B) \times C$ where U_A and U_B are the optical densities of the unknown at 251 mμ and 266 mμ respectively, S_A and S_B are the optical densities of the standard at 251 mμ and 266 mμ and C is the concentration of the standard.

Standards are prepared by treating a known concentration of papaverine in the same manner as the unknowns. An optical density of about 0.136 is obtained when 1 microgm. of papaverine is run through the procedure.

Urine. Papaverine was determined by the same procedure as described for plasma except that the heptane extract was shaken with 4 ml. 0.1 *N* HCl.

Tissues. Homogenize the tissue in a Waring blendor with 5 volumes of 0.1 *N* HCl. Transfer an aliquot of the homogenate to a 60 ml. glass-stoppered bottle containing 0.1 ml. 10 *N* NaOH and proceed as described above except that the papaverine is extracted into 5 ml. of 0.1 *N* HCl.

Papaverine added to biological material was recovered with adequate precision (95 ± 5 per cent).

Specificity of the method. Possible interference of metabolic products of papaverine in the plasma procedure was examined by the technique of comparative distribution ratios. Plasma was obtained 2 hours after the oral administration of 5 mgm./kgm. of papaverine hydrochloride to two human subjects and the apparent papaverine was extracted into heptane in the manner described in the above procedure. The distribution ratios of the substance extracted from plasma were compared with authentic papaverine in a series of two-phase systems consisting of n-heptane containing 2 per cent isoamyl alcohol and buffers at various pH values. The results indicate that both compounds possessed the same solubility characteristics and were presumably the same compound (table 1).

[1] Preliminary reports of this work appeared in Fed. Proc., **15:** 585, 1956; and Experientia XIII/8, 319, 1957.

[2] All solvents (reagent grades) were successively washed with 1 *N* NaOH, 1 *N* HCl and two washings with water.

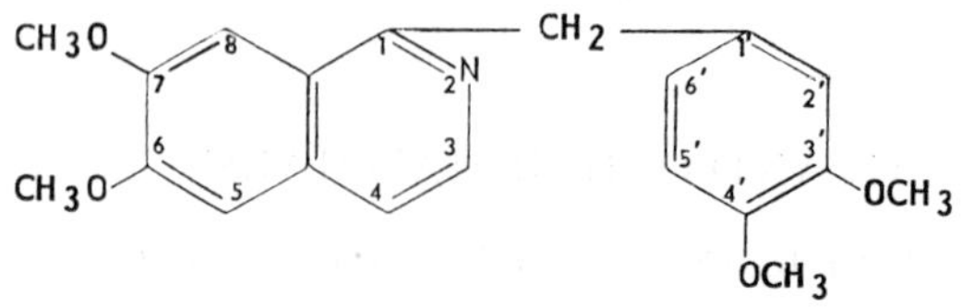

FIG. 1. Structural formula of papaverine.

TABLE 1

The distribution of papaverine and apparent papaverine between heptane and water at various pH values

Apparent papaverine from pooled plasma of two subjects receiving the drug was extracted into heptane containing 2 per cent isoamyl alcohol. Aliquots of the plasma extract and authentic papaverine in heptane isoamyl alcohol mixture were shaken with buffers at various pH values. The distribution is expressed as the ratio of the amount of drug remaining in the organic phase to total compound.

pH	Apparent Papaverine	Authentic Papaverine
6.0	0.82	0.78
5.6	0.63	0.60
5.1	0.38	0.39

Estimation of phenolic metabolites of papaverine. Phenolic metabolites of papaverine are extracted into 10 volumes ethylene dichloride[2] at pH 7–8 and then returned to 0.1 *N* HCl. Since several synthetic phenolic analogues of papaverine were found to have the same molecular extinction in 0.1 *N* HCl as papaverine at 251 mμ and 266 mμ readings were taken at these wave lengths. About 95 per cent of the phenolic metabolites found in urine were recovered, using this procedure.

Formaldehyde was determined by a procedure described previously (Axelrod, 1955).

Paper chromatography. Phenolic metabolites of papaverine were applied to Whatman No. 1 paper and developed by ascending chromatography with a mixture of 100 ml. butanol and 4 ml. acetic acid which was saturated with water. The compounds were visualized with potassium iodoplatinate reagent (Munier and Macheboeuf, 1949).

Measurement of biological half-life. Biological half-life of papaverine was determined from the plasma levels of the drug at various time intervals in man and dog. In mice the biological half-life was determined in the whole animal. The mice (NIH stock) were sacrificed 20 minutes after the intraperitoneal administration of papaverine hydrochloride and the drug concentration was determined in the whole animal after homogenizing with 4 volumes of 0.1 *N* HCl. The biological half-life of papaverine was determined graphically on semi-log paper by plotting the concentration of the compound at zero time and at 20 minutes.

Preparation of tissue samples for enzyme studies. Animals were stunned, exsanguinated and the tissues were removed immediately and chilled. Tissue slices were prepared using a Stadie-Riggs slicer. Two hundred mgm. of tissue were incubated with 0.6 micromol. papaverine and 4 ml. Krebs-Ringer bicarbonate buffer in a Dubnoff shaking incubator at 37° C., using 95 per cent O_2 and 5 per cent CO_2 as the gaseous phase. Following incubation, the contents of vessels were homogenized and an aliquot removed for analysis. Liver microsomes and soluble supernatant fraction were prepared by homogenizing liver with 5 volumes of 0.1 *M* phosphate buffer pH 7.4 at 0° C. using a glass homogenizer and then centrifuging at 9000 × *g* in a refrigerated centrifuge. Microsomes were obtained by differential centrifugation in isotonic KCl (Schneider, 1948).

Materials. 1-(3,-Methoxy-4,-hydroxybenzyl) 6, 7-dimethoxyisoquinoline and other phenolic analogues of papaverine were kindly supplied by Dr. Gerhard Billek, Chemisches Laboratorium der Universität, Wien. Triphosphopyridine nucleotide (TPN), diphosphopyridine nucleotide (DPN) of about 90 per cent purity and bacterial β-glucuronidase were obtained from Sigma Chemical Company, St. Louis, Missouri. Uridine diphosphoglucuronic acid (UDP-glucuronic acid) was prepared enzymatically from uridine diphosphoglucose (Pabst), DPN and uridine diphosphoglucose dehydrogenase (Strominger *et al.*, 1954).

RESULTS. *Plasma levels of papaverine in man.* Three human subjects were given 3 mgm./kgm. of papaverine hydrochloride intravenously and orally on different days. After oral administration, peak plasma levels were obtained in 1 to 2 hours, after which the concentration closely approximated those following intravenous administration. A typical experiment is shown in figure 2. These results indicate that the absorption from the gastrointestinal tract is relatively rapid and essentially complete. The biological half-life of the drug in man was found to range from 90 to 120 minutes. Approximately the same results were obtained with an analogue of papaverine, 1-(3′-methoxy-4′-ethoxybenzyl) 6,7-dimethoxy-3-methylisoquinoline (Paveril).[3]

Plasma levels of papaverine were studied in

[3] Paveril (Lilly) was determined by the same procedure as described for papaverine.

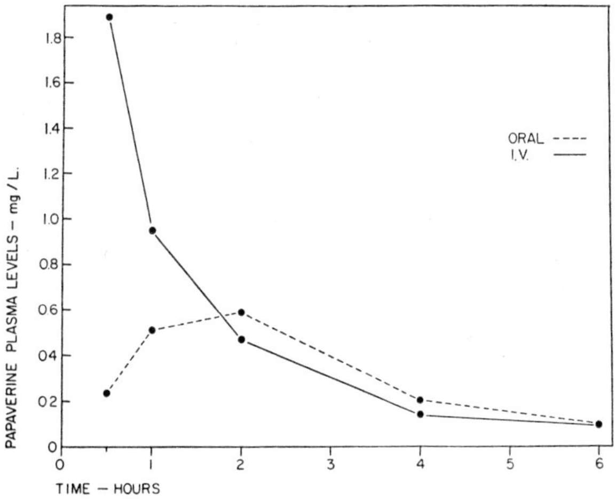

FIG. 2. Plasma levels of papaverine in man after oral and intravenous administration of 3 mgm./kgm. of the drug.

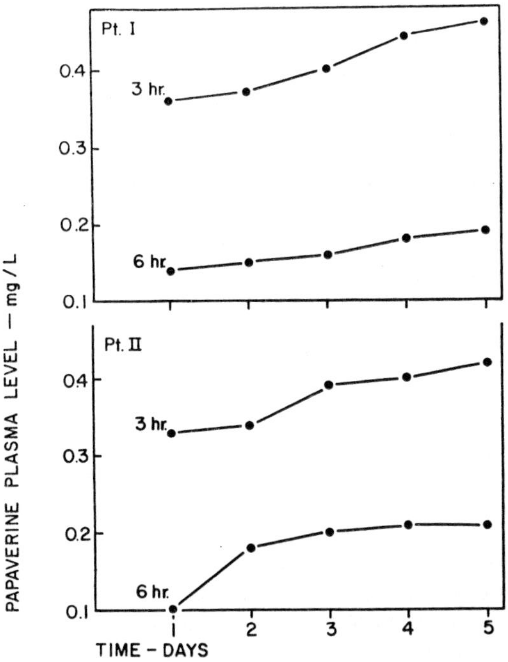

FIG. 3. Plasma levels of papaverine in man after the repeated administration of the drug. Each subject was given 200 mgm. of papaverine hydrochloride orally every 6 hours. Plasma levels were determined 3 and 6 hours after the first dose each day.

two human subjects who were given 200 mgm. of papaverine hydrochloride orally every 6 hours for 5 days. Plasma was assayed for the drug 3 and 6 hours after the first dose each day. A slight accumulation of the drug was found by the fifth day (figure 3).

TABLE 2

Tissue distribution of papaverine in the dog

Each animal received 35 mgm./kgm. papaverine hydrochloride by intravenous infusion over a period of one hour. The tissues were examined one hour after the end of the infusion.

Organ or Tissue	Papaverine	
	Dog 1	Dog 2
	mgm./kgm. of organ or tissue	
Plasma	17	14
Liver	82	68
Spleen	17	15
Kidney	28	23
Intestine	18	19
Lung	22	19
Heart	20	20
Brain	20	20
Muscle	17	13
Bile	19	19
Fat	71	63

Tissue distribution of papaverine in the dog. Two dogs were given an intravenous infusion of 35 mgm./kgm. of papaverine hydrochloride over a period of 1 hour and the tissues were examined for the drug 1 hour after the end of the infusion. Papaverine was found to be highly localized in liver and fat, and more or less uniformly distributed throughout the other tissues (table 2).

The binding of papaverine to the proteins of plasma was examined after dialysis at 37°C. for 20 hours through Visking membranes against isotonic buffer at pH 7.4. At a plasma concentra-

TABLE 3

Requirements for enzymatic metabolism of papaverine

Complete system contained microsomes and dialyzed soluble fraction obtained from 250 mgm. rabbit liver, 0.2 micromole TPN, 25 micromoles $MgCl_2$, 50 micromoles nicotinamide, 1 ml. pH 7.4 phosphate buffer (0.5 *M*), 0.5 micromole papaverine hydrochloride and water to make a final volume of 4 ml. After incubating for 2 hours at 37° C. the reaction mixture was assayed for papaverine.

	Papaverine Metabolized
	micromoles
Complete system	0.40
TPN omitted	0.05
DPN substituted for TPN	0.01
Oxygen omitted	0.00
Soluble fraction omitted	0.00
Microsomes omitted	0.00
Microsomes + TPNH* (2 micromoles)	0.25

* TPNH was added in 5 portions over a period of 90 minutes since this coenzyme disappeared rapidly even in the absence of substrate.

tion of 1 mgm./l., about 87 per cent of the drug was bound to the nondiffusible constituents of the plasma, while at 100 mgm./l. about 66 per cent of the drug was bound.

Urinary excretion of papaverine. Three human subjects received 3 mgm./kgm. of papaverine hydrochloride intravenously and orally on different days and the urine was collected for 24 hours. Less than 1 per cent of the unchanged drug was found in the urine, indicating it was almost completely metabolized in the body.

The site of metabolic transformation of papaverine. Experiments described above showed that papaverine was almost entirely transformed in the body. The site of metabolism was determined by measuring the disappearance of papaverine after its incubation with guinea pig or rabbit liver, brain, kidney, spleen and diaphragm slices at 37° C. in Krebs-Ringer bicarbonate. After two hours of incubation the liver and spleen metabolized 90 per cent and 10 per cent of the drug, respectively. In the remaining tissues the papaverine was recovered unchanged.

Requirements for enzymatic transformation of papaverine. Incubating rabbit liver homogenates with papaverine resulted in a negligible disappearance of the compound. However, when the liver homogenates or microsomes plus soluble fraction were fortified with TPN and nicotinamide, a substantial increase in the metabolism of papaverine was observed (table 3). When DPN was substituted for TPN, activity was markedly reduced. Microsomes and soluble supernatant fractions were found to be as active as the whole homogenate. Little activity was found when microsomes and soluble supernatant fraction were used alone.

When a TPNH generating enzyme system or chemically prepared TPNH was added to the microsomes, these cofactors were found to be about half as effective as the soluble supernatant and TPN (table 3). These observations indicated that the metabolism of papaverine was catalyzed by an enzyme system in the microsomes that required TPNH, oxygen and other cofactors present in the soluble supernatant.

TABLE 4

Balance study on the enzymatic demethylation of papaverine

Microsomes and soluble fraction obtained from 1 gram of rabbit liver were incubated at 37° C. with 1.0 micromole TPN, 25 micromoles $MgCl_2$, 50 micromoles nicotinamide, 100 micromoles neutralized semicarbazide hydrochloride, 5 ml. pH 7.4 phosphate buffer, 3.0 micromoles papaverine hydrochloride and water to make a final volume of 10 ml. After 2 hours of incubation the reaction mixture was analyzed for papaverine and formaldehyde.

Expt. No.	Papaverine Metabolized	Formaldehyde Formed
	micromoles	*micromoles*
1	2.3	2.2
2	2.3	2.6
3	2.3	2.4

Since numerous methoxy substituted compounds are cleaved *in vitro* to yield phenolic products and formaldehyde (Axelrod, 1956), it appeared likely that papaverine might undergo an analogous transformation. After incubating papaverine with the microsomal preparation and semicarbazide (to trap formaldehyde), one mole of formaldehyde was formed for each mole of papaverine metabolized (table 4). After precipitating the proteins with trichloracetic acid, the teaction mixture was examined for phenolic metabolites with Folin-Ciocalteu reagent (1927). Phenolic material was found to be present when the protein-free supernatant solution was treated with phenolic reagents.

A microsomal enzyme system requiring TPNH and oxygen was first described for the deamination of amphetamine (Axelrod, 1954a). Subsequently, it was found that TPNH dependent enzyme systems can carry out many metabolic reactions, such as demethylation of sympathomimetic amines (Axelrod, 1954b), hydroxylation of aromatic compounds (Mitoma and Udenfriend, 1955), side chain oxidation of barbiturates (Cooper and Brodie, 1955), and the cleavage of aromatic ethers (Axelrod, 1956). From the results described above, it appears that the same general mechanism is involved in the cleavage of the methoxy groups of papaverine.

Transformation of papaverine to phenolic metabolites in vivo. Eight guinea pigs received 100 mgm./kgm. of papaverine intraperitoneally and the urine was collected for 24 hours. The pooled urine was adjusted to pH 7.0 to 8.0 and extracted twice with three volumes of ether. After shaking the organic solvent with 0.1 *N* HCl, a considerable amount of material was found in the acid extract which reacted with a number of phenolic reagents. This material had ultraviolet absorption spectra (maxima, 251 mμ, 310 mμ; minimum, 266 mμ) similar to papaverine. Heating the urine in 1 *N* HCl at 100° C. produced a marked increase in the amount of phenolic material.

The phenolic metabolites present in guinea pig urine were isolated as follows: after heating the urine in 1 *N* HCl in a boiling water bath for 1 hour, the hydrolysate was adjusted to pH 7 to 8 and extracted with 5 volumes of ether. The ether extract was reduced to a small volume under nitrogen and the phenolic material was returned to 1 *N* HCl. The material showing an absorption peak at 251 mμ was subjected to a 24 transfer countercurrent distribution, using equal volumes of ethylene dichloride and pH 3.9 citrate buffer (0.1 *M*). After the countercurrent distribution the material which absorbed light at 251 mμ was determined in each tube. The resulting distribution curve indicated that at least two phenolic products were present. The contents of tubes 13 to 24 which contained about 25 per cent of the total phenolic material present in the original urine were pooled, adjusted to pH 7.0, and shaken with ethylene dichloride. After reducing the ethylene dichloride extract to a small volume the material absorbing at 251 mμ was distributed in 24 tubes with ethylene dichloride and pH 4.5 citrate buffer (0.1 *M*). From the resulting distribution, it appeared that at least two phenolic products were present. No further attempts were made to characterize these products.

The contents of tubes 0 to 12 from the first countercurrent distribution were pooled and the phenolic material was extracted into ethylene dichloride at pH 7.0. After subjecting this material to a 24 transfer countercurrent distribution with ethylene dichloride and pH 3.3 citrate buffer (0.1 *M*) the resulting distribution extract indicated the presence of a single phenolic product. Using a binominal expansion in the manner described by Williamson and Craig (1947), it was calculated that this metabolite represented about 70 per cent of the total phenolic material present in the guinea pig urine. Tubes 10 to 16 were pooled and the phenolic metabolite was extracted into ethylene dichloride at pH 7.0. After evaporating the ethylene dichloride *in vacuo*, the resulting material was recrystallized twice from ethanol, yielding white crystals which melted at 162 to 164° C. An authentic sample of 1-(3′-methoxy-4′-hydroxybenzyl)-6,7-dimethoxyisoquinoline, (4′-hydroxy papaverine), melted at 162 to 164° C. and a mixed melting point of the two compounds showed no depression. The ultraviolet absorption and fluorescence spectra of the isolated metabolite and 4′-hydroxy papaverine were identical. Additional evidence for the identity of the phenolic metabolite was obtained by paper chromatography, using the solvent system described under METHODS. Both the authentic and apparent compounds had the same R_f (0.69). The distribution ratios of the isolated and synthetic compound between various buffers and ethylene dichloride were the same.

The transformation of papaverine to phenolic metabolites was examined in two human subjects who received 1 gm. of the drug orally. Urine was collected for 24 hours and examined for the presence of phenolic compounds, using the procedure described under METHODS. Only traces of phenolic material were found. When the urine was made 1 *N* with respect to HCl and autoclaved at 20 lb. pressure for 2 hours, considerable amounts of phenolic metabolites were found. These transformation products represented about 60 per cent of the administered papaverine.

TABLE 5

Enzymatic synthesis of 4′-hydroxy papaverine glucosiduronic acid

Washed microsomes obtained from 300 mgm. of guinea pig liver were incubated at 37° C. for 25 minutes with 0.2 ml. pH 7.8 phosphate (0.5 *M*) buffer, 25 micromoles $MgCl_2$, 0.15 micromole 4′-hydroxy papaverine and water to make a final volume of 1.5 ml.

Additions	4′-Hydroxy papaverine	
	Disappearing on Incubation*	Recovered with β-Glucuronidase†
	micromoles	*micromoles*
None	0.010	0.000
UDP-glucuronic acid‡ (0.27)	0.135	0.140

* 4′-Hydroxy papaverine was extracted into ethylene dichloride and determined spectrophotometrically at 251 and 266 mμ as described under METHODS.

† Reaction mixture was extracted after incubation to remove free phenol; the aqueous residue was then incubated with bacterial β-glucuronidase (500 units) at 37° C. for 3 hours and phenol extracted again with ethylene dichloride and measured as described under METHODS.

‡ Generated enzymatically from UDPG with UDPG dehydrogenase and DPN (Strominger *et al.*, 1954).

TABLE 6

Species differences in the metabolism of papaverine

Urines were collected for 48 hours after the administration of papaverine hydrochloride. The proportion of the various urinary products is expressed in percentage of the amount of papaverine administered.

Species	Papaverine	Free Phenolic§ Metabolites	Conjugated¶ Phenolic Metabolites
	%	%	%
Man*	0.5	0.5	64
Rat†	0.5	2.9	45
Guinea pig†	0.7	18.0	56
Dog‡	0.5	1.6	7.1

* 10 mgm./kgm. papaverine hydrochloride given orally.

† 50 mgm./kgm. papaverine hydrochloride given intraperitoneally.

‡ 15 mgm./kgm. papaverine hydrochloride given intravenously.

§ Phenolic metabolites were extracted into ethylene dichloride and determined spectrophotometrically as described under METHODS.

¶ Represents the differences between the phenolic metabolites before and after acid hydrolysis.

Phenolic metabolites obtained after hydrolyzing the urine were extracted with ether as described above and subjected to a 24 transfer countercurrent distribution with equal volumes of ethylene dichloride and pH 3.4 citrate buffer (0.1 *M*). The distribution curve indicated the presence of at least 2 phenolic products. The material present in tubes 4 to 16, representing about 70 per cent of the total phenolic material, had the same ultraviolet and fluorescence spectra as 4′-hydroxy papaverine. Both the authentic and apparent 4′-hydroxy papaverine obtained from human urine had the same R_f (0.69) on paper chromatograms and distribution ratios in a number of buffer-solvent systems.

Nature and mechanism of formation of conjugated phenolic metabolites. Phenolic metabolites of papaverine were found to be excreted mainly in the bound form. Autoclaving of conjugated metabolites at 20 lb. pressure in 1 *N* HCl for 2 hours resulted in the complete hydrolysis of these compounds. When a urine sample containing 60 microgm. of bound phenolic metabolites was incubated with bacterial β-glucuronidase (5000 units) at pH 6.0 for 18 hours at 37°C. about 75 per cent of the conjugated phenolic metabolites were liberated, indicating that these compounds were bound to glucuronic acid.

Previous studies have shown that glucuronides can be synthesized by cell-free preparations in the presence of UDP-glucuronic acid (Dutton and Storey, 1953; and Strominger *et al.*, 1954). Incubating liver microsomes with UDP-glucuronic acid and 4′-hydroxy papaverine, the major transformation product of papaverine, resulted in the disappearance of this compound (table 5). After extracting the residual phenolic compound with ethylene dichloride, the aqueous residue was incubated with β-glucuronidase and assayed for liberated phenol. This treatment resulted in a quantitative recovery of 4′-hydroxy papaverine. These observations were taken as evidence that the phenolic metabolite which disappeared upon incubation with liver microsomes and UDP-glucuronic acid was converted to a glucosiduronic acid of 4′-hydroxy papaverine.

Fate of papaverine in a number of animal species. The urinary excretion of papaverine and its metabolic products were examined in man, rat, dog and guinea pig (table 6). All species excreted only negligible amounts of unchanged drug, indicating that it underwent almost complete metabolic alteration. With the exception of the dog, the major route of biotransformation involved O-demethylation to yield phenolic metabolites. These phenolic products were excreted mainly as conjugates. Using countercurrent distribution techniques described above, the major phenolic product (about 70 per cent of the phenols) was identified as 4′-hydroxy papaverine in man and guinea pig.

Considerable species differences in the rate of metabolism of papaverine was observed. The biologic half-lives in man, dog and mouse were 100, 35 and 8 minutes, respectively.

SUMMARY AND CONCLUSIONS

A specific and sensitive method for the estimation of papaverine in biologic material is described.

Papaverine is completely absorbed from the gastrointestinal tract of man. Negligible amounts of the drug are excreted unchanged in the urine indicating almost complete metabolic alteration. Papaverine is highly localized in liver and fat of the dog and uniformly distributed in other tissues. The biologic half-life of the drug ranges from 8 minutes in the mouse to 100 minutes in man.

The principle site of metabolism of papaverine is in the liver. An enzyme system in liver microsomes which cleaves papaverine to yield phenolic metabolites and formaldehyde is described.

About 60 per cent of administered papaverine is excreted as glucuronide conjugates of phenolic metabolites in man and the guinea pig. At least 3 phenolic metabolites were formed; the major one was identified as 4′-hydroxy papaverine. Considerable species differences in the metabolism of papaverine was found.

The glucosiduronic acid of 4′-hydroxy papaverine is formed by an enzyme in liver microsomes that can transfer glucuronic acid from UDP-glucuronic acid to 4′-hydroxy papaverine.

REFERENCES

Axelrod, J.: This Journal, **110:** 2, 1954a.
Axelrod, J.: Fed. Proc., **13:** 332, 1954b.
Axelrod, J.: This Journal, **114:** 430, 1955.
Axelrod, J.: Biochem. J., **63:** 634, 1956.
Cooper, J. R., and Brodie, B. B.: This Journal, **114:** 409, 1955.
Dutton, G. J., and Storey, I. D. E.: Biochem. J. **53:** xxvii, 1953.
Elek, S. R., and Bergman, H. C.: J. Appl. Physiol., **6:** 168, 1953.
Folin, O., and Ciocalteu, V.: J. Biol. Chem., **73:** 627, 1927.
Levy, J.: Bull. Soc. chim. biol., **27:** 578, 1945.
Mitoma, C., and Udenfriend, S.: This Journal, **113:** 40, 1955.
Munier, R., and Macheboeuf, M.: Bull. Soc. chim. biol.: **31:** 1144, 1949.
Schneider, W. C.: J. Biol. Chem.: **176:** 259, 1948.
Strominger, J. L., Kalckar, H. M., Axelrod, J., and Maxwell, E. S.: J. Amer. Chem. Soc., **76:** 6411, 1954.
Williamson, B., and Craig, L. C.: J. Biol. Chem., **168:** 687, 1947.
Zahn, K.: Biochem. Ztschr. **68:** 444, 1915.

8052

STUDIES ON THE BIOLOGICAL DISPOSITION OF STREPTOVARICIN (DALACIN)[1], A NEW ANTIBIOTIC

DONALD P. WALLACH AND JOHN G. WAGNER

With the technical assistance of N. J. Crittenden and W. C. Bell

Departments of Pharmacology and Product Research and Development, The Upjohn Company, Kalamazoo, Michigan

Received for publication May 23, 1958

Siminoff *et al.* (1957) have reported the discovery and biological activity of streptovaricin, a new antibiotic isolated from *Streptomyces spectabilis* n. sp., an actinomycete found in a sample of soil collected in Dallas, Texas. The interest in this antibiotic arises from its marked *in vitro* and *in vivo* activity against *M. tuberculosis*.

Streptovaricin is isolated from fermentation beers as a yellow-orange material consisting of a number of very similar antibiotic components, 5 of which have been individually isolated and designated as streptovaricins A, B, C, D, and E. Rhuland *et al.* (1957) demonstrated highest activity for streptovaricin C, followed by streptovaricin B, in the tuberculous mouse. The other components are either inactive, or represent such a small percentage of the fermentation product that they have not been investigated further. For these reasons the major share of the work to be reported in this paper was carried out with a partially purified preparation which contained 60 per cent streptovaricin C, 10 per cent streptovaricin B, and 30 per cent inert material. Where other preparations of streptovaricin were used, these are indicated in the text.

The chemical structure of the streptovaricin components is unknown at the present time. As reported by Whitfield *et al.* (1957) the material is soluble in alcohols, lower molecular weight acetates and ketones, methylene chloride and chloroform. Its solubility in water is 0.7 mgm./ml. It is virtually insoluble in hexane, ether, carbon tetrachloride and benzene. The antibiotic complex is alkali-labile; practically all activity is lost over a period of 3 days at pH 7.8. The material gives positive ferric chloride and iodoform tests and negative reactions in the Benedict, ninhydrin, Molish, Zimmerman, and Liebermann tests.

MATERIALS AND METHODS. When blood assays are performed, the following procedure is employed. A 12 to 15 ml. blood sample is drawn and transferred to a 20-ml. lusteroid centrifuge tube. The sample is left standing for 30 to 45 minutes at room temperature to assure complete clotting, after which it is centrifuged at 3000 × *g* at 0 to 3°C for 10 minutes. All subsequent operations are carried out in the cold.

A 6-ml. aliquot of serum is withdrawn from the centrifuged sample and placed in a clean 60-ml. separatory funnel. To this aliquot is immediately added 30 ml. (5 volumes) of cold reagent grade chloroform. The funnel is then closed and vigorously shaken for a minimum of 30 seconds. The phases are allowed to separate and the opaque chloroform layer is transferred to another 60-ml. separatory funnel containing approximately 30 ml. of cold water. The contents of the funnel are vigorously shaken for about 5 seconds. When the phases have separated, the solvent phase should appear perfectly clear. An alternative, though slower, procedure is to clarify the chloroform extract by filtration through dry filter paper.

A 25-ml. aliquot of the clarified chloroform extract is transferred to a 50-ml. round bottom flask. The flask is then attached to a high vacuum manifold. To avoid bumping a slow stream of air is allowed to bubble into the flask through a capillary tube which reaches almost to the bottom of the flask. Evaporation is rapid. The chloroform vapor is condensed in 2 dry ice-ethanol traps between the vacuum manifold and the pump. An 8 or 10 place manifold is about the maximum practical number for the usual size laboratory pump. The dry residue, with a minimum of contaminating lipids, is equivalent to the streptovaricin in 5 ml. of serum.

When tissue determinations are made this

[1] Dalacin is the trademark applied to streptovaricin by The Upjohn Company.

method is modified as follows. Twenty grams of tissue are homogenized with 80 ml. of water in a Waring blendor for 3 to 4 minutes at top speed. The homogenate is then filtered through cheesecloth to remove fibrous material and a 12-ml. aliquot equivalent to 2.4 gms. of tissue is pipetted into a 125-ml. separatory funnel. Sixty ml. of cold chloroform are added and the contents of the funnel vigorously shaken for at least 30 seconds. The phases are allowed to separate and the chloroform extract is filtered through dry Whatman #40 filter paper to remove insoluble material. A 50-ml. aliquot equivalent to 2.0 gm. of tissue is then measured into a 100-ml. round bottom flask and evaporated in the same manner as described for serum samples.

The dry residue from either serum or tissue is then dissolved in absolute alcohol in appropriate volume to dissolve all the material in the flask, and to bring the concentration of antibiotic within a range of 0.5 to 5.0 microgm./ml. of solution.

A microbiological assay is carried out essentially as described by Perry *et al.* (1957). Eight hundredths of a ml. of the alcohol solution is applied to 12.7 mm. Schleicher and Schuell paper discs on a glass plate, after which the discs are dried for 20 to 30 minutes at room temperature. The dry disc is then applied to an agar plate seeded with *S. lutea* PCI 1001 and immediately moistened with 0.05 ml. of 0.1 *M* potassium phosphate buffer pH 6.0. Four discs are used for each serum extract. The assay plates are then incubated at 37°C for 16 to 18 hours. At this time good growth of the organism is evident and the zones of inhibition around the discs are measured to the nearest 0.5 mm. The concentration of antibiotic is determined from a standard curve prepared from assays on samples of known concentration run concurrently with the unknown samples and plotted as zone size versus log concentration. This method obviously measures total antimicrobial activity in blood and tissues and would not differentiate active antibiotic conversion products in blood and tissues.

A series of control tests were run on serum samples containing known amounts of streptovaricin using the procedures described. The average recovery was found to be 80 per cent with 95 per cent confidence limits of ±10 per cent[2]. Results with all tissues hereinafter described have indicated the same recovery.

RESULTS. *Gastrointestinal absorption of streptovaricin in dogs.* Eleven dogs were divided into 3 groups of 3 dogs each and 1 group of 2 dogs and were fasted for 16 to 18 hours. Then each dog in a group was given 50 ml. of 0.1 *N* HCl via stomach tube to insure uniform gastric pH. This was followed by a capsule containing a dose of streptovaricin complex equivalent to 50 mgm./kgm. of body weight. Blood samples were taken at the indicated times and allowed to clot as described. After centrifugation, a 3-ml. aliquot of serum was removed from each sample; the aliquots were pooled and assayed by the described procedures. The results as shown in table 1 reveal that with the dose employed antibiotic serum concentrations of a relatively low magnitude are obtained and that these are present for a 12-hour period.

TABLE 1

Average serum levels of streptovaricin complex following an oral dose of 50 mgm./kgm. body weight to 11 dogs*

Hour	Microgm./ml. of Serum
0	0
1	0.6 ± 0.3†
2	1.6 ± 0.4
3	2.2 ± 0.3
4	2.3 ± 0.6
5	2.7 ± 0.6
6	2.2 ± 0.8
8	1.0 ± 0.5
12	0.4 ± 0.2

* Contains all antibiotic components amounting to 50 to 60 per cent of the material and 40 to 50 per cent inert impurities.

† Standard error.

Because of the projected importance of the oral route of administration for this drug, the sites of gastrointestinal absorption were investigated as follows. Eight dogs fasted for 48 hours were anesthetized with intravenous injections of 20 mgm./kgm. of thiopental and 250 mgm./kgm. of barbital. The abdomen of each animal was opened and the several indicated segments of the gastrointestinal tract were cut and tied at one end. An aqueous suspension of streptovaricin complex containing 25 mgm./ml. equivalent to a dose of 50 mgm./kgm. body weight was introduced and the other end of the segment tied off. The abdomen of each dog was then closed and blood samples from arterial cannulas were taken at hourly intervals and assayed. The highest serum levels of streptovaricin were observed when

[2] The values for streptovaricin reported in this paper are uncorrected for this assay error.

TABLE 2

Half-life values for streptovaricin in the serum of normal dogs following intravenous administration

Figure	Curve	Dog No.	Dose	Time Range*	Concentration Range	Correlation Coefficient of Regression Line†	Half-Life‡
			mgm./kgm.	*minutes*	*mgm./ml. of serum*		*minutes*
1	C		5	15 to 60	0.9 to 2	−0.925§	48
1	B		10	15 to 90	1 to 6	−0.840¶	35
1	A	247	20	1 to 30	10 to 28	—	20
2	D	246	20	1 to 30	8 to 24	—	18
2	E	248	20	1 to 30	6 to 25	—	15
							Avg. 27‖
1	C[1]		5	60 to 240	0.2 to 0.9	−0.999§	78
1	B[1]		10	105 to 360	0.09 to 0.9	−0.970§	74
1	A[1]	247	20	60 to 300	1 to 7	−0.986§	119
2	D[1]	246	20	30 to 300	2 to 8	−0.989§	142
2	E[1]	248	20	30 to 300	0.7 to 7	−0.993§	79
							Avg. 98

* The time range over which the half-life was calculated.

† The correlation coefficient of the regression, log (serum level) versus time.

‡ Half-life = 0.693/−(2.303) (slope) where "slope" is the slope of the log (serum level) versus time curve.

§ Significant at P = 0.001

¶ Significant at P = 0.01

‖ There is some evidence of negative correlation of this "secondary" half-life with the dose administered, or in other words, positive correlation of the corresponding rate constant with dose. There is insufficient data to confirm such a relationship.

absorption took place in the small intestine and duodenum. Absorption was appreciably less from the large intestine, and negligible absorption took place from the stomach.

At the conclusion of these experiments the tied-off segments of the gut in one "stomach," "duodenal," "small intestine" and "large intestine" dog were excised and opened, and the contents were carefully removed. The gut wall was thoroughly washed in ethanol and the washings were added to the gut contents. The entire material was then made up to a definite volume in ethanol, thoroughly mixed and a filtered aliquot diluted appropriately for the microbiological assay. The analysis showed 91 per cent of the antibiotic had disappeared from the stomach, 74 per cent from the duodenum, 70 per cent from the small intestine below the duodenum and 60 per cent from the large intestine.

E. R. Garrett (personal communication) has studied the rates of degradation of various streptovaricin components in 25 per cent aqueous ethanol at 30.3°C as a function of pH. He reported that the half-life of streptovaricin C is less than 5.8 hours at pH 1. At pH 2, the half-life was found to be 43 hours. While the pH of the gastric contents was not measured, extensive degradation of the antibiotic must have taken place as negligible blood levels in the two "stomach" dogs were observed. The absorption from the other segments is probably lower than indicated, but the precise value is difficult to assess due to our inability to distinguish between inactivated nonabsorbed drug, and that which was absorbed. The figure for disappearance from the duodenum is also compromised to some degree by biliary excretion of streptovaricin.

It would appear, however, that the antibiotic is absorbed throughout the entire gastrointestinal tract with the possible exception of the stomach. The data also indicate that, for its length, the duodenum is the most efficient site of absorption

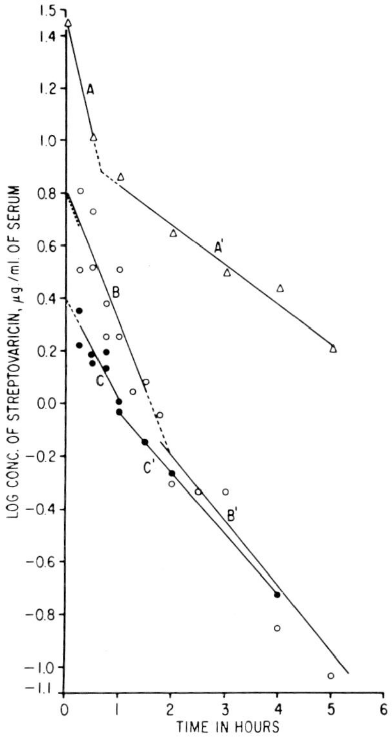

FIG. 1. First order plots of streptovaricin elimination from the blood of normal dogs.

followed by the rest of the small intestine and then the large intestine.

Serum levels resulting from intravenous administration of streptovaricin in the dog. The mechanisms of streptovaricin distribution and elimination were studied using the intravenous route of administration. The partially purified preparation of streptovaricin C (see introduction) was dissolved in 45 per cent aqueous ethanol at a concentration of 50 mgm./ml. Injections of this solution were given within a period of 1 minute in the cephalic vein of the forearm, and blood samples were taken from the external jugular vein at intervals of 1, 30 and 60 minutes. Samples were taken at hourly intervals thereafter.

If it is assumed that serum volume is equivalent to 4 per cent of body weight, 80 to 90 per cent of an intravenously administered dose of streptovaricin disappears from the blood within 1 minute. This initial rate of loss was not measured since the first blood sample was taken 1 minute in most experiments and 15 minutes in 2 experiments after injection, as shown in table 2. Hence the "primary" half-life was not measured. The serum concentration of streptovaricin in microgm./ml. were converted to logarithms and plotted. The first order plots are shown in fig. 1. Each first order plot of measured streptovaricin

TABLE 3

Comparison of rates of loss of streptovaricin from the serum of normal and nephrectomized dogs following intravenous administration of a dose of 20 mgm./kgm. in 45 per cent ethanol-water

Figure	Curve	Dog No. and State	Time Range*	Concentration Range	Correlation Coefficient of Regression Line†	Slope of Line	Ratio of Slopes	Half-Life‡
			minutes	*mgm./kgm. of serum*				*minutes*
2	D	246 (normal)	1 to 30	8 to 24	—	−0.0164	1.6/1	18
2	F	246 (nephrectomized)	1 to 60	8 to 35	—	−0.0103		29
2	D^1	246 (normal)	30 to 300	2 to 8	−0.989§	−0.0021	1.3/1	142
2	F^1	246 (nephrectomized)	60 to 300	2 to 8	−0.953¶	−0.0016		194
2	E	248 (normal)	1 to 30	6 to 25	—	−0.0205	1.6/1	15
2	G	248 (nephrectomized)	1 to 60	5 to 32	—	−0.0127		24
2	E^1	248 (normal)	30 to 300	0.7 to 7	−0.993§	−0.0038	2.4/1	79
2	G^1	248 (nephrectomized)	120 to 360	1 to 3	−0.875‖	−0.0016		187

* The time range over which the half-life was calculated.

† The correlation coefficient of the regression, log (serum level) *versus* time.

‡ Half-life = 0.692/−2.303 (slope), where "slope" is the slope of the log (serum level) *versus* time curve.

§ Significant at P = 0.001.

¶ Significant at P = 0.01.

‖ Significant at P = 0.05.

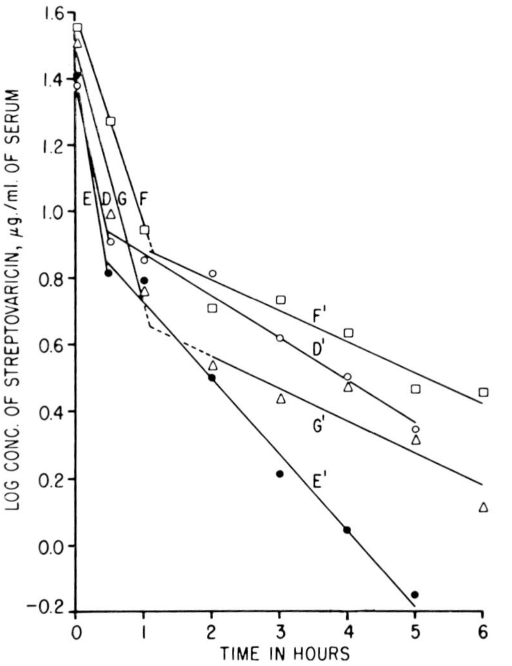

FIG. 2. First order plots of streptovaricin elimination from the blood of normal and bilaterally nephrectomized dogs.

TABLE 4

Serum levels of streptovaricin (microgm./ml.) after i.v. administration of 20 mgm./kgm.

Dog No.	1	2	3	4	5
Time Sacrificed	5 min.	1 hr.	2 hr.	3 hr.	4 hr.
Time Post Injection					
60 sec.	92.0	44.8	41.75	15.58	90.4
5 min.	14.2	—	—	—	—
30 min.	—	8.0	7.86	2.34	3.0
1 hr.	—	4.84	5.87	1.32	2.7
2 hr.	—	—	3.9	0.71	1.36
3 hr.	—	—	—	0.35	0.47
4 hr.	—	—	—	—	0.21

elimination from the blood stream is readily resolvable into 2 straight lines of differing slope. The points were fitted by the method of "least squares" where possible; if only 2 points were available, the slope was calculated directly. From the first segment with steepest slope an average half life of 27 minutes was calculated for normal unanesthetized dogs; this is termed the average "secondary half-life."

From the second segment of these first order plots, an average half-life of 98 minutes was calculated and is termed the "tertiary half-life." These rates are not significantly affected by the vehicle in which the drug is given.

Experiments were also performed to compare the rate of clearance from the blood of normal dogs and the rate of clearance from the blood of the same dogs following bilateral nephrectomy. The results are shown in table 3 and fig. 2. The data indicate that streptovaricin is cleared from the blood of normal dogs 1.3 to 2.4 times faster than from the blood of nephrectomized dogs. The amount of streptovaricin in the blood, however, at the times these differences were measured represents only a small fraction of the total dose administered intravenously. While part of this difference in rate of disappearance of streptovaricin from the blood may well be due to the effects of the anesthetic, it is apparent that renal excretion does not account for the rapid decline in blood levels of this drug.

Tissue levels of streptovaricin after intravenous and oral administration of streptovaricin in the dog. To investigate the tissue levels of streptovaricin after intravenous administration each of 5 dogs was given a dose of 20 mgm./kgm. as a solution containing 50 mgm./ml. in 45 per cent ethanol. Blood samples were taken at the indicated times for assay. The results are shown in table 4.

At the terminal hour, each dog was bled and then was sacrificed with an intravenous injection of magnesium sulfate. The heart, lungs, liver, kidneys and spleen were removed. A sample of small intestine, carefully cleaned, was assayed as "smooth muscle." A sample of skeletal muscle was also removed. The contents of the gall bladder were saved, along with a sample of cerebrospinal fluid and aqueous humor. The results of the assays expressed as microgm. of streptovaricin/gm. of wet tissue are shown in column "a" of table 5. The total amounts of streptovaricin in each organ is shown in column "b" of table 5.

While the data presented must be interpreted cautiously as only one animal for each time interval was used, it can be seen from the data in table 6 that 5 minutes after injection only 60 per cent of the drug can be accounted for. In 1 hour, approximately two-thirds of the drug has disappeared and 3 to 4 hours post injection less than 4 per cent remains. When the ratio of tissue level

TABLE 5

Concentration and total quantity of streptovaricin in tissues after the intravenous dose of 20 mgm./kgm. of 70 per cent streptovaricin

Dog No.	1		2		3		4		5	
Time Sacrificed	5 min.		1 hr.		2 hr.		3 hr.		4 hr.	
Weight	13.2 kgm.		11.5 kgm.		15.7 kgm.		11.8 kgm.		13.2 kgm.	
Mgm. of Antibiotic Activity Given	185 mgm.		160 mgm.		220 mgm.		165 mgm.		185 mgm.	
Organ	a	b	a	b	a	b	a	b	a	b
Spleen	47.5	0.97	5.9	0.18	3.9	0.43	0.1	0.04	0.4	0.02
Liver	43.1	16.50	13.0	3.53	8.4	3.09	1.5	0.53	0.8	0.39
Kidney	43.5	2.19	8.7	0.35	5.4	0.35	1.0	0.05	0.6	0.05
Heart	37.5	3.86	6.3	0.38	2.2	0.22	0.7	0.06	0.1	0.02
Lungs	116.0	9.55	5.4	0.38	5.7	0.71	1.0	0.09	0	0
Skeletal muscle*	3.6	21.8	5.7	33.2	4.0	47.3	0.6	3.82	0.3	2.32
"Smooth muscle"*	13.3	8.75	6.3	3.62	6.0	4.72	1.9	1.12	0.7	0.44
Terminal serum*	14.2	48.6	4.8	2.23	3.9	2.45	0.3	0.16	0.2	0.11
Bile*	130.0	0.19	125.0	6.62	138.0	3.37	47.0	0.57	24.8	3.86
Cerebrospinal fluid	3.7	—	1.6	—	—	—	0	—	0	—
Aqueous humor	2.0	—	1.11	—	0.7	—	0.4	—	0.5	—
Total Recovery										
mgm	112.4		50.84		62.64		6.44		7.19	
per cent of dose	60.75		31.55		28.47		3.90		3.88	

a) Microgms. of streptovaricin/gm. wet weight of tissue.

b) Total mgm. of streptovaricin in organ.

* Total values estimated on the basis of 50 per cent, 5 per cent and 4 per cent of body weight respectively.

† Cystic bile only.

TABLE 6

Serum levels of streptovaricin (mgm./ml.) after oral administration of streptovaricin complex, 50 mgm./kgm.

Dog No.	1	2	3
Time Sacrificed	2 hr.	4 hr.	6 hr.
Time Post Adminstration			
1	0	0.5	0
2	0.6	0.9	1.7
3		3.0	2.1
4		3.7	1.4
5			0.8
6			0.6

to serum level of streptovaricin was calculated, the highest ratio was found for liver. The drug was also markedly concentrated in the bile.

These experiments were repeated on 3 dogs using the oral route of administration. Each animal was fasted for 18 hours and then given 50 ml. of 0.1 *N* HCl prior to a capsule containing streptovaricin complex equivalent to a dose of 50 mgm./kgm. Blood samples were taken at the times indicated and assayed; these data are shown in table 6. Immediately after the terminal blood sample was taken, each dog was sacrificed with an injection of magnesium sulfate and the same tissues were removed and analyzed. The results are shown in table 7. The peak values seen at 4 hours are indicative of a continuous absorption of the antibiotic at a faster rate than the drug is eliminated through the kidney, the bile or by enzyme degradation.

There was no significant concentration of the antibiotic in any one organ which would explain its rapid disappearance from the blood; this was true after both intravenous and oral administration. The extremely rapid rate of diffusion of streptovaricin is shown by its appearance in the spinal fluid and aqueous humor of the eye as early as 5 minutes after an i.v. dose. The high

TABLE 7

Tissue levels of streptovaricin in experimental dogs after oral administration of 50 per cent biologically active streptovaricin complex at a dose of 50 mgm./kgm.

Dog No.	1		2		3	
Time Sacrificed	2 hr.		4 hr.		6 hr.	
Weight	14.4 kgm.		13.8 kgm.		9.0 kgm.	
Mgm. of Antibiotic Activity Given	360 mgm.		345 mgm.		225 mgm.	
Organ	a	b	a	b	a	b
Spleen	1.4	0.07	4.6	0.45	0.9	0.04
Liver	6.9	2.21	15.8	5.26	3.4	0.70
Kidney	1.7	C.12	7.9	0.45	1.4	0.05
Heart	0.9	0.09	3.8	0.33	0.7	0.05
Lungs	1.3	0.11	2.1	0.23	1.0	0.07
Skeletal muscle*	4.2	30.6	7.2	49.7	0.9	4.05
"Smooth Muscle"*	66.5	47.9	20.0	13.8	1.1	0.51
Terminal Serum*	0.60	0.34	3.7	2.04	0.62	0.37
Bile	67.5	0.23	171.0	1.28	43.7	1.97
Cerebrospinal Fluid	0	—	0	—	0	—
Aqueous Humor	0	—	0.57	—	3.7	—
Total Recovery						
mgm.	81.7		73.5		7.8	
per cent of dose	22.7		21.5		3.46	

a) Microgms. of streptovaricin/gm. wet weight of tissue.
b) Total mgm. of streptovaricin in organ.
* Total values estimated on the basis of 50 per cent, 5 per cent and 4 per cent of body weight respectively.

value for "smooth muscle" is interesting and may represent absorbed drug in the gut mucosa.

Biliary and renal excretion of dalacin. The extent of renal and biliary excretion was investigated beginning with a pilot experiment as follows. A dog was anesthetized with 20 mgm./kgm. of thiopental and 250 mgm./kgm. of barbital. The duodenum was opened and a polyethylene cannula was inserted into the common bile duct. When good bile flow was evident, the dog was given an intravenous injection of 20 mgm./kgm. of 70 per cent streptovaricin in 45 per cent ethanol. Blood and bile samples were taken at the times indicated in table 8. The bile was diluted with absolute alcohol and appropriate concentrations were applied to paper discs in the same fashion as other samples. At the conclusion of the experiment the entire contents of the urinary bladder were removed, lyophilized and made up to a volume of 100 ml. An aliquot of this solution was extracted with chloroform and assayed. The results of this study are included in table 8 as experiment 1. In a second experiment 2 female dogs (#2 and #3) were anesthetized and operated as before. A Foley catheter was inserted into the urinary bladder and hourly samples of urine were collected. After each sample was removed, the bladder was washed with 20 ml. of water and the washings were added to the sample. The urine was then extracted with chloroform and the extracts assayed in the usual fashion. Results are shown in table 8. It is apparent that while the antibiotic is concentrated to a marked degree in the bile, the total excretion of streptovaricin by this route and also through the kidney accounts for a minor portion of the administered dose.

Discussion. The data demonstrate that streptovaricin is absorbed throughout the entire gastrointestinal tract with the possible exception of the stomach. While it is impossible to quantitate accurately the extent of gastrointestinal absorption due to our inability to distinguish between absorbed versus degraded antibiotic, the following considerations lead to the conclusion that the drug is absorbed to a considerable degree from the gut.

After intravenous administration of streptovaricin there is a rapid decline in serum and tissue levels such that 3 hours post injection, less than 4 per cent of the total dose can be accounted for. In contrast, following oral administration serum levels of streptovaricin persist at nearly peak levels for the 3- to 6-hour period after administration, and tissue levels at 2 and 4 hours account for approximately 20 per cent of the dose. Thus, instead of the precipitous decline in serum levels observed after a single intravenous injection, after oral administration serum levels remain relatively constant over a period of several hours. Tissue levels increase to a maximum at approximately 4 hours followed by a decrease observed at 6 hours. Since rapid destruction of the antibiotic occurs after intravenous and oral administration, the fact that after an oral dose serum and tissue levels steadily increase for at least a 4-hour period must mean that continuous absorption from the gut occurs at a rate above and beyond the rates of elimination and degradation.

Calculations on the rates of elimination of streptovaricin from the blood of dogs following intravenous administration show that 80 to 90 per cent of the dose disappears in the first minute. A true half-life for this primary period cannot be calculated. In the second period of 1 minute to approximately 90 minutes the average half-life of 27 minutes was calculated. The half-life values

TABLE 8

Biliary and renal excretion of streptovaricin

Dog No.	1			2			3		
Antibiotic Activity Administered	185 mgm.			185 mgm.			210 mgm.		
Hour	Serum Conc.	Total Antibiotic in Bile	Total Antibiotic in Urine	Serum Conc.	Total Antibiotic in Bile	Total Antibiotic in Urine	Serum Conc.	Total Antibiotic in Bile	Total Antibiotic in Urine
	μgm./ml.	*mgm.*	*mgm.*	*μgm./ml.*	*mgm.*	*mgm.*	*μgm./ml.*	*mgm.*	*mgm.*
0	0	0	0	0	0	0	0	0	0
1 min.	47	—	—	104.5	—	—	77	—	—
30 min.	27.3	—	—	16.5	—	—	9.5	—	—
1 hr.	18.2	3.20	—	7.5	0.90	1.15	5.7	1.74	2.10
2 hr.	14.0	1.80	—	3.0	0.70	0.77	2.7	2.88	1.00
3 hr.	9.6	2.01	—	4.5	0.84	0.45	2.6	1.19	0.89
4 hr.	7.4	2.70	—	1.8	1.10	0.29	1.6	0.80	1.18
5 hr.	5.1	2.21	—	—	0.02	0.64	1.3	0.57	0.45
				Expt. terminated					
6 hr.	5.1	2.30	12.28	—	—	—	3.5	0.38	0.43
	Expt. terminated								
8 hr.	—	—	—	—	—	—	4.5	0.55	0.59
12 hr.	—	—	—	—	—	—	1.9	0.24	0.54
Total Amt. in Cystic Bile		0			0			1.84	
Total Amt. Excr. in Bile and Urine		14.22	12.28		3.56	3.3		10.19	7.18
Amt. Excr. as per cent of Dose Adm.		7.7	6.6		1.9	1.8		4.9	3.4

for the tertiary period of 90 minutes to complete disappearance was found to be 98 minutes.

Plough *et al.* (1956) reported average half-lives for thiopental in the plasma of dogs of 4 minutes in the 0 to 10 minutes range post injection. In the period 10 to 45 minutes the average half-life was 32 minutes. In the subsequent period of 45 minutes to complete disappearance of the drug, the calculated half-life was 188 minutes. It is thus apparent that the rate of disappearance of streptovaricin from the blood is considerably faster than that of thiopental.

Streptovaricin is practically insoluble in fat and it is not taken up by the cellular elements of blood. The data show that no one organ concentrated the drug to the degree necessary to account for its rapid disappearance. Urinary and biliary excretion of the unchanged antibiotic account for insignificant percentages of the administered dose. Therefore, the rapid decline in blood and tissue levels of streptovaricin must be due to a notably rapid and efficient enzymic destruction.

SUMMARY

Streptovaricin has been shown to be well absorbed from all parts of the digestive tract of dogs with the possible exception of the stomach. Following intravenous administration antibiotic activity disappears from the blood at a considerably faster rate than thiopental. Tissue levels also decline at a very rapid rate. The antibiotic is not excreted to a significant degree in the urine and bile, nor is it stored in tissues to an appreciable degree.

ACKNOWLEDGEMENTS. The authors wish to thank Dr. W. A. Freyburger and Dr. P. H. Seay for their help with some of the surgical procedures, Dr. W. T. Sokolski for providing agar plates, Dr. O. S. Carpenter for some of the statistical analyses and Dr. M. J. Vander Brook and Dr. M. E. Greig for advice and help in the preparation of the manuscript.

REFERENCES

PERRY, J. J., SOKOLSKI, W. T., BURCH, M. R., AND FOLKERTSMA, J. P.: Antibiotics Annual, 1957–1958, Medical Encyclopedia Co., N. Y., 1958 (in press).

PLOUGH, I. C., WALDSTEIN, S. S., BARILA, T. G., AND GOLDBAUM, L. R.: THIS JOURNAL, **116**: 486, 1956.

RHULAND, L. E., STERN, K. F., AND REAMES, H. R.: Am. Rev. Tuberc., **75**: 588, 1957.

SIMINOFF, P., SMITH, R. M., SOKOLSKI, W. T., AND SAVAGE, G. M.: Am. Rev. Tuberc., **75**: 576, 1957.

WHITFIELD, G. B., OLSON, E. C., HERR, R. R., FOX, J. A., BERGY, M. E., AND BOYACK, G. A.: Am. Rev. Tuberc., **75**: 584, 1957.

8053

COMPARISON OF THE VASCULAR ACTIONS OF 1,1-DIMETHYL-4-PHENYLPIPERAZINIUM AND TETRAMETHYLAMMONIUM[1]

MARTIN M. WINBURY

Scientific Research Division, Department of Pharmacology, Schering Corporation, Bloomfield, New Jersey

Received for publication March 28, 1958

The potent ganglionic stimulating activity of 1,1-dimethyl-4-phenylpiperazinium (DMPP) was first demonstrated by Chen, Portman and Wickel (1951) and Chen and Parcell (1954). An investigation of the cardiovascular actions of DMPP by Page and McCubbin (1953a, b) indicated that the DMPP vasopressor response results from several actions which include stimulation of peripheral sympathetic ganglia and stimulation of the adrenal glands to release epinephrine (Epi) and norepinephrine (levarterenol) (nor-Epi). They found no *direct* action on the blood vessels of the denervated hind limb of the dog, but observed a vasoconstrictor effect in the innervated kidney. However, in a recent study (Winbury, Wolf and Tabachnick, 1958), DMPP was found to have a direct vasodilator action on the dog hind limb.

Because of the interest in DMPP as a relatively "pure" ganglionic stimulant, a comparison of the vascular effects of DMPP with another ganglionic stimulant, tetramethylammonium (TMA), seemed warranted. This report describes the effects of these compounds on blood pressure and blood flow following intravenous and intraarterial administration. Autonomic stimulating and blocking agents were used in attempts to determine the pharmacological mechanisms involved.

METHODS. A total of 34 dogs was used in this study. In the majority of experiments, the animals were anesthetized with sodium thiopental (Pentothal), 20 to 30 mgm./kgm. i.v., followed by *alpha*-chloralose, 60 to 80 mgm./kgm. i.v. Additional doses of 10 to 20 mgm. of chloralose were given as needed to maintain a steady state of anesthesia. In a few experiments, sodium pentobarbital (Nembutal), 30 mgm./kgm. i.v., was employed for anesthesia.

The rate of blood flow in the femoral artery was determined with a recording rotameter (Shipley and Wilson, 1951). The inflow to the rotameter was connected to the central end of a sectioned carotid or femoral artery. The outflow from the rotameter was connected to the peripheral end of a sectioned femoral artery. The blood pressure was recorded with a pressure transducer at the inflow tubing to the rotameter close to the arterial cannula. The blood pressure and blood flow were recorded simultaneously on a direct writing electronic recorder. In some of the experiments, positive pressure artificial respiration was used to reduce phasic changes in blood flow.

Heparin was employed as the anticoagulant (initial intravenous dose: 1400 units/kgm.; supplemental dose after several hours: 350 units/kgm.). Pontamine Fast Pink BL frequently was employed to supplement the action of the heparin (10 to 25 ml. of a 5 per cent solution i.v. slowly, Winbury *et al.*, 1950).

Intravenous injections were made into the cannulated femoral or jugular vein. Intraarterial injections were made into the outflow tubing from the rotameter close to the cannula in the peripheral end of the artery. For the intraarterial studies, the compounds were dissolved in 0.9 per cent sodium chloride and administered in volumes of less than 0.2 ml. In each experiment, the intravenous and intraarterial actions of TMA were compared with those of DMPP.

In several experiments on the intraarterial action of the compounds, the hind limb was denervated one-half to one hour previous to the injection of drugs by sectioning the sciatic nerve plexus and femoral nerve. The femoral artery was sectioned during the cannulation procedure. According to Clonninger and Green (1955) this procedure eliminates the sympathetic supply to the limb.

RESULTS. Although TMA and DMPP produce the same general effects on the vascular

[1] A preliminary report of some of this work was presented at the 1957 Fall meeting of the American Society for Pharmacology and Experimental Therapeutics in Baltimore, Maryland.

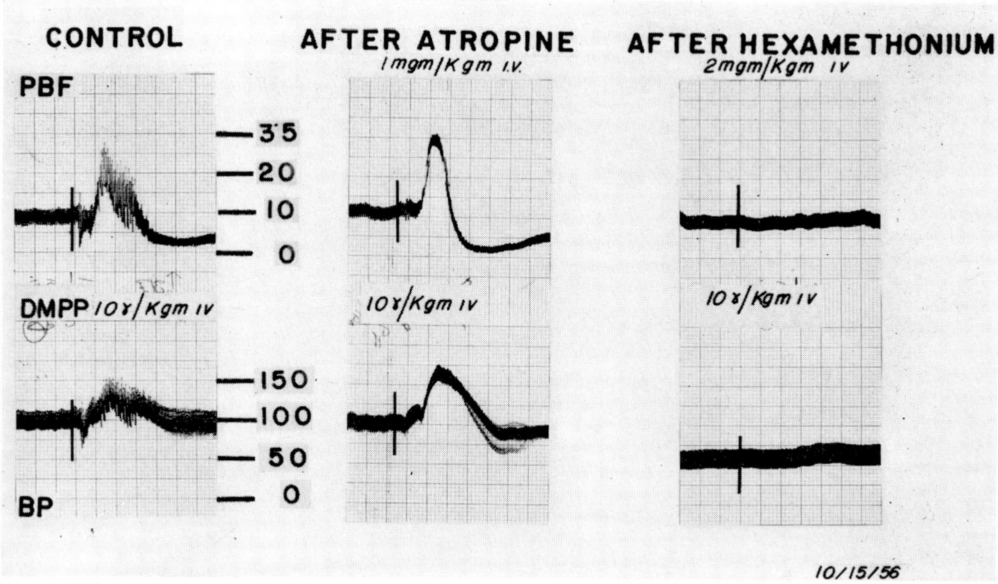

FIG. 1. Effect of atropine and hexamethonium on the response to intravenous injection of DMPP. PBF is femoral blood flow rate (ml./min.); BP is systemic blood pressure (mm. Hg). The heavy vertical bar indicates the point of injection. Each heavy time line represents 20 sec. Note absence of initial hypotensive effect in BP record after atropine.

system, there are fundamental differences in the pharmacological mechanisms involved. TMA shows two types of autonomic cholinergic stimulatory action (ganglionic and peripheral) while DMPP shows primarily ganglionic stimulating action. Intravenous injection of TMA or DMPP produced a rise in blood pressure which was blocked by hexamethonium (ganglionic stimulation). Intraarterial injection of TMA produced a local vasodilatation which was blocked by atropine (cholinergic-like stimulation). Intraarterial injection of DMPP most frequently produced dilatation, but this response was blocked by hexamethonium and not by atropine (possibly ganglionic stimulation).

I. Effects of intravenous administration. A. Depressor and pressor response: TMA and DMPP produced qualitatively similar effects on intravenous injection. A typical response consisted of two phases: 1) an initial transient depressor effect followed by 2) a sharp and more prolonged pressor response (fig. 1, 2 and 3; control tracings). The brief depressor response was associated with bradycardia while the initial stage of the pressor response was associated with tachycardia. These effects were produced by a dose of 5 to 10 microgm./kgm. of DMPP and 40 to 80 microgm./kgm. of TMA. Lower doses revealed a difference between the two compounds; DMPP elicited no effect but TMA produced a depressor response only, similar to that of acetylcholine (ACh).

B. Changes in blood flow: The pattern of changes in blood flow was similar to that observed on blood pressure, namely, a slight decline followed by a sharp rise in flow. However, in spite of the elevated blood pressure, the flow rate rapidly declined from the peak to below the control level (fig. 1, 2 and 3). The initial phases of the flow response probably are due to the alterations in blood pressure; the sharp decline in flow rate probably is due to a local vasoconstriction resulting from stimulation of the sympathetic vasomotor ganglia and from the circulating epinephrine (Epi) and norepinephrine (nor-Epi) released from the adrenal glands (Page and McCubbin, 1953a) by DMPP.

C. Elimination of the depressor response by peripheral cholinergic effector blockade: Atropine, 1 mgm./kgm. i.v., eliminated the initial depressor and bradycardic effect of both compounds (fig. 1); the pressor response was usually enhanced. Subsequent administration of hexamethonium blocked the remaining pressor effect (see section on ganglionic blockade, I D).

It is interesting to note that after atropine

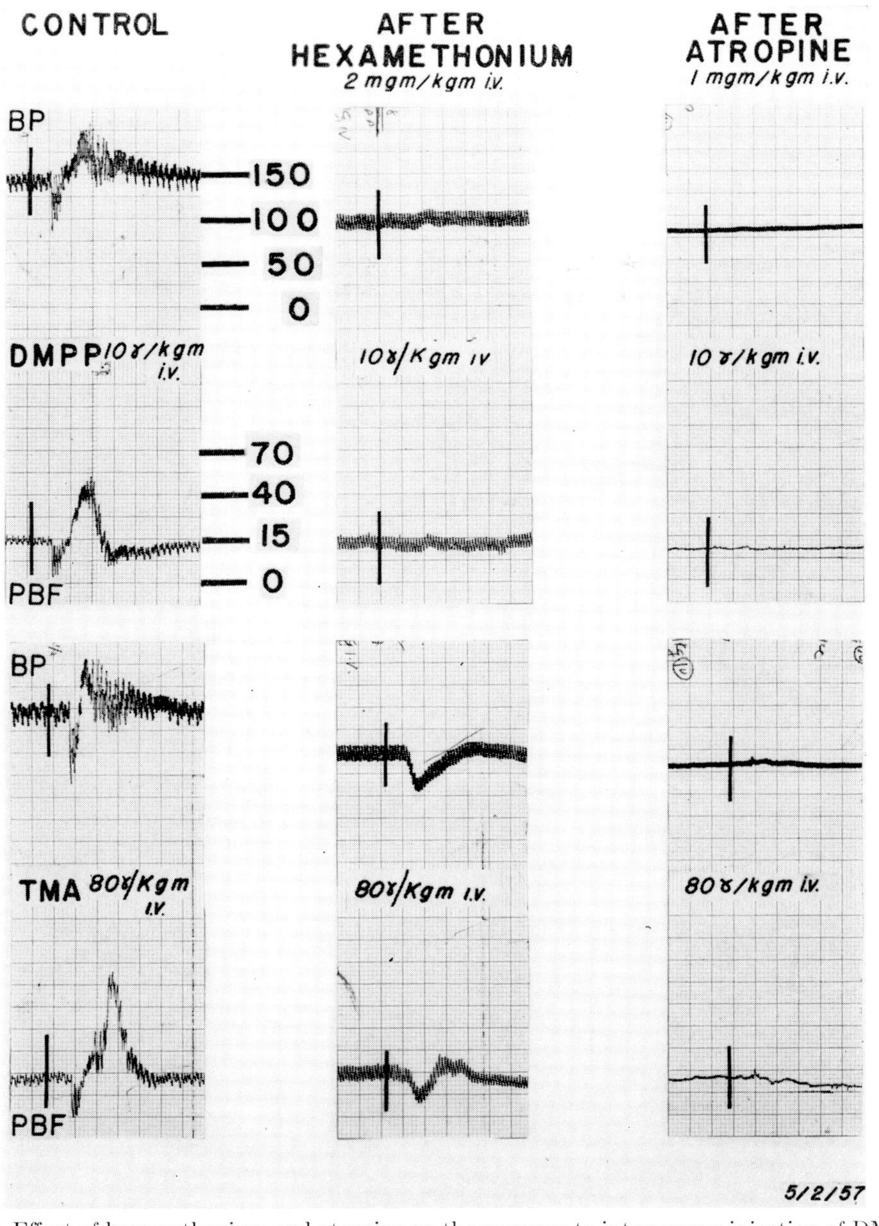

FIG. 2. Effect of hexamethonium and atropine on the response to intravenous injection of DMPP and TMA.

PBF is femoral blood flow rate; BP is systemic blood pressure. Remainder of legend as in fig. 1. Note preservation of hypotensive effect of TMA after hexamethonium.

blockade, the vasoconstriction which follows the peak flow rate was more pronounced.

D. Elimination of the entire response to DMPP and the pressor response to TMA by ganglionic blockade: Hexamethonium, 2 mgm./kgm. i.v., blocked the intravenous effect of DMPP completely, but *only* the pressor effect of TMA (fig. 2). The depressor component of TMA occurred at the same time as it did during the control period. This indicates that there merely was a preservation of the initial depressor component of the TMA response, and not a "reversal" phenomenon. Atropine subsequently blocked this depressor action.

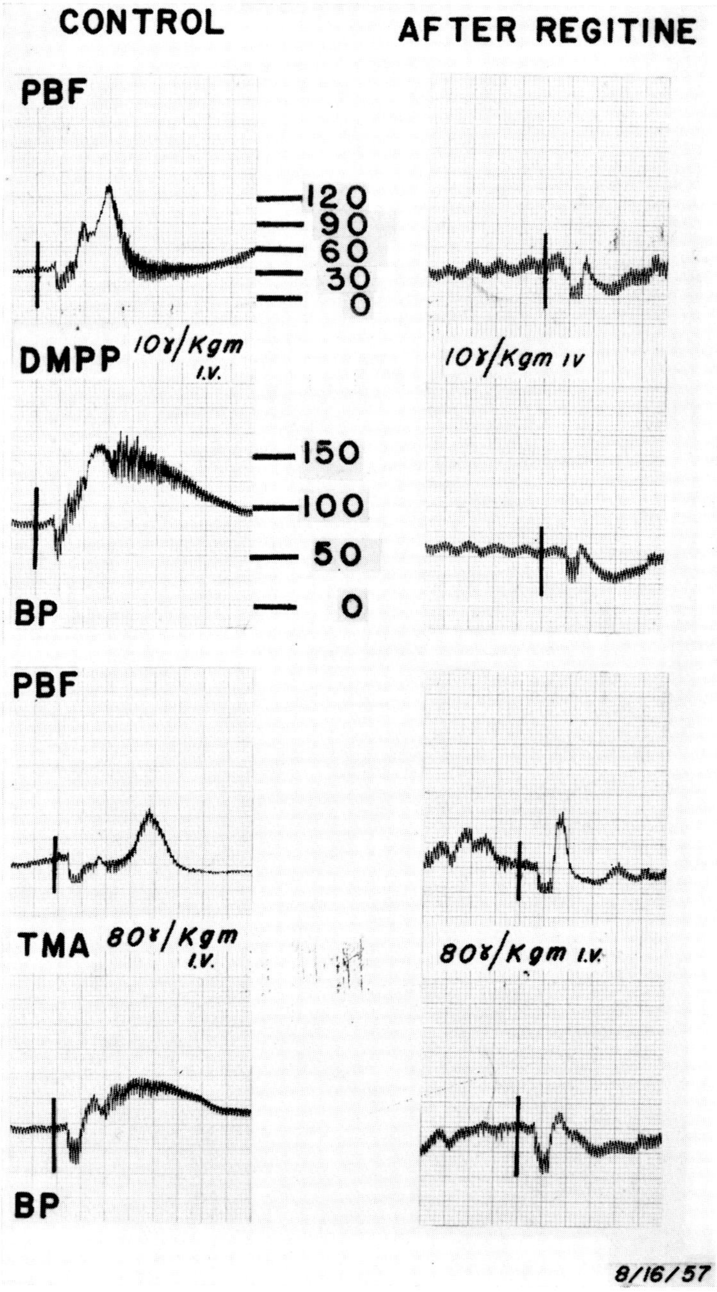

FIG. 3. Effect of phentolamine (Regitine), 2 mgm./kgm. i.v., on the response to intravenous injection of DMPP and TMA.

PBF is femoral blood flow rate; BP is systemic blood pressure. Remainder of legend as in fig. 1.

E. Reversal of pressor response by adrenergic effector blockade: Phentolamine (Regitine), 2 mgm./kgm. i.v., or azapetine (Ilidar), 2 to 6 mgm./kgm. i.v., reversed the pressor response to DMPP or TMA but did not alter the depressor response (fig. 3). Thus, a two-stage decline in pressure resulted. The first decline was rapid and corresponds to the initial depressor response observed before adrenergic blockade. The second stage, a more prolonged decline, was

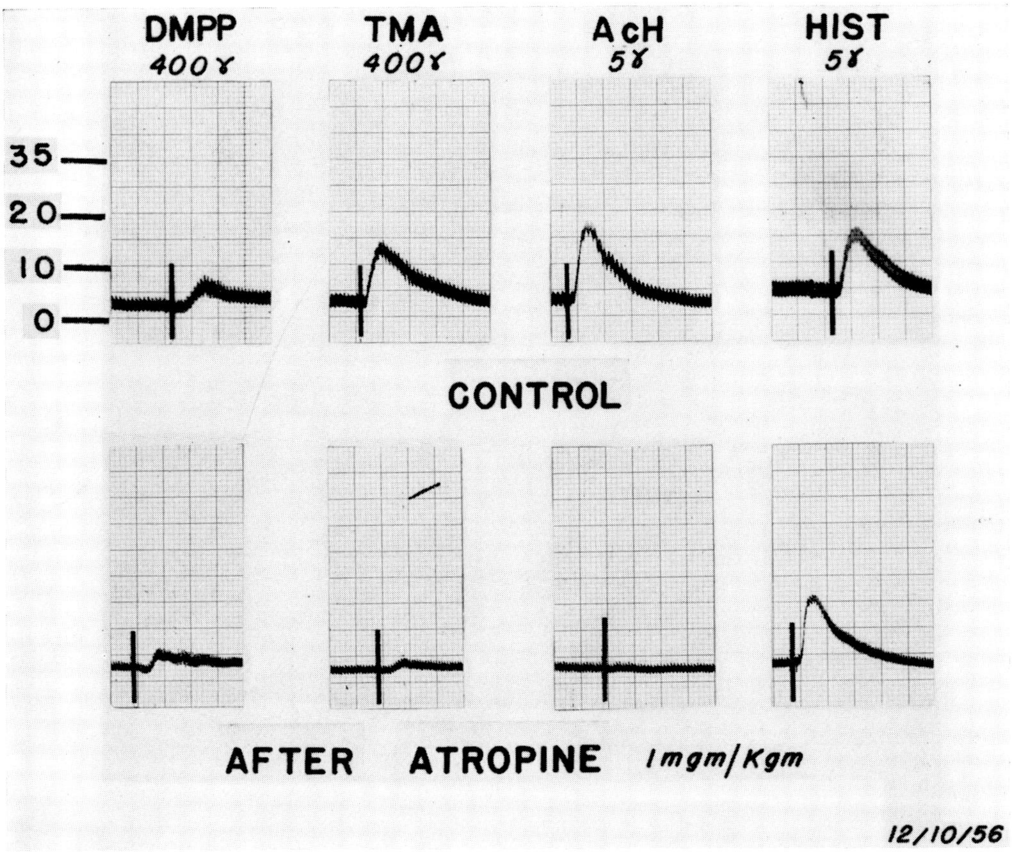

FIG. 4. Effect of atropine on the vasodilatation produced by intraarterial injection of DMPP, TMA, ACh and Hist.

The records show the changes in femoral artery blood flow rate. Scale is in ml./min. Remainder of legend as in fig. 1.

probably associated with a "reversal" of the action of the epinephrine and norepinephrine released at the adrenergic vasomotor endings and from the adrenal glands (see section II F).

F. Mechanism of depressor and pressor response: Since hexamethonium eliminated both the depressor and pressor effects of DMPP, it is likely that ganglionic stimulation is involved in both phases of the DMPP response. On the other hand, the response to TMA involved peripheral cholinergic effector site stimulation (cholinomimetic action) in addition to ganglionic stimulation. The initial depressor response to TMA probably results primarily from the cholinomimetic action. The facts that tend to confirm this are: 1) the depressor response is not blocked by hexamethonium but is blocked by atropine and 2) low doses of TMA produced only hypotension (like ACh). The pressor response to TMA involves ganglionic stimulation like DMPP.

II. Effects of intraarterial administration. A. Dilator response to intraarterial TMA: Effective doses (100 to 400 microgm., total dose) always produced an increase in blood flow (vasodilatation) with no change in arterial pressure. A typical response consisted of a rapid rise in flow rate with a gradual decline to control levels (fig. 4, 5, 6 and 7). No constrictor response was observed.

B. Dilator and constrictor response to intraarterial DMPP: The usual response to DMPP (100 to 500 microgm., total dose) was vasodilatation, but in a few animals vasoconstriction was observed at the start of an experiment. The dilator response (fig. 4, 5 and 6) persisted throughout the experiment unless blocking agents were used (see below). The constrictor response (fig. 7) did not persist and changed to a dilator response as the experiment progressed. The dilatation produced by DMPP was similar to that of TMA

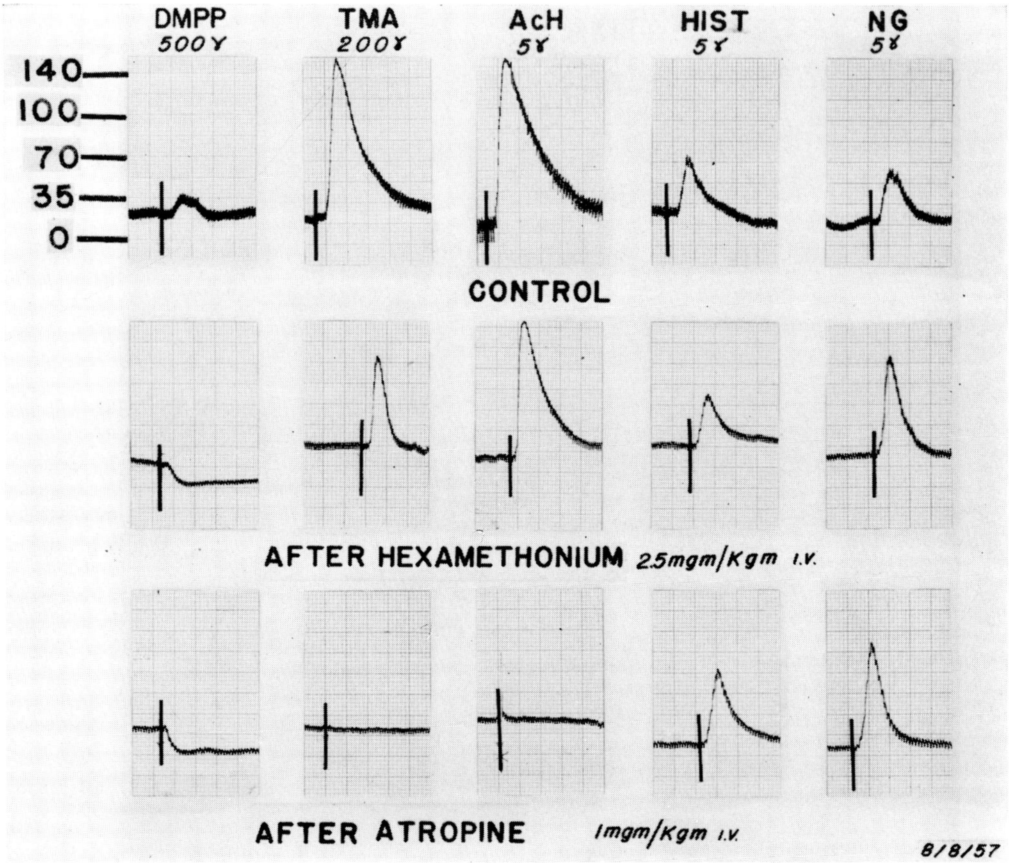

FIG. 5. Effect of hexamethonium and atropine on the vasodilatation produced by intraarterial injection of DMPP, TMA, ACh, Hist and nitroglycerine (NG).

Remainder of legend as in fig. 1. Note vasoconstriction of DMPP after hexamethonium.

but it was never possible to produce as great a maximal response with DMPP because systemic effects[2] intervened at higher doses.

C. Local vascular actions of other compounds: Other compounds that consistently produced vasodilatation, on intraarterial injection, like that of TMA are: ACh (0.5 to 10 microgm.); histamine (Hist, 1 to 10 microgm.); nitroglycerine (NG, 5 microgm.) and isoproterenol (Isuprel, 0.25 to 1 microgm.). Intraarterial injection of Epi or nor-Epi (1 to 5 microgm.) usually produced vasoconstriction.

D. Elimination of dilator response to intraarterial TMA and ACh by cholinergic effector blockade: Atropine, 1 mgm./kgm. i.v., blocked the vasodilator effect of TMA and ACh (fig. 4). There was no "reversal" to a constrictor effect. The actions of DMPP, Hist, Isuprel or NG were not affected.

E. Elimination of dilator response to intraarterial DMPP by ganglionic blockade; appearance of constrictor response: Hexamethonium, 2 to 3 mgm./kgm. i.v., blocked the vasodilator effect of DMPP; in fact, a vasoconstrictor response appeared in almost every case (fig. 5). The dilator responses to TMA and ACh were not affected by hexamethonium, but were eliminated by the subsequent administration of atropine. The fact that Hist and NG were active after ganglionic and peripheral cholinergic blockade indicated that the vascular bed was capable of dilatation.

F. Reduction of dilator response to intra-

[2] In addition to the local dilator action, the intraarterial injection of DMPP also produced systemic effects, in some of the animals, on reaching the general circulation. The systemic response, observed 30 to 40 seconds after the intraarterial injection, was identical with the systemic response following intravenous injection and consisted of a rise in blood pressure and flow rate.

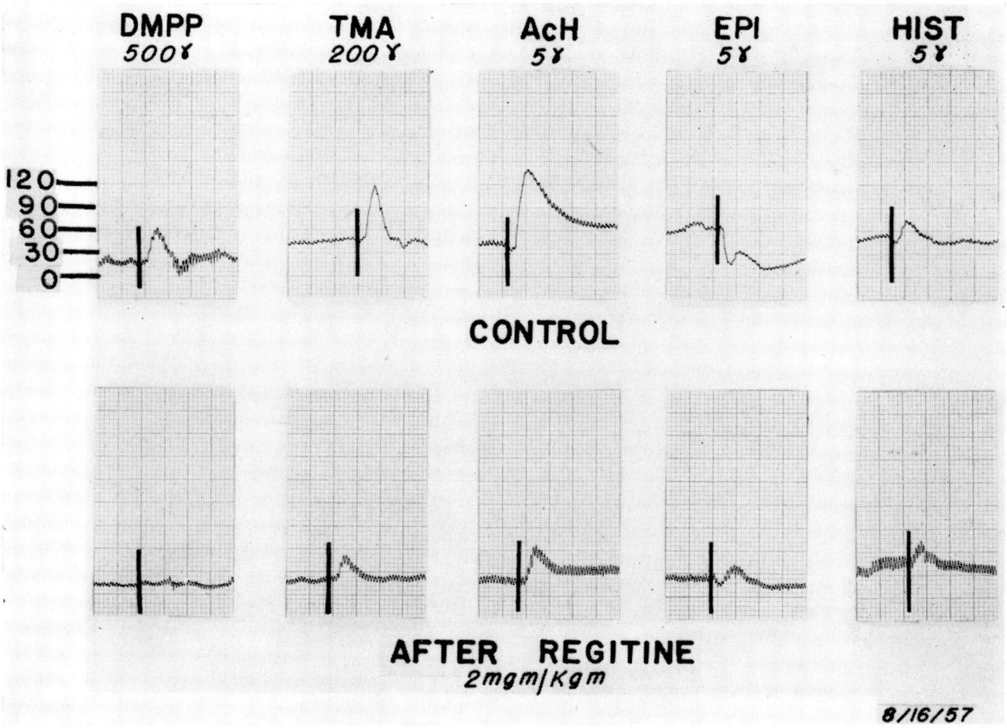

FIG. 6. Effect of phentolamine (Regitine) on the response to intraarterial injection of DMPP, TMA, ACh, Epi and Hist. Remainder of legend as in fig. 1.

arterial DMPP by adrenergic effector blockade: Regitine, 2 mgm./kgm. i.v., or Ilidar, 2 to 6 mgm./kgm. i.v., reduced or blocked the dilator response to DMPP in some experiments. However, this blocking action was not as consistent as that of hexamethonium. The dose of adrenergic blocking agent required to eliminate the dilator effect of DMPP frequently reversed the constrictor effect of Epi (fig. 6) and reduced that of nor-Epi. On the other hand, the dilator response to Isuprel was not altered.

G. Persistence of vasoconstrictor response to intraarterial DMPP which appears after ganglionic blockade: The vasoconstriction produced by DMPP in animals treated with hexamethonium was not blocked by subsequent treatment with atropine or more hexamethonium (fig. 5).

H. Effect of reduction in vascular tone on dilator action of intraarterial DMPP: It seemed possible that the appearance of the local dilator or constrictor response to DMPP could be related to the state of vascular tone, *i.e.* dilator when tone was normal (control state) and constrictor when tone was reduced (after hexamethonium). To test this hypothesis, the vascular tone was reduced by a mechanism other than ganglionic blockade. Vasodilatation was produced in the test limb by intraarterial infusion of NG (200 and 400 microgm./min.) or Hist (16 microgm./min.), and DMPP was injected before, during, and after the infusion. The dilator response to intraarterial DMPP was not altered significantly during the NG or Hist infusion, indicating that the "reversal" by hexamethonium was not due to a reduction in vascular tone.

I. Effect of acute denervation on dilator response to intraarterial DMPP and TMA: Page and McCubbin (1953a) indicated that DMPP had no effect on the denervated hind limb. Since the results described in the previous sections were obtained from studies on limbs with an intact innervation, it was of interest to determine if denervation would alter any of these responses. Two types of studies were carried out in different groups of animals. In one group, the compounds were compared in a normal and a denervated limb. In the other group, the response was determined in the same limb before

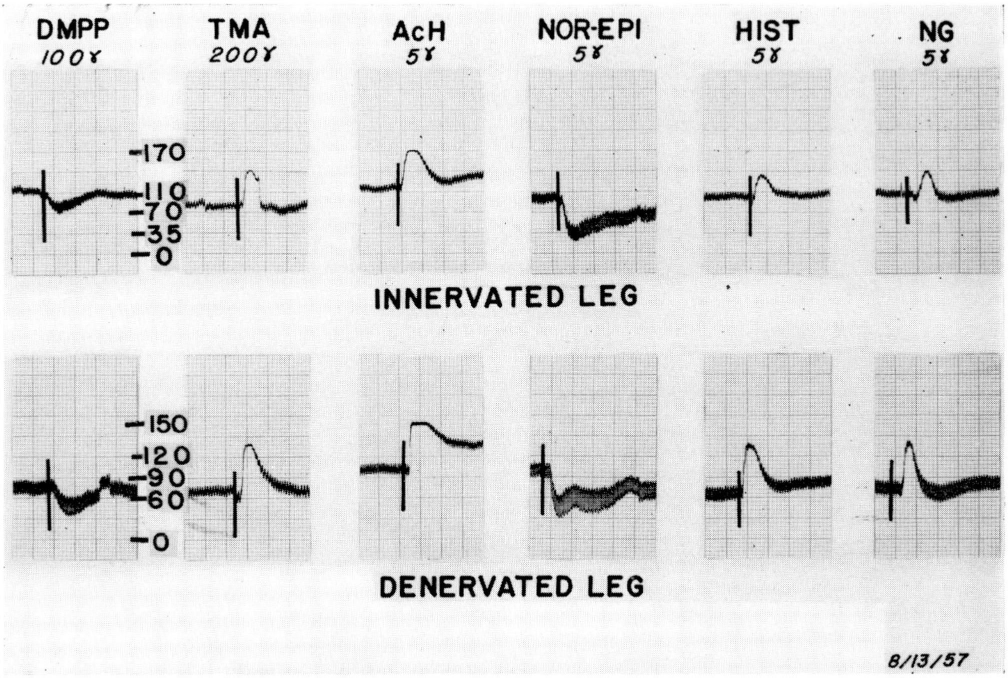

FIG. 7. Comparison of response in a normal and denervated hind limb in same animal.
The sciatic nerve plexus and femoral nerve were sectioned about 45 minutes before injections were started. Compounds by intraarterial injection. Remainder of legend as in fig. 1. Note vasoconstrictor effect of DMPP.

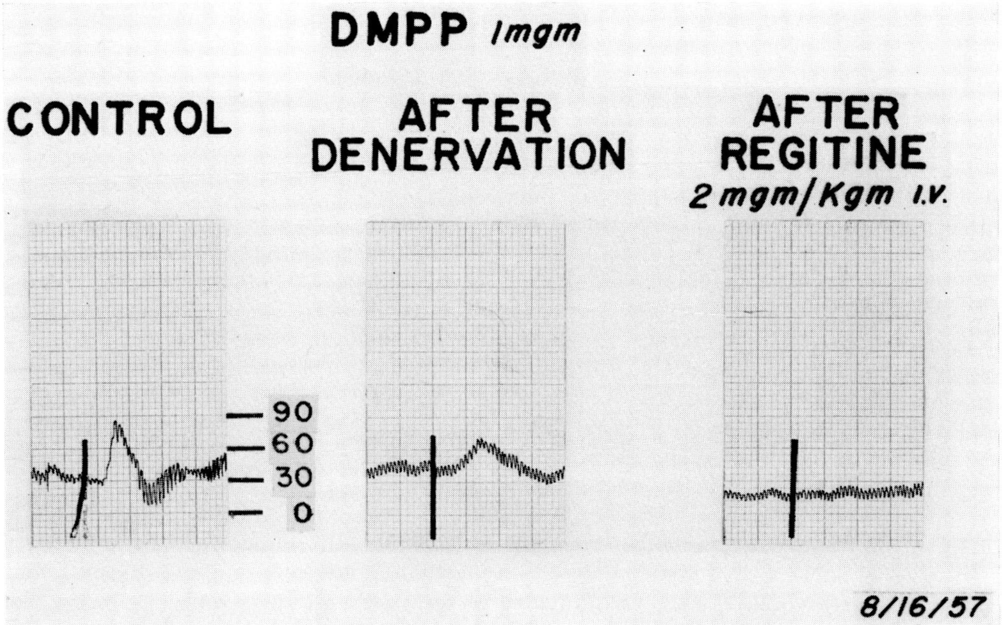

FIG. 8. Comparison of vasodilator response to DMPP before and after denervation-blockade by phentolamine (Regitine).
Denervation performed between first and second panel. Regitine given between second and third panel. DMPP by intraarterial route. Remainder of legend as in fig. 1.

and after denervation. The results illustrated in figures 7 and 8 demonstrate that denervation did not alter the dilator response to TMA or DMPP nor the occasional constrictor response to DMPP. The responses to other vasodilator or vasoconstrictor agents also were not altered. The slight reduction in the dilator action of DMPP after denervation in figure 8 is well within the variation found under normal circumstances.

J. Mechanism of dilator response to TMA: The local dilator action of TMA is pharmacologically identical to that of ACh, *i.e.* peripheral cholinergic effector site stimulation. Both compounds were blocked by atropine but not by hexamethonium, Regitine or Ilidar. It is unlikely that TMA has a local effect analogous to that of DMPP since there was no appearance of an atropine "resistant" vasodilatation. This would be expected if any ganglionic effect contributed to the response.

K. Interrelation of dilator and constrictor response to DMPP: Analysis of the local actions of DMPP, previously cited (table 1), suggested that DMPP had both a dilator and constrictor action; the total response was the sum of the two opposing effects. Under control conditions the dilator action predominated and masked the constrictor action. Hexamethonium, Regitine or Ilidar appeared to block *only* the dilator action and hence unmasked the constrictor action. The latter was resistant to cholinergic and ganglionic blockade.

L. Mechanism of the dilator response to DMPP: There is little doubt that the mechanism involved in the dilator action of DMPP is located in the periphery since acute denervation did not alter this action.

The blockade of the dilator response by hexamethonium suggests that ganglionic stimulation may be involved. This might be considered as supporting the concept of *peripheral ganglion cells* (for review of this subject see Folkow, 1955, 1956). The studies of Kottegoda (1953) and Ginzel and Kottegoda (1953) on nicotine also support this view. They demonstrated that nicotine produced a constrictor effect or, in the presence of tolazoline (Priscoline), a dilator effect, in the normal or chronic sympathectomized rabbit ear which was blocked by hexamethonium.

If an analogy can be drawn with nicotine, *axon reflexes* are another possible mechanism

TABLE 1

Effect of autonomic blocking agents on the intravenous and intraarterial responses to TMA and DMPP

Compound and Route	Control Response	Effect of Blocking Agents		
		Atropine	Hexamethonium	Regitine
Intravenous				
TMA	Depressor	Block	None	None
	Pressor	Enhanced	Block	Reversed
DMPP	Depressor	Block	Block	None
	Pressor	Enhanced	Block	Reversed
Intraarterial				
TMA	Dilator	Block	None	None
DMPP	Dilator	None	Reversed	Block?*
DMPP after hexamethonium	Constrictor	None	None	—
ACh	Dilator	Block	None	None
Epi	Constrictor	None	None	Reversed
Isuprel	Dilator	None	None	None
Hist	Dilator	None	None	None

* Regitine reduced or blocked the dilator response to DMPP in some, but not all experiments.

(Folkow, 1955, 1956). The experiments of Hilton (1953) indicate that nicotine can elicit a local constriction and a local dilation in the muscle of the cat hind limb by axon reflexes. The constrictor response was blocked by chronic sympathectomy and reversed by Regitine suggesting an axon reflex in adrenergic sympathetic fibers. The dilator response was reduced by hexamethonium, chronic denervation or treatment with botulinium toxin suggesting that part of the response is due to an axon reflex in cholinergic vasodilator fibers.

The possibility of *direct action on the smooth muscle* must not be overlooked. The doses of DMPP required to produce the local dilator response were high and may have produced nonspecific stimulation. Certainly, the blockade of the dilator response in some animals by antiadrenergic agents suggests that the "*beta* receptors" of Ahlquist (1948) could somehow be involved.

CONCLUSIONS. TMA and DMPP have many similarities in action on the vascular system. However, it was possible to demonstrate differences in the mechanisms involved by means of cholinergic, ganglionic or adrenergic blockade (table 1). TMA has ganglionic stimulating and cholinomimetic actions, a fact established by the original work of Burn and Dale (1915). The intravenous effects of TMA involve both actions, while the intraarterial effect is cholinomimetic.

DMPP appears to act as a "pure" ganglionic stimulant. Hexamethonium blocked both the depressor and pressor response to intravenous injection and the vasodilator response to intraarterial injection.

The apparent disparity between the results for the intraarterial action of DMPP reported in this communication and those of Page and McCubbin (1953a) may be explained by a difference in the dose range employed. The above investigators found that the intraarterial injection of 50 to 100 microgm. produced no effect on the blood flow in the hind limb. In the present investigation, 100 to 500 microgm. weie required to produce the vasodilator response.

SUMMARY

The vascular actions of 1,1-dimethyl-4-phenylpiperazinium (DMPP) and tetramethylammonium (TMA) were compared in anesthetized dogs. Intravenous injection of both agents produced an initial transient fall in blood pressure followed by a more prolonged rise in pressure.

Hexamethonium blocked both phases of the DMPP action but the hypotensive phase of TMA persisted; this was subsequently blocked by atropine. The hypotensive phase of both compounds was selectively blocked by atropine whereas the hypertensive phase of both compounds was selectively blocked by Regitine.

Intraarterial injection of TMA into the hind limb produced local vasodilation which was blocked by atropine but not by hexamethonium. DMPP most frequently produced local vasodilation on intraarterial injection but vasoconstriction was observed in a few animals at the start of the experiment. This later changed to vasodilatation. The dilator response to DMPP was blocked or converted to a constrictor response by hexamethonium, Regitine and Ilidar, but not by atropine. Acute denervation of the limb did not alter the response to DMPP or TMA.

The results indicate that TMA can stimulate both at the autonomic ganglia and at the peripheral cholinergic effector sites (cholinomimetic action). The mechanism of the local vasodilator action of DMPP is not clear except that it is located in the periphery. It was suggested that it may involve peripheral ganglion cells, an axon reflex or direct stimulation of the smooth muscle in the vessel walls.

ACKNOWLEDGMENT. The author wishes to thank Joanne K. Wolf and Lorraine M. Hausler for aid in completing these studies.

REFERENCES

AHLQUIST, R. P.: Am. J. Physiol., **153:** 586, 1948.
BURN, J. H., AND DALE, H. H.: THIS JOURNAL, **6:** 417, 1915.
CHEN, G., AND PARCELL, R. F.: Arch. internat. pharmacodyn., **97:** 186, 1954.
CHEN, G., PORTMAN, R., AND WICKEL, A.: THIS JOURNAL, **103:** 330, 1951.
CLONNINGER, G. L., AND GREEN, H. D.: Am. J. Physiol., **181:** 258, 1955.
FOLKOW, B.: The Control of the Circulation, Supplemental Volume, pp. 1–86, Wm. Dawson and Sons Ltd., London, 1956.
FOLKOW, B.: Physiol. Rev., **35:** 629, 1955.
GINZEL, K. H., AND KOTTEGODA, S. R.: Brit. J. Pharmacol., **8:** 348, 1953.
HILTON, S. M.: J. Physiol., **123:** 289, 1953.
KOTTEGODA, S. R.: Brit. J. Pharmacol., **8:** 156, 1953.
PAGE, I. H., AND McCUBBIN, J. W.: Am. J. Med., **15:** 675, 1953a.
PAGE, I. H., AND McCUBBIN, J. W.: Am. J. Physiol., **173:** 411, 1953b.
SHIPLEY, R. E., AND WILSON, C.: Proc. Soc. Exper. Biol. & Med., **78:** 724, 1951.
WINBURY, M. M., MICHIELS, P. M., HAMBOURGER, W. E., STOCKFISCH, W. J., AND COOK, D. L.: THIS JOURNAL, **99:** 343, 1950.
WINBURY, M. M., WOLF, J. K., AND TABACHNICK, I. I. A.: THIS JOURNAL, **122:** 207, 1958.

ACTION OF CIGARETTE SMOKE ON CARDIOVASCULAR HEMODYNAMICS AND OXYGEN UTILIZATION IN THE DOG[1, 2]

GERALD A. KIEN,[3] NORMAN LASKER AND THEODORE R. SHERROD

Department of Pharmacology, University of Illinois College of Medicine, Chicago

Received for publication March 24, 1958

Although the hemodynamic responses to cigarette smoking have been studied extensively, both by animal experimentation and clinical investigation, there still remains considerable controversy as to the degree or even the existence of deleterious effects. It has been generally agreed that the most important pharmacologically active substance in cigarette smoke is nicotine (Lehmann, 1908; Baumberger, 1923). It has also been shown that in special situations, such as high altitude flying with low oxygen tension environments, carbon monoxide may also exhibit an appreciable effect on the circulatory system (Barach *et al.*, 1941). Smoking one cigarette results in the absorption of 1 to 4 mgm. of nicotine and in a carbon monoxide blood level of approximately 5 per cent (Baumberger, 1923). The absorption of nicotine results initially in a brief but marked bradycardia. This has been attributed to stimulation of the cardiac vagal ganglia. Following this response, stimulation of the adrenal medulla, as well as the peripheral sympathetic ganglia, occurs (Acheson, 1955). It has been demonstrated by Kiser *et al.* (1956) that the administration of nicotine results in a marked elevation in the epinephrine level of the circulating blood. The release of posterior pituitary hormone due to stimulation of the supraoptic nuclei by nicotine has been demonstrated by Burn and associates (1945). These actions of nicotine result in a transient pressor response.

There are many conflicting reports concerning the action of cigarette smoke on the myocardium and the coronary vasculature. The observation of tobacco-induced angina pectoris by Moschowitz (1928) and Ralli and Oppenheimer (1928), of tobacco-induced electrocardiographic changes by Bryant and Wood (1947) and Russek *et al.* (1955), and of tobacco-induced ballistocardiographic deterioration by Davis *et al.* (1953, 1956) and Henderson (1953) have led to the development of several theories concerning the mechanism of action of cigarette smoke on the myocardium. These investigators postulate that cigarette smoke inhalation results in either a constriction of the coronary arteries or an increase in the work load of the heart beyond the capacity of the coronary arteries to supply the necessary metabolic requirements.

In spite of the numerous investigations concerning the action of cigarette smoke on the myocardium, it is apparent that there are many questions as yet unanswered. The effect of tobacco smoke on the myocardium, cardiac hemodynamics and coronary blood flow is not clear and the many clinical manifestations are likewise not well understood. It is for this reason that it seemed worthwhile to study the time course of the hemodynamic changes in the myocardium, including cardiac work, coronary blood flow and oxygen metabolism, using the anesthetized open-chest dog.

METHODS. Dogs weighing 15 to 25 kgm. were anesthetized intraperitoneally with pentobarbital sodium (30 mgm./kgm. body weight). A tracheal cannula was inserted and the dog maintained on room air by means of a positive pressure respirator. A metal sound of small diameter was inserted into the ascending aorta by way of a carotid artery and blood pressure was measured by means of a Statham blood pressure transducer.

Coronary blood flow was measured with a recording rotameter (Shipley and Wilson, 1951), which was interposed between a femoral artery and the circumflex branch of the left coronary artery. The open-chest dogs were prepared in a manner similar to that described by Winbury *et*

[1] Presented in part before the Society of Experimental Biology and Medicine, Chicago, Illinois, April, 1957.

[2] This investigation was supported in part by a grant from the National Heart Institute, National Institutes of Health.

[3] A portion of these studies was used by Gerald Kien as partial fulfillment of the requirements for the degree of Master of Science at the University of Illinois College of Medicine, Chicago, Illinois.

al. (1950). Heparin sodium[4] (10 mgm./kgm. body weight) was used as the anticoagulant.

Blood pressure, coronary blood flow and several leads of the electrocardiogram were recorded simultaneously on either a Grass or Sanborn multichannel recorder. Cardiac output was determined by the direct Fick procedure. The work of the left ventricle was determined by the following formula (Gregg, 1950): $W = QR + mV^2/2g$, in which W = work of the left ventricle in gm. meters per beat, Q = mean cardiac output in ml. per beat, R = mean aortic blood pressure in meters of Hg, m = mass of blood ejected in gm. per beat, g = gravity factor, 9.8, V = velocity of the blood as it leaves the ventricle in ml. per second.

Cardiac oxygen consumption per minute was measured as the product of the coronary blood flow per minute and the coronary arteriovenous oxygen difference. Coronary venous blood samples were obtained through a soft Koroseal catheter, which was inserted about 1 cm. into the distal end of the great cardiac vein by way of the external jugular vein, the superior vena cava and the coronary sinus. The catheter was guided by manipulation of the heart and its position was confirmed at the termination of each experiment. Coronary venous blood was allowed to flow freely from the catheter and returned to the animal at frequent intervals via a femoral vein. Arterial blood samples were collected from the thoracic aorta with a catheter inserted through a femoral artery. Arterial and venous blood samples were collected simultaneously under anaerobic conditions in glycerinized glass syringes to which mercury was added to facilitate mixing of the cells. Blood samples were immediately refrigerated until analyzed for blood oxygen, both by the method of Van Slyke and Neill (1924) and also by the spectrophotometric method of Nahas (1950).

Cigarette smoke was administered to the dog by placing a standard brand "Kingsize" non-filtered cigarette in a holder adapted to fit the inflow arm of the positive pressure respirator pump. The pump was adjusted to deliver 5 intermittent aliquots of cigarette smoke over a 30 second period with the total quantity of smoke delivered being 1200 to 1500 ml. The cigarette was then removed and the dog again respired with room air.

Withdrawal of the blood samples and measurements of cardiac work were started 1 minute prior to administration of cigarette smoke and continued at 30 second intervals for a 5 minute period or until blood pressure, coronary flow and the electrocardiogram returned to control levels. The blood withdrawn was replaced by an equal quantity of heparinized blood from a donor dog.

Nicotine alkaloid (20 microgm./kgm. body weight) was injected via a femoral vein, and similar studies were done as described for cigarette smoke.

All statistical analyses were made on the basis of paired analysis of control and experimental values obtained at the time of the maximal change in the electrocardiogram.

RESULTS. Figure 1 illustrates the effects of cigarette smoke inhalation on the blood pressure and electrocardiogram of the open-chest anesthetized dog. Following the administration of 1200 to 1500 ml. of cigarette smoke, there usually occurred a marked sinus bradycardia of short duration. This was followed by an increase in blood pressure. There was considerable variation in the degree of the pressor response and in a series of 12 dogs, this varied from 12 to 120 mm. Hg, with a mean increase of 600 mm. Hg. Electrocardiographic changes varied from a depression or inversion of the T-wave to lengthy periods of cardiac arrhythmias in all animals. The electrocardiographic alterations were most frequently observed during the pressor response and occasionally during the period of bradycardia. No correlation was observed between the magnitude of the blood pressure increase and the severity of the electrocardiographic alterations. In many instances electrocardiographic alterations accompanied only a slight increase in blood pressure.

Bilateral vagotomy prior to administration of cigarette smoke failed to alter the extent of the decrease in heart rate. Pretreatment with atropine sulfate (1.0 mgm./kgm. body weight) completely prevented the bradycardia but had no effect on the subsequent cardiac arrhythmias. The pressor response could be prevented entirely by pretreating the animal with piperoxan HCl (Benodain) (2.0 to 4.0 mgm./kgm. body weight); but, again, this did not alter the nature or severity of the electrocardiographic alterations. Denervation of the adrenals or bilateral adrenalectomy significantly reduced the pressor response and cardiac arrhythmias elicited by inhalation of cigarette smoke. Pretreatment with tetraethylammonium chloride (10 mgm./kgm. body weight) completely abolished all cardiovascular responses to cigarette smoke.

Table 1 summarizes the effects of cigarette smoke inhalation on cardiac dynamics and myocardial oxygen consumption at the time of the

[4] The heparin was kindly supplied by Armour Laboratories, Chicago, Illinois.

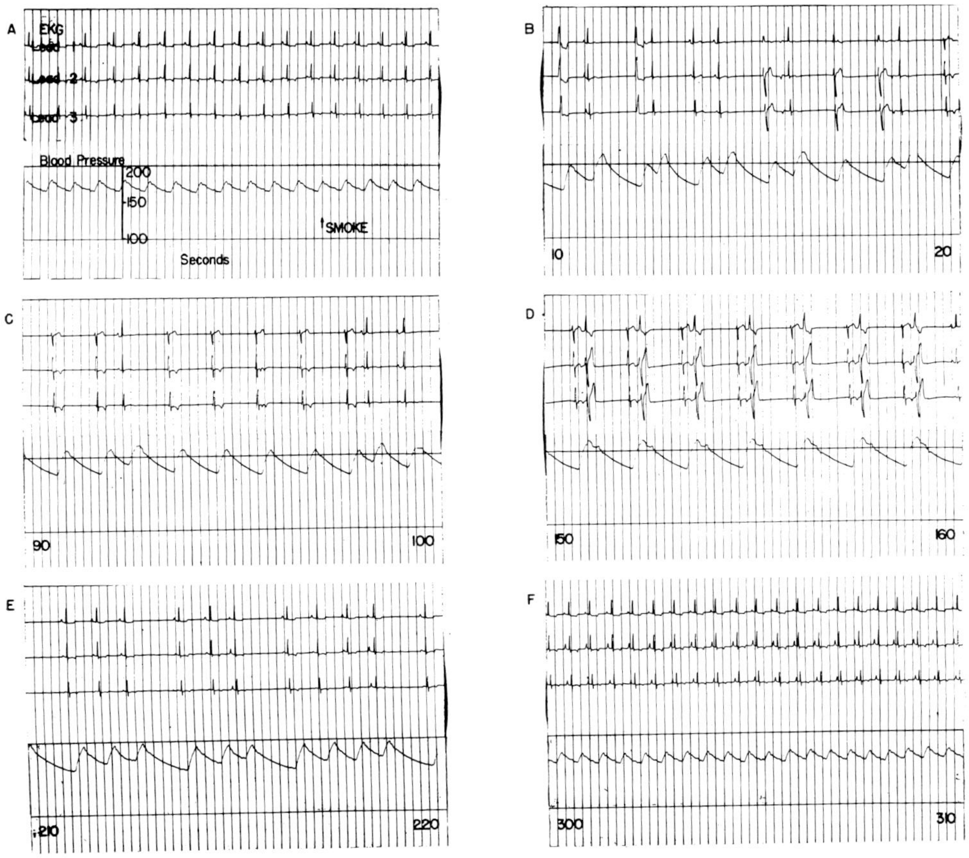

FIG. 1. Blood pressure and electrocardiographic changes due to cigarette smoke.

Cigarette smoke was administered in quantities of 1200 to 1500 ml. over a 30-second period as indicated in section A. Sections B through F represent consecutive 10 second portions of the subsequent recording. The increase in blood pressure averaged 50 mm. Hg. The occurrence of a sinus bradycardia, a nodal rhythm, and ectopic ventricular systoles were typical responses for this quantity of cigarette smoke.

maximal electrocardiographic changes. In all experiments there was an increase in cardiac work (P = <.05). In only 7 of the experiments, however, could this increase be considered significant, as compared to the variation of duplicate control measurements in a given animal. In all experiments in which there was a significant increase in cardiac work, there was a significant increase in cardiac oxygen utilization (P = <.01). In 2 cases, however, the increase in cardiac oxygen utilization occurred in the absence of a significant change in cardiac work. No relationship could be found between the changes in cardiac work and cardiac oxygen utilization, either with respect to each other or to their original levels. There was no consistent effect noted on heart rate (P = >.1) or coronary arteriovenous oxygen difference. Cardiac output (P = <.05), coronary blood flow (P = <.001) and blood pressure (P = <.001) increased in all experiments, but there appeared to be considerable variation in the magnitude of the increases.

Table 2 summarizes the effects of intravenous injection of nicotine alkaloid (20 microgm./kgm.) on cardiac dynamics and myocardial oxygen consumption at the time of the maximal electrocardiographic alterations. As with the administration of cigarette smoke, this quantity of nicotine resulted in electrocardiographic alterations ranging from apical premature contractions to multifocal ventricular extrasystoles. Cardiac work increased significantly in all experiments (P = 0.05), as did cardiac oxygen consumption (P = 0.05). No relationship could be found be-

TABLE 1

The effect of cigarette smoke (1200 to 1500 ml.) on the dynamics and oxygen utilization of the heart during maximal electrocardiographic alterations

Exp. No.	Cardiac Work		Oxygen Usage		Blood Pressure		Cardiac Output		Coronary Flow		Heart Rate	
	Control	Change	Control	Change	Control	Change	Control	Change	Control	Change	Control	Change
	kgm. m./min.		*ml./min.*		*mm. Hg*		*ml./min.*		*ml./min.*		*beats/min.*	
1	1.43	+3.55*	6.48	+0.66*	67	+46	1347	+1685	65	+11	150	+50
2	1.77	+0.11	4.39	+1.47*	53	+4	2417	−36	44	+12	80	0
3	0.90	+6.05*	4.07	+2.19*	33	+68	1966	+2489	36	+26	138	−12
4	0.67	+0.02	0.68	+0.53*	49	+6	789	−188	17	+5	156	−15
5	0.81	+1.71*	0.95	+0.99*	68	+10	847	+1000	17	+14	110	+40
6	0.69	+0.02	1.45	+0.20	41	+9	1149	−20	23	+9	132	−20
7	0.37	+0.76*	1.75	+1.95*	42	+20	636	+650	21	+23	120	−50
8	0.36	+0.19	0.52	+0.13	34	+10	845	+290	23	+3	84	−18
9	0.57	+0.61*	0.93	+0.20*	49	+5	996	+20	40	+5	70	+30
10	1.85	+1.97*	4.02	+1.32*	55	+30	2100	+900	40	+20	130	+10
11	1.64	+1.45*	3.76	+0.57*	60	+30	1910	+820	30	+9	140	−14
P	<.05		<.01		<.001		<.05		<.001		>.1	

* Change in cardiac work or oxygen utilization greater than twice the variation observed in duplicate control measurements.

TABLE 2

The effect of nicotine (20 microgm./kgm.) on the dynamics and oxygen utilization of the heart during maximal electrocardiographic alterations

Exp. No.	Cardiac Work		Oxygen Usage		Blood Fresure		Cardiac Output		Coronary Flow		Heart Rate	
	Control	Change	Control	Change	Control	Change	Control	Change	Control	Change	Control	Change
	kgm. m./min.		*ml./min.*		*mm. Hg*		*ml./min.*		*ml./min.*		*beats/min.*	
1	1.74	+4.81*	5.76	+0.61*	73	+44	1720	+2115	46	+30	100	+10
2	1.61	+0.58*	8.09	+0.52*	85	+14	1391	+237	94	+4	140	−10
3	1.83	+5.76*	8.26	+1.04*	90	+123	1500	+1100	88	+58	130	−20
4	2.81	+0.45*	5.80	+0.95*	60	0	3415	+515	57	+8	170	0
5	1.88	+2.33*	1.31	+3.06*	58	+50	1087	+870	28	+46	140	0
P	.05		.05		>.1		<.05		<.05		>.1	

* Change on cardiac work or oxygen utilization greater than twice the variation observed in duplicate control measurements.

tween the increases in cardiac work and cardiac oxygen consumption, either with respect to each other or to their original levels. There was considerable variability in the changes of blood pressure (P = >.1), cardiac output (P = <.05), coronary flow (P = <.05) and heart rate (P = >.1).

Figures 2 and 3 represent the time course of the hemodynamic changes subsequent to inhalation of 1200 to 1500 ml. of cigarette smoke over a 30 second period. As can be seen in figure 2, inhalation of cigarette smoke resulted in an increase in cardiac work, which reached a maximum 100 seconds after the termination of smoke administration. After 200 seconds, cardiac work was again at control values. Immediately upon administration of cigarette smoke, there was a marked increase in the oxygen saturation of the coronary venous blood. Arterial oxygen saturation did not change significantly. Cigarette smoke, therefore, caused a brief but considerable decrease in the cardiac oxygen consumption, which was reflected as an appreciable decrease in the coronary arteriovenous oxygen difference.

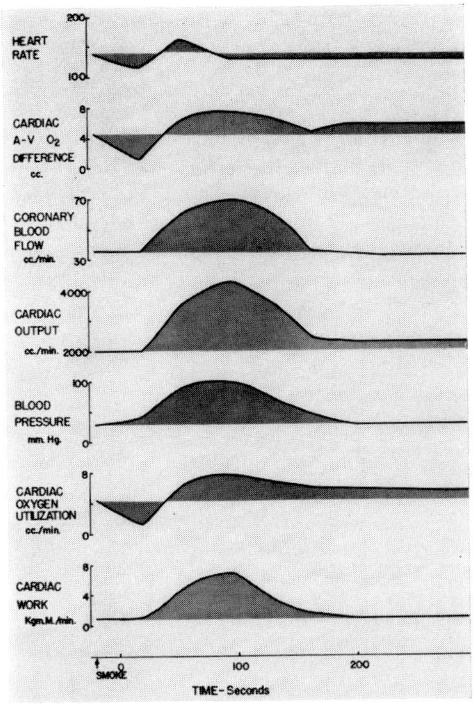

FIG. 2. The time course of the hemodynamic changes subsequent to administration of 1200 to 1500 ml. of cigarette smoke to an open-chest anesthetized dog.

Coronary blood flow increased and remained above control levels throughout the experiment. The initial decrease in cardiac oxygen utilization was followed by a long-lasting increase, extending throughout the remainder of the experiment. There was no apparent primary effect of cigarette smoke on the coronary circulation and changes in coronary blood flow seemed to be entirely due to changes in cardiac output and blood pressure. In response to cigarette smoke, there was an initial bradycardia followed by a brief tachycardia. The heart rate then fell below control values.

A comparison of three experiments which represents the greatest variations in the magnitude of response is illustrated in figure 3. Smoke was administered over a 30 second period in equal quantities in these animals. Cardiac work increased markedly in the first experiment, less in the second and not at all in the third. In all three experiments there was an early decrease in cardiac oxygen utilization. In the second experiment, however, the decrease was not below control values. It is interesting to note that regard-

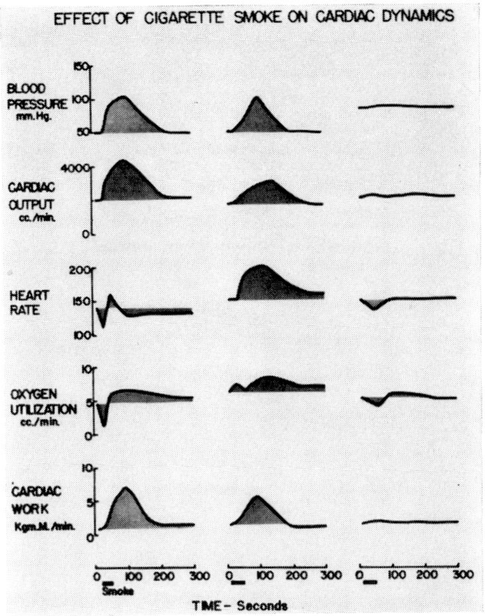

FIG. 3. The time course of the hemodynamic changes subsequent to the administration of 1200 to 1500 ml. of cigarette smoke to three open-chest anesthetized dogs.

This figure compares three experiments in which the changes in cardiac work varied from no effect to a marked increase.

less of the change in the level of cardiac work, there occurred, nevertheless, a decrease in the cardiac oxygen utilization. In all cases, the decreased oxygen utilization by the heart was reflected as a brief but considerable increase in the oxygen saturation of the coronary venous blood. In all of the experiments, administration of cigarette smoke resulted in marked variations in the electrocardiographic pattern. The degree of the electrocardiographic alterations did not seem to depend upon the absolute change in blood pressure or cardiac output, and, therefore, appeared to be independent of changes in the work of the heart. There was, however, a close relationship between the onset of the electrocardiographic alterations and the magnitude of the decrease in the cardiac oxygen utilization. Administration of nicotine alkaloid (20 microgm./kgm. body weight) resulted in hemodynamic and metabolic changes similar to those resulting from the administration of cigarette smoke. Figure 4 represents such an experiment in which the most pronounced electrocardiographic alterations occurred in close relationship to the decrease in cardiac oxygen consumption.

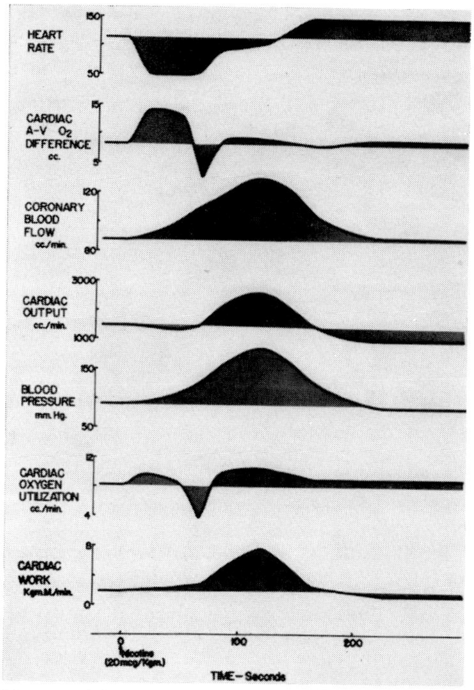

FIG. 4. The time course of the hemodynamic changes subsequent to the administration of 20 microgm./kgm. body weight of nicotine alkaloid.

DISCUSSION. It is apparent that there are marked cardiac disturbances following administration of cigarette smoke to the experimental animal. The occurrence of tobacco-induced angina pectoris has been reported by many clinical investigators. Moschowitz (1928) reported 4 cases of angina pectoris due to cigarette smoking. It was postulated that tobacco smoke caused generalized vasoconstriction in which the coronary arteries were involved. That tobacco smoke may cause spasm of the coronary arteries was reported by Cornwall (1934) and Bryant and Wood (1947). Boyle *et al.* (1947) found that administration of nicotine in two individuals with coronary artery disease resulted in angina pectoris. Ralli and Oppenheimer (1928) reported that in patients predisposed to angina pectoris smoking first caused peripheral vasoconstriction followed by a rise in blood pressure. Since the pressor response immediately preceded the onset of precordial pain, it was postulated that the coronary arteries participated in the general vasoconstriction which caused the pressor response.

Bryant and Wood (1947) and Russek *et al.* (1955) studied the electrocardiographic effects of cigarette smoking in patients with coronary artery disease. Russek *et al.* reported electrocardiographic changes in 15 of 37 patients which could not be reversed by sublingual administration of nitroglycerine. Bellet *et al.* (1941) found that lower doses of nicotine were required to produce electrocardiographic changes after myocardial damage due to coronary artery ligation in the open-chest dog.

Ballistocardiographic evidence of myocardial changes due to cigarette smoking is extensive. Henderson (1953) and Mandelbaum and Mandelbaum (1952) found that the presence or absence of heart disease affected the incidence of ballistocardiographic deterioration due to cigarette smoke; the incidence being markedly greater in cardiac patients. Davis *et al.* (1953, 1956) confirmed these findings. The changes in myocardial function responsible for the occurrence of ballistocardiographic deterioration, electrocardiographic alterations or the onset of angina pectoris is not known.

Although a decrease in coronary blood flow due to coronary artery constriction has been suggested as a possible cause of the myocardial effects of cigarette smoke, there is no evidence to justify this hypothesis. Laubry *et al.* (1933) measured the coronary flow in the isolated perfused rabbit heart and found that nicotine caused an increase in flow. Only in toxic doses was there a diminution in the rate of coronary flow. Dietrich and Schimert (1939) found that nicotine in a dose range from 0.01 to 25 mgm. caused an increase in coronary blood flow. Schmitthenner (1956) found that an increased coronary blood flow resulted from administration of nicotine to the anesthetized dog. Recently Bargerson *et al.* (1957) found that cigarette smoking results in an increase in coronary blood flow in man. On the basis of these data, it is doubtful that the effects of cigarette smoke on the myocardium are due to constriction of the coronary arteries.

The cardiac effects of cigarette smoke have also been attributed to an increase in the cardiac work load as a consequence of an increased blood pressure and heart rate. The data by Henderson (1953) and Levy *et al.* (1947), however, show that an increase in cardiac work was not consistent with the observed changes in cardiac function. In the present study of the maximal changes due to cigarette smoke inhalation, a significant increase in cardiac work occurred in only 4 of the 9 animals. Nevertheless, major electrocardiographic alterations occurred in all animals, and no correlation between the magnitude of the electrocardiographic effects and the degree of change in cardiac work was noted. Although an increase in cardiac work may contribute to the severity of the cardiac effects of smoking, it is doubtful that this is the sole responsible factor, since it is not consistent with the observed responses.

Investigations of Burn (1945, 1953), Bulbring (1949), and Walker (1949) suggest that the myocardial effects of cigarette smoke inhalation, or injection of nicotine, are due to the release of posterior pituitary hormone with its subsequent pressor and coronary constrictor actions. It is doubtful that this can be the sole cause of the observed effects, since electrocardiographic alterations have been shown to occur almost immediately after the first inhalation of cigarette smoke.

In the series of experiments measuring the time course of the hemodynamic changes following administration of cigarette smoke, there was considerable variability in the magnitude of the responses, but, in general, the effects were directionally similar. In 4 of the animals studied in which cigarette smoke was administered, there was a marked increase in both blood pressure and cardiac output, resulting in a marked increase in cardiac work. Coronary blood flow increased in these cases and seemed to follow increases in blood pressure and cardiac output. In one experiment in which there was no significant change in either blood pressure or cardiac output and, hence, no change in cardiac work, there was no increase in coronary blood flow. However, it was found that in all animals, regardless of the degree or even the existence of change in either blood pressure, cardiac output or coronary blood flow, there was a marked increase in the oxygen saturation of the coronary venous blood. This effect was of short duration and usually occurred soon after the administration of smoke. The arterial blood oxygen saturation did not vary significantly from control values. The net cause of this response appeared to be a brief but marked decrease in the oxygen utilization by the myocardium. In 4 of the animals there was a decrease in the cardiac oxygen utilization in the presence of a greatly increased cardiac work load. It is interesting to note that even in the experiments in which there were no significant changes in blood pressure or cardiac output, and, hence, no changes in cardiac work, there was also a decrease in myocardial oxygen utilization. That this is no doubt harmful to adequate cardiac function is suggested by the simultaneous occurrence of marked cardiac irregularities, as evidenced by the electrocardiographic studies.

Administration of nicotine alkaloid (20 microgm./kgm. body weight) resulted in dynamic and metabolic changes similar to the changes elicited with cigarette smoke inhalation.

It is suggested that the decrease in the cardiac oxygen consumption is the primary factor involved in the production of the electrocardiographic disturbances and cardiac arrhythmias incident to cigarette smoke inhalation or injection of nicotine. It would seem that this could also be the factor involved in the precipitation of "tobacco angina pectoris" so frequently associated with cigarette smoking.

SUMMARY

The cardiovascular effect of cigarette smoke was studied in the open-chest anesthetized dog. Observations of blood pressure, cardiac output, coronary blood flow, coronary arteriovenous oxygen difference, and the electrocardiogram were made. In addition, cardiac work and cardiac oxygen utilization were calculated.

The maximal cardiovascular effects of cigarette smoke were measured in the open-chest anesthetized dog. Extreme variability of response was observed. A lack of correlation was observed between the onset of the electrocardiographic effects and the changes in cardiac work. Coronary blood flow increased and appeared to follow the changes in blood pressure and cardiac output. It is suggested that the electrocardiographic disturbances subsequent to inhalation of cigarette smoke are not due entirely to increases in cardiac work. It is also suggested that coronary vasoconstriction does not result as a consequence of cigarette smoke inhalation.

A study of the time course of the hemodynamic changes subsequent to inhalation of cigarette smoke indicates that a brief but marked decrease in the oxygen consumption of the heart occurs in a close time relationship to the electrocardiographic disturbances. This decrease in the oxygen consumption of the heart appears invariably, and it is suggested that this factor is of prime importance in the development of the observed cardiac irregularities. It is further suggested that this may be of importance in the precipitation of "tobacco angina pectoris."

The effects of cigarette smoke can be duplicated by intravenous injection of nicotine alkaloid.

REFERENCES

ACHESON, G. H.: Pharmacology in Medicine, Drill, V. A., editor, McGraw-Hill Inc., New York, 1955.

BARACH, A. L., ECKMAN, M., AND MOLOMUT, N.: Am. J. M. Sci., **202:** 336, 1941.

BARGERON, L. M., EHMKE, D., GONLUBOL, F., CASTELLANOS, A., SIEGEL, A., AND BIND, R. J.: Circulation, **15:** 251, 1957.

BAUMBERGER, J. P.: THIS JOURNAL, **21:** 35, 1923.

BELLET, S., KIRSHBAUM, A., MEADE, R. H., AND SCHWARTZ, L.: Am. J. M. Sci., **201:** 40, 1941.

BOYLE, M. N., WEGRIA, R., CATHCART, R. T., NICKERSON, R. T., AND LEVY, R. L.: Am. Heart J., **34:** 65, 1947.

BULBRING, E., BURN, H. H., AND WALKER, J. M.: Quart. J. Med., **18:** NSV69, 1949.

BRYANT, M. J., AND WOOD, J. E.: Am. Heart J., **34:** 20, 1947.

BURN, J. H.: Am. Heart J., **46:** 529, 1953.

BURN, J. H., TRULOVE, L. N., AND BURN, I.: Brit. Med. J., **1:** 403, 1945.

CORNWALL, E. C.: Medical Times, **62:** 209, 1934.

DAVIS, F. W., SCARBOROUGH, W. R., MASON, R. E., SINGEWALD, M. L., AND BARKER, B. M.: Am. Heart J., **46:** 529, 1953.

DAVIS, F. W., SCARBOROUGH, W. R., MASON, R. E., SINGEWALD, M. L., AND BARKER, B. M.: Am. Heart J., **51:** 165, 1956.

DEITRICH, S., AND SCHIMERT, G.: Ztschr. klin. Med., **135:** 718, 1939.

GREGG, D. E.: Coronary Circulation in Health and Disease, Lea and Febiger, Philadelphia, 1950.

HENDERSON, C. B.: Brit. Med. J., **15:** 278, 1953.

KISER, J. C., BOOHER, W. T., AND WATTS, D. T.: Arch. int. Pharmacodyn., **105:** 403, 1956.

LAUBRY, C., WALSER, J., AND DEGAUDE, L.: Bull. Acad. Med., **109:** 595, 1933.

LEHMANN, K. B.: Munchen. med. Wchnschr., **55:** 723, 1908.

LEVY, R. L., MATHERS, J. A. L., MUELLER, A. A. AND NICKERSON, J. L.: J. A. M. A. **135:** 417, 1947.

MANDELBAUM, H., AND MANDELBAUM, R. A.: Circulation, **5:** 885, 1952.

MOSCHOWITZ, E.: J. A. M. A., **90:** 733, 1928.

NAHAS, G. G.: Am. J. Physiol., **163:** 737, 1950.

RALLI, E. P., AND OPPENHEIMER, B. S.: Proc. Soc. Exper. Biol. & Med., **26:** 9, 1928.

RUSSEK, H. I., ZOHMAN, B. L., AND DORSET, U. J.: J. A. M. A., **157:** 7, 1955.

SCHMITTHENNER, J. E., FORTE, I., REIGEL, C., AND HAFKENSCHIEL, J. H.: Internat. Physiol. Cong., XX, 1956.

SHIPLEY, R. A., AND WILSON, C.: Proc. Soc. Exper. Biol. & Med., **78:** 727, 1951.

VAN SLYKE, D. D., AND NEILL, J. M.: J. Biol. Chem., **61:** 523, 1924.

WALKER, J. M.: Quart. J. Med., **18:** 51, 1949.

WINBURY, M. M., MICHIELS, P. M., HAMBOURGER, W. E., STOCKFISCH, W. J., AND COOK, D. L.: THIS JOURNAL, **99:** 343, 1950.

FACTORS INFLUENCING CONTRACTION IN GLYCERINATED MYOCARDIAL FIBERS[1, 2]

F. NORMAN BRIGGS[3]

Department of Pharmacology, Harvard Medical School, Boston, Massachusetts

Received for publication April 10, 1958

The precise mechanism by which adenosinetriphosphate (ATP) causes actomyosin to shorten or develop tension is unknown. It is possible, however, to study this interaction and the factors which influence it by studying the amount of tension obtained under controlled conditions. To simplify the system cardiac muscle can be treated with glycerin to destroy the membrane (Taeschler and Bing, 1953) and to remove the water-soluble glycolytic enzymes. Such glycerinated muscle cannot be made to contract or develop tension except by the addition of a nucleosidetriphosphate, ATP being the physiologically occurring one and the one most studied. By fixing a small bundle of glycerinated cardiac fibers to a tensiometer it is then possible to measure the amount of tension produced when ATP is added and to determine the influence of environment on the tension. Experimental study of glycerinated cardiac muscle (Taeschler and Bing, 1953; Ranney, 1955; Hawkins and Smith, 1956) has not been sufficiently extensive to allow one to be certain which factors are most important in determining tension. A decrease in intracellular potassium has been postulated by Hajdu (1953) and Szent-Györgyi (1953) as the mechanism of *treppe* potentiation (Bowditch, 1871) and poststimulation potentiation (Langendorff, 1885). Whether this or some other environmental factor is important in determining tension is the object of the following study.

METHODS. Hearts from dogs exsanguinated under ether anesthesia were rapidly removed and chilled in ice water. Small strips of trabecular muscle were cut from the left ventricle, extracted with 50 per cent (v/v) water-glycerol buffered to pH 7.4 with phosphate and stored at −18°C. The length of time the fibers were extracted in each experiment is presented in the appropriate figure or table.

Tension generation was measured with a sensitive (0.3 mgm.) pseudoisometric tensiometer (maximum shortening 8 per cent of the "rest length") similar to that described by Weber (1951). In all experiments each fiber bundle was tested at each experimental point, *i.e.* at each ATP concentration or each pH *etc.* so that all data are comparable. In going from one point to the next each fiber was subjected to a small quick stretch and quick release so that a truly new tension was obtained for each point (Briggs and Portzehl, 1957). Tension is expressed as per cent of maximum tension obtained with each fiber. Table 1 shows, for each investigation, the absolute tension (gm./cm.^{2}) observed when the average tension was at a maximum. All fibers in the group did not, however, necessarily reach their maximum value at the same experimental point. The cross sectional area of the fibers, assuming a cylindrical shape, was calculated from the optically measured fiber diameters. The fiber bundles averaged 140 μ in diameter. The medium in which the fibers developed tension was always made up such that the ionic strength was 0.16, the buffer strength was 0.02 *M*, and the magnesium concentration was 0.002 *M*. The ionic strength was adjusted to 0.16 by varying the concentration of KCl. All experiments were carried out at room temperature (approx. 24°C.) in an air-conditioned laboratory. Small variation in temperature produces only small changes in tension (Weber, 1951).

RESULTS. *Tension generated in glycerinated myocardial fibers.* Effect of ATP concentration: The cardiac fibers used in these experiments were extracted with glycerol-water for one to two months. There was little difference in the maximum tension developed by the fibers when the ATP concentration was varied between 0.5 *mM* and 10 *mM*. This is shown graphically in figure 1. However, with the lower ATP concentrations

[1] These results were presented in part at the Federation Meetings in Philadelphia, April, 1958.

[2] This work was supported by a grant from the U. S. Public Health Service (H-2205).

[3] Present address: Department of Physiology, Tufts University School of Medicine, Boston.

TABLE 1

Table of maximum tensions

Glycerinated myocardial fibers. Room temperature.

Experiment	No. of Fibers	Tension
		gm./cm.^{2} ± *S.B.*
Figure 1: ATP, $1 \times 10^{-3}M$	8	90 ± 11
Figure 1: ATP, $5 \times 10^{-3}M$; Ca, $2 \times 10^{-3}M$	4	91 ± 15
Figure 2: pH 9.0	5	82 ± 19
Figure 2: pH 9.0; Ca, $2 \times 10^{-3}M$	4	82 ± 7
Figure 2: pH 9.0; EDTA treated; Ca, $2 \times 10^{-3}M$	4	112 ± 27
Figure 3: ATP, $1 \times 10^{-3}M$; K^+	4	88 ± 18
Table 2: ATP, $1 \times 10^{-3}M$	4	151 ± 54

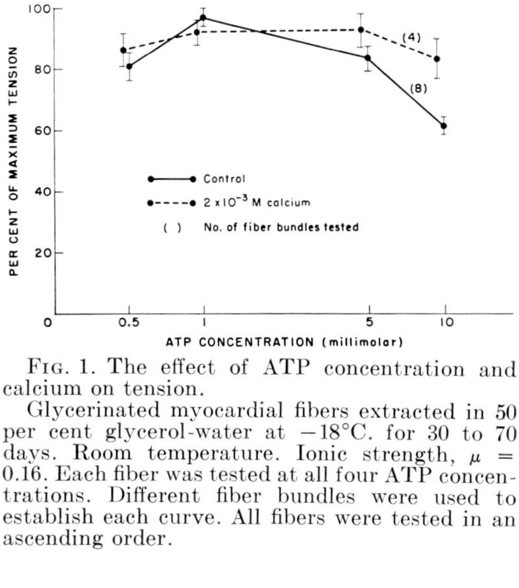

FIG. 1. The effect of ATP concentration and calcium on tension.

Glycerinated myocardial fibers extracted in 50 per cent glycerol-water at −18°C. for 30 to 70 days. Room temperature. Ionic strength, $\mu = 0.16$. Each fiber was tested at all four ATP concentrations. Different fiber bundles were used to establish each curve. All fibers were tested in an ascending order.

up to 20 minutes were required for the tension to reach its maximum, whereas with the higher concentrations it was reached more rapidly. Tension at $1 \times 10^{-2}M$ ATP was lower than that developed at lower ATP concentrations, suggesting that such a concentration is either over-optimal for cardiac actomyosin or that some Marsh-Bendall relaxing factor (Bendall, 1953) survived the extraction procedure. The latter explanation seems most likely as the addition of calcium, a potent antagonist of Marsh-Bendall factor, abolished the decrease.

One would expect that at low ATP concentration less tension would be developed in the fiber bundle as ATP would be unable to diffuse

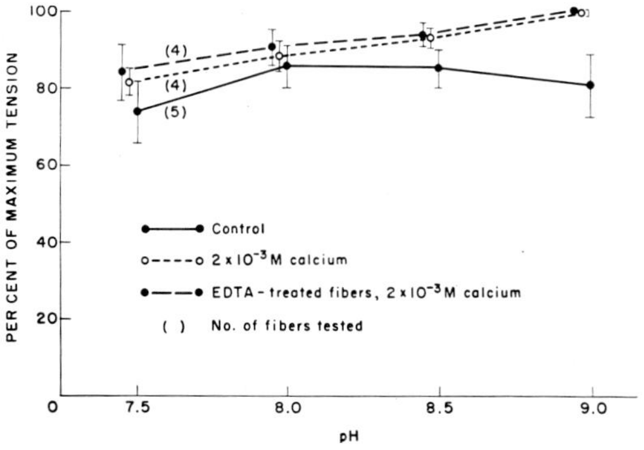

FIG. 2. The effect of pH, calcium and ethylenediaminetetraacetic acid (EDTA) plus calcium on tension.

Glycerinated myocardial fibers extracted in 50 per cent glycerol-water at −18°C. for 13 to 16 days. Room temperature. Ionic strength, $\mu = 0.16$. Each fiber was tested at all four pH's. Different fiber bundles were used to establish each curve. All fibers were tested in an ascending order.

throughout the fiber. The length of the diffusion path at which the ATP concentration becomes zero can be estimated from the Meyerhof formula (1930). The diffusion constant for ATP in muscle has been found to be 2×10^{-8} cm.^{2}/sec. (Hasselbach, 1952) and the adenosinetriphosphatase activity of glycerinated myocardial myofibrils is 0.1 micromol. of ATP/min. mgm. protein (personal observation). With these values for ATP splitting and diffusion, one can calculate, for a fiber bundle of 140 μ (micra) diameter, that when the ATP concentration in the medium is 5×10^{-4} M a rim only 13 μ in thickness would contain ATP. Such fiber bundles would thus have only 33 per cent of the total protein exposed to ATP and contributing to tension. However, the cardiac fibers developed nearly maximal tension at 5×10^{-4} M ATP. Such results could best be explained if an ATP restituting system were present. That myokinase was performing this function was shown by causing fibers to contract in the presence of ADP rather than ATP. The tension obtained ranged from 70 to 82 per cent of that produced by equivalent amounts of ATP. The myokinase present in the glycerinated heart fibers thus made ATP available to all the protein in the fiber bundle allowing all elements to contribute to the generation of tension.

Effect of pH and calcium. Figure 2 shows the effect of pH on the steady-state tension produced by 5×10^{-3} M ATP. Since the experiments performed with phosphate or glycine buffer gave comparable results, the data obtained with either

TABLE 2

*Effect of ionic strength on tension**

Ionic strength..	0.054	0.129	0.195	0.252	0.302
Per cent of maximum tension.......	92.1	99.6	88.0	69.8	49.5
Standard error.	2.9	0.5	3.6	4.8	3.6

* Glycerinated myocardial fibers extracted 43 days in 50 per cent glycerol-water at −18°C. Room temp. Each fiber was tested at all five ionic strengths. Four fibers were tested. All fibers were tested in an ascending order.

buffer were combined. The effect of calcium was also investigated under these same conditions. No influence on tension was found. The addition of calcium to fibers pretreated with ethylenediaminetetraacetic acid (EDTA) likewise did not produce depression of tension as reported by Ranney (1955).

Effect of ionic strength. Table 2 shows that tension was little affected at ionic strengths from 0.05 to 0.20. At strengths of 0.25 and 0.30 tension was progressively diminished to 50 per cent of maximum. If the ionic strength of the intracellular fluid of heart muscle is calculated from the sum of electrolyte concentrations (Benson *et al.*, 1956), nucleotide concentrations (Khairallah and Mommaerts, 1953) and phosphocreatine concentrations (Harvey, 1955) a value of 0.16 is obtained. Thus an accumulation of intracellular sodium or potassium greater than 40 mEq. would have to occur before it would significantly depress tension by a direct action on the contractile apparatus.

Effect of sodium ion on tension. With each cardiac fiber bundle a direct comparison was made between tension in the presence of sodium ion and tension in the presence of potassium ion. One-half of the experiments were started in potassium-containing media and the other half in sodium-containing media. The results and the amount of sodium or potassium at each ATP concentration are shown graphically in figure 3. The discrepancy between the concentrations of sodium and potassium at the high ATP concentrations is a consequence of the use of sodium-ATP in all experiments. Analysis of the data shows that tension in the presence of sodium averaged 5 per cent less than in the presence of potassium. The probability that this difference is due to chance is less than 0.001 (Student's t-test).

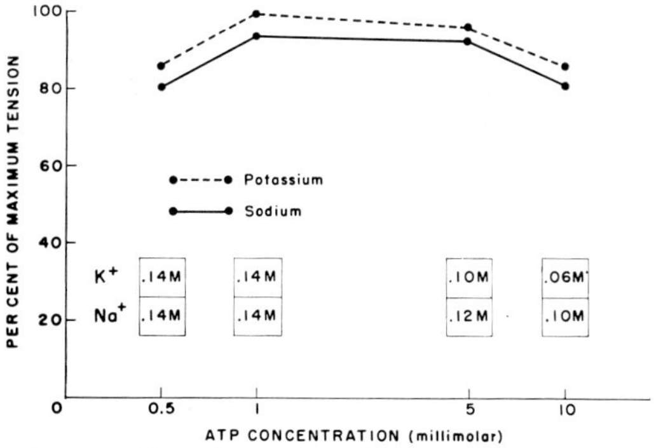

FIG. 3. The effect of sodium ion on tension. Glycerinated myocardial fibers extracted in 50 per cent glycerol-water at −18°C. for 12 days. Room temperature. Ionic strength, $\mu = 0.16$. One-half the fibers were tested first in sodium medium and then potassium medium while the other half were tested first in potassium medium and then in sodium medium. The results did not depend upon which sequence was used.

DISCUSSION. The response of glycerinated cardiac muscle to ATP suggests that contraction in heart muscle is fundamentally identical with contraction in skeletal muscle. The most striking quantitative difference was the maximum tension developed. The value of 100 gm./cm.^{2} (table 1) is only 1/10 the value observed in skeletal muscle under similar conditions of ionic strength, pH and ATP concentration (Briggs and Portzehl, 1957). As in the case of skeletal muscle (Briggs and Portzehl, 1957) the development of tension by cardiac muscle fibers was found to be independent of ATP concentration over a wide range of concentrations. Any attempt to relate cardiac failure to low ATP levels would have to take this observation into account.

The use of steady-state tensions to study muscular contraction may lead to false conclusions, for physiological development of tension most likely never reaches such a steady-state condition. Weber and Hasselbach (1954) and more recently Tonomura and Kitagawa (1957) have demonstrated that the ATP-ase activity of actomyosin or myosin solutions during the first few seconds of exposure to ATP exceeds the steady-state activity by about five times. Further, this initial rate of hydrolysis depends more upon ATP concentration than does steady-state hydrolysis. If tension generation depends upon the hydrolysis of ATP, then under physiological circumstances, *i.e.* over a period of approximately 0.1 second, the tension developed may depend much more on ATP concentration than is indicated in the steady-state conditions studied here.

In contrast to the experiments of Ranney (1955), no inhibition of tension by sodium or calcium could be demonstrated. Studies with glycerinated skeletal muscle have also shown that neither sodium (Weber, 1951) nor calcium inhibits, except under the special condition where the calcium to magnesium ratio is very high (Bowen, 1951). Ranney's results are not explicable on such a basis since his investigations were carried out with a Ca/Mg ratio of 1 or less.

In their studies of the *treppe* phenomenon Szent-Györgyi (1953) and Hajdu (1953) found that the development of maximum tension was associated with a decrease in intracellular cation concentration of about 8 mEq. per 1. They suggest that the low intracellular cation concentration favors contraction by a direct effect on actomyosin just as low salt concentration favors superprecipitation of actomyosin. However, in the glycerinated heart muscle preparation, where the actomyosin is organized as in the living tissue, varying the salt concentration of the medium above and below physiological levels produces little effect upon tension.

Attempts have also been made to determine if salt accumulation occurs in cardiac failure. High salt concentration favors the dissociation of actomyosin. Benson *et al.* (1956) found an average increase of 19 and 31 mEq. of alkali ion in experimentally produced heart failure. Statistical analysis of their data shows the increases to be statistically not significant. In the glycerinated heart fiber increases in ionic strength of 20 to 30 mEq. above the physiological level did not significantly depress tension. The experiments described in this paper do not imply that changes in intracellular ion concentrations are not important to contraction in the intact heart; they do, however, indicate that such changes do not exert their influence through a direct effect on actomyosin.

SUMMARY

Studies have been made of a number of factors which might influence the amount of tension generated in glycerinated myocardial fibers by ATP. ATP concentrations from $5 \times 10^{-4}M$ to $1 \times 10^{-2}M$ were about equally effective in generating similar degrees of tension. An increase of pH from 7.5 to 9.0 was associated with slight increase in generated tension. Calcium was not found to inhibit the generation of tension, and when sodium was the principal cation the amount of tension generated was only 5 per cent less than the tension generated when potassium was the principal cation. The tension generated was not significantly influenced by ionic strengths from 0.05 to 0.20. At ionic strengths of 0.25 and 0.30, tension was progressively diminished to 50 per cent of maximum. The significance of these results for various theories of how ions influence contraction are discussed.

ACKNOWLEDGMENT. The author wishes to acknowledge the very excellent technical assistance given by Miss Regis King in all aspects of these investigations.

REFERENCES

BENDALL, I. R.: J. Physiol., **121:** 232, 1953.
BENSON, E. S., FREIER, E. F., HALLAWAY, B. E., AND JOHNSON, M. J.: Am. J. Physiol., **187:** 483, 1956.
BOWDITCH, H. P. Ludwigs Arb., **VI:** 139, 1871.
BOWEN, W. J.: Am. J. Physiol., **165:** 10, 1951.
BRIGGS, F. N., AND PORTZEHL, H.: Biochim. et biophys. acta, **24:** 482, 1957.
HAJDU, S.: Am. J. Physiol., **174:** 371, 1953.
HARVEY, S. C.: Am. J. Physiol., **183:** 559, 1955.
HASSELBACH, W.: Ztschr. Naturforsch., **76:** 334, 1952.
HAWKINS, L. W., AND SMITH, J. R.: Am. J. Physiol., **186:** 304, 1956.
LANGENDORFF, O.: Arch. Physiol. Leipz., **284:** 1885.
MEYERHOF, O.: Die chemischen Vorgänge im Muskel und ihr Zusammenhand mit Arbeitsleistung und Wärmebildung, Springer, Berlin, 1930.
KHAIRALLAH, P. A., AND MOMMAERTS, W. F. H. M.: Circulation Res., **1:** 8, 1953.
RANNEY, R. E.: Am. J. Physiol., **183:** 197, 1955.
SZENT-GYÖRGYI, A.: Chemical physiology of contraction in body and heart muscle, Academic Press, New York, 1953.
TAESCHLER, M., AND BING, R. J.: Circulation Res., **1:** 129, 1953.
TONOMURA, Y., AND KITAGAWA, S.: Biochim. biophys. acta, **26:** 15, 1957.
WEBER, A.: Biochim. biophys. acta, **7:** 214, 1951.
WEBER, A., AND HASSELBACH, W.: Biochim biophys. acta, **15:** 237, 1954.

8056

TEMPERATURE AND RESTING POTENTIAL OF DIAPHRAGM MUSCLE IN A CO_2-BICARBONATE MEDIUM

R. CREESE, N. W. SCHOLES[1] AND D. B. TAYLOR

With the technical assistance of Darrell Zinn

Department of Pharmacology, University of California Medical Center, Los Angeles

Received for publication June 10, 1958

The resting potential of frog muscle in the presence of a high concentration of potassium phosphate has been found to be proportional to the absolute temperature (Ling and Woodbury, 1949). Under these conditions the potassium content of the muscle was probably unchanged. These results, while of considerable theoretical importance, are not necessarily applicable to tissues in physiological salt solutions such as Krebs fluid in which the buffer system is formed by carbon dioxide and bicarbonate. The present results showed no detectable changes in the resting potential of rat muscle between 15° and 39°C., and the change on dropping to 5°C. was small and not significant.

There is a further reason for the study of the effect of temperature. The action of *d*-tubocurarine is altered in a complex manner by temperature changes, and the paralyzing effect on isolated rat diaphragm muscle is a minimum at 26°C., being greater above and below this temperature (Holmes, Jenden and Taylor, 1951). The constancy of the resting potential under these conditions is of value in the study of curarization, because it eliminates a variable from these experiments.

METHODS. *Saline*. The composition was (*mM*): Na^+ 144, K^+ 5.0, Ca^{++} 1.3, Mg^{++} 1.2, Cl^- 125, HCO_3^- 25, SO_4^{--} 1.2. The solution was gassed with a mixture containing 5 per cent carbon dioxide in oxygen, giving a pH close to 7.4 at body temperature. *d*-Tubocurarine chloride was used in some cases in a concentration of 5 microgm./ml.

Temperature control. The organ baths were jacketed, and water was circulated around them by means of a pump. Two reservoirs were maintained as heat exchangers, and were connected in such a way that one or the other could be included in the circuit at any time. This permitted rapid change between two set temperatures as required. Recording thermometers were placed in the organ bath close to the tissue.

Tissue dissection. Albino rats weighing about 200 gm. each were used. The diaphragm was exposed, and the pleura was rapidly stripped away from the central portion of the left diaphragm. Omission of this process was found to increase greatly the difficulty of penetration of microelectrodes in this part of the muscle. The diaphragmatic pleura is loose in this region, and a lower portion of the left lung is frequently found partly invaginated between the heart and the diaphragm. If this portion of lung is pulled out, the pleura can be gripped by forceps and removed from a portion of the muscle, the process being extended towards the rib margin. Sometimes the outer cells appear to be damaged by this procedure (see below). The hemidiaphragm is then rapidly removed to a shallow bath so that the remaining dissection can be continued in oxygenated saline.

The muscle was attached to a simple plastic frame and then transferred to a plastic organ bath which was designed for microelectrode recording. The diaphragm muscle was held in a verticle position with ribs uppermost and pleural surface towards the microelectrode. The tendon was tied by a thread to the frame, and the ribs were attached to threads which passed over the side of the organ bath and were fastened to a weight of 50 gm. It was found that a smaller weight did not keep the muscle sufficiently rigid for satisfactory impaling with microelectrodes. The muscle was placed vertically because it was easier to ensure satisfactory oxygenation from below in this position.

Microelectrode technique. The methods resembled those of Nastuk and Hodgkin (1950). Micropipettes filled with 2.5 *M* KCl were used, having a resistance of 20 to 30 megohms. The micropipettes were about 7 cm. in length, and were prepared by a machine from glass capillary tubes (Kimble) of 0.7 mm. diameter, with wall

[1] Public Health Service Research Fellow of the National Institute of Neurological Diseases and Blindness.

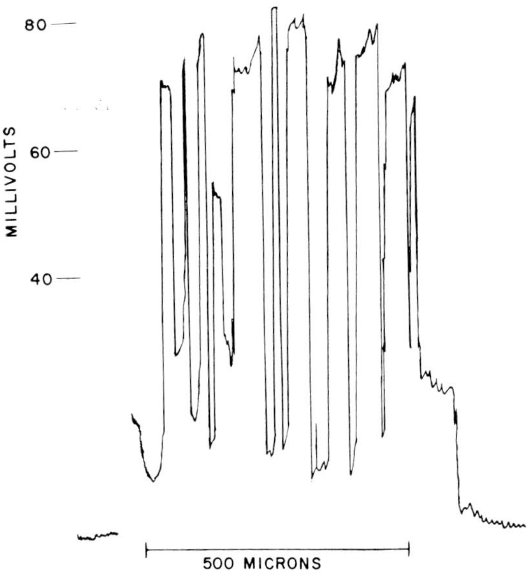

FIG. 1. Resting potentials of diaphragm muscle. The microelectrode was pushed steadily through the tissue. The deflexions produced as the electrode enters and leaves the fibers were recorded by a pen writer. Read from right to left. Upward deflexion indicates a potential which is negative with respect to the solution.

thickness about 0.2 mm. One end of the micropipette was clamped in a plastic holder containing agar jelly (1.5 per cent, with 2.5 *M* KCl). The micropipette approached the tissue at an angle of 42° with the vertical muscle. A chlorided silver wire, about 2 cm. long, connected the agar jelly with the grid of the tube used as cathode follower (see below). The microelectrode assembly and cathode follower components were mounted on a microscope rack which permitted coarse and fine movement in the direction of the microelectrode. A simple swivel device allowed an electrode to dip into the organ bath or into a nearby beaker, so that electrodes were easily changed. The microscope rack containing cathode follower and microelectrode was mounted on a universal adjustable milling table, which allowed all movements in a horizontal plane. The muscle was viewed by a dissection microscope through the front face of the plastic organ bath. This face was plane, unjacketed and polished. The muscle was illuminated from the side by means of a slit lamp whose light was focused on to the tissue. The tip of the microelectrode could be guided to the same fiber for repeated impaling if necessary. A synchronous motor was used to rotate the fine adjustment of the microscope rack so that the microelectrode was pushed slowly through the whole tissue at a speed of 0.37 mm./min.

The cathode follower was formed by a Raytheon CK 5886 subminiature pentode, energized by small mercury batteries. The anode current was 5 to 6 microamp., and the cathode resistance was 650 k ohms. In conditions of low humidity, produced by a stream of dry air or by other means, the grid current could be held below 10^{-14} amp., as measured by inserting a resistance of 10^{12} ohms in the grid circuit. In humid conditions, the grid current may be 10^{-12} amp. The output was led to a cathode ray oscilloscope, and also to a Leeds and Northrup pen recorder having a high impedance with a rise time of 0.5 second. The solution in the bath was earthed as usual. The recording system was calibrated with known potentials from a Weston cell. No corrections have been made in the results to allow for the liquid junction between the cell contents and the electrolyte inside the micropipette. The methods were somewhat similar to those used earlier (Creese *et al.*, 1957).

RESULTS. *Records from pen writer.* Figure 1 shows the deflexions obtained when a microelectrode is pushed slowly through the whole substance of a diaphragm muscle. Each deflexion presumably represents the resting potential of a single fiber, and each such penetration gives a sample of potentials. Records were only accepted in which there was no change in base line when the needle returned to saline, and also no change in the resistance of the microelectrode. The first cell frequently shows a low potential, possibly due to damage caused by stripping off the pleura. Penetration of the pleura on the far side of the preparation (left side in figure 1) is often accompanied by breaking of the electrodes, and the forward movement of the electrode is usually stopped just before this point. The microelectrode tip is of the order of 0.5 micron, but as the tissue is penetrated, the shaft of the microelectrode, which is wider, necessarily penetrates the fibers. Some damage may be caused, for penetration again at exactly the same point reveals cells with low voltages, whereas penetration through an adjacent layer shows cells which appear normal.

Figure 1 shows that the potentials recorded when the electrode tip was between cells are low but rarely become zero. The explanation for this is not known. The potential varies somewhat while the microelectrode is penetrating the fiber, and for the purpose of comparing measurements under different conditions, it was decided to take the highest deflexion as indicating the resting potential.

TABLE 1

Temperature and resting potential (mV) of rat diaphragm fibers

27°C.	39°C.	15°C.	27°C.	5°C.	39°C.	Number
79.7	79.1		77.3			50
	73.0		69.7		72.1	50
80.4	77.1		78.3			50
	74.2		74.4		73.4	50
		84.3	83.4			100
78.3		76.9				100
	73.8			71.0		50
				73.9	74.2	50

Each line shows results on one muscle. Figures give means (*mV*) after equilibration for 2 hours at successive temperatures; read from left to right. There is little change in mean values. The last column gives the approximate number of fibers measured at each temperature.

TABLE 2

Temp. °C.	Mean *mV*	S.D.	Mean as %	No. of Fibers	No. of Muscles
39	74.7	±7.25	100	528	6
27	76.4	±9.20	99.8	825	6
15	80.5	±10.35	99.5	195	2
5	72.7	±6.45	97.9	100	2

The fourth column gives the results expressed as a percentage of the value at 39°C. as obtained from table 1 for each pair of temperatures (see text).

Constancy with time. The general procedure consisted in recording the resting potentials of some 50 cells at one temperature, then changing to a second temperature, allowing at least 2 hours for equilibration and then 50 more cells were impaled. The temperature was finally restored to the original value and results from 50 more cells were obtained after further equilibration.

Table 1 lists the mean values, and shows the results after successive recording at different temperatures. The table should be read from left to right. The first line shows that the mean value was 79.7 *mV* at 27°C., changing to 79.1 *mV* at 39°C., and was 77.3 *mV* when the temperature was returned to 27°C. (the standard deviations are listed later). There would seem to be little change in the mean value. The first 4 results are of interest in that they compare the results at the same temperature after a lapse of some 6 hours. It can be seen that in these 4 cases, the mean value is similar to that obtained earlier, being on the average some 1.5 *mV* lower after 6 hours. This might be due to some damage following repeated penetration, but in any case it shows that there is little change in the potentials with time. The potassium content is also steady (Creese, 1954).

The effect of temperature. Change of temperature between 39°C. and 5°C. produced little effect on the resting potential. Table 2 lists the means and standard deviations at 4 temperatures while figure 2 shows in histogram form the deviation of the measured potentials at 39°C. and 5°C. The fourth column expresses the mean values as a percentage of the value at 39°C., and it can be seen that the differences are very small. These percentages were obtained as follows. In the first line of table 1 the mean of all values at 27°C. is 78.5 *mV*, which is 99.2 per cent of the mean value at 39°C. The mean for the first 4 lines gives 99.8 per cent for 27°C., and this is listed in table 2. Similarly, the value at 15°C., was expressed as a percentage of that at 27°C., and hence as a percentage of the value at 39°C. Values at 5°C. and 39°C. were compared directly.

Figure 3 shows the mean potentials, expressed as a percentage of the value at 39°C., plotted against temperature, with the standard deviation also shown. The weighted regression coefficient has a slope of + 0.0430 per cent per degree centigrade. The standard deviation of the regression coefficient is 0.0290, and this may be used when evaluating the significance of difference between coefficients (Fisher, 1950). P was >0.1 by the t-test, so the results do not reveal a significant effect of temperature under these circumstances. If only the measurements between 15°C. and 39°C. are considered, the regression coefficient is only +0.0146 with standard deviation 0.0372 and $P > 0.4$.

The dotted line in figure 3 shows the slope calculated from the Nernst equation on the assumption that the resting potential is proportional to the absolute temperature and that other factors remained constant. The slope would then be +0.321 per cent per degree centigrade (taking the value at 39°C. as 100), and by a t-test the difference between this line and that found experimentally is large and not fortuitous ($P < 0.001$). This does not, of course, invalidate the Nernst equation, the predictions of which regarding the effects of temperature are only applicable to conditions in which the internal

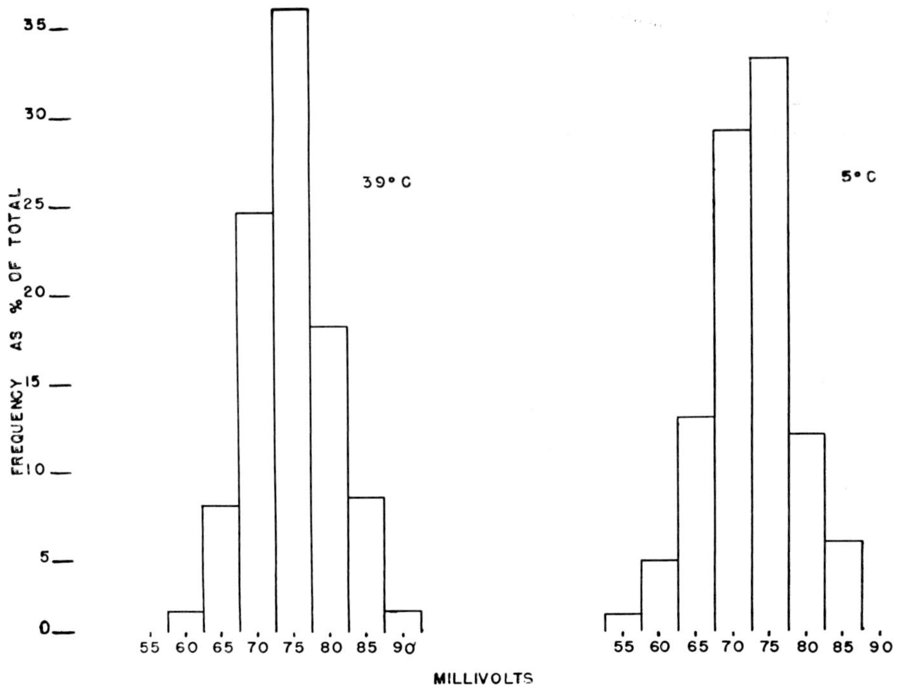

FIG. 2. Histograms showing distribution of resting potentials of 528 fibers recorded at 39° C. and resting potentials of 100 fibers recorded at 5° C.

The mean values are not appreciably different (see also table 2).

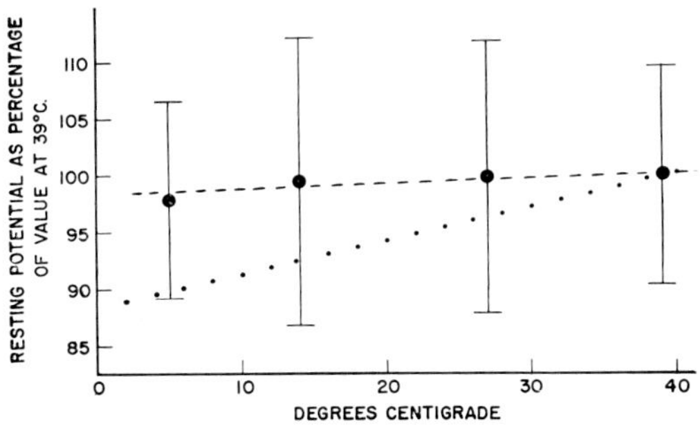

FIG. 3. Effect of temperature on resting potential.

Results are expressed as a percentage of the value at 39°C., as compared for each pair of temperatures. The limits give the standard deviations. The broken line gives the regression, while the dotted line gives the slope expected if the potential were proportional to the absolute temperature.

and external ionic environment remain constant, but it suggests that the situation is more complex when Krebs fluid is used.

DISCUSSION. *Effect of temperature on the CO_2-bicarbonate system.* A fall of temperature will increase the solubility of carbon dioxide and lower the pH. Table 3 gives the calculated pH for various temperatures in a solution of 0.154 ionic strength containing 25 *mM* bicarbonate equilibrated with 5 per cent CO_2. Let the buffer equation be expressed as:

$$pH = -\log K_{(s)} + \log (HCO_3^-) - \log n - \log S - \log ((B - p)/B).$$

TABLE 3

Effect of temperature on CO_2-bicarbonate system

Mixed saline containing 25 *mM* bicarbonate with ionic strength 0.154 is equilibrated with 5 per cent CO_2.

Temp.	Vapor Pressure	Henry's Law Constant	$-\log K_{(s)}$*	Calculated pH
	mm. Hg	*moles/atmos.*		
0	4.6	0.0736	6.316	7.15
5	6.5	0.0617	6.255	7.17
10	9.2	0.0516	6.174	7.17
15	12.7	0.0438	6.128	7.19
20	17.4	0.0377	6.116	7.25
25	23.6	0.0332	6.084	7.28
30	31.7	0.0290	6.057	7.31
35	42.0	0.0258	6.036	7.35
38	49.8	0.0242	6.027	7.37
40	55.0	0.0231	6.021	7.39

* $K_{(s)}$ is the ionization function.

$K_{(s)}$ is the ionization function (H^+) x (HCO_3^-)/(CO_2) using molal concentrations. $K_{(s)}$ is defined by Harned and Bonner (1945) and listed at various temperatures for 0.1 and 0.2 molal NaCl. Values for 0.154 molal NaCl were obtained by interpolation and are given in table 3; they are assumed to hold for the saline used. (HCO_3^-) is taken to be 0.025; n is the fraction of carbon dioxide in the mixture, and is 0.05. S is Henry's law coefficient for carbon dioxide in saline, expressed in moles per atmosphere. Values of S for various temperatures and concentrations of sodium chloride have been measured by Harned and Davis (1943), and figures interpolated for 0.154 *M* NaCl are shown in table 3. B is the atmospheric pressure and p the vapor pressure of the saline. Values of p for solutions of water and for 2.5 per cent sodium chloride are given in International Critical Tables for various temperatures, and figures for 0.9 per cent sodium chloride, obtained by interpolation, are listed in table 3.

It is assumed that the solution is brought into equilibrium with carbon dioxide the partial pressure of which can be calculated from the percentage in the gas tank. The gas mixture must be bubbled into the saline to oxygenate the tissue, and it is known that this process may force excess gas into solution and introduce hydrostatic and other errors (Cady, Elsey and Berger, 1922; Harned and Davis, 1943). However, the pH measured with a glass electrode under the above conditions at body temperature usually differed by no more than 0.05 unit from the calculated value, and table 3 should show the trend with temperature.

It can be seen from table 3 that a fall of temperature from 39° C. to 5° C. almost trebles the carbon dioxide concentration and lowers the pH by about 0.2 units. It is possible that these complex environmental changes serve to mask or compensate other effects of temperature. It is known that frog sciatic nerve responds to an increase in the partial pressure of carbon dioxide by a polarization, followed later by a slow depolarization (Shanes, 1948).

The effect of temperature on the action of curare. The studies of Fatt and Katz (1951) on frog muscle have shown that the resting potential of the muscle fiber is equal to that of the end-plate region, and that the end-plate potential is an approximately linear function of the resting potential. If these findings are generally applicable, then it seems that search should be made elsewhere for an explanation of temperature effects on the action of *d*-tubocurarine.

Information on the effect of temperature on the end-plate potential of isolated cat tenuissimus muscle is provided by the studies of Boyd and Martin (1956b). They found that a fall of temperature from 37° C. to 22° C. increased the amplitude of the end-plate potential when transmission was blocked by magnesium, and this was considered largely due to an increase in quantum content of transmitter. The amplitude and direction of spontaneous miniature end-plate potentials was also generally increased, while the frequency was decreased (Boyd and Martin, 1956a). Liley (1956) also found that the frequency of spontaneous miniature end-plate potentials in the rat diaphragm was decreased with temperature, being a minimum at about 25° C. These results suggest the need of a study of the effect of temperature on the liberation of acetylcholine. The action of temperature seems, however, to be complex, for in the presence of curare a fall of temperature to 22° C. decreases the amplitude of the end-plate potential in cat muscle (Boyd and Martin, 1956b). This suggests a more potent action of curare at lower temperatures and contrasts with the fact that curare activity approaches a minimum at this temperature (Holmes *et al.*, 1951).

It is of interest that Kostial and Vouk (1956) have found no change in the liberation of acetylcholine in the isolated superior cervical ganglion of the cat in the temperature range from 20° C. to 40° C., while no change in depolarization produced by acetylcholine on the superior cervical ganglia of the rat was detected between 2° C. and 38° C. (Pascoe, 1956).

SUMMARY

The effect of temperature on the isolated rat diaphragm in a carbon-dioxide-bicarbonate medium has been studied with intracellular electrodes. The electrode was pushed through the whole substance of the tissue and the electrical deflexions were recorded by a pen writer.

Mean potentials showed little change after at least 6 hours.

In this medium there was no change in the mean resting potential between 39° C. and 15° C. Lowering the temperature to 5° C. gave a small and insignificant fall of resting potential.

The effects of temperature on the carbon-dioxide-bicarbonate system are summarized.

ACKNOWLEDGMENTS. This research was supported by a grant from the U. S. Public Health Service, Number B-738.

It is a pleasure to acknowledge the help received from Dr. Xenia Mackne and from Mr. P. B. Hollander regarding the use of microelectrodes.

The slit lamp was kindly given by Spratt Optical Company, Los Angeles.

Some of the material of this report has been incorporated into a thesis presented to the University of California by one of us (N.W.S.).

REFERENCES

BOYD, I. A., AND MARTIN, A. R.: J. Physiol., **132:** 61, 1956a.
BOYD, I. A., AND MARTIN, A. R.: J. Physiol., **132:** 74, 1956b.
CADY, H. P., ELSEY, H. M., AND BERGER, E. V.: J. Amer. Chem. Soc., **44:** 1456, 1922.
CREESE, R.: Proc. Roy. Soc. London s.B., **142:** 497, 1954.
CREESE, R., DILLON, J. B., MARSHALL, J., SABAWALA, P. B., SCHNEIDER, D. J., TAYLOR, D. B., AND ZINN, D. E.: THIS JOURNAL, **119:** 485, 1957.
FISHER, R. A.: Statistical Methods for Research Workers, Chap. 5, 11th ed., Hafner Pub. Co., New York, 1950.
FATT, P., AND KATZ, B.: J. Physiol., **115:** 320, 1951.
HARNED, H. S., AND DAVIS, R.: J. Amer. Chem. Soc., **65:** 2030, 1943.
HARNED, H. S., AND BONNER, F. T.: J. Amer. Chem. Soc., **67:** 1026, 1945.
HOLMES, P. E. B., JENDEN, D. J., AND TAYLOR, D. B.: THIS JOURNAL, **103:** 382, 1951.
International Critical Tables, 1929, Vol. 3. McGraw-Hill, New York.
KOSTIAL, K., AND VOUK, V. B.: J. Physiol., **132:** 239, 1956.
LILEY, A. W.: J. Physiol., **132:** 650, 1956.
LING, G., AND WOODBURY, J. W.: J. Cell. & Comp. Physiol., **34:** 407, 1949.
NASTUK, W. L., AND HODGKIN, A. L.: J. Cell. & Comp. Physiol., **35:** 39, 1950.
PASCOE, J. E.: J. Physiol., **132:** 242, 1956.
SHANES, A. M.: Am. J. Physiol., **153:** 93, 1948.

8057

ANTIARRHYTHMICS. QUINIDINE-LIKE ACTIVITY OF SOME ATARAXIC AGENTS[1, 2]

R. B. ARORA

Department of Pharmacology, All India Institute of Medical Sciences, New Delhi 3, India

Received for publication May 14, 1958

It was adduced by Arora and Das (1956) that antiveratrinic action is a property common to a large number of synthetic and natural drugs which combat experimental cardiac arrhythmias. Of the tranquilizing agents, reserpine and alseroxylon (Rauwiloid) exhibit marked antagonism to veratridine (Arora, 1956). It was, therefore, deemed expedient to determine if they also possess antiarrhythmic properties. Benactyzine and meprobamate, recently categorized as ataraxics, were also included in these investigations to assess their antiveratrinic and antiarrhythmic properties.

Since no single antiarrhythmic assay procedure can predict adequately the over-all activity of a compound, a combination of test procedures was employed. Quinidine sulfate was used for comparison.

Materials and methods.[3] One per cent solutions of reserpine, alseroxylon, benactyzine and meprobamate were used throughout.

1. *Isolated rabbit atria.* The method developed by Dawes (1946) was used. Adult albino rabbits (1 to 2 kgm.) were killed by a blow on the head. The heart was removed immediately and placed in oxygenated Ringer-Locke solution. After washing the chambers free of blood, the atria were isolated and quickly transferred to an organ bath containing oxygenated Ringer-Locke solution at 29°C. The electrode arrangement was the same as used by Dawes. After the atrium had been immersed in the bath for 30 minutes, it was stimulated periodically for 15 seconds by break shocks of increasing frequency until a point was reached where the atrium no longer responded to every stimulus. This was recorded as "maximal response rate" (considered to be the reciprocal of the refractory period). Ten minutes after the addition of a drug to the bath the maximal response rate was redetermined.

2. *Atrial arrhythmias.* Mongrel dogs of both sexes (8 to 13 kgm.) were anesthetized with pentobarbital (30 mgm./kgm. intravenously). Under positive pressure artificial respiration, the chest was opened to expose the right side of the heart. To permit free access to the right side of the atrium, the animal was rotated on its long axis so that the heart fell towards the left side. The split pericardium was sutured over the chest walls.

Atrial flutter: Atrial flutter was initiated in all experiments by the injury-stimulation procedure described by Rosenblueth and García Ramos (1947 a, b). A narrow band of atrial tissue connecting the superior and inferior vena cava was crushed by means of hemostats and stable flutter was produced by subsequent stimulation of the atrium with square waves (duration 1 millisecond, voltage 15 to 20, frequency 15 to 20 per second).

The drugs were injected after the flutter had continued for at least 35 minutes. Spontaneous reversions to normal of an arrhythmia of this duration were rare.

Aconitine-induced atrial fibrillation: Atrial fibrillation was produced in dogs after the method of Scherf (1947). In exactly the same manner as described above, the chest and pericardium were opened under pentobarbital anesthesia. A cotton pledget, soaked in 0.05 per cent solution of aconitine nitrate, was placed on the atrium. Within a few minutes, persistent atrial fibrillation was produced. The intravenous administration of the drug was continued until 1:1 rhythm with the rate below 200 beats per minute (endpoint) was reached. The "titration procedure" employed by Winbury and Hemmer (1955) was used, *i.e.*, 1 mgm./kgm. of the drug was injected intravenously every minute until reversion to normal sinus

[1] This investigation was supported by a grant-in-aid from the Indian Council of Medical Research.

[2] Presented in preliminary form in the Proceedings of the Indian Science Congress, 45th Session, January 1958, at Madras. The author is grateful to Mr. R. K. Manik, artist, A.I.I.M.S., New Delhi, for the help rendered in the preparation of graphs.

[3] Drugs were generously supplied by the following: benactyzine, Boots Pure Drug Company, Nottingham, England; reserpine, Ciba, Ltd., Bombay; meprobamate, Lederle Laboratories (India), Ltd., Bombay; alseroxylon, Riker Laboratories, Los Angeles, California.

rhythm occurred in flutter or "endpoint" was reached in fibrillation.

In addition to the bipolar Lead II, electrograms were recorded directly from the atrium and ventricle by a 3-channel Grass ink-writing oscillograph and Cardiopan II.

3. *Ventricular arrhythmias, following acute myocardial infarction.* The technique of two-stage ligation of the anterior descending branch of the left coronary artery as developed by Harris (1950) was employed.

Mongrel dogs of both sexes (12 to 18 kgm.) were anesthetized with pentobarbital 30 mgm./kgm. Under artificial respiration, the anterior descending branch of the left coronary artery was exposed via a small incision in the fourth intercostal space on the left side. The artery was freed from connective tissue and accompanying veins for a few mm. at a level 2 to 5 mm. distal to the margin of the left auricular appendage. A doubled ligature was passed under the artery and cut, thereby becoming two ligatures. One of the ligatures was then tied snugly but not tightly around the artery together with a No. 20 hypodermic needle. The needle was withdrawn immediately leaving the artery constricted but not closed. The second ligature was tightened 30 minutes later, totally occluding the artery. The chest wound was closed in layers and natural respiration restored. The animals were used in the unanesthetized state 18 to 24 hours after the operation when their electrocardiogram indicated complete dissociation of atrial and ventricular activity with nearly all beats ventricular in origin. The test compounds were administered (dosage ranging between 6 and 20 mgm./kgm.) intravenously, well diluted in 20 ml. of 5 per cent glucose in normal saline over a period of 5 minutes. The drug was repeated after 30 minutes if necessary. Electrocardiograms, bipolar Lead II, were recorded as in 2.

Antiveratrinic method: Male frogs (*Rana tigrina*) were used. Both sartorius muscles of an individual animal were prepared, suspended in twin chambers and attached to tension levers. The bath fluid was bicarbonate buffer solution (Krayer *et al.*, 1943) similar to that described by McLean and Hastings (1934). The method has been described in detail in a previous communication (Arora and Dandiya, 1956).

Supramaximal square wave shocks were applied to the muscle in the bath fluid. The intensity of the stimulus as a rule was 40 volts and the duration 0.5 millisecond. The "veratrine response" was produced by suspending the muscle in a concentration of 1:10 million veratridine.

By experimenting with various concentrations of the drug in the bath, the minimum concentration which was capable of preventing the veratrine

TABLE 1

Effect of drugs in cardiac arrhythmias

Number of Experiments	Drug	Dose	Results
	Isolated Rabbit Atrium		
			Average per cent reduction in maximal frequency
6	Quinidine	2.5×10^{-6}*	13.4
6	Reserpine	2.5×10^{-6}	9.4
6	Alseroxylon	2.5×10^{-6}	17.8
6	Benactyzine	2.5×10^{-6}	26.1
6	Meprobamate	2.5×10^{-6}	10.2
	Atrial Flutter		
		mgm./kgm.	
6	Quinidine	21.0	Reversion†
6	Reserpine	1.5	Reversion
6	Alseroxylon	6.7	Reversion
6	Benactyzine	2.1	Reversion
8	Meprobamate	25.0	No reversion
	Aconitine-induced Atrial Fibrillation		
		mgm./kgm.	
6	Quinidine	16.5	End point‡
6	Reserpine	12.0	End point
6	Alseroxylon	17.3	End point
6	Benactyzine	5.6	End point
8	Meprobamate	25.0	Not reached
	Ventricular Tachycardia Following Acute Myocardial Infarction		
		mgm./kgm.	*Reduction in ectopic rate*
6	Quinidine	20	¶
6	Reserpine	15	§
6	Alseroxylon	6	‖
6	Benactyzine	6	‖
6	Meprobamate	20	¶

* Concentration in bath.

† Reversion means restoration of normal sinus rhythm.

‡ End point is establishment of 1:1 rhythm, with heart rate below 200/min.

§ Reduction in total heart rate, no effect on ectopic rate.

¶ Reduction in total heart rate, 50 to 75 per cent reduction in ectopic rate maintained for more than 15 minutes.

‖ Reduction in total heart rate, 75 per cent reduction to complete suppression of ectopic activity, maintained for more than 15 minutes.

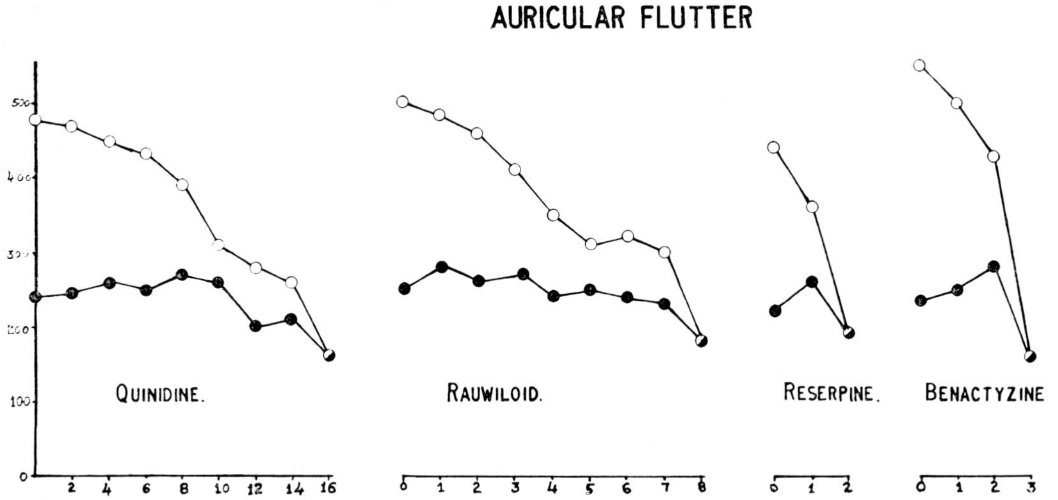

FIG. 1. Effect of quinidine, alseroxylon (Rauwiloid), reserpine and benactyzine in atrial flutter.

Ordinate: number of beats per minute of the atrium ---○--- and the ventricle ---●---. Abscissa: total dose in mgm./kgm. The compounds were injected intravenously at the rate of 1 mgm./kgm./minute. Each graph represents results from a different animal.

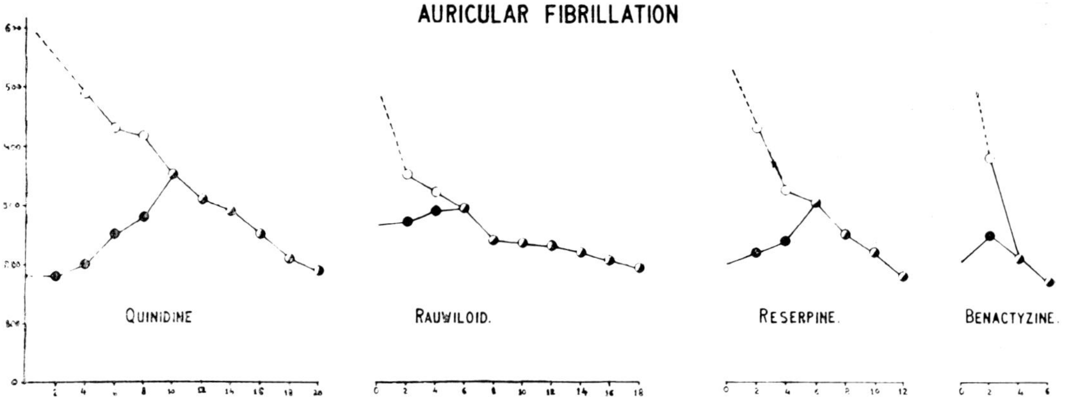

FIG. 2. Effect of quinidine, alseroxylon (Rauwiloid), reserpine and benactyzine in aconitine-evoked atrial fibrillation.

Ordinate: number of beats per minute of the atrium ---○--- and the ventricle ---●---. Abscissa: total dose in mgm./kgm. The compounds were injected intravenously at the rate of 1 mgm./kgm./minute. Each graph represents results from a different animal.

response and abolishing a fully developed veratrine response was found out. In the former case pretreatment of the muscle with the desired concentration of the drug was for 14 minutes.

In addition, specificity of the antiveratrinic effect was also tested. Following the complete abolition of a fully developed veratrine response by the test substance, the treated muscle was washed, sometimes more than twice, with bicarbonate buffer solution and 1:10 million veratridine was added to the bath. Development of the usual veratrine response showed that the action was a specific one (Arora, 1956).

RESULTS. *Action on atrial arrhythmias.* Preliminary experiments on the isolated rabbit atrium indicated that all the drugs studied *in vitro* caused lengthening of the refractory period. When compared to quinidine, benactyzine and alseroxylon were stronger, while reserpine and meprobamate were weaker in this respect (table 1).

In atrial flutter produced by the injury-stimulation procedure, the initial effect of the administration of these drugs was a decline in the atrial rate; ventricular rate followed no set pat-

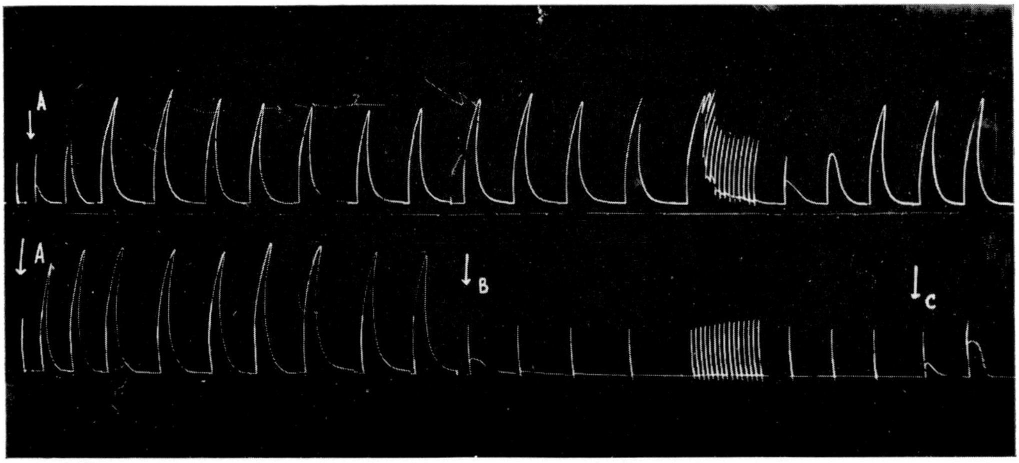

FIG. 3. The abolition of fully developed "veratrine response" by meprobamate.

Sartorius muscles suspended in twin chambers in a bath volume of 6 ml. of bicarbonate buffer solution attached to tension levers. Stimulation (40 volts, 0.5 millisec., square waves) and drum arrested for most of the two-minute interval between stimuli except where mentioned on the tracing when stimulation was at the rate of one per second. At signal "A" both the upper and lower muscles were exposed to 1:10 million veratridine. At signal "B" in the lower muscle a concentrated solution of meprobamate was added to make a 1:10,000 concentration of the drug in bicarbonate buffer solution. After 8 minutes, the veratrine response was completely abolished. At "C" the meprobamate solution in veratridine was removed from the bath of lower muscle and was replaced by a solution containing 1:10 million veratridine. For explanation, see text.

tern (fig. 1). With increasing doses there was sudden reversion to normal sinus rhythm. Reserpine, alseroxylon and benactyzine possessed greater activity than quinidine in this test procedure (table 1 and fig. 1). Meprobamate, however, showed no activity even when injected in doses as large as 25 mgm./kgm.

In aconitine-induced atrial arrhythmia, the endpoint was reached with all the drugs except meprobamate. Benactyzine was found to be more potent than any other drug in this respect (table 1 and fig. 2).

Meprobamate was successful in bringing about 1:1 rhythm in 2 of the 5 experiments but failed to reduce the rate below 200 beats per minute in any experiment.

Action on ventricular arrhythmias. Only such dogs were selected for determining the antiarrhythmic activity in which over 75 per cent of the heart beats were ventricular in origin and there was complete A-V dissociation with little evidence of atrial activity as characterized by the absence of P waves. A drug was considered to be effective in combating the arrhythmia if it produced and maintained reduction in the ectopic rate by more than 50 per cent for more than 15 minutes.

The typical response in the "coronary dog" to an effective dose of an active antiarrhythmic drug was as follows: a reduction in total rate and ectopic ventricular rate occurred first and, as the action progressed, sinus beats appeared, frequently as short runs of 5 or 6 beats. The rhythm then fluctuated between sinus and ventricular and then shifted to nearly continuous sinus rhythm. The duration of sinus rhythm varied in different experiments and lasted from a few minutes to an hour or more. Before the ventricular tachycardia fully returned, there were alternating phases of sinus and ventricular beats.

In the case of reserpine, ventricular ectopic activity was refractory even when the drug was administered up to a total dose of 15 mgm./kgm. There was, however, some reduction in the total rate. With this dose of reserpine, 3 out of the 6 dogs developed parkinsonian tremors of head and limbs.

The semi-quantitative scheme, as adopted by Clark and Cumming (1956) was employed for assessing the degree of antiarrhythmic activity of a compound. The results are summarized in table 1.

Antiveratrinic activity. Meprobamate was found ineffective in antagonizing the veratrine response in concentrations up to 1:30,000. In a concentration of 1:10,000, however, it prevented

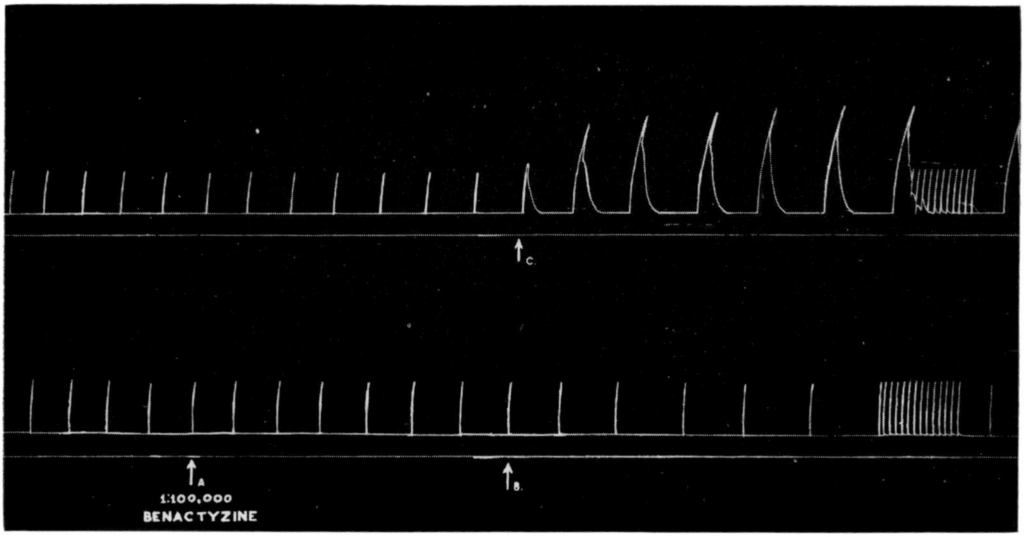

FIG. 4. The prevention of "veratrine response" by benactyzine.
At signal "A" the lower muscle was exposed to benactyzine 1:100,000. At signal "B" the solution in the bath of lower muscle was replaced by a solution containing benactyzine 1:100,000 and veratridine 1:10 million. Immediately after this at signal "C" the upper muscle was exposed to veratridine 1:10 million. For further explanation, see text.

the onset of the veratrine response in each of 6 experiments. It abolished it, as well, in 8 minutes in 5 out of 6 experiments (fig. 3).

Benactyzine in a concentration of 1:100,000 exhibited potent antiveratrinic activity (fig. 4). Like meprobamate, it resembled quinidine in that it not only abolished the veratrine response in 22 minutes in each of 6 experiments but also prevented it in each of 6 experiments.

With both meprobamate and benactyzine in effective concentrations, this was found to be a specific antiveratrinic effect.

DISCUSSION. The production of rapid, persistent, ectopic ventricular tachycardia by two-stage coronary ligation duplicates some of the major features exhibited by patients with myocardial infarction, in whom severe ventricular arrhythmia arises (Harris *et al.*, 1951, 1952). This arrhythmia may precipitate ventricular fibrillation (Harris and Guevara Rojas, 1943; Harris, 1948). If the intensity of the ectopic excitatory activity is reduced in the boundary of the infarct by drugs, the danger of an ectopic focus, frequently sufficiently great to produce the conditions required to initiate ventricular fibrillation, is effectively diminished (Harris *et al.*, 1952). Both benactyzine and alseroxylon have been found to be more effective than quinidine in suppressing such ectopic activity without exhibiting any demonstrable untoward side-effects in the unanesthetized coronary dog. They are equally successful in abolishing aconitine-induced atrial fibrillation as well as flutter produced by the injury-stimulation procedure in anesthetized dogs. These experimental atrial arrhythmias also simulate clinical disorders (Winbury and Hemmer, 1955).

The LD_{50}'s of these tranquilizing agents in mice are: benactyzine 100 mgm./kgm., i.p.; meprobamate 800 ± 15 mgm./kgm., i.p.; reserpine 28 ± 12 mgm./kgm., i.p.; and alseroxylon 45.6 mgm./kgm., i.p. The toxicity of benactyzine compares favorably with that of quinidine, the intraperitoneal LD_{50} of which was found by Dawes (1946) to be 135 mgm./kgm. in the same species. Meprobamate compares even more favorably; it is equally effective on ventricular arrhythmias but much less toxic than quinidine.

Chlorpromazine, an ataraxic agent, was shown to possess puissant antiarrhythmic activity (Arora, 1956). Recently it has been found more effective than quinidine in combating ventricular tachycardia following acute myocardial infarction (Arora, unpublished observations).

Keeping in mind these facts and the psychosomatic background of cardiac arrhythmias, which has lately been stressed by Katz and Pick (1956), it seems that these tranquilizing agents show sufficient promise to warrant clinical trials in selected cases.

It has been previously reported by Arora (1956) that alseroxylon, reserpine and chlorpromazine show strong antiveratrinic activity. The results of the present study indicate that benactyzine shares this property with these drugs. In their ability to combat established atrial arrhythmias produced experimentally, benactyzine, alseroxylon and reserpine compare favorably with quinidine while meprobamate is devoid of this activity. These observations strengthen the parallelism existing between the antiveratrinic and atrial antiarrhythmic actions of a compound which has been described previously by Arora and Das (1956) and Arora and Madan (1956 a, b).

Findings obtained in the present investigations also show that meprobamate increases the refractoriness of the atria but is unsuccessful in the treatment of experimental atrial arrhythmias. It, therefore, implies that the ability of a compound to lengthen refractory period may not be a correct guide to the assessment of its antiarrhythmic activity. Although this observation runs counter to the contention of Dawes (1946), it is in consonance with the observations of Van Dongen (1950).

SUMMARY

Alseroxylon, reserpine and benactyzine possess significant quinidine-like activity in prolonging the refractory period of isolated rabbit atria as well as in abolishing experimentally induced atrial fibrillation and flutter in anesthetized dogs. Meprobamate is not efficacious in the atrial arrhythmias although it shares the propensity of quinidine to increase atrial refractoriness. It, however, equals quinidine in the suppression of ectopic activity produced by 2-stage coronary ligation in unanesthetized dogs. In this test procedure, benactyzine and alseroxylon are stronger than quinidine while reserpine is considerably weaker.

REFERENCES

Arora, R. B.: Arch. internat. Pharmacodyn., **106**: 28, 1956.

Arora, R. B., and Dandiya, P. C.: This Journal, **118**: 230, 1956.

Arora, R. B., and Das, P. K.: Arch. internat. Pharmacodyn., **107**: 202, 1956.

Arora, R. B., and Madan, B. R.: Indian J. M. Res., **44**: 453, 1956a.

Arora, R. B., and Madan, B. R.: J. Indian M. A., **26**: 262, 1956b.

Clark, B. B., and Cumming, J. R.: Ann. New York Acad. Sci., **64**: 543, 1956.

Dawes, G. S.: Brit. J. Pharmacol., **1**: 90, 1946.

Harris, A. S.: Circulation, **1**: 1318, 1950.

Harris, A. S., Estandia, A., Ford, T. J., Smith, H. T., Olsen, R. W., and Tillotson, R. F.: Circulation, **5**: 551, 1952.

Harris, A. S., Estandia, A., Ford, T. J., and Tillotson, R. R.: Circulation, **4**: 522, 1951.

Harris, A. S., and Guevara Rojas, A.: Exper. Med. & Surg., **1**: 105, 1943.

Harris, A. S.: Am. Heart J., **35**: 895, 1948.

Katz, L. N., and Pick, A.: Clinical Electrocardiography, 2nd ed., Lea & Febiger, Philadelphia, 1956.

Krayer, O., Linstead, R. P., and Todd, D.: This Journal, **77**: 113, 1943.

McLean, F. C., and Hastings, A. B.: J. Biol. Chem., **107**: 337, 1934.

Rosenblueth, A., and García Ramos, J.: Arch. Inst. cardiol. Mexico, **17**: 1, 1947a.

Rosenblueth, A., and García Ramos, J.: Am. Heart J., **33**: 677, 1947b.

Scherf, D.: Proc. Soc. Exp. Biol. & Med., **64**: 233, 1947.

Van Dongen, K.: Arch. internat. Pharmacodyn., **81**: 129, 1950.

Winbury, M. M., and Hemmer, M. L.: This Journal, **113**: 402, 1955.

8058

SOME CARDIOVASCULAR EFFECTS OF NORETHANDROLONE (NILEVAR), TESTOSTERONE AND PROGESTERONE

C. GORDON VAN ARMAN AND VICTOR A. DRILL

Division of Biological Research, G. D. Searle & Co., Chicago 80, Illinois

Received for publication June 18, 1958

The steroid norethandrolone (Nilevar) is 17-ethyl-19-nortestosterone. Its chief property of therapeutic interest is an anabolic effect, that is, an ability to promote formation of tissue in general (Saunders and Drill, 1956). In this process, nitrogen and potassium are retained in the body. Norethandrolone is closely related chemically to testosterone, but has much weaker androgenic properties. Saunders, Colton and Drill (1957) have found that norethandrolone has certain progesterone-like actions in that it will bring about endometrial gland proliferation, when injected systemically or into the uterine lumen, in estrogen-primed rabbits. Progesterone itself had a negative inotropic action on perfused hearts in one study (Rubin and Salter, 1952), an action which was not seen with several other common steroids.

In the present work norethandrolone was studied in dogs for possible effects on auricular flutter, blood pressure, heart rate, ventricular arrhythmia and electrocardiogram. Progesterone and testosterone propionate were evaluated for effects on auricular flutter and blood pressure. Progesterone was used because it has some other properties similar to those of norethandrolone, and testosterone was used because it is close to norethandrolone in structure. All three compounds were perfused through the isolated rabbit heart to determine effects on the rate, rhythm and strength of contraction.

METHODS. *Auricular flutter.* The procedure of Rosenblueth and García Ramos (1947), as employed by Winbury and Hemmer (1955), was used with mongrel dogs weighing approximately 15 kgm. In most of the work the compounds, because of the relative insolubility in water, were given intramuscularly in oil instead of intravenously. Initially they were administered to a few animals intravenously in propylene glycol. Electrodes sewed onto the right atrium picked up the electrical impulses which were recorded on a Grass electroencephalograph. Control experiments with intravenous saline showed only 2 out of 23 spontaneous reversions to normal rhythm within a half-hour after initiation of the flutter.

Blood pressure was measured during the auricular flutter and cardiac output experiments, by means of a strain gauge transducer connected with a carotid artery.

Heart rate was recorded via Lead II of an electrocardiograph.

Effects on ventricular arrhythmia were measured by the method of Winbury and Hemmer (1955), which is essentially that of Harris (1950). Dogs were subjected to a 2-stage coronary ligation; the next day approximately 95 to 100 per cent of beats recorded electrocardiographically were of ectopic origin. Drugs like quinidine and procaine can revert these to normal sinus rhythm.

Perfusion of the isolated rabbit heart was essentially according to the method of Langendorff, as described by Burn (1952). Two bottles were set up containing Locke-Ringer solution (Sollman and Hanzlik, 1939); each led through a set of warming coils in a water bath to a two-way stopcock so that the contents of either bottle could be directed into the perfusion system. One bottle also contained the steroid in solution. An experiment was done in which both bottles contained only Locke-Ringer solution; switching from one bottle to another did not affect the heart.

Solubilities of the steroid in Locke-Ringer at 25°C., determined by ultraviolet absorption analysis, are as follows: norethandrolone 4.7 mgm./l., testosterone propionate 2.6 mgm./l., progesterone 4.3 mgm./l. All three compounds were tested at a concentration of 2.5 mgm./l.

RESULTS. *Auricular flutter.* Intravenous administration of norethandrolone in 20 per cent propylene glycol caused reversion to normal rhythm in 1 dog at 1.5 mgm./kgm., in another dog at 4 mgm./kgm., and in another at 5 mgm./kgm. Intramuscular administration of 10 mgm./kgm. of norethandrolone in corn oil was accomplished by injection into 3 or 4 different sites; if no reversion occurred within 30 minutes,

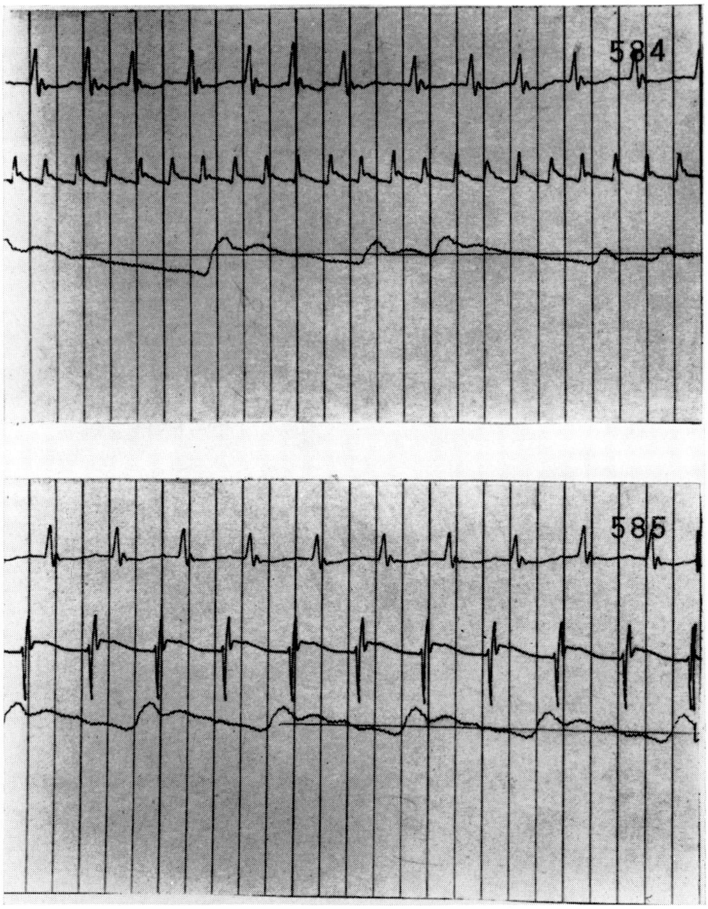

Fig. 1. Upper half of figure shows tracings taken from a dog before norethandrolone was given. Top line: Lead II electrocardiogram. Second line: Direct leads from the auricle. Third line: Pressure in femoral artery (mean 160 mm.).
Bottom half shows same tracings 14 minutes after 10 mgm./kgm. of norethandrolone was given intramuscularly. Mean blood pressure was unaltered.

another 10 mgm./kgm. was given; if no effect occurred within a further 30 minutes, the result was considered negative. Under such conditions norethandrolone caused reversion to normal rhythm in 5 of 6 dogs (see fig. 1 and table 1).

In addition, there were 3 trials (1 in each of 3 dogs) in which norethandrolone was given after a previously ineffective dose of 20 mgm./kgm. of testosterone. Norethandrolone caused reversion to normal rhythm in 1 dog at 10 mgm./kgm., in another at 20 mgm./kgm.; it was not active in the third dog at 20 mgm./kgm. There was also one trial, following a previous dose of progesterone, in which norethandrolone did not revert rhythm to normal after 20 mgm./kgm.

Testosterone propionate was administered intramuscularly as described above for norethandrolone, but without any effect on auricular flutter (table 1).

Progesterone given intramuscularly caused reversion of auricular flutter to normal rhythm in 5 of 6 dogs (table 1). In addition, there was 1 dog in which progesterone was ineffective despite the fact that norethandrolone had previously produced a reversion to normal rhythm. In a second dog, neither norethandrolone nor, later, progesterone produced a normal beat, at a dose of 20 mgm./kgm.

Blood pressure. After intravenous doses of norethandrolone in 20 per cent propylene glycol, the blood pressure fell; in 1 dog from 140 mm. of mercury to 92 mm. at a dose of 4 mgm./kgm., and in another dog from 125 to 102 mm. at a

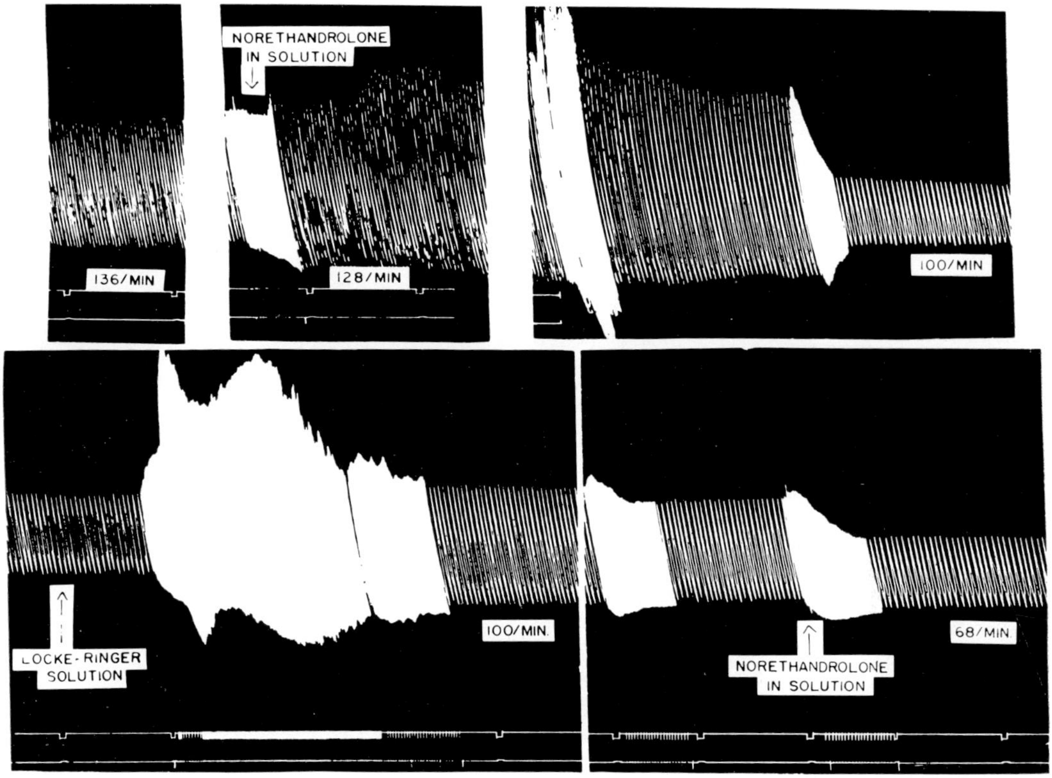

FIG. 2. Tracing from isolated rabbit heart.
Kymograph was run at slow and at fast speeds. Rate of beat is indicated.

dose of 5 mgm./kgm. The propylene glycol was not responsible for the effect.

On the other hand, with intramuscular doses in oil, in the flutter studies, no certain influence on blood pressure was detectable with norethandrolone, testosterone propionate or progesterone, at doses of 10 or 20 mgm./kgm.

Isolated rabbit heart. The phenomena elicited by all three steroids were similar. They were rather unexpected and do not appear to have a ready explanation. Three hearts were tested with norethandrolone, 4 with testosterone propionate, and 3 with progesterone. These all behaved in the same way (fig. 2). After the control period, at the time when the drug was given, a great stimulation of amplitude occurred. The heart beat strongly for several minutes. The amplitude then began to decrease and soon fell below the initial level to a clear depression. If the drug were continued, A-V block and cardiac arrest followed, as we observed in several experiments other than those described here. When perfusion with the control solution was begun again, the heart recovered and increased its contraction strength beyond control level, up to the treatment level, for a brief period. It then returned to a condition which appeared essentially normal; *i.e.*, to the pretreatment level. However, if the steroid were now again perfused through the heart, no stimulation occurred; instead the phase of depression began at once. Washing out the control solution merely resulted in a recovery to normal amplitude without any overshoot. Repeated doses produced a like effect. It is noteworthy that the rate of beat did not change suddenly with perfusion. It gradually became slower; *e.g.*, it decreased from 136 to 100 beats per minute over a 10-minute period. The perfusion rate likewise did not change greatly; *e.g.*, in an experiment with norethandrolone, a control rate of 10 ml. per minute was not altered by addition of the steroid to the perfusion.

Heart rate in unanesthetized dogs. In 1 normal

TABLE 1

Effects of norethandrolone, testosterone propionate and progesterone, administered intramuscularly in oil, on auricular flutter

	Nor-ethan-drolone*	Testosterone propionate	Proges-terone*
Number of dogs	6	7	6
Effective at 10 mgm./kgm.	3	1	2
Effective at 20 mgm./kgm.	2	1(?)†	3
Not effective at 20 mgm./kgm.	1	5	1
Total fraction effective	5/6	2/7 (or 1/7)	5/6

* In the following animals included in the above table, a flutter could not be reestablished after the drug had abolished it. Norethandrolone: 2 out of 3 at 10 mgm./kgm.; 1 out of 2 at 20 mgm./kgm. Progesterone: 1 out of 2 at 10 mgm./kgm.; 1 out of 3 at 20 mgm./kgm.

† Doubtful whether this reversion was caused by the drug.

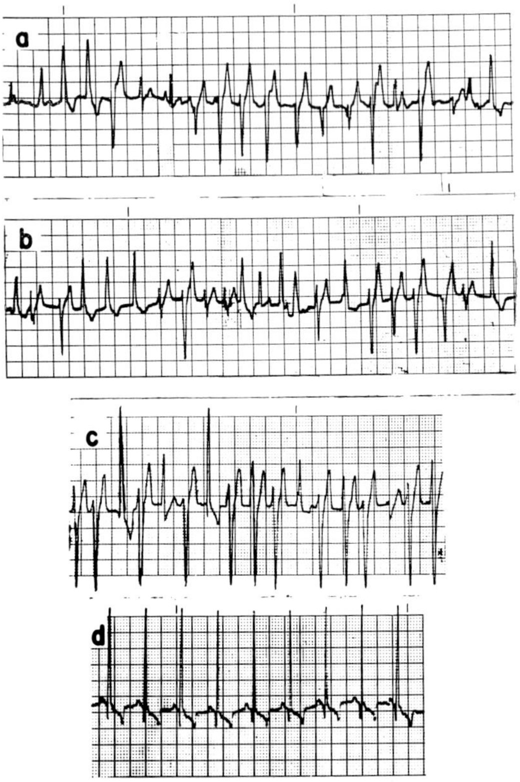

FIG. 3. (a) and (b) are tracings from Lead II from a dog with arrhythmia caused by ligation of the coronary artery; the control (a) is not different from (b) taken after treatment with norethandrolone at 10 mgm./kgm. subcutaneously; (c) is control record for (d) which shows the effect of procaine amide at 100 mgm./kgm. intravenously.

dog given norethandrolone intramuscularly in oil in several divided doses to a total of 12.5 mgm./kgm. over a period of 2 hours, no appreciable change in heart rate or electrocardiogram occurred. In another dog given a single dose of 10 mgm./kgm., no change occurred within 2 hours. With a massive dose, 50 mgm./kgm. intramuscularly, in a third dog, the rate rose from a control level of 65 beats per minute up to 104 for a half-hour, then fell to 72 for the next hour. During the next hour, the PR interval increased somewhat and returned to normal. A fourth dog given the same large dose responded with a slow fall in rate during 2 hours. This fall could be attributed to mere inactivity of the dog. In this dog the PR interval lengthened from 0.08 to 0.10 seconds, beginning at a half-hour and continuing through 2 hours. No studies of the effect of testosterone or progesterone on heart rate were made.

Ventricular arrhythmia. There were 3 trials with intravenous and 1 with intramuscular administration of norethandrolone. No consistent effect worthy of note became evident at doses of 10, 15 and 20 mgm./kgm. by the intravenous route and 12.5 mgm./kgm. by the intramuscular route (see fig. 3). In one dog, however, a moderate reduction in the percentage of ectopic beats occurred, along with temporary retching and slight prolongation of the PR interval.

DISCUSSION. One might suspect at first that reversion to normal rhythm could result secondarily from a decrease in myocardial contraction caused by a compound, instead of from the direct eurhythmic effects of the compound. However, there is no evidence here for any such decrease. A lowering of blood pressure may sometimes stop a flutter, but no appreciable lowering occurred in any of the studies following intramuscular administration.

The experiments on the isolated heart demonstrate that testosterone, progesterone and norethandrolone initially produce a stimulant effect followed by a depressant effect. Inasmuch as testosterone and progesterone do not show such an effect clinically, we conclude that the isolated rabbit heart, by this particular technique, does not correlate with the clinical actions of these substances. Our findings thus resemble those of Gowdey, Loynes and Waud (1950), who observed similar activity for testosterone and several other steroids. It is of interest that Nahum, Geller, Levine and Sikand (1951) found that progesterone lowered the threshold of excitability and produced extrasystoles in the intact dog heart.

Because norethandrolone and progesterone were both effective in stopping auricular flutter, and because testosterone was relatively less effective, one might suspect that it is the progesterone-like property of norethandrolone which confers upon it the eurhythmic potency.

The role of potassium and sodium in auricular flutter, and the possible changes in cardiac muscle cell permeability brought about by norethandrolone, lie entirely in the unexplored areas of the problem. The compound does produce a retention of potassium over a period of time, this retention being at least partially associated with the increased nitrogen retention and protein synthesis.

SUMMARY

Norethandrolone (17-ethyl-19-nortestosterone), testosterone propionate and progesterone all depress the amplitude of contraction of the isolated perfused rabbit heart.

Norethandrolone has appreciable potency in abolishing auricular flutter in dogs. Progesterone is approximately as effective as norethandrolone in this regard. Testosterone propionate does not show such activity to the same extent as the other two steroids.

Norethandrolone does not affect ventricular arrhythmia caused by coronary occlusion. It has negligible effects on blood pressure, heart rate and electrocardiogram, even at very large doses.

REFERENCES

BURN, J. H.: Practical Pharmacology, Blackwell Scientific Publications, Oxford, 1952.

GOWDEY, C. W., LOYNES, J. S., AND WAUD, R. A.: Fed. Proc., **9:** 277, 1950.

HARRIS, A. S.: Circulation, **1:** 1318, 1950.

NAHUM, L. H., GELLER, H. M., LEVINE, H., AND SIKAND, R. S.: Symposium on Steroids in Experimental and Clinical Practice, Blakiston Co., New York, 1951.

ROSENBLUETH, A., AND GARCÍA RAMOS, J.: Am. Heart J., **33:** 677, 1947.

RUBIN, B., AND SALTER, W. T.: THIS JOURNAL, **105:** 443, 1952.

SAUNDERS, F. J., AND DRILL, V. A.: Endocrinology, **58:** 567, 1956.

SAUNDERS, F. J., COLTON, F. B., AND DRILL, V. A.: Proc. Soc. Exper. Biol. & Med., **94:** 717, 1957.

SOLLMANN, T. H., AND HANZLIK, P. H.: Fundamentals of Experimental Pharmacology, 2nd ed., J. W. Stacey, Inc., San Francisco, 1939.

WINBURY, M. M., AND HEMMER, M. L.: THIS JOURNAL, **113:** 402, 1955.

8059

A STUDY OF THE PERIPHERAL AND CENTRAL ACTIONS OF DIBROMOPYRUVIC ACID[1]

WILLIAM R. MARTIN,[2] DANIEL H. ABDULIAN, KLAUS R. UNNA AND HARRIS BUSCH

Department of Pharmacology, University of Illinois College of Medicine, Chicago

Received for publication May 27, 1958

The findings of Busch *et al.* (1956) that halogenated pyruvic acid derivatives produce cholinergic effects, have provided an additional tool for the study of central cholinergic transmission. Early studies with the halogenated pyruvic acid derivatives demonstrated that central nervous system effects could be produced in doses of the same order of magnitude as those necessary to produce peripheral effects (Martin *et al.*, 1957). It appeared that halogenated pyruvic acids, unlike quaternary choline derivatives, could easily pass the blood brain barrier.

Dibromopyruvic acid was found to be the most potent of the halogenated pyruvic acid derivatives (Busch *et al.*, 1958) in producing cholinergic effects and for this reason was employed in these experiments. The purpose of this study is to characterize the nature of the peripheral and central actions of dibromopyruvic acid.

METHODS. Dibromopyruvic acid employed in these experiments was synthesized and characterized by Busch *et al.* (1958).

The *toxicity* and *analgetic* potency of dibromopyruvic acid was determined on female white mice of the Harlan strain weighing between 18 and 22 grams. The LD_{50} of dibromopyruvic acid was determined for the intravenous route and the animals were observed for 24 hours after injection. The analgetic $dose_{50}$ was determined with Bianchi and Franseschini's (1954) modification of the method of Haffner (1929). A 38-mm. serrafine of moderate strength was placed on the mouse's tail at the hairline, such that the tail lay midway between the extremes of the clamping surface. Most mice turn upon and attempt to dislodge the serrafine by biting it. A reactor is defined as one that bites the serrafine within thirty seconds after application. Mice were screened for reactors and only reactors were employed. The analgetic effects of dibromopyruvic acid were tested by this means 2, 5 and 15 minutes after intravenous injection and 30 minutes after subcutaneous injection.

The LD_{50} and AD_{50}, using 10 to 30 mice at 10 dose levels, were determined by the method of Litchfield and Wilcoxon (1949). Semiquantitative methods for the estimates of threshold for salivation and lacrimation were employed (Busch *et al.*, 1958).

Isolated rabbit ileum. The isolated rabbit ileal segments were suspended in a 30-ml. bath containing Krebs bicarbonate buffer at 37°C. The activity of the segment was recorded isotonically. The load on the muscle varied from 3 to 10 grams. The drugs were dissolved in 0.9 per cent NaCl and were added in a volume of 0.5 ml. to the bath.

Isolated heart. Cat hearts were perfused in a Langendorff apparatus with Ringer-Locke solution containing 1 gram of glucose per liter. After an adequate control was established, the perfusing fluid was switched to one containing a 1.0 or 5.0 mgm. per cent solution of dibromopyruvic acid dissolved in Ringer-Locke solution. To determine the reversibility of the effects produced by dibromopyruvic acid the heart was reperfused with the control Ringer-Locke solution.

Blood pressure, intestinal motility, electroencephalographic, electrocardiographic, and electromyographic activity were recorded from 12 unanesthetized spinal cats sectioned between C1 and C2 on a Grass eight-channel EEG, employing two balance demodulator units. The cats were surgically prepared under ether anesthesia and allowed to recover for at least 2 hours before continuing the experiments. The animals were maintained on artificial respiration. Bilateral vagotomy was performed in some experiments to eliminate any changes of vagal tone of central origin to the heart and upper gastrointestinal tract. The drugs were administered intravenously through a polyethylene catheter in the femoral vein. The blood pressure was detected from a polyethylene cannula in the femoral artery using a Statham strain gauge

[1] This investigation has been supported by grant B-983 from the U. S. Public Health Service and the Jane Coffin Childs Fund.

[2] Present address: National Institute of Mental Health, Addiction Research Center, U. S. Public Health Service, Lexington, Kentucky.

transducer and recorded on the EEG using a balance demodulator. Intestinal activity was recorded using a small balloon placed either in the duodenum or descending colon and hydraulically coupled to a water manometer; the gas filled portion of the manometer was coupled pneumatically to a Grass Model PT5 pressure transducer and the output of the transducer was recorded in the same manner as was employed for blood pressure. The EEG was recorded bipolarly from needle electrodes placed in the exposed calvarium. The ECG was taken from needle electrodes placed subcutaneously (Lead 1). An electromyogram was obtained with needle electrodes placed either in the hamstrings or quadriceps of the hindleg or the flexors of the forepaw. Needles were placed within 0.5 cm. of each other, and the electrical activity was recorded on the EEG.

Patellar reflex. These experiments were performed in unanesthetized spinal cats suspended in a frame by their intraspinous ligaments. The patellar reflex was elicited by a hammer tapping the patellar tendon once a second. Both sciatic nerves were exposed and Harvard electrodes were applied bilaterally. Inhibition and facilitation were produced by stimulating the ipsilateral and contralateral sciatic nerves respectively with a Labtronics stimulator delivering condenser discharge waves with a time constant of 1 millisecond and a frequency of 50 cycles/second. The stimulus was applied alternately to the ipsilateral and contralateral sciatic nerve for a 5 second period every minute. The strength of stimulation was varied such that the threshold voltage for inhibition and facilitation was determined. The knee jerk was recorded mechanically on an ink writing Bird Kymograph with the lower leg kicking against a spring. Blood pressure was recorded on the same record from the common carotid artery using a Statham strain gauge, an Offner type 131 DC amplifier and dynagraph pen. In some experiments the distal end of the cut common peroneal nerve was stimulated with a 250-cycle/second wave for 10 seconds and the force of contraction of the anterior tibial muscle recorded mechanically from the cut end of the tendon. The drugs were injected intravenously through a polyethylene cannula inserted into a tributary of the brachial vein.

RESULTS. *Pattern of effects of dibromopyruvic acid in the mouse.* Intravenous injection of dibromopyruvic acid produces a typical pattern of behavior in the mouse. Initially, there is a brief period of hyperexcitability which lasts approximately one minute. Within this first minute the animal exhibits salivation, lacrimation, urination, and defecation. These signs seem to be most intense several minutes after injection and gradually subside over a period of 10 minutes. They are readily depressed by atropine (2 mgm./kgm.), but are either unaffected or intensified by hexamethonium (2 mgm./kgm.). During the first 10 minutes the animals exhibited marked analgesia.

TABLE 1

Potency of dibromopyruvic acid in producing death (LD_{50}), analgesia (AD_{50}), salivation and lacrimation in mice without and with pretreatment with atropine

Values in parenthesis are 95 per cent confidence limits.

	Dibromopyruvic Acid	Dibromopyruvic Acid plus Atropine, 2 mgm/kgm.
	mgm./kgm.	*mgm./kgm.*
LD_{50}	90 (80.5–100)	125 (114.7–136.2)
AD_{50} (2 min.)	24.5 (16.9–35.5)	20 (12.2–32.8)
AD_{50} (5 min.)	68 (62–74)	50*
AD_{50} (15 min.)	no analgesia at 120	no analgesia at 150
Lacrimation (threshold)	5	no lacrimation at 150
Salivation (threshold)	10	no salivation at 150

* Approximation, since data were not homogeneous.

After the period in which the animal exhibits salivation and lacrimation, there is a progressive decrease in spontaneous activity of the mice, though they remain awake and can be easily stimulated to activity. After one or more hours following the injection of a lethal dose of the drugs, respiration becomes labored, there is evidence of a stasis of peripheral circulation inasmuch as the venous engorgement produced by milking the tail subsides very slowly, and shortly before death there are gasping respiratory movements that recur at a decreasing rate until the animal expires. Seizures have not been observed. Death ensued after 1 to 6 hours. Pretreatment of mice with atropine (2 mgm./kgm.) caused a small increase in the LD_{50} (table 1).

Because of the temporal relationship between the effects produced by this drug, it seemed useful to divide the effects into two syndromes. The first is characterized by lacrimation, salivation, urination, defecation, and analgesia, while the late effects are characterized by progressive cardiovascular and respiratory collapse.

Analgesia. The analgetic effects of dibromopyruvic acid have a rapid onset following intra-

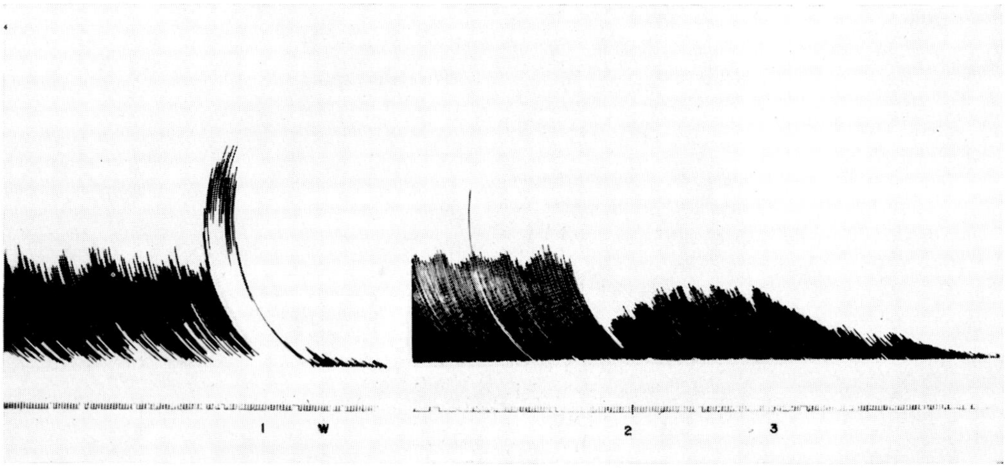

FIG. 1. Atropine antagonism of dibromopyruvic acid on rabbit ileum.

These illustrations were taken from a replicate series of ileal segments loaded with 3 grams. Dibromopyruvic acid in a concentration of 0.1 mgm./ml. (1) produced an increase in tone that disappeared with washing (W). In another segment atropine (2 microgm./ml.) (2) produced a decrease in the amplitude of spontaneous contraction and inhibited the stimulating action of dibromopyruvic acid (3) in a dose of 0.1 mgm./kgm. Following dibromopyruvic acid there was a progressive decrease in the amplitude of contractions. Time marks are 10 seconds.

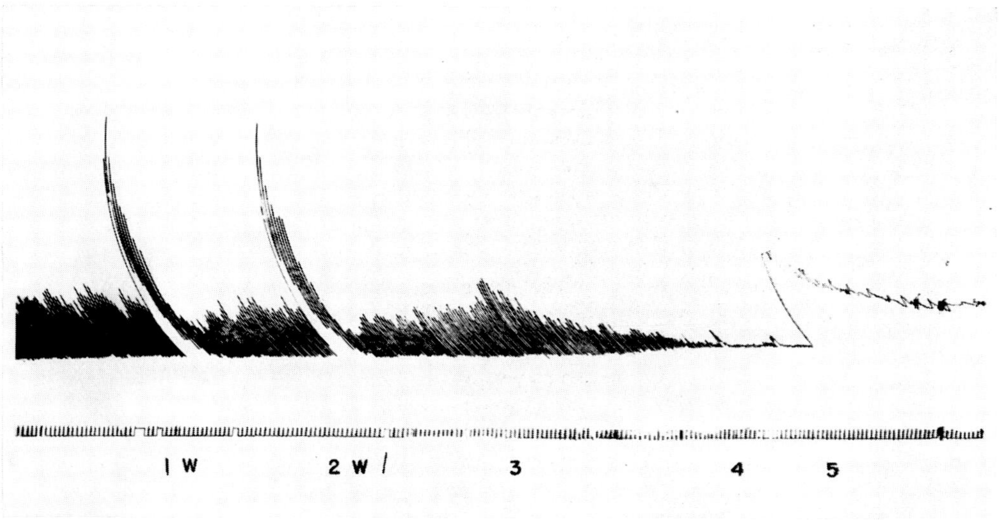

FIG. 2. The effects of dibromopyruvic acid on acetylcholine induced contractions of rabbit ileum.

Segment loaded with 5 grams. Acetylcholine in a concentration of 0.025 microgm./ml. produced concontractions at 1 and 2. Dibromopyruvic acid (0.1 mgm./ml.) (3) produced an initial increase in amplitude of contraction, which was followed by a progressive decrease in amplitude of contraction. Acetylcholine (0.025 microgm./ml.) (4) failed to produce any contraction, whereas 16.6 microgm./ml. of acetylcholine (5) produced a contracture. W = wash. Time marks 10 seconds.

venous administration and decay rapidly. Analgesia reached a maximum within 5 minutes and completely subsided within 15 minutes (table 1). Temporally, the cholinomimetic effects of this compound parallel its analgetic activity. Analgesia was also observed when dibromopyruvic acid was administered subcutaneously; however, the AD_{50} was greater (178 mgm./kgm.).

Gastrointestinal effects. Dibromopyruvic acid produces an increase in gastrointestinal activity in the unanesthetized spinal vagotomized cat, as well as in the intact mouse. Figure 3 illustrates the increase in duodenal tonus following 25

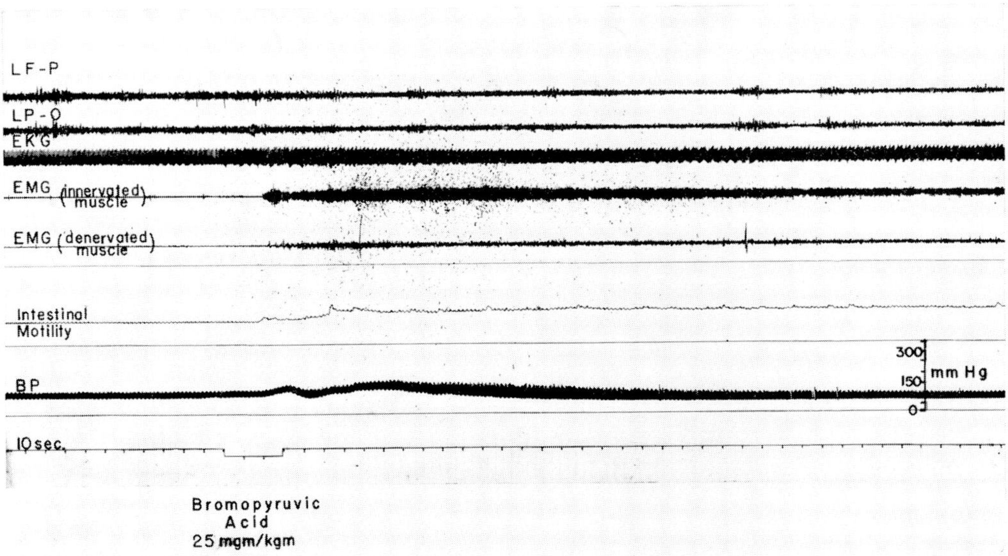

FIG. 3. The effect of dibromopyruvic acid on unanesthetized spinal vagotomized cat. Records taken on Grass EEG with paper speed of 0.5 cm./second. The tracings are EEG (LF–P = left frontal to parietal; LP–O = left parietal to occipital); ECG lead I; electromyogram (EMG) of an innervated and denervated hamstring muscle; intestinal motility and blood pressure (BP). Note the marked increase in electromyographic activity, intestinal tone, and blood pressure following dibromopyruvic acid.

mgm./kgm. of dibromopyruvic acid. An increase in activity was also observed in the descending colon. The stimulatory effects on both portions of the intestinal tract could be abolished or prevented by 1 to 2 mgm./kgm. of atropine.

The stimulatory action of dibromopyruvic acid was further studied on 60 segments of isolated rabbit ileum. Its effects were dependent upon the amount of loading of the segment. With a load of 5 or 10 grams, doses of 0.01 to 1.0 mgm./ml. of dibromopyruvic acid produced an increase in the amplitude of contraction with little or no increase in tone (figure 2), while the same doses caused a marked increase in tone when the strip was loaded with 3 grams (figure 1). Graded responses with a threshold of 0.01 mgm./ml. were obtained in 5 segments. These data indicate that dibromopyruvic acid is approximately $1/10{,}000$ as potent as acetylcholine. The contracting effects of dibromopyruvic acid on the rabbit ileum were antagonized by atropine (2 microgrm./ml.) as illustrated in figure 1. Neostigmine (0.16 microgrm./ml.) did not enhance the stimulatory effects. It was difficult to obtain dose response relationships because dibromopyruvic acid proved toxic to the segments of ileum. After the initial stimulatory effect, there was a progressive and irreversible decrease in spontaneous activity and in reactivity to acetylcholine (figure 2).

Effect on secretory glands. The threshold doses of dibromopyruvic acid necessary to produce salivation and lacrimation were 5.0 to 10 mgm./kgm. (table 1). The effects were further studied in the cat in which the mandibular and lingual branch of the trigeminal nerve was excised unilaterally. There was only a small difference in rate of production of saliva between the innervated and denervated submaxillary gland following 25 mgm./kgm. of dibromopyruvic acid.

Cardiovascular effects. The initial blood pressure changes produced by dibromopyruvic acid depend not only upon the dose but also on the rate of administration. Rapid administration in a spinal vagotomized cat resulted in a precipitous fall in blood pressure, while a slower administration of the same dose produced a rise in blood pressure (figure 3). During these early changes, which persisted for 1 to 10 minutes, dibromopyruvic acid always caused a tachycardia and in this respect differed from acetylcholine. The pressor response was not blocked by hexamethonium (1 to 2 mgm./kgm.) or mecamylamine (2 to 4 mgm./kgm.) indicating that it did not arise from stimulation of sympathetic ganglia. Twenty to 30 minutes following the

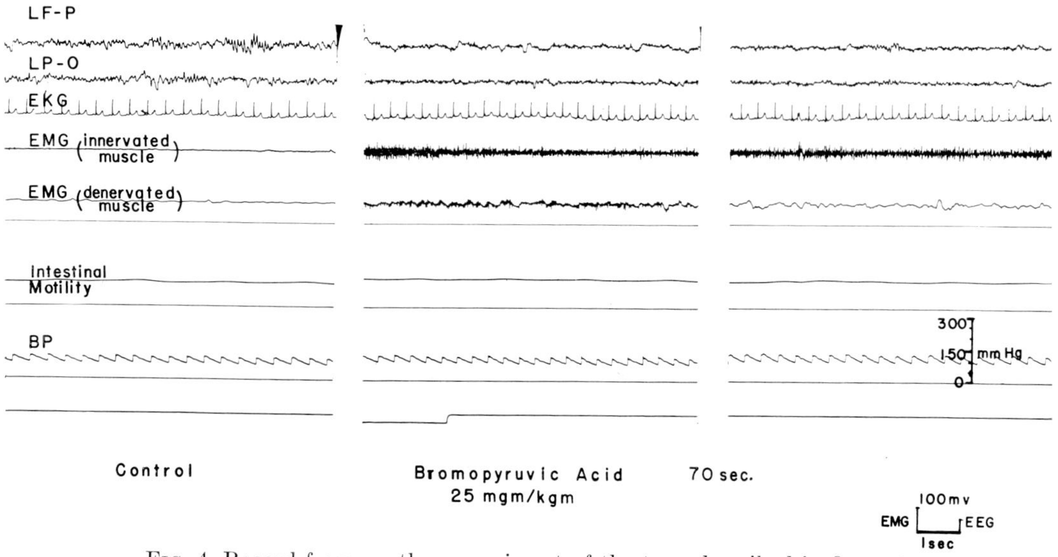

FIG. 4. Record from another experiment of the type described in figure 3. Paper speed is 3.0 cm./second. Attention is called to the activation of EEG and the increase in myographic activity that is well developed before injection of dibromopyruvic acid (25 mgm./kgm.) is complete.

injection of toxic doses of dibromopyruvic acid there was a gradual and progressive decrease in blood pressure, pulse pressure and pulse rate. These changes were accompanied by a progressive decrease in reactivity of the blood pressure to the pressor effects of epinephrine and levarterenol.

Perfusion of the isolated cat heart with 1 and 5 mgm. per cent solution of dibromopyruvic acid produced a decrease in contractile force, a slowing of rate and irregularities in rhythm that were irreversible.

Effects on the CNS. Immediately following the injection of dibromopyruvic acid the spinal cat exhibited biting movements and turning of the head, in addition to salivation and lacrimation. Below the section the animal showed flexor movements of the fore and hind limbs. Electromyograms obtained from innervated flexor muscles of 8 preparations, which were quiescent during the control period, demonstrated intense electromyographic activity following dibromopyruvic acid. On the other hand, the denervated muscle showed only a slight increase in electromyographic activity (figures 3 and 4), indicating that this activity was predominantly spinal in origin. The electromyographic activity recorded from the innervated extensor quadriceps muscle in 4 preparations was slight or absent during the control period in the unstretched muscle, but of larger amplitude when the muscle was placed on stretch. Dibromopyruvic acid (25 mgm./kgm.) had no effect on the electromyographic activity of the unstretched quadriceps muscle but caused a complete inhibition of activity in the muscle during stretch.

The increase of electromyographic activity of flexor muscles in the spinal cat was coincident with the onset of salivation, lacrimation, and increased intestinal motility (see figure 3) and had a duration of approximately 10 minutes. Atropine in doses of 1 to 4 mgm./kgm. did not antagonize the increase in electromyographic activity produced in innervated flexor muscles by dibromopyruvic acid, whereas mephenesin (50 mgm./kgm.) diminished or abolished the increased electromyographic activity.

The effects of dibromopyruvic acid (25 and 50 mgm./kgm.) on the patellar reflex were studied in 10 animals, 5 of which had been prepared to allow the simultaneous recording of the contraction of the anterior tibial muscle evoked by stimulation of the common peroneal nerve.

In 8 experiments the injection of dibromopyruvic acid was followed immediately by a marked or complete inhibition of the patellar reflex which had a duration of 1 to 4 minutes and was followed by a partial recovery (upper tracing of figure 5). Dibromopyruvic acid had little effect on the threshold of inhibition, while

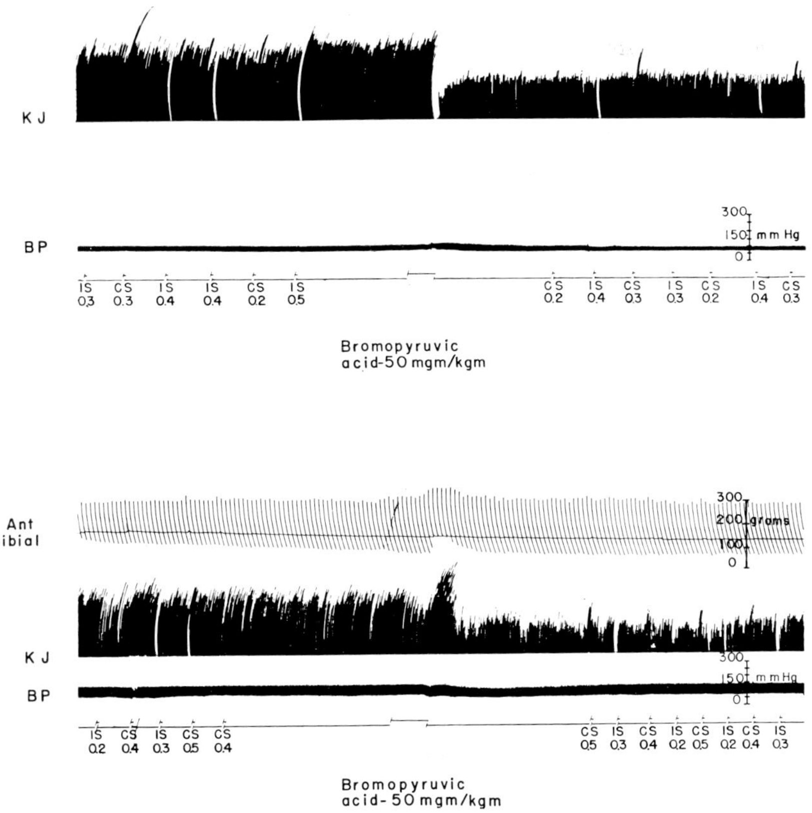

FIG. 5. The effect of dibromopyruvic acid on the patellar reflex and nerve muscle preparation of spinal cat.

Upper tracing illustrates complete inhibition of patellar reflex by dibromopyruvic acid (50 mgm./kgm.). In lower tracing dibromopyruvic acid (50 mgm./kgm.) produces an initial inhibition followed by facilitation which in turn is followed by a prolonged depression of the patellar reflex. The force of contraction of the anterior tibial muscle evoked by stimulation of the peroneal nerve is increased during the period of facilitation. KJ: patellar reflex, BP: blood pressure, Ant. tibial: anterior tibial muscle, CS: contralateral sciatic, IS: ipsilateral sciatic.

the threshold for facilitation was elevated. Because the elevation of threshold of facilitation persisted with the depression of the patellar reflex, depression of facilitation appears to be related to the toxic effects of dibromopyruvic acid.

In 2 experiments the inhibition of the patellar reflex produced by dibromopyruvic acid (50 mgm./kgm.) was followed by a transient increase in the amplitude of the patellar reflex (figure 5, lower tracing). In these 2 experiments there was a concomitant increase in the force of contraction of the anterior tibial muscle. In 3 other experiments in which the force of contraction of the anterior tibial muscle was measured, dibromopyruvic acid (50 mgm./kgm.) had no effect upon the amplitude of contraction. Because 50 mgm./kgm. of dibromopyruvic had an inconsistent effect on the contraction of the anterior tibial muscle evoked by stimulating the peroneal nerve while causing intense salivation and lacrimation, it is felt that the occasional enhancement of the patellar reflex indicates that the drug has slight nicotinic effects which may be related to its anticholinesterase activity (Busch *et al.*, 1958). Atropine (1 to 4 mgm./kgm.) did not alter the initial inhibition produced by dibromopyruvic acid. However, these doses caused an additional depression of the patellar reflex when administered several minutes after dibromopyruvic acid; this depression could be reversed by mephenesin (50 mgm./kgm.). Mephenesin, on the other hand, decreased or abolished the initial inhibitory action of dibromopyruvic acid.

Dibromopyruvic acid in doses of 25 and 50

mgm./kgm. produced activation of the EEG that was also concomitant with salivation, lacrimation, increased intestinal motility, and electromyographic activity. The activation, illustrated in the upper tracing of figure 4, persisted for approximately 10 minutes and could be abolished or prevented by atropine (1 to 4 mgm./kgm.). It was followed by a diminution of spontaneous activity until the cortex became isoelectric and unresponsive when doses of 50 mgm./kgm. or more were employed. Mephenesin (25 mgm./kgm.) did not alter the activation of the EEG produced by dibromopyruvic acid (25 and 50 mgm./kgm.).

Discussion. During the course of these experiments it became increasingly apparent that the halogenated pyruvic acids had two dissociable types of action. The first type of action appeared immediately following intravenous injection of these drugs and consisted of a syndrome of cholinergic effects of short duration, which were prevented by atropine and which subsided within 10 minutes. The second type of activity frequently became manifest slowly over the course of hours and consisted of a marked impairment of function and reactivity of many tissues and organs. These were not antagonized by atropine. The isolated cat heart and the isolated rabbit ileum were all quickly depressed by dibromopyruvic acid and became unreactive to epinephrine and acetylcholine respectively. The cardiovascular system of the spinal cat was progressively depressed by toxic doses of these drugs. The blood pressure and pulse pressure fell and the animal became unresponsive to large doses of epinephrine and levarterenol. Concomitantly with the failure of the cardiovascular system the central nervous system became unreactive. Evidence has been obtained that dibromopyruvic acid is a potent metabolic inhibitor and this may be the mechanism whereby these tissues are poisoned (Busch *et al.*, 1958).

The evidence suggests that the site of action of these drugs in producing salivation and lacrimation is the effector cell. The studies with surgical denervation clearly indicate that the site is not proximal to the ganglia and studies with ganglionic blocking agents strongly suggest that salivation and lacrimation are not due to ganglionic stimulation.

In explanation of the mode of action of dibromopyruvic acid, the following possibilities were considered: 1) dibromopyruvic acid may act as an anticholinesterase, 2) it may be involved in the synthesis of a labile cholinester, and 3) it may react with cholinergic receptors. Dibromopyruvic acid was 1:4000 as potent as neostigmine as an anticholinesterase; however, *in vivo* it was 1:400 as potent as neostigmine (Busch *et al.*, 1958). Dibromopyruvic acid did not potentiate the action of acetylcholine on the rabbit ileum; however, *in vivo* it potentiated the action of acetylcholine on the heart. Unlike neostigmine, it did not produce fasciculations of denervated skeletal muscle, or consistently potentiate the effect of stimulation of the nerve on the contraction of skeletal muscle. These data indicate that the anticholinesterase activity of dibromopyruvic acid is not primarily responsible for its cholinergic effects but may play a contributory role. Since neostigmine did not potentiate the action of dibromopyruvic acid on the isolated ileum, it is unlikely that the activity of dibromopyruvic is due to a labile cholinester which is hydrolyzed by cholinesterase. The fact that dibromopyruvic acid can cause an increase in tone of the isolated ileum in concentrations that are comparable to those necessary to produce cholinomimetic effects *in vivo* and that these contractions are blocked by atropine suggest that dibromopyruvic acid in itself possesses cholinelike activity. Studies on the peripheral action of this drug indicate that its spectrum of activity is similar to muscarine since it stimulates salivary glands, lacrimal glands and the gastrointestinal tract, but has little effect upon the myoneural junction. It differs from muscarine in that it does not produce bradycardia. It appears likely, therefore, that the muscarinic activity of dibromopyruvic acid is due to a reaction with cholinergic receptors.

Dibromopyruvic acid inhibits the patellar reflexes and in this respect resembles acetylcholine and nicotine (Schweitzer and Wright, 1937; Bulbring and Burn, 1941; and van Harrevald, 1953). Curtis *et al.* (1957) found that both nicotine and acetylcholine depress monosynaptic reflexes of both flexor and extensor muscles. These authors attribute the inhibition of the monosynaptic reflex arcs to stimulation of the inhibitory Renshaw cell which involves a nicotinic synapse. Preliminary experiments in this laboratory indicate that dibromopyruvic acid in doses of 10 to 25 mgm./kgm., given intravenously does not alter the firing rate of the Renshaw cell. The failure of dibromopyruvic acid to stimulate the nicotinic synapse of the Renshaw cell would indicate that the central action of this agent, like its peripheral action, is nonnicotinic. Since the inhibition of the patellar reflex produced by dibromopyruvic acid was not antagonized by atropine, it is suggested that there may be central nonnicotinic or muscarinic synapses that are not vulnerable to atropine. This type of synapse will be referred to as "nonnicotinic cholinergic." The site of action of dibromopyruvic acid responsible for its inhibitory action has not been determined; however, the most likely possibilities are that it excites "nonnicotinic cholinergic" inhibitory neurones or "nonnicotinic cholinergic" interneurones that have synaptic connection with inhibitory neurones.

In attempting to explain all of the early central actions of dibromopyruvic acid by one basic mechanism, it has been assumed that dibromopyruvic acid acts upon central synapses. It is possible that the pattern of alteration of central function produced by dibromopyruvic acid may be the consequence of other changes, such as stimulation of afferent nerves or changes in neuronal metabolism.

Consistent with the hypothesis that there are cholinergic interneurones are the observations that acetylcholine can cause flexor movements (Bulbring and Burn, 1941), that anticholinesterases increase flexor reflexes (Bulbring and Burn, 1941; Chennels *et al.*, 1949; Chennels *et al.*, 1951) and potentiate polysynaptic ventral root potentials (Skoglund, 1951; Taverner, 1954). Dibromopyruvic acid resembles acetylcholine and various anticholinesterases in that it produces flexor movements and increases the motor outflow of the spinal cord to flexor muscles which may be interpreted as additional evidence for "nonnicotinic cholinergic" central synapses. The fact that mephenesin antagonizes stimulation of flexor muscles and inhibition of the patellar reflex produced by dibromopyruvic acid indicates that both of these phenomena are mediated by interneurones.

Bulbring and Burn (1941) and Skoglund (1953) have demonstrated that atropine can depress excitatory central actions of acetylcholine and anticholinesterases. Eccles *et al.* (1954) found that atropine was ineffective in depressing the firing rate of the Renshaw cell. If the alterations of central excitability produced by acetylcholine, anticholinesterases and dibromopyruvic acid are due to a direct central action of these drugs, many experimental findings may be reconciled by assuming that there are at least three types of central cholinergic synapses: 1) "nicotinic cholinergic synapses": those stimulated by acetylcholine, nicotine and anticholinesterases and depressed by dihydro-*beta*-erythroidine but not by atropine, 2) "muscarinic cholinergic synapses": those stimulated by acetylcholine, anticholinesterases and dibromopyruvic acid and depressed by atropine, 3) "nonnicotinic cholinergic synapses": those stimulated by acetylcholine, anticholinesterases and dibromopyruvic acid but not depressed by atropine.

Dibromopyruvic acid resembles a wide variety of anticholinesterases in its ability to produce activation of the EEG. The fact that activation of the EEG produced by dibromopyruvic acid has a time course similar to the peripheral cholinergic and spinal cord effects of this drug suggests that there may be a common mechanism for the production of these effects. Previous studies with acetylcholine (Bonnet and Bremer, 1937; Bremer and Chatonnet, 1949; Longo and Silvestrini, 1957a) and anticholinesterases (Bradley and Elkes, 1957; Desmedt and LaGrutta, 1957; Funderburk and Case, 1951; Longo and Silvestrini, 1957b) have demonstrated that all of these drugs activate the EEG. Desmedt and LaGrutta (1957) have presented evidence that anticholinesterases, which are effective in blocking pseudocholinesterases, are more potent in activating the EEG than anticholinesterases which are effective against true cholinesterases. The demonstration that pseudocholinesterase is localized in glial cells, whereas true cholinesterase is predominantly in neuronal tissue (Koelle, 1955) and Desmedt and LaGrutta's (1957) observations suggest that activation of the EEG may be influenced by factors other than neuronal activity. However, the fact that dibromopyruvic acid activates the EEG indicates that there may be "nonnicotinic cholinergic" or "muscarinic" synapses involved in this phenomena. Atropine, which is ineffective in blocking the effects of dibromopyruvic acid on the spinal cord, is very effective in blocking activation of the EEG produced by dibromopyruvic acid.

The late effect of dibromopyruvic acid on the EEG, *i.e.*, a progressive depression of the spontaneous activity, is most probably due to inhibition of oxidative metabolism. Chenoweth and St. John (1947) and Hendershot and Chenoweth (1955) found that fluoroacetate and fluorobutyrate, which are structurally similar to β-halogenated pyruvic acid derivatives and which inhibit oxidative metabolism, produced both electroencephalographic and motoric seizure activity. Dibromopyruvic acid does not produce seizure activity in the intact animal nor has there been any electroencephalographic evidence of seizure activity.

Slaughter and Gross (1940) and Slaughter and Munsell (1940) showed that anticholinesterases potentiate analgetic effects of morphine and suggest that the activity of morphine may be in some way related to acetylcholine metabolism. More recently Knoll *et al.* (1953) have shown that neostigmine (Prostigmin) and choline displace morphine from plasma protein and believe that it is this action that accounts for the synergistic effects of parasympathomimetic drugs. No ready explanation exists for the analgetic action of dibromopyruvic acid. The time course of the analgesia closely parallels the cholinergic effects, and this suggests that the analgesia may involve a cholinergic mechanism, although recent experiments (Busch *et al.*, 1958) indicate that analgetic and cholinergic properties may be dissociated in other β-substituted pyruvic acid derivatives.

SUMMARY

Two actions of dibromopyruvic acid have been differentiated *in vivo* and *in vitro*; it produces a wide variety of cholinergic effects and is also toxic to all tissues and organ systems studied. The toxic effects have been related to its inhibitory action on oxidative metabolism. The *in vivo* and *in vitro* evidence indicates that dibromopyruvic acid produces its cholinergic activity by reacting with cholinergic receptors and that its anticholinesterase activity plays only a contributory role. Dibromopyruvic acid has been characterized as a drug with predominantly muscarinelike activity. It has been differentiated from muscarinelike drugs by its failure to produce bradycardia. Its actions on the central nervous system are similar to the actions of acetylcholine and anticholinesterases (as reported by other investigators). Because it possesses predominantly muscarinelike peripheral activity, its action on the central nervous system has been interpreted as evidence for the existence of nonnicotinic cholinergic synapses in the central nervous system. Atropine was ineffective in antagonizing the spinal cord activity of dibromopyruvic acid, while mephenesin was an effective antagonist. These observations have suggested that there are nonnicotinic cholinergic interneurones that are not depressed by atropine.

ACKNOWLEDGEMENT The authors wish to thank Mr. Newton E. Long for his assistance in the conduct of these experiments.

REFERENCES

BIANCHI, C., AND FRANSESCHINI, E. J.: Brit. J. Pharmacol., **9:** 280, 1954.

BONNET, V., AND BREMER, F.: C. R. Soc. Biol., **126:** 1271, 1937.

BRADLEY, P. B., AND ELKES, J.: Brain, **80:** 77, 1957.

BREMER, F., AND CHATONNET, J.: Arch. internat. physiol., **57:** 106, 1949.

BULBRING, E., AND BURN, J. H.: J. Physiol., **100:** 337, 1941.

BUSCH, H., MARTIN, W. R., NYHAN, W. L., AND ZARATZIAN, V.: Science, **124:** 981, 1956.

BUSCH, H., NAIR, P. V., FRANK, M., AND MARTIN, W. R.: THIS JOURNAL, **123:** 48, 1958.

CHENNELS, M., FLOYD, W. F., AND WRIGHT, S.: J. Physiol., **108:** 375, 1949.

CHENNELS, M., FLOYD, W. F., AND WRIGHT, S.: J. Physiol., **114:** 107, 1951.

CHENOWETH, M. B., AND ST. JOHN, E. F.: THIS JOURNAL, **90:** 76, 1947.

CURTIS, D. R., ECCLES, J. C., AND ECCLES, R. M.: J. Physiol., **136:** 420, 1957.

DESMEDT, J. E., AND LAGRUTTA, G.: J. Physiol., **136:** 20, 1957.

ECCLES, J. C., ECCLES, R. M., AND FATT, P.: J. Physiol., **131:** 154, 1956.

FUNDERBURK, H. W., AND CASE, T. J.: Electroencephalog. & Clin. Neurophysiol., **3:** 213, 1951.

HAFFNER, F.: Deutsche med. Wchnschr., **55:** 731, 1929.

HENDERSHOT, L. E., AND CHENOWETH, M. B.: THIS JOURNAL, **113:** 160, 1955.

KNOLL, J., KOMLOS, E., AND TARDOS, L.: Acta physiol. Hung., **4:** 131, 1953.

KOELLE, G. B.: THIS JOURNAL, **114:** 167, 1955.

LITCHFIELD, J. T., JR., AND WILCOXON, F.: THIS JOURNAL, **96:** 99, 1949.

LONGO, V. G., AND SILVESTRINI, B.: Proc. Soc. Exper. Biol. & Med., **95:** 43, 1957a.

LONGO, V. G., AND SILVESTRINI, B.: THIS JOURNAL, **120:** 160, 1957b.

MARTIN, W. R., BUSCH, H., NYHAN, W. L., AND ABDULIAN, D. H.: THIS JOURNAL, **119:** 165, 1957.

SCHWEITZER, A., AND WRIGHT, S.: J. Physiol., **89:** 384, 1937.

SKOGLUND, C. R.: The spinal cord, p. 195, Ciba Foundation Symposium, Churchill, London, 1953.

SLAUGHTER, D., AND GROSS, E. G.: THIS JOURNAL, **68:** 96, 1940.

SLAUGHTER, D., AND MUNSELL, D. W.: THIS JOURNAL, **68:** 104, 1940.

TAVERNER, D.: Brit. J. Pharmacol., **9:** 84, 1954.

VAN HARREVALD, A., AND FEIGEN, G. H.: J. Neurophysiol., **11:** 141, 1953.

8060

THE ANTI-TREMORINE EFFECT OF SOME DRUGS AS DETERMINED BY HAFFNER'S METHOD OF TESTING ANALGESIA IN MICE

GRAHAM CHEN

Research Laboratories, Parke, Davis & Company, Detroit, Michigan

Received for publication May 29, 1958

Tremorine, 1,4-dipyrrolidine-2-butyne, discovered by Everett and associates (1956), exerts a unique action on the central nervous system, producing sustained tremors, salivation, miosis and hypothermia in laboratory animals. On the basis of studies showing that atropine and some other agents effective against Parkinsonism are specific antagonists of Tremorine, tremors induced by the latter in rats have been employed for the evaluation of anti-Parkinsonism drugs (Blockus and Everett, 1957). In our experiments with this compound in mice, it was found that in addition to the signs and symptoms described by the previous investigators, the animals became less responsive to noxious stimuli, either mechanical or electric. The analgesic effect of Tremorine was discernible at doses which were insufficient to produce tremors, salivation, rigidity or other striking neurotoxic symptoms in mice. The extent of Tremorine-induced analgesia was in direct proportion to its dosage and could be antagonized by the anti-Parkinsonism drugs.

The site or mode of action of Tremorine in producing analgesia appears to be different from that of morphine. This is shown by the difference in antagonistic effects of atropine and nalorphine on analgesia induced by these two compounds.

The results obtained with Tremorine, various anti-Parkinsonism drugs and some centrally acting agents with morphine, nalorphine and atropine, by Haffner's method of testing analgesia (Haffner, 1929) are presented and discussed in this report.

METHODS. The simple procedure described by Bianchi and Franceschini (1954) was followed. It consists of applying an artery clip with thin rubber-covered tips to the root of the tail of a mouse for 30 seconds. Without analgesia, the animal will react to the noxious stimulus by biting the clip. In our experiments, male albino mice weighing 18 to 22 grams were given 5 mgm./kgm. of Tremorine·2HCl intramuscularly and, at the same time, a dose of the test compound (except reserpine) intraperitoneally. Reserpine was administered four hours prior to Tremorine. Analgesia was tested one hour later. The amount of Tremorine employed is a submaximal analgesic dose. The insoluble substance was administered as a fine suspension in gum-acacia solution. Three groups of 10 mice each were injected with 3 graded doses of the test drug. These doses would antagonize the analgesic effect of Tremorine in 10 to 90 per cent of the animals. The 50 per cent effective dose and the standard errors were estimated by the graphical method of Miller and Tainter (1944).

The mydriatic effects of the various compounds were compared by observing the duration of pupillary dilatation in mice (Pulewka, 1932). Four mice were used for each dose level of a test compound. The activity of atropine·SO_4 at 0.1 mgm./kgm. intramuscularly, giving a duration of effect of 3.5 to 4 hours, was taken as a comparative reference. The relative activity values were roughly estimated from the weight of the material required to produce approximately the same duration of mydriasis as 0.1 mgm./kgm. of atropine sulfate.

RESULTS AND DISCUSSION. The analgesic effect of Tremorine at various dose levels as determined by the quantal response in mice is shown by the data in section (A) of table 1. The 50 per cent effective dose (ED_{50}), estimated graphically by the probit-log dose linear relationship, is 1.45 ± 0.25 mgm./kgm. of Tremorine·2HCl. In the table are given also the results for morphine sulfate obtained in parallel experiments. The onset of analgesia induced by Tremorine is slower than that by morphine, but the duration of analgesia is longer (6 to 7 hours with Tremorine, 2 to 3 hours with morphine). Although the ED_{50} of Tremorine·2HCl is less than that of morphine·SO_4 (2.35 ± 0.44), on the basis of molecular equivalents, morphine·SO_4 (mol. wt. = 698) is more potent than Tremorine·2HCl (mol. wt. = 265.3).

TABLE 1

A comparison of the analgesic effects of Tremorine and morphine by Haffner's method in mice

Section (A)

(a)		(b)	
Tremorine·2HCl	No. with Analgesia/ No. Tested	Morphine·SO_4	No. with Analgesia/ No. Tested
mgm./kgm., 1 hr.		*mgm./kgm., ½ hr.*	
0.63	2/10	0.63	0/10
1.25	4/10	1.25	3/10
2.50	7/10	2.50	6/10
5.00	10/10	5.00	7/10
		10.00	10/10
ED_{50} ± S.E. = 1.45 ± 0.25		ED_{50} ± S.E. = 2.35 ± 0.44	

Section (B)

(a)			(b)		
Compound		No. with Analgesia/ No. Tested	Compound		No. with Analgesia/ No. Tested
mgm./kgm., 1 hr.			*mgm./kgm., ½ hr.*		
Tremorine HCl, (Alone)	5.0	10/10	Morphine SO_4, (Alone)	10.0	10/10
Tremorine HCl + Atropine SO_4	5.0 2.5	0/10	Morphine SO_4 + Atropine·SO_4	10.0 2.5	10/10
Tremorine·HCl + Atropine·SO_4	5.0 5.0	0/10	Morphine·SO_4 + Atropine·SO_4	10.0 5.0	9/10
Tremorine·HCl + Nalorphine	5.0 20.0	10/10	Morphine·SO_4 + Nalorphine	10.0 20.0	0/10

As shown by the other data in section (B) of the table, the analgesic effect of Tremorine may be antagonized by atropine but not by nalorphine. The opposite is the case in morphine-induced analgesia. Apparently the site or mode of action of the two compounds in producing analgesia is different.

It may be of interest to mention that neostigmine (Prostigmin) and some other anticholinesterase agents are capable of producing a slight increase in the pain threshold (Floodmark and Wrammer, 1945; Gross *et al.*, 1948). Atropine was found to prevent the rise of pain threshold produced by Prostigmine and to decrease the analgesic action of morphine (Christensen and Gross, 1948). The effect of atropine on morphine-induced analgesia, however, should be investigated further, for a potentiation of morphine analgesia by atropine has also been observed (De Jongh, 1954). In our experiment, intra-

TABLE 2

The anti-Tremorine effect of certain drugs as determined by Haffner's method of testing analgesia in mice

Compound*	Anti-Tremorine Effect	Relative Mydriatic Activity (Approx.)†
mgm./kgm., i.p.	*ED_{50} ± S.E.*	
Hyoscine·HBr	0.67 ± 0.13	1
Benztropine (Congentin)	1.16 ± 0.17	1/5
Benactyzine·HCl	1.98 ± 0.36	1/50
PU 220	1.98 ± 0.47	1/50
Atropine·SO_4	2.15 ± 0.24	1
PU 239	2.61 ± 0.55	1
Procyclidine·HCl (Kemadrin)	2.95 ± 0.60	1/50
Reserpine	3.3 ± 0.54	0
Trihexyphenidyl·HCl (Artane)	4.00 ± 0.75	1/20
Caramiphen·HCl (Parpanit)	4.50 ± 0.74	1/125
Promethazine·HCl (Phenergan)	10.2 ± 1.67	1/100
Diethazine·HCl (Diparcol)	14.3 ± 2.35	1/500
Chlorpromazine·HCl	15.4 ± 4.43	1/500
Diphenhydramine·HCl (Benadryl)	15.7 ± 2.57	1/125
Orphenadrine·HCl (Desipal)	16.5 ± 2.67	1/125
AH 47	19.5 ± 3.40	1/125
AH 883	19.2 ± 2.82	1/125
Diphenylhydantoin·Na	99.0 ± 20.1	1/500
Desoxyephedrine	Ineff. at 2	0
PM 1090	Ineff. at 5	0
Nalorphine	Ineff. at 20	0
Bromodiphenhydramine	Ineff. at 25	1/500
Tripelennamine	Ineff. at 25	1/500
Phenobarbital·Na	Ineff. at 25,50	0
Pentylenetetrazol	Ineff. at 30	0
Barbital·Na	Ineff. at 50,100	0
Meprobamate	Ineff. at 75,150	0
Zoxazolamine	Ineff. at 25,50	0

* PU 220 = 1-ethyl-3-pyrrolidinol, benzilate ester·HCl; PU 239 = 1,1-diethyl-3-pyrrolidinol, benzilate ester·Br; AH 47 = β-(benzhydryloxy)-ethyl diethylamine·HCl (Rigidyl); AH 883 = β-(2-chlorbenzhydryloxy)ethyl dimethylamine·HCl; and PM 1090 = α,α,β,β-tetramethylsuccinimide.

† 0 = no mydriatic effect at 50 mgm./kgm. intramuscularly.

muscular administration of 0.5 mgm./kgm. of physostigmine salicylate (a maximal tolerated dose) was ineffective in producing analgesia in mice. A study of the mechanism involved in Tremorine-induced analgesia might give an explanation to such conflicting findings and might also shed some light upon the mechanism of analgesia in general.

In table 2 are given the results obtained in mice by antagonism with the test compounds and Tremorine. In each experiment a control was conducted using the challenging dose of 5 mgm./kgm. of Tremorine·2HCl alone. In each instance an analgesic effect was shown in all ten animals. The effective agents are arranged in the order of decreasing potency in terms of the doses required to antagonize the analgesic action of Tremorine in 50 per cent of animals (ED_{50}). Bromodiphenhydramine (Ambodryl) and tripelennamine (Pyribenzamine) were ineffective at 25 mgm./kgm., and so were a number of CNS stimulants and depressants at minimal neurotoxic dosages as designated.

As shown by the anti-Tremorine effect and the relative mydriatic activity of the different compounds, it is significant that, although a mydriatic property is present in all the effective anti-Tremorine agents (except reserpine), their anti-Tremorine activities do not necessarily parallel their mydriatic activities. For instance, whereas diphenhydramine is 1/8 as effective as atropine in antagonizing Tremorine, its mydriatic activity is only 1/125 of that of the latter. Benactyzine as well as PU 220 are equal to atropine in anti-Tremorine activity but possess only 1/50 the activity of atropine in producing dilatation of mouse pupils. The same is also strikingly demonstrated by the data for PU 220 and PU 239, which are approximately equal in effect against Tremorine, although PU 239 has a mydriatic activity 50 times that of PU 220.

The anti-Tremorine effect of chlorpromazine was more marked, proportional to dosage, at levels less than 15 mgm./kgm.; however, it was less with increasing dosage. This is probably caused by a dual action of chlorpromazine at different dose levels (Himwich and Rinaldi, 1955; Rinaldi and Himwich 1955; Preston, 1956). Chlorpromazine has been shown to possess some anticholinergic activity and is said to be capable of potentiating the analgesic effect of morphine (Courvoisier *et al.*, 1952).

Reserpine, which is cholinergic in nature in some of its pharmacologic effects, was found to antagonize the analgesic action of Tremorine quantitatively with dosage. In spite of the fact that reserpine will produce a syndrome resembling Parkinsonism in man upon continuous administration of massive doses, at low dosages it may give a palliative effect toward Parkinsonism. That reserpine possesses both a depressing and a stimulating action on the central nervous system, depending upon the dose level, appears to support such a possibility (Chen and Bohner, 1956). The beneficial effect of reserpine in the management of some patients with Parkinsonism is probably, therefore, not entirely attributable to its effect on the psychic and emotional aspects of the disease (Constable and Doshay, 1956).

The other CNS depressants and stimulants were investigated at minimal neurotoxic doses. Among them, diphenylhydantoin (Dilantin) only was effective in abolishing analgesia due to Tremorine. Incidentally, Dilantin shows an anticholinergic action at high doses (Haury and Drake, 1940). It was found to be palliative in some patients with Parkinsonism (Shapera, 1940).

In conclusion, it may be stated that the drugs which have been successfully employed for the management of Parkinsonism were found to be capable of antagonizing the analgesic action of Tremorine quantitatively. The antagonism appears to be unique in that the anti-Tremorine activity of a compound does not necessarily parallel its mydriatic potency, and this anti-Tremorine property is not shared by the common CNS stimulants and depressants. No data are yet available in the literature setting forth the effect of these drugs on Tremorine-induced tremors. A comparison of the anti-Tremorine effects, as determined by analgesia and tremors, of these agents might reveal some information as to which phase or phases of the syndrome of Parkinsonism are best controlled by the different drugs.

SUMMARY

Tremorine has been shown to produce analgesia in mice by Haffner's method. The Tremorine-induced analgesia may be antagonized by hyoscine, atropine, and other drugs effective against Parkinsonism. Nalorphine, desoxyephedrine, phenobarbital and numerous CNS stimulants and depressants are ineffective at minimal neurotoxic dose levels. Antagonism against Tremorine-induced analgesia, as determined by

Haffner's method in mice, is suggested as a simple and reliable procedure for screening potential anti-Parkinsonism agents.

Acknowledgment. The writer is indebted to Mr. Charles R. Ensor for testing the analgesic effect of Tremorine in mice with electrical stimuli in some preliminary experiments.

REFERENCES

Bianchi, C., and Franceschini, J.: Brit. J. Pharmacol., **9:** 280, 1954.

Blockus, L. E., and Everett, G. M.: Fed. Proc., **16:** 283, 1957.

Chen, G., and Bohner, B.: This Journal, **117:** 142, 1956.

Christensen, E. M., and Gross, E. G.: J.A.M.A., **137:** 594, 1948.

Constable, K., and Doshay, L. J.: J. Am. M. Women's A., **11:** 165, 1956.

Couvoisier, S., Fournel, J., Ducrot, R., Kolsky, M., and Koetschet, P.: Arch. internat. pharmacodyn., **92:** 305, 1952.

De Jongh, D. K.: Acta. physiol. et pharmacol. neerl., **3:** 164, 1954.

Everett, G. M., Blockus, L. E., Sheppard, I. M., and Toman, J. E. P.: Fed Proc., **15:** 420, 1956.

Floodmark, S., and Wrammer, T.: Acta physiol. scandinav., **2:** 88, 1945.

Gross, E. G., Holland, H., Carter, H. R., Christensen, E. M.: Anesthesiology, **9:** 459, 1948.

Haffner, F.: Deutsche med. Wchnsch., **55:** 731, 1929.

Haury, V. G., and Drake, M. E.: This Journal, **68:** 36, 1940.

Himwich, H. E., and Rinaldi, F.: Yale J. Biol. & Med., **28:** 308, 1955.

Miller, L. C., and Tainter, M. L.: Proc. Soc. Exper. Biol. & Med., **57:** 261, 1944.

Preston, J. B.: This Journal, **118:** 100, 1956.

Pulewka, P.: Arch. exper. Path. u. Pharmakol., **168:** 307, 1932.

Rinaldi, F., and Himwich, H. E.: Dis. Nerv. System, **16:** 3, 1955.

Shapera, W.: Pittsburgh M. Bull., **29:** 732, 1940.

CHLORPROMAZINE II: THE EFFECTS OF CHLORPROMAZINE ON EVOKED POTENTIALS IN THE MIDBRAIN RETICULAR FORMATION[1, 2]

EDMUND W. J. DEMAAR,[3, 4] WILLIAM R. MARTIN[5] AND KLAUS R. UNNA

Department of Pharmacology, University of Illinois College of Medicine, Chicago 12

Received for publication May 19, 1958

Many investigators have found that chlorpromazine alters the EEG of cats and modifies the response of the EEG to a variety of alerting stimuli and drugs (*cf.* Martin *et al.*, 1958). Though the alterations of the activating response of the EEG produced in cats by pentobarbital resemble those produced by chlorpromazine with regard to elevation of threshold and shortening of the activating response, there is little difficulty in distinguishing barbiturate-induced alterations of the EEG in the cat from those produced by chlorpromazine. Barbiturates produce a large number of well-formed spindles as compared to the predominant 2- to 4-cycle/second high voltage activity and abortive or poorly formed spindles following chlorpromazine.

The behavioral changes produced by these two drugs are quite different. If an animal tends to become quiet and immobile under the influence of barbiturates, it is roused to activity with great difficulty. On the other hand, the immobility produced by chlorpromazine is not accompanied by a difficulty in arousal. In fact, frequently the transition from the quiet, immobile state to one of activity is so abrupt that one suspects the animal has not been asleep or unconscious.

Pentobarbital depresses the EEG activating response as well as potentials evoked in the medial reticular formation (French *et al.*, 1953a, b; Arduini and Arduini, 1954) and prolongs the recovery cycle of evoked potentials (King *et al.*, 1957). Chlorpromazine enhances the amplitude of single potentials evoked diffusely over the surface of the cortex, while it depresses the activating response (Martin *et al.*, 1958). This observation suggests that the depression of conduction through the reticular formation was incomplete.

The purpose of this paper is to describe the effects of chlorpromazine on potentials evoked in the medial reticular formation and compare them to changes produced by pentobarbital.

METHODS. Operative procedures were carried out under ether anesthesia. As the cats recovered from the anesthesia, a 0.1 per cent solution of succinylcholine was infused at a rate of about 0.5 ml./min., depending on the individual requirements of each animal, to obtain neuromuscular blockade and immobilization. Respiration was maintained by artificial means through a tracheal cannula. Body temperature, taken rectally, was kept at 37°C. by heat lamps. The ECG was recorded from leads taken from the forelegs. Femoral blood pressure was recorded by means of a Statham strain gauge. Drug effects were investigated two hours after the discontinuation of ether. The drugs employed were pentobarbital Na and chlorpromazine HCl. They were dissolved in 0.9 per cent saline and administered slowly through a cannula in the femoral vein.

EEG leads were taken from frontal, parietal and occipital areas by means of phonograph needles driven through the overlying bone with their tips just touching the cortex. The EEG usually shows low amplitude, high frequency activity. In those preparations in which the EEG shows a predominance of slow, high amplitude waves, a variety of activating stimuli could easily evoke high frequency activity. The pattern of the EEG was not noticeably changed by lightening or deepening the degree of muscular blockade produced by changes in the rate of infusion of succinylcholine. The EEG could be readily activated

[1] This investigation has been supported by grant B-983 from the National Institute of Health, Public Health Service.

[2] Preliminary reports were made at the 1956 proceedings of the Federation of American Societies for Experimental Biology and at the XX International Physiological Congress, Brussels, 1956.

[3] Fellow of the National Academy of Science.

[4] Present address: Department of Pharmacology, Emory University, Emory, Georgia.

[5] Present address: U. S. Public Health Service Hospital, National Institute of Mental Health, Addiction Research Center, U. S. Public Health Service, Lexington, Kentucky.

by stimulating all sites from which evoked potentials were recorded. The electrode position was verified by gross examination of the electrode tract in fixed brains in the majority of experiments.

Concentric bipolar electrodes were oriented stereotaxically in the vicinity of the red nucleus (Horsley-Clarke coordinates anterior 2, lateral 0.5 to 2, and depth −3 to −4). The ipsilateral undivided sciatic nerve was stimulated with a square wave type stimulus of one-millisecond duration. A stimulus strength of 4 to 9 volts was employed to give near maximal responses. Paired shocks were applied with delays ranging from 10 to 100 milliseconds. These stimuli were delivered through two serially connected isolation units energized by two Grass stimulators. The potentials thus evoked in the midbrain reticular formation were recorded from the central to the outer conductor of a concentric bipolar electrode. Potentials were amplified by a Grass preamplifier and photographed on a Dumont dual beam oscilloscope, using a triggered sweep. Because spontaneous activity precluded the possibility of using a fixed base line as a reference from which to measure the amplitude of the evoked potentials, the amplitude was measured from the point of deflection occurring at the proper time to the peak of the potential. This measurement assumed that the spontaneous potentials did not arise from the same neurons as the evoked potentials did and consequently that no occlusion occurred (see DISCUSSION).

Alterations in the amplitude of the single shock evoked potentials were expressed as the ratio of the mean of 20 potentials after drug-induced changes to the mean of 20 potentials evoked during the control periods. Paired responses were evoked in samples of 10, with one response being evoked every 20 seconds. The ordering of the series of ten shocks at various delays was randomized and each series was repeated two to four times. Every measurement from every series was used for construction of recovery cycles. The time period between samples was 5 or 10 minutes. In the determination of the recovery cycle of the potentials, the mean amplitude of the second potential was compared to the mean amplitude of the first. The ratio of the second to the first potential at delays of 10 to 100 milliseconds was compared before and after drug.

Results are based on experiments conducted on 23 cats. In order to have the entire sweep of the oscilloscope available for the display of both evoked potentials, the first potential, in many experiments, was positioned near the beginning of the sweep by adjusting the delay between the first stimulus and the synchronizing pulse. In such experiments an estimate of latency was made by adding the delay setting of the stimulator to the time from the beginning of the sweep to the appearance of the first action potential.

RESULTS. Two types of potentials evoked by single shocks to the sciatic nerve, which can be differentiated on the basis of their latency and recovery cycle, have been recorded in the medial reticular formation. The first type which will be referred to as the "fast" potential is illustrated in figure 1A. The latency of this response is from 10 to 20 milliseconds (see figure 1A and B) and the duration is usually from 10 to 20 milliseconds.

The second type of potential obtained will be referred to as the "slow" potential. Figure 3 is taken from an experiment in which only the "slow" potential could be evoked. The "slow" potential has a latency of approximately 40 milliseconds and a duration of over 40 milliseconds.

Figure 1B and C and the tracing of figure 2C illustrate the first and second potentials together. When the first and second type potentials are recorded together, the "fast" type is usually evoked by stimuli of equal or greater intensity than the "slow" type. However, in some locations, the "fast" potential may be the only one recorded. This is illustrated in figure 1A from an experiment in which varying the stimulus strength over a wide range failed to evoke the second type of potential.

The effect of chlorpromazine was studied first on the "slow" and "fast" single evoked potentials. Dose levels of 5 and 10 mgm./kgm. have been used. At these dose levels chlorpromazine increases the amplitude of the single evoked potential. In 10 experiments there was a mean increase of 21.5 per cent with a range of +110 per cent to −10 per cent, the decrease occurring in only one experiment. An example of this increase is illustrated in figure 2 in which paired stimuli are used.

The effect of chlorpromazine on the recovery cycle of both the "slow" and "fast" wave action potentials were studied. The time interval between paired shocks ranged from 10 to 100 milliseconds and was increased by steps of 10 or 20 milliseconds. The ratio of the amplitude of the second evoked potential of the pair to the amplitude of its own first potential at various

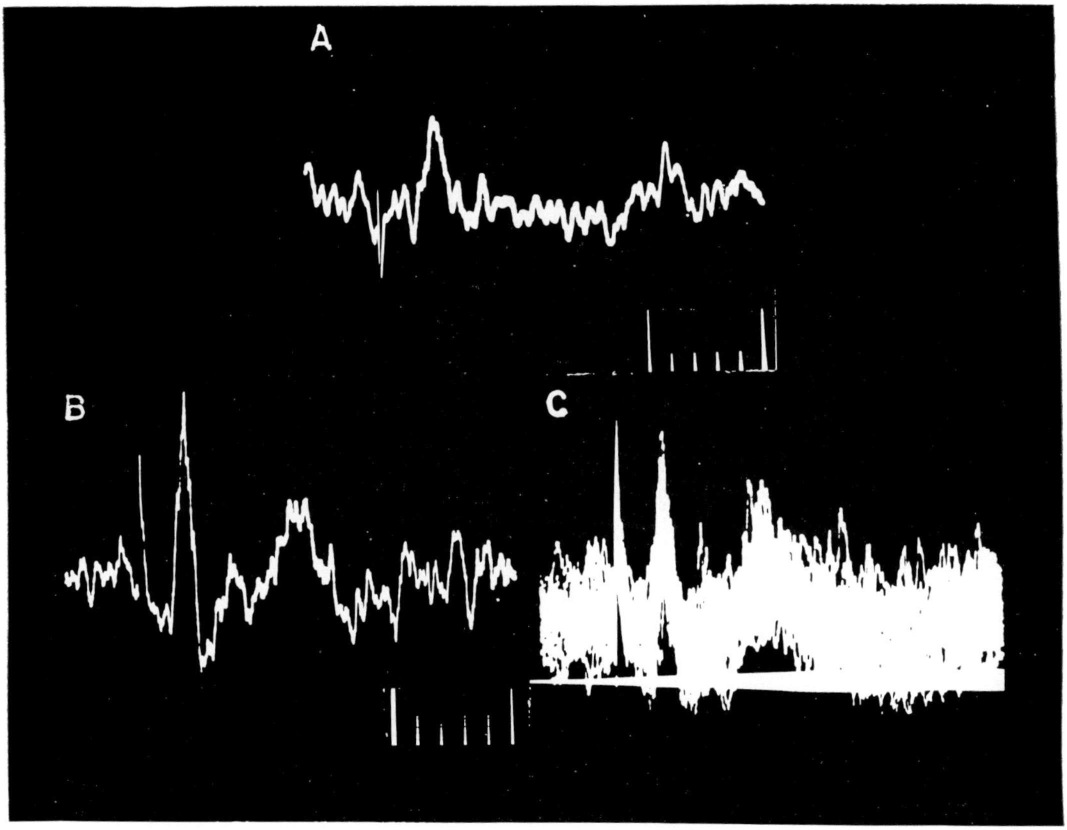

FIG. 1. Potentials evoked by sciatic nerve stimulation in the vicinity of the red nucleus of the cat. Tracing A obtained at A 1.5, L 1, V -4 illustrates a "fast" potential with a latency of 15 milliseconds and a duration of approximately 18 milliseconds. Tracing B obtained in another experiment at A 0, L 2, V -4 illustrates a "fast" and "slow" potential. The latency of the "fast" potential is 15 milliseconds and that of the "slow" potential approximately 50 milliseconds. The duration of the "fast" potential is 11 to 12 milliseconds and that of the "slow" over 40 milliseconds. C is a superposition of 20 consecutive tracings as illustrated in B. Time marks = 10 milliseconds.

delay intervals was used to determine the recovery cycle for each type of potential.

Figure 2 illustrates typical "fast" paired potentials evoked at various delays before and after chlorpromazine. Figure 4 summarizes the data of 8 experiments. The "fast" potential has an "absolute refractory" period of less than 12 milliseconds. There is a 50 per cent recovery of excitability at a delay interval of 15 milliseconds and a complete recovery of excitability occurs within 30 milliseconds. This is followed by a short period of supranormality and a prolonged period of subnormality (curve A, figure 4). The recovery cycle after doses of 5 and 10 mgm./kgm. of chlorpromazine is illustrated by curve C of figure 4. The "absolute refractory" period is still less than 12 milliseconds; however, the recovery at a delay of 15 milliseconds is now only 20 per cent and a 50 per cent recovery of excitability is found at a delay of 25 milliseconds. There was no demonstrable difference between the effects at the 5 and 10 mgm./kgm. dose level. Curve B of figure 4 is a plot of the data obtained after 1 mgm./kgm. of chlorpromazine. This dose failed to produce a significant effect.

Figure 3 illustrates a typical experiment on the effects of chlorpromazine on the amplitude of paired "slow" potentials evoked at various delays. The recovery cycle of the "slow" potential determined from a plot of the mean value of the ratios obtained of 10 experiments is shown in figure 5. Curve A illustrates the normal recovery cycle. There is an "absolute refractory" period of at least 20 milliseconds and a 50 per cent re-

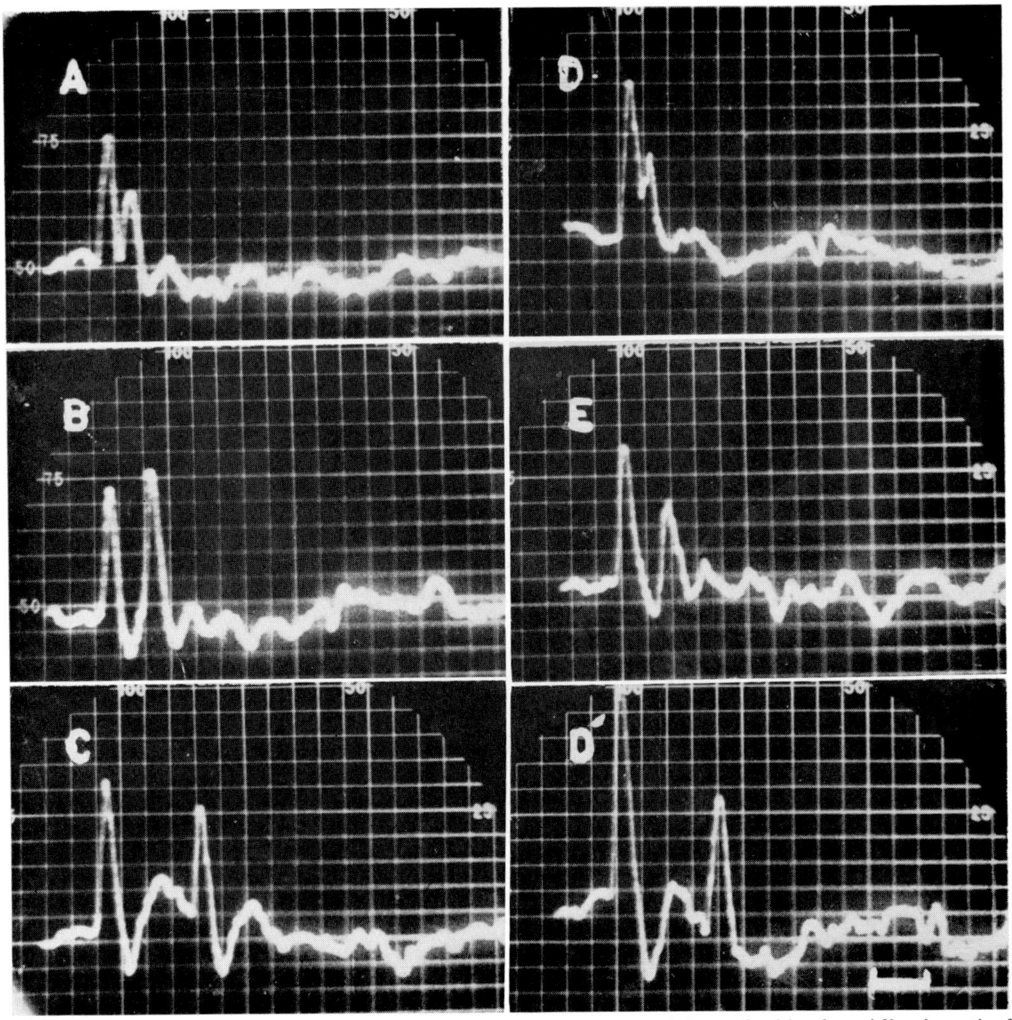

FIG. 2. The effect of chlorpromazine on "fast" and "slow" potentials evoked in the midbrain reticular formation by stimulation of the sciatic nerve.

All tracings demonstrate paired "fast" potentials while tracing C, in addition, shows paired "slow" potentials. The tracings of the left hand column were taken before chlorpromazine with delays of A = 15, B = 30, C = 70 milliseconds. The tracings of the right hand column were taken after chlorpromazine (10 mgm./kgm.) with delays of D = 15, E = 30, D = 70 milliseconds. The first "fast" potential after chlorpromazine is markedly increased in amplitude. The second "fast" potential is attenuated at a 15-millisecond delay and decreased in amplitude at a 30-millisecond delay. Time mark denotes 40 milliseconds.

covery of excitability after a delay of 32 milliseconds. At a delay of 70 milliseconds there is a complete recovery of excitability. This is followed by a transient period of supranormality. Chlorpromazine in doses of 5 and 10 mgm./kgm. abolishes or decreases the amplitude of the second potential when evoked within a delay period of 100 milliseconds. The recovery cycle after 10 mgm./kgm. of chlorpromazine is given by curve B of figure 5. There is no recovery of excitability at a delay of 40 milliseconds, and there is a 50 per cent recovery of excitability at a delay of 70 milliseconds. At a delay of over 100 milliseconds the ratio after chlorpromazine approaches the control value.

The effects of chlorpromazine in these doses have been compared to the effects of pentobarbital at the same dose levels. The "fast" action potential evoked by single or paired shocks was studied. Pentobarbital in a dose of

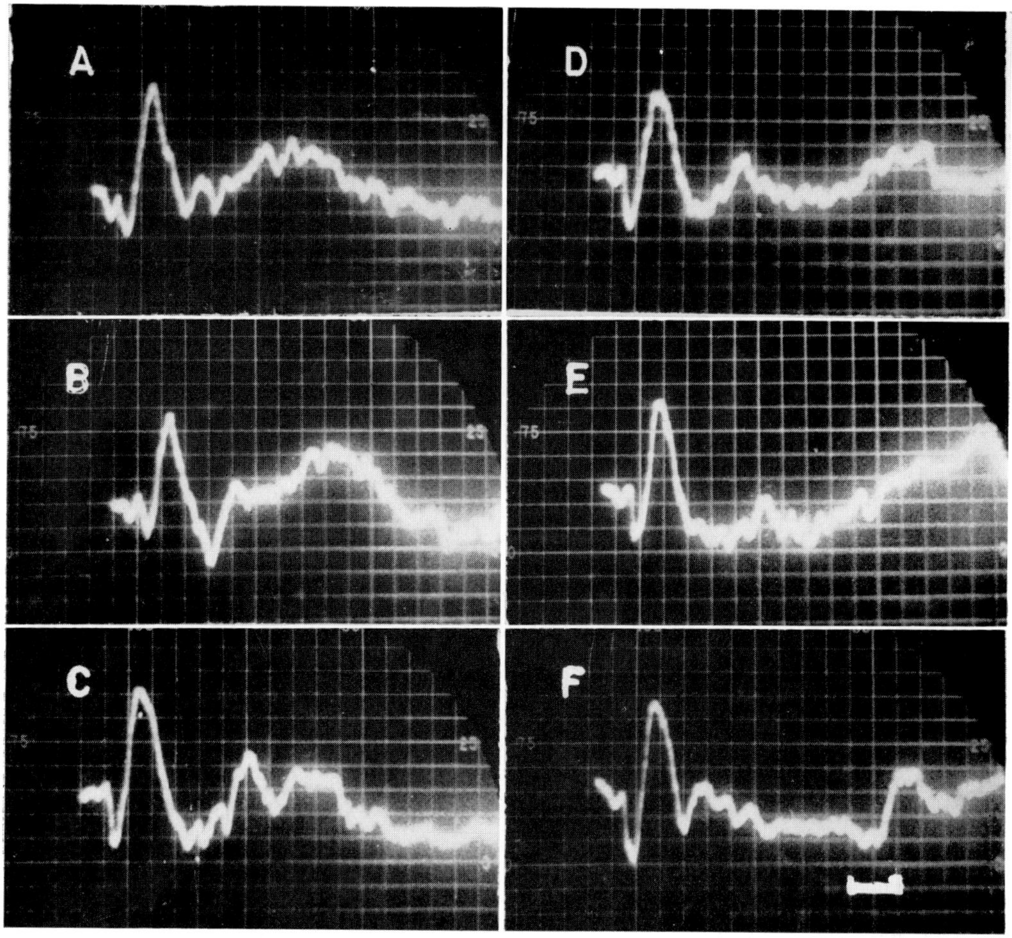

Fig. 3. The effect of chlorpromazine on "slow" potentials evoked in the midbrain reticular formation by stimulation of the sciatic nerve.

The tracings in the left hand column illustrate the paired "slow" potentials evoked before chlorpromazine. The second potential is absent at a delay of 20 milliseconds (A) but discernible at delays of 40 (B) and 70 milliseconds (C). Tracings in the right hand column illustrate paired "slow" potentials evoked after 10 mgm./kgm. of chlorpromazine. The second potential is absent at a delay of 20 (D), barely discernible at 70 milliseconds (E) but appears at a delay of 150 milliseconds (F). Time mark denotes 30 milliseconds.

5 mgm./kgm. induces a slight and consistent decrease in the amplitude of the single shock evoked potential (figure 6). After 10 to 15 mgm./kgm. the potentials are abolished, or very much diminished in amplitude. The appearance of spontaneous slow activity in this location after pentobarbital makes measurements of the evoked potential difficult. On the other hand, no marked change occurred in spontaneous activity recorded in this location after chlorpromazine.

The recovery cycle for the "fast" action potential obtained from the combined data of 4 experiments with pentobarbital is shown in figure 7. The control tracing A shows a 50 per cent recovery at a delay interval of 20 milliseconds and a nearly complete recovery at a delay of 40 milliseconds. A dose of 1 mgm./kgm. pentobarbital does not alter the recovery cycle. At the 5 mgm./kgm. dose level there is a 50 per cent recovery of excitability at a delay of 35 milliseconds and a return to control excitability at a delay of about 70 milliseconds.

Discussion. Evoked potentials have been employed by Starzl *et al.* (1951) and French *et al.* (1952, 1953a) to trace the pathway of the

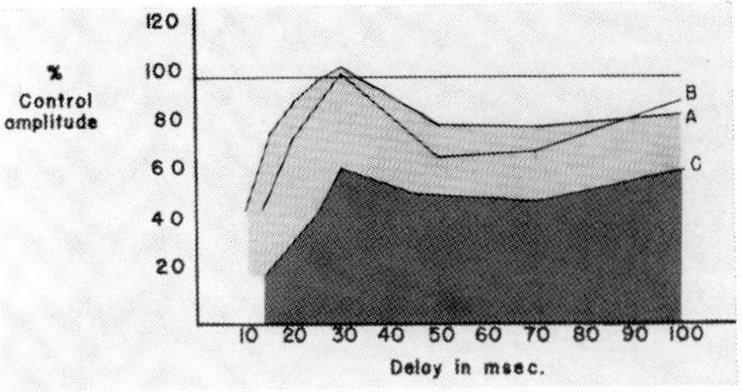

FIG. 4. The effect of chlorpromazine on the recovery cycle of the "fast" evoked potential.

Curve A represents the recovery cycle before chlorpromazine. There is a 50 per cent recovery of excitability at a delay interval of 15 milliseconds. Curve B represents the recovery cycle following 1 mgm./kgm. of chlorpromazine. Curve C represents the recovery cycle after 5 and 10 mgm./kgm. of chlorpromazine. There is a 50 per cent recovery of excitability at a delay of 25 milliseconds.

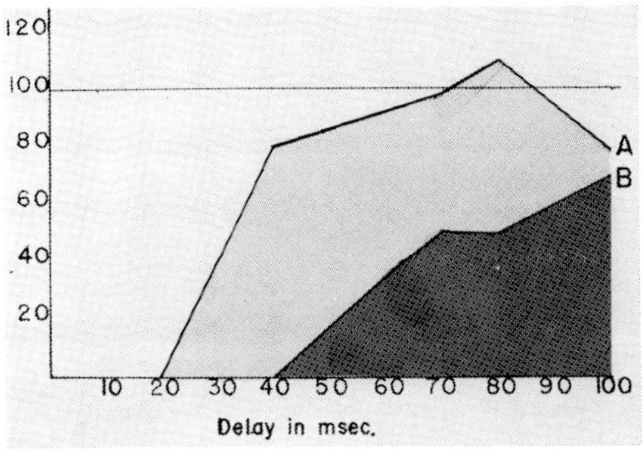

FIG. 5. The effect of chlorpromazine on the recovery cycle of the "slow" evoked potential.

The unit of the ordinate is per cent. Curve A represents the recovery cycle before chlorpromazine. There is a 50 per cent recovery of excitability at a delay of 32 milliseconds. Curve B represents the recovery cycle after 10 mgm./kgm. of chlorpromazine. A 50 per cent recovery of excitability is reached at a delay of 70 milliseconds.

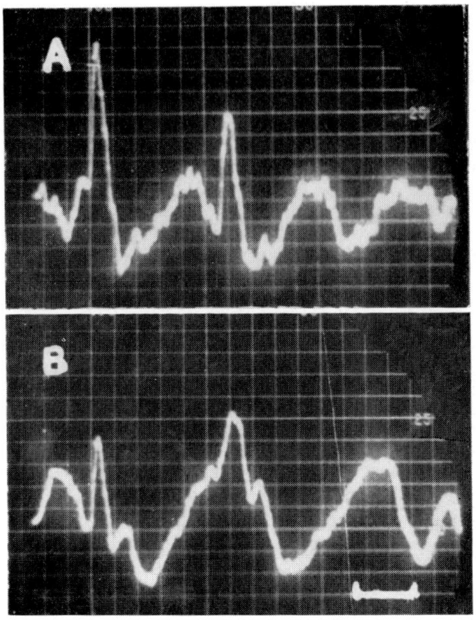

FIG. 6. The effect of pentobarbital on the "fast" potentials evoked in the midbrain reticular formation by stimulating the sciatic nerve.

Tracing A is a control record of two "fast" potentials evoked at a delay interval of 70 milliseconds. Tracing B demonstrates the depressions of the first and second potential at a delay of 70 milliseconds by 5 mgm./kgm. of pentobarbital. Time interval denotes 30 milliseconds.

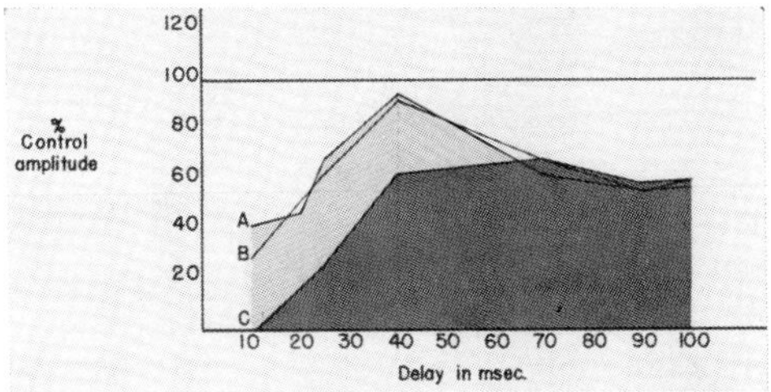

FIG. 7. The effect of pentobarbital on the recovery cycle of the "fast" evoked potential.

Curve A represents the recovery cycle before pentobarbital. There is a 50 per cent recovery of excitability at a delay interval of 20 milliseconds. Curve B shows the recovery cycle after 1 mgm./kgm. of pentobarbital, and curve C shows the recovery cycle after 5 mgm./kgm. of pentobarbital. Following 5 mgm./kgm. there is a 50 per cent recovery of excitability after a delay of 35 milliseconds.

activating system and subsequently by French *et al.* (1953b) and King *et al.* (1957) to study the action of anesthetic agents. Both the latency and wave form suggest that the activity, in these studies as well as ours, was recorded from units which were at least one synapse removed from the sensory inflow. In the region from which we have recorded, there are sites which on stimulation yield vasomotor responses, alteration of somatic reflexes, changes in respiration, alteration in intestinal activity, changes of excitability of sensory relay nuclei, as well as the activating response (*cf.* Dell, 1952). Within the confines of this system may be found large and small islands that produce antagonistic or agonistic effects. The evoked potentials recorded in the brain stem may result from the activity of interneurones that subserve any one or all of the above functions. Scheibel *et al.* (1955) have shown that several modalities of stimulation, capable of activating the EEG, may not stimulate the same neurones in the mesencephalon. Napolitano and

Longo (1957) have shown that the vegetative, somato-motoric and EEG changes produced by stimulating at a single position in the hypothalamus are not equally depressed by drugs and that one or the other function may be selectively depressed. Though the studies of Scheibel *et al.* (1955) and of Napolitano and Longo (1957) suggest that it may be possible to characterize neurones in the brain stem reticular formation on an anatomical and physiological basis, one cannot be certain that the activity recorded by our electrodes arises solely from corticipetal impulses of the activating system or that any drug alteration of evoked potentials implies depression of the activating system.

Aside from the physiological meaning of potentials evoked in the midbrain reticular formation, the relationship between the potentials recorded with large and small electrodes is not clear. Potentials evoked in the brain stem reticular formation have been recorded with macroelectrodes by several investigators. The latency of potentials recorded in the pontine and mesencephalic tegmentum by French *et al.* (1953a) was 13 to 23 milliseconds when evoked by sciatic nerve stimulation. A similar latency (12 to 20 milliseconds) was reported by Hernandez-Peon and Hagbarth (1955) in the midbrain tegmentum and medial reticular formation. The recovery cycle reported by King *et al.* (1957) for potentials evoked in the reticular formation showed an "absolute refractory" period of 10 milliseconds and 50 per cent recovery of excitability in 18 to 22 milliseconds.

Investigations conducted with microelectrodes on the reticular formation at the medullary or midbrain level have revealed several types of neuronal activity. Mollica *et al.* (1953) have described unit activity that may be recorded from the brain stem reticular formation either spontaneously or secondary to cerebellar polarization. The spontaneous activity consisted either of continuous slow or rapid spikes or bursts of activity. Cerebellar polarization increased the firing rate, inhibited the firing rate, or caused a unit to fire in bursts. Machne *et al.* (1955) observed, following peripheral nerve stimulation, bursts of unit activity in the midbrain tegmentum of a frequency of 100 to 300 spikes per second with a latency of 15 to 30 milliseconds. Other units demonstrated a much longer latency (85 milliseconds) and a lower rate of firing. Scheibel *et al.* (1955) found that the most common effect of sciatic nerve stimulation was an augmentation of firing rate of units in the bulbar mesencephalic tegmentum. Both Scheibel *et al.* (1955) and Amassian and Devito (1954) have described units in the reticular formation that respond after a short period with several spikes followed by a relatively quiet period, which in turn is followed after a long delay by a long burst of spikes. This delayed burst can be induced by I α and β fibers alone (Amassian and Devito, 1954). Amassian and Devito (1954) reported a wide range of latencies (12 to 80 milliseconds) of unit potentials evoked by peripheral nerve stimulation, as well as a wide range in the frequency of discharge of evoked spikes which varied from slight augmentation to 1000 spikes per second.

The "fast" potential that we have studied seems to be the same potential studied by French *et al.* (1953a, b) and King *et al.* (1957). The latency and recovery cycles are very similar. This "fast" potential of the medial reticular with a latency of 10 to 20 milliseconds is not conducted as rapidly as lemniscal potentials which have a latency of 5 and 8 milliseconds. There is ample evidence from studies on unit potentials that there are neurones in the brain stem reticular formation that have a latency of 40 or more milliseconds, as well as units that have latencies of 10 milliseconds. The "slow" potential that we have recorded may be derived from neurones that have a longer latency or perhaps from cells that have a diphasic response as have been reported by Scheibel *et al.* (1955) and Amassian and Devito (1954). It would be well to recall that Amassian and Devito (1954) could evoke the delayed response with impulses in the I α and β fibers and that the "slow" potential that we have studied could be evoked by stimuli equal to or smaller than those required to evoke the "fast" potential.

The fact that chlorpromazine increases the amplitude of a single evoked potential in the central core of the mesencephalon is not necessarily evidence that the excitability of this system has been increased. Many investigators (Mollica *et al.*, 1953; Lorente de No, 1953; Amassian and Devito, 1954; Machne *et al.*, 1955) have recorded from spontaneously firing units from the brain stem with small electrodes. Whether this firing is truly spontaneous or whether it is due to a tonic influence of other parts of the brain is unknown. It is known that the cerebral cortex (Baumgarten *et al.*, 1953; Hernandez-Peon and Hagbarth,

1955; French *et al.*, 1955; Adey *et al.*, 1957) and the cerebellum (Mollica *et al.*, 1953; Cooke and Snider, 1953) can send impulses to this system. These structures or others may exert a tonic influence on the cells of the medial reticular formation. Therefore, it seems possible that the increase in amplitude of a single evoked response following chlorpromazine may result from a diminution of the tonic influences that may bombard this system. The resulting effect would be a diminution of a steady tonic occlusion allowing the incoming signal to excite more neurones or to cause a greater excitation of neurones.

The periods of nonreactivity ("absolute refractory period") and the recovery periods reported are estimates based on the pooled data of a number of experiments. Each point illustrated in figures 4, 5 and 7 represents the mean of almost 100 determinations and in some instances of over 500 determinations. The variability not only of the ratio of the second potential to the first potential but also of the amplitude of single evoked potentials (see figure 1C) is large. We found, like King *et al.* (1957), that variability in the amplitude of evoked potentials is characteristic of this system. Recording of spontaneous activity in this system reveals activity of frequencies that range from below 10 to over 50 cycles per second. It is entirely possible that these potentials reflect a continuing state of changing excitability of the bulboreticular system and it may be that the recovery cycle of this system cannot be defined with precision even with methods different from those employed in this study.

The interval following the initial "fast" potential during which no response can be evoked is less than 12 milliseconds. This period is not markedly altered by chlorpromazine, although the rate of recovery is slowed. The period of time following the initial stimulus during which no response can be evoked for the "slow" potential is approximately 20 milliseconds; chlorpromazine increases this period to 40 milliseconds. These data suggest that the maximum frequency that can be accepted by the "fast" system is of the order of magnitude of 100 cycles/second (slightly greater than 83 cycles/second) and that chlorpromazine in doses up to 10 mgm./kgm. though attenuating signals of a frequency of 100 cycles/second does not markedly alter the maximum frequency that can be accepted by this system. On the other hand, the maximum frequency that the "slow" system can accept is 50 cycles/second and chlorpromazine decreases this to 25 cycles/second. Moruzzi and Magoun (1949) and Starzl *et al.* (1951) found that stimuli applied to the medial reticular formation had to have a frequency of at least 50 cycles per second in order to cause activation. It is interesting to speculate that if a moderately high frequency volley (of about 50 cycles/second) is necessary for the activating response and if this "slow" system is necessary for the activating response, then chlorpromazine could depress the activating response by diminishing the frequency response of this system.

Furthermore, activation may be more than one process and the activating system may not be functionally and/or anatomically homogenous. The alterations in the recovery cycle of the "fast" wave indicate that, though chlorpromazine prolongs the recovery cycle, the maximum acceptable frequency is not markedly altered in that the nonresponsive period for the parameters of stimulation employed was, before and after chlorpromazine, less than 12 seconds. This "fast" system may be responsible for the activation evoked from the more caudal sites (Martin *et al.*, 1958).

The finding that pentobarbital depresses the magnitude of evoked potentials in the medial reticular formation and prolongs the recovery cycle of the "fast" potential is confirmatory of earlier work (French *et al.*, 1952; Arduini and Arduini, 1954; King *et al.*, 1957). The marked depression of the single "fast" potential after pentobarbital differentiates its effect from that of chlorpromazine.

SUMMARY

The mechanism of depression of the activating system by chlorpromazine was investigated on potentials recorded in the reticular formation and evoked by stimulation of the sciatic nerve.

The latency, duration and recovery cycles of two types of evoked potentials, "slow" and "fast," recorded in the medial reticular formation, have been described and differentiated on the basis of their latency and recovery cycle.

Chlorpromazine enhanced the amplitude of single evoked "fast" and "slow" potentials and markedly slowed the rate of recovery of both the "fast" and "slow" potentials. The "absolute" refractory period for the "fast" potential was not measurably increased, whereas the "absolute" refractory period for the "slow" potential was markedly increased.

Pentobarbital decreased the amplitude of single evoked potentials. It increased the "absolute" refractory period and slowed the rate of recovery of the "fast" potential. The effects of pentobarbital were thus differentiated from the effects of chlorpromazine.

It is suggested that chlorpromazine may act selectively by depressing the frequency response of neurones responsible for the "slow" potential recorded in the medial reticular formation.

ACKNOWLEDGMENTS. We wish to acknowledge the assistance generously given in these experiments by Mr. Newton E. Long. Grateful appreciation is expressed for a generous supply of chlorpromazine to Dr. E. Fellows of Smith, Kline and French Laboratories.

REFERENCES

ADEY, W. R., SEGUNDO, J. S., AND LIVINGSTON, R. B.: J. Neurophysiol., **20:** 1, 1957.
AMASSIAN, V. E., AND DEVITO, R. V.: J. Neurophysiol., **17:** 575, 1954.
ARDUINI, A., AND ARDUINI, M. G.: THIS JOURNAL, **110:** 76, 1954.
BAUMGARTEN, R. V., MOLLICA, A., AND MORUZZI, G.: EEG Clin. Neurophysiol., Suppl., **3:** 68, 1953.
COOKE, P. M., AND SNIDER, R. S.: EEG Clin. Neurophysiol., **5:** 563, 1953.
DELL, P.: J. physiol. Paris, **44:** 471, 1952.
FRENCH, J. D., HERNANDEZ-PEON, R., AND LIVINGSTON, R. B.: J. Neurophysiol., **18:** 74, 1955.
FRENCH, J. D., VON AMERONGEN, F. K., AND MAGOUN, H. W.: Arch. Neurol. Psychiat., **68:** 577, 1952.
FRENCH, J. D., VERZEANO, M., AND MAGOUN, H. W.: Arch. Neurol. Psychiat., **69:** 505, 1953a.
FRENCH, J. D., VERZEANO, M., AND MAGOUN, H. W.: Arch. Neurol. Psychiat., **69:** 519, 1653b.
FRENCH, J. D., HERNANDEZ-PEON, R., AND LIVINGSTON, R. B.: J. Neurophysiol., **18:** 74, 1955.
HERNANDEZ-PEON, R., AND HAGBARTH, K. E.: J. Neurophysiol., **18:** 44, 1955.
KING, E. E., NAQUET, R., AND MAGOUN, H. W.: THIS JOURNAL, **119:** 48, 1957.
LORENTE DE NO, R.: Ciba Foundation Symposium, The Spinal Cord, p. 131, Churchill, London, 1953.
MACHNE, X., CALMA, I., AND MAGOUN, H. W.: J. Neurophysiol., **18:** 547, 1955.
MARTIN, W. R., DEMAAR, E. W. J., AND UNNA, K. R.: THIS JOURNAL, **122:** 342, 1958.
MOLLICA, A., MORUZZI, G., AND NAQUET, R.: EEG Clin. Neurophysiol., **5:** 571, 1953.
MORUZZI, G., AND MAGOUN, H. W.: EEG and Clin. Neurophysiol., **1:** 455, 1949.
NAPOLITANO, L., AND LONGO, V. G.: Arch. internat. pharmacodyn., **110:** 142, 1957.
SCHEIBEL, M., SCHEIBEL, A., MOLLICA, A., AND MORUZZI, G.: J. Neurophysiol., **18:** 309, 1955.
STARZL, T. E., TAYLOR, C. W., AND MAGOUN, H. W.: J. Neurophysiol., **14:** 479, 1951.

8062

IN VITRO ANAPHYLACTIC AND NONANAPHYLACTIC RESPONSES OF ORGANS OF IMMUNIZED GUINEA PIGS[1]

SEYMOUR KATSH[2]

Department of Embryology, Carnegie Institution of Washington, Baltimore, and Department of Pharmacology, University of Colorado Medical School, Denver

Received for publication May 23, 1958

Since the demonstrations by Schultz (1910) and Dale (1913) that the ileum and the uterus of the immunized guinea pig contracts when provoked with the specific antigen *in vitro*, the Schultz-Dale test has become a standard procedure for demonstrating organ anaphylaxis in hypersensitivity. Thus it has been found that, in addition to the ileum and the uterus, the tracheal system and the associated arteries, thereof, of sensitized guinea pigs also respond to the specific antigen *in vitro* (see review by Seegal, 1949).

Presumably because the common denominator of all of the organs studied is the possession of smooth muscle, it has come to be accepted that *all* smooth muscle containing organs of the sensitized animal contract upon provocation with the specific antigen (see, for example, Cushing and Campbell, 1957). This assumption is appealing because it appears to support and, in turn, to be supported by the theory that the smooth muscle itself is sensitized (Dale, 1956). However, both the assumption and the theory suffer from a lack of direct evidence and the large questions regarding the mechanism of anaphylaxis and a rational therapy still remain unanswered.

Our own work, as expressed recently (Katsh, 1958b), supports the view that antigen causes the antibody-containing cells (*i.e.*, lymphocytes, plasma cells) present in the shocked organ to release a factor which then stimulates the muscle to contract.

The current work provides evidence for this and against the assumption that all smooth muscle containing organs of the immunized guinea pig respond to antigen *in vitro*. The implications of the findings are discussed.

Materials and Methods. The guinea pigs used in these studies were kept in metal cages in an adequately ventilated and illuminated animal room. Food, which included standard laboratory rations plus ascorbic acid and greens, and water were available at all times.

This report is concerned with the observations on 105 animals. As shown in table 1, 10 animals were not injected, and these served as the uninjected controls. For the following groups, which were injected with adjuvant combined with antigen or adjuvant alone, detailed descriptions of the preparation of the emulsion containing antigen appear elsewhere (Katsh, 1958a). Therefore, only brief mention of these procedures will be made in each of the appropriate groups which follow.

Ten males were injected with adjuvant alone. The adjuvant consisted of paraffin oil, Arlacel A, and *Mycobacterium butyricum*, as described by Freund *et al.* (1953). A volume of 0.9 per cent saline was emulsified in an equal volume of the adjuvant. Each animal received 1 ml. of the emulsion intracutaneously in 4 to 7 sites in the nuchal region along the middorsal line.

Forty-three male guinea pigs were injected intracutaneously with an emulsion of homologous testicular homogenate in adjuvant. The homogenate was prepared by grinding freshly obtained or frozen-thawed and decapsulated adult guinea pig testicles in an equal volume (w/v) of 0.9 per cent saline in a glass hand homogenizer. A volume of the homogenate was then emulsified in an equal volume of adjuvant. The anaphylactogenicity of testicular material has been reported (Katsh, 1957, 1958a).

Ten male guinea pigs were injected with guinea pig sperm in adjuvant. The method of obtaining the sperm and the anaphylactogenicity of sperm has been described (Katsh, 1958a). About 10 to 15 mgm. (wet weight) of washed, epididymal sperm were suspended in 1 ml. of 0.9 per cent saline and

[1] This study was supported by funds made available by The Population Council, New York, N. Y.

[2] Present address: Department of Pharmacology, University of Colorado Medical Center, 4200 East Ninth Avenue, Denver 20.

then incorporated into the adjuvant and injected in the manner described above.

Ten male guinea pigs were injected with ovalbumin[3] in adjuvant. One to 2 mgm. of ovalbumin were dissolved in 1 ml. of 0.9 per cent saline and then incorporated into the adjuvant; 0.25 to 2.0 ml. of the emulsion was injected.

Twelve female guinea pigs were injected with homologous testis in adjuvant and 10 females received ovalbumin in adjuvant.

At the time of sacrifice, 17 to 60 days after injection, each animal was exsanguinated. Portions of the following organs were taken for histologic examination: ileum, vas deferens, seminal vesicle, epididymis, testis and uterus. Sections were made and stained for the demonstration of mast cells (Smith and Atkinson, 1956) and for routine histological purposes with a triple stain (Himes and Moriber, 1956) and with Heidenhain's azan method (Lillie, 1948).

Also at the time of sacrifice, 3- to 4-cm. segments of ileum, vas deferens, seminal vesicle and uterus were placed in individual beakers containing Locke's solution. The segments were tested for reaction to antigen while immersed in oxygenated Locke's solution in a constant temperature bath, maintained at 37.5° ± 0.5°C. The bath and its associated parts have been described in detail elsewhere (Katsh, 1958a).

Records were made on smoked paper with the aid of an electrically driven kymograph.

The ilea were tested in the following manner. Within 5 minutes after the segment was suspended, 0.25 ml. of a 10^{-5} *M* solution of acetylcholine (ACh) was injected slowly into the bath (yielding a final concentration of 0.25×10^{-6} *M* ACh). It had been found in previous experiments[4] that this amount of ACh induced a maximal contraction which was readily reversed by flushing the bath. Within 2 minutes thereafter, the ileum was tested for its reaction to one or several antigens which were not injected into the animal. For example, the ilea of guinea pigs injected with homologous testis or sperm were tested for their reaction to ovalbumin or to rabbit, bull or rooster sperm. Then the specific antigen was injected into the bath. After each contracture, the preparation was tested for desensitization by introducing subsequent doses of the antigen after repeated flushing of the bath to counteract the contraction produced by the provoking dose. When the preparation had been desensitized, its response to ACh or to histamine (10^{-5} to 10^{-4} *M*) was determined. In most cases, 2 or more segments of ileum from each animal were tested in this manner. More than 200 ileal segments were observed.

In 10 experiments, ileal segments of animals injected with homologous testis were tested daily for 3 to 5 days after storage of the segments in a refrigerator at 4°C.

In 10 cases, both open ends of the ileal segments were closed securely before suspension in the bath. This was done to determine if it was necessary for the antigen to make contact with the cells lining the lumen in order for contracture to occur.

The procedure for testing the uteri has been reported (Katsh, 1957, 1958a). The vas deferens and seminal vesicle were tested in the same manner as the ileum, except that each of these organs was permitted to reside in the bath for at least 10 minutes before the tests. In most instances, both vasa and both seminal vesicles from each animal were tested. A total of more than 110 tests of the accessory organs of reproduction were performed.

In the experiments in which the vasa deferentia and seminal vesicles were exposed to the antigen, the usual procedure was, as in the ileal studies, to inject the antigen into the bath fluid surrounding the tissue. In 14 trials, however, the antigen was injected into the lumina of the vasa deferentia and the seminal vesicles, and in 10 other cases the antigen was injected into the muscle of these organs *in vitro*.

Sperm for the experiments *in vitro* were secured from the epididymides and were washed and centrifuged as described (Katsh, 1958a). About 5 to 10 mgm., wet weight, of each variety of sperm was suspended in 4 ml. of Locke's solution. Between 0.5 and 1.0 ml of the suspension was introduced into the bath.

The ovalbumin for the studies *in vitro* was dissolved in Locke's solution to a concentration of 1 mgm./ml. One ml. of this solution was used to test the organs.

Contractures induced by antigen were rated as follows: If the contraction elicited was equal to the greatest tension that the muscle was capable of developing as judged by comparison with the effect of a standard dose of ACh, the response was given a rating of *4*. The minute contractions were rated as *−1*.

Results. It can be seen from table 1 that the animals which were not injected and those which were injected with adjuvant alone had

[3] Twice crystallized ovalbumin, OA 536, Worthington Biochemical Corp., Freehold, New Jersey.

[4] Extensive experiments on the effects of a variety of drugs and other materials were performed on isolated ilea, uteri, fallopian tubes, vasa deferentia, seminal vesicles, epididymides and penes of sensitized and nonsensitized guinea pigs. The scope of these investigations makes it impossible to present the results in this communication and, therefore, they will be reported elsewhere.

TABLE 1

Responses in vitro of the ilea, vasa deferentia (Vas), seminal vesicles (S.V.) and uteri of sensitized and nonsensitized guinea pigs

No. of Guinea Pigs	Material Injected	Response to Nonspecific Antigen*			No. of Animals Responding to Specific Antigen†			Response Rating to Specific Antigen		
		Ileum	Vas	S.V.	Ileum	Vas	S.V.	Ileum	Vas	S.V.
Males	*mgm./ml.*									
10	None	0	0	0	0	0	0	0	0	0
10	Adjuvant alone	0	0	0	0	0	0	0	0	0
43	Guinea pig testis in adjuvant (200–250 mgm.)	0	0	0	43	1	2	4	−1	−1
10	Guinea pig sperm in adjuvant (10–15 mgm.)	0	0	0	10	0	0	4	0	0
10	Ovalbumin in adjuvant (0.25–2.0 mgm.)	0	0	0	10	0	0	4	0	0
Females		Ileum	Uterus		Ileum	Uterus		Ileum	Uterus	
12	Guinea pig testis in adjuvant (200–250 mgm.)	0	0		12	12		4	4	
10	Ovalbumin in adjuvant (0.25–2.0 mgm.)	2	2		10	10		4	4	

* Nonspecific antigen refers to antigens other than those which were injected. For example, the organs of animals injected with homologous testis or sperm were tested with heterologous sperm or ovalbumin before provocation with the specific antigen.

† Specific antigen refers to the antigen with which the animal was injected. The organs of animals which were not injected or injected with adjuvant alone were tested with homologous and heterologous sperm and with ovalbumin.

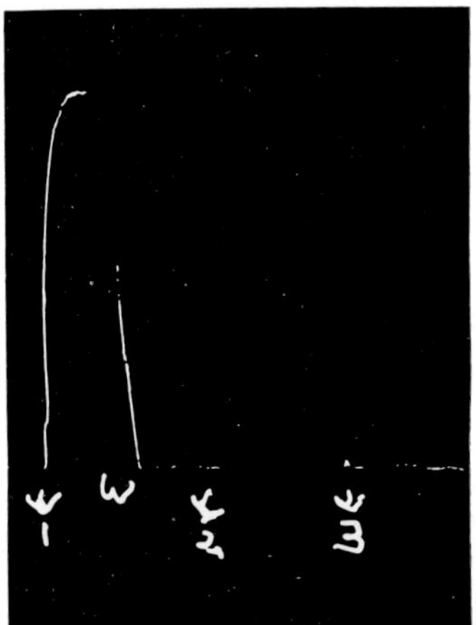

FIG. 1. Nonreactivity to antigen of the ileum of control guinea pigs.
At *1*, 0.25 ml. of 10^{-6} *M* acetylcholine induced contraction. Neither homologous (*2*) nor heterologous (*3*) sperm porduced an effect.

organs which were not responsive to homologous or heterologous sperm or to ovalbumin. The negative reaction of the ilea of control animals is illustrated by fig. 1. The ileum of an animal injected with adjuvant contracted after exposure to 0.25×10^{-6} *M* ACh, but the addition of homologous sperm (*2*) or albumin (*3*) was without effect.

Table 1 indicates that each of 43 males which was injected with guinea pig testis and each of the 10 guinea pigs which received homologous sperm possessed ilea which did not respond to heterologous sperm or to ovalbumin but did contract when homologous sperm was introduced into the bath. Fig. 2 illustrates the effect. In this figure, it can be seen that neither heterologous sperm (at *1*) nor ovalbumin (at *2*) induced contraction. Within 10 to 15 seconds after 1.0 ml. of an homologous sperm suspension was added (at *3*), the ileum was stimulated to contract. Flushing the bath 5 minutes later (W) did not completely reverse the reaction. Subsequent addition of guinea pig sperm did not cause further contraction. In most preparations, desensitization was accomplished only after 3 to 4 further additions of homologous sperm. Even though the desensitized preparations would not react to further exposure to sperm, they did contract in the presence of ACh or histamine (10^{-5} to 10^{-4} *M*).

Ilea that were stored at 4°C. for up to 5 days still responded to antigen, but the magnitude of response decreased with time. At the longest interval, 5 days, although the ilea re-

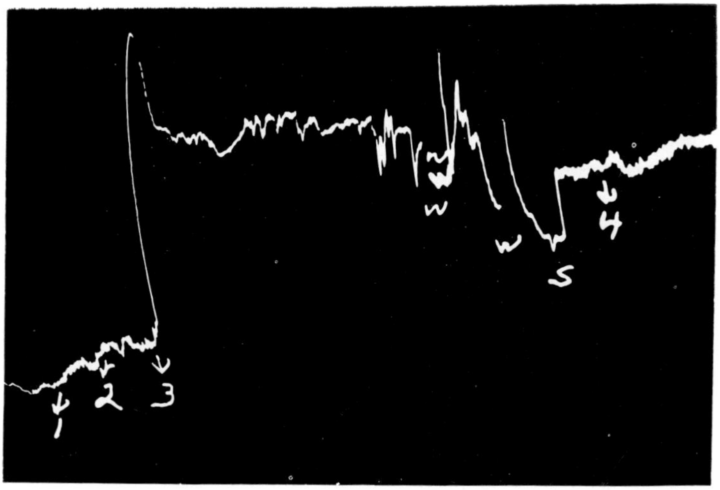

FIG. 2. The response to specific antigen of ileum of guinea pig injected with homologous testis or sperm.

At *1* and *2*, respectively, heterologous sperm and ovalbumin did not induce contraction. Ten to 20 seconds after the addition of homologous sperm, *3*, the ileum contracted maximally. Five minutes later the bath was flushed. The contracture was not reversed completely by washing (W). At *S* the drum was stopped and 10 minutes were permitted to elapse to allow time for equilibration. The ileum did not respond to a subsequent dose of antigen (*4*).

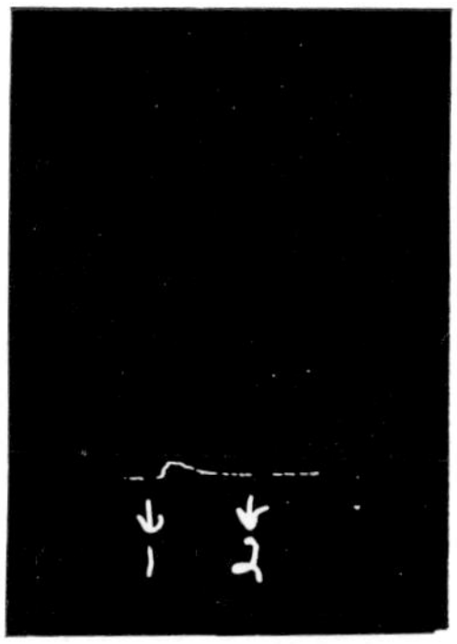

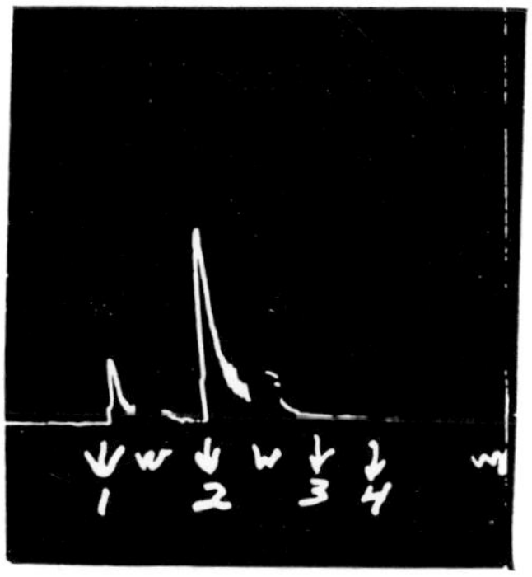

FIG. 3. Strongest of the 3 responses to antigen obtained in either the vasa deferentia or seminal vesicles of guinea pigs injected with homologous testis or sperm.

At *1*, the seminal vesicle was stimulated to contract slightly, and the preparation did not react to another exposure to the antigen, *2*.

FIG. 4. Responses of the vas deferens of guinea pigs injected with homologous testis or sperm.

At *1* and *2*, acetylcholine (10^{-5}, 10^{-4} *M*) elicited contractions. Ovalbumin (*3*) and homologous sperm (*4*) induced no observable effect.

sponded to antigen, no response to ACh was observed.

Ilea with lumina blocked to antigen by tying off the ends responded to antigen, but the height of contraction was not as great as similar untied segments.

In only 3 of the 43 males which were injected with testis or sperm was there any detectable reaction to the antigen on the part of the vasa deferentia and the seminal vesicles. These organs, however, did contract after the addition of ACh, histamine, or any of the other stimulants used. Fig. 3 represents an instance in which the seminal vesicle did contract after the addition of the specific antigen. In this figure, it can be seen that the response is a tiny contraction and that the contraction is not long maintained. Except for two other positive results, both rated as *−1*, none of the vasa deferentia or seminal vesicles exhibited any reaction to specific or nonspecific antigen. The organs did respond regularly to ACh (fig. 4). None of 10 males injected with sperm possessed accessory organs of reproduction that responded to antigen.

Table 1 also discloses that all of the 10 animals which were sensitized with ovalbumin had ilea which reacted *in vitro* to the antigen. Fig. 5 illustrates the response of the sensitized ileum to albumin and the lack of response to sperm.

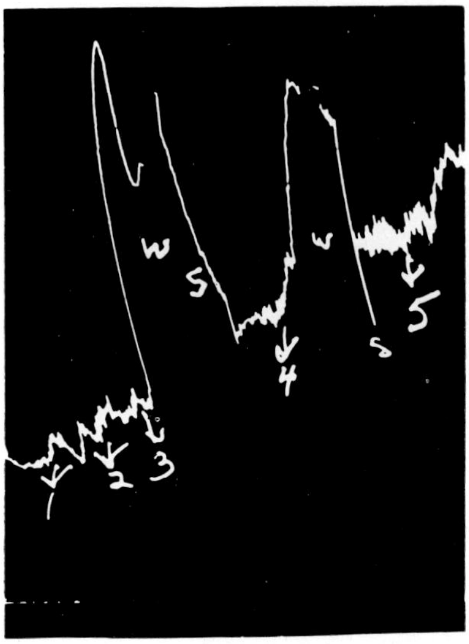

FIG. 5. Response of guinea pig ileum injected with ovalbumin.
At *1* and *2*, heteologous and homologous sperm, respectively, were placed in the bath. Contraction occurred after ovalbumin was added, *3*. The preparation was washed within 2 minutes but the contracture was not completely reversed by flushing the bath (W). At *S*, the drum was stopped to allow time for equilibration. At *4*, a second dose of albumin was administered and a contraction was elicited. This was repeated (*5*) and the contracture was smaller.

The vasa deferentia and the seminal vesicles of these animals did not respond to the specific antigen and were also insensitive to sperm. These organs were readily stimulated by ACh and histamine before and after trials with antigens (fig. 6).

Each of 12 females injected with homologous testis possessed ilea and uteri which reacted to homologous sperm and not to ovalbumin. The responses were rated as *4*. (This rating should not be confused with that employed in a previous study (Katsh, 1958a), because in the latter report *duration of contraction* and not *height of contraction* formed the basis for the rating scale.)

All of 10 females injected with ovalbumin had ilea and cornua which responded maximally to ovalbumin. In 2 cases the uteri and ilea were observed to react to homologous sperm. This reaction has been considered in a previous paper (Katsh, 1958a).

Histological observations. Ileum, vas deferens, seminal vesicle, uterus: The general histology of these organs has been well characterized in textbooks of histology. The outstanding similarity among these organs is the presence of a large quantity of smooth muscle, in which the vas deferens is particularly rich. In general, the muscle is arranged so that there is an inner circular layer and an outer longitudinal layer.

The major histological findings which are pertinent here are as follows: 1. The ileum and uterus contain large amounts of lymphoid

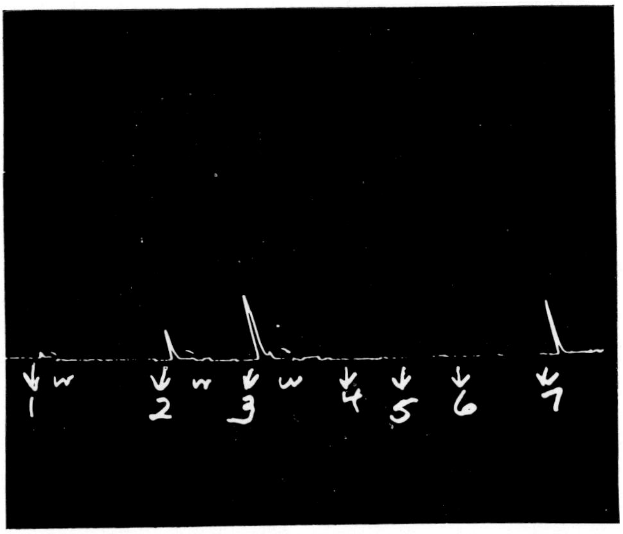

FIG. 6. The vas deferens of an animal injected with ovalbumin responded to acetylcholine (*1, 2, 3*) (10^{-7}–10^{-5} *M*) but not to homologous or heterologous sperm (*4, 5*) or to ovalbumin (*6*). The preparation was still sensitive to ACh, *7* (10^{-5} *M*).

tissue and lymphocytes, respectively, as well as macrophages and other white blood cellular elements including plasma cells and lymphocytes. These are the cell types that have been demonstrated to form antibodies (Ehrich, 1953). Cells concerned with antibody synthesis (plasma cells and lymphocytes) will hereafter be referred to in general terms as "cells of the antibody series." 2. Mast cells were found in the ileum, uterus, vas deferens and seminal vesicles. Mast cells have considerable importance in view of the histamine theory of muscle contraction following antigenic stimulation (see reference concerned with the Ciba Foundation Symposium on Histamine).

Testis: The testes of all animals injected with homologous testicular homogenate or with sperm were aspermatogenic. This reaction has been described in detail elsewhere (Freund *et al.*, 1953; Katsh and Bishop, in press). The aspermatogenic testes were found to be infiltrated with lymphocytes. The testes of all other animals were unaffected.

Discussion. The essential facts and conclusions revealed by the current investigations are as follows:

1. The insensitivity of the accessory organs of reproduction cannot be attributed to a difference in amount of muscle in these organs as compared with the ileum and uterus, for the vas deferens and seminal vesicle are heavily muscled and, on a unit basis, may even be more richly endowed with this tissue than either the ileum or the uterus. It is apparent, therefore, that the presence of smooth muscle alone is insufficient to insure demonstration of anaphylaxis in the Schultz-Dale test. It appears to be incorrect also to assume that *all* organs containing smooth muscle are sensitized in immunized guinea pigs.

2. The insensitivity of the accessory organs of reproduction cannot be ascribed to any known physiological difference between the smooth musculature of these organs as compared with that of the ileum and uterus. The same muscle stimulants (*e.g.*, ACh, histamine, anticholinesterases) elicited the same effects in all these organs. This information, together with the reports that the vas deferens and seminal vesicle contain well defined nerve-muscle units (Waddell, 1916; Macht, 1917; Gruber, 1933), relegates the nerve involvement theory of smooth muscle response in anaphylaxis (Geiger *et al.*, 1956; Geiger and Alpers, 1957) to an intermediary position in the chain of events leading to antigen-induced contracture.

3. The insensitivity of the vasa deferentia and seminal vesicles cannot be referred to an inaccessibility to antigen of reactive sites in these organs. Injection of antigen directly into the lumina and into the musculature of these organs *in vitro* did not produce an effect. Moreover, the corollary experiments in which the open ends of isolated ilea were tied off before exposure to antigen support the contention that inaccessibility of reactive sites is not tenable, since such ilea did respond.

4. The insensitivity of the vas deferens and seminal vesicle cannot be assigned to an absence of mast cells which are presumed to release histamine during antigenically induced contracture (see Dale, 1956), since mast cells were found in these organs. Therefore, the presence of mast cells together with smooth muscle is not enough in itself to insure that contracture will occur upon exposure to antigen.

Since available hypotheses regarding the mechanism of anaphylactic contracture cannot explain the observations and results, it is essential to propose a concept which can. The following formulation is based upon previous and current observations which reveal that the vas deferens and seminal vesicle, unlike the ileum and uterus, do not contain cells of the antibody series and is in harmony with the one clearly established fact underlying the anaphylactic response of smooth muscle-containing organs, namely, that unless the animal is sensitized, antigen is incapable of eliciting contracture, and, therefore, antibody is involved.

1. Antibodies to the specific antigen are brought to the organs by the cells of the antibody series via the circulatory system. Antibodies may also be synthesized by antibody-forming cells (*e.g.*, lymph nodes, Peyer's patches in the ileum) in the respective organs under stimulus of antigen brought to the organ.

2. After an approriate interval of time, during which antibody synthesis proceeds, a challenging dose of antigen administered to the sensitized organ (or animal) will induce a contracture in those organs containing smooth muscle and possessing cells of the antibody series, *i.e.*, ileum and uterus. Organs containing smooth muscle but not cells of the antibody series will not contract.

It is emphasized that, whereas organs such as the vas may not contract *in vitro* to antigen, they may do so *in vivo* by virtue of the antibody-containing cells coursing through them in the blood vessels. This explains the 3 instances in which the accessory organs were observed to contract *in vitro*, *i.e.*, the presence of such cells in the blood vessels of the segments.

3. The strength of contracture will depend upon the number of antibody-containing cells present in the organ as well as the number of antigenic units presented to the organ.

This explains the minute nature of the 3 contractions observed: a paucity of antibody cells available to combine with antigen.

4. Desensitization will be accomplished only after all combining sites of antibody have reacted with antigen.

This can explain why the ileum, which possesses so rich a supply of lymphoid tissue, requires several exposures (or prolonged exposure) to antigen for complete desensitization (figs. 2 and 5). The uterus, which contains fewer lymphoidal elements, is more easily desensitized than the ileum.

The hypothesis is consistent with the data, and, moreover, with the known facts concerning the mechanism of anaphylaxis. The fact that Schild (1939) has obtained antigen-induced contractures of the seminal vesicles of guinea pigs sensitized with ovalbumin is not in conflict with the current results. In Schild's experiments the animals were killed by a blow on the head and the tissues were removed and placed in the fluid. Under these circumstances the blood vessels of the seminal vesicles would not be emptied of their contents. Thus, cells of the antibody series present in the vessels of these segments can account for the responses obtained. In the current work, the animals were exsanguinated and the blood vessels of the accessory organs were free of formed elements. Consequently, there were no cells of the antibody series with which antigen could react.

The same hypothesis offers a rational interpretation of the specificity of damage in such conditions as aspermatogenesis. The current studies disclose that cells of the antibody series were abundant in these damaged gonads. Thus, organ specific damage after a single injection is self-generating because of the interaction between the cells of the antibody series and the antigen contained in that organ. Extrapolation of the concept to include uveitis (Collins, 1949), neuritis (Waksman and Adams, 1954), and encephalomyelitis (Lumsden, 1949) indicates a unity which is so intriguing as to warrant intensive examination.

SUMMARY

Guinea pigs were sensitized with homologous testis or sperm or with ovalbumin in adjuvant. Control animals were uninjected or were injected with adjuvant alone. Seventeen to 60 days later, the animals were sacrificed, and portions of the following organs were taken for histological study: ileum, vas deferens, seminal vesicle, epididymis, testis and uterus. Segments of ileum, uterus, vas deferens and seminal vesicle were suspended in a constant temperature bath. These organs were tested for their response to drugs, nonspecific antigen and specific antigen. It was found that none of the organs of the control animals responded to any of the antigens. Of 53 males injected with homologous testis or sperm, all had ilea which contracted maximally to homologous sperm but not to heterologous sperm or to ovalbumin. Of the 53 animals, only 3 instances of contraction to antigen in vasa deferentia or seminal vesicles were observed. In these 3 cases, the contraction was minute and transitory. All of 10 animals which received ovalbumin had ilea which contracted when provoked with antigen, and in no instance did the accessory organs of reproduction contract to antigen. All of 12 females injected with homologous testis and a similar number injected with ovalbumin had ilea and uteri which responded to specific antigen.

Histological examination revealed that the vasa deferentia and seminal vesicles were devoid of cells of the antibody series (plasma cells, lymphocytes), whereas the ileum was richly endowed with lymphoid tissue, and the uterus was heavily infiltrated with lymphocytes.

Since none of the available hypotheses explains the insensitivity of the vasa deferentia and seminal vesicles, a concept is proposed.

REFERENCES

Collins, R. C.: Am. J. Ophth., **32:** 1697, 1949.
Cushing, J. H., and Campbell, D. H.: Principles of Immunology, McGraw-Hill, Inc., New York, 1957.
Dale, H. H.: This Journal, **4:** 167, 1913.
Dale, H. H.: The Ciba Foundation Symposium on

Histamine, Little, Brown and Co., Boston, 1956.
EHRICH, W. E.: Blood Cells and Plasma Proteins, Chap. 4, Academic Press, New York, 1953.
FREUND, J., LIPTON, M. M., AND THOMPSON, G. E.: J. Exper. Med., **97:** 711, 1953.
GEIGER, W. B., HILL, E. M., AND THOMPSON, M.: Proc. Soc. Exp. Biol. & Med., **92:** 793, 1956.
GEIGER, W. B., AND ALPERS, H. S.: Science, **125:** 1141, 1957.
GRUBER, C. M.: Physiol. Rev., **13:** 497, 1933.
HIMES, M., AND MORIBER, L.: Stain Technol., **31:** 67, 1956.
KATSH, S.: Nature, **180:** 1047, 1957.
KATSH, S.: J. Exper. Med., **107:** 95, 1958a.
KATSH, S.: Ann. New York Acad. Sc. in press, 1958b.
KATSH, S., AND BISHOP, D. W.: J. Embryol. and Exp. Morph., **6:** 94, 1958.
LILLIE, R. D.: Histopathologic Technic, Blakiston Co., Phila., 1948.
LUMSDEN, C. E.: Brain, **72:** 517, 1949.
MACHT, D.: THIS JOURNAL, **9:** 121, 1917.
SCHILD, H. O.: J. Physiol., **95:** 393, 1939.
SCHULTZ, W. H.: THIS JOURNAL, **1:** 549, 1910.
SEEGAL, B. C.: Ann. New York Acad. Sc., **52:** 681, 1949.
SMITH, E. W., AND ATKINSON, W. B.: Science, **123:** 941, 1956.
WADDELL, J. A.: THIS JOURNAL, **8:** 551, 1916.
WAKSMAN, B. H., AND ADAMS, R. D.: Fed. Proc., **13:** 516, 1954.

8063

A MINIMUM ERROR TABLE FOR PARALLEL LINE BIOLOGICAL ASSAYS

MINDEL C. SHEPS AND KATHARINE H. HENDRIE

Department of Preventive Medicine, Harvard University Medical School, Boston, Massachusetts

Received for publication April 30, 1958

The precision of a parallel line biological assay is often described by the index $\lambda = s/b$, where s is the residual standard deviation per observation and b is the slope of the dose response regression line. As was pointed out by Gaddum (1953), λ (or its reciprocal, $L = 1/\lambda$) measures the innate precision of any method since it is nondimensional and independent of the number of assay subjects (N). λ is therefore considered as a characteristic of an assay method, which is particularly useful in comparisons between assay methods. All other things being equal, the method with a lower average value of λ is more precise.

An important additional factor is the number of assay subjects (Munson and Sheps, 1958). In many methods, the possibility of increasing the number of subjects may be sharply limited because of: a) technical difficulties met in preparing animals and keeping them alive, as when hypophysectomized adrenalectomized mice are used in an assay; b) difficulties of obtaining large amounts of unknown substance when it is found in low concentration in human blood, urine, or other body fluids; c) other factors such as space, expense, etc.

Formulas are available (Bliss, 1952; Gaddum, 1953) which relate the value of λ to the minimum variance of a log potency estimate (M) and to N. The calculations are performed in terms of the logarithms. If the investigator thinks in terms of error of a potency estimate itself (R), he must transform the answer by calculating the square root of the variance and converting it to its antilogarithm.

The calculations and transformations have been performed for the accompanying table which shows the relationship between three quantities: λ, the number of assay subjects and the minimum standard error of R, expressed as a percentage (Munson and Sheps, 1958). Thus, for a given value of λ, the table yields a more specific description of an assay method in ordinary percentage terms. It may be used to find the minimum standard error expressed as a per cent of a potency estimate for known values of λ and N, or alternatively to find the minimum number of assay subjects needed to achieve a desired level of precision. It will not give the error of an individual potency estimate, since this error is often greater than the minimum.

Derivation of the Table. When the assay slope is determined with relatively great precision, the formula for the confidence limits of M (Bliss, 1952, 1956; Gaddum, 1953) reduces to $M \pm ts_M$ where s_M is the standard error of M.

$$s_M = \lambda\sqrt{1/N_S + 1/N_U + (\bar{y}_U - \bar{y}_S)^2/b^2\Sigma x^2}$$

where: N_S and N_U are, respectively, the number of subjects on the reference standard and on the unknown, $\bar{y}_U$ and $\bar{y}_S$ the mean responses to the standard and the unknown and Σx^2 is the sum of the squared derivations of the log doses from their mean.

The smallest value that can be assumed by s_M (min. s_M) is achieved when $\bar{y}_U = \bar{y}_S$. In this case, min. $s_M = \lambda\sqrt{1/N_S + 1/N_U}$.

The difference between the min. s_M and the standard error of individual potency estimates varies with the absolute value of $\bar{y}_U - \bar{y}_S$ and inversely with the denominator $b^2\Sigma x^2$. The magnitude of the denominator depends on the total number of assay subjects and on the design of the assay. Therefore the min. s_M cannot be recommended as an approximate estimate of individual standard errors.

When considering the antilog of M, *i.e.*, the potency estimate itself, it is appropriate to consider the antilog of s_M also. Since addition of logarithms implies multiplication of antilogarithms, the results may be expressed as in the following example:

	Estimate of relative potency	Minimum standard error	Approximate "standard error limits"
In logarithms	0.25	0.10	$0.25 \pm 0.10 =$ 0.15 to 0.35
In antilogarithms	1.78	1.26	$1.78 \overset{\times}{\div} 1.26 =$ 1.41 to 2.24

The formula 100 (antilog min. $s_M - 1$) transforms min. s_M into a percentage of the potency estimate (Bliss, 1952). In the example, this is $100(1.26 - 1) = 26$ per cent.

The min. s_M was calculated for values of λ from 0.10 to 0.45 inclusive, and for values of N_S or N_U up to 100. It was then converted into a percentage of the potency estimate, *i.e.*, of the antilogarithm, and tabulated.

Use ot the Table. To enter the table, let N_S = the number of subjects on the reference standard and N_U = the number of subjects on the unknown. Calculate $N' = 2N_SN_U/(N_S + N_U)$. When N_S and N_U are equal, $N_S = N_U = N'$.

Examples: 1) In an assay where $\lambda = 0.20$ and $N_S = N_U = 6$, enter the table at row $N' = 6$ and column $\lambda = 0.20$. The minimum standard error is 30 per cent of the potency estimate.

2) If $\lambda = 0.35$, $N_S = 40$ and $N_U = 20$, from the formula $N' = 2(40)(20)/60 = 26.7$ For $N' = 26$ and $\lambda = 0.35$ the minimum standard error is shown in the table as 25 per cent of the potency estimate.

3) If $\lambda = 0.15$ and a minimum standard error of 15 per cent is desired, the table gives $N' = 12$ corresponding to these values. Therefore, if the method remains stable with $\lambda = 0.15$ the number of subjects should be at least $N_S = N_U = N' = 12$ to yield a minimum standard error of 15 per cent. If a fixed number N_S of subjects are treated with the reference standard, N_U may be calculated as $N_U = N'N_S/(2N_S - N')$. In the example, if $N_S = 20$, then $N_U = 12(20)/(40 - 12) = 240/28 = 8.6$. Therefore, at least 9 assay subjects must be treated with the unknown substance.

TABLE 1

Minimum standard error of a parallel line biological assay expressed as a percent of a potency estimate

N′	λ = s/b .10	.15	.20	.25	.30	.35	.40	.45	N′
2	26	41	58	78	100	124	151	182	2
3	21	33	46	60	76	93	112	134	3
4	18	28	39	50	63	77	92	108	4
5	16	24	34	44	55	66	79	93	5
6	14	22	30	39	49	59	70	82	6
7	13	20	28	36	45	54	64	73	7
8	12	19	26	33	41	50	58	68	8
9	11	18	24	31	38	46	54	63	9
10	11	17	23	29	36	43	51	59	10
11	10	16	22	28	34	41	48	56	11
12	10	15	21	26	33	39	46	53	12
13	9	15	20	25	31	37	43	50	13
14	9	14	19	24	30	36	42	48	14
15	9	13	18	23	29	34	40	46	15
16	8	13	18	23	28	33	39	44	16
17	8	13	17	22	27	32	37	43	17
18	8	12	17	21	26	31	36	41	18
19	8	12	16	21	25	30	35	40	19
20	8	12	16	20	24	29	34	39	20
22	7	11	15	19	23	28	32	37	22
24	7	10	14	18	22	26	30	35	24
26	7	10	14	17	21	25	29	33	26
28	6	10	13	17	20	24	28	32	28
30	6	9	13	16	20	23	27	31	30
35	6	9	12	15	18	21	25	28	35
40	5	8	11	14	17	20	23	26	40
45	5	8	10	13	16	19	21	24	45
50	5	7	10	12	15	18	20	23	50
55	4	7	9	12	14	17	19	22	55
60	4	7	9	11	13	16	18	21	60
65	4	6	8	11	13	15	18	20	65
70	4	6	8	10	12	15	17	19	70
80	4	6	8	10	12	14	16	18	80
90	4	5	7	9	11	13	15	17	90
100	3	5	7	8	10	12	14	16	100

$N' = 2N_SN_U/(N_S + N_U)$ where N_S and N_U are, respectively, the number of subjects on the reference standard and on the unknown.

SUMMARY

The calculation of the index λ in parallel line biological assays yields comparative information about the precision of the method. Further calculations and logarithmic transformations are needed to describe the minimum standard error of potency estimates derived in the assay with a given number of subjects, or alternatively to estimate the minimum number of assay subjects to achieve a desired minimum error.

The table presented in this paper obviates the need for such calculations. It shows directly the relationship between λ, the number of assay subjects and the minimum standard error expressed as a per cent of a potency estimate. Examples are given of the use of the table.

REFERENCES

Bliss, C. I.: The Statistics of Bioassay, Academic Press, Inc., New York, 1952.
Bliss, C. I.: Drug Standards, **24:** 33, 1956.
Gaddum, J. H.: Pharmacol. Rev., **5:** 87, 1953.
Munson, P. L. and Sheps, M. C.: Endocrinology, **62:** 173, 1958.

8064

PHARMACODYNAMIC ASPECTS OF ALLYL ALCOHOL TOXICITY[1]

JIRO K. KODAMA[2] AND CHARLES H. HINE

Department of Pharmacology and Experimental Therapeutics, University of California School of Medicine, San Francisco

Received for publication June 2, 1958

As early as 1891, Miessner recognized the unusual toxicity of allyl alcohol, and showed that it was bout 50 times as toxic to mice as its saturated analogue, propyl alcohol. Other data have indicated that allyl alcohol is between 15 and 60 times as toxic as propyl alcohol to various species, by various routes of administration (Smyth *et al.*, 1951, 1954; Dunlap *et al.*, 1958).

The characteristic pharmacologic and toxic effects of allyl alcohol have little relation to the route of administration, and include excessive secretion of the lacrimal, salivary, and gastroenteric glands, increased motility of the gastroenteric tract, generalized vasodilation, hemoconcentration, severe depression of blood pressure, pulmonary effusion, congestion of the viscera, and hepatic necrosis. The production of hepatic necrosis is noteworthy, since the simple saturated alcohols cause merely a moderate and reversible fat infiltration (von Oettingen, 1943; Drill, 1952). A distinctive feature of the necrosis is its locus in the periportal areas. Signs of hypnosis, commonly seen with saturated alcohols, are essentially absent; in fact, the intoxicated animals remain very sensitive to pain and sound, and appear apathetic rather than hypnotic in the usual sense.

Because of these interesting features, we felt that a pharmacodynamic investigation of allyl alcohol would be worthwhile. The purpose of our first study was to quantitate the metabolic impairment of selected organs from rats intoxicated with allyl alcohol. Respiration of tissue slices was used as the criterion of injury. An analytic method suitable for microdetermination of allyl alcohol in blood was then developed, which permitted both the estimation of the alcohol concentrations *in vivo* and a corollary comparison of hepatotoxic effects *in vivo* and *in vitro*. The possibility of histamine release was explored, since many of the signs of allyl alcohol poisoning resemble those produced by histamine. The hypothesis that an excessive discharge of the sympathoadrenal system, induced by the profound hypotensive action of allyl alcohol, played a significant role in the development of hepatic injury was investigated by protection studies with phenoxybenzamine (Dibenzyline) and hexamethonium. The relation of inhibition of tissue respiration to tissue swelling was also examined. Finally, we tested the thesis that this simple aliphatic alcohol might act by inhibition of sulfhydryl enzymes, such as the dehydrogenases, which are involved in numerous energy-yielding reactions and represent an important class of enzyme.

METHODS. *Oxygen uptake of tissues of intoxicated rats.* Male rats (90 to 150 gm.) of the Long-Evans strain were fasted overnight and given single doses of 60 or 120 mgm./kgm. of allyl alcohol intragastrically as a 10 per cent solution (w/v) in distilled water. The LD_{50} of allyl alcohol in this strain of rat is about 100 mgm./kgm. (Dunlap *et. al.*, 1958). The rats were decapitated one or two hours later, and the brain, liver and kidneys immediately removed and sliced in a moistened cold chamber for standard manometric measurement of oxygen uptake with the Warburg apparatus.

The liver and kidneys were sectioned with either the Martin slicer (1942) or the Stadie-Riggs (1944) microtome, and the cerebral slices were obtained with a razor and template. The tissue slices were weighed on a micro-torsion balance in amounts ranging from 70 to 130 mgm. of liver or kidney and 30 to 40 mgm. of cerebral cortex. The incubation medium was a modified Krebs-Ringer-phosphate solution (Elliott, Warren and James, 1947) with and without 0.1 *M* glucose.

Oxygen uptake was measured every 15 minutes at 37.2°C in a gas phase of 100 per cent oxygen,

[1] Supported in part by a grant from the Shell Development Company, Emeryville, California.

[2] This study formed part of a thesis submitted by this author and accepted by the University of California in partial fulfilment of the requirements for the degree of Doctor of Philosophy.

and the incubation period was arbitrarily set at 120 minutes. Mean rates of oxygen uptake and their standard error were calculated in terms of microl. of oxygen/mgm. wet weight of tissue/hour. Each mean value represented 6 to 12 observations and 3 to 4 rats. These means were compared by the Student "t" test, significance being assumed when P = <5 per cent.

Inhibition in vitro of oxygen uptake of rat tissues. The same Warburg technique was used, and the oxygen uptake of normal rat liver and kidney slices was measured every 15 minutes for 150 minutes. Immediately after the 30-minute reading, graded quantities of allyl alcohol were tipped from the side-arm of the Warburg flask into the incubation medium, producing final concentrations of 10^{-2}, 10^{-3}, 10^{-4} and 10^{-5} M/l. Five or six observations were made at each concentration.

Mean rates of oxygen uptake were calculated for each 15-minute interval. The total oxygen uptake during the 120-minute exposure was compared with that of the control slices. The total uptake and the molar concentration required for 50 per cent inhibition of the rate of oxygen uptake (I_{50}) were graphically estimated for each tissue.

Protection studies with Dibenzyline and hexamethonium. Twelve male rats (132 to 190 gm.) of the Long-Evans strain were randomized into four groups and fasted overnight. The first group of three served as an untreated control; the other groups received 120 mgm./kgm. of allyl alcohol intragastrically. Of these, three rats received only the alcohol; three received, 3 hours before the alcohol, an intramuscular injection of 10 mgm./kgm. of dibenzyline hydrochloride (4 per cent in equal parts of anhydrous ethanol and propylene glycol); and the last group received, one hour before the alcohol, 10 mgm./kgm. of hexamethonium chloride (2 per cent aqueous) intramuscularly. The rats were decapitated one hour after the allyl alcohol was administered.

The livers were removed and sliced as in the previous respiration studies, with one modification in technique. As low temperatures affect the osmotonicity of cells, probably by diminishing the metabolic activity of the cell membrane, the tissue and medium were not chilled as is customary during preparation. The entire procedure was performed rapidly at room temperature. Quadruplicate measurements of oxygen uptake were made for each liver. In order to estimate the degree of swelling of liver slices, the percentage of water in the slices was also measured in quadruplicate. Before and after the incubation period of 120 minutes, slices were drained on filter paper and weighed in tared aluminum foil before and after drying overnight at 105 to 110°C.

The following acute toxicity study was carried out to determine whether significant protection could be afforded by Dibenzyline against allyl alcohol. Twenty fasted rats, which had been injected intramuscularly with 10 mgm./kgm. of Dibenzyline hydrochloride three hours previously, and 20 untreated rats, were given 120 mgm./kgm. of allyl alcohol intragastrically. Gross signs of toxicity, time of death and number of deaths were observed in both groups for a period of 5 days. The mean time of death and the standard error of the mean were calculated for each group for statistical comparison.

Studies on tissue swelling in vitro. This experiment was intended to determine whether liver slices exposed *in vitro* to allyl alcohol would swell in correspondence with the degree of respiratory inhibition previously found, and whether propyl alcohol would produce similar results.

Rat liver slices were exposed to 2.5×10^{-4} and 2.5×10^{-5} M allyl alcohol for 60 and 90 minutes. These concentrations were selected to produce significant inhibition of oxygen uptake both above and below the 50 per cent level of inhibition. The rate of oxygen uptake and percentage water content were determined in duplicate at the end of the exposure period. In similar fashion, slices were exposed to 2.5×10^{-1} M propyl alcohol for 120 minutes, and the rate of oxygen uptake and percentage of water determined in quadruplicate.

Effect of allyl alcohol on blood pressure, respiration and plasma histamine levels. A mongrel dog (11 kgm.), anesthetized with 30 mgm./kgm. of sodium pentobarbital and heparinized with 300 units/kgm. of heparin sodium, was conventionally prepared for measurement of carotid blood pressure and respiration, and given 40 mgm./kgm. of allyl alcohol intravenously. The blood pressure and respiration were measured over a period of several hours.

Blood samples were taken from the femoral vein just before administration of the allyl alcohol and 1.7, 9 and 40 minutes afterward. The samples were drawn with a siliconized 10-ml. syringe and immediately transferred with care to siliconized centrifuge tubes, chilled with crushed ice to minimize nonspecific histamine release (Gaddum, 1949), and then centrifuged at 3000 r.p.m. for 20 minutes at 5°C. Histamine was extracted from the plasma by the method of Code (1937), and plasma containing a known amount of histamine was run as a control. The histamine in the eluates was assayed on guinea-pig ileum suspended in Tyrode solution containing 1 mgm./l. of atropine sulfate. Hematocrit determinations were also made on each sample.

Dehydrogenase inhibition in vitro. The inhibition of various dehydrogenases of rat liver by allyl alcohol, propyl alcohol and acrolein was studied by the method of Kun and Abood (1949) for colorimetric estimation of succinic dehydrogenase with TTC (2,3,5-triphenyltetrazolium chloride). The substrates used with the liver homogenate were the sodium salts of succinic, pyruvic, isocitric and glutamic acids.

Microquantitation of allyl alcohol. Allyl alcohol is oxidized by diffusion into a solution of potassium dichromate in sulfuric acid. The amber color of unreduced dichromate was found to be unsatisfactory for conventional direct spectrophotometry, since this method is not sensitive enough to detect the allyl alcohol present in small amounts of rat blood. Therefore, the unreacted dichromate is reacted with potassium iodide, liberating iodine. The blue color resulting from reaction of the iodine with starch is measured spectrophotometrically. In place of the standard Conway cells, a similar microdiffusion unit was assembled, consisting of a small Paar weighing bottle (with an outside-ground cap) of approximately 4-ml. capacity to the base of the neck, and a 1-ml. microbeaker. Among the advantages of this unit are: the small air volume within the cell, ease of handling and cleaning, and an excellent seal with minimum amounts of silicone grease.

The materials used were as follows: potassium dichromate, 0.1026 N in H_2SO_4 15.5 N; standard solutions of allyl alcohol in distilled water and rat blood, 2 to 8 microgm./0.1 ml.; potassium iodide, 0.2 N; and starch solution, 0.25 per cent.

Using a micropipette, 0.025 ml. of the dichromate solution was placed in the inner chamber; 0.1 ml. of allyl alcohol standard was placed in the outer chamber. Diffusion proceeded overnight (20 to 24 hours) at 50°C. The contents of the inner chamber were then washed out with 1 ml. of water, three times. These washings were added to 80 ml. of distilled water in a 100-ml. volumetric flask, and 5.0 ml. of potassium iodide were added. The flask was held in boiling water for 30 minutes. After rapid cooling with tap water, 3 ml. of starch solution were added, and water to make 100 ml. Color formation was allowed to progress for 30 minutes, and was then measured at 575 mμ with the Coleman Jr. Spectrophotometer, using a cuvette with a 1-cm. light path. The mean optical density with confidence limits of ± 1 S.D. was calculated for each set of readings.

Certain precautions must be observed when employing this method. 1) The excess dichromate extracted from the sulfuric acid should be diluted (in these experiments it was diluted to about 80 ml.) before the potassium iodide is added, to minimize the reaction between iodide and acid, which can liberate iodine. 2) The heated solution should be cooled to about room temperature before starch is added, as the intensity of the color varies with temperature. 3) Since the intensity of color increases with time, the measurement should be made at a set time after the addition of starch (30 minutes, in these experiments).

Quantitation of blood levels of allyl alcohol following intragastric or intravenous administration. Male rats (280 to 390 gm.) of the Long-Evans strain were given allyl alcohol, 10 per cent (w/v) in physiologic saline, in single doses of 120 mgm./kgm. intragastrically or 30 mgm./kgm. intravenously. Only the rats receiving intragastric instillation were fasted (overnight). Other rats were given the same solution by constant intravenous infusion at the rate of 42, 68 and 100 mgm./kgm./hour, or a 3.9 per cent solution at 23 and 24 mgm./kgm./hour. The total volume of solution infused never exceeded 0.75 ml. The solution was infused into the femoral vein through a polyethylene catheter, using the constant-metering device previously described by Hine and his associates (1953).

The rats were anesthetized with 45 mgm./kgm. of sodium pentobarbital (20 mgm./ml.) and light hypnosis was maintained with intramuscular doses of 5 mgm./kgm. as required. After laparotomy, a control blood sample of 0.1 or 0.2 ml. was taken; serial samples were taken from the portal vein after intragastric administration of the alcohol, and from the inferior vena cava after single intravenous injection and during the constant infusion. It would have been preferable to take all samples from the portal vein, but repeated samples were difficult to obtain in satisfactory volume from this small, sensitive vein. Since this experiment was designed to determine the rate of metabolism of allyl alcohol, the method was considered adequate, although as the alcohol was infused into the femoral vein, vena caval samples would misrepresent the circulating level if it were not constant.

Samples were drawn with a recalibrated 0.25-ml. syringe and 27-gauge needle, not more than 0.2 ml. at a time, and at a rate not exceeding 0.1 ml. in 10 seconds. If the amount of allyl alcohol in the sample was expected to exceed 8 microgm., duplicate or triplicate samples of smaller volume were also drawn. To preclude circulatory disturbance, the total volume of blood taken was less than 5 per cent of the total volume, assuming the total blood volume to be 7 per cent of the body weight. The amount of allyl alcohol in the samples was determined by the method described above. When the rats were killed for necropsy, sections of liver were taken for histologic study.

RESULTS. *Oxygen uptake of tissues of intoxicated rats.* There was no apparent effect on oxygen uptake of cerebral cortex slices when the rats had been dosed with either 60 or 120 mgm./kgm. of allyl alcohol. Uptake by liver slices, on the other hand, was severely inhibited at 120 mgm./kgm. While the results were statistically insignificant, there were consistent indications that 60 mgm./kgm. did produce slight inhibition, that inhibition was more pronounced one hour after treatment than at two hours, and that the presence of glucose in the medium reduced the inhibition. In contrast, oxygen uptake by kidney slices was significantly elevated at both dose levels. A summary of these results is given in table 1. The findings concerning rate of oxygen uptake followed the same general pattern.

Inhibition in vitro of oxygen uptake of rat tissues. There was no significant alteration in either the rate of oxygen uptake or total oxygen uptake by liver or kidney slices exposed to allyl alcohol in a concentration of 10^{-4} *M* or less. However, at 10^{-2} and 10^{-3} *M*, there was rapid and progressive decline in the rate of oxygen uptake of both tissues. In fact, the rate of uptake of liver slices exposed to 10^{-2} *M* was definitely decreased before the alcohol was tipped into the incubation medium, suggesting rapid diffusion. Increase in uptake by kidney slices did not appear at any time (figure 1). The concentrations of allyl alcohol producing 50 per cent inhibition of the rate of uptake were estimated to be 2.5×10^{-4} *M* (14.5 microgm. ml.) for liver and 1.0×10^{-3} *M* (58.0 microgm./ml.) for kidney. In other words, the metabolic processes involved in oxygen utilization were found to be about 4 times more sensitive in liver than in kidney. An apparent loss of intracellular chromogenic substances previously noted in liver slices was again evident in this experiment, occurring both in liver and kidney slices exposed to 10^{-2} and 10^{-3} *M* allyl alcohol.

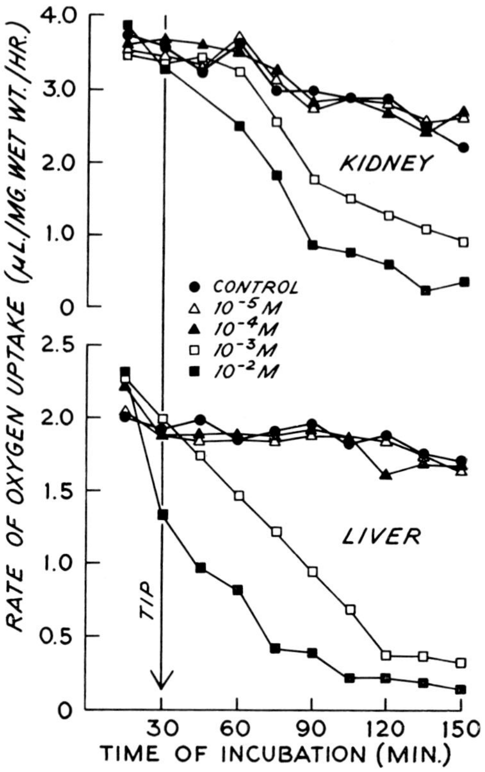

FIG. 1. Inhibition *in vitro* of oxygen uptake rates of rat tissue slices by allyl alcohol.

TABLE 1

Mean total oxygen uptake of tissue slices from rats intoxicated with allyl alcohol

Tissue	Dose	Hour of Sacrifice	Oxygen Uptake			
			Without glucose		With glucose	
	mgm./kgm.		*μl./mgm. 120 min.*	*% of control*	*μl./mgm. 120 min.*	*% of control*
Liver	0		3.96	100	3.83	100
	60	1	3.42	86	3.64	95
		2	3.66	92	3.74	98
	120	1	2.13*	54	2.14*	56
		2	2.42*	61	2.66*	70
Kidney	0		5.93	100	6.66	100
	60	1	6.72*	113	6.87	103
		2	7.41*	125	7.64*	115
	120	1	6.47	109	7.42*	111
		2	7.31*	123	7.25	109

* Significantly different from the control at P of 0.05.

In contrast, propyl alcohol at the inordinately high concentration of 2.5×10^{-1} *M* (1.5 mgm./ml.) produced only 28 per cent inhibition of the rate of oxygen uptake by the liver.

Protection studies with Dibenzyline and hexamethonium. The rates of oxygen uptake by liver slices for each experimental condition are shown graphically in figure 2. Both Dibenzyline and hexamethonium afforded highly significant protection against impairment of the liver respiration. A comparison of the initial rates of oxygen uptake of the treated groups with the control rate revealed that allyl alcohol produced 80 per cent inhibition of respiration, whereas with Dibenzyline and hexamethonium pretreatment

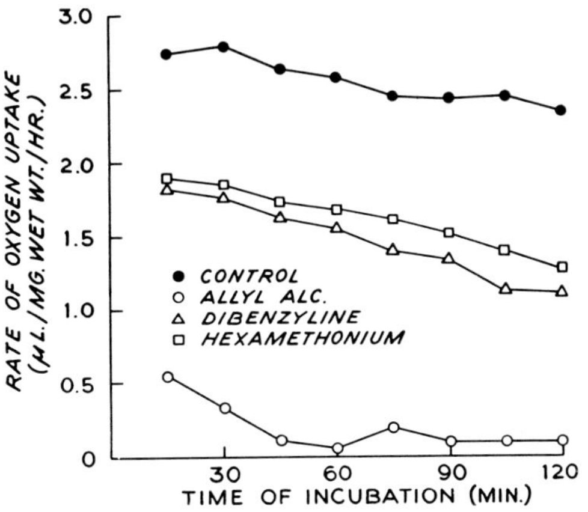

FIG. 2. Protective effects of Dibenzyline and hexamethonium against the depression of liver respiration of rats given allyl alcohol perorally.

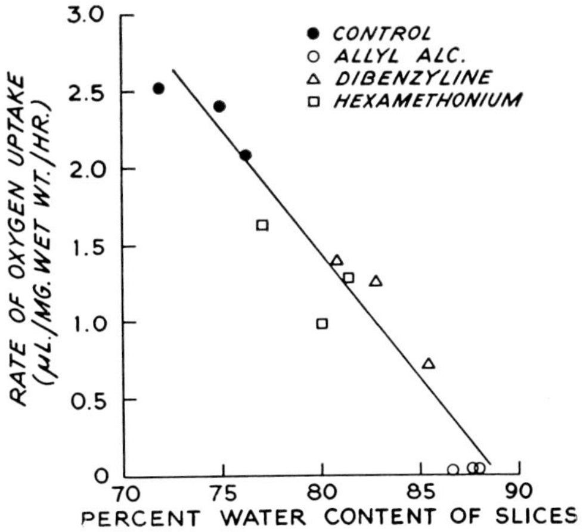

FIG. 3. Relationship between oxygen uptake and water content of liver slices from rats given allyl alcohol and prophylactic doses of Dibenzyline and hexamethonium.

the decrease was little more than 30 per cent. It was of interest to note that pretreatment with Dibenzyline or hexamethonium afforded partial protection against hepatic injury by allyl alcohol, as shown by the significant changes in oxygen uptake and water content. Higher doses of these drugs were not used because previous experience in this laboratory indicated that nearly optimum pharmacologic action could be achieved with the dose used.

An excellent linear relationship was found between the water content of the liver slices and the final rates of oxygen uptake (table 2, figure 3). Comparison with water content prior to incubation indicated that only slight swelling had occurred in the body one hour after alcohol administration, although respiration was decidedly depressed at the first reading of oxygen uptake. However, there was an unavoidable lapse of about 30 minutes between the placing of slices in the incubation medium and the taking of the first measurements, to allow for gassing of the Warburg flasks with oxygen, temperature equilibration within the water bath, and for the initial 15-minute period of oxygen uptake. Most of the swelling probably took place during this time interval, which would account for the initial low level of oxygen uptake.

Despite the appreciable protection afforded by Dibenzyline against liver injury by allyl alcohol, the acute toxicity study revealed no significant protection against the lethal action of allyl alcohol. The mortality in the untreated and pretreated rats was 15 and 14 of 20, respectively. The mean time of death for the rats pretreated with Dibenzyline was 263 ± 103 minutes, apparently later by 100 per cent than that of the untreated rats, 121 ± 20 minutes;

TABLE 2

Relationship between oxygen uptake and water uptake of liver slices from rats pretreated with Dibenzyline or hexamethonium and receiving allyl alcohol orally

Group	% Water Content		Oxygen Uptake*	
	Initial	Final	Initial	Final
Control	70.7 ± 1.1	74.3 ± 0.6	2.74 ± 0.04	2.34 ± 0.07
Allyl alcohol only	72.9 ± 0.9	87.3 ± 0.3	0.55 ± 0.05	0.11 ± 0.01
Allyl alcohol preceded by Dibenzyline	71.5 ± 0.4	82.9 ± 0.6	1.82 ± 0.14	1.12 ± 0.16
Allyl alcohol preceded by hexamethonium	70.5 ± 0.3	79.4 ± 0.5	1.89 ± 0.09	1.29 ± 0.25

* Microliters/mgm. wet weight per hour.

however, no statistical significance was found (Student "t" test). Qualitatively speaking, the severity of the toxic signs appeared somewhat less in the pretreated rats.

Studies on tissue swelling in vitro. Following exposure of liver slices *in vitro* to 2.5×10^{-4} M allyl alcohol, the final rates of oxygen uptake were 1.97 and 1.29 microl./mgm. wet weight/hour for 60 and 90 minutes, respectively (approximately 20 and 47 per cent inhibition), and the water content of the slices was 79.3 and 79.8 per cent, respectively. After exposure to 2.5×10^{-3} M for 60 and 90 minutes, the rates of oxygen uptake were 0.58 and 0.39 microl./mgm. wet weight/hour (76 and 83 per cent inhibition), and the water content was 83.8 and 83.5 per cent respectively. Exposure to propyl alcohol in the high concentration of 2.5×10^{-1} M for 120 minutes, on the other hand, produced only 28 per cent inhibition of respiratory rate, and only minimal swelling, while lower concentrations produced no effect. The water content was 76.9 per cent, while that of the control was 75.5 per cent.

These findings *in vitro* further substantiate the evidence that the impairment in oxygen uptake induced by allyl alcohol is intimately related to the abnormal swelling of the hepatic cells, and that the presence of an unsaturated bond imparts considerable biologic activity to the molecule.

Effect of allyl alcohol on blood pressure, respiration and plasma histamine levels. About 30 seconds after intravenous administration of 40 mgm./kgm. of allyl alcohol to a dog, the carotid blood pressure began a rapid drop of about 100 mm. Hg. It rose again slowly with time, but several hours later was still down 15 to 20 mm. There was a decided reduction in respiratory rate and amplitude during the period of maximum hypotension, followed by 5 to 8 minutes of hyperpnea (figure 4).

The low initial hematocrit reading (table 3) indicated anemia. Subsequent readings revealed increasing hemoconcentration. In addition, the samples taken at 1.7 and 9 minutes showed some hemolysis and increased sedimentation of erythrocytes. There was no increase in histamine in the serial blood samples, indicating that the depression of blood pressure and respiration, and the hemoconcentration, were not mediated by the endogenous liberation of histamine. When the histamine standard was submitted to the preliminary extraction procedure, together with the plasma samples, there was 80 to 90 per cent recovery. Kymograph tracings depicting the biologic assay of plasma histamine are shown in figure 5.

Dehydrogenase inhibition in vitro. Excessively high concentrations of allyl alcohol and propyl alcohol, ranging from 2×10^{-1} M to 1 M, were required before any appreciable inhibition

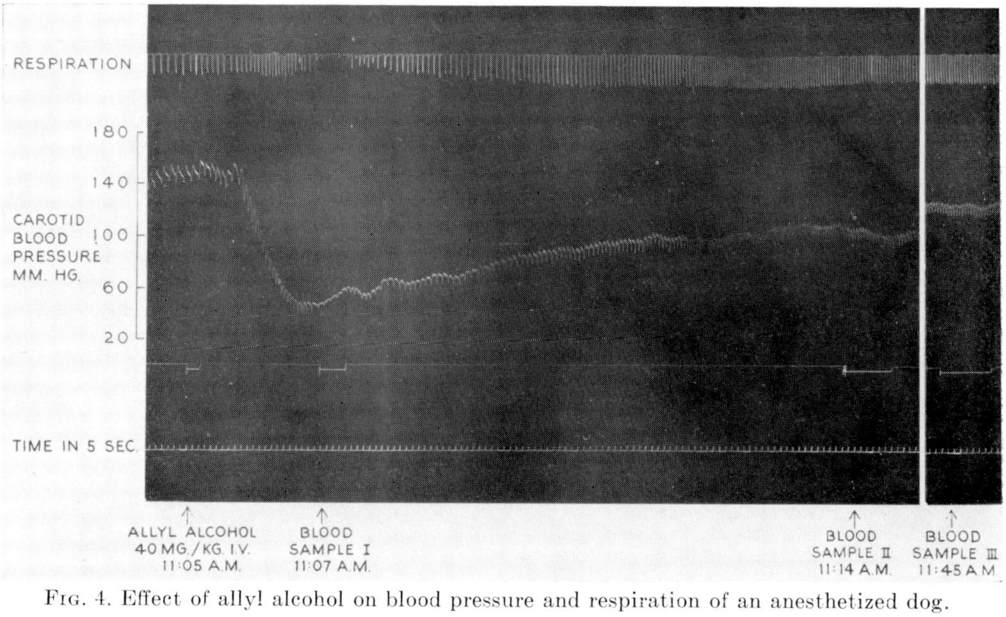

FIG. 4. Effect of allyl alcohol on blood pressure and respiration of an anesthetized dog.

TABLE 3

Alterations in carotid blood pressure, hematocrit and circulating plasma histamine in a dog given 40 mgm./kgm. of allyl alcohol intravenously

Minutes	Blood Pressure	Hematocrit	Plasma Histamine
	mm. Hg		*microgm./ml.*
0	148	0.32	0.078
1.7	40	0.30	0.076
9	142	0.44	0.040
40	126	0.48	0.064

of the various liver dehydrogenases occurred. Therefore, significant inhibition of dehydrogenases *in vivo* by allyl alcohol (and probably propyl alcohol) would be unlikely.

Acrolein was approximately a thousandfold more active; its relatively high potency may be attributable to its reactivity with sulfhydryl groups.

Microquantitation of allyl alcohol. The method devised was found to be about 50 times as sensitive as the standard dichromate method, since the changes in optical density per microgram of allyl alcohol were 0.0255 and 0.0005/O.D. units respectively. There was a good linear relationship between the alcohol concentration and the O.D. change, whether the alcohol was diffused from water or from rat blood (figure 6). Several determinations were made with allyl alcohol added directly to the dichromate solution and incubated overnight. The results were the same as when the alcohol was allowed to diffuse into the dichromate solution. No volatile interfering substance was detected in rat blood, even when the maximum volume of blood analyzed was 0.2 ml.

While the method as described was satisfactory for our purposes, the conditions were not necessarily optimum. For example, the concentrations of the reagents could probably be modified to increase the rate of reaction, and the incubation time might be shortened by raising the temperature or by adding a solute such as potassium carbonate to the alcohol to increase its diffusibility.

The partition coefficient of allyl alcohol be-

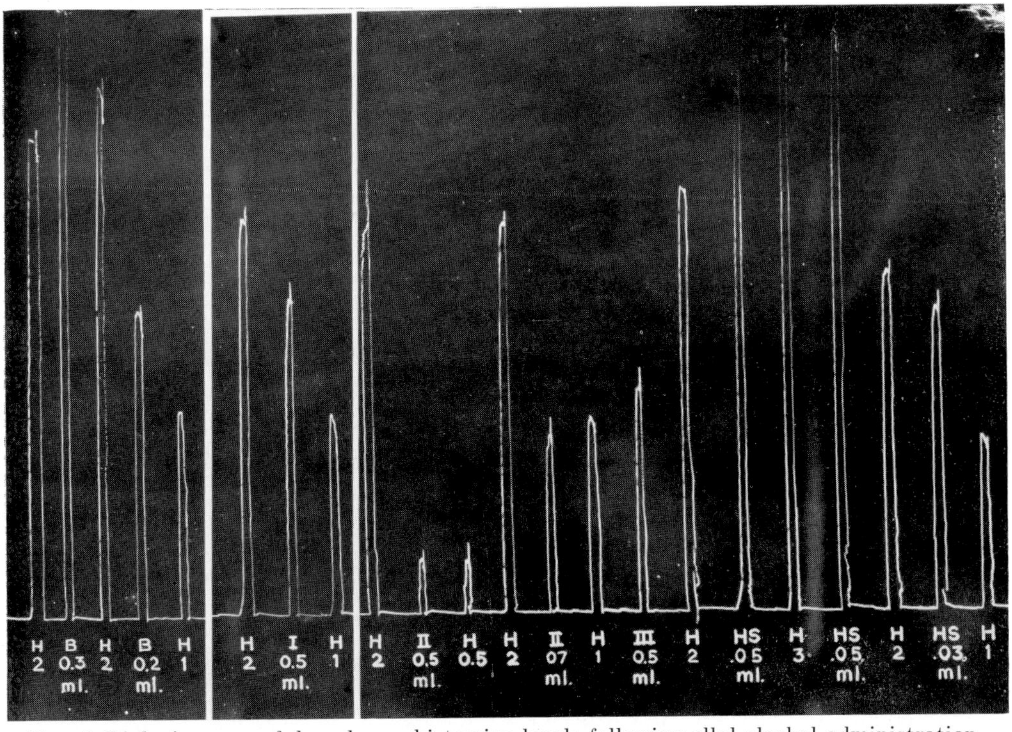

FIG. 5. Biologic assay of dog plasma-histamine levels following allyl alcohol administration. Guinea-pig ileum preparation in 15 ml. Tyrode solution containing 1 mgm./l. of atropine sulfate. H = histamine standard, microgm./l.; B = control plasma extract, ml.; I, II, III = serial plasma extracts, ml.; and HS = histamine standard carried through extraction, ml.

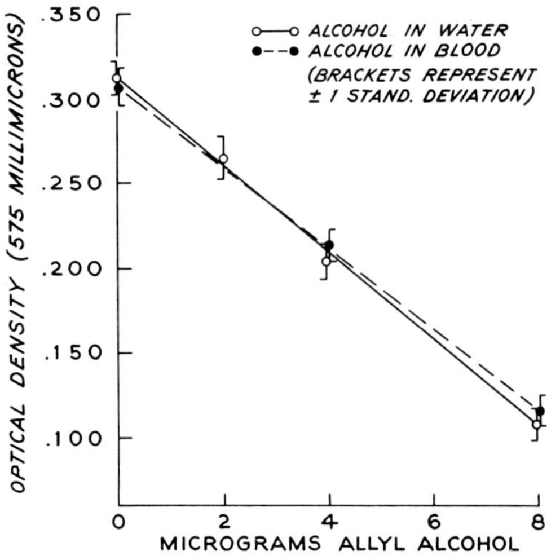

FIG. 6. Standard calibration curves, as determined by the modified dichromate method, for allyl alcohol in water and rat blood.

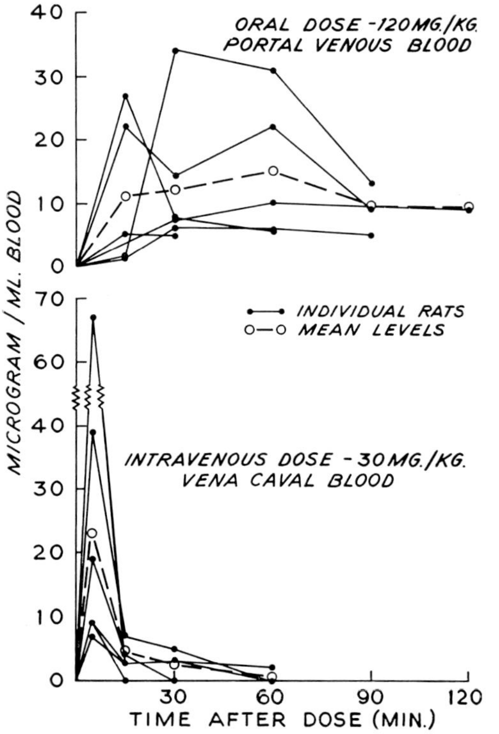

FIG. 7. Blood levels of allyl alcohol in rats following single oral and intravenous doses of this substance.

tween olive oil and water at 20°C. was found to be 0.116, which is appropriately between those of ethanol (0.035) and propanol (0.140) reported by Macy (1948).

Quantitation of blood levels of allyl alcohol following intragastric or intravenous administration. The mean levels of allyl alcohol in rats given a single intragastric dose of 120 mgm./kgm were found to range between 9 and 15 microgm./ml. during the 15 to 120 minutes after administration. Although individual values varied considerably, the maximum appeared at about 30 to 60 minutes (figure 7).

Administration of allyl alcohol was followed by profuse nasal and lacrimal secretion, moderate depression of respiration, and increase in gastroenteric motility leading to defecation of soft, watery feces. In 5 to 15 minutes there was visceral congestion with definite reduction in the caliber of larger visceral blood vessels, depression of respiration, and hypoxic color of circulating blood. Although there was slight improvement in the color of the blood and in the circulation and respiration after 20 to 30 minutes, no further improvement appeared during the remainder of the experimental period.

The mean levels in vena caval blood after the intravenous dose of 30 mgm./kgm. indicate rapid disappearance within 15 minutes, and almost complete disappearance in an hour, correlating well with the gross signs of intoxication (figure 7). Lacrimal and nasal hypersecretion, and respiratory and (apparent) circulatory depression, appeared in 15 to 30 seconds and decreased considerably after 5 to 15 minutes.

Since Aull and his associates (1956) found that the rat metabolized ethyl alcohol at the rate of 283 mgm./kgm./hour, the continuous infusion of allyl alcohol was initially set at 100 mgm./kgm./hour. The rat showed signs of severe shock and died after 10 minutes; the blood level of allyl alcohol rose precipitously. All viscera were congested, with mottled discoloration and hemorrhage in the liver, and scattered hemorrhages and apparent edema in the intestinal walls, particularly in the jejunum. Infusion rates of 42 and 68 mgm./kgm./hour were also excessive, as shown by an abrupt rise in blood alcohol after 30 minutes, and death at about 180 and 140 minutes, respectively. The gross appearance of the viscera was the same as with the infusion of 100 mgm./kgm./hour.

Respiration, oxygenation of blood and circulation throughout the larger abdominal vessels appeared satisfactory during the first 60 to 90 minutes of infusion with 23 or 24 mgm./kgm./

hour. Subsequently, there was increasing indication of circulatory insufficiency. The flow through the larger vessels seemed to decrease, although respiration still appeared adequate. The blood levels in these rats rose only slowly, indicating that metabolism was proceeding at about the rate of infusion (figure 8). Death occurred at 195 and 187 minutes, and congestion of the viscera was again the most striking finding. The hilar region of the liver from the rat infused with 24 mgm./kgm./hour appeared to be hemorrhagic in scattered areas.

Periportal necrosis was observed histologically in all the rats in this study, even in those given a single intravenous dose.

Discussion. Since allyl alcohol has been demonstrated to produce rapidly both a significant hepatic injury and a classical picture of shock with reduction of blood pressure and respiration, hemoconcentration, visceral congestion and terminal pulmonary edema, the question arises whether the shock could have been the predisposing factor for the hepatic injury.

That a relatively short period of hepatic anoxia can cause significant damage to the liver has been amply demonstrated by the studies of Wilhelmi *et al.* (1945) and Baker (1956). The former group found that when the blood supply to the liver of albino rats was restricted by ligation of the portal vein to that supplied by the hepatic artery, occlusion of the artery for 5, 15, 30, 60 and 120 minutes caused a progressive fall in the rate of respiration of liver slices *in vitro*. After 15 minutes of anoxia, the respiratory rate was reduced as much as 50 per cent, while 30 minutes of anoxia produced about 67 per cent reduction.

However, it was possible to reproduce under strict *in vitro* conditions (oxygen supplied in excess) such adverse changes as severe depression of oxygen consumption, abnormal tissue swelling and loss of intracellular chromogenic substances in rat liver slices, which also accompanied intoxication *in vivo*. The concentration of allyl alcohol producing 50 per cent inhibition of oxygen uptake *in vitro* was 14.5 microgm./ml., which compares favorably with the blood-alcohol levels, ranging from 9 to 15 microgm./ml., found in intoxication *in vivo*.

One would be inclined to favor a theory of direct action on the hepatic parenchyma over an indirect or vascular action. The fact that a

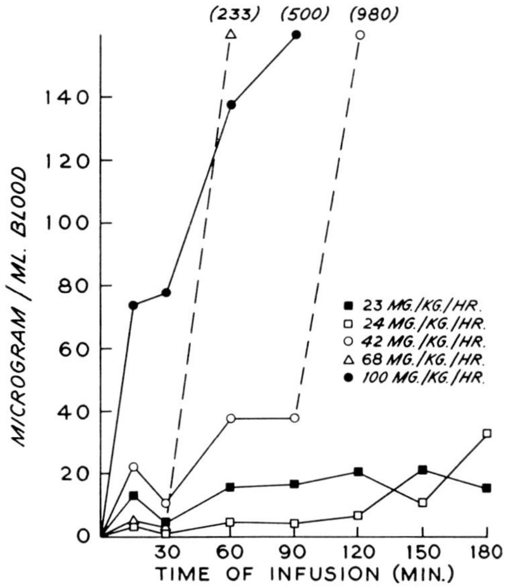

Fig. 8. Blood levels of allyl alcohol in rats during constant infusion of graded doses of this substance.

selective zonal necrosis developed, rather than a massive or focal necrosis (consistently seen by Baker in his studies on hepatic anoxia) would tend to favor direct action. On the other hand, the disclosure that prophylactic treatment with either Dibenzyline or hexamethonium can afford significant protection against liver injury implies that the influence of the sympathetic nervous system on the circulatory system does play a role in the genesis of hepatic injury by allyl alcohol.

It is pertinent to note that Jacobs and his associates (1956) concluded from their studies, wherein preliminary treatment with N,N′-dibenzyl-β-chlorethylamine HCl (Dibenamine) unequivocally protected rats against hemorrhagic shock, that the mechanism of protection seemed to lie in part in a better blood flow to the brain stem, permitting maintenance of normal respiration. Their conclusion is further substantiated by the finding that vasoconstriction by epinephrine also produced respiratory failure in rats (Nickerson *et al.*, 1950) and that Dibenamine prevented this (Raab and Humphreys, 1946). The effectiveness of adrenergic and ganglionic blocking agents in reducing the mortality in rats subjected to traumatic shock have also been adequately described (Levy, North and Wells, 1954; Ross and Herczeg, 1956). On the basis of these studies and the fact that significant protection against liver injury was obtained with Dibenzyline, the lack of protection against the lethal action of allyl alcohol was not anticipated. These results indicate that death following allyl alcohol intoxication was not primarily mediated by hepatic injury.

In conclusion, it can be postulated that allyl alcohol produces periportal hepatocellular injury by the following mechanism: The direct action on liver cells alters the membrane permeability, which is normally involved in the maintenance of intracellular hypertonicity. As a consequence, abnormal hepatocellular swelling, leakage of intracellular chromatogenic substances and then osmotic disruption of cell metabolism develop. Superimposed on the direct action, there is a vascular action which intensifies the hepatic damage. This may be either an intrahepatic decrease of blood flow to the periportal region (which is poorly vascularized in the rat) or, more probably, an extrahepatic effect. The extrahepatic effects of hypotension and hemoconcentration decrease blood flow to the liver, while oxygenation of the blood is decreased by inhibition of respiration secondary to concomitant decrease in blood flow to the respiratory center.

The primary cause of death is probably cardiovascular failure, which probably follows depression of the respiratory and vasomotor centers and a decrease in effective blood pressure.

It was considered possible that the toxicity of allyl alcohol is materially influenced by the metabolic production of acrolein, which is the most likely primary oxidation product of allyl alcohol. Comparison of the acute toxicity data for the two compounds, however, shows that acrolein is only slightly more toxic than allyl alcohol (Skog, 1950; Smyth *et al.*, 1954). Further, at least 8 to 19 mgm./kgm. of acrolein intravenously were necessary for a significant depression of blood pressure and respiration of dogs (Skog, 1952). The present studies revealed similar depression of both blood pressure and respiration with 40 mgm./kgm. of allyl alcohol.

On the other hand, if it could be assumed that the ratio between acrolein and allyl alcohol in blood following the administration of allyl alcohol was roughly similar to that found between acetaldehyde and ethanol following ethanol intoxication, where less than 1 mgm. per cent of acetaldehyde was found to 200 or 300 mgm. per cent of ethanol (Jacobsen, 1952), the existing blood concentration of acrolein would probably be too low for significance—particularly when one further considers that the rate of metabolism of allyl alcohol in the rat is considerably lower than that reported for ethyl alcohol.

In spite of the similar picture of shock and irritation of mucous membranes seen with acrolein and allyl alcohol, survey of the literature on acrolein and other lower aliphatic aldehydes revealed no evidence that they can produce periportal necrosis. In addition, the fact that the various biologic responses measured after exposure to allyl alcohol were elicited quite rapidly would favor the supposition that the toxic actions are inherent in the original alcoholic molecule. It would therefore be reasonable to conclude that a biotransformation of allyl alcohol to acrolein is not necessary to explain its high toxicity.

SUMMARY

Peroral administration of allyl alcohol to rats resulted in severe inhibition of oxygen uptake by the liver, moderate stimulation of oxygen uptake by the kidneys, and no alteration in oxygen uptake by the cerebral cortex, one and two hours after administration.

Studies of oxygen uptake *in vitro* showed that rat liver was about 4 times as sensitive to allyl alcohol as kidney, and although kidney oxygen consumption is presumably increased *in vivo*, no such increase was demonstrable *in vitro.*

Administration of either Dibenzyline or hexamethonium prior to allyl alcohol provided good protection against both tissue swelling and decrease in oxygen uptake of liver slices. The swelling was well correlated with the oxygen uptake. On the other hand, prophylactic treatment with Dibenzyline did not significantly alter the lethal effects of allyl alcohol.

Intravenous administration produced profound depression of a dog's blood pressure and respiration, and hemoconcentration, signs characteristic of histamine release. However, there was no evidence that allyl alcohol caused histamine release.

Liver dehydrogenases were not inhibited by allyl or propyl alcohol at levels possible *in vivo.* Inhibition by acrolein was 400 to 1000 times greater.

A method for microquantitation of allyl

alcohol is described. Mean blood levels ranged between 9 and 15 microgm./ml. during 120 minutes after oral administration of allyl alcohol. This concentration *in vivo* correlated well with the concentrations effective *in vitro* against tissue respiration. The alcohol disappeared rapidly after single intravenous injection, and was metabolized at about 23 mgm./kgm./hour during constant intravenous infusion.

A mechanism of toxic action is suggested.

ACKNOWLEDGMENT. The kind and helpful suggestions of Dr. V. C. Sutherland and Dr. F. H. Meyers of this Department are gratefully acknowledged by the authors. We also wish to express our appreciation to Dr. J. S. Wellington, Department of Pathology, for the histopathological studies.

REFERENCES

AULL, J. C., ROBERTS, W. J., AND KINARD, F. W.: Am. J. Physiol., **186**: 380, 1956.
BAKER, H. DE C.: J. Path. & Bact., **71**: 135, 1956.
CODE, C. F.: J. Physiol., **89**: 257, 1937.
DRILL, V. A.: Pharmacol. Rev., **4**: 1, 1952.
DUNLAP, M. K., KODAMA, J. K., ANDERSON, H. H., AND HINE, C. H.: A.M.A. Arch. Indust. H., in press.
ELLIOTT, H. W., WARREN, A. E., AND JAMES, H. P.: THIS JOURNAL, **91**: 98, 1947.
GADDUM, J. H.: J. Physiol., **108**: 467, 1949.
HINE, C. H., ANDERSON, H. H., MOON, H. D., KODAMA, J. K., MORSE, M., AND JACOBSEN, N. W.: Arch. Ind. Hyg. Occup. Med., **1**: 118, 1953.
JACOB, S., FRIEDMAN, E. W., LEVENSON, S., GLOTZER, P., FRANK, H. A., AND FINE, J.: Am. J. Physiol., **186**: 79, 1956.
JACOBSEN, E.: Pharmacol. Rev., **4**: 107, 1952.
KUN, E., AND ABOOD, L. G.: Science, **109**: 144, 1949.
LEVY, E. A., NORTH, W. C., AND WELLS, J. A.: THIS JOURNAL, **112**: 151, 1954.
MACY, R.: J. Ind. Hyg. Toxicol., **30**: 140, 1948.
MARTIN, A. W.: Endocrinol., **30**: 624, 1942.
MIESSNER: Berl. klin. Wchnschr., **28**: 813, 1891.
NICKERSON, M., BERGHOUT, J., AND HAMMERSTROM, R. N.: Am. J. Physiol., **160**: 479, 1950.
RAAB, W., AND HUMPHREYS, R. J.: THIS JOURNAL, **88**: 268, 1946.
ROSS, C. A., AND HERCZEG, S. A.: Proc. Soc. Exper. Biol. & Med., **91**: 196, 1956.
SKOG, E.: Acta pharmacol. et toxicol., **6**: 299, 1950.
SKOG, E.: Acta pharmacol. et toxicol., **8**: 275, 1952.
STADIE, W. C., AND RIGGS, B. C.: J. Biol. Chem., **154**: 669, 1944.
SMYTH, H. F., JR., CARPENTER, C. P., AND WEIL, C. S.: Arch. Ind. Hyg. Occup. Med., **4**: 119, 1951.
SMYTH, H. F., JR., CARPENTER, C. P., WEIL, C. S., AND POZZANI, U. C.: Arch. Ind. Hyg. Occup. Med., **10**: 61, 1954.
VON OETTINGEN, W. F.: Publ. Health Bull., **281**: 1943.
WILHELMI, A. E., RUSSELL, J. A., ENGEL, F. L., AND LONG, C. N. H.: Am. J. Physiol., **144**: 669, 1945.

ERRATUM

There is an error in the publication by A. E. TAKEMORI AND G. J. MANNERING, entitled "Metabolic N- and O-Demethylation of Morphine- and Morphinan-type Analgesics," which appeared in THIS JOURNAL, **123:** 171, (July) 1958.

The second of the two structural formulae in table 1 on page 172 should be:

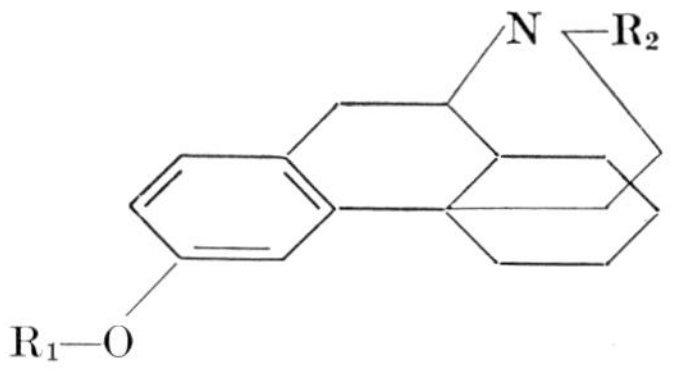

Morphinan series

8065

PROTEIN BINDING OF RADIOACTIVE DIGITOXIN[1, 2]

JAMES L. SPRATT[3, 4] AND GEORGE T. OKITA

Argonne Cancer Research Hospital, USAEC, and the Department of Pharmacology, The University of Chicago, Chicago, Illinois

Received for publication May 8, 1958

Studies by Lendle and Pusch (1935) and Haarman *et al.* (1940) have indicated that digitoxin is bound only to the albumin of the blood proteins. These investigators used human, horse and rabbit sera from which the proteins were fractionated by salt precipitation and electrodialysis. Drug binding was studied by exchange dialysis using Baljet's alkaline picrate reaction to quantitate digitoxin. Fawaz and Farah (1944), using salt fractionated proteins from rabbit serum, tested binding by exchange dialysis and checked the resulting solutions on protection of the isolated frog heart. They also found digitoxin to be bound by albumin. Farah, in later work, using the Baljet reaction test (Farah, 1945) obtained similar results. More recently, Rothlin and Kallenberger (1950), working with the isolated frog heart, reported that human serum albumin bound 2.2 μg of digitoxin per mg of protein.

Because of the limitations of methods available to previous investigators and the high dosage levels employed, we undertook a radioisotopic tracer study on protein binding of digitoxin. It was hoped that this study might contribute information concerning the possible role of serum proteins in the vascular transport of digitoxin.

MATERIALS AND METHODS. Both biosynthetically labeled C^{14}-digitoxin (Okita *et al.*, 1954) and self-radiation labeled H^3-digitoxin (Wilzbach, 1957; Spratt *et al.*, 1957) were used in this study. The methods used for the determination of unchanged drug and its metabolites by C^{14} radioassay have been described elsewhere (Okita *et al.*, 1953; Okita *et al.*, 1955). Tritium assay was performed using liquid scintillation spectrometry.

Starch block electrophoresis was selected as the method for studying drug-protein binding since it is considered to be one of the most gentle methods of manipulating macromolecules. For the proper evaluation of our data in the light of methods used by earlier investigators, drug binding by equilibrium dialysis of salt fractionated proteins was also employed. For purposes of comparison it was considered essential to include the latter method since it is known that proteins isolated by salt fractionation are nonhomogeneous.

Electrophoretic method. Both *in vitro* and *in vivo* studies were conducted. The experimental procedure adopted for the *in vitro* studies was as follows. A starch bed was prepared with potato starch (Fischer Scientific Co.) by mixing it with barbital buffer (pH 8.6, ionic strength 0.1) (McDonald *et al.*, 1953). When the starch bed had dried sufficiently, a perpendicular strip, 1 cm wide, was removed from the mid-section of the bed. The drug-protein sample was prepared by allowing 1 ml of fresh human plasma plus 1.3 or 2.7 μg of C^{14}-digitoxin to incubate at 37°C for 20 minutes. To this was added enough potato starch to form a slurry. The slurry was then poured into the excavation. The apparatus cover was bolted into place and a current of 10 mA and 450 V was generated across the carbon electrodes. The current was allowed to flow for 24 hours at 4°C.

At the termination of the run, the starch bed was allowed to dry and was cut into 1-cm segments. Each segment was extracted with 5 ml of saline, and an aliquot was assayed for protein content by the Folin-Ciocalteau tyrosine assay procedure as modified by Lowry *et al.* (1951).

The *in vivo* electrophoretic studies were performed using techniques similar to those outlined above for the *in vitro* studies. Normal male rats (160–180 g) were injected intravenously with 0.5 mg of H^3-digitoxin (76.8 μc/mg) in 0.5 ml of 40% ethanol. Blood serum was obtained by allowing

[1] This work was aided in part by grants to the Department of Pharmacology, University of Chicago, from the Life Insurance Medical Research Fund, from the Dr. Wallace C. and Clara A. Abbott Memorial Fund and from A.E.C. Contract No. AT (11-1)-45.

[2] Presented in part at the Annual Meetings of the Federation of American Societies for Experimental Biology, Chicago, Illinois, April, 1957 and Philadelphia, Pennsylvania, April, 1958.

[3] Submitted in partial fulfillment of the requirements for the degree of Doctor of Philosophy at the University of Chicago.

[4] This work was done while this author was a Predoctoral Research Fellow of the National Heart Institute.

drainage from the neck vessels into paraffinized centrifuge tubes without the addition of anticoagulants. The blood was allowed to clot for 30 minutes in an incubator at 37°C. It was then chilled and centrifuged. Serum was removed with a pipette and used directly. The water-soluble proteins of the myocardium were obtained by using an aliquot of the soluble supernate of the heart after differential cell fractionation (Spratt and Okita, 1958).

When the protein assays were completed, they were graphically illustrated. From these graphs it was determined where the appropriate cuts should be made with respect to protein separation. The remaining portions of the block segments were then combined with respect to protein content and were assayed for radiodigitoxin. It was found that the hot methanol extraction procedure reported elsewhere (Okita *et al.*, 1955) was quantitative with respect to recovery of digitoxin from this starch block system.

Salt fractionation and dialysis method. Fresh whole blood was collected from a single human donor 4 hours postprandially in paraffinized centrifuge tubes without the addition of anticoagulants. The blood was allowed to clot for 30 minutes at 37°C. It was then chilled and centrifuged. A serum aliquot was taken for whole serum studies and the remainder was fractionated as outlined in figure 1.

Each fraction was dialyzed for 18 hours against 6 liters of Locke's solution at 4°C. After dialysis, aliquots of each fraction were removed for protein (Svedberg and Sjogren, 1928), cholesterol (Foldes and Wilson, 1950) and phospholipid (Koch and Hanke, 1953) analyses and the remainder stored in the cold.

In addition to the assays performed to determine the total protein composition of these various fractions, we were also interested in determining what proteins were actually present, since it is generally conceded that salt fractionation usually yields rather heterogeneous fractions. Therefore, each protein fraction was analyzed using starch block electrophoresis, the methods of which were described in the previous section.

A modification of Farah's method (1945) was used to study binding and consisted of the following: 75 mg of protein sample plus either a "lethal dose" of 500 μg nonradioactive digitoxin or a "therapeutic dose" of 2 μg C^{14}-digitoxin in 15 ml of Locke's solution was dialyzed against 15 ml of Locke's solution at 4°C. Dialysis was continued until equilibrium was evident as indicated by determination of nonradioactive control samples. Assays for drug content were then performed on these solutions.

Nonradioactive digitoxin was determined by the method of Anderson and Chen (1946) utilizing the Raymond reaction. Since protein had a definite effect on the optical density determinations, protein-containing solutions were not assayed directly. Wanting a measure of total Raymond-reactive material to compare our results against those of previous investigators, we decided to make determinations of nonradioactive drug inside the bag by difference. The unchanged radioactive drug could be determined directly inside and outside the bags. Bound drug was determined from the concentration difference inside and outside the dialysis bags at equilibrium.

RESULTS. *In vitro zone electrophoresis.* Of 7 *in vitro* experiments of this nature, in only one

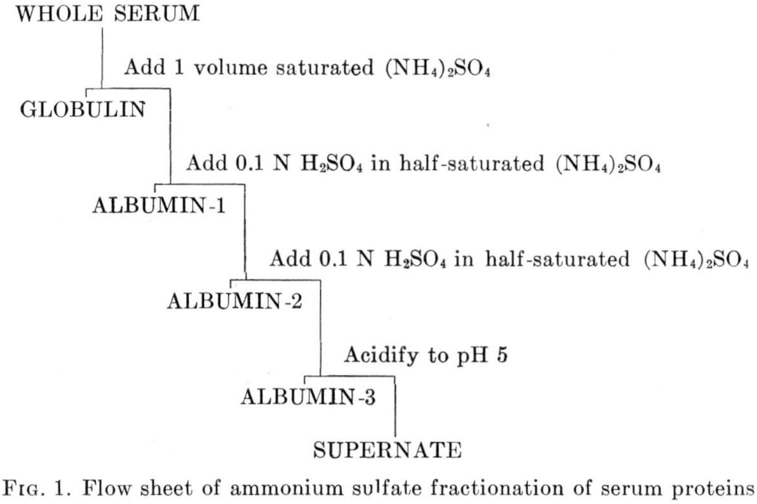

FIG. 1. Flow sheet of ammonium sulfate fractionation of serum proteins.

case were we able to detect any digitoxin associated with albumin. Figure 2 shows the results of a typical experiment. Unchanged digitoxin bound to migrating proteins was found in the *alpha-*, *beta-* and *gamma*-globulin fractions. A relatively larger amount of digitoxin was found at the application site (plus one segment on either side). However, some or all of this drug may not be associated with any protein because the drug *per se* does not migrate in this system.

The small amount of drug found to be associated with the *alpha-*, *beta-* and *gamma*-globulins is believed to represent bound drug. Various steroids have been shown to be bound by globulins (Roberts and Szego, 1955) and it would not appear strange to find digitoxin similarly bound.

To check on the possibility of digitoxin binding being associated with cholesterol content of serum proteins, a similar *in vitro* experiment was conducted wherein the relative cholesterol content of the various segments was determined using the method of Ackermann *et al.* (1954). Increased cholesterol content was noted in the vicinity of albumin and *beta*-globulin, which is the normal lipoprotein location. This experiment also showed the albumin to be devoid of bound drug. However, there did appear to be a slight binding affinity for both drug and metabolites by *beta*-globulin.

Zone electrophoresis of drug given in vivo. Since it has been shown that steroid binding by blood proteins can be dependent on factors in the *in vivo* environment (Roberts and Szego, 1955), electrophoretic studies were performed on blood obtained from 3 intravenously injected rats used for intracellular distribution studies (Spratt and Okita, 1958).

Upon electrophoresis of the serum from these rats, all 3 patterns showed more than 97% of the unchanged drug at the application site. Only trace amounts of drug were found associated with albumin or globulin constituents. Results of a typical experiment are given in figure 3.

The water-soluble myocardial proteins of two of the intravenously injected rats were also separated electrophoretically using the barbital buffer system. In both cases there did not appear to be any significant binding affinity for digitoxin elicited by the migrating proteins. However, the amounts of radioactive drug recovered at the site of application in these runs were so small (12 mμg and 2 mμg) that this observation can only be considered preliminary and does not necessarily negate the possibility of digitoxin-binding by myocardial proteins.

Equilibrium dialysis with salt-fractionated proteins. Our electrophoretic studies indicated the possibility that the disparity between the previously reported results and our own results could be due to differences in techniques. It was for this reason that protein-drug dialysis studies were performed. Table 1 is a listing of dosages used by some of the previous investigators as well as their assay methods. At the bottom of the table are the dosage levels which were used in the present study.

Table 2 gives the data obtained from the dialysis binding study performed on the various protein fractions obtained by ammonium sulfate fractionation. From the experiments using non-

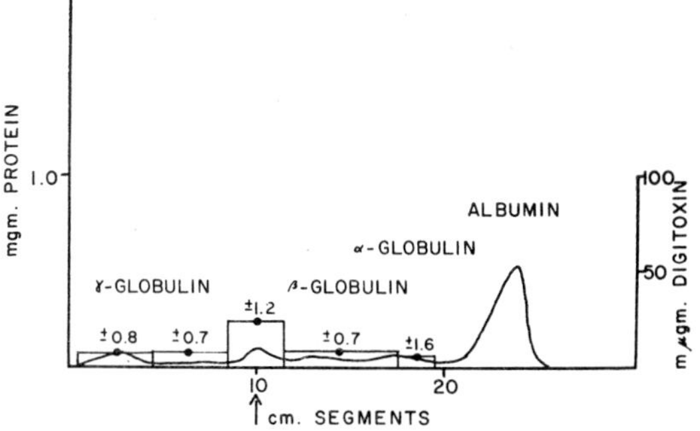

FIG. 2. *In vitro* plasma binding of C^{14}-digitoxin (1 ml plasma plus 2.7 μg C^{14}-digitoxin).
Drug-protein complex fractionated by starch block electrophoresis. Arrow indicates site of sample application. Amount of digitoxin represented by bar graph.

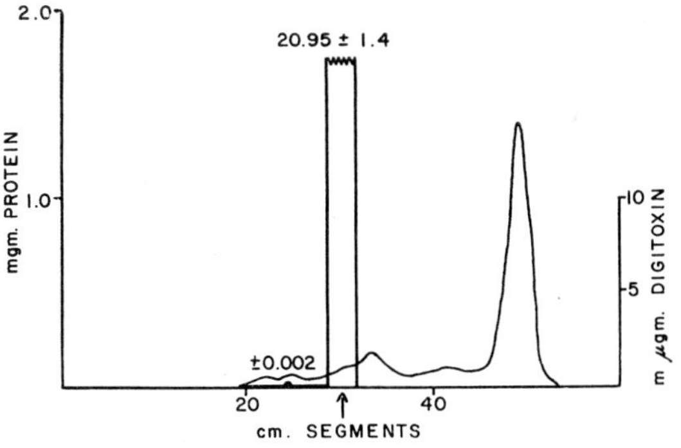

FIG. 3. *In vivo* serum binding of H^3-digitoxin.
Proteins fractionated by starch block electrophoresis. Amount of digitoxin represented by bar graph.

TABLE 1

Dosages and assays used in studying digitoxin binding by blood proteins

Investigator	Digitoxin (mg/g Protein)	Assay
Hoekstra (1931)	25	biological
Lendle and Pusch (1935)	1	colorimetric
Haarmann *et al.* (1940)	2	colorimetric
Farah (1945)	6.7	colorimetric
Rothlin and Kallenberger (1950)	5	biological
Nonradioactive in present study	6.7	colorimetric
Radioactive in present study	0.03	radioisotopic

TABLE 2

Digitoxin binding by serum protein components after salt fractionation (expressed as μg or μg equivalent digitoxin ± mean deviation bound per 75 mg of protein)

Fraction	Radioactive Digitoxin*			Nonradioactive Digitoxin† (Total Raymond positive)
	Unchanged	$CHCl_3$-soluble metabolites	Total radioactive	
Non-dialyzed serum	0.86 ± 0.13	0.18 ± 0.03	1.04 ± 0.10	329 ± 1
Dialyzed serum‡	0.54 ± 0.03	0.22 ± 0.01	0.75 ± 0.06	§
Total protein	0.98 ± 0.04	0.14 ± 0.02	1.11 ± 0.05	258 ± 2
Globulin	0.43 ± 0.04	0.14 ± 0.02	0.57 ± 0.03	252 ± 10
Albumin-1	0.39 ± 0.04	0.15 ± 0.01	0.54 ± 0.03	192 ± 14
Albumin-2	0.63 ± 0.07	0.10 ± 0.03	0.73 ± 0.10	269 ± 5
Albumin-3	0.76 ± 0.02	0.10 ± 0.01	0.86 ± 0.03	223 ± 24
Supernate	0.08 ± 0.08	0.05 ± 0.02	0.13 ± 0.07	10 ± 10
Blank	0.01 ± 0.01	0.00 ± 0.00	0.01 ± 0.01	6 ± 6

* 0.03 mg digitoxin per g protein.
† 6.7 mg digitoxin per g protein.
‡ mean of 3 runs, all others mean of 2 runs.
§ no determination.

radioactive drug (0.5 mg/75 mg of protein) there are no clear correlations between increase in albumin "purity" (albumin-1 to albumin-3) and drug binding. However, the radiotracer experiments utilizing "therapeutic" dosage levels demonstrate that there is an increase in the binding of microgram quantities of drug as one proceeds from the globulin to the albumin-3 fraction. No similar relationship is evident in the case of the chloroform-soluble metabolites. On a quantitative basis, the tracer results would indicate a binding of approximately 0.01 μg of digitoxin per mg of protein.

In an attempt to determine the extent of nonhomogeneity of the various protein fractions obtained with ammonium sulfate, the electrophoretic patterns of these fractions were determined. Figure 4 shows the results of such an experiment. When these data were compared on an equal weight basis (75 mg of protein was used per determination), it was quite clear that the *gamma*-globulin content decreased from the globulin to the albumin-3 fraction. On the other hand, the albumin content increased progressively from albumin-1 through albumin-3. Comparison of the *alpha*- and *beta*-globulin contents were somewhat more difficult to interpret since these peaks were not so readily resolved. All of the fractions showed a significant amount of heterogeneity. Although Fawaz and Farah's fractionation method (1944) was used, it must be remembered that salt fractionation is generally not a well-standardized procedure and therefore these data are not meant

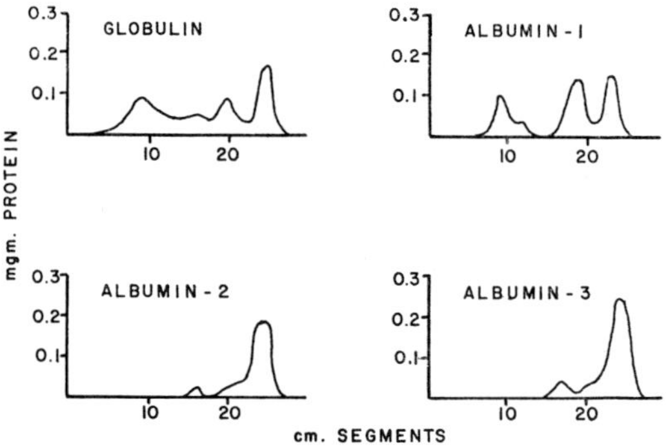

FIG. 4. Electrophoretic patterns of serum protein fractions isolated by salt-fractionation (equal weight basis).

to indicate any direct comparison with their fractions.

When the cholesterol and lipid-phosphorus contents of the fractions are expressed on an equivalent protein weight basis (table 3) an inverse association is found between drug binding and lipid content. Similar results were reported by Fawaz and Farah (1944).

During the course of these dialysis-binding studies we also concerned ourselves with the possible influence of the alkaline pH at which our electrophoretic determinations were performed. Hoekstra (1931) has reported that this alkaline pH is capable of splitting bound digitoxin from

TABLE 3

Composition of serum protein components after salt fractionation

Fraction	Protein	Cholesterol		Lipid Phosphorus	
	g %	mg %	mg per g protein	mg %	mg per g protein
Serum		124.9		5.2	
Total protein	6.76	119.3	17.7	4.9	0.7
Globulin	2.11	33.2	15.8	1.4	0.6
Albumin-1	0.90	26.9	29.9	1.3	1.4
Albumin-2	1.96	35.6	18.2	1.3	0.7
Albumin-3	1.22	7.2	5.9	0.5	0.4
Supernate	0.58	0.0		0.0	

serum proteins. Fawaz and Farah (1944), however, claim that this is not true. To test the validity of Hoekstra's observation, binding studies using whole serum were conducted at pH 7.4 and 8.6. No obvious effects of pH on drug-protein binding were noted.

DISCUSSION. Starch block electrophoresis was selected as the method of choice for studying protein binding of radioactive digitoxin. This method was selected since it is considered to be one of the most gentle methods for fractionating drug-protein complexes.

Contrary to the findings of earlier investigators, electrophoretic separation of both human *in vitro* and rat *in vivo* serum-drug preparations did not show binding of digitoxin by serum albumin. However, our findings from the equilibrium dialysis experiments of salt-fractionated proteins using radioactive digitoxin agree with those of previous reports. Namely, that as albumin is purified the binding of digitoxin increases.

A possible explanation for part of the differences noted between results obtained by the two methods may be due to binding of digitoxin by an unidentified protein component which coprecipitates with albumin during salt fractionation. If this component had an electrical charge different from albumin, the two would not migrate together on a starch block electrophoretic bed.

The cholesterol and phospholipid composition of salt-fractionated serum proteins (table 3) suggests that there is an inverse association between drug binding and lipid content. With an increase in radioactive digitoxin binding from globulin to albumin-3 fractions there is a decrease in lipid content.

It should be pointed out that the bound drug levels reported by previous investigators are very high if one is to attach *in vivo* significance to them. Haarmann *et al.* (1940) claims binding of 9 μg of digitoxin per mg of protein. Rothlin and Kallenberger (1950) found 2.2 μg of digitoxin bound per mg purified human serum albumin. However, *in vivo* application of this figure is not feasible since it might imply that a normal man could bind 300 mg of the drug without significant pharmacological effect. Using doses within the "therapeutic" range, our data indicate that 1 mg of rat serum protein will bind 0.01 μg of digitoxin.

On the basis of these studies we cannot definitely state the specific protein(s) with which digitoxin is associated. However, it is believed that our data lay open to question the interpretations of previous investigators of this problem. A number of the methods available to these investigators are subject to various criticisms. Among these may be listed the use of bioassay, the use of nonspecific color reactions, high dosage levels, and heterogenous proteins in some cases. These criticisms may help to explain the differences between our data and those of previous investigators.

SUMMARY

Using zone electrophoresis, digitoxin binding by serum albumin could not be demonstrated.

Using salt precipitation and dialysis methods, results obtained in the radiotracer portion of the present study agree qualitatively but not quantitatively with those of previous workers who found that digitoxin binding by serum proteins is correlated with albumin content of protein fractions.

When doses within the "therapeutic" range are used, 1 mg of rat serum protein will bind 0.01 μg of digitoxin.

ACKNOWLEDGMENTS. The authors wish to express their appreciation to Dr. E. Mika and the Department of Botany, University of Chicago, for making available time and facilities for the growing of radioactive *Digitalis purpurea L.* and to Dr. K. Wilzbach of Argonne National Laboratory and Dr. W. G. Brown of the Department of Chemistry, University of Chicago, for tritiating the digitoxin used in this study.

REFERENCES

ACKERMANN, P. G., TORO, G. AND KOUNTZ, W. B.: J. Lab. clin. Med. **44:** 517, 1954.

ANDERSON, R. C. AND CHEN, K. K.: J. Amer. pharm. Ass., Sci. Ed. **35:** 353, 1946.

FARAH, A.: THIS JOURNAL **83:** 143, 1945.

FAWAZ, G. AND FARAH, A.: THIS JOURNAL **80:** 193, 1944.

FOLDES, F. F. AND WILSON, B. C.: Analyt. Chem. **22:** 1210, 1950.

HAARMANN, W., HAGEMEIR, A. AND LENDLE, L.: Arch. exp. Path. Pharmak. **194:** 205, 1940.

HOEKSTRA, R. A.: Arch. exp. Path. Pharmak. **162:** 649, 1931.

KOCH, F. C. AND HANKE, M. E.: Practical Methods in Biochemistry, 6th ed., Williams & Wilkins Co., Baltimore, 1953.

LENDLE, L. AND PUSCH, P.: Arch. exp. Path. Pharmak. **177:** 550, 1935.

LOWRY, O. H., ROSEBROUGH, N. J., FARR, A. L. AND RANDALL, R. J.: J. biol. Chem. **193:** 256, 1951.

MCDONALD, H. J., LAPPE, R. J., MARBACH, E. P., SPITZER, R. H. AND URBIN, M. C.: Clin. Chemist **5:** 51, 1953.

OKITA, G. T., KELSEY, F. E., TALSO, P. J., SMITH, L. B. AND GEILING, E. M. K.: Circulation **7:** 161, 1953.

OKITA, G. T., KELSEY, F. E., WALASZEK, E. J. AND GEILING, E. M. K.: THIS JOURNAL **110:** 244, 1954.

OKITA, G. T., TALSO, P. J., CURRY, J. H., JR., SMITH, F. D., JR. AND GEILING, E. M. K.: THIS JOURNAL, **113:** 376, 1955.

ROBERTS, S. AND SZEGO, C. M.: Annu. Rev. Biochem. **24:** 543, 1955.

ROTHLIN, E. AND KALLENBERGER, A.: Arch. int. Pharmacodyn. **81:** 520, 1950.

SPRATT, J. L., OKITA, G. T. AND GEILING, E. M. K.: Int. J. App. Rad. Isotopes **2:** 167, 1957.

SPRATT, J. L., AND OKITA, G. T.: THIS JOURNAL **124:** 115, 1958.

SVEDBERG, T. AND SJOGREN, B.: J. Amer. chem. Soc. **50:** 3318, 1928.

WILZBACH, K. E.: J. Amer. chem. Soc. **79:** 1013, 1957.

8066

SUBCELLULAR LOCALIZATION OF RADIOACTIVE DIGITOXIN[1, 2]

JAMES L. SPRATT[3, 4] AND GEORGE T. OKITA

Argonne Cancer Research Hospital, USAEC, and the Department of Pharmacology, The University of Chicago, Chicago, Illinois

Received for publication May 8, 1958

Although much information has been obtained concerning the pharmacodynamic actions of digitalis glycosides, no satisfactory explanation has been presented which adequately explains the action of these compounds at the cellular level. In an attempt to gain insight into the intracellular locus of action of cardiac glycosides and the manner in which intracellular particulates interact to effect myocardial contraction, it was considered of interest to study the subcellular localization of digitoxin.

Two reports on the intracellular distribution of digitoxin have appeared. St. George, Friedman and Ishida (1953), using Long-Evans rats injected intravenously, report that digitoxin is localized in the soluble supernate of both heart and liver cells. Harvey and Pieper (1955) have reported the intracellular distribution of radioactive digitoxin in perfused guinea pig hearts. When nonradioactive drug was used to clear the vascular space of radioactive drug, the soluble supernates of these hearts accounted for only 12% of the recovered radioactivity.

The basis of the differences between these two reports appears to be well-summarized by Harvey and Pieper (1955). They suggest that the differences in results may be due to species differences or to the nonspecificity of one or both assay methods used for determining digitoxin.

MATERIALS AND METHODS. Biosynthetically-labeled C^{14}-digitoxin (Okita *et al.*, 1954) and self-radiation-labeled H^3-digitoxin (Wilzbach, 1957; Spratt *et al.*, 1957) were used as radioisotopic tracers in conjunction with methods for the determination of unchanged drug and its metabolites (Okita *et al.*, 1953; Okita *et al.*, 1955a).

Cell fractionation procedure. For the *in vivo* studies, three male (Sprague-Dawley) rats weighing 160–180 g were used. Each animal was injected via the tail vein with 0.5 mg of H^3-digitoxin (76.8 μc/mg) in 0.5 ml 40% ethanol. Since a significant amount of digitoxin is taken up by the isolated rat heart in 20 minutes (Sjoerdsma and Fischer, 1951), the animals were sacrificed at this time interval after injection. Blood for protein binding studies (Spratt and Okita, 1958) was collected and the carcass then perfused with 200 ml of Ringer-Locke's solution containing 3 μg/ml of nonradioactive digitoxin.

At the termination of perfusion, the heart (ventricles), kidneys and liver were excised and rinsed in cold (0°C) Ringer-Locke's solution containing 3 μg per ml of nonradioactive digitoxin. The tissues were freed of adjacent tissue and the wet weight was taken. (From this point on, all procedures were performed at 4°C.) The heart was minced with a pair of scissors and ground in an ice-cooled glass mortar with 1 ml 0.25 *M* sucrose—0.0018 *M* $CaCl_2$ and 1 g acid-washed sand until finely comminuted (Cleland and Slater, 1953). The kidneys and liver were minced with a pair of scissors and transferred to ice-cold Tenbroeck homogenizers.

Each tissue was diluted with 0.25 *M* sucrose—0.0018 *M* $CaCl_2$ to make a 10% suspension. The kidneys and liver were homogenized with 30 passes using a motor-driven pestle. Microscopic examination showed disruption of at least 90% of the cells by means of this procedure. Each of the 3 suspensions was then strained through 4 layers of muslin to remove connective tissue. Three ml of each of the homogenates were then fractionated according to the two-phase sucrose system of Hogeboom *et al.* (1953), with mitochondria and microsomes being isolated as well as nuclei.

In addition to the above heart, kidney and

[1] This work was aided in part by grants to the Department of Pharmacology, University of Chicago, from the Life Insurance Medical Research Fund, from the Dr. Wallace C. and Clara A. Abbott Memorial Fund, and from A.E.C. contract No. AT (11-1)-45.

[2] Presented in part at the Fall Meeting of the American Society for Pharmacology and Experimental Therapeutics, Baltimore, Maryland, September, 1957.

[3] Submitted in partial fulfillment of the requirements for the degree of Doctor of Philosophy at the University of Chicago.

[4] This work was done while this author was a Predoctoral Research Fellow of the National Heart Institute.

liver fractionations, experiments were performed on liver aliquots using the following modifications in the fractionation procedure: a) 3 ml as above but with sucrose solutions containing nonradioactive digitoxin (0.3 μg per ml) to minimize the possibility of redistribution of drug after homogenization; b) 3 ml as above, the particulate fractions being washed with the same sucrose—$CaCl_2$ solutions as their original suspending media, in the same volumes, and at the same centrifugation rates and times; c) 3 ml as above, the particulate fractions being washed with the same sucrose—$CaCl_2$ solutions as their original suspending media (except that they also contained 0.3 μg per ml of nonradioactive digitoxin), in the same volumes, and at the same centrifugation rates and times.

The *in vitro* distribution studies were performed using rat liver slices that had been incubated for 15 min at 37°C in oxygenated Krebs-Ringer phosphate buffer (Umbreit *et al.*, 1949) containing C^{14}-digitoxin. The *in vitro* "dose" ranged from 1 μg/g to 3.75 μg/g. The fractionation procedure used was the same as that outlined for the *in vivo* studies.

In addition to these liver slice studies, we sought a check system by which the problem of contamination from intravascular and interstitial fluid could be avoided. For this, we chose to inject 2 Ehrlich-Ascites tumor mice intraperitoneally with 250 μg of C^{14}-digitoxin. Thirty minutes after injection the animals were sacrificed by cervical fracture, and the tumor cells were aspirated from the peritoneal cavity, washed, homogenized and fractionated according to the scheme outlined above.

Composition of cell fractions. The various components of the fractions were identified by their microscopic morphology and staining characteristics, using methyl green pyronin (Kay, 1953) and Janus green B. By using the double homogenization technique, only a very few intact cells were found in the nuclear fraction. Owing to the wide range of what have been descriptively termed different kinds of mitochondria, it was inevitable that some Janus green B positive material should be found in the nuclear and microsomal fractions. On the basis of microscopic examination this contamination was estimated to be only a few %. The mitochondrial fraction satisfied the classical description of mitochondria as elongate rods showing a strong stain with Janus green B and assuming spheroidal shape in hypotonic solutions.

In addition to the Janus green B staining, 2,3,4-triphenyltetrazolium chloride was used to measure succinic dehydrogenase (mitochondrial) activity of the various fractions (Kun and Abood, 1949) in a semiquantitative fashion. Our mitochondrial preparations showed maximum formazon precipitation, with little or none in other fractions.

Radioassay of cell fractions. Unchanged digitoxin in the various fractions was determined by means of the hot methanol extraction procedure of Okita *et al.* (1955a) with 2 mg of nonradioactive digitoxin per sample as carrier. The C^{14}-labeled drug was determined by internal gas-flow Geiger counters (Packard Instrument Co., model 200A).

A liquid scintillation spectrometry method was employed for the determination of H^3-digitoxin. The samples were counted on either of two liquid scintillation spectrometers (model 314 Tri-Carb, or model XC-2, Packard Instrument Co., La Grange, Illinois).

RESULTS. *Studies on rat liver slices.* The results of these studies are given in table 1. It can be seen that only in the third experiment did unchanged drug appear to be associated with any of the particulate fractions. The first two experiments showed all recoverable drug to be in the soluble supernate and the third experiment yielded 80 per cent of the unchanged drug in the soluble supernate.

Studies on Ehrlich-Ascites tumor cells. This system, which is devoid of vascular space (and also interstitial space, since the cells were washed 3 times before fractionation) showed 91% (1.1 μg) of the unchanged drug in the soluble

TABLE 1

Intracellular distribution of digitoxin in incubated rat liver slices (dose given as μg digitoxin/g tissue wet weight)

Fraction	Dose		
	1 μg/g	3 μg/g	3.75 μg/g
	μg-Digitoxin Recovered (± Standard Deviation)*		
Nuclei	0.00	0.00	0.20 ± 0.01
Mitochondria	0.00	0.00	0.15 ± 0.01
Microsomes	0.00	0.00	0.09 ± 0.02
Supernate	0.68 ±0.27	0.22 ±0.01	1.85 ± 0.05
Total	0.68	0.22	2.29
	% of Total Recovered		
Nuclei	0.0	0.0	8.9
Mitochondria	0.0	0.0	6.6
Microsomes	0.0	0.0	4.1
Supernate	100.0	100.0	80.5

$$* \text{ Standard deviation} = \sqrt{\frac{\Sigma d^2}{n-1}}$$

TABLE 2

H^3-digitoxin blood levels 20 minutes after intravenous injection (± standard deviation)

	Animal No. 1	Animal No. 2		Animal No. 3	
	Unchanged digitoxin	Unchanged digitoxin	$CHCl_3$-soluble metabolites	Unchanged digitoxin	$CHCl_3$-soluble metabolites
Serum (mμg/ml blood)	604.5 ± 36.3	248.6 ± 19.4	69.3 ± 0.8	34.9 ± 1.7	16.1 ± 1.4
RBC (mμg/ml blood)	280.6 ± 17.1	139.8 ± 7.0	19.9 ± 1.0	14.7 ± 1.0	7.1 ± 0.7
Whole blood (mμg/ml)	885.1 ± 40.4	388.4 ± 20.6	89.2 ± 1.0	49.6 ± 2.0	23.2 ± 1.4
Serum/RBC	2.15	1.78	3.48	2.37	2.27
mμg per total blood volume	6700.2	2734.3	628.0	392.8	183.7
% of injected dose remaining in vascular system	1.34	0.55	0.13	*	*

* Injection incomplete.

supernate. Of the particulate fractions only the nuclei showed any significant drug-binding.

Studies on intravenously-injected rats. Table 2 gives results obtained on blood level studies of these animals after injection with H^3-digitoxin. The data for serum and cells are expressed in terms of 1 ml whole blood assuming a hematocrit value of 0.46 (Spector, 1956). Total blood volume was calculated on the basis of 5.5% of body weight using a specific gravity of 1.054 (Spector, 1956). From these data it can be seen that within 20 minutes after a single intravenous injection, the rat almost completely clears its blood of digitoxin. It can also be seen that a significant amount of metabolism of the drug has occurred within this time interval, as evidenced by the chloroform-soluble metabolites which were determined for the second and third animals. It might be noted here that the low values for the third animal were due to incomplete injection into the vascular system. For this reason no figure is given for the % of injected dose remaining in this animal's vascular system.

Table 3 gives intracellular distribution data for the unchanged drug in terms of mean % ± standard deviation found in each fraction as based on the total found for the given tissue sample. The mean drug recoveries (excepting the third animal) were: heart, 105 μg; kidney, 255 μg; liver, 536 μg. The designation (+) indicates *with*, and (−) indicates *without* (*i.e.*, with or without washing of fractions, with or without drug in the suspending media).

In each case it can be seen that little or no unchanged drug is found in the various particulate fractions, whereas the majority is found in the soluble supernate. The same can be said for the chloroform-soluble metabolites that were determined for the second animal. From these data, no pronounced difference is found when nonradioactive drug is or is not present in the suspending media. Washing of the particulate fractions does remove drug from the solid material; however, the general distribution picture does not appear to change except for the lowering of these figures for the solid fractions.

TABLE 3

Intracellular distribution of unchanged H^3-digitoxin after a single intravenous injection (in mean % ± standard deviation)

Fraction	Heart −Wash, −Drug	Kidney −Wash, −Drug	Liver −Wash, −Drug
Nuclei	1.2 ± 1.57	0.3 ± 0.26	0.2 ± 0.22
Mitochondria	1.9 ± 1.68	3.4 ± 2.96	6.6 ± 3.58
Microsomes	5.4 ± 7.11	3.3 ± 3.59	1.6 ± 1.42
Supernate	90.8 ± 5.69	93.1 ± 0.44	91.7 ± 2.44
	Liver −Wash, +Drug	**Liver +Wash, −Drug**	**Liver +Wash, +Drug**
Nuclei	0.0 ± 0.07	0.0 ± 0.07	0.0 ± 0.00
Nuclei Wash		0.1 ± 0.17	0.0 ± 0.07
Mitochondria	5.2 ± 1.56	1.1 ± 0.95	0.5 ± 0.42
Mitochondria Wash		4.5 ± 1.72	3.9 ± 2.16
Microsomes	1.0 ± 0.95	0.3 ± 0.47	0.1 ± 0.24
Microsome Wash		1.7 ± 1.48	1.3 ± 1.15
Supernate	93.8 ± 2.18	92.4 ± 4.37	94.2 ± 3.82

Discussion. These intracellular distribution studies indicate that digitoxin is localized primarily in the soluble cytoplasm of the cell. Studies on both *in vitro* and *in vivo* systems yield similar results. The small amount of drug found associated with the particulate fractions appears to be due to soluble cytoplasm that has been trapped by particulate matter.

From our studies it is difficult to resolve all of the differences noted between the work of St. George *et al.* (1953) and Harvey and Pieper. However, some possible sources of conflict are suggested. St. George *et al.* measured cardiotonic activity. Harvey and Pieper measured ethanol-extractable radioactivity and could not find radioactivity in the residues after extraction. Since we have determined both unchanged drug and some of its metabolites, we feel that both of these groups undoubtedly measured a mixture of both digitoxin and its metabolites. Since we know that the drug:metabolite ratio is not constant throughout the body (Okita *et al.*, 1955b) it is unwarranted to describe this mixture as digitoxin. This is even more important when one takes cognizance of the recent work demonstrating that digitoxin is converted *in vivo* to digoxin by C_{12}-hydroxylation (Brown *et al.*, 1957).

The question of contamination from intravascular and interstitial fluids is another feature deserving attention. In the present study the animals for *in vivo* studies were exsanguinated and perfused before their tissues were fractionated. In addition to the absence of visible blood cells in the fractions, the blood levels clearly indicate that even if blood was not removed, it could not account for the drug found in the soluble supernate. Additional evidence indicating that the drug recoveries in the supernate were not caused by contamination from intravascular and interstitial fluids was the similarity in the pattern found with Ehrlich-Ascites tumor cells.

Since we did not conduct intracellular distribution studies on guinea pigs, the possibility that the differences found by St. George *et al.* and Harvey and Pieper may be due to a species difference still remains an open question.

The possibility of drug redistribution after homogenization is a factor which must be considered in any study where cell fractionation is utilized. Since a concentration gradient favorable to particulate binding was maintained in the experiments with media containing nonradioactive drug, it is doubtful that this has occurred. Autoradiographic studies on tissue sections could furnish further information on this question.

It is at present very difficult to ascribe a functional significance to our findings concerning the intracellular localization of digitoxin. Although the contractile elements of the myocardium are found in the soluble supernate, from preliminary experiments we could not demonstrate any strong binding affinity between these proteins and the drug (Spratt and Okita, 1958). In addition to these constituents, the soluble cytoplasm of mammalian cells contains a number of enzymes important in the biochemical energetics of the cell. Among these are all the anaerobic glycolytic enzymes. Snellman and Gelotte (1950) have reported that digitoxin is an inhibitor of adenosine deaminase, another enzyme found in this fraction. Further studies will be necessary to obtain a better understanding of our findings and their significance in attempting to understand the pharmacology of digitalis.

SUMMARY

The essential experimental findings of this study are listed as follows.

Twenty minutes after a single intravenous injection, the rat essentially clears its vascular system of digitoxin with a significant amount of metabolism of the parent compound.

Upon cell fractionation of *in vivo* preparations, over 90% of the unchanged digitoxin present in the cell is found in the soluble supernate of rat heart, kidney and liver cells. No marked quantitative binding could be demonstrated with any of the particulate fractions. The results of the *in vitro* experiments agree with the *in vivo* work.

Washing of the particulate fractions does lower the binding capacities of these fractions, but does not change the gross distribution picture.

The presence or absence of nonradioactive drug in the suspending media exerts no significant effect on the binding distribution.

ACKNOWLEDGMENTS. The authors wish to express their appreciation to Dr. E. Mika and the Department of Botany, University of Chicago, for making available time and facilities for the growing of radioactive *Digitalis purpurea L.*; and to Dr. K. Wilzbach of the Argonne National Laboratory and Dr. W. G. Brown of the Department of Chemistry, University of Chicago, for tritiating the digitoxin used in these studies.

REFERENCES

BROWN, B. T., WRIGHT, S. E. AND OKITA, G. T.: Nature **180:** 607, 1957.

Cleland, K. W. and Slater, E. C.: Biochem. J. **53:** 547, 1953.
Harvey, S. C. and Pieper, G. R.: This Journal **114:** 14, 1955.
Hogeboom, G. H., Schneider, W. C. and Streibich, M. J.: Cancer Res. **13:** 617, 1953.
Kay, R. M.: Stain Tech. **28:** 41, 1953.
Kun, E. and Abood, L. G.: Science **109:** 144, 1949.
Okita, G. T., Kelsey, F. E., Talso, P. J., Smith, L. B. and Geiling, E. M. K.: Circulation **7:** 161, 1953.
Okita, G. T., Kelsey, F. E., Walaszek, E. J. and Geiling, E. M. K.: This Journal **110:** 244, 1954.
Okita, G. T., Talso, P. J., Curry, J. H., Jr., Smith, F. D., Jr. and Geiling, E. M. K.: This Journal, **113:** 376, 1955.
Okita, G. T., Talso, P. J., Curry, J. H., Jr., Smith, F. D., Jr. and Geiling, E. M. K.: This Journal **115:** 371, 1955.
St. George, S., Friedman, M. and Ishida, T.: Proc. Soc. exp. Biol., N. Y. **83:** 318, 1953.
Sjoerdsma, A. and Fischer, C. S.: Circulation **4:** 100, 1951.
Snellman, O. and Gelotte, G.: Nature **165:** 604, 1950.
Spector, W. S.: Handbook of Biological Data, Saunders, Philadelphia, 1956.
Spratt, J. L., Okita, G. T. and Geiling, E. M. K.: Int. J. App. Rad. Isotopes **2:** 167, 1957.
Spratt, J. L. and Okita, G. T.: This Journal **124:** 109, 1958.
Umbreit, W. W., Burris, R. H. and Stauffer, J. F.: Manometric Techniques and Tissue Metabolism, Burgess, Minneapolis, 1949.
Wilzbach, K. E.: J. Amer. chem. Soc. **79:** 1013, 1957.

8067

REFLEXES FROM THE INTESTINAL MESENTERY ELICITED BY VERATRIDINE, ACETYLCHOLINE AND NICOTINE

WILLIAM K. RIKER

Department of Pharmacology, School of Medicine, University of Pennsylvania, Philadelphia, Pennsylvania

Received for publication June 16, 1958

The experiments described in this paper arose from the observation that a minute dose of veratridine, when injected into the superior mesenteric artery of a lightly anesthetized dog, regularly produced an immediate apnea associated with visible contraction of the abdominal muscles. The latter phenomenon has received considerable attention, particularly in the cat, and it has been established that manipulation of the mesentery and/or intestine causes reflex contraction of abdominal wall muscles and a slight rise in arterial blood pressure (Lewis and Kellgren, 1939; Downman and McSwiney, 1946; von Euler and Sjöstrand, 1947; Downman *et al.*, 1948). There was, however, no evidence concerning the existence of a respiratory reflex arising from this area until recently. Bean (1952) claimed that injection of sodium cyanide into the mesenteric vessels or application of cyanide on the peritoneal surface of the intestine, in dogs, produced an initial respiratory depression followed by augmentation. Toh *et al.* (1955) injected capsaicin into the cat's superior mesenteric artery and caused brief respiratory depression (not apnea) in two animals, while in two others respiratory stimulation ensued.

These findings, indicating that chemical agents may arouse either respiratory stimulant or depressant reflexes from the mesenteric circulation, suggested further study of the invariable apnea elicited from this area by intraarterial injection of veratridine.

MATERIALS AND METHODS. Male and female mongrel dogs, weighing between 10 and 15 kg, were used. Anesthesia consisted of morphine sulfate (2 mg/kg, s.c.) followed in approximately one hour by chloralose (80 to 90 mg/kg, i.v.). Arterial blood pressure was recorded by a mercury manometer, and respiration by a pneumograph and tambour. A similar tambour was connected to a water-filled balloon in the lumen of the intestine in those experiments in which intestinal motility was recorded. Intraarterial injections were made through a flexible plastic catheter, approximately 15 cm long and 1 mm in diameter, inserted into the superior mesenteric artery via a proximal jejunal arterial branch vessel. The dead space of the injection assembly was approximately 0.1 ml. The volume of the intraarterial injections was 0.2 ml in most instances, and rarely exceeded 0.5 ml. Injection of saline, in equal volume, was always used as a control.

When, in the latter stages of some experiments, it was desired to cut the splanchnic nerves these were isolated in the chest. Bilateral incisions were made in the posterior parts of the 8th or 9th intercostal spaces during artificial respiration, and the splanchnic nerves sectioned between the diaphragm and the last thoracic para-vertebral ganglion. The chest was then closed, the lungs were reexpanded, and spontaneous respiration was reestablished.

All drug doses indicated in the text and figures are total doses expressed as amounts of the salts, with the exception that veratridine and nicotine dosages are expressed as amounts of the bases.

RESULTS. *Inhibition of respiration.* Injections of veratridine into the superior mesenteric artery (i.a.) consistently results in apnea in expiration (fig. 1), the onset of which almost always occurs within 3 sec after beginning the injection. The apnea generally lasts for from 5 to 20 sec, during which time there is visible a sustained contraction of the muscles of the abdominal wall. In nearly all instances the minimal effective dose for eliciting the apnea is in the range of from 3 to 10 μg. Furthermore, the relatively rapid development of tachyphylaxis observed with intravenous injections of veratridine, as in the evocation of the Bezold-Jarisch reflex (Jarisch and Richter, 1939), is not evident here. With i.a. injections of equal doses of veratridine every 3 min the sixth injection is as effective as the first.

Following the apnea the sequence of respiratory events is variable. Some dogs resume

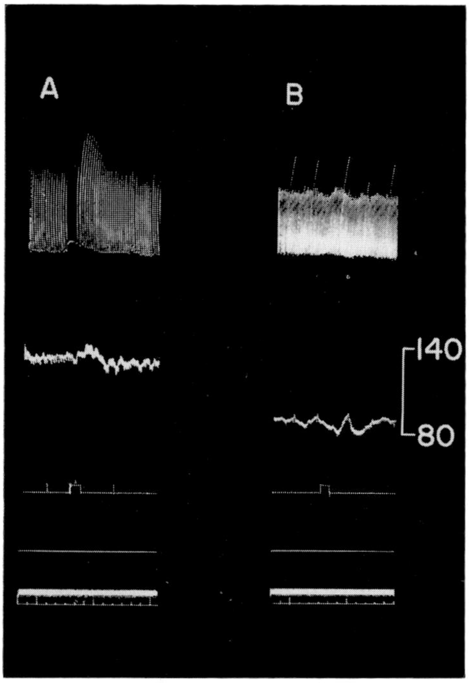

FIG. 1. Reflex apnea and its abolition by splanchnic section.

Record from above down: thoracic respiration, carotid blood pressure (scale at side in mm Hg in this and subsequent figures), signal, time in 10 sec intervals.

A. Apnea produced by veratridine, 10 μg i.a.

B. Veratridine, 10 μg i.a., after bilateral splanchnic section.

breathing in a pattern identical to that preceding the veratridine injection, while in others a brief period of hyperpnea ensues. Reactivity of the particular animal in relation to the depth of anesthesia is doubtless an important determinant of the pattern observed. Accordingly, it is conceivable that in the more reactive animal brief hyperpnea is a consequence of the slight anoxia and hypercarbia which develops during the apnea. In still another group of dogs the apnea is followed by marked inhibition of thoracic breathing, with the return to a control pattern of respiration taking several minutes. It has not been determined whether this prolonged response is maintained by veratridine-induced after-discharge in the afferent arm of the reflex pathway, or is a secondary response to the apnea. Nevertheless, this type of response is not a function of the dosage as it has been observed with as much as 40 μg, and as little as 3 μg of veratridine.

Acetylcholine (ACh) and nicotine are also effective in evoking reflex apnea (fig. 2). This apnea is of further interest since it might well represent the functional end-point of the action potentials recorded by Brown and Gray (1948) in sensory fibers in the cat's mesentery following i.a. injections of ACh and nicotine. Apnea does not occur, however, when epinephrine, isoproterenol, or sodium cyanide are injected into the superior mesenteric artery. In fact these agents, in doses as high as 200 μg, are without any immediate or remarkable effects on respiration.

The rapidity with which apnea supervened after i.a. administration of veratridine precluded its originating from stimulation of vagal afferents in the lungs and/or heart. Conclusive elimination of this possibility was shown by the persistence of the apneic response after bilateral cervical vagotomy. In addition, this procedure excluded the vagus nerves from consideration as afferent pathways. Instead, the afferent arm for this reflex inhibition of respiration was located in the splanchnic nerves. After bilateral section of these nerves it was no longer possible to elicit apnea with i.a. injection of veratridine (fig. 1).

Reflex inhibition of rhythmic contractions of the small intestine. During the initial stages of this investigation the rhythmic contractions of the small intestine were recorded in order to determine what change, if any, in respiratory function resulted from drug-induced inhibition or augmentation of these contractions. No respiratory change was exhibited but the results suggested that intestinal motility was reflexly altered by i.a. injection of veratridine. Demonstration of this reflex effect was then made by recording the rhythmic contractions of two widely separated segments of small intestine, surgically isolated from each other and from the rest of the intestine (fig. 3). Under these conditions a minimal effective dose of veratridine (3 to 10 μg), reaching only the distal segment, causes an immediate inhibition of the rhythmic contractions of the proximal segment of intestine (fig. 4B). This, therefore, reveals another reflex mechanism activated by amounts of veratridine equivalent to those which cause reflex apnea. Administration of ACh, i.a., confirmed the position of the catheter inasmuch as the characteristic action of this drug on intestinal smooth muscle was obvious only in the distal segment (fig. 4A). It may also be noted that ACh brings about reflex inhibition of the proximal segment (fig. 4A), as does nicotine; epinephrine and isoproterenol are ineffective.

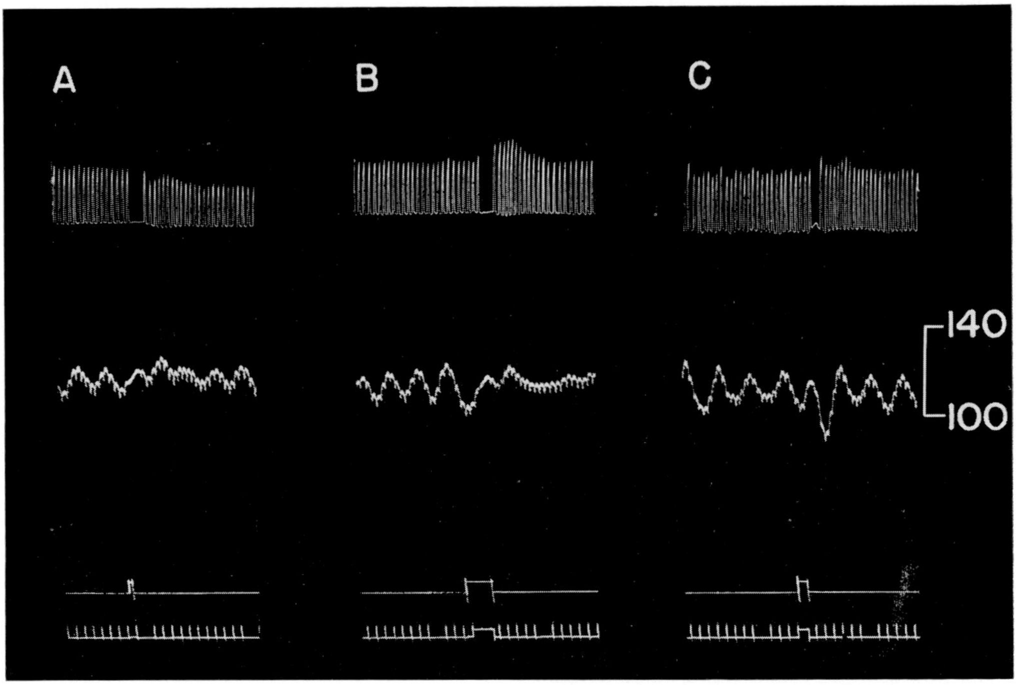

FIG. 2. Demonstration of reflex apnea produced by veratridine, ACh and nicotine. Record from above down: respiration and blood pressure as in fig. 1, signal, time in 5 sec intervals.
A. Veratridine i.a., 10 μg.
B. ACh i.a., 20 μg.
C. Nicotine i.a., 40 μg.

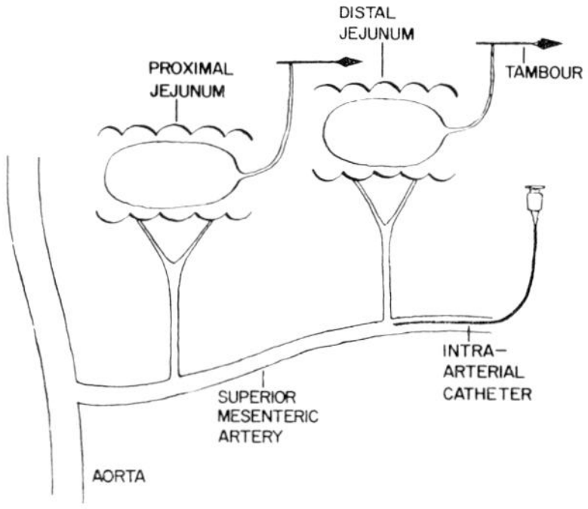

FIG. 3. Schematic representation of method used for demonstrating reflex intestinal inhibition.
Note that catheter tip is positioned near arterial branch to distal segment of small intestine. Mesentery has been omitted for simplicity.

The reflex intestinal inhibition induced by i.a. veratridine and ACh persisted unchanged after bilateral cervical vagotomy (fig. 4C) but was abolished after both splanchnic nerves were cut (fig. 4D). This would indicate that the splanchnics are the afferent pathway were it not for the fact that in sectioning these nerves the efferent arm for this reflex was also interrupted. Nevertheless, the results of splanchnic section do show that the intestinal inhibition is not an intrinsic, or intramesenteric, reflex.

It would be desirable to extend these experiments on spinal animals to determine whether the reflex intestinal inhibition involves mediation of the higher centers in the neuraxis or is solely a spinal reflex. Supporting the latter alternative would be the investigations of Downman and McSwiney (1946), in which the pressor and leg movement responses to visceral stimulation were shown to be spinal reflexes.

Locus of origin of veratridine-induced reflexes: physically-induced counterpart. It has been established that the veratridine-induced reflexes originate from all areas supplied by the superior mesenteric artery. Injections of veratridine were made into the intestinal branches of this artery at various points along the jejunum and ileum. Doses of the order of 1 to 3 μg regularly produced a brief apnea, regardless of the site of injection, indicating that the origin of the reflexes is not limited to any segmental area of the mesentery.

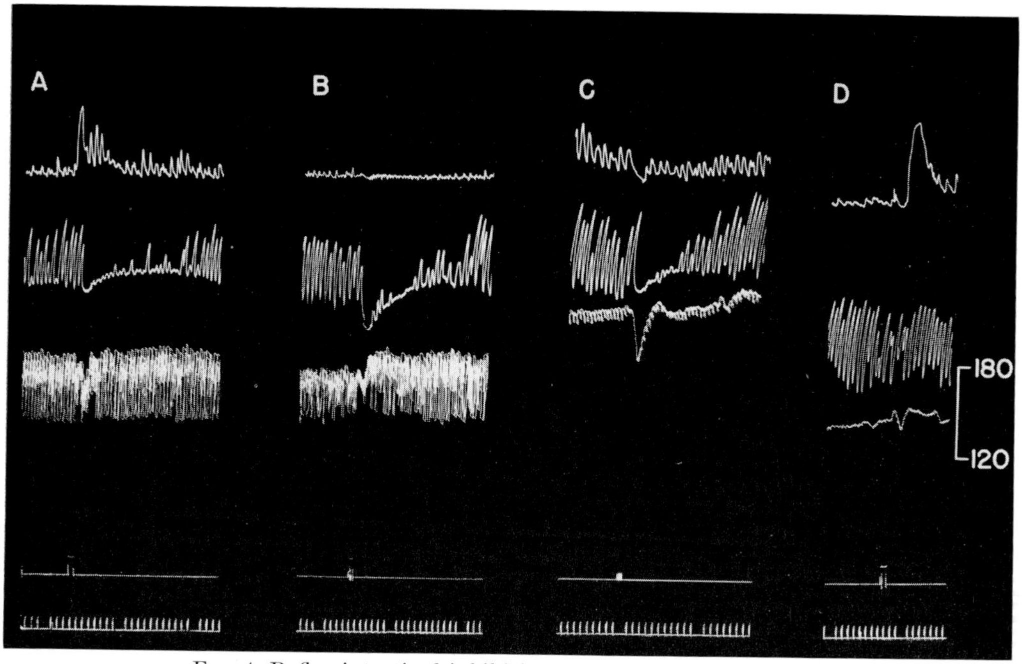

FIG. 4. Reflex intestinal inhibition and its afferent pathway.
Record from above down: motility in distal segment of intestine, motility in proximal segment, carotid blood pressure, signal, time in 5 sec intervals.
A. ACh i.a., 5 μg, to distal segment.
B. Veratridine i.a., 3 μg, to distal segment.
C. Same as B, after vagotomy. Note persistence of reflex inhibition of proximal segment.
D. Same as B, after splanchnic nerve section. Inhibition abolished.

The evidence for the location of the responsible afferent nerve-endings in the mesentery is inconclusive, but suggestive. Although topical application and injections of veratridine, in doses as high as 100 μg, into the muscularis or lumen of the small intestine fail to elicit apnea, there are obvious limitations to conclusions drawn from these results. Consequently further attempts at localization of the responsible receptor elements led to physical manipulation of the small intestine and mesentery. Thus, various distortions of the intestine produced spasmodic, gasping respiration, in contrast to which was the apnea in expiration which occurred following traction on either the jejunal or ileal mesentery. This strongly suggests that the point of origin of the veratridine-induced reflexes is in the intestinal mesentery; a conclusion which is further enhanced by the striking similarity of the responses to i.a. veratridine, i.a. ACh and traction on the mesentery (fig. 5).

Cardiovascular effects of intraarterial veratridine. The variability in the blood pressure responses to i.a. veratridine injections (table 1) presents a sharp contrast to the regularity with which the respiratory and intestinal reflexes are evoked. Moreover, the dose range indicated in table 1 extends beyond the minimal effective doses necessary for eliciting apnea and intestinal inhibition. This inconsistency in the blood pressure responses suggested a possible relation to either the apnea or alterations in heart rate. However, injections of equal doses of veratridine before and during artificial respiration produced comparable effects on the systemic blood pressure. Nor was a change in heart rate a contributory factor. In more than 40 electrocardiograms taken during the i.a. administration of veratridine, tachycardia was never observed and only 4 revealed a noteworthy bradycardia. In these 4 instances, however, the slowing occurred so late after the injections (20 to 30 sec) that it nullified any likelihood of being mediated through a mesenteric reflex.

Intraarterial injections of ACh and epinephrine are of interest here because, in contrast to veratridine, these agents exert potent effects on vascular smooth muscle. Hence, the local

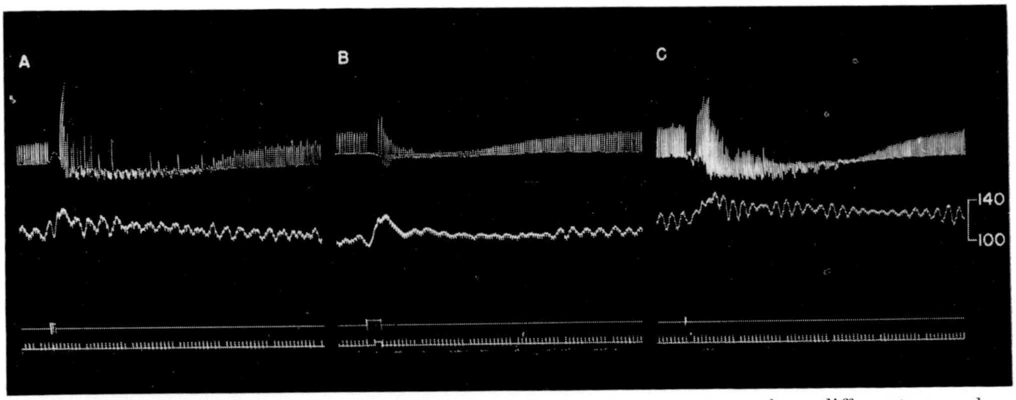

FIG. 5. Apnea followed by inhibition of thoracic respiration in response to three different procedures. Record from above down (as in fig. 2).
A. Veratridine i.a., 40 μg.
B. ACh i.a., 60 μg.
C. Traction on mesentery of small intestine.

TABLE 1

Blood pressure responses to i.a. veratridine

Summary of 107 injections in dose range 2 to 20 μg.

Injections		Response	Av. Change (mm Hg)
No.	Per cent		
60	56	Increase	+14
30	28	No change	—
17	16	Decrease	−14

action of these agents on the mesenteric vasculature might be expected to complicate the analysis of systemic blood pressure responses. It is significant, therefore, that i.a. injections of epinephrine, which did not produce reflex apnea or intestinal inhibition, had no remarkable effect on systemic blood pressure except when the doses were so high that a late systemic effect occurred. Equally important is the fact that i.a. injections of ACh, which decreased mesenteric arterial pressure, evoked essentially the same systemic blood pressure responses as did i.a. veratridine, including the pressor response.

Neither cervical vagotomy nor splanchnic section had a marked influence on the blood pressure changes due to i.a. veratridine injections. The vagus nerves definitely do not contribute significantly, if at all, whereas in 4 out of 6 animals splanchnic nerve section was followed by either a reduction in, or abolition of, the blood pressure response. However, the variability in the veratridine-induced pressure changes, even in a single animal, precludes other than a tenuous conclusion from these results. It suffices to say that the mutable character and the relatively small magnitude of the blood pressure responses permits the conclusion that a vasomotor reflex is not a significant component of the reflex effects of small doses of i.a. veratridine.

DISCUSSION. The preceding sections have illustrated that a well-developed reflex pattern originates from the stimulation of sensory nerve-endings in the mesentery of the small intestine. Moreover, it has been shown that these nerve-endings are susceptible to stimulation by i.a. injections of veratridine, ACh and nicotine. That these three drugs produce an identical reflex pattern is cause for brief comment. It is evident that the various reflex patterns elicited by i.a. injections of veratridine into different vascular beds arise from stimulation of several types of sensory nerve-endings (Aviado and Schmidt, 1955). Acetylcholine, too, is effective in exciting a wide variety of sensory receptors (Diamond, 1955). Therefore, neither veratridine nor ACh when given i.a., would appear to possess specificity as pharmacological tools for uncovering reflex responses. Indeed, West and Guzman (1957) have observed the triad of responses (hypotension, bradycardia and apnea) characteristic of the Bezold-Jarisch reflex following intracoronary injections of veratridine, ACh and nicotine. Although the lack of specificity of these agents does not detract from their usefulness it makes pertinent a consideration of the type of nerve-ending which is stimulated. It is this consideration, for the mesenteric reflexes, which is the purpose of this discussion.

The possibility that chemoreceptors[1] exist in the circulation of the superior mesenteric artery of the dog was suggested by the experiments of Bean (1952), in which topical and i.a. administration of cyanide led to initial depression, and then augmentation, of respiration. The initial depression conflicts with the customarily observed effect of cyanide on respiration. However, since cyanide is *sine qua non* in the detection of chemoreceptor tissue it was administered i.a. in the present investigation and shown to have no influence on respiration in the doses tested. These observations, and the well-known fact that carotid and aortic chemoreceptor denervation abolishes the respiratory stimulation caused by anoxia or intravenous cyanide (Schmidt and Comroe, 1940), preclude further consideration of mesenteric chemoreceptors. It is more likely that Bean, apparently using very large doses of cyanide, was stimulating pain endings. His observance of respiratory depression, rather than apnea, may have been related to the use of barbiturate anesthesia with consequent depression of synaptic transmission (Exley, 1954) along the reflex pathway.

Mesenteric pressoreceptors, or receptors sensitive to changes in the tone of the mesenteric vessels, are implied in the perfusion experiments of Gammon and Bronk (1935) and Heymans *et al.*, (1936). The former, working with the cat, concluded that the Pacinian corpuscles in the mesentery were responsive to the degree of distention of the mesenteric vessels. Heymans' group used a donor dog to perfuse a segment of intestine and mesentery in the recipient dog. Alterations in perfusion pressure led to a vasodilatation reflex in the peripheral and splenic vessels of the recipient animal. The absence of Pacinian corpuscles in the mesentery of the dog enhances the supposition that the reflex vasodilatation has a pressoreceptor origin. Therefore, a question existed as to whether the veratridine-sensitive elements in the present investigation were actually pressoreceptors. Resolution of the problem was made by i.a. administration of epinephrine and isoproterenol; the former constricting, the latter dilating, mesenteric vessels thereby changing mesenteric arterial pressure in opposite directions. These sympathomimetic amines failed to elicit not only reflex apnea, but also any immediate change in systemic arterial blood pressure and heart rate. Furthermore, ACh and isoproterenol produce the same directional change in mesenteric arterial pressure yet only the former elicits the reflex responses. It is necessary to point out also that the reflex responses to i.a. veratridine, ACh and nicotine consist of a profound, reproducible effect on respiration but a weak, variable effect on the circulation. In contrast, the pressoreceptor prototypes in the carotid sinuses and aortic arch are distinguished by their predominant effects on circulation, and minimal effects on respiration. It suffices to say that the veratridine-sensitive elements in the mesentery are not likely to be pressoreceptors.

Although the earlier literature on reflexes of intraabdominal origin does not mention a respiratory component it contains abundant demonstrations of the skeletal muscle contractions resulting from manipulation of abdominal viscera (Lewis and Kellgren, 1939; von Euler and Sjöstrand, 1947; Downman and McSwiney, 1946). It is of more than passing interest, therefore, that the apnea caused by injection of veratridine into the superior mesenteric artery is accompanied by a visible, sustained contraction of the muscles of the abdominal wall. From the teleological standpoint apnea and abdominal muscle contraction would be expected responses to abdominal pain; *i.e.*, an attempt to splint a painful viscus. However, the likelihood that the reflexes described in this paper arise from veratridine stimulation of nerve-endings concerned with pain sensation rests on ground more solid than that of teleology. Impulses characteristic of C fiber discharge were recorded in mesenteric nerve fibers by Gernandt and Zotterman (1946); these occurred upon pinching the gut of the cat and were believed to represent intestinal pain. Cannon (1933) used an implanted electrode to stimulate the intact splanchnic nerve and noted discomfort in the unanesthetized cat. More closely related to the present investigation is the work of Egami (1955) which reveals that ACh applied to the intestine appears to cause pain in the lightly anesthetized cat. These observations, together with the previous exclusion of chemoreceptors and presso-

[1] The term "chemoreceptor," in this discussion, is used in the strict sense of a sensory receptor responding to a decrease in arterial pO_2, the prototypes of which would be the carotid and aortic bodies.

receptors, support the hypothesis that stimulation of intramesenteric endings of pain fibers is responsible for the reflexes elicited by i.a. administration of veratridine, ACh and nicotine.

SUMMARY

Apnea and inhibition of the rhythmic contractions of the small intestine are shown to be reflex responses to injections of veratridine into the superior mesenteric artery of the anesthetized dog.

Acetylcholine and nicotine are also capable of eliciting these reflexes, whereas epinephrine, isoproterenol and sodium cyanide are not.

The reflex responses have their sole afferent pathway in the splanchnic nerves.

The hypothesis is advanced that the sensory nerve-endings being stimulated are the terminations of fibers subserving the sensation of pain.

ACKNOWLEDGMENT: The author is indebted to Dr. D. M. Aviado, Jr. for many helpful suggestions, and to Mr. A. Falk and Mr. N. Liebman for their excellent technical assistance.

REFERENCES

AVIADO, D. M., JR. AND SCHMIDT, C. F.: Physiol. Rev. **35:** 247, 1955.

BEAN, J. W.: Amer. J. Physiol. **171:** 522, 1952.

BROWN, G. L. AND GRAY, J. A. B.: J. Physiol. **107:** 306, 1948.

CANNON, B.: Amer. J. Physiol. **105:** 366, 1933.

DIAMOND, J.: J. Physiol. **130:** 513, 1955.

DOWNMAN, C. B. B. AND MCSWINEY, B. A.: J. Physiol. **105:** 80, 1946.

DOWNMAN, C. B. B. AND MCSWINEY, B. A. AND VASS, C. C. N.: J. Physiol. **107:** 97, 1948.

EGAMI, M.: Jap. J. Pharmacol. **4:** 160, 1955.

VON EULER, C. AND SJÖSTRAND, T.: Acta physiol. scand. **14:** 363, 1947.

EXLEY, K. A.: Brit. J. Pharmacol. **9:** 170, 1954.

GAMMON, G. D. AND BRONK, D. W.: Amer. J. Physiol. **114:** 77, 1935.

GERNANDT, B. G. AND ZOTTERMAN, Y.: Acta physiol. scand. **12:** 56, 1946.

HEYMANS, C., BOUCKAERT, J. J. AND WIERZUCHOWSKI, M.: C.R. Soc. Biol., Paris **123:** 286, 1936.

JARISCH, A. AND RICHTER, H.: Arch. exp. Path. Pharmak. **193:** 347, 1939.

LEWIS, T. AND KELLGREN, J. H.: Clin. Sci. **4:** 47, 1939.

SCHMIDT, C. F. AND COMROE, J. H., JR.: Physiol. Rev. **20:** 115, 1940.

TOH, C. C., LEE, T. S. AND KIANG, A. K.: Brit. J. Pharmacol. **10:** 175, 1955.

WEST, J. W. AND GUZMAN, S. V.: Fed. Proc. **16:** 136, 1957.

CONCERNING THE MECHANISMS OF THE CARDIOVASCULAR ACTIONS OF HEXAHYDRO-1-AZEPINEPROPIONAMIDOXIME (SU-4029)

R. A. MAXWELL, A. J. PLUMMER, A. I. DANIEL, F. SCHNEIDER AND H. POVALSKI

Research Department, CIBA Pharmaceutical Products Inc., Summit, New Jersey

Received for publication June 25, 1958

In recent communications (Mull *et al.*, 1957; Maxwell *et al.*, 1958) we have described the long-acting antihypertensive properties of hexahydro-1-azepinepropionamidoxime dihydrochloride (Su-4029). This compound did not markedly lower the arterial blood pressure of unanesthetized or anesthetized normotensive dogs but clearly depressed the arterial pressures of unanesthetized renal and neurogenic hypertensive dogs. The cardiovascular properties of Su-4029 could not be explained by known mechanisms but the site of action was determined to be, at least in part, in the efferent sympathetic periphery. We have directed our attention toward determining the mechanisms underlying this peripheral action of Su-4029 and the following is a report of our results.

METHODS. Mongrel dogs of both sexes, anesthetized with 30 mg/kg of Na pentobarbital intraperitoneally plus an intravenous drip of 0.1 mg/kg/min of this substance, were used. Blood pressures were recorded with the Anderson glass capsule manometer (1941).

A 10% stock solution of Dibenamine HCl (dibenzyl-β-chlorethylamine HCl) in propylene glycol was diluted with water just prior to use. All other drugs were administered in aqueous solution.

The levorotatory isomer of epinephrine (i.e. Epinephrine, U.S.P.) was used throughout the study. In the case of norepinephrine, however, the racemic mixture was employed.

RESULTS. *Effect of Su-4029 on the blockade produced by a "reversible" adrenergic blocking agent.* Three mg/kg of phentolamine HCl given intravenously markedly reduced the pressor response to norepinephrine and reversed the pressor response to epinephrine (fig. 1) in 7 dogs studied. Subsequent intravenous administration of 180 mg/kg of Su-4029 in a series of 30 and 60 mg/kg doses produced a stepwise return of the pressor response to norepinephrine to control dimensions in 4 dogs (fig. 1) and partially returned the pressor response in 3 dogs. The reversal of the epinephrine pressor response evoked by phentolamine was not affected in the 7 animals by these doses of Su-4029 (fig. 1). At the time that norepinephrine responses could be obtained, phentolamine was clearly blocking the pressor receptors for epinephrine. At this point the administration of a second dose of 3 mg/kg of phentolamine again produced complete blockade of the pressor response to norepinephrine.

The blockade of norepinephrine and the reversal of epinephrine pressor responses resulting from intravenous administration of 0.5 mg/kg of phentolamine were both antagonized by the subsequent injection of 30 mg/kg of Su-4029 in the 3 dogs studied.

To discover if phentolamine might exert an unequal blockade against epinephrine and norepinephrine, the doses of these 2 amines needed to overcome blockade by phentolamine were determined in 3 dogs. Control activities for the amines were determined at 4 μg/kg and 8 μg/kg. To elicit pressor responses of control magnitude after the administration of 0.5 mg/kg of phentolamine required a 4-fold increase for both amines. After 3 mg/kg of phentolamine a 12-fold increase in epinephrine and a 16-fold increase in norepinephrine were required. It seems that there was no great discrepancy in the degree of blockade produced by phentolamine against epinephrine and norepinephrine.

The depressor response to an intravenous injection of 1 μg/kg of isopropylarterenol (isoproterenol) was clearly augmented following the acute intravenous administration of 30 mg/kg of Su-4029 in 3 out of 4 dogs studied (fig. 2).

Effect of Su-4029 on the blockade produced by an "irreversible" adrenergic blocking agent. In the following experiments Dibenamine was ad-

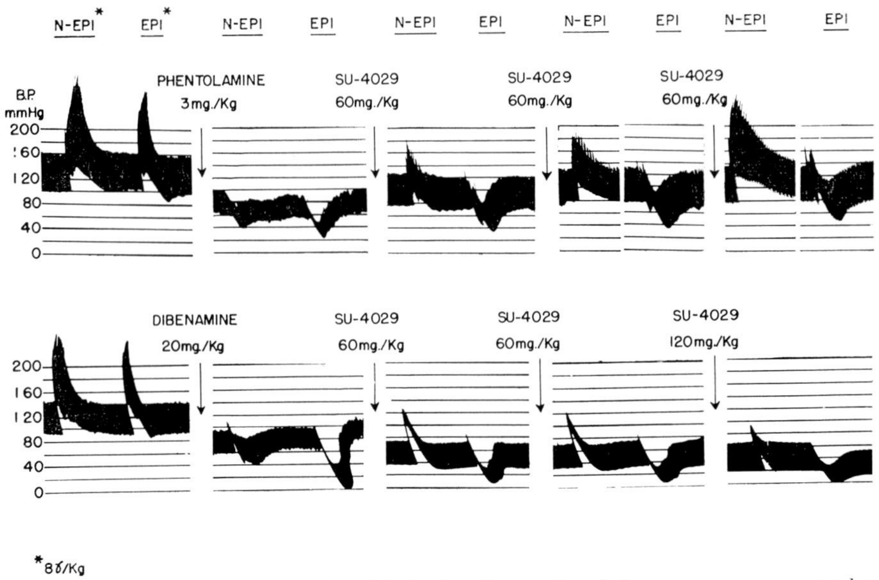

FIG. 1. The reversal of the phentolamine blockade of norepinephrine pressor responses by Su-4029. Also shown is the lack of effect of Su-4029 on the Dibenamine blockade of the norepinephrine pressor response. All drugs were administered intravenously.

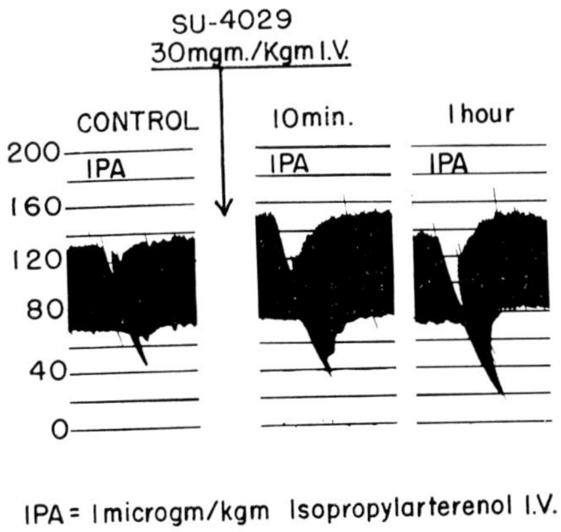

FIG. 2. The augmenting effect of acutely administered Su-4029 on the depressor action of isopropylarterenol.
All drugs administered intravenously.

ministered over a one-half hour period and then in order to insure complete blockade one and one-half to two hours were allowed to elapse between the end of administration and the resumption of the experiment. Ten to 20 mg/kg of Dibenamine profoundly reduced the pressor response to norepinephrine and reversed the response to epinephrine in the 7 dogs studied (fig. 1). The subsequent administration of a total of 180 to 240 mg/kg of Su-4029 in a series of 30 and 60 mg/kg doses did not unequivocally affect the blockade of norepinephrine and epinephrine pressor responses produced by Dibenamine (fig. 1) in any of the 7 dogs.

Time course of augmented epinephrine and norepinephrine pressor responses following acute Su-4029. In a previous communication (Maxwell *et al.*, 1958), it was reported that the pressor response to norepinephrine was markedly augmented at 3 days following the administration of 30 mg/kg of Su-4029 intravenously. The following concerns the acute effects of Su-4029 administration on the responses to norepinephrine and epinephrine.

Five to 10 minutes following the intravenous injection of 30 mg/kg of Su-4029 the pressor response to 4 μg/kg of norepinephrine was clearly enhanced (fig. 3), in 5 dogs studied. The pressor response to 4 μg/kg of epinephrine was also augmented but less markedly than the response to norepinephrine (fig. 3) in all 5 dogs. The responses to subsequent doses of norepinephrine and epinephrine were progressively diminished until at 2 hours the pressor responses were of the order of magnitude of those elicited before Su-4029 injection (fig. 3). Thus it would appear that augmentation of the pressor actions of norepinephrine and epinephrine reappears at some time between 2 hours and 3 days after administration of Su-4029.

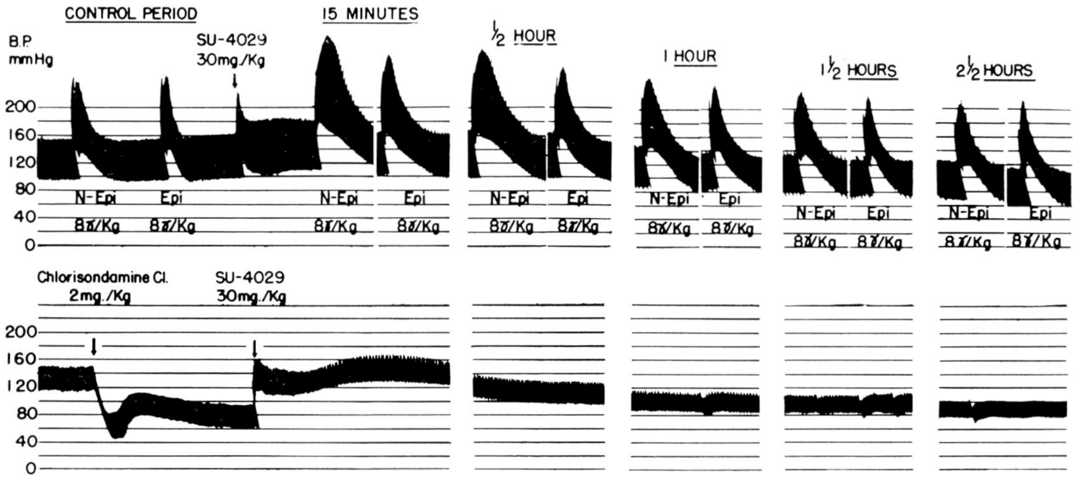

Fig. 3. Time course of the augmentation of norepinephrine and epinephrine pressor responses following Su-4029.
Also shown is the time course of the pressor response elicited by Su-4029 administration during the hypotension produced by a ganglionic blocking agent. All drugs were administered intravenously.

The pressor response elicited by 250 μg/kg of tyramine was markedly but not completely antagonized at 10 minutes and 1 hour after 30 mg/kg of Su-4029 (fig. 4).

Time course of pressor response produced by acute Su-4029 following a ganglionic blocking agent. Four normotensive anesthetized dogs were treated intravenously with 2 mg/kg of the ganglionic blocking agent, chlorisondamine chloride. Subsequent administration of 30 mg/kg of Su-4029 produced a sharp elevation of pressure of 40 to 60 mm Hg within a few minutes. The pressure gradually declined to approximately pre-Su-4029 levels during a one and one-half to two and one-half hour period (fig. 3). The time course of this pressor response closely paralleled the time course of the augmentation of norepinephrine and epinephrine observed after acute Su-4029 administration (compare fig. 3a with 3b).

Effect of Su-4029 on the chronically and acutely denervated nictitating membranes of the cat. It has been reported (Maxwell *et al.*, 1958) that Su-4029 produces a sustained contraction of the cat nictitating membrane. In an attempt to decide if this acute sympathetic-like action of Su-4029 was a direct or indirect action of Su-4029, 7 cats were subjected to unilateral excision of the superior cervical ganglion under pentobarbital anesthesia and then 5 to 6 days allowed to elapse. After this time the animals were anesthetized with 0.7 ml/kg of Dial-Urethane and

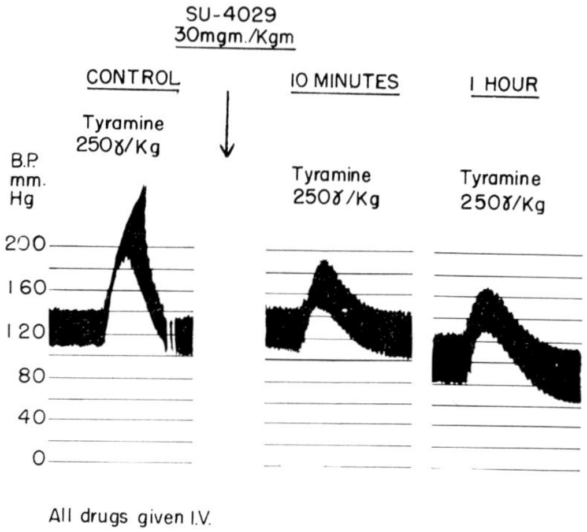

FIG. 4. Partial antagonism of the pressor response to tyramine following acute administration of Su-4029.

one-half inch of the vagosympathetic trunks of the nonoperated sides was resected. The animals were maintained on positive pressure respiration. Both nictitating membranes of each animal were attached to a set of isotonic lever systems which were carefully constructed to produce equal magnifications. The chronically denervated membrane was markedly hypersensitive to norepinephrine in all 7 cats as compared to the acutely denervated membranes (fig. 5). Despite this fact in 6 out of 7 animals administration of 30 mg/kg of Su-4029 resulted in a greater contraction of the acutely denervated membrane than of the chronically denervated membrane over a 3 hour period (fig. 5). In 5 of these animals with intact adrenals, the chronically denervated membrane was contracted more markedly than the acutely denervated one over the first 5 to 10 minutes (fig. 5). In 2 animals subjected to bilateral adrenalectomy this differential in initial response was not observed (fig. 5).

These results strongly indicated that the contractions of the nictitating membrane were not due to an indirect action via a mechanism involving a release of catechol amines from body depots and we assume a direct action for Su-4029. The subsequent administration of 3 mg/kg of phentolamine reduced the contraction of the nictitating membranes which demonstrated that the contracting effect of Su-4029 was occurring through a mechanism sensitive to interruption by adrenergic blocking agents.

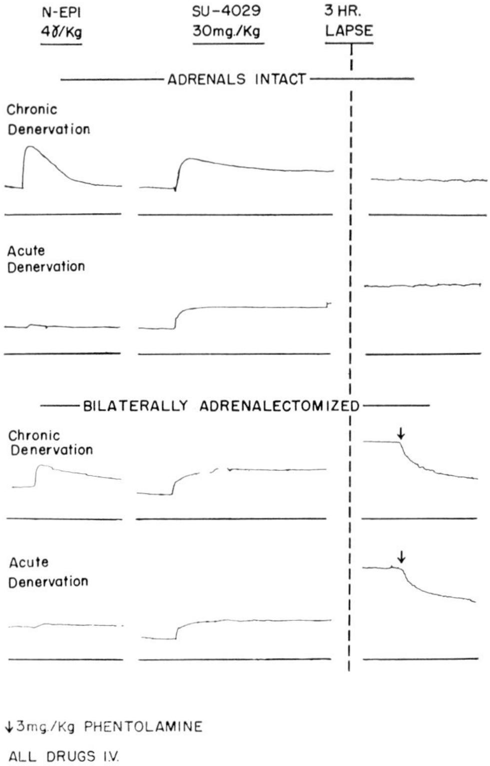

FIG. 5. The relative contracting effect of acutely administered Su-4029 on the chronically and acutely denervated nictitating membranes of the cat in the presence and absence of adrenal glands.

The lower tracing also shows the effect of phentolamine on the Su-4029 induced contraction.

Differential effects of Su-4029 pretreatment on pressor amine activity. The pressor response of a series of anesthetized dogs to the following series of amines was determined: phenylethylamine, 0.5 mg/kg; amphetamine sulfate, 0.5 mg/kg; Vonedrine HCl (phenylpropylmethylamine HCl), 0.5 mg/kg; methamphetamine HCl, 0.5 mg/kg; tyramine HCl, 1 mg/kg; Paredrine HBr (hydroxyamphetamine HBr), 0.25 mg/kg; Paredrinol HCl, 0.25 mg/kg; Propadrine HCl (phenylpropanolamine HCl), 0.5 mg/kg; ephedrine HCl, 0.6 mg/kg; norepinephrine HCl, 4 to 8 μg/kg; epinephrine bitartrate, 4 to 8 μg/kg; Cobefrin HCl (Nordefrine HCl), 4 μg/kg; Epinine HCl, 25 μg/kg; Neo-synephrine HCl (phenylephrine HCl), 0.1 mg/kg and Synephrine tartrate, 0.25 mg/kg. These doses were sufficient to produce a rise of at least 60 mm Hg mean blood pressure. In a second series 3 days after the intravenous administration of 30 mg/kg of Su-4029 to each animal, 30 dogs were anesthetized and the blood pressure response to the amines determined. The doses listed above were employed.

The pressor actions of norepinephrine, Cobefrine, Epinine, epinephrine, Neosynephrine and Synephrine were either not affected or were clearly augmented by Su-4029 (*e.g.*, fig. 6). These 6 amines are referred to as Group 1.

Pressor responses to Propadrine and ephedrine were blocked (*e.g.*, fig. 6). However, administration of a 10-fold dose of these 2 amines resulted in a pressor response which was indistinguishable from the rise in pressure ob-

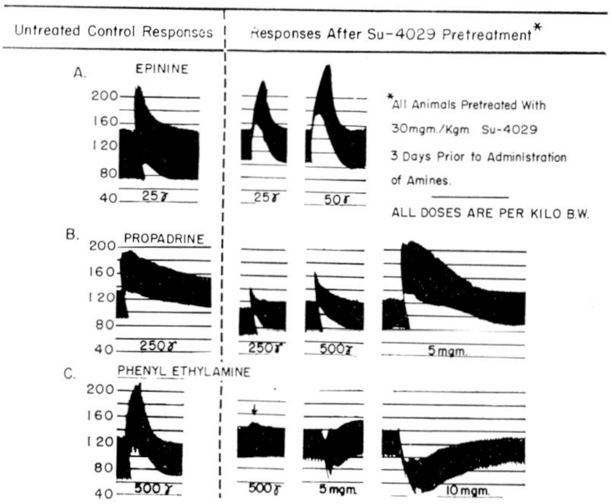

FIG. 6. Differential effect of Su-4029 pretreatment on the pressor response to several sympathomimetic pressor amines.

All drugs administered intravenously.

TABLE 1

Effect of Su-4029 on the pressor response to sympathomimetic amines

Not Blocked or Augmented (Group 1)	Reversibly Blocked (Group 2)	Irreversibly Blocked (Group 3)
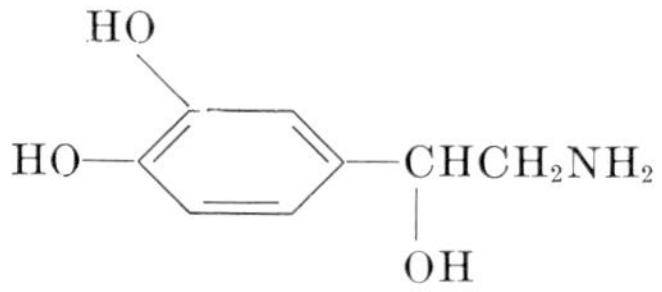 Norepinephrine		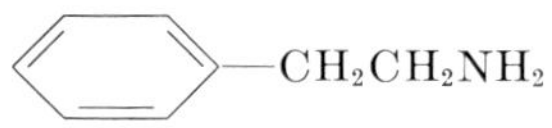 Phenylethylamine
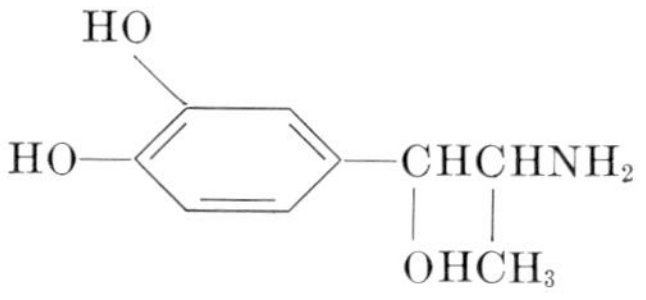 Cobefrine	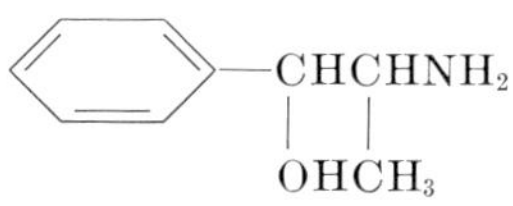 Propadrine	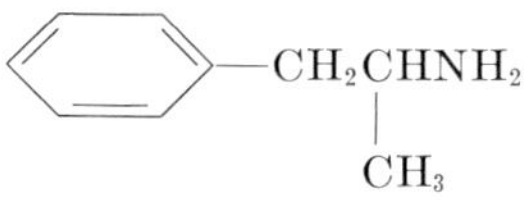 Amphetamine
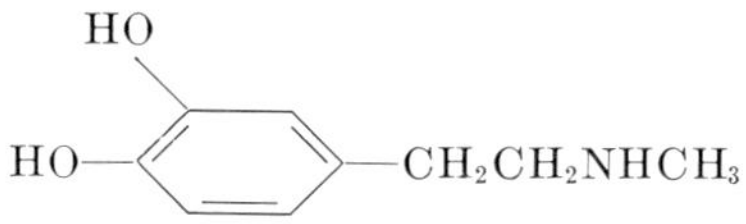 Epinine		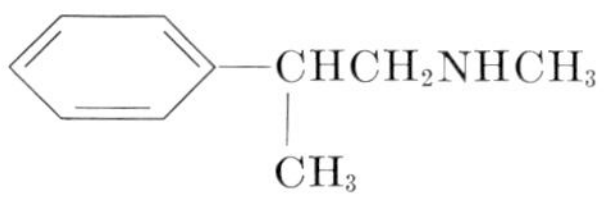 Vonedrine
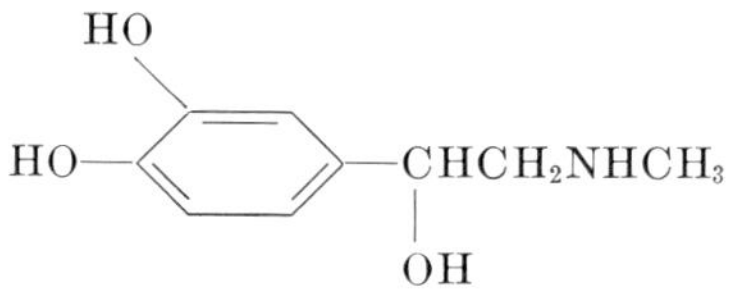 Epinephrine	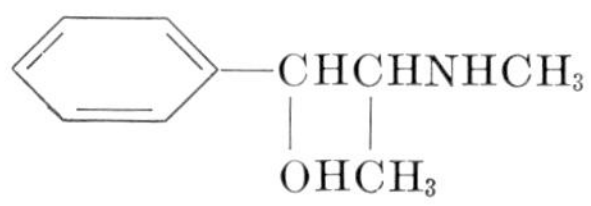 Ephedrine	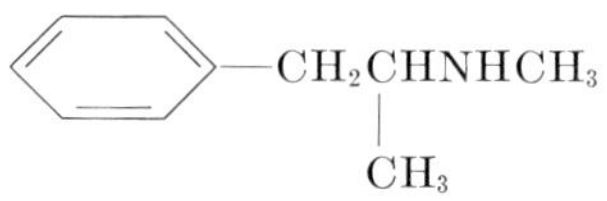 Methamphetamine
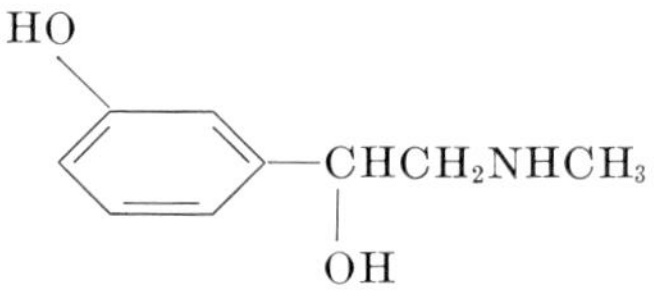 Neosynephrine		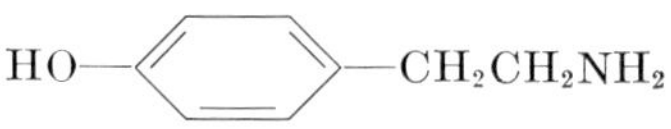 Tyramine
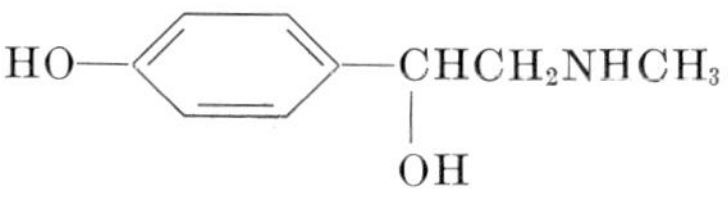 Synephrine		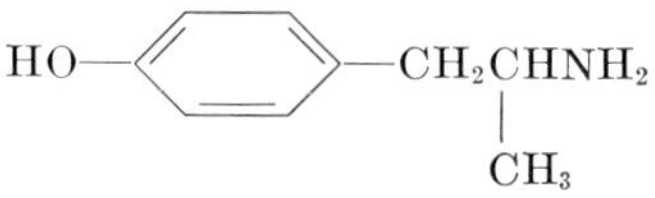 Paredrine
		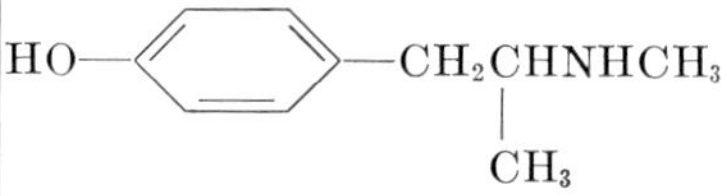 Paredrinol

served in the untreated animals (*e.g.*, fig. 6). These 2 agents comprise Group 2.

Pressor actions of phenylethylamine, amphetamine, Vonedrine, methamphetamine, tyramine, Paredrine and Paredrinol were completely blocked. Administration of 10 to 20 times the doses quoted above did not produce pressor responses but generally resulted in a depressor action (*e.g.*, fig. 6). These 7 amines are Group 3.

The amines fall into 3 structural categories (table 1). Group 1 includes compounds possessing *m* or *p* hydroxylation in the ring and compounds containing *m* or *p* hydroxylation or both on the ring plus *beta*-hydroxylation in the chain. Group 2 compounds are hydroxylated only on the *beta* carbon of the chain. Group 3 compounds have no hydroxylation or contain only a *p*-hydroxyl in the ring.

Effect of various agents on Su-4029 activity. In dogs pretreated intravenously 3 days earlier with 30 mg/kg of Su-4029, acute intravenous injections of the following agents were ineffective in altering the blocking effects of Su-4029 on carotid occlusion and amphetamine pressor responses: atropine sulfate, 1 mg/kg; choline-p-tolyl ether, 10 mg/kg; Metrazol (pentylenetetrazol), 3 mg/kg; naphazoline, 25 μg/kg; Antrenyl (oxyphenonium) 0.5 mg/kg; Prostigmin (neostigmine), 0.1 mg/kg and picrotoxin, 0.3 mg/kg.

Pretreatment with 200 mg/kg of iproniazid phosphate subcutaneously 18 hours prior to administration of 30 mg/kg of Su-4029 was effective in 3 out of 6 dogs in preventing the blockade of carotid occlusion pressor responses and partially preventing the block of amphetamine pressor responses. However, these high doses of iproniazid produced kidney damage and the combination of both drugs was lethal to 3 other animals. For this reason the study was discontinued.

Discussion. Fig. 7 is a hypothetical representation of an adrenergic motor receptor (*alpha* receptor of Ahlquist, 1948) designed only as an aid in interpreting our results. We have tried to make the structure as generalized as possible and therefore we have included a membrane barrier possessing selective permeability properties and then a series of metabolic steps interspersed between amine penetration of the membrane and the actual contractile process. Step 1 is considered to cover all biochemical actions prior to the step affected by adrenergic

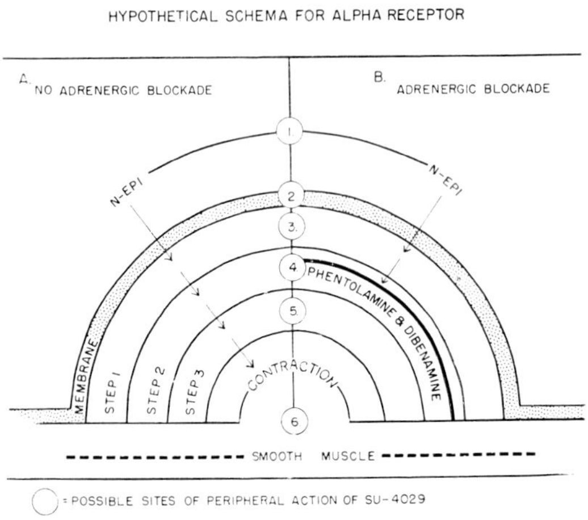

Fig. 7. Hypothetical schema for an adrenergic motor receptor.
See text for explanation.

blocking agents. Step 3 covers all biochemical actions which occur after the step affected by adrenergic blocking agents. The circled figures represent the possible sites of action of Su-4029. Site 1 represents any source of vasoactive amines, *e.g.*, adrenal medullae or nerve endings.

For the *acute* actions of Su-4029 we draw the following conclusions:

1) Since the phentolamine block of the norepinephrine pressor action is negated by Su-4029 and the blockade produced by Dibenamine is not, the action of Su-4029 is apparently not at site 5 or 6. We arrive at this conclusion because the adrenergic blocking agents phentolamine (Meier *et al.*, 1949) and Dibenamine (Nickerson and Goodman, 1947; Nickerson, 1949) are generally considered to act at the same site (Green, 1954; Goodman and Gilman, 1955; Furchgott, 1955; Fleckenstein, 1952). According to Goodman and Gilman (1955) the primary difference between the action of the *beta*-haloalkylamines, of which Dibenamine is a member, and that of other classes, which include phentolamine, is that the latter are bound to their site of action by relatively weaker forces, whereas the *beta*-haloalkylamines are attached by firm chemical bonds. If the action of Su-4029 were beyond the site of action of phentolamine and Dibenamine, the lack of a negating effect on the Dibenamine blockade is inexplicable. The relaxing action of phentolamine on the cat nictitating membrane which has been contracted by Su-4029 would also tend

to rule out a direct musculotropic action of Su-4029 at site 6.

2) It is possible that the negation of the phentolamine evoked norepinephrine blockade could be explained by Su-4029 induced release of amines from body depots, *e.g.*, nerve endings or adrenal medullae (*i.e.*, from site 1). Such a release of amines could partially counteract the blockade of phentolamine such that the subsequent introduction of exogenous norepinephrine would produce a marked rise in blood pressure. Likewise the contracting effect of Su-4029 on the cat nictitating membrane might be explained by a release of amines from depot sites. However, such an action of Su-4029 at site 1 seems unlikely since following the administration of Su-4029 the chronically denervated nictitating membrane of the cat, which is markedly hypersensitive to norepinephrine and epinephrine contracts less than the acutely denervated membrane which is relatively highly insensitive to norepinephrine. The fact that the acutely denervated membrane contracts so markedly and for such a long period is in itself evidence that the effect would require large quantities of active amines, almost certainly larger than the amount available from the nerve endings in the nictitating membrane *per se*. Furthermore, our evidence in adrenalectomized animals demonstrates that the greatest amine depots, the adrenal medullae, play only a very minor part in this Su-4029 evoked contraction of the nictitating membrane. Thus we infer that the effect of Su-4029 is probably a direct action on the receptor substance.

3) It is also possible that the negation of the phentolamine evoked norepinephrine blockade could be explained by an action of Su-4029 which increases the penetrability of norepinephrine through the membrane (site 2) or an action which increases the efficacy of norepinephrine at site 3. Actions such as this could also explain the augmented response to injected norepinephrine which occurs immediately following Su-4029 administration. However, the retraction of the cat nictitating membrane cannot be explained in this way since this is apparently due to a direct action of Su-4029. Our data do not permit us to exclude decisively such actions at site 2 and 3. The nature of the changes whether produced at site 2, 3 or 4 must be quite complex and need to explain not only the sympathetic-like actions but also the partial depression of tyramine pressor responses seen immediately after Su-4029 administration.

It has been demonstrated that the pressor response of the vascular system to norepinephrine is increased immediately after Su-4029 to a greater extent than is the sensitivity to epinephrine. Likewise, the depressor effect of epinephrine seen after relatively low doses of phentolamine is only partially reversed following a dose of Su-4029 which completely restores the pressor response to norepinephrine. This differential in restoration of norepinephrine and epinephrine pressor responses induced by Su-4029 administration during phentolamine blockade cannot be explained by a greater affinity of phentolamine for the areas of the *alpha* receptors sensitive to epinephrine than for the areas sensitive to norepinephrine since by experimentation we could not detect any large discrepancy in such affinities. However, the fact that the depressor response of isopropylarterenol is augmented by Su-4029 would indicate that *beta*-receptors (inhibitory receptors) are also sensitized. Epinephrine, as is well known, stimulates both the *alpha* and *beta* receptors. The differential in action between norepinephrine and epinephrine following Su-4029 treatment might well be explained by the double site of epinephrine action. The possibility also remains that the alterations produced by Su-4029 make *alpha* receptors in general more sensitive to the terminal-NH_2 of norepinephrine than to the —$NHCH_3$ of epinephrine.

There is a striking parallelism between the 3 classifications of pressor amine activity seen 3 days after Su-4029 administration and the classifications of amines reported by Fleckenstein and Burn (1953). These authors and Fleckenstein and Stöckle (1955) have shown that pressor amines which contract the innervated nictitating membrane fall into 3 groups when tested for their effect on the chronically denervated nictitating membranes of the cat: 1) pyrocatechol derivatives containing the structure

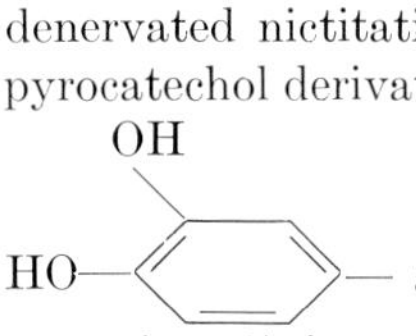

— are augmented following denervation; 2) intermediate group containing the structure

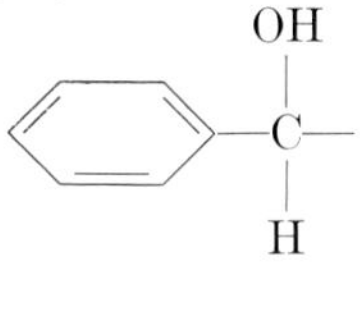

— are not significantly

affected and 3) neurosympathomimetics containing the structure 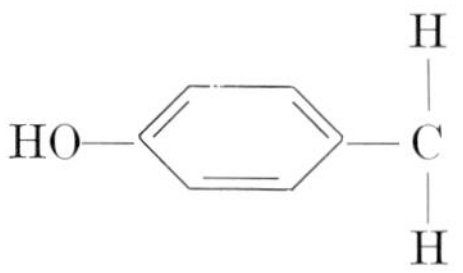 or 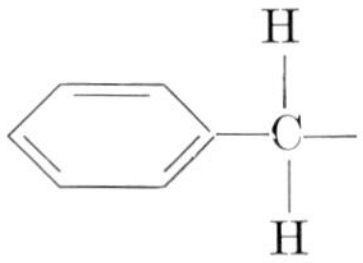 are blocked. The fact that exactly the same 3 classifications can be demonstrated following cocaine pretreatment has led Fleckenstein and Stöckle (1955) to postulate that cocaine produces a "pharmacological denervation." It is tempting to speculate that Su-4029 is also a "pharmacological denervator." However, where Fleckenstein and Stöckle (1955) have not presented evidence for an effect of cocaine on the receptor substance and explain the effects of cocaine and denervation in terms of effects on nerve functioning, we have presented evidence that the Su-4029, at least in the acute phase of its actions, affects directly those cardiovascular areas sensitive to phentolamine and Dibenamine, *i.e.*, presumably the *alpha* receptor substance. If we are permitted to assume that the long-term peripheral effects of Su-4029 are an extension of the early actions we have just discussed and to make the simplifying assumptions (1) that all 3 classes of amines attack directly the *alpha* receptors and (2) that the action of Su-4029 in the receptor substance which results in a sensitization to the amines in Group 1 is the same as that which produces a desensitization of these receptors to Group 2 and 3 amines, we can then descriptively refer to the efferent peripheral action of Su-4029 as a "deformation" of cardiovascular *alpha* receptor substance.

SUMMARY

The blockade of norepinephrine produced by the "reversible" adrenergic blocking agent phentolamine is negated by Su-4029. The blockade of norepinephrine produced by the "irreversible" blocking agent Dibenamine is not negated by Su-4029. Since phentolamine and Dibenamine are generally considered to function at the same locus in the adrenergic receptor substance these facts indicate that Su-4029 may have an action in the substance of the *alpha* receptors and that it may be at the same site as that affected by Dibenamine and phentolamine. The responses to a series of pressor phenylalkylamines following Su-4029 pretreatment fall into 3 categories: 1) irreversibly blocked are the amines with no or only *p*-hydroxylation; 2) reversibly blocked are the amines with hydroxylation on the carbon adjacent to the ring, *i.e.*, the *beta* carbon; and 3) not blocked or augmented are the amines with *m* and *p*-hydroxylation or *m* or *p* plus *beta*-hydroxylation. It is suggested that part of the action, at least, of Su-4029 is to "deform" that portion of the *alpha* receptor substance which is affected by adrenergic blocking agents such as phentolamine and Dibenamine.

REFERENCES

Ahlquist, R. P.: Amer. J. Physiol. **153:** 586, 1948.

Anderson, F. F.: J. Lab. clin. Med. **26:** 1520, 1941.

Fleckenstein, A.: Brit. J. Pharmacol. **7:** 553, 1952.

Fleckenstein, A. and Burn, J. H.: Brit. J. Pharmacol. **8:** 69, 1953.

Fleckenstein, A. and Stöckle, D.: Arch. exp. Path. Pharmak. **224:** 401, 1955.

Furchgott, R. F.: Pharm. Rev. **7:** 183, 1955.

Goodman, L. and Gilman, A.: The Pharmacological Basis of Therapeutics, 2nd ed., The Macmillan Company, New York, 1955.

Green, H. D.: Pharmacology in Medicine, Drill, V. A., ed., McGraw Hill Company, New York, 1954.

Maxwell, R. A., Ross, S. and Plummer, A. J.: This Journal **123:** 128, 1958.

Meier, R., Yonkman, F. F., Craver, B. N. and Gross, F.: Proc. Soc. exp. Biol., N.Y. **71:** 70, 1949.

Mull, R. P., Maxwell, R. A. and Plummer, A. J.: Nature, **180:** 1200, 1957.

Nickerson, M.: This Journal **95** II: 27, 1949.

Nickerson, M. and Goodman, L. S.: This Journal **89:** 167, 1947.

8069

THE EFFECT OF ATROPINE UPON MAMMALIAN STRIATED MUSCLE

CAROLINE TUM-SUDEN

Neurology Branch, U. S. Army Chemical Warfare Laboratories, Army Chemical Center, Maryland

Received for publication March 31, 1958

The insusceptibility of the neuromuscular junction in mammalian striated muscle to atropine under experimental conditions (Duke-Elder and Duke-Elder, 1930; Simonart and Simonart, 1935a, b; Dale *et al.*, 1935) suggested a situation similar in some respects to that encountered in demonstrating the response of this junction to acetylcholine. As shown by Brown *et al.* (1936), the neuromuscular junction responds to small doses of acetylcholine injected intraarterially but not to moderate amounts given intravenously. It was decided, therefore, to reinvestigate the problem using relatively close intraarterial injections for the administration of atropine to nerve-muscle preparations of the dog and cat. For the preliminary studies, the extrinsic ocular muscle was chosen because of its reputed similarity to striated muscle of the lower vertebrates with respect to drug reactions (Duke-Elder and Duke-Elder, 1930). To confirm occasional reports of the competitive action of atropine upon striated muscle response to nerve stimulation, the study was extended to include typical skeletal muscle of the dog, cat and monkey (Feng, 1936; Brown, 1937; Hougs and Andersen, 1954).

METHODS. By a lateral approach, the inferior oblique muscle and its nerve were isolated with every precaution to preserve the circulation, in a series of 30 dogs. The isotonic contractions (50 to 70% of maximum) were recorded kymographically in response to repetitive pulses delivered from a Grass Stimulator and applied at a frequency of from 0.5 to 2/sec.

All drugs were injected by way of the cannulated central stump of the temporal or lingual artery into the uninterrupted peripheral distribution of the external carotid artery. For comparative purposes the effect of acetylcholine (ACh) was observed before and at intervals after the injection of atropine sulfate. In some preparations ACh was given during omission of the stimulus as well.

In the preparations of the anterior tibial muscle of 20 dogs, 9 cats and 6 monkeys only the tendinous portion was exposed for kymographic recording of the isometric contractions in response to stimulation of the peroneal nerve similar to that in the ocular preparation. All accessory side branches in the vicinity of the popliteal artery were ligated except the posterior femoral artery which was cannulated for drug administration. To avoid unpredictable variations and to increase the sensitivity as advised by Brown (1937, 1938), the central circulation was occluded temporarily during injection. In agreement with the latter's advice and observations, this technique in itself did not produce any immediate and significant change in muscle activity but enhanced the response to rapid injections of small volumes of the drugs. Consequently in the skeletal muscle preparations the injections constituted relatively close rather than relatively distant arterial injections which anatomical conditions imposed upon the ocular muscle preparations.

All doses were on a per kilogram basis and in concentrations such that the total volume injected for the usual doses of atropine employed (0.1 to 2.0 mg) ranged around 0.5 ml, followed immediately by a saline wash injection. Saline control injections, which were without effect, were run initially and frequently during the course of each experiment as a check on the injection system. In both preparations the blood pressure was recorded manometrically.

RESULTS. *Inferior oblique muscle.* Upon injection of atropine, 1 to 5 mg/kg, the maximum reduction in twitch amplitude, amounting to 20 to 80%, was attained within 10 to 15 sec of the injection and was roughly proportional to the dose. The degree of inhibition varied widely from preparation to preparation, but for complete block of all response to nerve stimulation dosages around 10 mg/kg were required. With such amounts recovery was prolonged, but with doses in the range of 1 to 5 mg/kg an apparently complete recovery was attained within 1 to 2 min. However, repeated injections of atropine increased the duration and magnitude of block although apparent recovery from a previous injection had been established and maintained for many minutes (residual effect). Intervals of 30 to 60 min between injections were required to obtain comparable effects from the same dose (fig. 1).

Amounts of atropine which had little or no effect upon the indirect response to electrical stimulation readily inhibited the typical brief, tetanic contraction in response to the injection of ACh (10 to 50 μg/kg). In contrast to the apparent brief action of atropine upon muscle response to nerve stimulation the time required for recovery of the ACh contraction after atropine block was 30 to 60 min, a period of time which closely coincided with that of its residual effect upon transmission (fig. 1A).

Anterior tibialis muscle. The characteristics of atropine inhibition of typical skeletal muscle response to nerve stimulation were the same as observed for the extraocular muscle. The sensitivities cannot be compared because of the distance factor for the intraarterial injection sites, but it seemed that any difference with respect to atropine was much smaller than that which obtained for ACh.

At the routine stimulus frequency of 0.5/sec, injections of atropine into the reduced and temporarily occluded circulation to the tibial muscle group inhibited the indirect response at times as much as 30% with dosages of 100 μg/kg and up to 98% with doses of 1 and 2 mg/kg. The average sensitivity of the muscle to atropine block under experimental conditions is presented in fig. 2. Although the deviations ranged from 9.0 to 17.26%, the individual variability seemed much less than that reported by others (Luco and Altamirano, 1943). In an isolated preparation of the anterior tibial muscle the effective doses were about one-half those obtained above. Furthermore, at higher frequencies of stimulation sensitivity to atropine increased. During partial tetanus at a frequency of 50/sec, 25 μg/kg of atropine briefly abolished the signs of individual twitch and lowered the over-all height of the tetanic plateau (fig. 3). At 5 per sec, a substantial block occurred with 50 μg/kg. The speed of apparent recovery from atropine block and the duration of a residual effect for up to an hour in typical skeletal muscle are comparable to those observed in the extraocular muscle preparation. Likewise, atropine inhibition of the effect of from

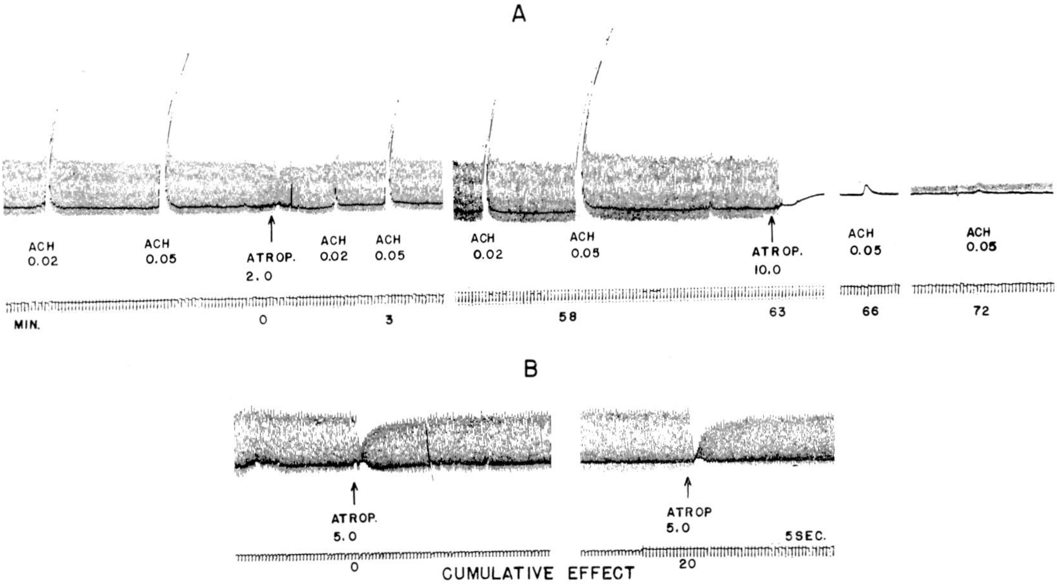

FIG. 1. Atropine block of cholinergic responses of striated ocular muscle (dog).

A. Showing a small and fleeting effect of atropine (2.0 mg/kg) upon response to nerve stimulation at 0-time; compare with the effect upon the response to injected ACh. Duration ACh antagonism, 58 min. At 63 min from 0-time injection of 10 mg/kg of atropine eliminated all response to nerve stimulation; maximum effect upon ACh delayed.

B. Atropine inhibition of the response to nerve stimulation showing the cumulative (residual) effect upon repeating the initial injection (5 mg/kg) 20 min later.

Stimulus to nerve at 0.5/sec; dosages, mg/kg, intraarterial.

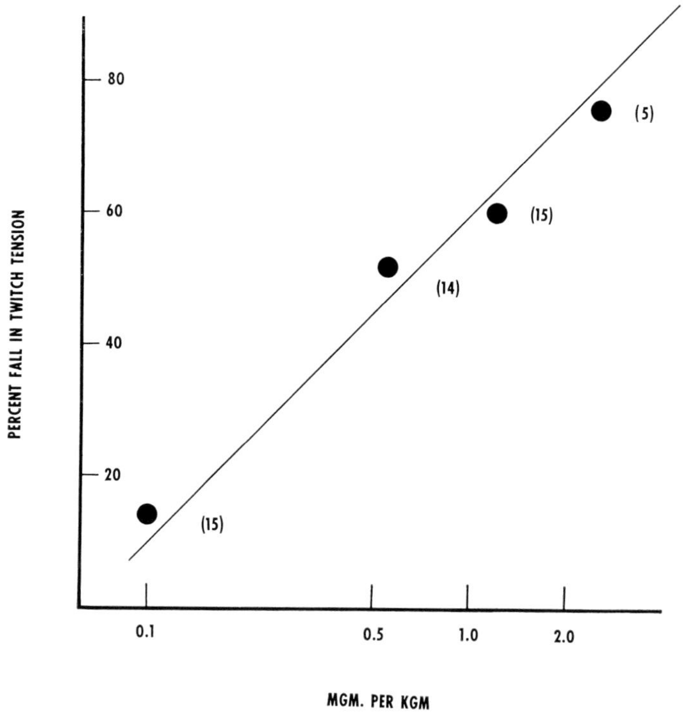

FIG. 2. Average % reduction of the indirect response of skeletal muscle (dog) following intraarterial injections of atropine in amounts ranging from 0.1 to 2.0 mg/kg.

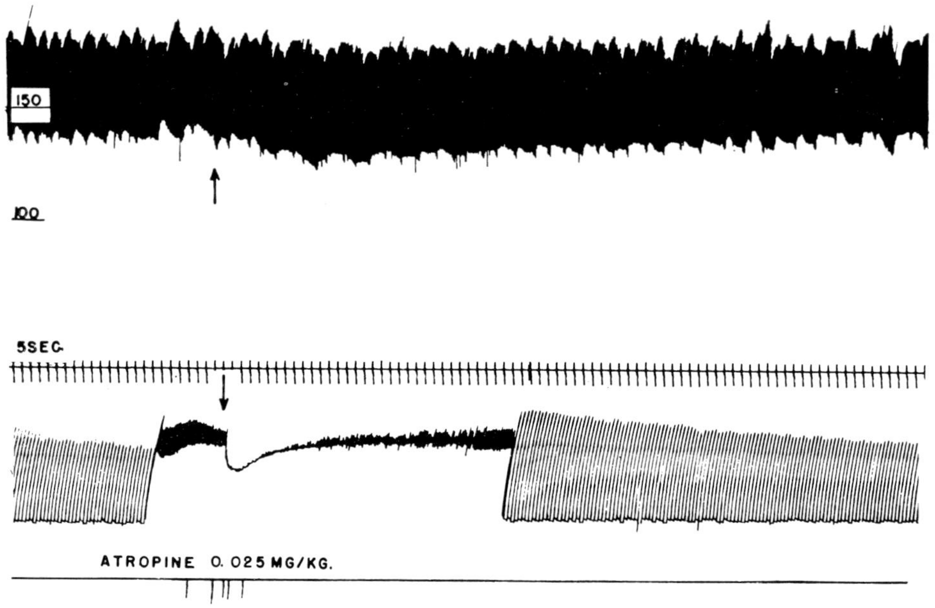

FIG. 3. Atropine effect on anterior tibial muscle response to nerve stimulation at 50/sec. At arrow, injection of 0.025 mg/kg atropine, intraarterially. Recovery practically complete in 2½ to 3 min from time of injection. Upper record, blood pressure.

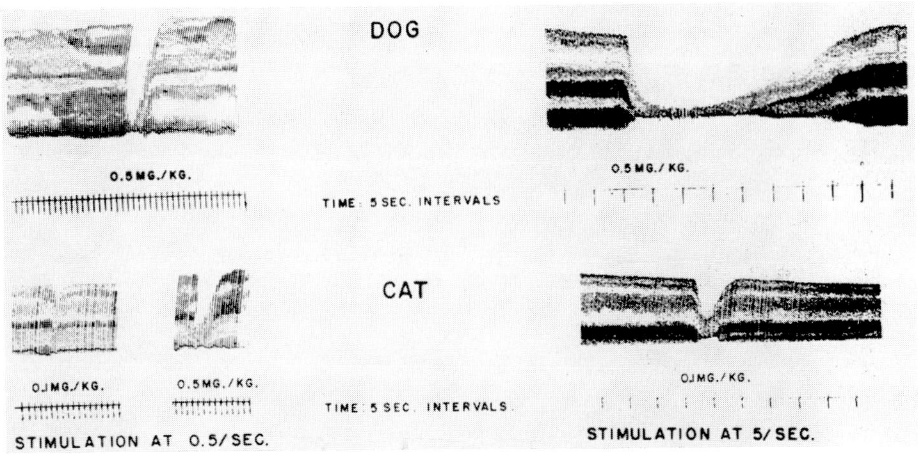

FIG. 4. Atropine block of transmission in mammalian skeletal muscle. Intraarterial injections; anterior tibialis preparations in the dog and cat.

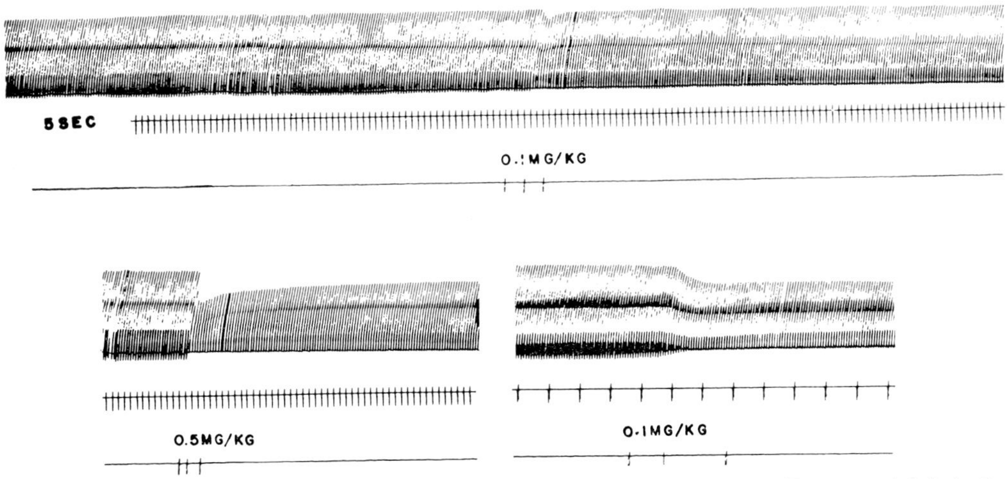

FIG. 5. Atropine block of transmission in mammalian skeletal muscle. Intraarterial injections. Anterior tibialis preparation in the monkey (*Rhesus macacus*). Second signal, time of injection.

5 to 100 µg/kg of ACh confirmed the fact that antagonism of exogenous ACh was evident for more than half an hour after twitch tension had regained control levels.

In the cat and monkey (*Rhesus macacus*), the effect of atropine upon the indirect response did not differ significantly from that of the dog, but in the monkey the poor condition of the animals did not permit a thorough study (fig. 4, 5).

Effect of anticholinesterase. In 2 pilot experiments on dogs recovering from large doses of isopropyl methylphosphonofluoridate (Sarin, GB), the response of the ocular muscle to nerve stimulation returned. Following atropine, however, it was noted that recovery from inhibition was abnormally prolonged. Therefore, the effect of atropine upon transmission in skeletal muscle after potentiating doses of eserine, isofluorophate (diisopropyl fluorophosphate, DFP) and GB was observed in 3 or 4 experiments each using the following dosages per kg: 0.5 to 2.0 mg of eserine; 100 µg of DFP; and 3 to 10 µg of GB. After potentiation of the indirect response was established, atropine was injected in amounts of 1 to 2 mg/kg. The immediate fall in tension was equal to and occasionally greater than that in the untreated muscle. However, the striking and consistent difference was the abrupt termination of the rapid recovery phase at a level significantly lower than that of the potentiated twitch heights.

The twitch tension then remained depressed for minutes (figs. 6, 7). The time for complete recovery to the potentiated control level required from 30 to 60 min after 1 to 2 mg/kg of atropine in contrast to the untreated muscle. An injection of atropine 1 or 2 hours later upon recovery from eserine, again produced a typical brief block as in the untreated muscle. In preparations receiving GB or DFP, atropine inhibition displaying the two phases of block could be reproduced upon *complete* recovery from the first injection of atropine, that is, after an interval of about 1 hour.

In all experiments of this group, following the administration of potentiating amounts of one of the anticholinesterases, the inhibitory effect of atropine upon the neuromuscular junction was enhanced, as evidenced by delayed recovery. The effect was apparently a manifestation of atropine antagonism of excess ACh rather than any direct increase in sensitivity of the neuromuscular junction as it corresponded in time with the periods in which the cumulative action of atropine was demonstrable in both skeletal and ocular muscle.

Further substantiation of an increased response to atropine block after an injection of any one of the anticholinesterases was noted upon *intravenous* injection. In 7 preparations an average fall of 19% in twitch tension occurred in response to 10 mg/kg of atropine, an amount ineffective upon transmission in normal skeletal muscle.

DISCUSSION. The difference between atropine antagonism of endogenous and exogenous ACh at the neuromuscular junction in striated muscle appears to be primarily a matter of accessibility of the drug to the transmitting substance according to the so-called "Proximity Theory" of Dale (Dale and Gaddum, 1930; Dale *et al.*, 1936).

Brief atropine block of the response of mammalian striated muscle to nerve stimulation is demonstrable upon intraarterial injection in proportion to the amount given and in dosages which are pharmacologically significant, but not deleterious to the animal. The residual action of atropine upon the muscle response to nerve stimulation, the depression of the reaction to injected ACh, and the reduction of the indirect response after potentiation by anticholinesterase for a similar period of time all indicate the speci-

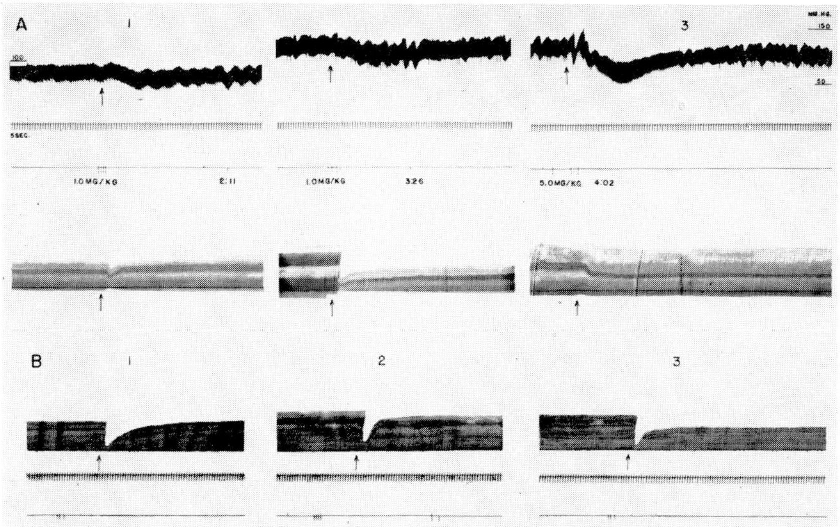

FIG. 6. Effect of sarin (GB) and of DFP on atropine block of striated muscle in the dog.

In A, the inhibitory effect of 1.0 mg/kg of atropine, intraarterially, upon the muscle response to nerve stimulation is shown in the column on the left and is to be compared with the prolonged effect obtained after potentiation of the twitch response following intraarterial injection of 0.01 mg/kg of GB (middle column). GB injected during interval between columns 1 and 2. On the right is shown a slight inhibitory effect of 5.0 mg/kg of atropine, given intravenously after potentiation, an amount ineffective in normal muscle. Top row, blood pressure; lower row, myogram.

In B, the myograms in the left and middle columns show the effects of atropine before and after a potentiating dose of DFP (0.1 mg/kg.) Column on the right shows the cumulative effect of a third injection. Intervals between injections, 35 to 40 min.

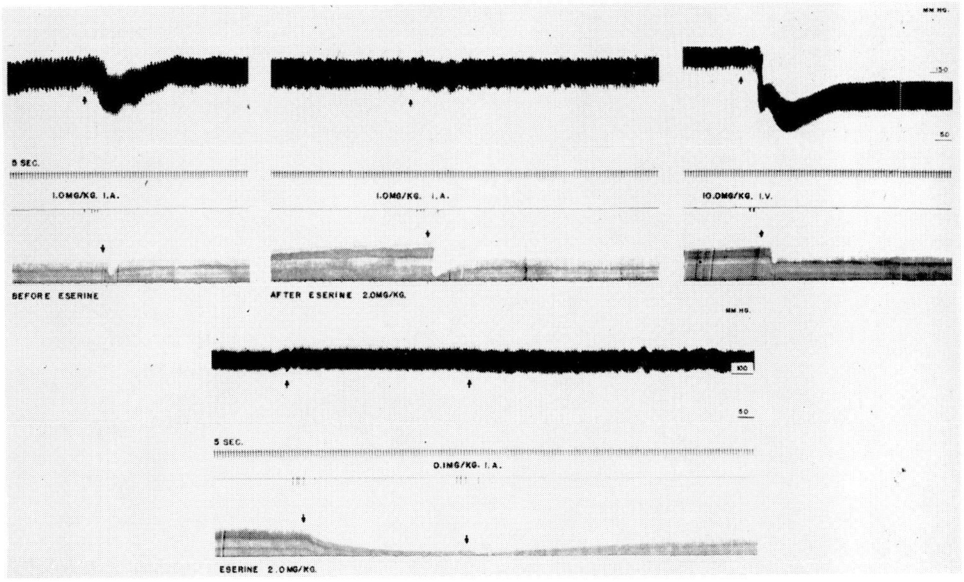

FIG. 7. Atropine inhibition of the dog anterior tibial muscle response to nerve stimulation before and after eserine.

As in fig. 6, the middle column of upper record shows the increased duration and degree of atropine block during potentiation of the twitch response upon recovery from a depressant amount of eserine. On the right is shown atropine inhibition upon intravenous injection of 10 mg/kg, an amount ineffective in preparations not receiving an anticholinesterase. Maximum fall in twitch tension precedes that of the blood pressure (upper row).

Lower record shows the inhibitory effect of 0.1 mg/kg of atropine injected intraarterially during eserine depression of the twitch response.

ficity of the competitive effect of atropine upon this cholinergic junction. In support of this viewpoint, studies of the reaction of voluntary muscle to ACh, whether the response to ACh was elicited peripherally or centrally, at spinal or at cortical levels, have all shown that the duration of atropine block lasted about 1 hour (Brown, 1937; Abdon, 1940; McKail *et al.*, 1940–41; Calma and Wright, 1944–45). The time course of atropine-ACh competition in muscle so reported also agrees with that disclosed by atropine assays in muscle and studies on atropine metabolism (Tønnesen, 1948; Goslin *et al.*, 1955; Evertsbusch and Geiling, 1956).

Previous failures to obtain conclusive evidence of atropine block of the response to nerve stimulation in somatic muscle may be attributed in part to the failure to recognize its prompt and brief action. Abdon (1940–41) allowed 15 to 45 min to elapse before testing the indirect response in the intact, atropinized rabbit and frog. In both species he was unable to confirm Brown (1937), who obtained an inhibition of the response to nerve stimulation after close intraarterial injection of 100 mg of atropine in the gastrocnemius preparation of the frog. By rough calculation, the effective atropine dosage per kg for the frog according to the figures, 100 μg/100–200 g body weight, was around 0.5 to 1.0 mg/kg. This dosage produced 50 to 70% reduction in twitch tension of the dog tibial muscle. As the dosages are of the same order of magnitude, there may not be as marked a difference in atropine susceptibility of the neuromuscular junction in different striated muscles as there is to ACh and the relative ease with which it is antagonized.

It is of interest to note that by adapting the methods used on the experimental animal by Brown (1936, 1937) to elicit ACh responses and utilized in this study to demonstrate atropine inhibition of transmission in striated muscle, Ward and Jager (personal communication) and Grob and Harvey (personal communication) have demonstrated pharmacologic effects of atropine upon the motor end-plate of the muscles of the arm in man.

SUMMARY

In isometric preparations of the tibialis anticus muscle of the cat, dog and monkey, relatively close intraarterial injections of atropine produce an immediate and transient inhibition of the response of voluntary muscle to nerve stimulation. Sensitivity varies widely, 1 to 2 mg/kg producing 50 to 100% block.

Following the recovery of the response to nerve stimulation the residual amount of atropine in muscle exerts a cumulative action up to 30 min or longer. Inhibition of the reaction to injected ACh is demonstrable during this period of time after the apparent recovery of the response to nerve stimulation.

After injection of potentiating amounts of one of the anticholinesterase agents the manifestation of atropine block is greatly prolonged, namely for a period of 30 to 60 min, in contrast to 1 or 2 min in the normal muscle.

The minimal, effective, intraarterial dosages of atropine to block the responses to nerve stimulation at frequencies of 50/sec, 5/sec, and 0.5/sec are respectively 25 mg/kg, 50 mg/kg and 100 mg/kg in normal muscle.

After a potentiating amount of an anticholinesterase 10 mg/kg of atropine *intravenously* exerts a slight inhibitory effect.

In isotonic preparations of the normal striated ocular muscles the responses to nerve stimulation and to ACh are inhibited similarly as in skeletal muscle by relatively distant intraarterial injections of atropine.

The results do not indicate any great difference in the susceptibility to atropine inhibition of the responses to nerve stimulation in typical and in atypical mammalian striated muscle such as obtained with respect to *injected* ACh.

ACKNOWLEDGMENT. The author is indebted to Dr. A. S. Marrazzi and to Dr. E. Ross Hart for suggesting this study and for their kindly interest in the problem.

REFERENCES

ABDON, N. C.: Acta physiol. scand. **1:** 153, 1940.
BROWN, G. L., DALE, H. H. AND FELDBERG, W. J.: J. Physiol. **87:** 394, 1936.
BROWN, G. L.: J. Physiol. **89:** 438, 1937.
BROWN, G. L.: J. Physiol. **92:** 22P, 1938.
CALMA, I. AND WRIGHT, S.: J. Physiol. **103:** 93, 1944–45.
DALE, H. H. AND GADDUM, J. H.: J. Physiol. **70:** 109, 1930.
DALE, H. H., FELDBERG, W. J. AND VOGT, A. M.: J. Physiol. **86:** 353, 1936.
DUKE-ELDER, E. S. AND DUKE-ELDER, P. M.: Proc. roy. Soc. London B **107:** 332, 1930.
EVERTSBUSCH, V. AND GEILING, E. M. K.: Arch. int. Pharmocodyn. **115:** 175, 1956.
FENG, T. P.: Chin. J. Physiol. **10:** 513, 1936.
GOSLIN, R. N., CABOUREL, J. D., KALSER, S. C. AND WILLS, J. H.: THIS JOURNAL **115:** 217, 1955.
HOUGS, W. AND ANDERSEN, E. W.: Acta pharm. tox. Kbh., **10:** 227, 1954.
LUCO, G. V. AND ALTAMIRANO, M.: Amer. J. Physiol. **139:** 520, 1943.
MCKAIL, R. A., OBRADOR, S. AND WILSON, W. C.: J. Physiol. **99:** 312, 1940–41.
SIMONART, A. AND SIMONART, E.: Arch. int. Pharmacodyn. **49:** 302, 1935a.
SIMONART, A. AND SIMONART, E.: Arch. int. Pharmacodyn. **51:** 76, 1935b.
TØNNESEN, MOGENS: Acta pharm. tox. Kbh., **4:** 367, 1948.

8070

THE EFFECT OF ATROPINE UPON SKELETAL MUSCLE IN THE GOAT WITH MYOTONIA CONGENITA

CAROLINE TUM-SUDEN AND ROBERT M. STOUFER

Neurology Branch, Clinical Research Division, U. S. Army Chemical Warfare Laboratories, Army Chemical Center, Maryland

Received for publication March 31, 1958

The donation of a small herd of goats with varying degrees of myotonia congenita provided an opportunity to investigate the susceptibility to atropine of mammalian muscle with an inherent supersensitivity to acetylcholine (ACh).

According to current concepts of the fundamental defect in myotonia, the abnormality resides in heightened irritability of the muscle fiber's membrane (Brown and Harvey, 1939; Buchtal and Clemmensen, 1941; Sanderson and Adey, 1952; Walton, 1952; Norris and Chatfield, 1955; Floyd *et al.*, 1955; Geschwind and Simpson, 1955) and not in abnormalities of the components of the cholinergic system (Poncher and Wade, 1939). Consequently, there has been little interest in the reactions of the myotonic muscle to atropine, especially since that drug has been shown to be of little clinical value (Kechsner and Finesilver, 1924–25; Bremer and Mage, 1929; Lanari, 1936, 1939; Kolb, 1938; Garai, 1954).

As the reactivity of an effector to ACh has been considered to be a determinant of the ability of atropine to inhibit the response to exogenous (injected) ACh and, by inference, to endogenous ACh liberated by nerve (Abdon, 1940; Luco and Altamirano, 1943), it was of interest to find out whether there is any correlation between the sensitivity of the myotonic muscle to ACh and its susceptibility to atropine.

METHODS. Essentially the same preparation, procedures and saline controls were employed as in previous experiments (tum-Suden, 1958), for comparison of the effects of intraarterial injections of atropine upon repeated isometric contractions of the tibial group of muscles in the myotonic goat (7 experiments) with that of the normal goat (11 experiments).

Surgical anesthesia was induced by intraperitoneal injection of 45 to 50 mg/kg of pentobarbital sodium followed after an hour by a slow intravenous injection of 1.2 mg/kg of 15% sodium barbital. This procedure, together with manometric recording of the blood pressure, helped to detect and control rumen stasis and the development of circulatory embarrassment in the recumbent, anesthetized goat. All injections of experimental drugs were given intraarterially upon a per kilogram basis.

In addition to routine study of the twitch response to low frequencies of stimulation (0.2 and 0.5/sec), the tetanus elicited by a frequency of 50/sec for a period of 5 sec was recorded at intervals of about 15 min. Occasionally a single pair of 5-sec tetani were tested 5 min apart. By means of Adrian-Bronk type concentric electrodes, the muscle potentials evoked by tetanic activation were led directly to a Grass (P5) Preamplifier for single-ended amplification and thence displayed upon a Dumont 322 Type Oscilloscope. Photographic recordings were made at a film speed of 100 mm per sec. As in the study of the extraocular skeletal muscle preparations of the dog (tum-Suden, 1958), the changes in response to injections of acetylcholine and of atropine after anticholinesterase were checked.

Attempts were made to demonstrate the immediate effect of intravenous administration of atropine upon the clinical state of the unanesthetized, myotonic goat. The speed and degree of the "warm-up" phenomenon (Kolb, 1938) after periods of monitored rest and the changes in the ability of the goats to take a low (6 to 9 inch) jump were observed before and after atropine over a period of 6 weeks.

Assays were conducted on the muscle for cholinesterase activity. The entire anterior tibial muscle of the opposite leg was removed immediately after induction of surgical anesthesia and analyzed by the colorimetric method of Hestrin (1949) as adapted by Fleischer (1954) and Harrison (unpublished).

RESULTS. *Twitch.* Atropine had the same inhibitory effect on twitch responses in goats, whether myotonic or normal, that it had in species studied previously (tum-Suden, 1958) and was not

TABLE 1

The effect of intraarterial injections of atropine upon the response of skeletal muscle to nerve stimulation in the myotonic goat compared to that of the normal goat and of the normal dog

Average Per Cent Fall in Twitch Tension

Atropine mg per kg	Myotonic goat %	S.D.	#	Normal goat %	S.D.	#	Normal dog %	S.D.	#
0.1	11.1	± 10.15	(3)	9.3	± 6.08	(4)	13.6	± 9.00	(10)
0.2	24.7	± 12.39	(4)	19.4	± 10.25	(5)	—		
0.5	48.2	± 12.32	(6)	41.5	± 16.34	(7)	51.0	± 12.84	(15)
1.0	66.9	± 8.90	(7)	64.4	± 11.45	(11)	63.0	± 17.26	(14)
2.0	—			—			78.0	± 12.90	(5)

Regression Curves

Myotonic goat $y = 65.14 + 60.50 \log x$.

Normal goat $y = 62.64 + 60.22 \log x$.

Normal dog $y = 66.26 + 56.33 \log x$.

Average Time for Approximately 100% Recovery

Atropine mg/kg	Normal	Myotonic
0.1	25″	25″
0.25	42″	35″
0.5	6′	4′
1.0	10′	10′

attributable either to the saline injected or to the method of injection. The average per cent inhibition of twitch tension and the approximate times for recovery for the dosage range used are given in table 1. The weighted regression curves for the average per cent reduction in twitch amplitude for this range of doses are given in fig. 1. Cumulative effects of atropine were also conspicuous in these muscles.

Tetanus. In each of two experiments, the differences between the normal and the myotonic goat muscle responses to 5-sec tetanization of the nerve at frequencies of 50 per sec were essentially the same as described by Brown and Harvey (1939). The myotonic muscle as compared to the normal showed more evidence of treppe, no decline of the plateau during stimulation and delayed relaxation up to 30 sec. During the initial 2 to 3 sec of stimulation, a volley of irregular, asynchronous potentials was superimposed upon the rhythmic polyphasic electrical response which gradually subsided towards the end of the period of stimulation, at which time the pattern of the electrical effect resembled that of the normal discharge.

Within 30 to 50 sec of an intraarterial injection of atropine (0.5 or 1.0 mg/kg) the initial tension attained during tetanization of the *normal* muscle was reduced and rapidly declined to a much lower level than before injection. The mechanical change was accompanied by some reduction in the amplitude of the potentials. Periodic tests showed that the effect of atropine was not eliminated completely until nearly one hour later (fig. 3A).

Under the same experimental conditions there was little if any change in the amplitude of the mechanical contraction of the *myotonic* muscle. Treppe or a slow, continued rise in tension occurred during stimulation. On the cessation of the stimulus, however, inhibition due to atropine was evidenced by the observation that relaxation was greatly accelerated. In the electromyogram the initial volley of extraneous potentials was reduced greatly in degree and duration. Within 0.3 sec, or less, a simple polyphasic potential pattern was established, similar to the normal discharge. As in the normal muscle, about one hour was required to eliminate the mechanical and electrical signs of atropine block (fig. 2, 3A).

Acetylcholine reactions. Acetylcholine (ACh), 1 μg and 10 μg/kg, was much more effective in the myotonic goat preparations than in the normal preparations. When injected intraarterially during continual indirect activation of the muscle at frequencies of 0.5/sec, the amplitude of the ACh contraction of the myotonic muscle not only approached the maximum twitch tension but lasted up to 30 sec compared to the brief response in the normal goat muscle. The differential sensitivity to ACh in these preparations was not diminished by continued activation of the myotonic muscle at frequencies of 0.5 per sec and at intensities near maximum. Moreover, in the 6 goats receiving ACh the clinical symptoms ranged from minimum to severe, so that the dosages used did not disclose any correlation between the sensitivity to ACh and the degree of myotonia. Following 1.0 mg/kg of atropine, the response to ACh was inhibited electrically and mechanically for 30 min or more (fig. 4).

Anticholinesterase reactions. After the intraarterial administration of 0.1 mg/kg of diisopropyl fluorophosphate (DFP) or 0.025 to 0.15 mg/kg of eserine the duration of atropine inhibition of the response to repetitive nerve stimulation was prolonged up to 30 to 60 min in myotonic and in normal preparations. Both showed the same features as seen in the skeletal muscle preparation

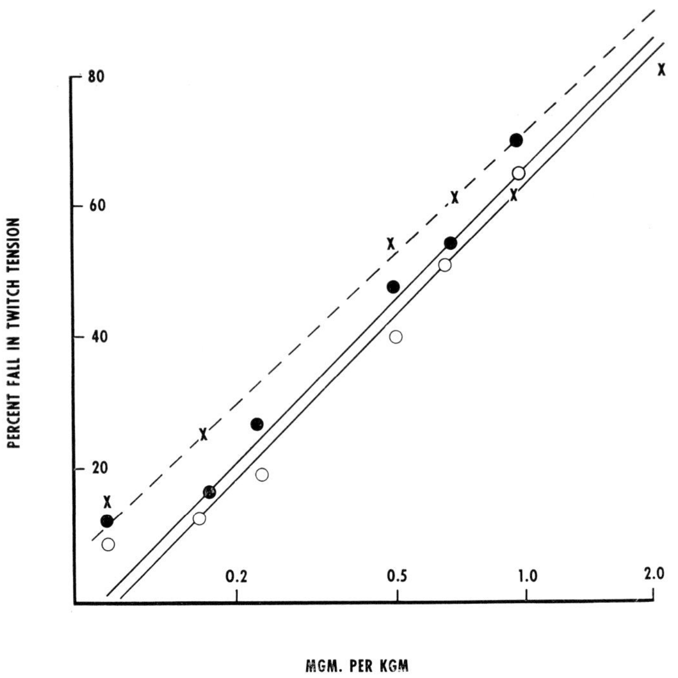

FIG. 1. Comparison of the dose response of the anterior tibial muscle preparation of the normal goat with that of the myotonic goat and normal dog to intraarterial injections of atropine.

Ordinate: Per cent loss of twitch tension; abscissa mg/kg atropine sulfate. Symbols: × = normal dog; ○ = normal goat; ● = myotonic goat.

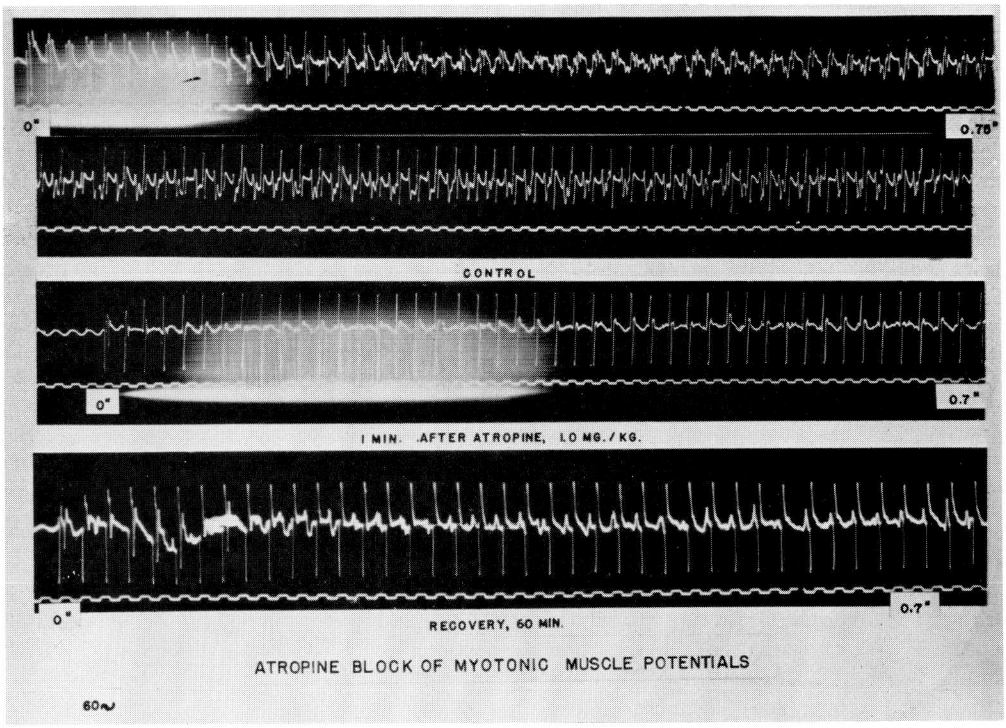

FIG. 2. Electromyogram of myotonic goat muscle at the onset of 5 sec tetanus; stimulation through nerve at 50 per sec.

Before injection note the extraneous, asynchronous potentials which persist for more than 2 sec (lower strip of control record) and compare with the regularity of the electrical pattern after the injection of 1.0 mg/kg atropine. Note the marked reduction of the extraneous potentials, the increase in spike amplitudes and the duration of atropine inhibition.

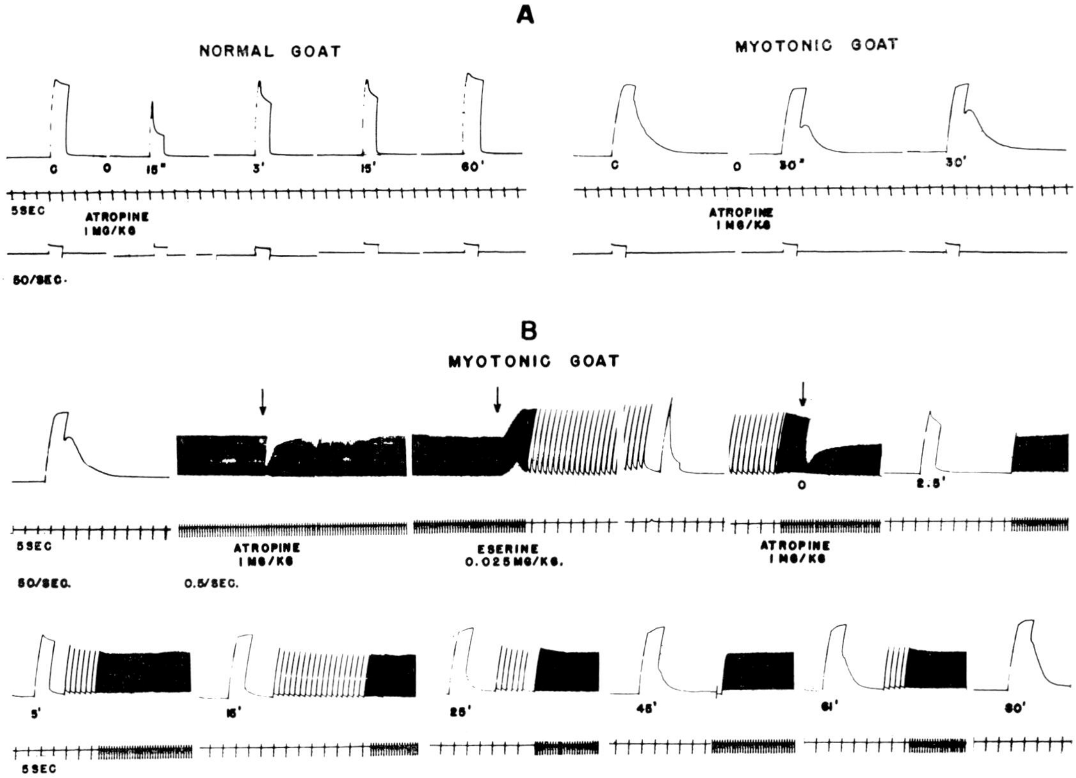

FIG. 3. A. Effect of intraarterial atropine upon the responses of the normal and myotonic muscle activated through nerve at 50/sec for 5 seconds.
B. Effect of intraarterial atropine upon the responses of myotonic muscle activated through nerve at 0.5 and at 50/sec after potentiation of the indirect response by eserine.

of the dog. The results of these few experiments are given in table 2 for ease of comparison.

The enhancement of atropine block after some inactivation of muscle cholinesterase (ChE) in the experiments employing repetitive twitch technique was substantiated also for the tetanized eserinized muscle in one experiment. Atropine (1.0 mg/kg) shortened the relaxation time by 60% in the untreated myotonic preparation. After eserine followed by atropine, however, the response to stimulation at 50/sec was like the normal, showing rapid and complete relaxation on cessation of the stimuli and the small decline in tension like the normal during the period of stimulation. During the ensuing 70 min, relaxation gradually became more delayed and treppe more prominent (fig. 3B).

The aggravation of symptoms in myotonia congenita as reported clinically upon administration of Prostigmin (neostigmine) and similar pharmacological agents (Kennedy and Wolf, 1937; Kolb, 1938) was evident in the reactions of the myotonic preparations to eserine and to DFP. The potentiation of the twitch tension after 0.1 mg/kg intraarterially of DFP was consistently greater than that observed in the normal goat muscle preparation. Twitch responses were superimposed upon an initial tetanic type of contraction which was not present in the normal goat and dog myograms upon injection of anticholinesterase. When eserine was given to effect potentiation in the experiments on the myotonic goat, the amounts required to produce marked potentiation were at most one-half those required by the normal muscle (table 2).

Muscle cholinesterase determinations. The analyses of the specimens of the distal half of the hamstring muscles and of the entire anterior tibial muscles of the normal goat and of the myotonic goat were made by Dr. B. Harrison. The results showed no difference between the normal goat muscle and that of the myotonic goat muscle in the values for % hydrolysis attained after 60 min (table 3).

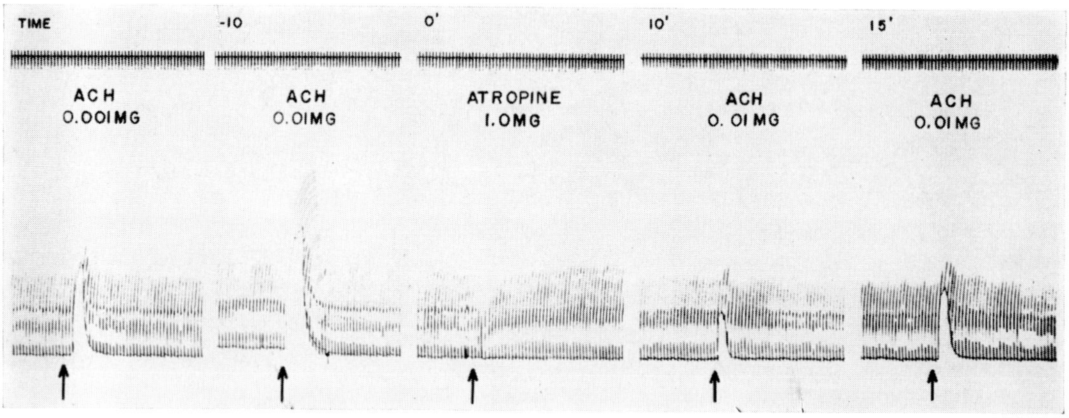

FIG. 4. Effect of relatively close intraarterial injections of ACh upon the responses of the anterior tibial muscle preparation in the goat with myotonia congenita before and after an intraarterial injection of atropine. Dosages, mg/kg.

Note that the recovery from atropine block of response to injected ACh is greatly prolonged as compared to the response to stimulation through nerve.

TABLE 2

Atropine block of the isometric contraction of skeletal muscle to nerve stimulation after administration of an anticholinesterase in the normal and myotonic preparations

Anticholinesterase	Normal					Myotonic			
	None		Eserine		DFP	None	Eserine		DFP
mg/kg, anti-ChE	0		0.15	0.5	0.1	0	0.025	0.05	0.1
Per cent change before atropine	0		+40	+20*	+21	0	+75	+43	+42
mg/kg, atropine	0.5	1.0	0.5	1.0	1.0	1.0	1.0	1.0	1.0
Per cent change, A, immediate	−47		−52			−72	−84		
	−54			−85		−61		−66	
		−65			−58	−62†			−74
B, 10 min later	0	0	−50	−70	−50	0	−33	−45	−50

* Initial change, −40%, potentiation upon recovery.

† Average of 3 experiments; others 1 experiment each.

Observations on the unanesthetized goat. Atropine, 0.1 mg/kg, was given intravenously to 2 males and 1 female with severe myotonia to check the possibility that any beneficial effect might be immediate and too short-lasting to be detected 15 min later according to the procedure used by Kolb (1938).

After prolonged inactivity two male goats fell, from rigidity of all body muscles, immediately upon attempting to run. Atropine was then rapidly injected intravenously. Within 15 sec the goats regained their feet with agility and freedom of all body movements, including the neck and eye muscles. The rapidity of the change and the nimbleness attained seemed to exceed that observed after complete "warm-up." All attempts to duplicate these results during the next few weeks failed and in other tests (hurdle jumps) signs of some slight improvement were questionable. The adaptability of the goat with myotonia (in distinction to "warm-up") to repeated performances and the precipitation of a sudden "freeze" after continuous, vigorous activity upon an unpredictable startle-reaction increased the difficulty in establishing control situations and attributing slight improvements to drug action. Even after 1.0 mg/kg was given to the female, improvement of the myotonic condition was not apparent. The ease with which secretions were blocked and rumen stasis was developed after these intravenous amounts of atropine contraindicated the use of larger doses.

DISCUSSION. In the striated muscle preparations of the goat as well as the dog, cat and mon-

TABLE 3

Cholinesterase activity in goat muscle

Specimen	Average Per Cent Hydrolysis at 60 min per 100 mg Muscle*	
	Normal	Myotonic
Anterior tibial	22.75 ± 0.395; S.E. = 0.197	23.73 ± 6.22; S.E. = 3.11
Hamstring	13.75 ± 1.87; S.E. = 0.935	15.00 ± 2.74; S.E. = 1.54†

Values are average of 4 determinations.

* Initial available substrate, 4 μmol ACh per 100 mg, wet wt., of tissue.

† Three determinations only.

key, the continuous activation through nerve at frequencies of from 0.5 to 2/sec favored the detection of the brief inhibitory effect of atropine and presented fewer complications than the study of single twitch or the responses to higher frequencies of stimulation. Nevertheless, brief periodic tetanization disclosed significant differences between the responses of normal and myotonic muscle to nerve stimulation and some distinctive features of atropine inhibition in myotonia (improved relaxation).

The responses of the normal and pathological mammalian striated muscle to nerve stimulation were equally subject to atropine inhibition, as regards dosage effects, duration and general characteristics and, therefore, showed little evidence of any correlation with differences in sensitivity of the muscle to exogenous (injected) ACh. The failure to show any gross difference between the ACh-sensitive, myotonic muscle and the ACh-insensitive, normal muscle as regards the magnitude and duration of atropine block of the response to slow, repetitive nerve stimulation also supports the impression mentioned in the previous report (tum-Suden, 1958) that the atropine susceptibility of the ACh-sensitive extraocular muscle is probably of the same order of magnitude as that of typical skeletal muscle.

However, both injected ACh and excess ACh, produced by inactivation of ChE, were blocked more effectively by atropine than endogenous ACh according to the interpretation given to the prolonged inhibitory action of atropine upon the response to injected ACh and the enhanced duration of atropine block after administration of an anti-ChE.

Explanations for the differences between typical skeletal muscle, atypical striated muscle as in the eye and pathological striated muscle as occurs after denervation or in myotonia, with respect to reactivity to ACh and its significance, remains at a speculative stage (Feldberg, 1945, 1951; Tiegs, 1953; Kuffler, 1955). It might be noted that the striated ocular muscles which possess a proprioceptive reflex system like the somatic gamma efferent system in goat and man (Cooper *et al.*, 1955) is not only, normally, uniquely sensitive to injected ACh but also displays the myotonic reaction and contracture under abnormal conditions (Brown and Harvey, 1941). Consequently the sensitivity to ACh is not necessarily indicative of abnormalities or "primitive" properties of muscle.

Likewise the ACh sensitivity in myotonia has not been correlated with any abnormality of the mediator system, contrary to the report of low cholinesterase values (Minz and Passouant, 1945). The normal values for ChE activity reported here for the total muscle provide additional as well as more reliable data than those on biopsy fragments. The evidence for normal ChE activity and for normal reactivity to atropine in the myotonic muscle of the goat supports the current opinion that the defect resides in the hyperirritability or instability of the muscle fiber *per se* to mechanical as well as to chemical stimuli (Brown and Harvey, 1939; Floyd *et al.* 1955).

SUMMARY

Intraarterial injections of atropine (0.1 mg to 1.0 mg/kg) promptly reduce the isometric twitch tension of the striated muscle of the goat with myotonia congenita; rapid recovery follows.

The effects of intraarterial injections of atropine (0.5 mg and 1.0 mg/kg) upon brief tetanus of the skeletal muscle of the myotonic goat are primarily those of temporarily improving the speed and completeness of relaxation, by reducing the initial frequency and duration of the asynchronous volley of muscle action potentials.

In the unanesthetized goat with myotonia

congenita, functional benefit from intravenous injections of atropine (0.1 mg and 1.0 mg/kg) could not be proven.

The susceptibility of myotonic goat muscle to atropine does not differ from that of normal goat muscle, but the sensitivity of myotonic muscle to injected acetylcholine and to anticholinesterase agents is greater than that of normal goat muscle.

The cholinesterase levels of normal and of myotonic goat muscle do not differ significantly.

These observations do not support explanation of the symptoms in myotonia congenita by either lowered cholinesterase activity or some other direct abnormality of the chemical mediator system in responses to nerve stimulation.

ACKNOWLEDGMENTS. The author gratefully acknowledges the suggestion of Dr. A. S. Marrazzi that she investigate the reaction of myotonic muscle to atropine and his efforts in procuring the herd of goats kindly donated by Hoffmann-LaRoche, Inc., New Jersey.

To Dr. Bernice Harrison the author is indebted for her generous work and expert determinations of muscle cholinesterase.

REFERENCES

ABDON, N. O.: Acta physiol. scand. **1:** 153, 1940.
BREMER, F. AND MAGE, G.: C. R. Soc. Biol., Paris **102:** 336, 1929.
BROWN, G. L. AND HARVEY, A. M.: Brain **62:** 341, 1939.
BROWN, G. L. AND HARVEY, A. M.: J. Physiol. **99:** 379, 1941.
BUCHTAL, F. AND CLEMMENSEN, SV.: Acta psychiat., Kbh. **16:** 389, 1941.
COOPER, S., DANIEL, P. M. AND WITTERIDGE, D.: Brain **78:** 564, 1955.
FELDBERG, W.: Physiol. Rev. **25:** 596, 1945.
FELDBERG, W.: Brit. med J. **1713:** 967, 1951.
FLEISCHER, J. H. AND POPE, E. J.: Arch. indust. Hyg. **9:** 323, 1954.
FLOYD, W. F., KENT, P. AND PAGE, F.: Electroenceph. clin. Neurophysiol. **7:** 621, 1955.
GARAI, O.: J. Neurol. Psychiat. **17:** 83, 1954.
GESCHWIND, N. AND SIMPSON, J. A.: Brain **78:** 81, 1955.
HESTRIN, S.: J. biol. Chem. **180:** 249, 1949.
KECHSNER, M. AND FINESILVER, B.: J. Neurol. Psychopath. **5:** 341, 1924–25.
KENNEDY, F. AND WOLF, A.: Arch. Neurol. Psychiat., Chicago **37:** 68, 1937.
KOLB, L. C.: Johns Hopk. Hosp. Bull. **63:** 221, 1938.
KUFFLER, S. W.: Amer. J. phys. Med. **34:** 161, 1955.
KUFFLER, S. W.: Amer. J. phys. Med. **34:** 180, 1955.
LANARI, A.: Rev. Soc. argent. Biol. **12:** 207, 1936.
LANARI, A.: Arch. int. Pharmacodyn. **61:** 360 1939.
LUCO, G. V. AND ALTAMIRANO, M.: Amer. J. Physiol. **139:** 520, 1943.
MINZ, B. AND PASSOUANT, P.: Rev. canad. Biol. **4:** 510, 1945.
NORRIS, F. H. AND CHATFIELD, P. O.: Electroenceph. clin. Neurophysiol. **76:** 391, 1955.
PONCHER, H. G. AND WADE, H. W.: Arch. Neurol. Psychiat., Chicago **41:** 1127, 1939.
SANDERSON, K. V. AND ADEY, W. R.: J. Neurol. Psychiat. **15:** 200, 1952.
TIEGS, O. W.: Physiol. Rev. **33:** 90, 1953.
TUM-SUDEN, C.: THIS JOURNAL **124:** 135, 1958.
WALTON, J. N.: J. Neurol. Psychiat. **15:** 219, 1952.

8071

THE ANTICONVULSANT ACTIONS OF METHAZOLAMIDE (A CARBONIC ANHYDRASE INHIBITOR) AND DIPHENYLHYDANTOIN[1]

WILLIAM D. GRAY, CHARLES E. RAUH, ARNOLD C. OSTERBERG AND LILLIAN M. LIPCHUCK

Experimental Therapeutics Research Section, Research Division, American Cyanamid Company, Pearl River, New York

Received for publication July 5, 1958

Fundamental knowledge about the mechanism of action of anticonvulsant drugs is scant. At the cellular level, the carbonic anhydrase inhibitors, acetazolamide[2] and methazolamide, are the only anticonvulsants the effect of which can be related to an action on a specific enzyme, carbonic anhydrase. Considerable evidence has been presented by Millichap, Woodbury and Goodman (1955) and Gray *et al.* (1957) implicating the inhibition of carbonic anhydrase, particularly that in brain, in the anticonvulsant action of carbonic anhydrase inhibitors. Anticonvulsants of this class are invaluable tools for investigating the physiology of experimental seizures. Pertinent to the question of the mechanism of action at the physiological level, it was thought to be of interest to compare the anticonvulsant effect associated with carbonic anhydrase inhibition to that of diphenylhydantoin and to look for possible qualitative differences. Diphenylhydantoin has been stated to have no effect on carbonic anhydrase in the brains of mice (Millichap, Woodbury and Goodman, 1955). Methazolamide was chosen over acetazolamide because it gives a much higher concentration of carbonic anhydrase inhibitor in mouse brain than an equal dose of the latter (Gray *et al.*, 1957); it is also a more potent anticonvulsant agent in rats and mice. The structural formula of methazolamide, synthesized by Young *et al.* (1956), has been shown in a previous communication (Gray *et al.*, 1957).

METHODS. Royal Hart male albino rats, 120 to 150 g, and albino Manor Farm male mice, 18 to 24 g, were used in all experiments except where indicated. They had been in the laboratory one week prior to use and were housed in air-conditioned quarters, temperature 76°F and relative humidity 50 to 60%. Free access to food and water was allowed until just prior to the experiment. Drugs were administered orally in a homogenized 2% starch suspension. Mice received 0.5 ml/20 g and rats 1.0 ml/100 g of body weight. Sodium salts of methazolamide and acetazolamide for intravenous use were prepared by the addition of 1.0 and 1.6 equivalents of sodium hydroxide per mole of drug respectively and made up to volume with distilled water. Sodium diphenylhydantoin was rendered sufficiently soluble by adjusting to pH 11 with sodium hydroxide. Only freshly prepared solutions were used. The volume injected via the tail vein was 0.25 ml/20 g of body weight.

The anticonvulsant activities of sodium diphenylhydantoin, methazolamide and occasionally acetazolamide were compared at times of peak effect (2 to 3 hours), using the following criteria: 1) ED_{50} for abolition of the tonic extensor component of the maximal electroshock seizure pattern in rats by the technique of Toman *et al.* (1946) and in mice by the modification introduced by Swinyard *et al.* (1952); 2) CS_{50} for maximal electroshock seizures in normal and hyponatremic mice; 3) prevention of "minimal" pentylenetetrazol (Swinyard *et al.*, 1952) and 4) "psychomotor" seizures (Toman, 1951). Forty to 60 mice and 20 to 30 rats were used for each ED_{50} or CS_{50} determination and 10 mice in each of the other procedures. The ED_{50} is the amount of the drug (mg/kg) estmated to be necessary for the prevention of seizures in 50% of the population. The CS_{50} is the current in milliamperes estimated to be necessary for the production of seizures in 50% of the population.

Acute hyponatremia was produced in mice by the intraperitoneal administration of isosmolar glucose (5.5%), 2 ml/20 g of body weight, a procedure which markedly lowers the extracellular sodium concentration (Darrow and Yannet, 1935) and electroshock seizure threshold (Swinyard, 1949; Brown, 1953). The drugs were administered orally 1 hour before the glucose was given so that

[1] This work has been reported in part in Fed. Proc. **15:** 430, 1956, and in abstracts in THIS JOURNAL **119:** 173, 1957, and **122:** 27A, 1958.

[2] The American Cyanamid Company trademark for acetazolamide is Diamox.

their times of peak effect coincided with the time of maximum hyperexcitability which is 2 hours in mice. In all experiments involving normal and hyponatremic mice, groups treated with methazolamide, sodium diphenylhydantoin, and 2% starch were run in parallel. The increase in the CS_{50} for maximal seizures in the mice given the anticonvulsants was determined by subtracting the CS_{50} of the parallel starch-treated group from those of the groups treated with the anticonvulsants. It was thought advisable to operate on increments rather than on absolute values because of the hyperexcitability brought about by hyponatremia.

The anticonvulsant action of mixtures of methazolamide and sodium diphenylhydantoin were assessed according to an experimental design of Wilcoxon (personal communication). Mixtures of the drugs in various proportions were prepared in 2% starch and administered orally. Since the peak effect of each drug occurred in 2 to 3 hours, the ED_{50} of each drug and combination for abolition of the tonic extensor component of the maximal electroshock seizure were determined 3 hours after administration. The following equation predicts the ED_{50} of any combination of two drugs which have additive effects: $\frac{\%A}{ED_{50A}} + \frac{\%B}{ED_{50B}} = \frac{100}{ED_{50AB}}$, where %A refers to the percentage of A in the mixture and %B must equal 100—%A.

In the experiments designed to study the possible development of tolerance to the anticonvulsant effects of methazolamide and sodium diphenylhydantoin, the mice and rats used were from populations having a common age, weight, sex and strain and were housed in the laboratory under identical conditions for the duration of the experiment.

The effect of reserpine on the anticonvulsant actions of methazolamide and sodium diphenylhydantoin against maximal electroshock seizures was investigated in the following manner. Reserpine was solubilized by the addition of 1.0 ml of 2% aqueous citric acid to 0.45 ml of propylene glycol-alkaloid (10 mg) suspension. A clear solution was obtained upon warming. Distilled water was then added to make a total volume of 100 ml. One-half to 4 mg/kg of reserpine or an equivalent volume of the vehicle were given intraperitoneally to separate groups of mice 24 hours prior to the oral administration of methazolamide or sodium diphenylhydantoin.

The effect of sodium chloride administration on the anticonvulsant activity of 15 mg/kg of methazolamide and 10 mg/kg of sodium diphenylhydantoin, their approximate ED_{50}'s for anticonvulsant effect on maximal seizures, was investigated in the following manner. Three hours prior to electroshock, the anticonvulsants were given; 10 minutes prior to electroshock, one-half of the mice treated with the anticonvulsants received intravenously 0.2 ml/20 g of an 8% sodium chloride solution equivalent to 800 mg/kg. The other half received an equivalent volume of 0.9% saline. The CS_{50}'s for maximal seizures were then determined. In an identical manner, the effect of 800 mg/kg of sodium chloride *per se* on the CS_{50} for maximal seizures was investigated in mice treated with 2% starch. The effect of this amount of sodium chloride (800 mg/kg) on the ED_{50} of methazolamide was also investigated.

The effect of acidosis on activity and duration of action was investigated in mice given 0.5 ml/20 g of a 2% solution of ammonium chloride orally. This amount, 500 mg/kg, was administered 2 hours and again 1 hour before the intravenous administration of the anticonvulsants. Parallel groups of mice received equivalent amounts of distilled water before drug administration. When duration of anticonvulsant effect was of prime interest, an additional dose of 250 mg/kg of ammonium chloride was administered at the time of drug administration and 1 hour later. Control mice received an equivalent amount of distilled water at these times. In a similar fashion, the effect of ammonium chloride administration *per se* on the maximal seizure pattern and the CS_{50} for such seizures was investigated. In order to make the amount of electrolyte injected comparable to that introduced when methazolamide was injected, 50 mg/kg of the sodium salt of the N^5 tertiary butyl analogue of methazolamide, 5-acetylimino-4-methyl-Δ^2-1,3,4-thiadiazoline-2-N-*t*-butylsulfonamide (CL17,262) were administered. The sodium salt was prepared by the addition of 1.0 equivalent of sodium hydroxide per mole of drug. The pK of this compound is similar to that of methazolamide. It has no *in vitro* carbonic anhydrase inhibitory activity and no anticonvulsant activity at the dose used.

The *in vitro* carbonic anhydrase inhibitory activity of sodium diphenylhydantoin was determined by the method of Maren *et al.* (1954). Ten mg were dissolved in distilled water. One ml of this solution containing 100 μg of sodium diphenylhydantoin had activity less than 0.0001 that of methazolamide or acetazolamide.

The concentrations of inhibitor in the brains and plasmas of mice following the administration of methazolamide were determined by methods previously described (Maren *et al.*, 1954; Gray *et al.*, 1957).

Statistical procedures were those of Litchfield and Wilcoxon (1949).

RESULTS. *Action on experimental seizures.* Table 1 shows the potencies of methazolamide, acetazolamide and sodium diphenylhydantoin against maximal electroshock seizures. Like diphenylhydantoin, the carbonic anhydrase inhibitors have the ability to modify the electroshock seizure pattern in rats and mice. Methazolamide is three to four times more active than acetazolamide in mice and about twice as potent in rats. Three other determinations of the ED_{50} of methazolamide were made other than that shown in the table; the values in mg/kg were 26 (22–31), 20 (16–24), and 13 (10–19). The intravenous ED_{50} was found to be 18 (15–22). The figures in parentheses are the P = 0.05 confidence limits.

The dose-effect curves of the carbonic anhydrase inhibitors do not differ from parallelism in mice and rats. In both animals, the dose-effect curves of methazolamide and acetazolamide are not parallel with those of sodium diphenylhydantoin, the latter having much steeper slopes. Consequently, potency ratios depend on the level of response. At the ED_{50} level in mice, methazolamide and sodium diphenylhydantoin are about equivalent in activity. At the ED_{95} level, sodium diphenylhydantoin is about two and one-half times more potent. In rats, methazolamide is about ten times more active.

The carbonic anhydrase inhibitors are similar to diphenylhydantoin in having no effect on "minimal" pentylenetetrazol and "psychomotor" seizures in mice. The median ataxic dose of sodium diphenylhydantoin, 80 mg/kg orally, had no action on these seizures. Methazolamide had no effect on "minimal" pentylenetetrazol seizures at 700 mg/kg orally; acetazolamide was inactive at 500 mg/kg. No effect on "psychomotor" seizures was shown by 500 mg/kg and 400 mg/kg of methazolamide and acetazolamide, respectively, given orally to mice.

No symptoms other than diuresis were observed following the oral administration of the carbonic anhydrase inhibitors up to 2 g/kg.

When methazolamide and sodium diphenylhydantoin were given orally to mice in amounts approximating their ED_{95} level of effect against maximal electroshock seizures, the maximum effect of both agents occurred at 2 hours. The activity of sodium diphenylhydantoin persisted up to 24 hours after drug administration; no effect was demonstrable 14 hours after the administration of methazolamide.

TABLE 1

The potencies of methazolamide, acetazolamide and sodium diphenylhydantoin against maximal electroshock seizures in rats and mice

Agent*	Oral ED_{50} and P = 0.05 Confidence Limits	
	Rats	Mice
	mg/kg	*mg/kg*
Methazolamide	2.4	14
	(1.7–3.4)†	(12–16)†
Acetazolamide	6.0	49
	(3.9–9.3)	(37–65)
Sodium diphenyl-hydantoin	26	13
	(17–42)	(12–14)

* Methazolamide is significantly more active than acetazolamide at P = 0.05. No tests of significance were made between the carbonic anhydrase inhibitors and diphenylhydantoin; dose-effect curves are not parallel.

† Figures in parentheses are the P = 0.05 confidence limits.

The effect on brain excitability of normal and hyponatremic mice. Sodium diphenylhydantoin increases the CS_{50} for maximal seizures in both normal and hyponatremic mice to a much greater extent than methazolamide. Figure 1 shows the increase in CS_{50} in milliamperes at various dose levels. At 15 mg/kg, which is the ED_{50} range for alteration of seizure pattern, the increases in the CS_{50} in the mice treated with sodium diphenylhydantoin were greater than 500 mA. In normal and hyponatremic mice administered 15 mg/kg of methazolamide, the increases in the CS_{50} were 59 and 13 mA, respectively. Hyponatremia appeared to reduce the anticonvulsant effectiveness of sodium diphenylhydantoin at all dose levels above 5 mg/kg. At 15 mg/kg, the CS_{50} under both conditions could not be determined (>500 mA). Above about 10 mg/kg, the effectiveness of methazolamide appeared to be reduced in hyponatremic mice.

The anticonvulsant effect of mixtures of methazolamide and sodium diphenylhydantoin. The anticonvulsant activity of mixtures of these agents appeared to be additive in their effect on the maximal electroshock seizure pattern. No significant enhancement or reduction of activity were demonstrated (figure 2). The nonparallelism of the dose-response curves complicates the prediction of the effect of combinations of the two drugs.

Studies on tolerance. Table 2 summarizes an experiment designed to test the possible development of tolerance to the anticonvulsant effect of methazolamide upon repeated administration. On the fifth day, the anticonvulsant activities of methazolamide and sodium diphenylhydantoin were considerably reduced in mice which had received nothing, starch, or the ED_{50} of the drug the first 4 days. The ED_{50}'s in these groups of mice did not differ from each other but were significantly different from the ED_{50} determined in a separate group of mice on the first day of the experiment. This altered reactivity to methazolamide and sodium diphenylhydantoin was not associated with prior drug treatment. Rats, on the other hand, did not show any altered responsiveness to the repeated administration of methazolamide (table 3). The ED_{50} values of methazolamide on the fifth day in rats which had received nothing, starch, or methazolamide on the 4 previous days did not differ from each other or the ED_{50} determined in a separate group of rats on the first day of the experiment. In another experiment, the administration of ten times the ED_{50} for 3 days did not result in any altered response to the anticonvulsant effect of methazolamide.

Experiments of longer duration or with multiple administration in mice failed to demonstrate a change in reactivity that could be the result of drug treatment. In mice which had received the ED_{50} of methazolamide for 11 days, the degree of protection following the administration of the ED_{50} on the twelfth day did not differ from that observed in mice treated with starch for the previous 11 days, or from the degree of protection in mice which received nothing but the ED_{50} of the drug on the first day of the experiment. The degree of protection was significantly less in these three groups than that observed in a group of mice administered the ED_{50} on the first day of the experiment. Similar results were obtained with diphenylhydantoin. In an experiment in which groups of mice were treated twice daily for 5 days with the ED_{50}'s of methazolamide, acetazolamide, or sodium diphenylhydantoin, the degree of protection observed on the fifth day did not differ from that of mice treated with starch twice daily

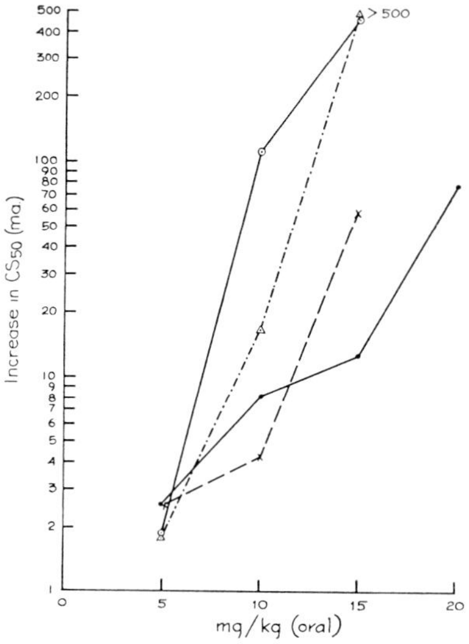

FIG. 1. The increase in CS_{50} (mA) for maximal electroshock seizures in normal and hyponatremic male mice (Armer). The increase is expressed as the difference between the CS_{50} of treated and the starch control group.

	normal	hyponatremia
methazolamide	X- - -X	•——•
sodium diphenylhydantoin	⊙——⊙	△-•-•-△

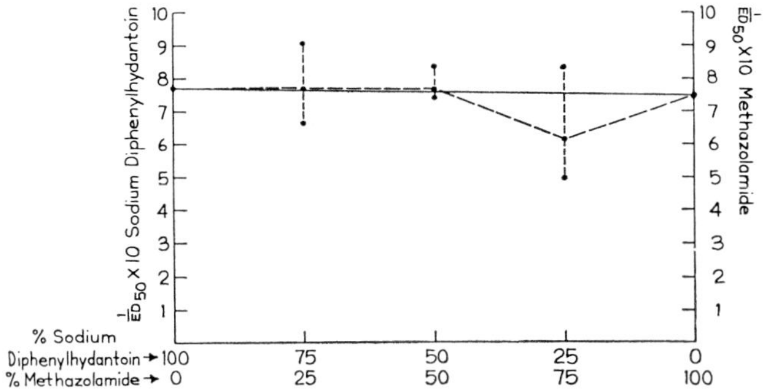

FIG. 2. The anticonvulsant activity of combinations of methazolamide and sodium diphenylhydantoin; maximal electroshock seizures in mice. •——• predicted effect; •- - -• observed effect and P = 0.05 confidence limits.

TABLE 2

The effect of repeated oral administration of either methazolamide or diphenylhydantoin on their anticonvulsant activity in mice (maximal electroshock seizures)

Group	Treatment Schedule—Day					Methazolamide		Diphenylhydantoin	
	1	2	3	4	5	ED_{50}	No. of mice	ED_{50}	No. of mice
						mg/kg		*mg/kg*	
A	DX	—	—	—	—	26 (22–31)*	120	11.0 (9.7–12.4)*	80
B	—	—	—	—	DX	58 (42–81)	40	17.0 (14.4–20.0)	40
C	D	D	D	D	DX	64 (49–83)	80	16.4 (14.9–18.1)	60
D	S	S	S	S	DX	48 (38–60)	80	16.0 (13.8–18.6)	80

D—Methazolamide, 20 mg/kg (ED_{50}) or diphenylhydantoin, 10 mg/kg (ED_{50}).
DX—Anticonvulsant in graded doses followed by determination of ED_{50}.
S—Starch, 2%.
—No treatment.
* Significantly different from other groups at P = 0.05. The figures in parentheses are the P = 0.05 confidence limits.

for the first 4 days and given the ED_{50} of the drug in question twice on the fifth day of the experiment. The degree of protection observed in mice given 100 mg/kg of methazolamide twice daily 8 hours apart and shocked on the fourth day 3 hours after a dose of 100 mg/kg did not differ from that found in mice which had been given starch twice daily for 3 days and 100 mg/kg on the fourth day of the treatment.

The effect of electrolyte administration. Eight hundred mg/kg of sodium chloride administered intravenously to mice 10 minutes prior to electroshock reduced the anticonvulsant effectiveness of methazolamide. The CS_{50} for maximal seizures in mice treated with 15 mg/kg of methazolamide was reduced from 52 (49–55) to 22 (18–29) mA (figure 3). As was anticipated from the work of others (Swinyard *et al.*, 1955), the CS_{50} in mice administered this amount of sodium chloride and starch was significantly greater (P = 0.05) than the CS_{50} in mice treated with 2% starch and injected with 0.2 ml/20 g of 0.9% saline. However, reduction in CS_{50} was not unique for methazolamide since 800 mg/kg of sodium chloride similarly reduced the anticonvulsant effectiveness of sodium diphenylhydantoin (figure 4). The ED_{50} in mg/kg of methazolamide was increased from 15 (11–19) to 30 (25–38); the effect on the ED_{50} of sodium diphenylhydantoin was not investigated.

The effect of reserpine on the anticonvulsant effect of methazolamide and sodium diphenylhydantoin. Figure 5 shows that reserpine more effectively antagonizes the anticonvulsant effect of methazolamide than that of sodium diphenylhydantoin. In mice which had received 0.5 mg/kg of reserpine 24 hours previously, the ED_{50} of methazolamide was increased about twofold. About an eightfold increase in ED_{50} was found in mice which had received 1 mg/kg. Five hundred mg/kg of methazolamide were ineffective in modifying the seizure pattern in mice treated with 2 and 4 mg/kg of reserpine intraperitoneally 24 hours previously. The ED_{50} of sodium diphenylhydantoin was increased to a much lesser extent in mice treated with reserpine. In mice which had received 4 mg/kg of reserpine, the ED_{50} was about two and

TABLE 3

The effect of repeated oral administration of methazolamide on its anticonvulsant activity in rats

(maximal electroshock seizures)

Group	No. of Rats	Treatment Schedule—Day					ED_{50} and P = 0.05 Confidence Limits*
		1	2	3	4	5	
							mg/kg
A	40	DX	—	—	—	—	2.8 (1.8–4.2)
B	40	—	—	—	—	DX	3.4 (2.4–4.7)
C	40	D	D	D	D	DX	2.7 (1.4–5.0)
D	40	S	S	S	S	DX	3.7 (2.1–6.5)

D—Methazolamide, 3 mg/kg (ED_{50}).
DX—Methazolamide in graded doses followed by determination of ED_{50}.
S—Starch, 2%.
—No treatment.
* There are no differences of statistical significance (P = 0.05) amongst the groups.

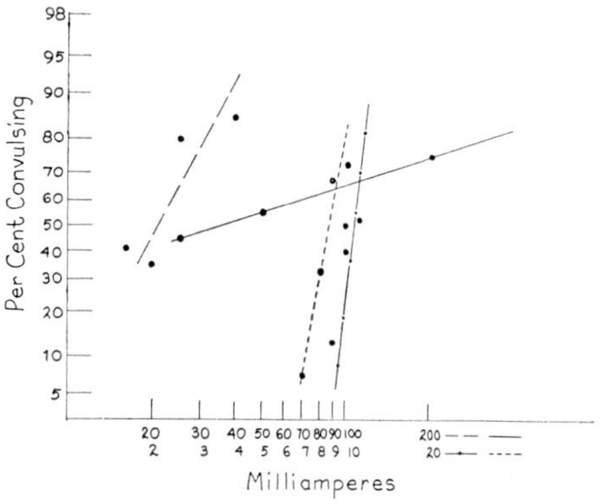

FIG. 3. The effect of 800 mg/kg of sodium chloride on the CS_{50} (mA) for maximal electroshock seizures in mice treated orally with 15 mg/kg of methazolamide; a separate group of 10 mice was used at each point. The 800 mg/kg of sodium chloride and the 0.2 ml/20 g of 0.9% sodium chloride were administered intravenously 10 minutes prior to electroshock. The latter treatment does not differ from starch alone. ——— methazolamide; 0.2 ml/20 g of 0.9% sodium chloride. CS_{50} = 52 (49–55). — — methazolamide; 800 mg/kg of sodium chloride. CS_{50} = 22 (18–29). —•— 0.5 ml/20 g of 2% starch; 800 mg/kg of sodium chloride. CS_{50} = 10.7 (10–11.5). - - - - 0.5 ml/20 g of 2% starch; 0.2 ml/20 g of 0.9% sodium chloride. CS_{50} = 8.8 (8.3–9.4). The figures in parentheses are the P = 0.05 confidence limits.

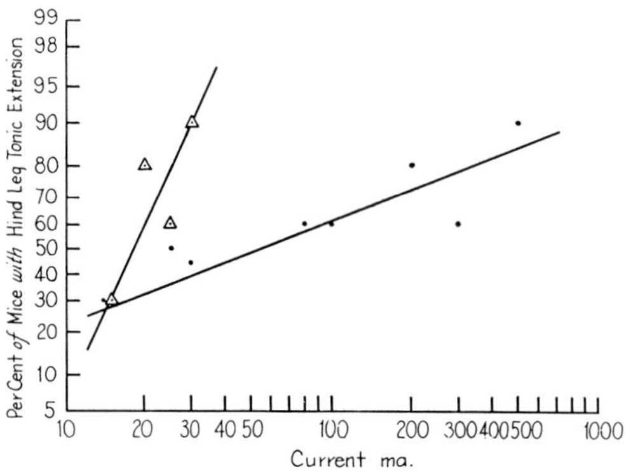

FIG. 4. The effect of 800 mg/kg of sodium chloride on the CS_{50} (mA) for maximal electroshock seizures in mice treated orally with 10 mg/kg of sodium diphenylhydantoin; a separate group of 10 to 20 mice was used at each point. The 800 mg/kg of sodium chloride and the 0.2 ml/20 g of 0.9% sodium chloride were administered intravenously 10 minutes prior to electroshock. •——• sodium diphenylhydantoin; 0.2 ml/20 g of 0.9% sodium chloride. CS_{50} = 52 (33–81). △——△ sodium diphenylhydantoin; 800 mg/kg of sodium chloride. CS_{50} = 19 (16–22). The figures in parentheses are the P = 0.05 confidence limits.

one-half times greater than the ED_{50} found in mice which had received the vehicle 24 hours previously. Similar to sodium diphenylhydantoin, the ED_{50}'s of phenobarbital, phenacemide and glutethimide were increased about twofold in mice treated with 2 mg/kg of reserpine.

The enhancement and prolongation of the anticonvulsant effect of methazolamide and sodium diphenylhydantoin by ammonium chloride. Figure 6 shows the time course of the development of the anticonvulsant effect of methazolamide in normal mice and in mice made acidotic by the administration of ammonium chloride. The main effects are the shift in time of maximum effect from two to three hours to one-half hour after drug administration and the prolongation of anticonvulsant activity. The decline in the anticonvulsant effect in acidotic mice one to four hours after administration is an occasional observation; no explanation is available. It has been shown that the potency of methazolamide is increased about threefold one-half hour after its intravenous administration to acidotic mice (Gray *et al.*, 1957).

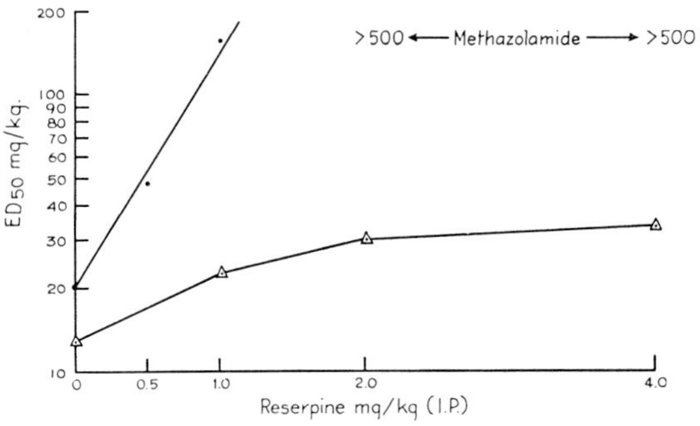

FIG. 5. The effect of reserpine on the anticonvulsant activity of methazolamide •——• and sodium diphenylhydantoin △——△ administered orally to mice; maximal electroshock seizures. Reserpine was administered intraperitoneally 24 hours prior to the administration of the anticonvulsants. Methazolamide, 500 mg/kg, was ineffective in mice treated with 2 and 4 mg/kg of reserpine.

The anticonvulsant activity of sodium diphenylhydantoin is strikingly augmented and prolonged by ammonium chloride administration (figure 7). With the same schedule of ammonium chloride administration as used in this experiment, the degree of protection in mice administered 50 mg/kg of methazolamide intravenously was 100% 8 hours after administration. In mice given distilled water instead of ammonium chloride, none was protected 8 hours after the administration of methazolamide.

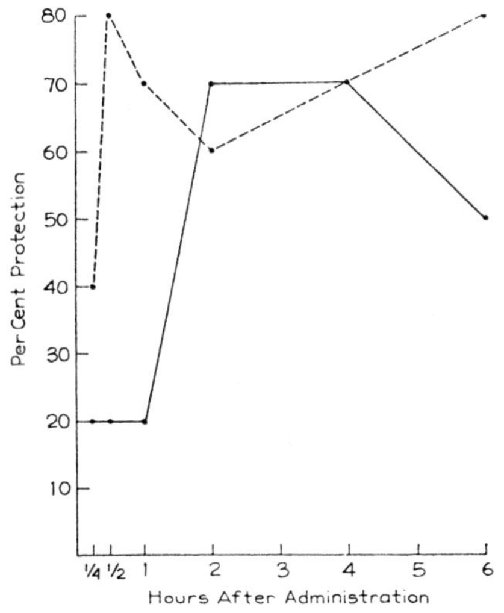

FIG. 6. The effect of ammonium chloride on the onset and duration of the anticonvulsant effect of 50 mg/kg of methazolamide administered intravenously to mice; maximal electroshock seizures; a separate group of 10 mice was used at each point. Five hundred mg/kg of ammonium chloride and 0.5 ml/20 g of distilled water were each given 2 hours and 1 hour before methazolamide. This treatment *per se* has no effect on seizure pattern. •----• ammonium chloride •——• distilled water.

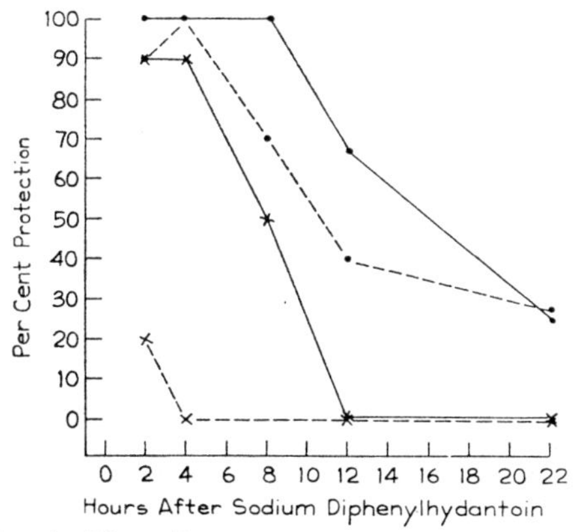

FIG. 7. The enhancement and prolongation by ammonium chloride of the anticonvulsant effect of sodium diphenylhydantoin administered intravenously at 10 mg/kg —— and at 5 mg/kg ----; maximal electroshock seizures, 10 mice per point (separate groups). ● mice received ammonium chloride in 4 divided oral doses; 500 mg/kg at 2 hours and at 1 hour before sodium diphenylhydantoin, and 250 mg/kg at the time of sodium diphenylhydantoin administration and 1 hour later. × mice received equivalent volumes of distilled water orally at corresponding time intervals. The final water and ammonium chloride treatments were omitted for mice scheduled to be shocked 1 hour after sodium diphenylhydantoin administration.

Ammonium chloride in amounts of 1 to 1.5 g/kg has only a minimal effect on the maximal electroshock seizure pattern. The tonic extensor component was abolished in about 10% of the mice shocked at the usual stimulus strength of 50 mA. Table 4 shows that large amounts of ammonium chloride decrease brain excitability, determined by the CS_{50} for maximal seizures. The CS_{50} was significantly increased at all times investigated.

Absorption: brain and plasma inhibitor concentrations. Comparison of plasma levels (figure 8) following oral and intravenous administration of 20 mg/kg of methazolamide to mice shows excellent absorption from the gastrointestinal tract. The decrease in plasma inhibitor concentration is more rapid when the drug is administered by the

TABLE 4

The effect of ammonium chloride administration on the CS_{50} for maximal electroshock seizures in mice

Time after CL 17,262* Administration 50 mg/kg i.v.	The CS_{50}(mA) and P = 0.05 Confidence Limits in Mice Treated as Indicated	
	Ammonium chloride†	Distilled water
hours		
1	12.6 (11.6–13.6)	8.1 (6.7–9.7)
2	13.8 (12.6–15.0)	8.5 (7.1–10.1)
4	18.0 (15.6–20.7)	9.0 (7.3–11.0)
7	27.5 (15.2–49.5)	8.9 (7.4–10.6)
7	14.3‡ (11.0–18.5)	

* CL 17,262 is the N^5 tertiary butyl derivative of methazolamide and is inactive as a carbonic anhydrase inhibitor. The final ammonium chloride and water treatments were omitted for mice scheduled to be shocked 1 hour after the administration of CL 17,262.

† Ammonium chloride was administered orally as follows: 500 mg/kg 2 hours and 1 hour before CL 17,262; 250 mg/kg at the time of CL 17,262 administration and 1 hour later; control mice received equivalent volumes of distilled water. Separate groups of mice were used for each determination.

‡ A second experiment on the following day.

After each time interval, the CS_{50} in mice treated with ammonium chloride differed from that of the corresponding water controls at P = 0.05.

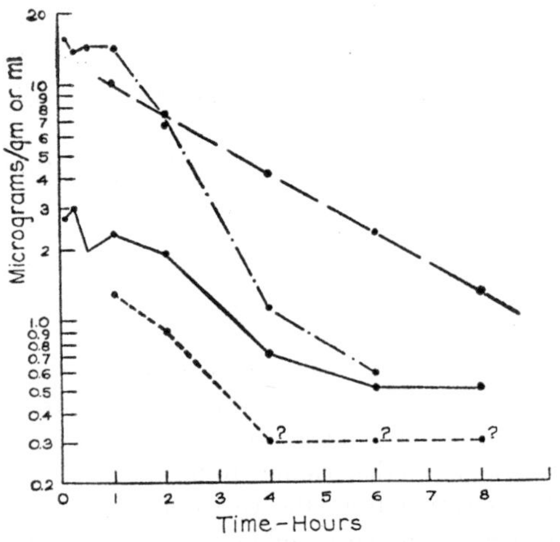

FIG. 8. Brain and plasma inhibitor concentrations following the administration of 20 mg/kg of methazolamide to mice. Each point is the mean derived from 3 mice. Beginning at the fourth hour after oral administration, the inhibitor concentration in brain is essentially zero.

	intravenous	oral
Brain	———	- - - -
Plasma	—•—	— —

intravenous rather than the oral route. The half-life by the former route is 1.1 hours. Of particular interest is the rapid penetration into the brain, the maximum concentration of inhibitor (approximately 3 $\mu g/g$) being achieved 5 minutes or less after intravenous administration. The concentration of inhibitor in brain persists longer after intravenous than after oral administration, even though the plasma level of inhibitor is better sustained with the oral route of administration.

DISCUSSION. This investigation has shown that methazolamide and diphenylhydantoin are qualitatively similar in the following respects: both 1) cause abolition of the tonic extensor component of the maximal electroshock seizure; 2) cause elevation of the CS_{50} for such seizures in normal mice and in mice in which the excitability of the brain is increased by hyponatremia; 3) show enhancement and prolongation of their anticonvulsant activity by ammonium chloride; 4) show reduction of anticonvulsant activity by sodium chloride; 5) show lack of effect against "minimal" pentylenetetrazol and "psychomotor" seizures in mice. The important differences found to date are: 1) reserpine has marked ability to antagonize the anticonvulsant effect of methazolamide but only a relatively weak antagonistic action on that of diphenylhydantoin; 2) methazolamide inhibits carbonic anhydrase while sodium diphenylhydantoin has no such action; 3) methazolamide (as well as acetazolamide) is more potent in rats than in mice; the reverse is true of sodium diphenylhydantoin.

The rapid and apparently complete absorption of methazolamide from the gastrointestinal tract of the mouse shows that the difference in potency of this agent in rats and mice cannot be explained on the basis of poorer absorption in the latter species. It also penetrates with ease and in quantity into the brains of mice. The reason for the difference in oral potency of sodium diphenylhydantoin in the two species is not clear. It may be that this drug is better absorbed in mice than in rats when given orally. Data in this laboratory show that the intravenous and oral ED_{50}'s against maximal electroshock seizures in mice are identical (12 (11–14) vs. 13 (12–14)). Swinyard *et al.* (1952) found that there was no difference in the potency of sodium diphenylhydantoin when given subcutaneously to rats and mice. Harned *et al.* (1903) found little difference in anticonvulsant potency by the oral and intraperitoneal routes in rats. However, the difference in lethality found by these investigators would indicate relatively poor oral absorption in rats. On the other hand, the analytical data of Dill *et al.* (1956) indicate that sodium diphenylhydantoin is well absorbed when given orally to rats.

The data on the concentration of inhibitor in the brains of mice following the intravenous administration of methazolamide confirms the previous finding that there is a considerable discrepancy in time between maximum brain concentration and maximum anticonvulsant effect (Gray *et al.*, 1957).

Although the inhibitor concentration in plasma following oral administration is well sustained, the inhibitor concentration in brain falls faster than when the intravenous route is used. A possible explanation of this is that intravenous administration of the drug establishes immediately a higher gradient between plasma and brain than occurs with oral administration. The consequence of this is a higher concentration of the inhibitor in brain than is achieved by oral administration, a differential which persists during the period of diminishing plasma concentration. It should be pointed out that since the concentration of inhibitor in brain following oral administration begins at a lower level, in a comparatively short time, around the fourth hour, it is in the range of the limit of the sensitivity of the method (0.5 μg/ml or g) where the analytical error is relatively large.

Tolerance has been claimed to develop to the anticonvulsant effect of acetazolamide in mice (Woodbury and Rollins, 1954; Millichap, Thatcher and Williams, 1955) and in rats (Koch and Woodbury, 1958). Our results showing 1) the constancy of the anticonvulsant activity of methazolamide in rats, and 2) that the anticonvulsant effect of methazolamide, acetazolamide and sodium diphenylhydantoin is reduced to a similar degree in mice treated with the drugs, starch, or receiving no treatment at all, cast considerable doubt on the validity of this conclusion. Mice under conditions yet to be defined undergo a change in the direction of reduced reactivity with time. It is necessary in tolerance studies, particularly in mice, to include in the experimental design parallel groups treated with the vehicle or receiving no treatment at all, but in which the effect of the agent is studied at the end of the experimental period. Control groups such as these have not been included in the experiments of Woodbury and Rollins (1954); Millichap, Thatcher and Williams (1955); or Koch and Woodbury (1958). The difficulty of distinguishing between drug-induced and time- or manipulative-induced changes in reactivity without such control groups is obvious.

The effect of repeated administration on the anticonvulsant effect of acetazolamide in rats has not been studied in this laboratory. It would appear highly unlikely that methazolamide and acetazolamide differ with respect to the development of tolerance.

Millichap (1956) is definite on the development of tolerance to the anticonvulsant effect of acetazolamide in man. Others (Bergstrom *et al.*, 1952; Merlis, 1954; Lombroso *et al.*, 1956; Ansell and Clarke, 1956) do not mention it. It may be assumed that either it was not a problem or that any escape from control observed was not considered peculiar to acetazolamide.

The basis of the anticonvulsant augmenting effect of ammonium chloride is not known. The primary event is assumed to be metabolic acidosis. Neither the concentration nor the persistence of inhibitor in the brains of mice following methazolamide administration is affected by ammonium chloride treatment (Gray, unpublished observations). Millichap, Thatcher and Williams (1955) have stated that the enhancement of the anticonvulsant activity of acetazolamide in mice by ammonium chloride was not associated with an increase in the degree of inhibition of brain carbonic anhydrase.

It has been shown that the concentration of sodium in plasma or extracellular fluid is correlated with the level of brain excitability (Swinyard, 1949; Davenport, 1949; Woodbury and Davenport, 1949; Woodbury *et al.*, 1950). Woodbury (1954) and Timiras *et al.* (1954) have shown particularly that the ratio

extracellular Na : intracellular Na

in the brain is intimately involved in the excitability of the brain to electroshock seizures. An increase in the ratio is associated with a decrease in brain excitability. A decrease in the ratio is associated with the opposite effect. Sodium chloride administration was investigated for the purpose of comparing the effect of such treatment on the anticonvulsant effects of methazolamide and diphenylhydantoin: the former is known to affect electrolyte metabolism; the latter was thought to be devoid of such activity. More recently, it has been shown by Woodbury (1955) that in normal rats, diphenylhydantoin decreased both the total and the intracellular concentration of brain sodium and increased the rate of movement of radiosodium into and out of brain cells. The ratio of extracellular to intracellular brain sodium was increased. The effect of carbonic anhydrase inhibition on brain electrolytes requires elucidation. Preliminary experiments of Millichap, Woodbury and Goodman (1955) have shown that acetazolamide in mice causes a decrease in the total brain sodium and an increase in the ratio of brain intracellular to brain extracellular potassium concentration. No data were given on sodium partition. That sodium chloride administration affected the anticonvulsant activity of both agents in the same direction is perhaps not as unexpected as it first seemed. What was unexpected, particularly in the case of diphenylhydantoin, is that the effect was one of reduced effectiveness instead of being additive. It has been postulated (Woodbury, 1955) that diphenylhydantoin acts to suppress or modify convulsions by stimulating metabolic processes involved in the active extrusion of sodium from brain cells; the resultant increase in the ratio of extracellular to intracellular sodium decreases the susceptibility to seizure-activating processes. A further increase in extracellular sodium concentration brought about by sodium chloride administration would be expected to cause an enhancement of anticonvulsant effectiveness. The observed opposite effect is an enigma requiring further research. It should be pointed out that there is no evidence that the administration of 800 mg/kg of sodium chloride causes hypernatremia in mice treated with methazolamide or diphenylhydantoin. These data have yet to be obtained. The slow administration of this quantity of sodium chloride did not have any adverse effect. Hematuria was not observed and it is assumed that hemolysis did not occur. Further research is planned to determine whether the ability to reduce the effectiveness of anticonvulsant drugs is specific for sodium. There is a similarity between the increased susceptibility of mice treated with diphenylhydantoin or methazolamide to electroshock following sodium chloride administration and the increased susceptibility of hypernatremic mice to "minimal" pentylenetetrazol seizures (Swinyard *et al.*, 1955).

Anticonvulsants may have an effect on experimental seizures by increasing seizure threshold, by preventing seizure spread, or by both mechanisms. Reserpine reduces seizure latency and this facilitatory effect on seizure spread has been considered to be the result of the breakdown of inhibitory processes in the brain (Toman *et al.*, 1957). The tonic extensor phase of the seizure represents maximal interneuronal facilitation (Goodman and Gilman, 1955). Chen *et al.* (1954) were the first to describe the facilitatory effect of reserpine on experimental seizures. Toman and Goodman (1948) have postulated and Toman (1949) and Chen and Ensor (1954) have presented some evidence that the principal effect of diphenylhydantoin is to prevent seizure spread. Toman found that diphenylhydantoin had little effect on the threshold and recovery process of frog peripheral nerve but was very effective in preventing the reduction in threshold and spontaneous firing produced by immersion in isotonic neutral sodium phosphate solutions. It also prevented the appearance of repetitive firing in normal nerves subjected to supramaximal shocks. Chen and Ensor found that diphenylhydantoin competitively antagonized the facilitatory action of reserpine on supramaximal electroshock seizures. Recently, Esplin (1957) has shown that diphenylhydantoin reduces posttetanic potentiation and has proposed that posttetanic potentiation is involved in the spread of seizure discharge and that reduction of posttetanic potentiation by diphenylhydantoin is intimately related to its anticonvulsant action. When this admittedly incomplete evidence is considered with the observation that reserpine is much more effective in antagonizing the anticonvulsant effect of methazolamide than that of diphenylhydantoin, it may be inferred that carbonic anhydrase inhibition may have only a minor effect on seizure spread. It would be hazardous to conclude that the additive effect of mixtures of methazolamide and sodium diphenylhydantoin against maximal electroshock seizures implies a similar action. Variables such as differences in absorption, distribution, excretion and metabolism complicate any such interpretation. The differences in the slopes of the dose-effect curves of the carbonic anhydrase inhibitors and sodium diphenylhydantoin against maximal electroshock seizures may be interpreted as evidence of a dissimilar action at the physiological level (Finney, 1947). There is no ready explanation as to why methazolamide approaches sodium diphenylhydantoin in ability to modify seizure pattern in mice and yet is far inferior to it in effect on the excitability of mouse brain as measured by the CS_{50} for maximal electroshock seizures. The reason may be a lack of effect on seizure spread. The electroshock techniques used in this study, however, cannot discriminate between an effect on seizure threshold and seizure spread.

On the basis of studies on the electroshock seizure patterns in young animals, Millichap (1957, 1958) has suggested that brain carbonic anhydrase and its specific catalytic activity may be essential for the propagation of the seizure discharge. Because there are undoubtedly a multiplicity of other enzymes increasing in amounts in the growing brain, it might be difficult to establish a unique role for carbonic anhydrase in the propagation of the seizure discharge.

The spinal cord contains carbonic anhydrase (Ashby, 1944). Its role in the function of the central nervous system is unknown. At the supraspinal level, the evidence is considerable that the inhibition of carbonic anhydrase in brain is intimately connected with the anticonvulsant effect of carbonic anhydrase inhibitors (Millichap,

Woodbury and Goodman, 1955; Gray *et al.*, 1957). Whether the inhibition of carbonic anhydrase at the spinal level participates in this effect needs to be examined. Preliminary experiments have shown that the intravenous administration of methazolamide to intact cats under chloralose anesthesia causes a prompt inhibition of the patellar reflex; diphenylhydantoin shows no effect or a slight enhancement. This effect of methazolamide is central not peripheral (Gray, unpublished observations). Experiments are in progress to elucidate the effects of methazolamide on transmission in the spinal cord. Davenport (1946) reported that thiophene-2-sulfonamide had no effect on the knee jerk or the crossed extensor reflex. The discrepancy may be due to the fact that thiophene-2-sulfonamide is a rather weak carbonic anhydrase inhibitor, having about one-eighth the activity of acetazolamide (R. R. Roepke, personal communication), and its penetration into the central nervous system may be much less than that of methazolamide.

SUMMARY

The anticonvulsant actions of the carbonic anhydrase inhibitor, methazolamide, and diphenylhydantoin show the following similarities: both 1) cause abolition of the tonic extensor component of the maximal electroshock seizure; 2) cause elevation of the CS_{50} for such seizures in normal and hyponatremic mice; 3) show enhancement and prolongation of their anticonvulsant effect against maximal electroshock seizures by ammonium chloride; 4) show reduction of anticonvulsant activity by sodium chloride; 5) show lack of effect against "minimal" pentylenetetrazol and "psychomotor" seizures in mice. The important differences found to date are: 1) reserpine has marked ability to antagonize the anticonvulsant effect of methazolamide but only a relatively weak antagonistic action on that of diphenylhydantoin; 2) methazolamide inhibits carbonic anhydrase while sodium diphenylhydantoin has no such action; 3) methazolamide is more potent in rats than in mice; the reverse is true of sodium diphenylhydantoin.

The absence of parallelism between the dose-effect curves of the two agents against maximal electroshock seizures makes quantitative comparisons difficult. At the ED_{50} level of response in mice, the two drugs are about equipotent; at the ED_{95} level, sodium diphenylhydantoin is about two and one-half times more active. The potency of methazolamide is about ten times that of sodium diphenylhydantoin in rats. Combinations of the two drugs appear to have an additive effect against maximal electroshock seizures in mice. In ability to elevate the CS_{50} for maximal electroshock seizures in normal and hyponatremic mice, sodium diphenylhydantoin is the far more effective agent. Methazolamide is three to four times more potent than acetazolamide against maximal electroshock seizures in mice; it is about twice as active in rats.

Rats do not develop a tolerance to the anticonvulsant effect of methazolamide. The anticonvulsant effectiveness of methazolamide, acetazolamide and sodium diphenylhydantoin is reduced to an equal degree in mice treated with the drugs, starch, or receiving no treatment at all. This reduction in the anticonvulsant effect of these drugs in mice does not appear to be due to the development of tolerance since it appears to be independent of prior drug treatment.

Methazolamide is well absorbed from the gastrointestinal tract of the mouse; following intravenous administration, maximum concentration of inhibitor in the brains of mice is achieved within 5 minutes.

From the marked ability of reserpine to antagonize the anticonvulsant action of methazolamide, it is inferred that the anticonvulsant action of carbonic anhydrase inhibition differs from that of diphenylhydantoin in having a comparatively weak effect on seizure spread.

ACKNOWLEDGMENT. We wish to thank Dr. George M. Sisson for the determinations of inhibitor concentrations, and Mrs. Margaret Ronsberg for her assistance in certain aspects of this investigation.

REFERENCES

ANSELL, B. AND CLARKE, E.: Brit. med. J. **I** (4968): 650, 1956.
ASHBY, W.: J. biol. Chem. **152:** 235, 1944.
BERGSTROM, W. H., GARZOLI, R. F., LOMBROSO, C., DAVIDSON, D. T. AND WALLACE, W. M.: Amer. J. Dis. Child. **84:** 771, 1952.
BROWN, W. C.: Epilepsia, third series **2:** 127, 1953.
CHEN, G. AND ENSOR, C. R.: Proc. Soc. exp. Biol., N.Y. **87:** 602, 1954.
CHEN, G., ENSOR, C. R. AND BOHNER, B.: Proc. Soc. exp. Biol., N.Y. **86:** 507, 1954.
DARROW, D. C. AND YANNET, H.: J. clin. Invest. **14:** 266, 1935.
DAVENPORT, H. W.: J. Neurophysiol. **9:** 41, 1946.
DAVENPORT, V. D.: Amer. J. Physiol. **156:** 322, 1949.

DILL, W. A., KAZENKO, A., WOLF, L. M. AND GLAZKO, A. J.: THIS JOURNAL **118:** 270, 1956.
ESPLIN, D. W.: THIS JOURNAL **120:** 301, 1957.
FINNEY, D. J.: Probit Analysis, The University Press, Cambridge, 1947.
GOODMAN, L. S. AND GILMAN, A.: The Pharmacological Basis of Therapeutics, 2nd ed., The Macmillan Company, New York, 1955.
GRAY, W. D., MAREN, T. H., SISSON, G. M. AND SMITH, F. H.: THIS JOURNAL **121:** 160, 1957.
HARNED, B. K., CUNNINGHAM, R. W., CLARK, M. C., HINE, C. H., KANE, M. M., SMITH, F. H., JR., VESSEY, R. E., YUDA, N. N. AND ZABRANSKY, F. W.: THIS JOURNAL **107:** 403, 1953.
KOCH, A. AND WOODBURY, D. M.: THIS JOURNAL **122:** 335, 1958.
LITCHFIELD, J. T., JR. AND WILCOXON, F.: THIS JOURNAL **96:** 99, 1949.
LOMBROSO, C. T., DAVIDSON, D. T., JR. AND GROSSI-BIANCHI, M. L.: J. Amer. med. Ass. **160:** 268, 1956.
MAREN, T. H., ASH, V. I. AND BAILEY, E. M., JR.: Johns Hopk. Hosp. Bull. **95:** 244, 1954.
MERLIS, S.: Neurology **4:** 863, 1954.
MILLICHAP, J. G.: Neurology **6:** 552, 1956.
MILLICHAP, J. G.: Proc. Soc. exp. Biol., N.Y. **96:** 125, 1957.
MILLICHAP, J. G.: Proc. Soc. exp. Biol. N.Y. **97:** 606, 1958.
MILLICHAP, J. G., THATCHER, L. D. AND WILLIAMS, P. M.: Fed. Proc. **14:** 370, 1955.
MILLICHAP, J. G., WOODBURY, D. M. AND GOODMAN, L. S.: THIS JOURNAL **115:** 251, 1955.
SWINYARD, E. A.: Amer. J. Physiol. **156:** 163, 1949.
SWINYARD, E. A., BROWN, W. C. AND GOODMAN, L. S.: THIS JOURNAL **106:** 319, 1952.
SWINYARD, E. A., SCHIFFMAN, D. O. AND GOODMAN, L. S.: THIS JOURNAL **114:** 160, 1955.
TIMIRAS, P. S., WOODBURY, D. M. AND GOODMAN, L. S.: THIS JOURNAL **112:** 80, 1954.
TOMAN, J. E. P.: Electroenceph. clin. Neurophysiol. **1:** 33, 1949.
TOMAN, J. E. P., EVERETT, G. M. AND JEANS, R. F.: Tranquilizing Drugs, ed. by Himwich, H. E., American Association for the Advancement of Science, Publication No. 46, p. 23, Washington, D. C., 1957.
TOMAN, J. E. P. AND GOODMAN, L. S.: Physiol. Rev. **28:** 409, 1948.
TOMAN, J. E. P.: Neurology **1:** 444, 1951.
TOMAN, J. E. P., SWINYARD, E. A. AND GOODMAN, L. S.: J. Neurophysiol. **9:** 231, 1946.
WOODBURY, D. M. AND DAVENPORT, V. D.: Amer. J. Physiol. **157:** 234, 1949.
WOODBURY, D. M., CHENG, C. P., SAYERS, G. AND GOODMAN, L. S.: Amer. J. Physiol. **160:** 217, 1950.
WOODBURY, D. M.: Recent Progress in Hormone Research, Pincus, G., ed. **10:** 65, Academic Press, Inc., New York, 1954.
WOODBURY, D. M. AND ROLLINS, L. T.: Fed. Proc. **13:** 418, 1954.
WOODBURY, D. M.: THIS JOURNAL **115:** 74, 1955.
YOUNG, R. W., WOOD, K. H., EICHLER, J. A., VAUGHAN, J. R., JR. AND ANDERSON, G. W.: J. Amer. Chem. Soc. **78:** 4649, 1956.

8072

EFFECTS OF ANTICONVULSANT DRUGS ON RECOVERY TIME FROM TONIC-CLONIC SEIZURES IN MICE AND RATS[1]

DAVID H. TEDESCHI[2] AND EWART A. SWINYARD

Departments of Pharmacology, University of Utah College of Pharmacy and College of Medicine, Salt Lake City, Utah

Received for publication May 22, 1958

The effects of anticonvulsant agents on postictal recovery time have been studied by several investigators. Toman *et al.* (1946) reported less central impairment and more rapid recovery from clonic seizures elicited by supramaximal electroshock stimulation in diphenylhydantoin-treated rats than from tonic-clonic seizures elicited in untreated rats. Subsequently, Woodbury *et al.* (1948) found that the duration of postseizure depression of various central nervous system functions was significantly decreased following clonic seizures evoked by supramaximal electroshock stimulation in diphenylhydantoin-treated cats. Since both of these studies compared recovery from a drug-modified (clonic) seizure with recovery from a maximal (tonic-clonic) seizure, they contribute little to our understanding of how anticonvulsant drugs influence the postseizure recovery process *per se*. Therefore, it was thought important to investigate the effects of anticonvulsant drugs on recovery time from *tonic-clonic* seizures. The effects of diphenylhydantoin on recovery time from such seizures elicited in mice have been reported previously (Tedeschi *et al.*, 1956a). The present report is an extension of this work in which seven clinically useful anticonvulsant drugs have been investigated in both mice and rats.

METHODS. Adult male albino mice obtained from Carworth Farms (CF # 1 strain) and adult male albino rats (Sprague-Dawley strain) were used as experimental animals. The drugs tested were as follows: 5,5-diphenylhydantoin sodium (Dilantin Sodium); 3-methyl-5-phenyl-5-ethylhydantoin (Mesantoin); 5-ethyl-5-phenylbarbiturate sodium (phenobarbitalsodium); 5-ethyl-1-methyl-5-phenylbarbiturate (mephobarbital, Mebaral); 3,5,5-trimethyloxazolidine-2,4-dione (trimethadione, Tridione); 3,5-dimethyl-5-ethyloxazolidine-2,4-dione (paramethadione, Paradione); and phenylacetylurea (phenacemide, Phenurone). In the experiments on *rats*, Dilantin, phenobarbital and Tridione were administered subcutaneously in aqueous solution; Mesantoin and Paradione were administered subcutaneously in propylene glycol;[3] and Mebaral and Phenurone were administered orally in 10% acacia solution. In the experiments on *mice*, all drugs were administered orally in 10% acacia solution. The time of peak anticonvulsant effect was determined for each drug by the maximal electroshock seizure (MES) test. The details of this test as employed in mice and rats and the special features of the electroshock apparatus have been described in detail elsewhere (Swinyard, 1949; Swinyard *et al.*, 1952; Woodbury and Davenport, 1952) and need not be repeated here. A dose-response curve was determined for each drug by the MES test at the time of peak anticonvulsant effect. The dose of each anticonvulsant drug tested for effects on seizure pattern, seizure duration and recovery time was selected from the aforementioned dose-response curve. The doses employed in *rats* were all approximately ED_{20}'s as measured by the MES test (*i.e.*, the dose which prevented the hindleg tonic-extensor component in 20% of rats tested); the doses employed in *mice* were all approximately ED_5's by this same test. The mean durations of hindleg tonic flexion and extension, terminal generalized clonus and total seizure were determined in both mice and rats, and the standard deviations of the means were calculated. Animals which failed to exhibit the hindleg tonic-extensor component after the first electroshock were not used either for seizure

[1] This investigation was supported by a grant (B-381) from the National Institute of Neurological Diseases and Blindness, National Institutes of Health, U. S. Public Health Service.

[2] Present address: Smith, Kline & French Laboratories, Philadelphia.

[3] The amounts of propylene glycol used were shown not to alter significantly the pattern and the duration of maximal electroshock seizures or the recovery time.

pattern measurements or for recovery time determinations. The time (RT_{50}) required for 50% of mice to recover the ability to exhibit a second tonic-clonic seizure, regardless of duration of components, after a first maximal convulsion was determined by the method of Litchfield and Wilcoxon (1949). The endpoints employed for the measurement of seizure pattern and the procedure employed for the determination of RT_{50} have been described elsewhere (Toman *et al.*, 1946; Tedeschi *et al.*, 1956b).

RESULTS. The effects of anticonvulsant drugs on MES pattern, duration, and RT_{50} in *rats* are summarized in table 1. All of the drugs tested produced the same qualitative effects on seizure pattern in that they increased the mean durations of hindleg tonic flexion and decreased the mean durations of hindleg tonic extension, terminal clonus and total convulsion. In general, the extent to which seizure pattern was modified by the various drugs was remarkably similar. Thus, recovery time was measured from tonic-clonic seizures of approximately equal severity. All of the drugs tested significantly increased RT_{50}, but the extent to which recovery time was increased varied considerably from drug to drug. For example, phenobarbital increased RT_{50} by 260%, whereas Mebaral increased RT_{50} by only 40%.

The effects of anticonvulsant drugs on MES pattern, duration and RT_{50} in *mice* are shown in table 2. As may be seen from the table, the effects of anticonvulsant drugs on the mean durations of hindleg tonic flexion and extension were qualitatively the same in mice as previously indicated for rats. Thus, the mean durations of tonic flexion were increased and the mean durations of tonic extension were decreased. In contrast to their effects in rats, however, all of the drugs tested increased the duration of terminal clonus in mice. Paradione and Tridione decreased total seizure duration in mice, whereas the remaining compounds increased total seizure duration. All of the anticonvulsants tested significantly increased RT_{50} for mice. The extent to which recovery time was increased varied from drug to drug, but in mice there was considerably less variation between drugs. For example, Paradione, the most effective agent, increased RT_{50} by 153%, whereas Tridione, the least active, increased RT_{50} by 110%.

TABLE 1

Effects of anticonvulsant drugs on MES pattern, seizure duration and RT_{50} in rats

Treatment	Dose‡	Time of Peak Effect	Mean Duration of Seizure Components, Seconds*: Hindleg tonic: Flexion	Hindleg tonic: Extension	Clonus	Total Duration	RT_{50}†
	mg/kg	*hr*				*sec*	*min*
Dilantin	6	½	3.84 ± .20	5.74 ± .24§	5.24 ± .17§	14.84 ± .15§	15.3 (12.0–19.4)
Control	—	—	3.60 ± .12	6.60 ± .18	6.09 ± .19	16.30 ± .17	10.9 (9.2–12.9)
Mesantoin	3	2	4.24 ± .12	4.97 ± .14	3.26 ± .10	12.46 ± .11	21.2 (16.8–26.7)
Control	—	—	3.23 ± .13	6.03 ± .18	4.37 ± .12	13.72 ± .11	9.2 (7.5–11.3)
Phenobarbital	6	2	4.95 ± .17	5.49 ± .23	3.24 ± .14	13.68 ± .13	37.0 (25.7–53.3)
Control	—	—	3.25 ± .12	6.40 ± .20	5.02 ± .14	14.67 ± .13	10.3 (9.0–11.8)
Mebaral	6	3½	3.96 ± .18	5.22 ± .26	3.43 ± .21	12.61 ± .26§	12.9 (10.1–16.5)
Control	—	—	3.23 ± .13	6.03 ± .18	4.37 ± .12	13.72 ± .11	9.2 (7.5–11.3)
Tridione	300	1	3.77 ± .13	5.35 ± .14	2.95 ± .10	12.13 ± .16	20.0 (16.7–24.0)
Control	—	—	3.23 ± .13	6.03 ± .18	4.37 ± .12	13.72 ± .11	9.2 (7.5–11.3)
Paradione	100	1	4.40 ± .14	4.31 ± .18	2.95 ± .10	12.27 ± .14	34.1 (26.2–44.3)
Control	—	—	3.41 ± .12	6.28 ± .20	4.37 ± .12	14.47 ± .13	11.6 (9.0–15.1)
Phenurone	10	3	4.41 ± .17	5.21 ± .20	4.52 ± .15	14.13 ± .16	19.8 (15.3–25.7)
Control	—	—	3.25 ± .12	6.40 ± .20	5.02 ± .14	14.67 ± .13	10.3 (9.0–11.8)

* ± Standard deviation of the mean.

† Figures in parentheses represent 95% fiducial limits.

‡ Approximately an ED_{20} by MES test.

§ Not significantly different from controls ($P > .05$).

TABLE 2

Effects of anticonvulsant drugs on MES pattern, seizure duration and RT_{50} in mice

Treatment	Dose‡	Time of Peak Effect	Mean Duration of Seizure Components, Seconds*: Hindleg tonic: Flexion	Hindleg tonic: Extension	Clonus	Total Duration	RT_{50}†
	mg/kg	*hr*				*sec*	*sec*
Dilantin	1	3	2.59 ± .12	11.43 ± .49	11.21 ± .63	24.31 ± .94§	160 (130–197)
Control	—	—	1.69 ± .05	13.94 ± .32	8.17 ± .32	23.17 ± .76	68 (63–73)
Mesantoin	35	3	3.01 ± .14	10.75 ± .42	12.53 ± .74	26.29 ± .71	165 (144–190)
Control	—	—	1.69 ± .05	13.94 ± .32	8.17 ± .32	23.17 ± .76	68 (63–73)
Phenobarbital	15	3	3.25 ± .17	12.37 ± .34§	10.82 ± .46§	26.43 ± .65	160 (140–182)
Control	—	—	1.81 ± .05	12.95 ± .33	9.69 ± .45	24.47 ± .50	70 (65–76)
Mebaral	25	3	2.92 ± .12	10.21 ± .39	14.15 ± .88	27.14 ± .85	153 (141–166)
Control	—	—	1.69 ± .05	13.94 ± .32	8.17 ± .32	23.17 ± .76	68 (63–73)
Tridione	1050	3	2.47 ± .15	5.80 ± .28	10.85 ± .54	19.08 ± .52	143 (127–162)
Control	—	—	1.69 ± .05	13.94 ± .32	8.17 ± .32	23.17 ± .76	68 (63–73)
Paradione	390	¾	2.80 ± .16	7.13 ± .43	8.35 ± .43	18.28 ± .41	202 (185–220)
Control	—	—	1.57 ± .07	13.20 ± .45	6.70 ± .43	21.47 ± .58	80 (70–89)
Phenurone	95	1	3.30 ± .20	10.23 ± .61	12.29 ± 1.07	25.82 ± .94	150 (132–171)
Control	—	—	1.69 ± .05	13.94 ± .32	8.17 ± .32	23.17 ± .76	68 (63–73)

* ± Standard deviation of the mean.
† Figures in parentheses represent 95% fiducial limits.
‡ Approximately an ED_5 by MES test.
§ Not significantly different from control ($P > .05$).

DISCUSSION. Since animals which failed to exhibit the hindleg tonic-clonic extensor component after the first electroshock were discarded and not included in the seizure pattern measurements, a critical comparison of the mean durations of the various seizure components is unwarranted. Nevertheless, certain general alterations in seizure pattern require brief mention. The tendency toward an increase in mean flexion duration and a decrease in mean extension duration is in agreement with previous observations on the effect of anticonvulsant drugs on MES pattern (Toman *et al.*, 1946; Tedeschi *et al.*, 1956b). Drug treatment decreased the duration of terminal clonus in rats, whereas, except for Tridione and Paradione, it tended to increase the duration of this component in mice. Tridione and Paradione decreased the mean duration of terminal clonus in mice. This latter observation suggests that the effect of an anticonvulsant drug on the duration of terminal clonus varies with the drug and the dose. This suggestion is supported by the fact that doses of Dilantin which prevent the tonic-extensor component of maximal seizures in rats have been shown to prolong markedly the duration of terminal clonus in this species (Toman *et al.*, 1946).

Drug treatment decreased the mean durations of hindleg tonic extension only 17 and 29% in rats and mice, respectively. Thus, the recovery time measurements reported herein were conducted in animals capable of exhibiting seizures which were predominantly maximal in character.

The data indicate that all drugs included in this study increased RT_{50} in both rats and mice. The order of decreasing effect on RT_{50} in *rats* was: phenobarbital > Paradione > Mesantoin > Tridione > Phenurone > Dilantin > Mebaral. The order of decreasing effect on RT_{50} in *mice* was: Paradione > Mesantoin > Dilantin > phenobarbital > Mebaral > Phenurone > Tridione. There is no obvious correlation between the order of ranking in the two species. There is no apparent quantitative relation between ability to prolong postictal recovery and either anticonvulsant activity or antiepileptic specificity.

The prolongation of postictal recovery by anticonvulsant drugs observed in these studies contrasts sharply with reports by previous investigators. Toman and co-workers (1946) reported that the rate of recovery from Dilantin-modified seizures in rats was more rapid than from control maximal tonic-clonic seizures. Similarly, Woodbury and colleagues (1948) reported that Dilantin reduced the duration of depression of central nervous system function after electroshock in cats. Since both of these studies compared recovery from drug modified clonic seizures with recovery from tonic-clonic seizures, it must be concluded that their observations do not reflect the true effect of anticonvulsant drugs on the recovery process.

The factors which influence recovery time, as measured in the present experiments, are numerous and complex. One important factor concerns the relation between initial seizure severity and recovery time. Considerable evidence has been accumulated which suggests that the rate of recovery from a seizure is related to the severity of the seizure, and that recovery from very severe seizures requires a longer period of time than is required for recovery from relatively mild seizures (Tedeschi *et al.*, 1956; Laffan *et al.*, 1957; Tedeschi, unpublished). With the introduction of an anticonvulsant drug, the influence of initial seizure severity on recovery time becomes more complicated. Not only does the drug influence the severity of the initial seizure, but it also acts to influence the recovery processes. The end result, therefore, is dependent on the degree of effect exerted on each component. In the experiments reported above, the compounds tested only slightly decreased the severity of the initial seizure, as shown by the increased duration of flexion and decreased duration of extension, yet all of the compounds significantly prolonged recovery time. Since a diminished initial seizure severity would have resulted in a shortened rather than a prolonged recovery time, it must be concluded that these drugs act directly on recovery processes.

SUMMARY

Seven clinically useful anticonvulsant drugs were tested for their effects on maximal electroshock seizure (MES) pattern and recovery time from maximal (tonic-clonic) seizures. The doses tested in rats were approximate ED_{20}'s by the MES test; those tested in mice were approximate ED_5's by this same test. Since only minor changes in maximal seizure pattern were produced by the doses of drugs employed, recovery time from maximal seizures was measured. All of the compounds tested significantly prolonged recovery time. The significance of these results is discussed.

REFERENCES

LAFAN, R. J., SWINYARD, E. A. AND GOODMAN, L. S.: Arch. int. Pharmacodyn. **111**: 60, 1957.
LITCHFIELD, J. T., JR. AND WILCOXON, F.: THIS JOURNAL **96**: 99, 1949.
SWINYARD, E. A.: J. Amer. pharm. Ass., Sci. Ed. **38**: 201, 1949.
SWINYARD, E. A., BROWN, W. C. AND GOODMAN, L. S.: THIS JOURNAL **106**: 319, 1952.
TEDESCHI, D. H., SWINYARD, E. A. AND GOODMAN, L. S.: Proc. Soc. exp. Biol., N.Y. **93**: 379, 1956a.
TEDESCHI, D. H., SWINYARD, E. A. AND GOODMAN, L. S.: THIS JOURNAL **116**: 107, 1956b.
TOMAN, J. E. P., SWINYARD, E. A. AND GOODMAN, L. S.: J. Neurophysiol. **9**: 331, 1946.
WOODBURY, L. A. AND DAVENPORT, V. D.: Arch. int. Pharmacodyn. **92**: 97, 1952.
WOODBURY, J. W., SIMONS, J., EVANS, R., BURTON, T. Y. AND TOMAN, J. E. P.: Amer. J. Physiol. **155**: 479, 1948.

8073

SOME EFFECTS OF ANALGESIC AND ANALGESIC-ANTAGONIST DRUGS ON INTESTINAL MOTILITY[1, 2]

GRACE W. GRAY

Department of Pharmacology, Marquette University School of Medicine, Milwaukee 3, Wisconsin

Received for publication June 21, 1958

This investigation comprised a study of the effects of 4 analgesic drugs and 2 analgesic-antagonists on intestinal motility, employing both *in vitro* and *in vivo* techniques. Possible mechanisms of the observed drug actions were further investigated using autonomic agents as pharmacologic tools. Finally, a quantitative study of analgesic antagonism with respect to intestinal tone *in vivo* was attempted.

MATERIALS AND GENERAL METHODS. *I. Drugs.* The analgesic drugs studied were morphine sulfate, levorphan tartrate (Levo-Dromoran), alphaprodine hydrochloride (Nisentil), and dihydrocodeine bitartrate. The analgesic-antagonists were nalorphine hydrochloride (Nalline) and levallorphan tartrate (Lorphan). The drugs were always administered in aqueous solution and all doses or concentrations cited refer to their salts.

II. In vitro studies. Experiments were performed to determine the effects of various concentrations of the analgesic and antagonist drugs on spontaneous activity of isolated segments of jejunum from rabbits and from 6- to 11-day old puppies. A modified Magnus technique was employed, with intestinal strips each suspended in 50 ml of continuously aerated Tyrode's solution at 37° C in a metal-free multiple smooth muscle bath apparatus. Separate fresh intestinal strips were employed not only for each drug but also for each drug concentration studied, and all experiments were repeated on tissues from more than 1 animal of each species used. Drug solutions were injected directly into the baths in amounts which would provide the desired final concentrations without altering bath volume by more than 1%. Control strips receiving equal volumes of distilled water were also run. The reversibility and reproducibility of all drug effects were tested by double washout and subsequent reexposure.

The effects of the experimental drugs on artificially induced spasms of intestine *in vitro* were also investigated. The spasmogenic agents and species employed were 10^{-7} and 10^{-8} g/ml methacholine chloride (rabbit jejunum), 10^{-4} and 2×10^{-5} g/ml barium chloride (rabbit jejunum), 10^{-6} and 10^{-7} g/ml histamine dihydrochloride (guinea pig ileum), 10^{-7} g/ml serotonin (5-hydroxytryptamine creatinine sulfate) (puppy jejunum) and "intestinal bio-dialysate"[3] (puppy jejunum). The higher concentrations of the first 3 spasmogenic agents were selected to produce near-maximal spasm of the intestinal strips; all other concentrations were selected to produce submaximal spasm. In running these experiments, 3 to 7 control spasms, separated by double washout, were produced in each intestinal strip, followed by a final spasm in the presence of the experimental drug (after response to experimental drug had stabilized). The height of the final spasm was compared with the mean control spasm height, and any difference found was considered significant only if it exceeded the range of variation among all control spasms in the same intestinal segment.

III. In vivo studies. With the exception of preliminary acute experiments, all of the *in vivo* studies were performed with 15 trained unanesthetized Thiry-Vella loop dogs. Thirteen were "double-loop" animals with 2 loops prepared from adjacent segments of jejunum; one being normally innervated and the other extrinsically denervated at the mesenteric vascular pedicle.[4]

---

[1] A preliminary report of part of this investigation appeared in abstract form in THIS JOURNAL **116:** 24, 1956.

[2] Supported by funds generously supplied by Hoffmann-LaRoche Inc., and by Abbott Laboratories.

[3] "Intestinal bio-dialysate" was prepared by allowing small intestine (with lumen washed out), from the same animal used to supply the test segments, to stand in 100 ml aerated Tyrode's solution at room temperature for 3 hours. Aliquots (usually 1 or 2 ml) of this Tyrode's solution, without further purification, were then injected into the baths to produce spasm of the intestinal strips. The presence in the "bio-dialysate" of amounts of histamine, serotonin or cholinergic substances great enough to contribute significantly to the spasmogenic effect was ruled out pharmacologically, and it was presumed that the stimulating substance(s) present might be "substance P" and/or "darmstoff."

[4] "Mesenteric denervation" was performed according to the method of Youmans (1949), with

The dogs were of both sexes, various breeds and ranged in size from 14 to 32 kg. They were immunized against distemper, kept free of internal and external parasites, housed in individual kennels and had *ad libitum* access to food (Fromm Dog Food Cubes) and water. Throughout the study, the dogs were always handled and the experiments performed by one person. To preclude the development of drug tolerance, the animals were never used more frequently than every 2 days (when small drug doses were employed) or once a week (when higher dose levels were being studied), and occasionally were given rest periods of 1 to 3 months duration. In each experimental series, an attempt was made to employ as many different dogs as possible, and no single animal was used more than twice in any series.

In the case of the "double-loop" dogs, simultaneous recordings were made from both loops during each experiment. Recording of loop intraluminal pressure and segmental contractile pattern was accomplished by means of air-filled finger cot balloons on urethral catheters, which were connected to bromoform manometers with ink-writing floats. An initial recording pressure of 3 to 5 cm bromoform was employed. During each experiment, a 15 to 30 minute period of normal motility was recorded prior to drug administration, and the recording was continued for 45 to 120 minutes after drug administration All drugs were given by rapid intravenous injection through a 26-gauge needle. Regardless of the dose levels being studied, a constant injection volume of 0.1 ml/kg was employed for each dose of analgesic drug or antagonist, and dosage was expressed in μM/kg (or μEq/kg in the case of morphine).

RESULTS *I. In vitro studies. A. Effects of analgesic and antagonist drugs on spontaneous activity of intestinal segments.* The experimental drugs, in final concentrations of 10^{-6} to 10^{-3} g/ml, were tested for their effects on spontaneous activity of isolated segments of rabbit and puppy jejunum. The observed responses are summarized in table 1. Several points deserve comment. 1) As has been reported by others (Gruber *et al.*, 1950; Randall and Lehman, 1950; Winter *et al.*, 1954), the concentrations of these agents required to affect activity of intestine *in vitro* were high. 2) At all concentrations tested, the effects of all of the drugs were rapidly reversible with washout, with the single exception of levallorphan 10^{-4} g/ml in which case recovery occurred somewhat more slowly with persisting irregularities in contractile pattern. 3) The experiments with rabbit jejunal segments were performed first. The *in vitro* drug responses with this species were difficult to correlate with the known intestinal actions of the drugs *in vivo*. For example, whereas morphine and nalorphine had qualitatively opposite effects *in vitro* throughout the range of effective concentrations, levorphan and levallorphan had similar effects. This discrepancy prompted the use of another species (puppy) which was found to behave quite differently. Both morphine and levorphan caused stimulation or spasm of puppy intestinal segments, and both nalorphine and levallorphan caused depression or paralysis. 4) With respect to relative *in vitro* potencies, levorphan and dihydrocodeine stimulated intestine of both species at lower concentrations than did morphine. 5) Alphaprodine depressed activity of the intestinal strips in both species. 6) Both rabbit and puppy intestinal segments exhibited "tachyphylaxis" to the actions of all of the drugs upon repeated exposure, the tolerance development being most marked in puppy intestine. Occasionally reversal, rather than tachyphylaxis, was exhibited upon repeated exposure to the antagonist drugs.

B. Antagonism in vitro. A preliminary attempt was made to utilize the *in vitro* preparation in the study of analgesic drug antagonism. Rabbit jejunal strips were exposed to equal mixtures (by weight) of morphine and nalorphine, of morphine and levallorphan, of levorphan and nalorphine and of levorphan and levallorphan in total drug concentrations of 10^{-6}, 10^{-5}, 10^{-4} and 10^{-3} g/ml. The studies were not pursued further since (as reported in table 1) analgesic and antagonist effects *in vitro* were sometimes indistinguishable, and tachyphylaxis or reversal precluded more than 1 drug exposure per intestinal segment.

C. Effects of analgesic and antagonist drugs on induced spasms of intestinal segments. The experimental drugs, in all concentrations cited in table 1, were tested for possible blocking or potentiating effects on artificially induced spasms of intestine *in vitro*. At the higher concentrations, all of the drugs produced nonspecific depression of the induced spasms, with the exceptions that morphine and dihydrocodeine failed to depress

the purpose of isolating the loop of jejunum from postganglionic sympathetic and preganglionic parasympathetic efferent fibers, as well as from all afferent connections with the central nervous system.

TABLE 1

Effects of analgesic and antagonist drugs on spontaneous activity of intestine in vitro

Drug	Final Conc.	Effect on Tone and/or Contractile Amplitude				
		Rabbit jejunum		Puppy jejunum		
		1st exposure	2nd exposure	1st exposure	2nd exposure	3rd exposure
	g/ml					
Morphine	10^{-6}	0	0	0	0	0
	10^{-5}	0	0	0	0	↓
	10^{-4}	↑ ↑	↑	↑ ↑	↑	↑
	10^{-3}	↑ ↑	↑ ↑	Spasm	↑	↑
Nalorphine	10^{-6}	↓	0	0	0	0
	10^{-5}	↓	0	↓	0	0
	10^{-4}	↓	↑	↓	0	0
	10^{-3}	Rapid paralysis	Rapid paralysis	Brief ↑, paralysis	Brief ↑, paralysis	Brief ↑, paralysis
Levorphan†	10^{-6}	↑	0	0	0	0
	10^{-5}	↑ ↑	↑	↑ ↑ ↑	↑ ↑	↑
	10^{-4}	Brief ↑ ↑, paralysis	Gradual paralysis	Brief ↑ ↑ ↑, spasm	↑ ↑	↑
Levallorphan	10^{-6}	↑	0	↓	0	0
	10^{-5}	↑ ↑*	↑†	↓	↑	↑
	10^{-4}	Brief ↑ ↑, paralysis	Rapid paralysis	Brief ↑, paralysis	Rapid paralysis	Rapid paralysis
Alphaprodine	10^{-6}	0	0	↓	0	
	10^{-5}	0	0	↓ ↓	↓	
	10^{-4}	Immediate paralysis	Rapid paralysis	Rapid paralysis	Gradual paralysis	
Dihydrocodeine	10^{-6}	0	0	0	0	
	10^{-5}	↑	0	↑ ↑	0	
	10^{-4}	↑ ↑	↑	Spasm	↑ ↑	
	10^{-3}	↑ ↑ ↑	↑ ↑	Spasm	Spasm	

0 = no effect.
↑ = slight; ↑ ↑ = moderate; ↑ ↑ ↑ = marked — increase in tone and/or contractile amplitude.
↓ = slight; ↓ ↓ = moderate — decrease in tone and/or contractile amplitude.
Spasm = sustained maximal contraction of tissue.
Paralysis = inhibition of rhythmic contractions with tissue in relaxed state.
† also tested on rabbit jejunal segments stored 24 hours in Tyrode's at 4° C with identical results.
* irregularities in contractile pattern.

greatly the barium, serotonin and "bio-dialysate" spasms, and alphaprodine failed to depress serotonin spasm. At lower concentrations, the experimental drugs exhibited no marked or selective blocking or potentiating effects on the induced spasms, with the exceptions of apparent potentiation of submaximal barium spasm by levallorphan and depression of serotonin spasm by nalorphine.

It was also observed that repeated exposure of an intestinal segment to a spasmogenic agent frequently altered the subsequent response of that segment to analgesic or antagonist drug, from the expected response as reported in table 1. This was usually manifested as sensitization or desensitization, without any change in the qualitative nature of the response. However, repeated exposure of puppy jejunal segments to either serotonin or "bio-dialysate" caused the tissue to respond to alphaprodine with hyperactivity or spasm, rather than the depression or paralysis ordinarily produced by alphaprodine *in vitro*.

II. In vivo studies. A. Preliminary acute experiments. Preliminary experiments were performed with 7 dogs under light sodium pentobarbital anesthesia, recording carotid blood pressure, respiratory excursions (pneumograph) and jejunal motility (water-filled balloon-tambour system). Spontaneous intestinal activity was present in these experiments but was poor compared to that routinely observed in the untraumatized, unanesthetized dog. Morphine, levorphan and levallorphan were administered intravenously, and the following observations with respect to intestinal activity were made: 1) Generally a dose of 0.5 mg/kg of analgesic, as the first drug administered, was required to produce increased intestinal tone or contractile activity. 2) Levallorphan (0.05 to 0.1 mg/kg), as the first drug administered, always produced mild depression of intestinal tone and contractions. Occasionally 0.5 mg/kg caused complete cessation of recorded activity, but more commonly it produced no further depression than did the lower doses. 3) When levallorphan was administered during analgesic-induced intestinal hyperactivity, the usual minimal antagonistic dose was 0.1 mg/kg. The effect of levallorphan under these conditions was of brief duration (5 to 15 minutes) in sharp contrast to the prolonged action of the analgesic drugs (30 to $>$ 90 minutes). 4) In one animal, in which the rhythmic contractions of the sphincter of Oddi (stimulated by continuous neostigmine infusion) were recorded, the effects of morphine and levallorphan were identical to those described for jejunal motility.

B. Effects of analgesic drugs. Experiments were performed in which analgesics, as the only drugs administered, were studied for their effects on intestinal tone[5] and contractile pattern in trained unanesthetized Thiry-Vella loop dogs. Although similar studies have been made by other investigators (Gruber *et al.*, 1950; Hart and McCawley, 1944; Krueger and Gay, 1933; Randall and Lehman, 1948; Randall and Lehman, 1950; Young *et al.*, 1955), the present experiments were deemed essential as controls for subsequent drug antagonism studies. Dose levels were selected as follows: The smallest dose of levorphan which would produce, in every case, an increase in intestinal loop tone was first determined and found to be 0.01 μM/kg. The dose of morphine which corresponded most closely in intestinal effects to the levorphan dose was then determined and found to be 0.015 μEq/kg. These dose levels and 10-fold multiples of them were selected for study. In the cases of dihydrocodeine and alphaprodine, dose levels of 0.045 μM/kg and 10-fold multiples thereof were chosen arbitrarily. The results are presented in table 2, and figure 1 illustrates recordings of typical responses to levorphan.

The most consistent response to intravenous administration of any of the analgesic drugs was an immediate and abrupt increase in intestinal loop tone, in some cases of sufficient magnitude to be classified as partial or complete loop spasm. As an index of duration of elevated intestinal tone, the endpoint of first return to predrug level was selected, and it will be observed from the table that there was considerable variation in duration, especially at the higher dose levels. In a small proportion of the experiments, steadily progressive failure of loop tone and contractile amplitude followed the initial tone stimulation produced by the analgesic drugs.

In some of the experiments, periodically recurrent abnormal motility waves were observed to begin at varying time intervals (but never immediately) after drug administration. These peculiar patterns, which have not been observed by the author in normal intestinal loop recordings, were designated "P waves." They resembled slow, wavelike intestinal spasms lasting about 1 minute, during which the normal 10 to 15 per minute segmental contractions were absent. Whether or not the "P waves" were propagated phenomena or propulsive in function was not established.

There were no striking or consistent differences between innervated and extrinsically denervated intestinal loops with respect to any of the afore-

[5] The term "tone" is employed to indicate the intraballoon pressure (reflecting intestinal intraluminal pressure) at the relaxation phase of each segmental contraction of the intestinal loop.

TABLE 2

Effects of analgesic drugs in Thiry-Vella loop dogs

Drug	Dose	No. of Expts.*	Loop Recordings†	Incidence Among Loop Recordings of: Increased loop tone	Partial or complete loop spasm	Progressive failure of loop activity	"P waves"	Mean Minutes Duration of Loop Hypertonicity (and range)	Other Observations§ (Incidence = 100% of expts. except where stated otherwise): Initial	Delayed
	$\mu M/kg$									
Levorphan	0.01	16	IN	16/16	3/16			12		
			DE	11/11	5/11	2/11		14		
		(10)	total	27/27	8/27	2/27	0/27	13(2–32)		
	0.1	16	IN	16/16	8/16	1/16	5/16	40	panting, slight nausea (2/16 expts.)	mild sedation
			DE	10/10	5/10	3/10	5/10	24		
		(10)	total	26/26	13/26	4/26	10/26	35(10->65)		
	1.0	10	IN	10/10	3/10	1/10	5/10	23	panting, dysphoria (1/10 expts.)	marked sedation, defecation after experiment terminated.
			DE	7/7	1/7	3/7	3/7	30		
		(6)	total	17/17	4/17	4/17	8/17	26(2->67)		
Morphine	0.015††	13	IN	12/12	7/12			12		
			DE	9/9	2/9		2/9	11		
		(10)	total	21/21	9/21	0/21	2/21	12(3–41)		
	0.15††	6	IN	6/6	6/6		1/6	20	panting, nausea (4/6 expts., vomiting (2/6 expts.), dysphoria (1/6 expts.)	mild sedation
			DE	4/4	4/4	1/4	2/4	17		
		(5)	total	10/10	10/10	1/10	3/10	18(4–38)		
Dihydrocodeine	0.045	8	IN	2/8						
			DE	1/6						
		(7)	total	3/14	0/14	0/14	0/14	2(0–14)		
	0.45	9	IN	9/9	4/9			10		
			DE	7/7	3/7		2/7	7		
		(8)	total	16/16	7/16	0/16	2/16	9(2–20)		
	4.5	6	IN	6/6	4/6		2/6	41	panting, peripheral vasodilation (4/6 expts.), slight nausea (3/6 expts.), dysphoria (2/6 expts.)	mild sedation (3/6 expts.)
			DE	5/5	4/5		2/5	31		
		(5)	total	11/11	8/11	0/11	4/11	36(1->78)		
Alphaprodine	0.045	6	IN	1/6						
			DE	3/5						
		(6)	total	4/11	0/11	0/11	0/11	2(0–7)		
	0.45–0.9	11	IN	10/10	5/10			17		brief mild sedation (6/11 expts.)
			DE	9/9	4/9		2/9	17		
		(6)	total	19/19	9/19	0/19	2/19	17(4–41)		
	4.5	6	IN	5/5	5/5			41	panting, salivation (4/6 expts.), dysphoria (3/6 expts.), peripheral vasodilation (3/6 expts.), skin twitching (3/6 expts.)	brief sedation: mild—(3/6 expts.), marked—(3/6 expts.)
			DE	5/5	4/5			14		
		(4)	total	10/10	9/10	0/10	0/10	27(3–62)		

* Parentheses indicate number of different dogs employed.

† IN = innervated loops, DE = denervated loops.

‡ μEq/kg.

§ Mild sedation = tendency to sleep more than usual during recording, but normal alertness and playfulness when aroused. Marked sedation = asleep during recording, and groggy or disoriented, but not ataxic, upon arousal. Dysphoria = evidence of apprehension, malaise or pain.

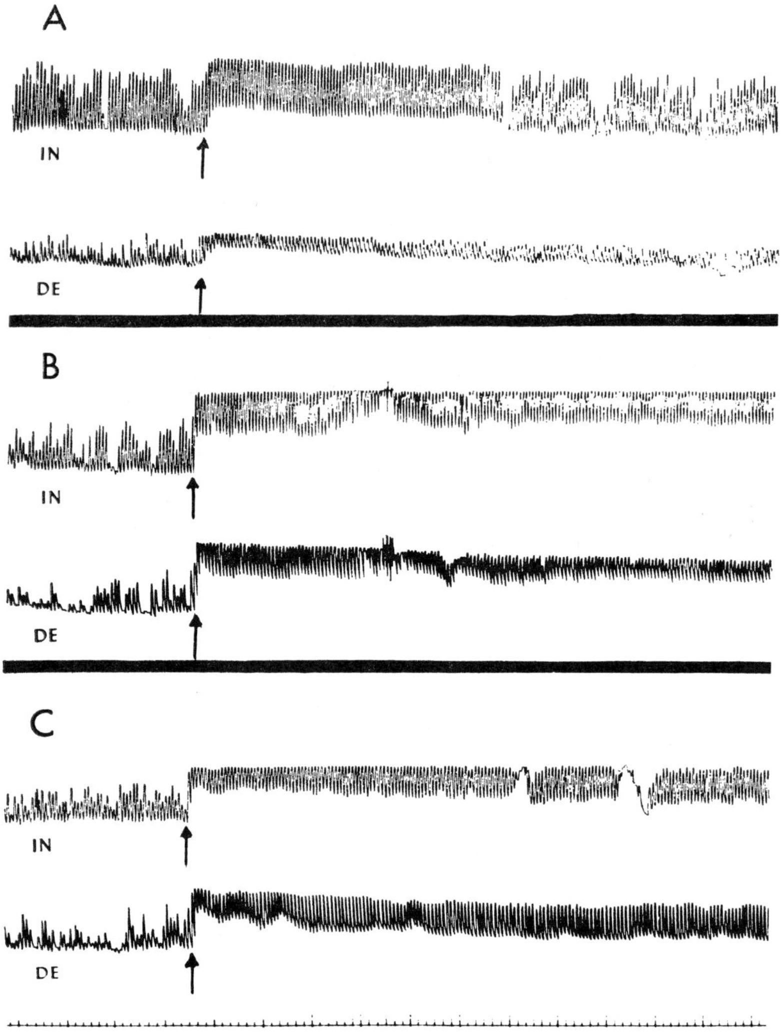

FIG. 1 Effects of various doses of levorphan on jejunal Thiry-Vella loop activity in separate experiments on the same dog.
Note partial spasm in B and C, and "P wave" in C.
A = 0.01 μM/kg i.v.; B = 0.1 μM/kg i.v.; C = 1.0 μM/kg i.v.; IN = innervated loop; DE = extrinsically denervated loop; ↑ = time of injection. Time signal: 10 sec.

mentioned indices of response to the analgesic drugs.

In comparing the various drugs and dose levels studied, the following generalizations were made. 1) All of the drugs produced intestinal loop hypertonicity at i.v. dose levels too low to cause nausea, vomiting, sedation or any other effects seen at higher dose levels. 2) Morphine and levorphan appeared to possess roughly equal potencies with respect to intestinal loop effects, and also with respect to sedation. As the dose levels of levorphan were increased 10- and 100-fold, the magnitude and duration of intestinal hypertonicity did not increase proportionally, but appeared instead to become self-limited. Indeed, some dogs who characteristically responded with prolonged intestinal spasm to 0.1 μM/kg, evidenced only brief and mild hypertonicity after 1.0 μM/kg. Morphine was not studied over a 100-fold dose range because of the severity of side effects at the 10-fold dose. 3) The incidence of "P waves" increased progressively with increasing dose levels of each analgesic drug except alphaprodine. 4) Dihydrocodeine, in these experiments, exhibited about 1/30 the intestinal spasmogenic and sedative potency of morphine. 5) Alphaprodine possessed intestinal stimulating potency roughly equal to dihydrocodeine, but somewhat greater C.N.S. depressant activity than the latter. 6) When sedation occurred following administration of any of the analgesic drugs, it was of prolonged duration excepting in the case of alphaprodine, whose C.N.S. depressant action lasted less than 1 hour at the dose levels studied.

C. Effects of analgesic-antagonist drugs. Experiments similar to those described in *B* above were performed to investigate the effects of the antagonists, levallorphan and nalorphine, on intestinal loop tone and contractile pattern. The results are presented in table 3, and figure 2 illustrates recordings of responses to levallorphan.

It was quite evident during these experiments that intestinal responses to the antagonists were far less consistent than were responses to the analgesic drugs, and the inconsistency seemed definitely to be due to interanimal variation since each dog responded similarly to repeated doses. Also in contrast to analgesic drug effects, some typical differences between responses of innervated and denervated loops were found.

Even the highest dose levels of the antagonists produced changes in intestinal tone in only about

TABLE 3

Effects of analgesic-antagonist drugs in Thiry-Vella loop dogs

Drug	Dose	No. of Expts.*	Loop Recordings†	Incidence Among Loop Recordings of: Effect on tone			Effect on contractile amplitude and/or frequency			Stabilization	"P waves"	Other Observations
				no effect	increase	decrease	no effect	increase	decrease			
	μM/kg											
Levallorphan	0.01	9	IN	8/9		1/9	7/9		2/9			
			DE	6/7	1/7		6/7		1/7		1/7	
		(9)	total	14/16	1/16	1/16	13/16	0/16	3/16	0/16	1/16	
	0.1	13	IN	10/13	1/13	2/13	10/13		3/13	3/13	7/13	
			DE	7/9		2/9	2/9		7/9		3/9	
		(9)	total	17/22	1/22	4/22	12/22	0/22	10/22	3/22	10/22	
	1.0	19	IN	11/19	7/19	1/19	12/19		7/19	5/19	11/19	mild sedation
			DE	7/13		6/13	4/13		9/13	1/13	9/13	(3/19 expts.)
		(11)	total	18/32	7/32	7/32	16/32	0/32	16/32	6/32	20/32	
	2.0–4.0	8	IN	3/7	4/7		4/7	2/7	1/7	6/7	7/7	initial dysphoria (1/8 expts.),
			DE	3/6		3/6	3/6		3/6		5/6	mild sedation
		(4)	total	6/13	4/13	3/13	7/13	2/13	4/13	6/13	12/13	(4/8 expts.)
Nalorphine	0.015	10	IN	4/9	5/9		6/9	2/9	1/9		2/9	
			DE	4/7	3/7		6/7		1/7			
		(9)	total	8/16	8/16	0/16	12/16	2/16	2/16	0/16	2/16	
	0.15	9	IN	4/9	2/9	3/9	6/9		3/9	2/9	1/9	
			DE	3/6	3/6		3/6		3/6		1/6	
		(8)	total	7/15	5/15	3/15	9/15	0/15	6/15	2/15	2/15	
	1.5	10	IN	5/10	2/10	3/10	5/10		5/10	4/10	5/10	mild sedation
			DE	2/7	3/7	2/7	2/7		5/7		3/7	(4/10 expts.)
		(9)	total	7/17	5/17	5/17	7/17	0/17	10/17	4/17	8/17	

* Parentheses indicate number of different dogs employed.

† IN = innervated loops, DE = denervated loops.

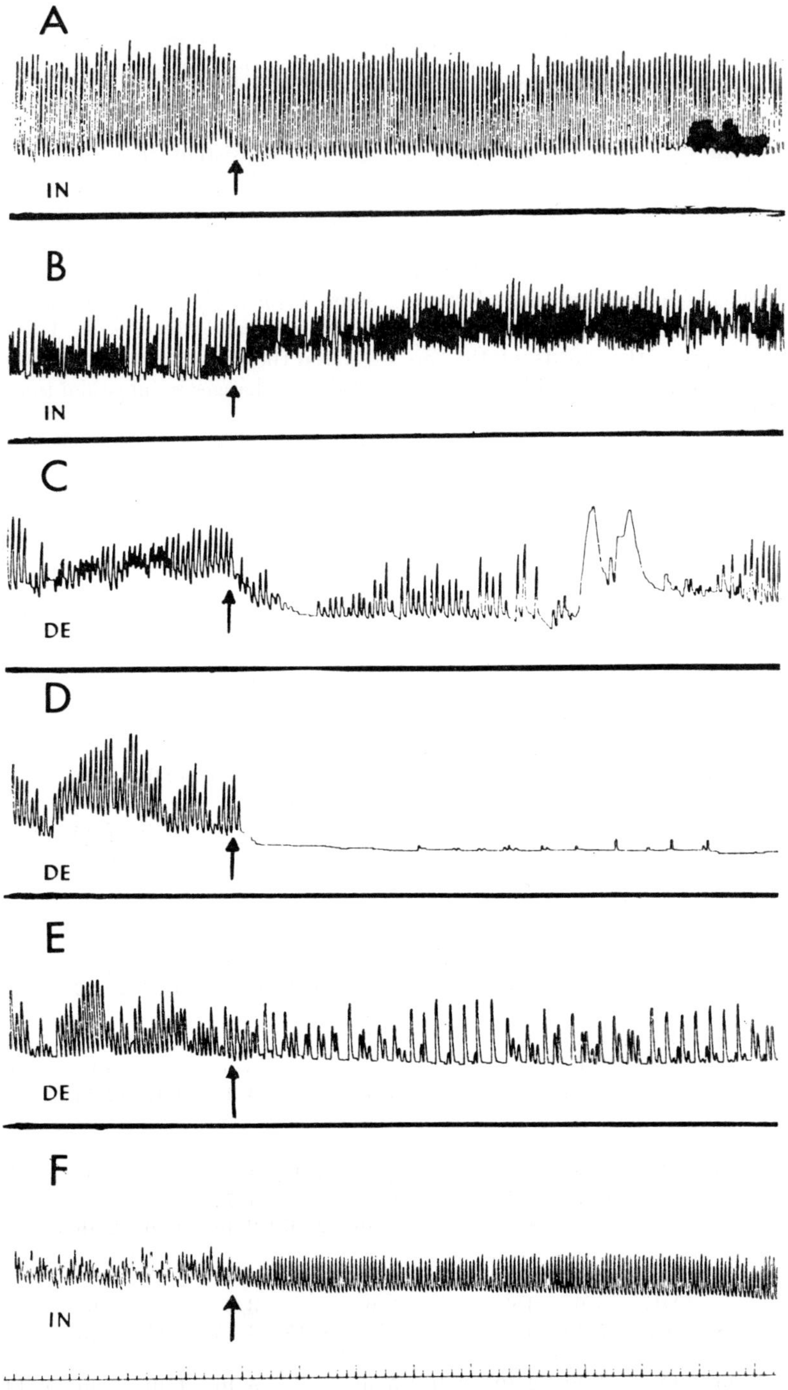

FIG. 2. Effects of levallorphan, 1.0 μM/kg i.v., on jejunal Thiry-Vella loop activity in dogs; several experiments selected to illustrate variation in type of response.

Note: no effect in A; increased tone in B; decreased tone and "P wave" in C; complete inhibition in D; decreased contractile frequency in E; stabilization in F.

IN = innervated loop; DE = extrinsically denervated loop; ↑ = time of injection. Time signal: 10 sec.

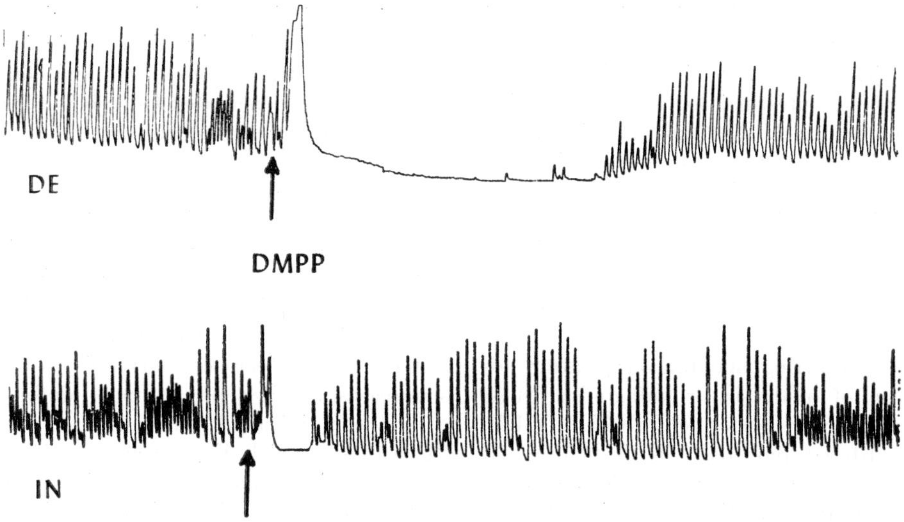

FIG. 3. Effect of DMPP, 250 μg i.v., on activity of jejunal Thiry-Vella loops in the dog. IN = innervated loop; DE = extrinsically denervated loop; ↑ = time of injection.

one-half of the experiments. When tone was affected, it was increased or decreased with approximately equal frequency. (However, the higher doses of levallorphan tended to cause increased intestinal tone primarily in innervated loops and decreased tone primarily in denervated loops, whereas little difference between innervated and denervated loop tone response was evident with nalorphine.) Tone increases were always mild and usually brief in duration (1 to 10 minutes). Tone decreases varied from mild to marked and frequently were more prolonged (10 to 75 minutes) in duration.

The antagonist drugs affected contractile amplitude and/or frequency with an incidence similar to effects on tone, but tone and contractions were often affected independently of each other. In the case of intestinal contractions, however, both of the antagonists caused depression much more frequently than stimulation, and this effect was evidenced more often by denervated than by innervated loops. The degree of depression of the contractile mechanism varied from mild to complete inhibition, and the effect was frequently prolonged in duration and sometimes delayed in onset.

In some experiments the antagonist drugs produced a striking change in contractile pattern (stabilization) which was characterized by markedly increased uniformity of tone and contractile amplitude. Stabilization was observed, with one exception, in innervated loops only.

Administration of the antagonists resulted in the occurrence of periodic "P waves" (described in *B* above), the incidence of which was at least as great as observed with the analgesic drugs, and increased progressively with increasing dosage.

With respect to C.N.S. depression, the antagonists exhibited much lower potency in dogs than did their analgesic analogues, but mild sedation was evident in some cases at the higher dose levels.

D. Autonomic drug experiments. Experiments were carried out to determine the interrelationships, if any, between certain autonomic drug effects on intestinal loop activity and the effects of the analgesic and antagonist drugs. The autonomic agents employed were the ganglionic stimulant DMPP[6], hexamethonium chloride and atropine sulfate. Control recordings were obtained from each of the dogs of the effects of each of the autonomic drugs administered alone.

1) When DMPP was injected intravenously in appropriate dosage (usually 150 to 250 μg) in dogs with innervated and denervated intestinal loops, an interesting complex of brief responses occurred (see figure 3). During the first circulation time the dogs exhibited intense hyperpnea, brief spasm of the denervated intestinal loops and usually no marked change in innervated loop activity. During the second circulation time, evidence of adrenal medullary

[6] 1,1-dimethyl-4-phenylpiperazinium iodide.

discharge supervened, with blanching of buccal and intestinal mucosae, bradycardia and complete inhibition of activity in both innervated and denervated intestinal loops, the inhibition being more prolonged in the hypersensitive denervated loops. This response may be elicited repeatedly in the same animal, and has been employed routinely by the author as a pharmacologic test for the persistence of chronic denervation in dog intestinal loop preparations.

Because of the similarity in appearance of DMPP denervated loop spasm and the periodic "P waves" occurring spontaneously after administration of analgesic or antagonist drugs, 15 experiments were performed in which DMPP was administered repeatedly both before and after a dose of 1.0 to 4.0 μM/kg levallorphan. The results were suggestive of possible DMPP blocking effect by levallorphan in some of the animals, but this was highly inconsistent. No potentiation of DMPP responses by levallorphan was observed, and spontaneously occurring "P waves" were similar in appearance and frequency to those usually seen after levallorphan administration alone.

2) Control hexamethonium administrations (1 mg of ion/kg i. v.) caused depression of intestinal loop tone, contractile amplitude and contractile frequency, the response being more pronounced and prolonged in denervated than in innervated loops. In addition, the dogs exhibited drying of nasal, salivary and intestinal secretions, and relaxation of the nictitating membrane. This dose of hexamethonium was also capable of blocking completely the response, described above, to DMPP.

In order to investigate further the possibility that intestinal "P waves" might be ganglionic in origin, 6 experiments were performed in which hexamethonium was administered 7 to 35 minutes after a dose of 1.0 or 2.0 μM/kg levallorphan, when "P waves" had started to appear. Regardless of the character of intestinal activity resulting from levallorphan administration (see section *C* above), hexamethonium effected no further change in any of the 10 loop recordings obtained. Typical "P waves" continued to appear after hexamethonium administration in all cases. It was concluded that intestinal loop motility under the influence of levallorphan is resistant to depression by hexamethonium, and that levallorphan-induced "P waves" are not prevented by the ganglionic blocking agent.

3) In control experiments, atropine sulfate (0.5 mg i.v.) produced a decrease in intestinal loop tone, contractile amplitude and contractile frequency, the denervated loops being markedly hypersensitive to the depressant action of the drug.

Eleven experiments were then performed in which atropine was administered 4 to 30 minutes after levallorphan (1.0 μM/kg), nalorphine (1.0 μM/kg) or levorphan (0.1 μM/kg). Under these conditions, atropine failed to depress intestinal tone in either innervated or denervated loops, although it did decrease contractile frequency in some cases. Furthermore, atropine administration consistently initiated the immediate onset of "P waves," which then recurred with greater regularity and frequency (5 to 8 minute intervals) than was characteristic for the analgesic or antagonist drugs in the absence of atropine. Thus it appeared that intestinal loop motility, under the influence of the analgesics or antagonists, exhibits resistance to the tone depressant action of atropine, and the latter drug not only fails to prevent, but strikingly enhances the occurrence of "P waves."

Nine additional experiments were run in which the order of drug administration was reversed. Levallorphan (1.0 μM/kg) was administered either 4 minutes after atropine (when intestinal motility was depressed), or 30 to 50 minutes after atropine (when intestinal motility had "recovered" from the depressant effect of atropine). At both time intervals, levallorphan stimulated intestinal tone in every case, and usually it increased contractile amplitude and frequency as well. The onset and frequency of "P waves," however, was not different from that usually observed for levallorphan in the absence of atropine.

E. Antagonism studies. Beal and Shapiro (1953), Gruber and Gruber (1953) and Hart and McCawley (1944) have demonstrated antagonism of analgesic-induced intestinal spasm by nalorphine in man and the dog, but published data on the nature of this antagonism are lacking. Studies were therefore carried out to determine the quantitative characteristics of antagonism of analgesic drug effect on intestinal loop tone in the dog. Nalorphine was tested against 2 dose levels of morphine, and levallorphan against 3 dose levels of levorphan, 1 of alphaprodine, and 1 of dihydrocodeine. For each dose level of analgesic drug employed, 3 to 5 molar dose ratios of

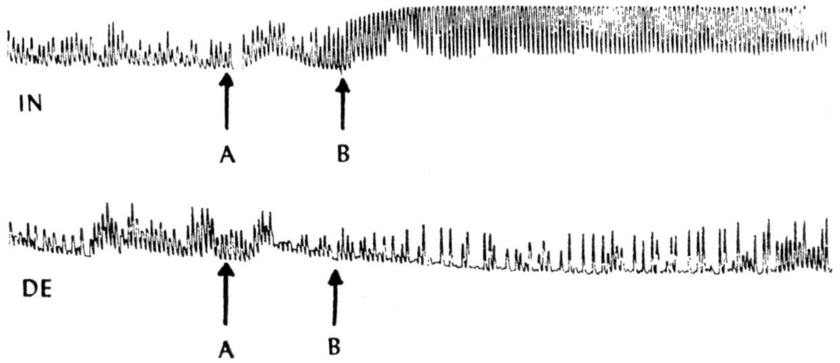

Fig. 4. Antagonism of levorphan effect on jejunal Thiry-Vella loop tone by prior administration o levallorphan.
Note complete antagonism in denervated loop, incomplete antagonism in innervated loop.
A = levallorphan, 0.05 μM/kg i.v.; B = levorphan, 1.0 μM/kg i.v.; IN = innervated loop; DE = extrinsically denervated loop.

analgesic to antagonist were studied, and at least 10 experiments were performed at each dose ratio. Figure 4 illustrates one such experiment. Since the doses of antagonists to be employed occasionally produced mild changes in intestinal motility pattern (see section *C* above), and in order to distinguish between these and analgesic drug effects, a standard procedure was followed in every experiment. This consisted of injecting the antagonist approximately 60 seconds prior to the injection of the analgesic drug.

It was apparent from the analgesic drug experiments (reported in *B* above) that the *in vivo* intestinal preparation does not yield analgesic drug effect data suitable for construction of graded dose-response curves and, therefore, an all-or-none criterion of analgesic drug antagonism in this preparation was necessarily chosen. The criterion selected for successful antagonism was complete prevention of any visible change whatsoever in loop tone during the first 5 minutes following administration of the analgesic drug. In analyzing the results, the records of all experiments were evaluated several times, in random order, and without knowledge of which drugs or dose levels had been employed. Results (see table 4) in each dose-ratio series were expressed as number of loop recordings in which complete antagonism was evident (numerator) over total number of loop recordings obtained at that dose ratio (denominator). The data were further separated into results obtained with innervated and with denervated loops.

Three dose ratio series were also run in which the order of drug administration was reversed, the antagonist being given 60 seconds *after* the analgesic. The criterion of antagonism employed here was the abrupt return of loop tone to normal following injection of the antagonist. The results are labelled "Reverse order series" in the table, and indicate that the order of administration of levorphan and levallorphan did not influence the effective antagonistic dose of the latter.

It was observed during these experiments that the duration of blocking action of the antagonists was considerably shorter than the duration of spasmogenic action of the higher dose levels of the analgesic drugs, and at these high analgesic dose levels the dogs exhibited delayed loop hypertonicity even though complete antagonism was evident initially. Also, the very small doses of antagonist necessary to prevent analgesic-induced intestinal loop spasm apparently were insufficient to antagonize the sedation produced by higher dose levels of the analgesic drugs (see section *B* above), but adequate to prevent nausea and vomiting. Antagonism of intestinal effects of analgesics was limited to those mechanisms controlling tone and did not involve the "P waves," which occurred with the same frequency in these experiments as in those in which the same doses of analgesic drugs were administered alone.

No consistent discrepancy between the behavior of innervated and denervated loops was observed in the antagonism studies.

With respect to the quantitative aspects of antagonism, the data fail to support the concept of critical and constant analgesic-to-antagonist dose ratios. (Effective antagonistic ratios varied 100-fold as the dose levels of analgesic drug were varied over a 100-fold range.) Instead, the abso-

TABLE 4

Results of antagonism studies

Analgesic Drug and Dose ($\mu M/kg$)	Antagonist Drug and Dose ($\mu M/kg$)	Molar Ratio of Analgesic to Antagonist	Incidence of Complete Antagonism		
			Innervated loops	Denervated loops	Total loops
Levorphan	Levallorphan				
	0.05	1:5	10/10	4/7	14/17
	0.01	1:1	5/10	1/5	6/15
0.01	0.005	1:0.5	1/10	2/6	3/16
	0.0025	1:0.25	1/10	1/5	2/15
	0.001	1:0.1	0/11	0/8	0/19
Levorphan	Levallorphan				
	0.1	1:1	10/10	6/8	16/18
0.1	0.05	1:0.5	10/10	4/5	14/15
	0.01	1:0.1	2/10	0/7	2/17
	0.005	1:0.05	1/10	0/8	1/18
Levorphan	Levallorphan				
0.1 (Reverse order	0.1	1:1	10/11	7/8	17/19
series)	0.05	1:0.5	10/10	7/7	17/17
	0.01	1:0.1	3/10	2/8	5/18
Levorphan	Levallorphan				
	0.1	1:0.1	7/10	5/6	12/16
	0.05	1:0.05	7/10	2/5	9/15
1.0	0.01	1:0.01	3/10	1/6	4/16
	0.005	1:0.005	2/10	0/6	2/16
	0.001	1:0.001	0/10	0/7	0/17
Morphine	Nalorphine				
0.015 μEq/kg	0.075	1:5	9/10	6/7	15/17
	0.015	1:1	3/11	4/8	7/19
	0.0075	1:0.5	2/10	0/6	2/16
	0.0037	1:0.25	0/10	0/7	0/17
Morphine	Nalorphine				
0.15 μEq/kg	0.075	1:0.5	10/10	4/6	14/16
	0.015	1:0.1	3/11	5/8	8/19
	0.0075	1:0.05	1/11	1/7	2/18
Dihydrocodeine	Levallorphan				
	0.05	1:0.11	9/10	7/8	16/18
0.45	0.01	1:0.022	8/10	3/8	11/18
	0.005	1:0.011	3/10	0/8	3/18
Alphaprodine	Levallorphan				
	0.05	1:0.11	10/10	8/8	18/18
0.45	0.01	1:0.022	7/11	4/9	11/20
	0.005	1:0.011	1/10	3/9	4/19

lute amount of antagonist drug necessary for initial prevention or reversal of intestinal loop spasm remained remarkably constant, regardless of the particular analgesic drug employed, the dose (over a 100-fold range) of analgesic administered or the order of administration. In these experiments, the effective dose of antagonist (producing complete antagonism in two-thirds of the cases in a series) was between 0.01 and 0.05 μM/kg for levallorphan, and between 0.015 and 0.075 μM/kg for nalorphine.

Discussion. Analysis of the nature of a particular drug antagonism has been most satisfactorily based upon data providing dose-response curves for the agonist in the absence of, and in the presence of various concentrations of the antagonist. The experiments reported here on analgesic antagonism with respect to intestinal tone *in vivo* could not yield data of this type. The present studies did demonstrate, however, that effective ratios of analgesic to antagonist increased progressively as the dose levels of the analgesic drugs were increased, and this behavior is not typical of simple competitive reversible antagonism. The very high, and seemingly absolute, affinity of the antagonist drugs for intestinal receptors is of considerable theoretical interest, but it should be borne in mind that practical utilization of such drug antagonism behavior is limited, in the case of the analgesic antagonists, by their demonstrably brief duration of blocking effect.

The type of drug antagonism behavior reported here for intestinal effects of analgesic drugs may extend to other actions of the opiates as well. Miller *et al.* (1955) studied levallorphan antagonism of morphine-induced depression of respiratory minute volume in rabbits, and observed that the ratio of antagonist to analgesic necessary to restore equally depressed minute volumes to control level was 2:4 when morphine dose levels of 4 mg/kg were employed, but was 5:32 when morphine dose levels of 32 mg/kg were used. Pertinent also are the observations of Axelrod and Cochin (1957) on the rat liver microsomal N-demethylating enzyme system, which these authors have proposed may serve as a model for the analgesic receptor sites. They stated that nalorphine inhibition of morphine N-demethylation in this system appeared to be noncompetitive in nature.

The similarity of analgesic drug responses in normally innervated and extrinsically denervated Thiry-Vella loops clearly divorces the locus of intestinal spasmogenic effect from the central nervous system. Less clear is the interpretation of the relationship between dose of analgesic and magnitude or duration of effect. The intestinal responses to levorphan over a 100-fold dosage range suggested a self-limiting or even self-antagonizing characteristic of effect on tone as dose levels were increased. Whether this may legitimately be considered evidence for a masked biphasic action, or for 2 types of unequally sensitive analgesic receptors in the intestine, is difficult to say. However, intestinal responses to the antagonist drugs afforded unquestionable evidence of capacity (within the opiate chemical group) both to stimulate and to depress intestinal tone and contractions.

Regarding the various types of observed intestinal responses to the antagonist drugs, it is interesting to note the dichotomy between the brief durations of intestinal hypertonicity or analgesic-antagonizing action (when these were elicited), and the prolonged durations of intestinal inhibition and persistence of "P waves" (when these were elicited by the same dosage levels)—further evidence for the possible multiplicity of intestinal functions or types of receptors affected by the antagonist drugs.

The recurrent "P waves" which appeared in recordings of Thiry-Vella loop activity following administration of either the analgesic drugs, the antagonists or both, may be similar to the morphine-induced "peristaltic waves" described by Krueger (1933), which he demonstrated to be propagated phenomena by means of multiple balloons in a Thiry-Vella loop. However, Fromherz and Pellmont (1952) reported depression by analgesic drugs of the peristaltic reflex in guinea pig ileum *in situ* and reversal of this depression by levallorphan.

Results obtained with the several experimental preparations employed in this study were sufficiently divergent to warrant comment. The high sensitivity of the Thiry-Vella loop dogs to intestinal effects of analgesic and antagonist drugs stood in marked contrast to the relative insensitivity of the acute dog preparation and the isolated tissue preparation. And the differences were not limited to quantitative ones. Whereas the antagonist drugs were consistently depressant to intestinal motility in the acute dogs, this was not true in the Thiry-Vella loop dogs. *In vitro* there were additional discrepancies in the qualitative nature of intestinal responses to many of the drugs, related to species employed and to prior exposure of the tissues to the same or different drugs. The validity and applicability of conclusions drawn from any given experimental preparation are thus understood to be appropriately limited.

SUMMARY

Four analgesic drugs (morphine, levorphan, alphaprodine, dihydrocodeine) and 2 analgesic-antagonists (nalorphine, levallorphan) were studied for their effects on intestinal motility *in vitro* and *in vivo.*

In experiments with isolated rabbit and puppy jejunum, responses to each drug were determined, and were shown to be reversible with washout and to vary with drug concentration, with species and with previous exposure of the tissues to the same or different drugs. As a group, the analgesics and antagonists failed to exhibit significant blocking or potentiating action on spasms of isolated intestine induced by barium, histamine, methacholine, serotonin or "bio-dialysate."

Experiments with trained unanesthetized Thiry-Vella loop dogs demonstrated the following: 1) The unanesthetized dog was far more sensitive to intestinal effects of intravenous analgesic drugs than was the acute anesthetized dog preparation or the *in vitro* preparation and intestinal hypertonicity or spasm was elicited consistently at subsedative and subnauseant dosage by each analgesic studied. 2) Innervated and extrinsically denervated intestinal loops responded similarly to analgesic drugs. 3) Dihydrocodeine and alphaprodine exhibited approximately 1/30 the intestinal spasmogenic potency of morphine. 4) When intestinal responses to analgesic-antagonist drugs were elicited, their nature varied from one animal to another and between innervated and denervated loops. 5) Administration of either the analgesics or the antagonists caused recurrent abnormal motility patterns ("P waves") to appear in recordings from both innervated and denervated loops. 6) Experiments with autonomic agents failed to reveal the cause of the analgesic or antagonist-induced "P waves," but did demonstrate some interesting interactions of the 2 drug groups. 7) Results of antagonism studies with respect to intestinal tone failed to support the concept of critical and constant analgesic-to-antagonist dose ratios. Instead, the absolute amount of antagonist drug necessary for initial prevention or reversal of analgesic-induced intestinal hypertonicity remained remarkably constant, regardless of the particular analgesic drug employed, dose (over a 100-fold range) of analgesic administered or order of administration.

ACKNOWLEDGMENTS. I should like to express my grateful appreciation to Miss Alice Stellmacher who assisted with the surgery and the running of the isolated tissue studies, and to the Marquette Art and Photography Department who prepared the figures. Thanks are extended also to the following for supplies of drugs used in this investigation: Dr. M. J. Schiffrin, Hoffmann-LaRoche Inc.; Dr. Rodney P. Gwinn, Abbott Laboratories; Dr. Graham Chen, Parke, Davis & Co.; Dr. Frederick K. Heath, Merck & Co., Inc.; Dr. M. E. Speeter, Upjohn Co.

REFERENCES

AXELROD, J. AND COCHIN, J.: THIS JOURNAL **121:** 107, 1957.
BEAL, J. M. AND SHAPIRO, H.: Surgery **33:** 65, 1953.
FROMHERZ, K. AND PELLMONT, B.: Experientia **8:** 394, 1952.
GRUBER, C. M. JR., LEE, K. S. AND GRUBER, C. M.: THIS JOURNAL **99:** 317, 1950.
GRUBER, C. M. JR. AND GRUBER, C. M.: THIS JOURNAL **109:** 157, 1953.
HART, E. R. AND MCCAWLEY, E. L.: THIS JOURNAL **82:** 339, 1944.
KRUEGER, H.: THIS JOURNAL **48:** 280, 1933.
KRUEGER, H. AND GAY, H.: THIS JOURNAL **48:** 279, 1933.
MILLER, J. W., GILFOIL, T. M. AND SHIDEMAN, F. E.: THIS JOURNAL **115:** 350, 1955.
RANDALL, L. O. AND LEHMAN, G.: THIS JOURNAL **93:** 314, 1948.
RANDALL, L. O. AND LEHMAN, G.: THIS JOURNAL **99:** 163, 1950.
WINTER, C. A., ORAHOVATS, P. D., FLATAKER, L., LEHMAN, E. G. AND LEHMAN, J. T.: THIS JOURNAL **111:** 152, 1954.
YOUMANS, W. B.: Nervous and Neurohumoral Regulation of Intestinal Motility, Interscience Publishers, Inc., New York, 1949.
YOUNG, D. C., VANDERPLOEG, R. A., FEATHERSTONE, R. M. AND GROSS, E. G.: THIS JOURNAL **114:** 33, 1955.

8074

THE EFFECT OF ESTROGENS ON UTERINE BLOOD FLOW IN THE RAT

SUMNER M. KALMAN

Department of Pharmacology, Stanford University School of Medicine, Stanford, California

Received for publication April 14, 1958

Recent studies on the fractionation of cardiac output in rats have led to a convenient tracer technique for the estimation of blood flow rates to various organs (Sapirstein, 1956). The method is based upon the principle that for a short time after introduction of a foreign substance into the animal's blood stream it will enter the arterial circulation of an organ without appearing in the venous outflow from that organ. Interesting data regarding redistribution of blood flow after a meal have been obtained by Reininger and Sapirstein (1957) using this method.

The material reported here shows how this useful technique may be applied to an organ where blood flow is not easily measured by classical methods. The rat uterus is quite small, particularly after ovariectomy. The arterial supply to each uterine horn comes from two arteries, the ovarian and the superior vesical, which anastomose in the mesovarium (Greene, 1955). In the ovariectomized rat the situation is altered by the operation which cuts off the supply from the ovarian artery. It is understandable that previous studies of uterine blood flow in experimental animals have been of a qualitative nature. The status of the problem may be assessed from Reynolds' book on the uterus (1949) wherein he reiterates the general impression that estrogens enhance uterine blood flow and induce a hyperemia characterized by a high level of oxygen saturation. He also states that "direct measurement of the blood flow at this time, (*i.e.*, after estrogen treatment) during anestrus and other nongravid conditions, has not, however, been made." A fairly extensive search of the literature has not uncovered any direct measurements of uterine blood flow in the ovariectomized rat or changes in flow rate induced by estrogen.

METHODS. Adult, ovariectomized Long-Evans rats were used. They weighed 200 to 250 g. Experimental animals were injected with 2 μg of ethinyl estradiol intravenously 4 hours before sacrifice. Controls received an intravenous injection of saline, the vehicle for hormone administration. About 5 minutes before sacrifice each rat was given an intraperitoneal injection of 5 to 8 mg of pentobarbital per 100 g. This is a high dose but it was found necessary to achieve an adequate degree of anesthesia. The rest of the procedure was essentially the same as that employed by Sapirstein (1956). The jugular vein was cannulated, a tracer substance was injected rapidly and this was followed by an injection of saturated KCl solution to stop the heart. Two different tracers were used, Na^{22} as $Na^{22}Cl$, and in a few cases I^{131} as NaI^{131}. Both were given in a volume of 0.1 ml in isotonic saline. About 3 microcuries of Na^{22} tracer were given to each animal. Larger amounts of I^{131} were used but smaller activities could have been employed. Tissues were removed, blotted on moist filter paper to remove excess blood and placed into small tared vials. Weights were obtained on an analytical balance, and radioactivity was determined in a well-type scintillation detector. Both kidneys of each animal were used *in toto* for assay of their radioactivity. The uterus was also counted, as a whole organ. For intestinal radioactivity a sample of distal large intestine was excised. Where "specific activity" is mentioned this term refers to counts per minute per mg wet tissue weight.

RESULTS. Table 1 presents raw data showing total counts per organ for uterus and kidney and then the fraction of the injected radioactivity which this represents. Variation encountered in this table is due largely to the fact that the uterus of the ovariectomized rat was of quite different size from animal to animal, depending upon how much of each horn was lost during operation and upon how big the uterus was at the time of operation. Nevertheless the differences between control and hormone-treated animals are highly significant with regard to uterine blood flow. No comparable effect on kidney blood flow is noted.

In table 2 an attempt has been made to make animals more nearly comparable by relating specific activities of each organ, uterus and kidney, to a third organ, the intestine. Ratios of specific activities between kidney and intestine do not change with treatment, but there is a striking change when treated uterus is compared to control uterus in this manner. Blood flow is seen to increase about 3 times when it is calculated in this way.

Several minor points are apparent also in the tables. For example, in table 1 no difference is

TABLE 1

Effect of estrogen on the portion of the rat's cardiac output distributed between kidney and the uterus

Rats were ovariectomized.

Rat No.	Time of Sacrifice	Total CPM*		% Injected Isotope	
		Uterus	Kidney	Uterus	Kidney
	seconds				
Group 1 (Control)					
1‡	30	16,640	748,978	.043	1.92
2	30	459	40,746	.027	2.42
3‡	30	1,184	92,579	.014	1.15
4‡	30	3,062	268,711	.036	3.18
5	30	934	80,050	.035	2.96
6	30	1,431	109,917	.049	3.78
7	45	1,972	50,314	.060	1.53
8	55	1,765	72,058	.051	2·09
9	15	1,027	100,525	.030	2.90
Mean	—	—	—	.0344§	2.44¶
†Group 2 (Estrogen)					
10	30	2,816	37,232	0.24	3.15
11‡	30	36,821	689,232	0.094	1.77
12‡	30	4,768	93,957	0.056	1.11
13	30	10,004	140,873	0.37	5.22
14	30	9,307	82,735	0.28	2.52
15	45	6,781	63,591	0.21	1.94
16	15	5,548	72,586	0.16	2.10
17	15	3,386	82,718	0.098	2.40
Mean	—	—	—	0.189§	2.53¶

* "Total CPM" refers to the whole uterus (column 3) and to *both* kidneys (column 4).

† This group received 2 μg of ethinyl estradiol 4 hours before sacrifice.

‡ These rats received I^{131}, all others received Na^{22}.

§ "t" = 4.52, which for 15 degrees of freedom is significant beyond the 1% level. Student's "t" test.

¶ The difference between these means is not significant.

No corrections have been made in this table or in table 2 for different whole animal weights.

TABLE 2

Ratio of specific activities of tissues with and without estrogen treatment

Specific activities are expressed as counts per minute per mg of wet tissue weight.

Rat No.*	Specific Activities			Ratios of Spec. Activity	
	Uterus	Kidney	Intestine	Uterus/Int.	Kidney/Int.
Group 1 (Control)					
1	231	452	268	0.86	1.69
2	7.07	24.9	8.15	0.87	3.06
3	13.0	51.4	11.3	1.15	4.55
4	36.5	149	47.9	0.76	3.11
5	13.2	43.2	16.5	0.80	2.62
6	27.6	62.9	29.3	0.94	2.15
7	22.7	26.7	17.9	1.27	1.49
8	20.7	38.5	20.8	0.99	1.85
9	16.8	61.6	18.5	0.91	3.33
Mean	—	—	—	0.95†	2.65‡
Group 2 (Estrogen)					
10	18.5	21.6	6.37	2.90	3.39
11	286	377	112	2.55	3.37
12	35.7	52.8	14.5	2.46	3.64
13	66.6	67.3	22.9	2.91	2.94
14	69.5	44.0	18.3	3.80	2.40
15	48.2	37.7	17.4	2.77	2.17
16	60.7	51.4	18.9	3.21	2.72
17	55.1	57.3	16.3	3.38	3.52
Mean	—	—	—	3.00†	3.02‡

* These are the same rats that supplied the material for table 1.

† The "t" value for the difference between these means is 12.93 which is significant beyond the 0.1% level.

‡ The difference between these means is not significant.

apparent in the results where the heart was stopped at different times after isotope injection. This is an essential part of the principle of the method as noted by Sapirstein (1956). Also of interest is the fact that different isotopes, I^{131} and Na^{22}, give quite comparable results. Incidentally, renal blood flow in this series of experiments is less than that reported by Sapirstein (1956). This may be due to use of a larger dose of anesthetic in the experiments reported here.

A third tracer substance, K^{42}, given as K^{42} Cl was employed to check the results obtained with

Na^{22} and I^{131}. Sixteen rats were used; 8 served as controls and 8 were treated with estrogen. Results corresponded closely with those described above for the other tracer materials. The only discrepancy noted was a greater uptake of potassium by the kidneys than was obtained with the sodium or iodide ion. Here again no extra-uterine effect of estrogen on blood flow could be demonstrated.

DISCUSSION. From these studies it is possible to make a quantitative estimate of estrogen effects on uterine blood flow. In the ovariectomized animal a physiological dose of estrogen brought about a 3-fold increase in uterine blood flow 4 hours after hormone injection. This increase in blood flow, measured as specific activity, is not due to an increase in the size of the vascular pool (Kalman, 1955; Kalman and Lowenstein, 1958). The size of the vascular pool seems to keep pace with the increase in tissue water content, and a correction is made for this fact when radioactivity is expressed on the basis of tissue wet weight.

An absolute value of blood flow through the uterus can be estimated from known values for rat cardiac output (Bullard, 1956). If we use Bullard's value of 210 ml/kg, then the 200 g rat will have an output of about 40 ml/min. The uterus gets approximately 0.045% of this, or 0.018 ml/min. Following estrogen injection this increases to about 0.2% or 0.08 ml/min.

It is likely that this remarkable change in blood supply is due to alterations in tissue metabolism, since metabolic changes are quite apparent within this interval after hormone injection (Szego and Roberts, 1953). Products of metabolism and altered pH probably induce a vasodilatation of arterioles. However, one cannot exclude the possibility of a direct estrogenic effect on uterine blood vessels.

SUMMARY

The administration of estrogen to adult, ovariectomized rats resulted in a 3-fold increase in uterine blood flow. Measurements were made at 4 hours after hormone administration in these animals and in a control group. Blood flow was estimated by a recently-introduced method which is based upon the early fractionation of a tracer material introduced into the rat's blood stream.

ACKNOWLEDGMENTS. The author would like to thank Mrs. Margaret Lombrozo for assistance with the experimental work. These experiments were supported by a grant from the U. S. Public Health Service.

REFERENCES

BULLARD, R. W.: Fed. Proc. **15:** 28, 1956.
GREENE, E. C.: Anatomy of the Rat, Hafner, New York, 1955.
KALMAN, S. M.: THIS JOURNAL **115:** 442, 1955.
KALMAN, S. M. AND LOWENSTEIN, J. M.: THIS JOURNAL **122:** 163, 1958.
REININGER, E. J. AND SAPIRSTEIN, L. A.: Science **126:** 1176, 1957.
REYNOLDS, S. R. M.: Physiology of the Uterus, 2nd ed., Hoeber, New York, 1949.
SAPIRSTEIN, L. A.: Circulation Res. **4:** 689, 1956.
SZEGO, C. M. AND ROBERTS, S.: Recent Prog. in Hormone Res. **8:** 419, 1953.

HEART LESIONS IN MICE CAUSED BY TREATMENT WITH BISHYDROXYCOUMARIN (DICUMAROL)[1]

F. I. DESSAU, S. KLEIN, L. LIPCHUCK, J. O'GRADY AND J. TSALIKIS

Department of Experimental Pathology, Experimental Therapeutics Research Section, Research Division, American Cyanamid Company

Received for publication May 5, 1958

The occurrence of myocarditis with necrosis and hemorrhage in rats and mice given purified diets containing sulfaguanidine was reported previously (Dessau *et al.*, 1954). Earlier unpublished experiments in rats had suggested that a complete dietary lack of vitamin E was essential for induction of these lesions. It was noted, however, that damage to the heart muscle was invariably associated with evidence of hemorrhage and this suggested the possible role of vitamin K. Systematic investigation in mice of the factors concerned led to the conclusion in the above report that a dietary lack of both vitamins E and K was necessary for the production of myocarditis in mice fed a purified diet containing sulfaguanidine. The role of vitamin K deficiency seemed the more definite one although there had been no suggestion of even an indirect relationship of vitamin-K deficiency to injury to the heart muscle prior to our experience.

If the role of vitamin K deficiency was correctly interpreted, it followed that the same type of heart lesions should be produced by incorporation of a vitamin K antagonist into the diet. As we did not find evidence of this kind in the literature, we decided to investigate the effect on the heart of feeding large doses of bishydroxycoumarin (Dicumarol) to mice. Prevention of a Dicumarol effect by vitamin K_1 and Menadione was also part of the experimental plan.

A similar approach was not possible in the case of vitamin E, as no antagonist to this vitamin is known. Therefore, the experiments with vitamin E reported here deal only with its action on the Dicumarol effect and with possible modification or enchancement of the effect of vitamin K by vitamin E.

[1] Presented in part at the 1957 Fall Meeting of the American Society for Pharmacology and Experimental Therapeutics, Baltimore, Md.

Materials and methods. *Animals and animal maintenance.* Male albino mice from Carworth Farms, Inc., were used throughout. They were weanling age, weighing about 12 to 14 g at the start of the experiment. Mice were kept in wire cages with mesh floors (stainless steel), in groups of 10, for a period of 5 weeks.

Diets and compounds used. In experiments III-2, V, VI, XI, XII, XIII, XV and XVI ground mouse pellets (Wayne Lab. Blox "R") were used. In all other experiments the same purified diet was used which had been employed in the sulfaguanidine experiments.

Dicumarol (Abbott Laboratories Lot No. 628-7434) was mixed with the diet. The vitamin K used was vitamin K_1, Merck Laboratories No. 52153; the Menadione (2-methyl-1,4,naphthoquinone), was a preparation from the Bound Brook Laboratories of the American Cyanamid Co. (Calco No. 53303). Vitamin E was given as *d-α*-tocopherol-acetate (DPi—Batch No. E7155). All diets were fed *ad lib.*

Observations during life. Data were recorded on food intake (daily), incidence of externally visible subcutaneous hemorrhage and time of death.

Post-mortem techniques. Mice dead before the termination of the experiment were autopsied as soon as possible. The survivors were killed by chloroform inhalation after 35 days of treatment. At autopsy, the cranial, thoracic and abdominal cavities were opened and inspected for occurrence of hemorrhages.

Histological studies were limited to the heart, which was examined in every mouse. Fixation was done in aqueous 4% formaldehyde. Paraffin sections were cut 6μ in thickness and stained with hematoxylin-eosin. Sections were made through an anteroposterior plane around the longitudinal axis of the heart to include apical and basal portions of both ventricles and auricles.

Method of evaluation of heart lesions. Sections (at least 4 per mouse) were scored as positive for lesions when necrosis, hemorrhage and leukocytic

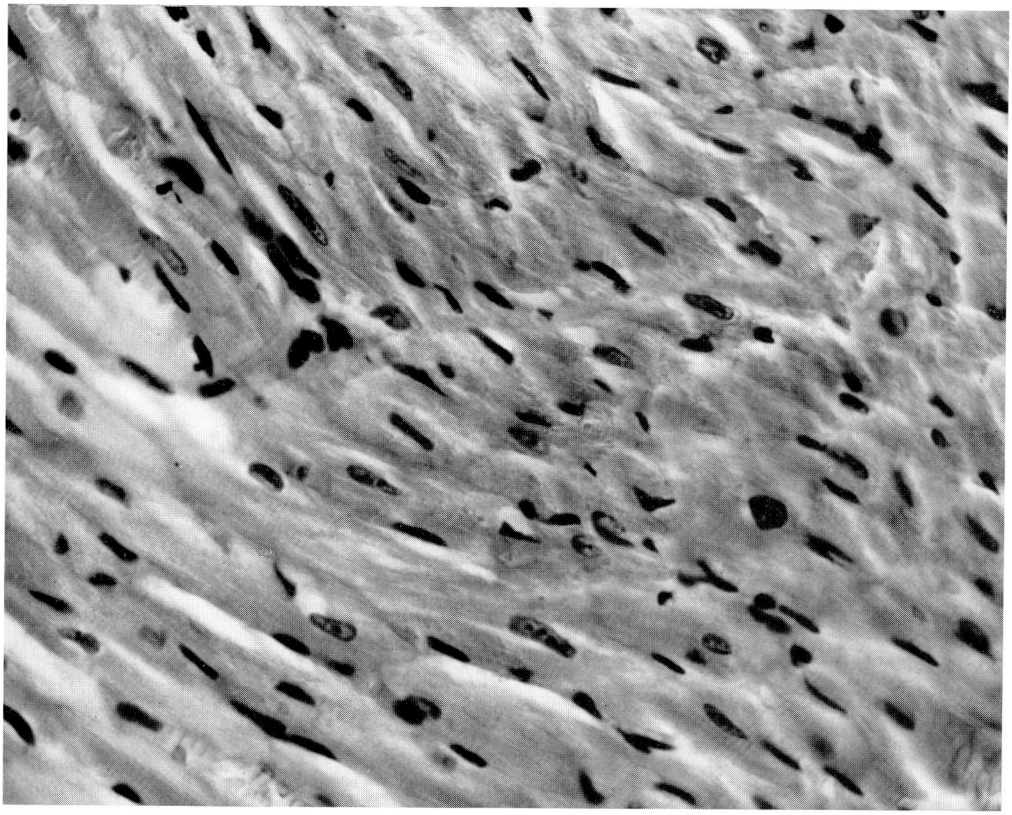

FIG. 1. Heart muscle of untreated control mouse.
Hematoxylin-eosin stain of 6μ section (450×). Note continuity of fibers, absence of leukocytes.

infiltration were seen in any part of the ventricular myocardium (figs. 1 and 2). Pigment, monocytic infiltration and fibrosis as evidence of previous hemorrhage and necrosis were also scored as positive. Whenever only 1 or 2 characteristics of these triads were encountered a negative score was given. Any of these, excepting necrosis, was observed alone in a number of cases. Only the incidence of heart lesions, scored as positive, is included in the tables in which results are summarized. Other observations, *e.g.*, the incidence of hemorrhages in other organs, are not included.

RESULTS. *Effect of Dicumarol alone.* In all cases with heart lesions there was evidence of hemorrhage in the heart muscle, often on gross inspection. The cellular reaction observed was related to the age of the lesion with polymorphonuclear leukocytes being in evidence in the early stages, after 4 to 6 days of treatment; while monocytic elements were more common afterward. Fibrosis with hemosiderin deposits was seen in later stages of treatment with Dicumarol. Necrosis was usually focal in character, but at times occupied large areas of the interventricular or the outer walls of the ventricles without predilection for regions either near the apex or the base. Hemorrhages seemed to originate from capillaries. Blood extravasates were seen in the epicardium, myocardium and subendocardial areas without evidence of tears or defects in the walls of arteries or venules.

Table 1 indicates that a dosage of 150 to 200 mg/kg of diet was required to produce these lesions in more than one-third of the experimental animals. The lowest dose level at which heart lesions were obtained was 40 mg/kg of diet. At a dose level of 150 to 200 mg/kg, 50% of the mice died within 6 days when kept on the purified diet, and within 8 days when fed ground pellets.

Effect of vitamin E. The effect of vitamin E on the incidence of Dicumarol-induced heart lesions

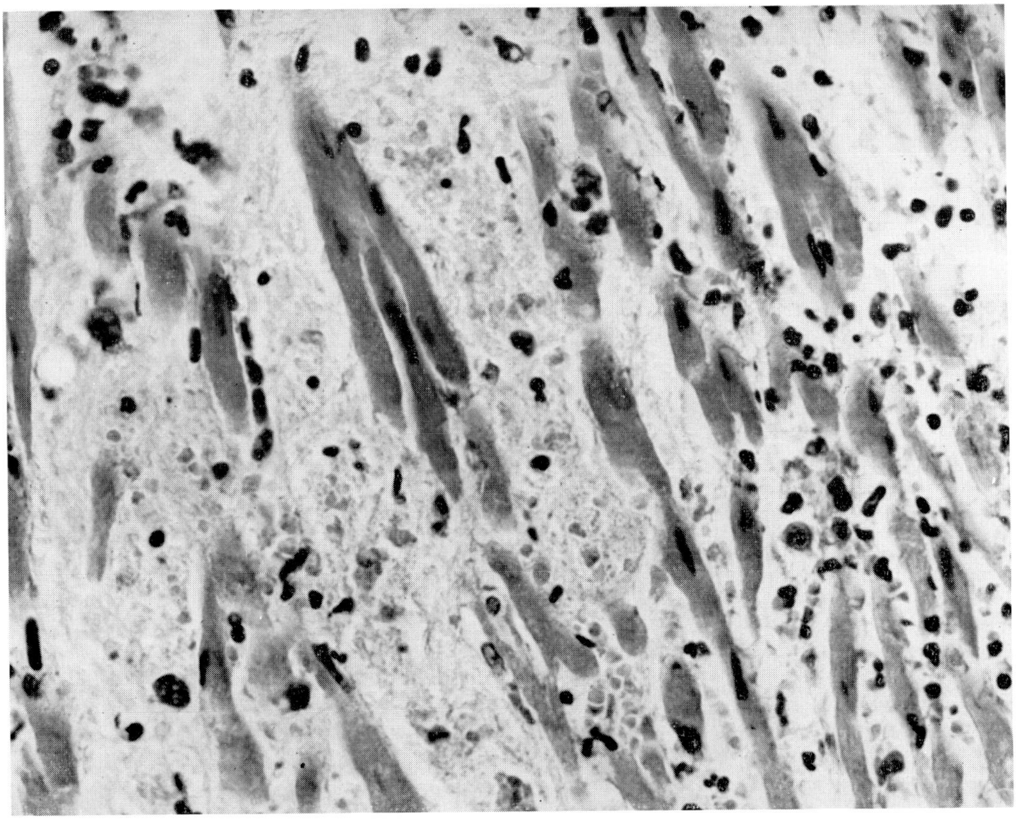

FIG. 2. Heart muscle of mouse fed 200 mg of Dicumarol/kg of diet. Hematoxylin-eosin stain of 6μ section (450×). Note disruption and necrosis of muscle fibers, leukocytic infiltration and wide separation of fibers due to hemorrhage.

was observed in 6 different experiments (V to X, not shown in tables). In 2 experiments (V and VI) with groups of 47 to 50 mice, a daily dose of vitamin E of 1 mg given subcutaneously 5 times per week failed to show any influence on the effect of both a 200 mg and 300 mg/kg diet level of Dicumarol. Groups of the same size were used in 3 dietary experiments. In 2 experiments (VII and VIII), the diet level of vitamin E was 250 mg/kg with 100 mg of Dicumarol/kg of diet in one and 200 mg in the other. In another experiment (X) 2,000 mg of vitamin E were added to 1 kg of a diet containing 200 mg of Dicumarol. This same level of Dicumarol was also applied in a dietary experiment (IX) during which groups of 17 to 20 mice each were given vitamin E at levels of 200 to 1,600 mg/kg diet at 2-fold dilutions. There was a complete lack of protective action by vitamin E at all levels.

Effects of vitamin K_1, Menadione and Menadione plus vitamin E. Table 2 contains data which show that vitamin K_1 (2 g/kg diet) gives complete protection from the effect of Dicumarol (200 mg/kg diet). It also shows the protective effect of graded dose levels. Complete suppression of the effect of a diet containing 200 mg/kg of Dicumarol was observed at the 400 mg/kg level of vitamin K_1.

Table 3 contains data regarding the prevention of the effect of 100 and 200 mg/kg diet of Dicumarol by Menadione. Menadione was found to be inferior to vitamin K_1, 800 mg of Menadione not sufficing to give full protection.

The possibility of a synergistic effect of vitamin E with Menadione was explored. Partial protection was given by 400 mg of Menadione/kg diet from the effect of 200 mg of Dicumarol. There were heart lesions in 6 of 23 mice in the Menadione-treated group as against 14 out of 25 in the mice receiving Dicumarol only. Adding

TABLE 1

Incidence of heart lesions in mice receiving Dicumarol

Purified diet in all experimental groups excepting III-2.

Expt.	Dose of Dicumarol		Mice with Heart Lesions
	mg/kg of diet	*mg/kg of mouse*	
I	0	0	0/25
	50	10	3/25
	100	20	6/25
	200	40	11/25
II	0	0	0/25
	10	2	0/25
	20	4	0/25
	40	8	4/25
III-1	200	40	10/50
-2	200	40	9/50
IV	0	0	0/19
	50	10	2/20
	100	20	3/19
	150	30	9/20
	200	40	7/19

2,000 mg of vitamin E to 1 kg of diet did not improve the effectiveness of 400 mg of Menadione against the effect of 200 mg Dicumarol. Heart muscle lesions were found in 10 of 25 mice.

DISCUSSION. *Dicumarol effect.* The lesions produced in the heart muscle of mice by means of treatment with Dicumarol were identical in appearance with those previously observed in mice kept on sulfaguanidine-supplemented purified diets deficient in vitamins K and E. The production of similar lesions in mice both on purified or on pellet diets not supplemented with sulfaguanidine, but with Dicumarol, was further confirmation of the causative role of vitamin K deficiency in the origin of these lesions.

In regard to the pathogenesis of these lesions, it has been evident in all experiments that no damage to the myocardium was encountered, unless it had been preceded by hemorrhage. While hemorrhage without necrosis was observed, there was no case of necrosis without some evidence of hemorrhage. Leukocytic infiltration, varying in degree, was always present whenever there was necrosis.

The role of vitamin K deficiency. Production of heart muscle lesions by means of Dicumarol seemed to be confirmation of the assumption that the lesions observed in mice kept on sulfaguanidine-supplemented, vitamin K-free rations had a causal relationship to vitamin K deficiency. The fact that addition to the diet of either vitamin K_1 or Menadione in adequate dosage prevented the Dicumarol effect seemed additional proof of this causal relationship. The occurrence of heart lesions was prevented to the extent that hemorrhages were prevented.

Prevention of hemorrhages and heart lesions was achieved with smaller doses of vitamin K_1 than of Menadione. This is in agreement with the well-known superiority of vitamin K_1 over Menadione in nullifying the anticoagulant effect of Dicumarol (Collentine and Quick, 1951).

The role of vitamin E. The data presented in this report demonstrated the failure of vitamin E (d-α-tocopherol-acetate) to influence the Dicumarol effect. Also, it did not modify in any way the action of Menadione on the Dicumarol effect. This failure of vitamin E to influence a vitamin K deficiency caused by a vitamin K antagonist, Dicumarol, is in contrast to the previously ob-

TABLE 2

Effect of vitamin K_1 in preventing heart lesions caused by Dicumarol

Dicumarol, 200 mg/kg of purified diet.

Expt.	Vitamin K_1	Mice with Heart Lesions
	mg/kg of diet	
XI*	0	7/25
	0.2	5/25
	2	8/25
	20	6/25
XII*	0	5/25
	20	4/25
	200	3/25
XIII*	0	10/25
	2,000	0/25
XIV†	0	8/12
	200	3/19
	400	0/20
	800	0/20
	1,600	0/20

* Ground pellet diet.

† Purified diet.

TABLE 3

Effect of Menadione on Dicumarol-induced heart lesions

Dicumarol: 200 mg/kg of diet in XV, XVI, XVIII; 100 mg/kg in XVII.

Expt.	Menadione	Mice with Heart Lesions
	mg/kg of diet	
XV*	0	8/25
	2	5/25
	20	10/24
	200	6/25
XVI*	0	12/25
	20	8/25
	200	9/25
	2,000	2/23
XVII†	0	11/20
	200	2/19
	400	2/19
	800	2/19
	1,600	1/20
XVIII†	0	11/15
	200	9/14
	400	9/16
	800	3/16
	1,600	0/19

* Ground pellet diet.

† Purified diet.

served role of vitamin E in the case of the vitamin K deficiency obtained in mice kept on a sulfaguanidine-supplemented purified diet. Possibly this discrepancy might be resolved if it could be shown that the effect of vitamin E was on the intestinal flora, favoring conditions for the preservation of vitamin-K-producing organisms in the presence of sulfaguanidine.

Relation to other forms of experimental myocardial injury. Myocardial injury has been obtained infrequently in mice, experimentally. It has been observed in the course of experimental virus infections, especially of the encephalomyocarditis group (Schmidt, 1948). None of these has been characterized by hemorrhages. Myocardial damage obtained by dietary means has been described by Highman and Daft (1951) in mice fed a low protein diet deficient in choline. Focal lesions throughout the ventricular myocardium showed hyalinization, necrosis and calcification of muscle fibers with little or no inflammatory reaction. There was no evidence of hemorrhage having been associated with these lesions.

Relation to problems of therapy. The question arises to what extent the data presented affect the use of Dicumarol-like anticoagulants in human medicine. The smallest dose at which some heart lesions have been observed in these mice was calculated at 8 mg/kg daily for 35 days. The dose in the human recommended for initial treatment is 200 to 300 mg, the recommended maintenance dose 100 to 200 mg daily (U.S.P. XV, pp. 96–97, 1955). It is open to question whether comparison of human and mouse doses is meaningful in this case. As occurrence of heart lesions in mice after Dicumarol is dependent upon occurrence of hemorrhage, similar lesions would be expected to occur in the human only after hemorrhage. Therefore, in man, a dosage should be avoided which would lead to hemorrhage. In clinical medicine periodic evaluation of prothrombin in blood plasma is used as an aid in avoiding this complication. The ability of vitamin K_1 and of Menadione in adequate doses to nullify the effect of Dicumarol-like anticoagulants has proved most useful in anticoagulant therapy and is also demonstrated in our mouse experiments.

If there is reason to fear uncontrollable overdosage, the clinician has the alternative of using heparin. Heparin, in unpublished experiments, failed to induce heart lesions in mice even with excessive doses (20 to 140 mg/kg) which caused hemorrhage at the site of injection.

Need for further investigation. The relation of the myocardial damage observed to the clotting defect, and the question of damage to the capillary wall by Dicumarol (Quick, 1946) are deserving of further study. This is also true of the similarity and dissimilarity of the observed effect to the heart muscle damage obtained by means of proteolytic enzymes (Kellner and Robertson, 1954). A protective effect by vitamin C (Link, 1945) might be explored. Studies with other anticoagulants, use of Dicumarol in other species and production of chronic myocardial damage by adequate dosing of Dicumarol also would seem desirable.

SUMMARY

Dicumarol added to either purified or pellet diets, at levels from 40 to 200 mg/kg diet, induced heart muscle lesions in mice resembling those observed in mice kept on sulfaguanidine-supplemented purified diets.

Vitamin E supplements to the diet did not modify the effect of Dicumarol (200 mg/kg), while this effect was prevented by vitamin K_1 at 2 times, or Menadione at 8 times the dietary level of Dicumarol.

The addition of vitamin E to a diet containing Menadione at twice the level of Dicumarol did not alter the effect of Dicumarol.

REFERENCES

Collentine, G. E. and Quick, A. J.: Amer. J. med. Sci. **222**: 7, 1951.
Dessau, F. I., Klein, S. and Lipchuck, L.: Proc. Soc. exp. Biol., N. Y. **87**: 522, 1954.
Highman, B. and Daft, F. S.: A.M.A.Arch Path. **52**: 221, 1951.
Kellner, A. and Robertson, T.: J. exp. Med. **99**: 387, 1954.
Link, K. P.: Proc. Chic. Inst. Med. **15**: 370, 1945.
Quick, A. J.: Proc. Chic. Inst. Med. **16**: 94, 1946.
Schmidt, E. C. H.: Amer. J. Path. **24**: 97, 1948.

8076

THE RELATIONSHIP BETWEEN IPRONIAZID METABOLISM AND THE DURATION OF ITS EFFECT ON MONOAMINE OXIDASE

SIDNEY HESS, HERBERT WEISSBACH, BETTY G. REDFIELD AND SIDNEY UDENFRIEND

Laboratory of Chemical Pharmacology and Laboratory of Clinical Biochemistry, National Heart Institute, National Institutes of Health, Public Health Service, U. S. Department of Health, Education, and Welfare, Bethesda, Maryland

Received for publication June 6, 1958

To determine the significance of the role played by amines such as serotonin, epinephrine and norepinephrine in the body and especially in the nervous system, methods or compounds are required which will affect their formation or metabolism. One such compound, iproniazid (1-isonicotinyl-2-isopropyl hydrazine, Marsilid) has been found useful as an inhibitor of monoamine oxidase (MAO) (Zeller *et al.*, 1952; Udenfriend *et al.*, 1957a, b; Davison, 1957; and Weissbach *et al.*, 1957).

Studies on the physiological distribution and metabolism of this drug are essential in order to obtain more information on its mechanism of action. We have developed a relatively specific assay for Marsilid and have modified the method for isonicotinic acid, its major pyridine end product (DeRitter, 1952), to include determinations of the compound in tissues.

Evidence will be presented that iproniazid administered to rats intraperitoneally quickly enters the brain and other tissues, inhibits MAO activity and quickly disappears. However, MAO inhibition persists for several days after no detectable quantity of drug can be distinguished. The work of Rubin *et al.* (1952) has been extended to show that there is no accumulation of isonicotinic acid in any of the tissues.

MATERIALS AND METHODS. Serotonin in tissues was measured by methods previously described (Udenfriend *et al.*, 1955; Bogdanski *et al.*, 1956). MAO activity was determined by measuring serotonin disappearance using a modification of the method described earlier by Sjoerdsma *et al.* (1955). The tissue removed from the animal immediately after death was homogenized in 2 volumes of cold water and kept cold until used. The incubation beakers contained 0.5 ml of homogenate (166 mg of tissue), 0.5 ml of 0.5 M phosphate buffer pH 7.4 and 1 mg of serotonin plus enough water to make a total volume of 3.5 ml. The beakers were incubated at 37° C in air. Serotonin analysis employing the usual α-nitroso-β-naphthol reagent was made on 0.5 ml aliquots removed at various times; MAO activity was reflected by the disappearance of serotonin.

Iproniazid was assayed by adding 1 ml of tissue homogenate (1 g of tissue + 2 ml of cold water) or plasma to 0.5 g of NaCl in a glass-stoppered shaking-tube. One ml of phosphate buffer pH 8 was added to adjust the final pH between 7.2 and 8.0, then 6 ml of n-butanol were added. The mixture was shaken for 10 minutes, centrifugated and 5 ml of the alcohol layer were transferred to a clean shaking-tube containing 2.5 ml of 0.1 N HCl and 10 ml of n-heptane. The tube was shaken for 4 minutes, centrifugated and 1.0 ml of the lower acid layer added to 1 ml of phosphate buffer pH 8, in a test tube; 0.5 ml of water and finally 0.05 ml of Folin and Ciocalteu (1927) phosphotungstic-phosphomolybdic acid color reagent were added. The solution was allowed to stand for 10 minutes and the optical density at 625 mμ was measured. Blank values were determined on the tissues of a number of normal animals and found to range from 10 to 14 μg/g of tissue and 5 to 10 μg/ml of plasma; the averages were subtracted from the values obtained using test animals. The distributions of iproniazid between the various solvents employed in the extraction were such that approximately 70% appeared in the final extract. When standards were prepared by carrying known amounts of iproniazid through the entire extraction procedure recoveries were essentially quantitative (90 to 110%).

Isonicotinic acid was assayed by shaking 1 ml of tissue homogenate (1 g of tissue in 2 ml of cold water) or plasma, 2 ml of water, 10 ml of n-butanol and 0.4 ml of a solution of 1% Hyamine 1622[1] in n-butanol in a 40-ml glass-stoppered shaking tube

[1] Hyamine 1622 (phemerol chloride, benzethonium chloride) as the free base (benzyldimethyl {2- [2-(p-1,1,3,3-tetramethylbutylphenoxy) ethoxy] -ethyl} ammonium hydroxide) was kindly supplied by Dr. F. Eisenberg, Jr. (1957).

for 10 minutes. The solution was centrifugated and 10 ml of the alcohol layer were transferred to a clean shaking tube containing 1 ml of borate buffer pH 8.5 (Hess *et al.*, 1956), 3 ml of water and 10 ml of n-heptane. After shaking for 4 minutes the solution was again centrifugated and 1 ml of the aqueous layer was used to complete the assay essentially according to the method of Mueller and Fox (1951) using 5% CNBr in water and allowing the chromogen to develop for 3½ minutes. Normal tissue blanks were determined as above and the averages were subtracted from the values obtained with the tissues from the test rats. The colors developed with a given tissue were relatively constant but varied from type to type. Thus, the color developed from normal plasma was equivalent to 2 μg of isonicotinic acid per ml while normal brain and muscle produced a color equivalent to <25 μg of isonicotinic acid; liver blanks were fairly high (<50 μg/g). Recoveries of known amounts of isonicotinic acid (50 to 1000 μg) added to normal tissues averaged 75 to 90% of standards carried through the entire extraction procedure.

Specificity of Methods. The specificity of the assays for iproniazid and for isonicotinic acid was determined by chromatography of plasma extracts obtained 20 minutes after administering iproniazid to rats. The extracts were chromatographed using the ascending technique, Whatman #1 paper with n-propanol-water (4 + 1). The paper was dried in air, exposed to the vapors of CNBr for about 10 minutes and then sprayed with 0.25% benzidine solution in 50% ethanol (Huebner, 1951). Mixtures containing both iproniazid and isonicotinic acid varying between 50 and 1000 μg added to normal tissue homogenates could be measured in each other's presence without interference. By chromatographing the extracts containing both compounds it was shown that small amounts of isonicotinic acid were present in the extracts obtained by the iproniazid method. However, isonicotinic acid did not react with the Folin reagent. The extracts obtained by the isonicotinic acid method were found to be almost completely free from iproniazid.

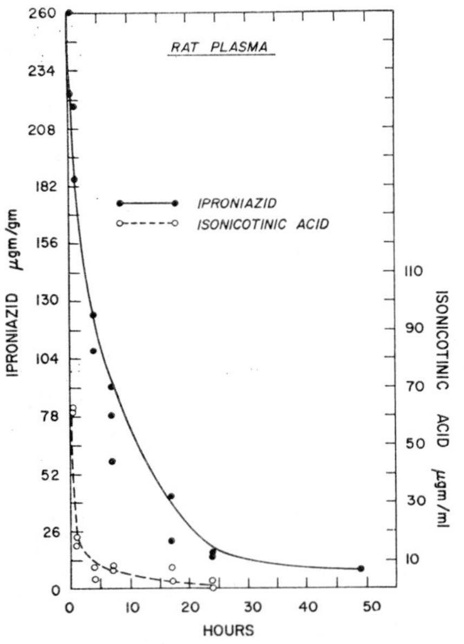

FIG. 1. Rat plasma levels of iproniazid and isonicotinic acid at various time intervals after receiving iproniazid (195 mg/kg) intraperitoneally.
Each point represents the combined plasma from 2 animals.

Although the color reaction was generally used to assay iproniazid in the experiments described here, the intense ultraviolet absorption of the pyridine compounds made it possible to corroborate the assay by an independent method. Iproniazid in dilute acid exhibits maximal absorption at 265 mμ. Pyridine compounds containing a hydrazine moiety (for example iproniazid, isoniazid, etc.) exhibit a shift in ultraviolet absorption in alkaline solution, with a new peak appearing at 310 mμ. By adding 1 ml of the final acid extract to 1.8 ml of water and 0.2 ml of N NaOH and measuring the optical density immediately at 310 mμ it was possible to measure iproniazid by this alternate method. The results of the colorimetric determinations for iproniazid were found to agree with those obtained by measurement of ultraviolet absorption.

RESULTS. *Disposition of iproniazid and its metabolite in rat tissues.* Male albino rats weighing 200 g received 195 mg/kg of iproniazid intraperitoneally. At various times thereafter blood samples were taken by cardiac puncture, the animals were then sacrificed and the tissues removed at once. The drug level reached a maximum in the plasma within 20 minutes after injection and persisted in this medium in measurable amounts for 24 hours; trace quantities, less than 10 μg/ml, were detectable 48 hours after injection (fig. 1).

The drug entered the brain, liver and muscle rapidly. A maximum concentration of 156 μg/g of tissue was found in the brain 20 minutes after the administration (fig. 2; table 1). The level fell slowly for the first hour, then more rapidly until at 17 hours the concentration of drug remaining was barely significant. Twenty-four hours after administration there was no detectable drug in

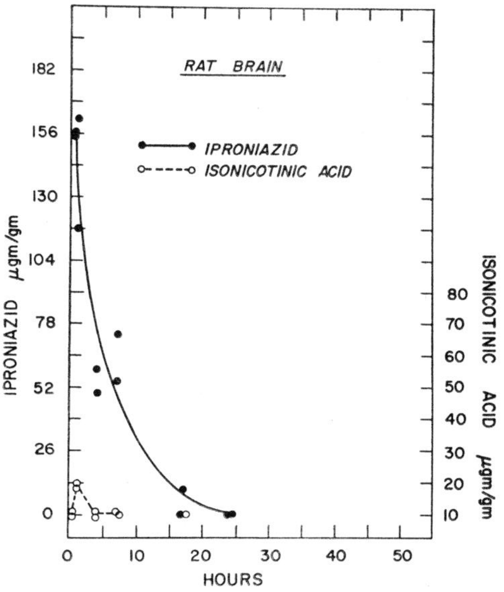

FIG. 2. Rat brain levels of iproniazid and isonicotinic acid at various time intervals after receiving iproniazid (195 mg/kg) intraperitoneally.
Each point represents the pooled homogenates from 2 animals.

the brain. The concentration changes in the livers and muscles of these animals emulated the brain concentration except that the values obtained in the liver were uniformly higher than those in any of the other tissues.

The change in concentration of isonicotinic acid in the plasma followed the variations in concentration of the parent drug (table 2). It reached a level of 62 µg/ml of plasma 20 minutes after administration and declined to trace quantities, less than 3 µg/ml, in 24 hours. Brain, on the other hand, contained a detectable amount in the 1-hour sample only. Liver and muscle exhibited the highest concentrations 1 hour after the dose was administered; no detectable levels were found in either tissue 24 hours later. There was no evidence that iproniazid or isonicotinic acid was stored in any of the tissues studied.

Monoamine oxidase activity. The MAO activity was also measured in the brain and liver homogenates prepared from the rats used in the study of the disposition of iproniazid. It may be seen (figs. 3, 4) that the ability of the tissues to metabolize the amine is impaired almost at once, both tissues being affected to a similar degree. Marked inhibition persisted for 5 to 6 days in both tissues, an extended period after the drug *per se* had apparently disappeared from the animal (table 1). The data suggest that inhibition in brain may persist longer than it does in liver. However, further studies are required to verify this point.

TABLE 1

Distribution of iproniazid in tissues of rats killed at various time intervals after receiving the drug (195 mg/kg) intraperitoneally, each value representing the average of 4 animals

Time	Iproniazid µg/g			
	Brain	Liver	Muscle	Plasma
Hours				
0.3	156	212	127	245
1	140	181	130	202
4	53	104	88	115
7	65	82	79	84
24	0	0	0	15
48	0	0	0	<10

TABLE 2

Distribution of isonicotinic acid in tissues of rats killed at various time intervals after receiving iproniazid (195 mg/kg) intraperitoneally, each value representing the average of 4 animals

Time	Isonicotinic Acid µg/g			
	Brain	Liver	Muscle	Plasma
Hours				
0.3	0	56	5	62
1	9	66	16	17
4	0	35	0	5
7	0	20	0	7
24	0	0	0	<3

Disappearance of iproniazid in the mouse. In a single exploratory experiment whole mice were analyzed for residual iproniazid to determine if the drug was concentrated in tissues other than those assayed as given in table 2. Mice weighing 20 g each received 325 mg/kg of iproniazid intraperitoneally; after various time intervals individual mice were dropped into an electric blendor containing 100 ml of 0.1 N HCl and homogenized. Two ml of the homogenate were used for the iproniazid assay. The results of this experiment are summarized in fig. 5. It may be seen that the concentration fell steadily and the drug did not appear to be stored in the animal.

DISCUSSION. The extended period after the last trace of iproniazid had apparently disappeared and before the MAO activity had returned

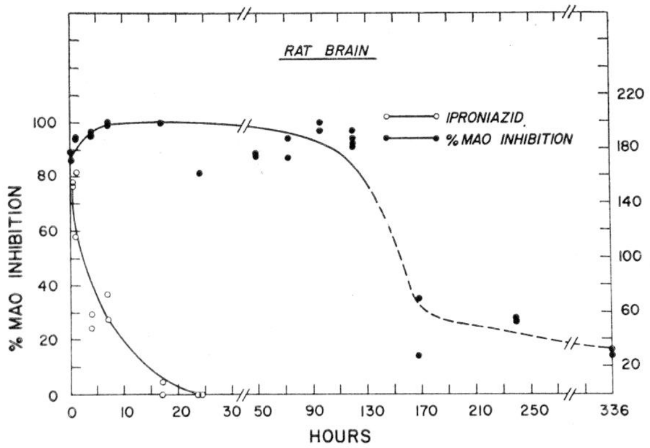

FIG. 3. Monoamine oxidase inhibition and concentration of iproniazid in rat brain at various time intervals after administering iproniazid (195 mg/kg) intraperitoneally.
Each point represents the pooled homogenates from 2 animals.

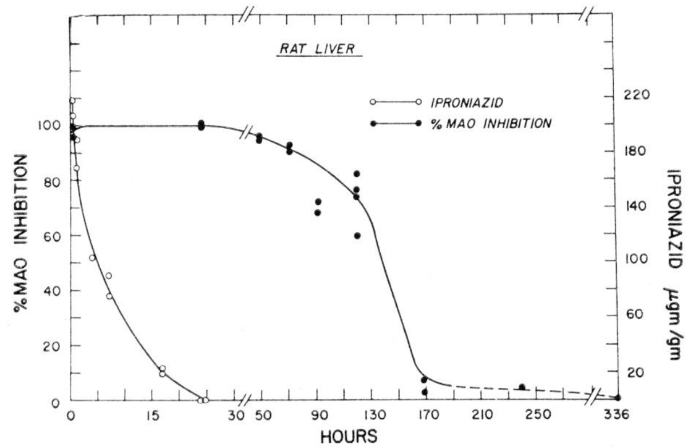

FIG. 4. Monoamine oxidase inhibition and concentration of iproniazid in rat liver at various time intervals after administering iproniazid (195 mg/kg) intraperitoneally.
Each point represents the pooled homogenates from 2 animals.

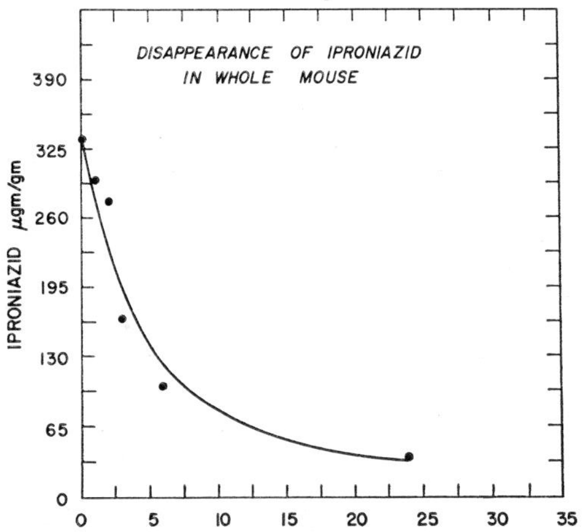

FIG. 5. Concentration of iproniazid in whole mice killed at various time intervals after receiving 325 mg/kg of the drug intraperitoneally.
Each point represents an average of 2 to 3 animals. All replicate values agreed within 10%.

to normal represents a pattern that is rather familiar. The relationship of MAO to primary amines may be compared to the relationship of cholinesterase to acetylcholine. The action of diisopropylfluorophosphate is known to be irreversible and long lasting (Mackworth and Webb, 1948) in a manner similar to iproniazid. Studies *in vitro* have indicated that iproniazid is an irreversible and noncompetitive inhibitor of MAO (Zeller *et al.*, 1955).

As in the case of cholinesterase, reversible MAO inhibitors can also be obtained (Freter *et al.*, 1958). A comparable study of the action of the reversible MAO inhibitor, harmaline, has also been carried out (Udenfriend *et al.*, unpublished results). With this compound the inhibition ended with the disappearance of the drug from the tissues. The finding of a persistent action of a drug after the compound can no longer be detected in the tissues is significant in elucidating the mechanism of its action. A similar persistence of action has been shown in the case of reserpine (Hess *et al.*, 1956). For such a phenomenon one must consider the alternative possibilities: (a) The enzyme or biological system may be totally destroyed and the period of inactivation represents a period of resynthesis of the system. (b) The prolonged inactivation of the enzyme may be caused by some simple product of degradation, or the drug itself may be incorporated irreversibly in a tissue catalyst required for the synthesis or action of the enzyme. There was a suggestion of the latter possibility since the concentration of iproniazid (table 1) and to a lesser extent isonicotinic acid (table 2) persisted in the plasma for some time after the compounds could no longer be detected in any of the tissues. However, the amounts found were rather small and further work is continuing along this line.

The possibility that the decrease in iproniazid was accompanied by a concomitant increase of some metabolic product was investigated. The major end product, isonicotinic acid, did not accumulate in any of the tissues examined and indeed, paralleled the concentration changes of the parent drug.

Although the highest concentrations of iproniazid and of the metabolic product, isonicotinic acid, were found in the liver, efforts to degrade the former using liver slices, homogenates, or subcellular fractions have thus far been uniformly unsuccessful.

SUMMARY

Iproniazid, administered intraperitoneally to rats, readily entered the brain and other tissues of the body, reaching a maximum concentration within 1 hour after administration of the drug. The concentration of the compound fell steadily until at 24 hours none could be detected in the brain, liver, or muscle. The drug persisted in trace amounts in the plasma for 48 hours although no storage depots could be discovered. The major end product, isonicotinic acid, was found in each of the tissues above in concentrations that paralleled the levels of the parent drug and again no storage depot could be found.

MAO inhibition was initiated within the first half-hour after the dose was administered, and was essentially complete for 5 to 6 days, long after the last trace of drug or metabolite had disappeared.

ACKNOWLEDGMENT. We wish to thank Hoffmann-La Roche, Inc., for the generous supplies of iproniazid.

REFERENCES

BOGDANSKI, D. F., PLETSCHER, A., BRODIE, B. B. AND UDENFRIEND, S.: THIS JOURNAL **117:** 82, 1956.
DAVISON, A. N.: Biochem. J. **67:** 316, 1957.
DERITTER, E., DREKTER, L., SCHEINER, J. AND RUBIN, S. H.: Proc. Soc. exp. Biol., N. Y. **79:** 654, 1952.
EISENBERG, F., JR.: Conference on Liquid Scintillation Counting, Northwestern Univ., Aug., 1957, in press.
FOLIN, O. AND CIOCALTEU, V.: J. biol. Chem. **73:** 627, 1927.
FRETER, K., WEISSBACH, H., REDFIELD, B. G., UDENFRIEND, S. AND WITKOP, B.: J. Amer. chem. Soc. **80:** 983, 1958.
HESS, S. M., SHORE, P. A. AND BRODIE, B. B.: THIS JOURNAL **118:** 84, 1956.
HUEBNER, C. F.: Nature **167:** 119, 1951.
MACKWORTH, J. F. AND WEBB, E. C.: Biochem. J. **42:** 91, 1948.
MUELLER, A. AND FOX, S. H.: J. Amer. pharm. Ass., Sci. Ed. **40:** 513, 1951.
RUBIN, S. H., DREKTER, L., SCHEINER, J. AND DERITTER, E.: Dis. Chest **21:** 439, 1952.
SJOERDSMA, A., SMITH, T. E., STEVENSON, T. D. AND UDENFRIEND, S.: Proc. Soc. exp. Biol., N. Y. **89:** 36, 1955.
UDENFRIEND, S., WEISSBACH, H. AND CLARK, C. T.: J. biol. Chem. **215:** 337, 1955.
UDENFRIEND, S., WEISSBACH, H. AND BOGDANSKI, D. F.: J. biol. Chem. **224:** 803, 1957a.
UDENFRIEND, S., WEISSBACH, H. AND BOGDANSKI, D. F.: THIS JOURNAL **120:** 255, 1957b.
WEISSBACH, H., REDFIELD, B. G AND UDENFRIEND, S.: J. biol. Chem. **229:** 953, 1957.
ZELLER, E. A., BARSKY, J. AND BERMAN, E. R.: J. biol. Chem. **214:** 267, 1955.

8077

THE INFLUENCE OF VARIOUS FACTORS ON THE ENZYMATIC CONVERSION OF ORGANIC THIOPHOSPHATES TO ANTICHOLINESTERASE AGENTS[1]

SHELDON D. MURPHY[2] AND KENNETH P. DuBOIS

Department of Pharmacology, University of Chicago, Chicago 37, Illinois

Received for publication June 3, 1958

Several investigators (Diggle and Gage, 1951; Myers *et al.*, 1952; Gage, 1953; Metcalf and March, 1953; Davison, 1955; DuBois *et al.*, 1957) have demonstrated that purified organic thiophosphates are ineffective or extremely weak inhibitors of cholinesterase *in vitro* but are metabolized by the liver of mammals to their corresponding oxygen analogues which are potent anticholinesterase agents. Previous studies in this laboratory (Murphy and DuBois, 1957a) resulted in the development and application of a quantitative method for measuring the activity of a pyridine nucleotide-linked enzyme system of liver microsomes which catalyzes this metabolic activation. One of the most interesting observations made during our initial studies on this enzyme system was the finding that the livers of male rats exhibit 2 to 3 times more activity than do the livers of female rats. This finding stimulated our interest in conducting further studies on the influence of sex, age and other factors on the enzymatic conversion of cholinergic organic thiophosphates to their corresponding oxygen analogues.

The experiments described in the present communication demonstrated that such variables as age, sex, the administration of hormones and carcinogenic hydrocarbons and some other factors exert a marked influence on the activity of the enzyme system which catalyzes the conversion of the dimethoxy ester of benzotriazine dithiophosphoric acid (guthion, DBD) and ethyl *p*-nitrophenyl thionobenzenephosphonate (EPN) to active anticholinesterase agents. The results demonstrated the necessity of giving careful consideration to factors which influence the metabolism of cholinergic thiophosphates when pharmacological and toxicological studies of a quantitative nature are conducted on this group of toxic agents. The enzyme system which catalyzes the oxidation of organic thiophosphates to toxic metabolites is similar in its intracellular location, coenzyme requirements, susceptibility to carcinogenic hydrocarbons and sex differences in activity to the enzymes which catalyze the reductive and oxidative changes in a number of chemical agents (Mueller and Miller, 1949, 1953; Brodie *et al.*, 1955; Conney, Miller and Miller, 1956, 1957; Axelrod, 1956). It therefore seems possible that the findings made during the present study are applicable to the metabolism of several other classes of chemical agents by the microsomal enzymes of liver.

MATERIALS AND METHODS. Weanling or adult (180 to 300 g) Sprague-Dawley rats and Carworth Farms mice (20 to 30 g) were used for these experiments. The animals were housed in air-conditioned rooms maintained at 68 to 75°F and were fed Rockland Rat Diet unless otherwise indicated. For the enzyme assays the animals were sacrificed by decapitation and the livers were quickly removed, weighed and homogenized in cold water. Solutions (0.1 M) of guthion and EPN were prepared by dissolving the compounds in warm ethanol and the alcoholic solutions were then diluted with distilled water. Conversion of the thiophosphates to their active metabolites was accomplished by the method previously developed in this laboratory (Murphy and DuBois, 1957a). For the conversion reaction each Warburg flask contained 0.4 ml of 0.1 M phosphate buffer (pH 7.2), 0.3 ml of nicotinamide (1×10^{-3} M), 0.5 ml of diphosphopyridine nucleotide (1 mg/ml), 0.1 or 0.2 ml of an aqueous liver homogenate (2.5%), 0.3 ml aqueous thiophosphate solutions (1×10^{-4} M guthion or 1×10^{-3} M EPN) and sufficient water to make a final volume of 3.0 ml. This mixture was incubated for 10 minutes at 38°C. The amount of active metabolite formed was determined by measuring the inhibition of rat brain cholinesterase (DuBois and

[1] This investigation was supported by a research grant (G-3349 C6) from the Division of Research Grants, National Institutes of Health, U. S. Public Health Service.

[2] University of Chicago Fellow.

Mangun, 1947) produced by a 0.6 ml aliquot of the reaction mixture. The enzyme activity was expressed in terms of arbitrary units of active metabolite formed per 5 mg of fresh liver per hour and was calculated using the procedures described in previous communications (Murphy and DuBois, 1956; DuBois *et al.*, 1957) from this laboratory. Steroid hormones were dissolved in sesame oil and administered subcutaneously. Carcinogenic hydrocarbons were dissolved in warm corn oil and administered intraperitoneally and aqueous solutions of ethionine, methionine and β-diethylaminoethyl diphenylpropylacetate were administered by the same route.

RESULTS. *Age and sex differences in enzyme activity.* In a previous communication (Murphy and DuBois, 1957a) we reported that the activity of the enzyme system responsible for the conversion of guthion to a potent anticholinesterase agent was 2 to 3 times greater in the livers of adult male rats than in females. A similar sex difference was noted in the present investigation when EPN was used as the substrate as shown by the data in table 1. The sex difference in enzyme activity appeared to be due to an actual difference in the enzyme concentration or to a firmly bound activator in the livers of male rats because the difference in activity still existed in washed microsomes from the livers of male and female rats. Furthermore, when liver homogenates from male and female rats were mixed no greater than additive activity was observed and the addition of a boiled homogenate of male rat liver to a fresh homogenate of liver from females did not result in any stimulation of the enzyme activity. A boiled homogenate of female rat liver failed to inhibit the activity of a fresh homogenate of male rat liver.

The rather large sex difference in the thiophosphate-oxidizing activity of rat livers and the apparent absence of an activator in the livers of male rats or an inhibitor in the livers of females suggested that the synthesis of the enzyme might be under hormonal control. It was felt that some information on this possibility could be obtained by measuring the enzyme activity of the livers of male and female rats at various intervals between the time of birth and maturity. The results of assays performed at intervals on livers of rats 14 to 60 days old are shown in figure 1, in which each point on the curves is the average of measurements performed on the livers of 4 to 8 rats.

TABLE 1

Sex difference in the oxidation of organic thiophosphates by rat liver

Thiophosphate	Sex	Number of Animals	Enzyme Activity (Units)*
Guthion	F	19	4.2 ± 0.6
Guthion	M	32	10.3 ± 1.0
EPN	F	4	4.35 ± 0.5
EPN	M	5	9.6 ± 2.0

* Figures represent average values ± average deviation from the mean.

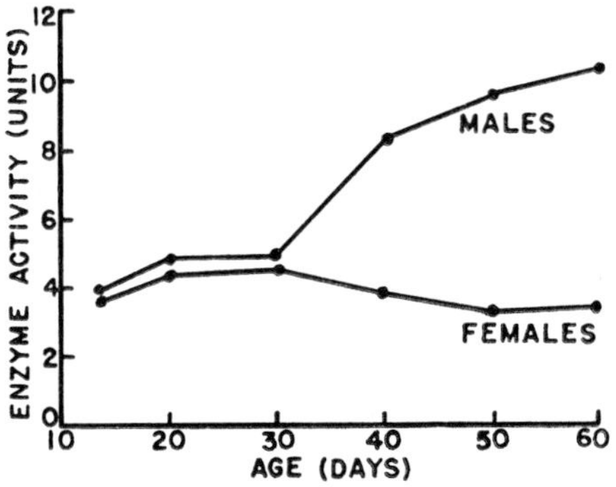

FIG. 1. Influence of age on the magnitude of the sex difference in the activity of the enzyme in rat liver which oxidizes guthion.

The data in figure 1 show that the livers of both male and female rats exhibit low and essentially equal enzyme activity within the age range of 14 to 30 days. The enzyme activity of the livers of male rats began to increase after 30 days of age and reached normal adult levels by the end of 60 days but the activity of the livers of females remained low and relatively constant throughout the entire observation period. It is interesting to note that the increase in the enzyme activity of the livers of males corresponds with the approximate time of onset of puberty in male rats (Farris, 1942). These experiments provide indirect evidence in support of the possibility that the concentration of the thiophosphate-oxidizing enzyme in the livers of male rats is controlled in some manner by androgens.

The effect of sex hormones and castration on the thiophosphate-oxidizing enzyme. Additional experiments were conducted in an effort to obtain direct evidence concerning the influence of sex hormones *in vivo* on the concentration of the enzyme which catalyzes the oxidation of thio-

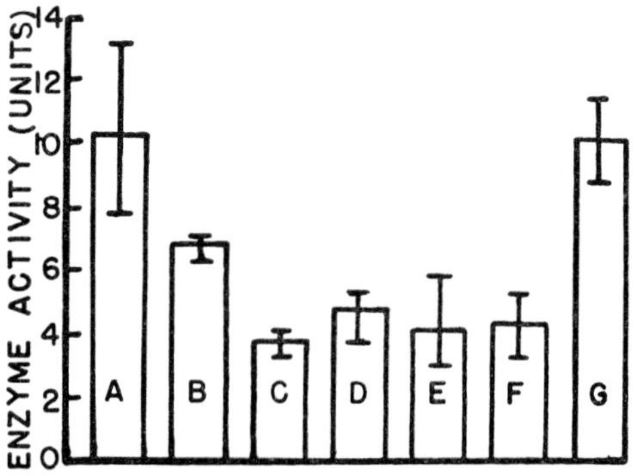

FIG. 2. Influence of hormones and castration on the sex difference in activity of the thiophosphate-oxidizing enzyme of rat liver.

Bars represent average of assays performed on the livers of at least 4 animals; bracketed lines represent the range of values obtained. Guthion was used as the substrate. A, Normal adult males. B, Adult males given 0.5 mg/kg/day of diethylstilbestrol for 30 days. C, Adult males given 2 mg/kg/day of progesterone for 30 days. D, Males castrated at 26 days of age and assayed at 60 days of age. E, Normal adult females. F, Females assayed 6 weeks after ovariectomy. G, Adult females given 1 mg/kg/day of testosterone propionate for 6 weeks.

phosphates. Thus, groups each containing 4 male rats were given diethylstilbestrol or progesterone daily by the subcutaneous route for 30 days and females received testosterone propionate for 42 days. The animals were sacrificed 24 hours after the last injection and the enzyme activity of the livers was measured. Another group of males was castrated at 26 days of age and sacrificed at 60 days of age and a group of adult females was ovariectomized and sacrificed 42 days later for enzyme assays. The effects of the various treatments on the thiophosphate-oxidizing enzyme activity of the liver are shown in figure 2, in which the average and range of values are presented for each group of animals.

The daily administration of 1 mg/kg of testosterone propionate to adult female rats for a period of 6 weeks resulted in an increase in the activity of the thiophosphate-oxidizing enzyme to 238% of normal. Thus prolonged treatment with testosterone increased the activity of the enzyme in the livers of female rats to the normal level of adult males. In another experiment daily administration of testosterone to groups of 4 males and 4 females was begun at 5 days of age. The animals were sacrificed 15 days later. The livers of males and females contained 6.8 and 6.6 units of enzyme activity respectively as compared with values of 4.9 and 4.4 units for untreated normal rats of the same age. The increase in enzyme activity observed after prolonged treatment of young male and female rats and adult females with testosterone appears to be due to an increase in the enzyme concentration rather than to activation of existing enzyme because we have previously found (Murphy and DuBois, 1957b) that testosterone as well as several other naturally occurring and synthetic steroid hormones are effective inhibitors of the enzyme *in vitro*.

Additional evidence indicating a stimulation of enzyme synthesis by androgens was obtained by experiments on castrated rats. When a group of 4 male rats was castrated at the age of 26 days and sacrificed at 60 days of age it was observed that castration completely prevented the increase in enzyme activity which normally occurs (figure 1). Thus, the average enzyme activity of the livers of these animals was 4.8 units (figure 2) as compared with 10.2 units for normal males of the same age. The average enzyme activity of the livers of 3 adult male rats at 21 days after castration was 24% lower than that of normal adult males. The activity of the thiophosphate-oxidizing enzyme of the livers of adult females did not exhibit any change from normal at 6 weeks following bilateral ovariectomy.

The daily administration of 0.5 mg/kg of diethylstilbestrol or 2 mg/kg of progesterone for 30 days decreased the enzyme activity of the livers of adult male rats to the extent of 35% and 64% respectively, as shown in figure 2. When the compounds were administered for only 15 days approximately one-half as much depression of enzyme activity occurred. Administration of only 2 daily doses of the hormones caused no detectable change in enzyme activity. The livers of male rats sacrificed 6 hours after the intraperitoneal injection of large doses of diethylstilbestrol (20 mg/kg) or progesterone (50 mg/kg) did not exhibit any reduction in enzyme activity. When daily administration of diethylstilbestrol (0.5 mg/kg) or progesterone (2 mg/kg) to male rats was started at the age of 25 days the increase in the enzyme activity of the livers which normally begins at that age failed to occur. These hormones thus appear to inhibit the synthesis of the thiophosphate-oxidizing enzyme *in vivo* rather that merely depressing its activity as they do *in vitro*.

The results of these experiments indicate that androgens are responsible for the initial stimulation of the enzyme activity in young male rats and for maintenance of the activity at an elevated level in adult males. The experiments also indicate that some female hormones are capable of depressing the synthesis of the enzyme. However, since the enzyme activity of the livers of ovariectomized females was no greater than that of controls, it appears that endogenous female hormones are of lesser importance than androgens in the regulation of the enzyme activity in the liver.

Activity of the thiophosphate-oxidizing enzyme in regenerating rat liver. Measurements of the thiophosphate-oxidizing enzyme in the regenerating livers of partially hepatectomized male rats were undertaken to ascertain whether the enzyme concentration was at a low level during the period of rapid growth. For this experiment groups of adult rats were sacrificed for enzyme assays at various intervals after partial hepatectomy. The results of these measurements are shown in figure 3, in which each point on the curve is the average of measurements on the livers of 4 animals. At 4 days after partial hepatectomy the enzyme activity of the liver was only 20% of normal. Comparison of liver to body weight ratios indicated that approximately 85% regeneration of the liver weight occurred in 4 days and return of the enzyme activity to normal levels is, therefore, much slower than growth of the tissue. The time required for regeneration of the thiophosphate-oxidizing enzyme is greater than that reported for a number of mitochondrial enzymes (Novikoff and Potter, 1948; Greenbaum *et al.*, 1954) and a microsome enzyme, glucose-6-phosphatase (Weber and Cantero, 1955) in regenerating liver. As indicated below, the regenerating liver resembled that of weanling male rats in responsiveness to chemical agents capable of increasing enzyme activity. The partially hepatectomized male rat may, therefore, constitute a useful preparation for future studies on the role of microsome enzymes in determining the susceptibility of animals to various chemical agents which are metabolized by these enzyme systems.

Influence of carcinogenic hydrocarbons on the thiophosphate oxidizing enzyme. Conney, Miller and Miller (1956, 1957) have reported that the administration of certain carcinogenic hydrocarbons to weanling male rats markedly increases the ability of the liver to demethylate and reduce aminoazo dyes and to hydroxylate benzpyrene.

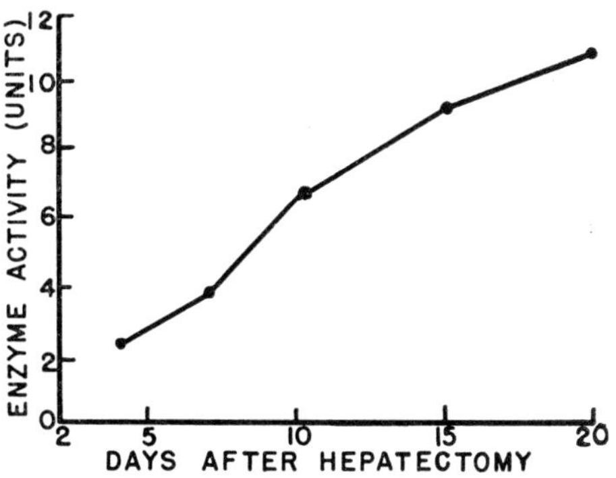

FIG. 3. Rate of oxidation of guthion to an anticholinesterase agent by the regenerating livers of partially hepatectomized male rats.

TABLE 2

*Influence of 3-methylcholanthrene on the enzymatic oxidation of guthion by rat liver**

Description of Animals	Number Treated	Enzyme Activity (Units)	
		Appropriate controls	Hydrocarbon treated
Males, 25 days of age	3	4.9 ± 0.7	10.1 ± 0.2
Males, normal adult	5	10.3 ± 1.0	13.9 ± 1.3
Males, adult, 4 days after partial hepatectomy	4	2.3 ± 0.3	9.4 ± 1.3
Females, normal adult	5	4.2 ± 0.6	10.5 ± 0.8

* Animals were sacrificed and assays were performed 24 hours after the intraperitoneal administration of 25 mg/kg of 3-methylcholanthrene.

They attributed this effect to an actual increase in the concentration of the microsomal enzymes which catalyze these reactions. Since the enzyme system responsible for the oxidation of thiophosphates is similar in certain respects to the enzymes involved in azo dye metabolism, we investigated the effect of carcinogenic hydrocarbons on its activity in rat liver. As shown in table 2 the intraperitoneal administration of 25 mg/kg of 3-methylcholanthrene caused an increase in the enzyme activity of weanling male rats to twice the normal level in 24 hours. The low enzyme activity of the regenerating livers of adult males and the livers of normal adult females was also markedly increased whereas only a small increase

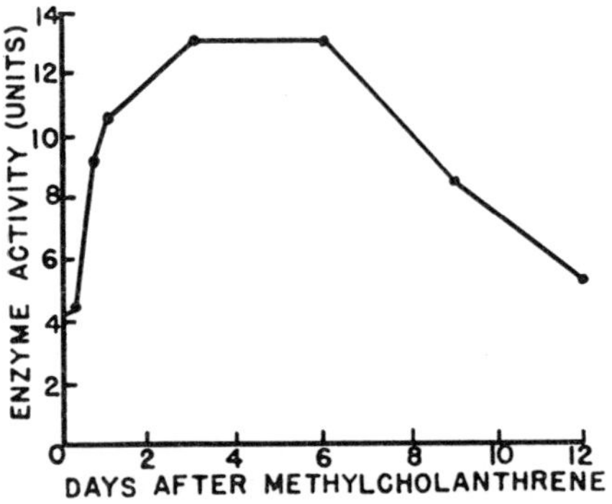

FIG. 4. The extent and duration of the increase in activity of the thiophosphate-oxidizing enzyme of the livers of female rats given a single dose of 25 mg/kg of 3-methylcholanthrene.
The substrate was guthion.

was noted in the activity of the livers of adult males. Increasing the dose of methylcholanthrene to 50 mg/kg did not result in any further increase in enzyme activity in any of the groups. The administration of less than 25 mg/kg of methylcholanthrene frequently resulted in marked increases in enzyme activity; however, the results were less consistent and a dose of 25 mg/kg was therefore chosen for subsequent experiments.

Further experiments demonstrated that the intraperitoneal administration of 25 mg/kg of 1,2,5,6-dibenzanthracene or 3,4-benzpyrene to adult female rats caused an increase in the thiophosphate-oxidizing enzyme activity from a normal level of 4.2 units to 9.5 and 9.1 units respectively in 24 hours. The addition of the hydrocarbons to an *in vitro* system caused no increase in the enzyme activity of the liver of female rats. A species difference in the response to carcinogenic hydrocarbons was observed since the administration of as much as 50 mg/kg of methylcholanthrene had no effect on the enzyme activity of the livers of adult male and female mice.

Conney *et al.* (1956) reported that ethionine completely inhibited the methylcholanthrene-induced increase in demethylase activity of the livers of young male rats and that the effect of ethionine could be blocked by the simultaneous administration of methionine. In the present study it was found that the intraperitoneal administration of 100 mg/kg of *dl*-ethionine 1 hour before methylcholanthrene completely inhibited the methylcholanthrene-induced increase in the activity of the thiophosphate-oxidizing enzyme in the livers of adult female rats and the regenerating livers of partially hepatectomized males. The simultaneous administration of 100 mg/kg of methionine only reduced the effectiveness of ethionine by 22%. The same amount of ethionine decreased the stimulation of enzyme activity only 20% when it was given 48 hours before methylcholanthrene.

To ascertain the duration of the increase in enzyme activity caused by the carcinogenic hydrocarbons a series of adult female rats was given 25 mg/kg of methylcholanthrene and groups each containing 4 animals were sacrificed at various intervals. As shown in figure 4 a rapid increase in enzyme activity occurred during the first 24 hours after injection of the hydrocarbon. The maximum increase in activity was observed at 3 days after treatment and the activity was maintained at the maximal level for about 6 days after which time a gradual decrease to normal occurred. A second dose of methylcholanthrene administered 18 days after the initial dose caused the same amount of increase as the initial treatment. In another experiment a second dose of methylcholanthrene given 3 days after the first dose caused a further pronounced increase in enzyme activity to 18.1 units in 3 days. Thus maintenance of a high concentration of the hydrocarbon in the liver results in continued increases in enzyme activity. Daily injection of several purine and pyrimidine antagonists for 5 days prior to treatment with methylcholanthrene failed to prevent the increase in enzyme activity induced by the latter compound which indicated that interference with nucleic acid metabolism does not affect the ability of methylcholanthrene to stimulate the synthesis of the thiophosphate-oxidizing enzyme.

Since methylcholanthrene increases the capacity of the liver to convert thiophosphates to their oxygen analogues, it was anticipated that it would increase the toxicity of at least some of the thiophosphates. Evidence in support of this possibility was obtained by toxicity and anticholinesterase measurements on rats which received guthion after treatment with methylcholanthrene. The average cholinesterase activity of the brains and submaxillary glands of 6 normal adult female rats was inhibited 45.9 and 28.7% respectively at 30 minutes after the intraperitoneal administration of 2 mg/kg of guthion. However, when the same dose of guthion was given to 5 female rats 48 hours after the administration of 25 mg/kg of methylcholanthrene the activity of brain and submaxillary was inhibited 69.9 and 47.3% in 30 minutes. The cholinesterase activity of the tissues of animals which received only methylcholanthrene did not differ significantly from that of untreated controls.

It was anticipated that the increased enzyme activity produced in female rats by the administration of methylcholanthrene would increase their susceptibility to cholinergic thiophosphates. This was shown to be the case by determining the LD_{50} of guthion to female rats which had been treated 48 hours previously with methylcholanthrene. The approximate LD_{50} of guthion to these animals was 2.8 mg/kg as compared with 5.7 mg/kg for normal female rats. Thus, methylcholanthrene produced approximately the same percentage increase in susceptibility to thiophosphates and in the activity of the thiophosphate-oxidizing enzyme.

Effect of protein-free diets on the methylcholanthrene-induced increase in the thiophosphate-oxidizing enzyme. The experiments described above indicated that methylcholanthrene stimulates the synthesis of the enzyme which catalyzes the oxidation of thiophosphates rather than increasing the catalytic activity of existing enzyme. To obtain further information on this point groups of rats were fed a protein-free diet and one containing 18% casein as described by Byerrum and DuBois (1947). It was found that the average enzyme activity of the livers of 4 adult male rats fed a protein-free diet for 4 weeks decreased from a normal level of 10.2 units to 2.5 units. The activity of the livers of 4 adult females fed a protein-free diet for 4 weeks was only 5.4 units at 24 hours after the administration of 25 mg/kg of methylcholanthrene as compared to 8.4 units for methylcholanthrene-treated females maintained on a diet containing 18% casein. The results of these experiments give further support to the idea that the high enzyme activity of the livers of adult males and of methylcholanthrene-treated females is due to an actual difference in the concentration of enzyme rather than to a nonprotein activator. Baxter *et al.* (1957) have reported that starvation increases the enzymatic oxidation of sulfide by the livers of rats. To determine whether a similar effect occurs in the case of thiophosphate oxidation assays were performed on the livers of rats fasted for a period of 50 hours. It was observed that the oxidation of guthion by the livers of 4 fasted male rats was inhibited to the extent of 30%. Thus prolonged fasting results in a decrease in the activity of the enzyme responsible for the oxidation of organic thiophosphates in contrast to the increase in sulfide oxidizing ability of the livers produced by the same treatment.

Influence of β-diethylaminoethyl diphenylpropylacetate (SKF 525A) on the susceptibility of rats to guthion. In previous studies it was found that β-diethylaminoethyl diphenylpropylacetate (SKF 525A) is an effective inhibitor of the enzyme which catalyzes the oxidation of EPN (Murphy and DuBois, 1956) and guthion (Murphy and DuBois, 1957a) to their corresponding oxygen analogues. In view of the ability of methylcholanthrene to increase the activity of the thiophosphate-oxidizing enzyme as well as the susceptibility of rats to guthion it seemed likely that inhibition of the enzyme would decrease the susceptibility of rats to cholinergic thiophosphates. This possibility was tested by the administration of 20 mg/kg of SKF 525A followed in 40 minutes by a sublethal dose of 2 mg/kg of guthion. Both compounds were given to female rats by the intraperitoneal route. At 30 minutes after the injection of guthion the animals were sacrificed for cholinesterase measurements. The brain and submaxillary glands of animals treated with guthion and SKF 525A exhibited an average of 7% inhibition of cholinesterase activity as compared with an average of 45.9 and 28.7% inhibition, respectively, in the tissues of animals receiving only guthion. Toxicity tests demonstrated that 20 mg/kg of SKF 525A completely protected female rats against the lethal action of approximately twice the LD_{50} of guthion (10 mg/kg). Seventy % mortality occurred in a group of rats which received 20 mg/kg of guthion and the enzyme inhibitor but the onset of symptoms was delayed and no deaths occurred until several hours after administration of guthion in contrast to the rapidly fatal action (10 to 20 minutes) of guthion in untreated animals. The results of these experiments provided further evidence for the strategic role of the thiophosphate-oxidizing enzyme of the liver in determining the toxicity of organic thiophosphates.

Discussion. The results of the present investigation have demonstrated that the activity of the microsomal enzyme of rat liver which catalyzes the conversion of guthion and EPN to potent anticholinesterase agents is influenced by factors such as age, sex, dietary protein intake and exposure to carcinogenic hydrocarbons. The livers of adult male rats normally contain 2 to 3 times as much enzyme as do the livers of adult females. A similar sex difference has been observed in the conversion of S-(1,2-dicarbethoxyethyl)-O,O-dimethylphosphorodithioate (malathion) to an anticholinesterase agent when appropriate measures were taken to prevent the coincident hydrolytic destruction of the active metabolite and its parent compound (Murphy and DuBois, 1957c). Although other compounds have not been subjected to detailed studies, it is likely that the oxidation of all cholinergic thiophosphates to their oxygen analogues is catalyzed by the same enzyme system. Thus the findings described in this communication are probably applicable to other cholinergic thiophosphates.

The activity of the thiophosphate-oxidizing enzyme of male rat liver begins to increase at an age which corresponds with the approximate age of puberty and appears to be due to an actual increase in enzyme concentration. Enzyme assays performed on the livers of castrated and sex hormone-treated animals indicated that androgens are responsible for the stimulation and maintenance of the high enzyme concentration in the livers of male rats. In contrast to the apparent ability of testosterone to stimulate enzyme synthesis *in vivo* it inhibits the activity of the enzyme *in vitro* (Murphy and DuBois, 1957b). March and Elliott (1954) observed a sex difference in the metabolism of morphine and other investigators have described similar sex differences in the oxidation of hexobarbital (Quinn *et al.*, 1954) and the demethylation of narcotic drugs (Axelrod, 1956) by microsomal enzymes of rat liver. Rubin (1957) has shown that the concentration of the enzyme in liver which catalyzes the *beta* hydroxylation of certain 3-keto steroids is stimulated by testosterone administration and decreased by castration. This similarity to the thiophosphate-oxidizing enzyme indicates a possible relationship between the enzyme systems which catalyze the metabolism of foreign chemicals and those which function normally in the metabolism of steroid hormones. The information obtained during the present study on the sex differences in the activity of the enzyme which oxidizes thiophosphates and the factors responsible for this difference may be applicable to a number of drug metabolism reactions catalyzed by enzymes present in liver microsomes.

The data presented in this communication show that the ability of the livers of adult male rats to oxidize thiophosphates to their corresponding oxygen analogues greatly exceeds that of young males and young and adult females. Since the toxicity of thiophosphates is dependent upon metabolic conversion to the oxygen analogues it would be anticipated, on the basis of the results of enzyme assays alone, that male rats would be more susceptible than females to the acute toxic action of cholinergic thiophosphates. However, numerous previous studies in this and other laboratories have shown that females are more susceptible to thiophosphates than males. In recent measurements of the toxicity of EPN (unpublished) we found that the LD_{50} for this compound was 5.9 and 5 mg/kg for weanling male and female rats, respectively, as compared with 26 mg/kg for adult males and 7.8 mg/kg for adult females. It seems probable that the greater resistance of adult male rats is due either to a more rapid detoxification which overshadows the effect of the higher activity of the enzyme which converts thiophosphates to their toxic oxygen analogues or to a regulatory influence of an endogenous inhibitor, possibly a hormone, which controls the activity of the converting enzyme *in vivo*. The existence of an extrahepatic site of conversion of thiophosphates to toxic metabolites in female rats was considered as another possible explanation for the sex difference in toxicity. However, assays on brain, kidney, cardiac muscle, skeletal muscle, adrenals, ovaries and uteri of female rats indicated that the metabolic conversion does not occur in these tissues. The recent observation (Murphy and DuBois, 1957c) that malathion is detoxified 4 times faster by the livers of male rats than by the livers of females supports the possibility that more rapid detoxification is the major factor responsible for the greater resistance of males; however, sufficient information concerning the relative rates of detoxification of other thiophosphates in males and females is not yet available to permit an extrapolation of these findings to all other agents of this class.

The low activity of the thiophosphate-oxidizing enzyme in the livers of young male rats and the abrupt increase in activity which occurs between the ages of 30 and 60 days indicates that careful consideration should be given to the age of animals used for comparison of susceptibility to agents which are converted *in vivo* to metabolites with greater or lesser toxicity than the parent compound. In the past most comparisons of this type have utilized rats exceeding 30 to 60 days of age but it is clear from the results of the present study that marked differences can be overlooked unless animals of the proper age are employed. It is noteworthy that the greatest individual variations in enzyme activity in male rats are observed during the period when the enzyme is undergoing an increase in concentration to the adult level. As a result, considerable individual differences in susceptibility to thiophosphates, and perhaps other agents which are metabolized by microsomal enzymes, can be expected during the same period. The ability of some carcinogenic hydrocarbons and sex hormones to increase the activity of the thiophosphate-oxidizing enzyme, apparently through stimulaing its synthesis, seems worthy of further study from the standpoint of the specific mechanisms involved. It should be noted that, although the polycylic aromatic hydrocarbons used in the present study are potent carcinogens, previous studies by Conney *et al.* (1956) have indicated that the ability of hydrocarbons to increase the activity of other microsome enzymes is apparently not related to their carcinogenicity. It is perhaps also noteworthy that the liver to body weight ratio did not exhibit a significant change from an average normal value of 3.3% in 24 hours after administration of methylcholanthrene or after treatment of the animals with steroids. Thus changes in enzyme activity per mg of tissue are indicative of changes in the activity of the whole liver. The results of the present investigation have provided some information on the mechanisms responsible for age and sex differences and other factors which influence susceptibility to cholinergic thiophosphates. The findings suggest that further research along similar lines may aid in gaining an understanding of the reasons for age, sex, species and individual differences in susceptibility to drugs and other chemical agents which have been observed frequently but have not been adequately explained.

SUMMARY

A detailed study was performed on the age and sex differences in the activity of the enzyme in the livers of rats which catalyzes the oxidation of thiophosphates. It was found that the enzyme activity of the livers of adult males was 2 to 3 times greater than that of adult females of the same age. No sex difference in enzyme activity was noted in animals less than 30 days of age but the activity of the livers of male rats exhibited an abrupt increase between 30 and 60 days of age which corresponds to the age of puberty in male rats. The low enzyme activity of the livers of adult females and young males was increased by prolonged administration of testosterone and the high activity of the livers of adult males was decreased by castration and by the prolonged administration of progesterone and diethylstilbestrol. The results of these experiments indicated that sex hormones influence the synthesis of the thiophosphate-oxidizing enzyme.

The activity of the thiophosphate-oxidizing enzyme of the regenerating livers of male rats was markedly decreased at 4 days after partial hepatectomy but gradually returned to the normal level within 20 days. The low enzyme activity of the livers of adult females, weanling males and partially hepatectomized males is increased to the level of adult males at 24 hours after the administration of 25 mg/kg of 3-methylcholanthrene. 3,4-benzpyrene and 1,2,5,6-dibenzanthracene also increased the activity of the livers of adult female rats. The administration of ethionine inhibited the response to the hydrocarbons. The inhibition of cholinesterase caused by the intraperitoneal administration of 2 mg/kg of guthion was increased by approximately 50% at 48 hours after injection of methylcholanthrene. The intraperitoneal administration of 20 mg/kg of β-diethylaminoethyl diphenylpropylacetate (SKF 525A) 40 minutes before injection of 2 mg/kg of guthion markedly decreased the inhibition of cholinesterase and reduced susceptibility to the acute toxicity of guthion. These effects are explainable on the basis of the ability of SKF 525A to inhibit the enzymatic oxidation of thiophosphates.

Feeding a protein-free diet to adult male rats reduced the ability of the liver to convert guthion to an anticholinesterase agent by 75%. The increase in activity of the thiophosphate-oxidizing enzyme which occurs after the administration of carcinogenic hydrocarbons was inhibited when the animals were fed a protein-free diet.

REFERENCES

Axelrod, J.: This Journal **117:** 322, 1956.
Baxter, C. F., Van Reen, R. and Rosenberg, C.: Proc. Soc. exp. Biol., N. Y. **96:** 159, 1957.
Brodie, B. B., Axelrod, J., Cooper, J. R., Gaudette, L., La Du, B. N., Mitoma, C. and Udenfriend, S.: Science **121:** 603, 1955.

BYERRUM, R. U. AND DUBOIS, K. P.: THIS JOURNAL **90:** 321, 1947.

CONNEY, A. H., MILLER, E. C. AND MILLER, J. A.: Cancer Res. **16:** 450, 1956.

CONNEY, A. H., MILLER, E. C. AND MILLER, J. A.: J. biol. Chem. **228:** 753, 1957.

DAVISON, A. N.: Biochem. J. **61:** 203, 1955.

DIGGLE, W. M. AND GAGE, J. C.: Biochem. J. **49:** 491, 1951.

DUBOIS, K. P. AND MANGUN, G. H.: Proc. Soc. exp. Biol., N. Y. **64:** 137, 1947.

DUBOIS, K. P., THRUSH, D. R. AND MURPHY, S. D.: THIS JOURNAL **119:** 208, 1957.

FARRIS, E. J.: in The Rat in Laboratory Investigations, Griffith, J. Q. and Farris, E. J., editors, p. 3, J. B. Lippincott Co., 1942.

GAGE, J. C.: Biochem. J. **54:** 426, 1953.

GREENBAUM, A. L., GREENWOOD, F. C. AND HARKNESS, R. D.: J. Physiol. **125:** 251, 1954.

MARCH, C. H. AND ELLIOTT, H. W.: Proc. Soc. exp. Biol., N. Y. **86:** 494, 1954.

METCALF, R. L. AND MARCH, R. B.: Ann. ent. Soc. Amer. **46:** 63, 1953.

MUELLER, G. C. AND MILLER, J. A.: J. biol. Chem. **180:** 1125, 1949.

MUELLER, G. C. AND MILLER, J. A.: J. biol. Chem. **202:** 579, 1953.

MURPHY, S. D. AND DUBOIS, K. P.: Fed. Proc. **15:** 462, 1956.

MURPHY, S. D. AND DUBOIS, K. P.: THIS JOURNAL **119:** 572, 1957a.

MURPHY, S. D. AND DUBOIS, K. P.: Fed. Proc. **16:** 324, 1957b.

MURPHY, S. D. AND DUBOIS, K. P.: Proc. Soc. exp. Biol., N. Y. **96:** 813, 1957c.

MYERS, D. K., MENDEL, B., GERSMANN, H. R. AND KETELAAR, J. A. A.: Nature **170:** 805, 1952.

NOVIKOFF, A. E. AND POTTER, V. R.: J. biol. Chem. **173:** 223, 1948.

QUINN, G. P., AXELROD, J. AND BRODIE, B. B.: Fed. Proc. **13:** 395, 1954.

TUBIN, B. L.: J. biol. Chem. **227:** 917, 1957.

WEBER, G. AND CANTERO, A.: Cancer Res. **15:** 679, 1955.

8078

THE HIGH ENERGY PHOSPHATE CONTENT OF CARDIAC MUSCLE UNDER VARIOUS EXPERIMENTAL CONDITIONS WHICH ALTER CONTRACTILE STRENGTH[1]

ROBERT F. FURCHGOTT[2] AND TAISIJA DE GUBAREFF[3]

Department of Pharmacology, Washington University School of Medicine, St. Louis, Missouri

Received for publication June 20, 1958

Changes in the strength of contraction of heart muscle can be brought about by a wide variety of drugs and also by alterations in experimental conditions. In attempting to elucidate the mechanism by which a drug or an alteration of experimental conditions produces a change in strength, it is important to find out whether any changes in the concentrations of high energy phosphate compounds of the cardiac muscle have also occurred. Since these compounds, which include adenosine triphosphate (ATP), adenosine diphosphate (ADP) and creatine phosphate (CP), either directly or indirectly supply the energy used for contraction, a change in their concentrations might under some circumstances be responsible for a change in contractile strength.

In the present investigation we have determined the concentrations of ATP, ADP, AMP (adenylic acid), CP and IP (inorganic phosphate) of isolated, electrically driven left atria of guinea pigs under standard experimental conditions, and also under altered experimental conditions and in the presence of a number of drugs which affect contractile strength. Our principal finding is that in many instances marked changes in contractile strength may occur without significant changes in concentrations of these high energy phosphate compounds.

METHODS. *The atrial preparation and apparatus.* The guinea pigs used weighed from 400 to 700 g each. They were fed on a diet of Purina rabbit chow supplemented with green vegetables or a solution of vitamin C. For each experiment a guinea pig was first anesthetized by intraperitoneal injection of sodium pentobarbital, and its heart was then rapidly excised and placed in a small beaker containing Krebs solution (Krebs and Henzeleit, 1932) at room temperature, through which was bubbled 95% O_2–5% CO_2. The ventricles were cut away from the atria, and the atria were placed in a petri dish also containing oxygenated Krebs solution. With a fine, sharp-pointed scissors, the left atrium was separated from the right and any adhering pieces of blood vessels, fat, connective tissue and ventricular muscle were carefully trimmed off.

One silk thread was securely tied around a small bit of tissue at the tip of the left atrium, held between the points of a pair of fine-tipped forceps, and a second thread was similarly tied at the base of the atrium. Each thread was then tied in the form of a loop of about 2 mm diameter. During the procedure described above, which required about 10 minutes from the time of removal of the heart, the atrium was kept under oxygenated Krebs solution except for brief intervals.

The left atrium was mounted in a rectangular glass muscle chamber, illustrated in fig. 1. The loop at the base of the atrium was passed over the silver hook projecting down from the lucite support, while a one-gram silver weight with a hook was attached to the loop at the tip of the atrium. The silver weight was a rectangular piece about 0.4 mm thick, with a central pinhole about 0.1 mm in diameter, on which the image of the filament of the light source was focused. Displacement of the weight by the contracting atrium could be followed by observing the movement of the bright image of the pinhole on a ruled screen under dim light. Magnification by the optical lever was about fourteenfold. Although no attempt was made to make photokymographic records of the movement of the image, it would have been possible to do so with the usual type of continuous drive, recording camera.

[1] This work was supported by grants from the American Heart Association and the St. Louis Heart Association. A report on part of the work was presented at the meeting of the American Society for Pharmacology and Experimental Therapeutics, September, 1953 (Furchgott *et al.*, 1954).

[2] Present address: Department of Pharmacology, State University of New York College of Medicine at New York City, Brooklyn 3, N. Y.

[3] Present address: Department of Physiology, Washington University School of Medicine, St. Louis, Missouri.

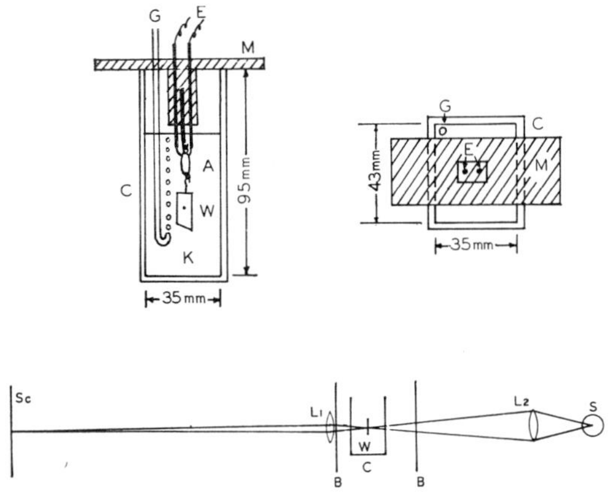

FIG. 1. Upper figures: Diagram of muscle chamber from front (left) and top (right). C, glass chamber with optically flat walls. K, Krebs-bicarbonate solution to 100 ml level. G, inlet for 95% O_2–5% CO_2. M, lucite support for electrodes and upper hook. E, fine silver wire stimulating electrodes, insulated with polyethylene tubing and "chlorided" at exposed tips touching atrium. A, left atrium. W, flat silver weight with pinhole. Lower figure: Diagram of optical lever for isotonic contractions. S, light source, 6 volt automobile headlight in metal housing with air vents and circular exit diaphragm. L_2, lens for focusing image of source on pinhole. W, silver weight with pinhole. L_1, lens for focusing image of pinhole on screen. Sc, screen of millimeter-ruled graph paper mounted on stiff cardboard. C, muscle chamber. B, glass walls of constant temperature water bath.

The muscle chamber was mounted in a constant temperature water bath, so that the chamber wall farthest from the light source was parallel to and within several mm of the outer wall of the water bath. The temperature of the water bath was 37°C unless stated otherwise. The oxygenated Krebs-bicarbonate solution was at a pH of 7.4 and contained 0.01 *M* glucose.

Electrical stimulation of the left atrium was accomplished with a Grass S4A stimulator, set to deliver a "biphasic" pulse of 1 millisecond duration. The intensity of the stimulus was set about 10% above threshold and was usually around 1 volt. Frequency of stimulation was 1 per second unless otherwise stated.

In any experiment contraction height was recorded at appropriate intervals. At the end of an experiment the atrium with weight attached was suddenly lifted from the muscle chamber and plunged into liquid nitrogen contained in an insulated beaker. The atrium was in air for no longer than 3 to 4 seconds. During this period contractions due to stimulation through the electrodes, which were still in contact with the atrium, were observed directly, and the atrium was plunged into the liquid nitrogen about a half second after the last beat.

Preparation of tissue extract. The atrium, while still in liquid N_2 was taken to a −20°C cold room, where it was weighed in the frozen state on a torsion balance. Before the weighing, the attached threads and the small bits of tissue to which they were tied were cut off and any adhering frozen Krebs solution was carefully scraped off. The weights of different atria ranged from about 40 to 90 mg. Occasionally an atrium was extracted immediately after being weighed, but usually it was stored for 18 to 24 hours at −20°C before being extracted. Extraction was carried out in a cold room with the procedure recently described in detail by us (Furchgott and de Gubareff, 1956a). In brief, the frozen tissue was first converted to a fine powder in a stainless steel pulverizer at dry-ice temperature. It was then extracted at 0°C with 1 ml of 0.3 *M* perchloric acid (PCA). Five ml of water at 0°C were then added and the mixture was centrifuged in the cold room. The supernatant extract was decanted into a test tube in an ice bath. Two ml of the extract were transferred to a second tube in the ice bath and 80 mm^3 of .004 *M* $CuSO_4$ were added. This portion of extract was used for the determination of IP and CP, while the remaining portion (with no added $CuSO_4$) was used for the enzymatic determination of ATP, ADP and AMP.

Analysis of IP and CP. The method used for determination of these compounds was a modification of the Fiske and Subbarow procedure recently described by us (Furchgott and de Gubareff, 1956a). The advantage of the method is that both IP and CP are determined sucessively on the same aliquot of solution during a continuous run in a Beckman spectrophotometer. Analyses were carried out within 1 hour after the end of the extraction procedure, during which period there was no significant hydrolysis of CP as long as the extracts were kept at 0°C. Duplicate, and sometimes triplicate determinations were made on all extracts, with 200 mm^3 of copper-treated solution being used for each determination.

Analysis of ATP, ADP, AMP. The method used for determination of these compounds was a modification of the combined enzymatic and spectrophotometric method of Kalckar (1947a, b), which will be referred to as the Kalckar "deaminase method." To Greiner (1952) should go the credit for first applying this highly specific method to small samples of cardiac muscle.

A measured quantity (2 to 3 ml) of that portion of the extract with no added $CuSO_4$ was brought to a pH between 6.5 and 7.5 by titration with 1 *N* NaOH, in a glass electrode assembly at room temperature. (The portion of extract containing

$CuSO_4$ cannot be used for analysis of adenine nucleotides by Kalckar's method since the Cu^{++} inhibits the enzymatic reactions.) To the neutralized extract was added one tenth of its volume of 1 *M* sodium succinate buffer at pH 6.0, giving a final pH of approximately 6.1. The buffered extract was then stored at 0°C until analyzed. Although the analysis was generally carried out on the same day as the preparation of the extract, it was possible to keep the buffered extract overnight in the cold without detectable changes in the ATP, ADP, or AMP concentrations.

To each of 4 fused silica cells (1 cm optical path and approximately 1 ml total capacity) in a standard Beckman cell carrier were added respectively water, an aliquot of a blank solution of succinate buffered PCA and 2 aliquots of buffered extract. The aliquots of blank solution and extract were delivered with the same constriction pipette[4] and ranged from 400 to 500 mm^3. The cell carrier was placed in a Beckman DU spectrophotometer, which had the upper half of the window between the cell and prism compartments occluded with a strip of opaque black paper so that the beam did not extend above the solutions in the cells. The spectrophotometer was set at 265 mμ, and optical density (O.D.) readings were made with the water cell set at zero O.D.

Before beginning the addition of enzymes to the cells containing blank solution and extract, 3 to 4 mm^3 of 1 *M* $MgCl_2$ were added. Successive additions of enzymes were then made in the same order used by Greiner (1952) in his determinations of the adenine nucleotides of cat papillary muscle. However, a comparison of the time course of his spectrophotometric changes with ours (compare his fig. 1 with our fig. 2) indicates that our enzyme preparations were more active and gave less "blank absorption." In our experiments, the decrease in O.D. after addition of adenylic acid deaminase was complete within 2 to 4 minutes; the decrease after addition of myokinase within 15 to 20 minutes; and the decrease after addition of adenylpyrophosphatase within 6 to 8 minutes. Each enzyme solution, in a measured volume usually ranging from from 1 to 5 mm^3, was delivered rapidly with a constriction pipette below the surface of the solution in the cell, and then rapidly mixed by air bubbles blown out of the pipette before it was withdrawn. Readings were made at intervals after each addition until no further decrease in O.D. occurred over a period of 3 to 5 minutes (fig. 2).

Adenylic acid deaminase was prepared by procedure A of Kalckar (1947b). The final precipitate was dissolved in 1.2 *M* ammonium sulfate solution,

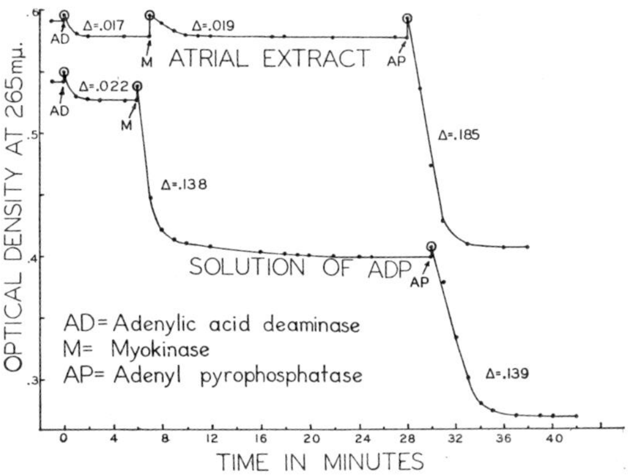

FIG. 2. Enzymatic determination of AMP, ADP, and ATP.

Upper curve was obtained with succinate buffered PCA extract of left atrium of guinea pig, and lower curve with succinate buffered PCA solution of commercial sodium ADP. Each Δ value gives fall in optical density after addition of enzyme. Optical density value immediately after addition of each enzyme (circled points) was calculated from change brought about by similar addition of enzyme to a succinate buffered PCA blank. Concentrations in μ*M* per ml of solution are obtained as follows: AMP = (Δ after AD)/7.34; ADP = (2 × Δ after M)/7.34; ATP = (Δ after AP − Δ after M)/7.34. Note that the ADP solution used contained a small amount of AMP as an impurity, but negligible ATP.

and any further dilutions were also made with the same solution. When stored at 2°C in such a solution the enzyme lost little activity over a period of several months.

Myokinase and adenylpyrophosphatase were also prepared by procedures very similar to those described by Kalckar (1947b.) Preparations of myokinase were used only if they were sufficiently active to complete the conversion of ADP to AMP and ATP within 20 minutes and exhibited negligible adenosine triphosphatase activity over that period. In the case of preparations of potato adenylpyrophosphatase, the solution of the final fraction was heated at 60°C for 20 minutes in order to inactivate AMP-phosphatase, which was always present as a contaminant. If this latter enzyme is not inactivated, it gives rise to erroneously low values for ATP, since it converts a fraction of the AMP formed from ATP to adenosine, which is not deaminated by the adenylic acid deaminase. Both myokinase and adenylpyrophosphatase preparations were stored at 2°C. The activity of the former declined to levels unsuitable for analytical use over a period of 1 to 3 months, while the activity of the latter was maintained for a year or more.

The concentrations of AMP, ADP and ATP in a tissue extract were calculated from the changes in O.D. at 265 mμ (corrected for enzyme absorption)

[4] In the present work all additions of solutions were made with constriction pipettes of the Lang-Levy type (Levy, 1936).

as indicated in fig. 2. The factor 7.34, which represents the fall in optical density per μM of adenine nucleotide deaminated per ml was obtained with a standard solution of purified sodium ATP (Pabst) which gave a molecular extinction coefficient of 13,100 at the 265 mμ setting on the Beckman spectrophotometer used and an O.D. decrease of 56% after addition of adenylic acid deaminase and adenylpyrophosphatase. The concentrations of adenine nucleotides in an atrium were obtained by multiplying the concentrations found in its extract by the proper dilution factors.

Analysis of high energy phosphate of ATP and ADP. The concentration of labile high energy phosphate of ATP and ADP, termed adenylpyrophosphate (APP), can be directly calculated from the results of the spectrophotometric analysis described above (2 such phosphates for ATP and 1 for ADP.)

However, in a number of experiments the APP concentration was also determined by analyzing aliquots of extract for IP before and after treatment with adenylpyrophosphatase. The increase in IP produced by the enzyme was taken as a measure of the APP present. The procedure was carried out in a Beckman spectrophotometer adapted for microdeterminations, using the Fiske and Subbarow method for phosphate analysis (Furchgott and de Gubareff, 1956a). To duplicate 200 mm^3 aliquots of neutralized extract were added 1.7 mm^3 of 1 M succinate buffer of pH 6.0 and 1.7 mm^3 of adenylpyrophosphatase. After 10 minutes (a sufficient time for complete hydrolysis of the pyrophosphate of ATP and ADP) 25 mm^3 of 5 N H_2SO_4 and 40 mm^3 of Fiske and Subbarow mixture were added and the optical density was read after 5 to 10 minutes at 660 mμ. A second set of duplicate aliquots was subjected to the same procedure, except that no enzyme was added. Appropriate blank solutions and IP standards were used both in the procedure with enzyme added and in that with no enzyme added.

In addition to determining APP concentration with the two enzymatic methods described above, a third method based on the acid-heat hydrolysis of the pyrophosphate of ATP and ADP was also sometimes used. 400 mm^3 of extract and 100 mm^3 of 5 N H_2SO_4 were mixed in a 5-ml test tube which was then placed in boiling water bath for 15 minutes. The mixture was then diluted with 500 mm^3 of H_2O, and duplicate 200 mm^3 aliquots were analyzed for phosphate with the Fiske and Subbarow method. Again a Beckman spectrophotometer adapted for microdeterminations was used and

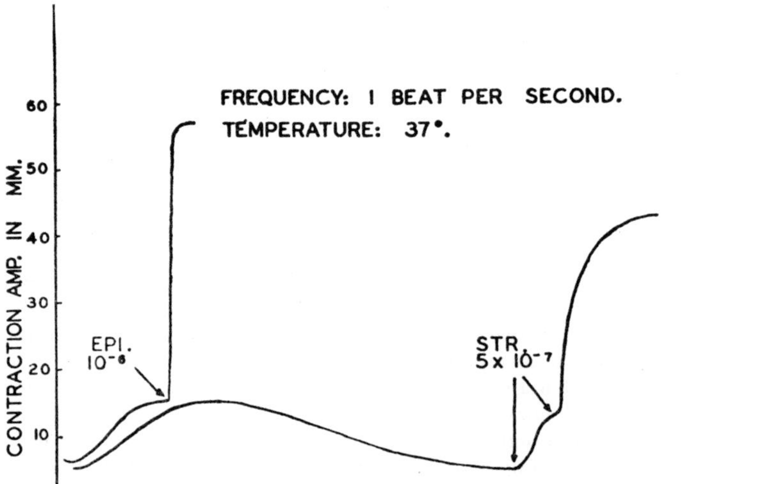

FIG. 3. Time course of typical experiments with electrically driven left atria of guinea pig. Ordinate scale gives time after mounting atrium in muscle chamber. Abscissa scale gives amplitude of isotonic contractions magnified (14×) by optical lever. Both curves show rise in contraction amplitude during the "initial incubation period." In one experiment (upper curve) epinephrine was added after contraction had attained "initial maximal amplitude," and atrium was frozen for analysis after epinephrine had produced its maximal increase. In the other experiment the attainment of "initial maximal amplitude" was followed by a gradual decrease in amplitude over the "hypodynamic period," which was terminated by the addition of strophanthin-K to the atrium in "spontaneous failure." Two additions of strophanthin, to give a final concentration of 10^{-6}, were required in this experiment to produce a maximal response, following which the atrium was frozen for analysis.

an appropriate blank solution and IP standard were carried through the same procedure as the extract. The difference between the total inorganic phosphate in an extract after acid-heat hydrolysis and the inorganic phosphate (IP + CP) before such treatment was taken as a measure of the APP present.

RESULTS. *General behavior of atria.* In Krebs bicarbonate medium at 37°C the isolated left atrium of the guinea pig usually exhibits no spontaneous contractions. In the present study any atrium exhibiting such contractions was discarded. Once an atrium was mounted in the muscle chamber and electrically driven at one beat per second, its contraction amplitude slowly rose, reaching a maximum usually after about 40 to 100 minutes (fig. 3). This maximum will be referred to as the "initial maximal amplitude" and the period over which it was attained and maintained will be referred to as the "initial incubation period." Once the initial maximal amplitude was attained, it was occasionally maintained for an hour or more, but usually it was followed within 15 to 30 minutes by a gradual decrease in amplitude. When the amplitude had fallen to 65% or less of the initial maximal amplitude the atrium was considered to be in "experimental failure." The period over which the amplitude was gradually decreasing will be referred to as the "hypodynamic period."

In Krebs bicarbonate solution at room temperature (25°–28°C) a gradual rise in contraction amplitude also occurred during an initial incubation period, just as at 37°C. However, at the lower temperature, once the amplitude had attained its initial maximal level, it usually stayed essentially at that level for several hours. The average initial maximal amplitude attained at room temperature was approximately twice as high as that attained at 37°C.

Both at room temperature and at 37°C isolated guinea pig atria, like several other isolated mammalian cardiac preparations (Kruta, 1937; Dale, 1932; Cattell and Gold, 1955; Katzung *et al.*, 1957), exhibit an increase in contraction amplitude with increase in frequency of contraction over a fairly wide frequency range (fig. 4). Although a detailed report on this "positive frequency effect" is to be the subject of a separate paper by the present authors, it should be noted here that this effect can be overcome by such

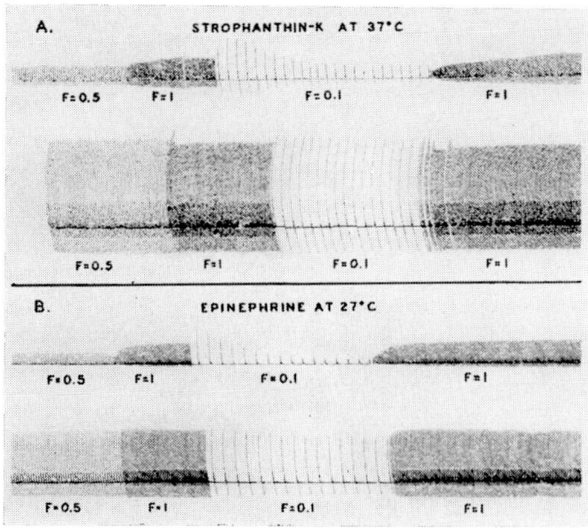

FIG. 4. Typical experiments showing effects of variations in frequency (F indicates frequency in beats per second) on amplitude of contraction at body temperature and room temperature, before and after addition of drugs with marked positive inotropic activity.

In both experiments recording was made with an ink-writing isotonic lever, exerting one gram tension on the left atrium of guinea pig suspended in oxygenated Krebs solution in a small muscle chamber. A. Contraction pattern before (upper record) and 30 min after (lower record) addition of 2×10^{-6} strophanthin-K at 37°C. B. Contraction pattern before (upper record) and 5 min after (lower record) addition of 10^{-6} epinephrine at 27°C. Note in both experiments the ability of these drugs to overcome "positive frequency effect."

positive inotropic agents as cardiac glycosides, epinephrine and certain other sympathomimetic amines, or extra $CaCl_2$ (Furchgott and Sleator, 1954; Furchgott and de Gubareff, 1956b). In the presence of an optimal concentration of one of these agents, contraction amplitude is increased to essentially the same maximal level over a wide range of frequencies, and the overshoot of amplitude of the first beats on switching from high to low frequency and the undershoot of the first beats on switching from low to high frequency largely disappear (fig. 4). It was therefore found useful to occasionally test all atria at a low frequency (1 per 10 sec) as well as at the standard frequency (1 per sec) following the addition of cardiac glycosides and other agents with strong positive inotropic action. When such an agent added had successfully eliminated the "positive frequency effect," it could be safely assumed that the atrium was being maximally stimulated.

Atria before failure. The results of the analyses on "control" atria frozen at a time when the initial maximal amplitude had been attained are given in the first section of table 1. All concentra-

TABLE 1

High energy phosphates and adenine nucleotides of guinea pig left atria at 37°C prior to failure, during failure and after restoration from failure with strophanthin-K

Treatment and Functional State: Prior to Failure (Controls)	Initial Incubation Period: Duration (min)	Initial Incubation Period: Max. ampl. (mm)	Concn. in μM Phosphate per g Moist Tissue: IP	CP	APP* by deaminase	APP* by APP-ase	APP* By acid hydrolysis	Adenine Nucleotides μM/g Moist Tissue: ATP	ADP	AMP
C-1	75	10	4.68	5.00	4.82	5.34	5.19	2.27	.28	.17
C-2	78	14	5.77	4.38	5.76	5.80	5.85	2.51	.74	.18
C-3	85	12	6.52	3.61	5.44	5.98	5.67	2.43	.58	.22
C-4	66	9	7.32	4.26	5.15	5.05	4.82	2.40	.35	.31
C-5	105	4	6.90	4.76	5.43	5.55	5.39	2.45	.43	.23
C-6	60	11	6.35	3.84	5.79			2.63	.53	.25
C-7	63	9	5.91	4.35	5.14	5.44	5.44	2.33	.48	.22
C-8	45	19	7.05	3.78	4.84			2.26	.34	.26
C-9	74	17	6.05	3.51	4.48			2.13	.22	.21
C-10	46	10	5.81	4.40	5.73			2.74	.25	.26
Mean	69.7	11.5	6.24	4.19	5.26	5.53	5.39	2.41	.43	.23
± SE_M	±5.7	±1.4	±.24	±.16	±.14	±.14	±.15	±.06	±.06	±.01

During Failure	Initial Incubation Period: Duration (min)	Initial Incubation Period: Max. ampl. (mm)	Hypodynamic Period: Duration (min)	Hypodynamic Period: Relative ampl.†	IP	CP	APP by deaminase	APP by APP-ase	APP By acid hydrolysis	ATP	ADP	AMP
F-1	42	28	148	.18	7.80	4.30	5.05	4.90	4.90	2.21	.62	.16
F-2	155	8	195	.41	6.75	4.42	4.51	4.81	5.02	2.01	.50	.15
F-3	55	11	180	.45	5.78	3.74	4.61	5.09	4.59	2.16	.28	.15
F-4	45	17	259	.65	5.95	4.49	4.94	5.33	5.01	2.24	.49	.14
F-5	95	20	120	.45	6.39	3.92	4.63	4.78	4.55	2.14	.34	.20
F-6	59	32	204	.38	5.00	4.85	5.82	6.10	5.80	2.71	.40	.14
F-7	65	9	96	.33	7.02	4.32	4.68	5.00	4.92	1.94	.76	.18
Mean	73.9	17.9	171.7	.41	6.38	4.29	4.89	5.14	4.97	2.20	.49	.16
± SE_M	±15.1	±3.6	±20.8	±.05	±.34	±.14	±.17	±.17	±.16	±.09	±.06	±.01

After Restoration from Failure	Initial Incubation Period: Duration (min)	Initial Incubation Period: Max. ampl. (mm)	Hypodynamic Period: Duration (min)	Hypodynamic Period: Relative ampl.†	Period of Restoration with Strophanthin-K: Final concn. $\times 10^{-6}$	Period of Restoration: Duration (min)	Period of Restoration: Relative ampl.†	IP	CP	APP by deaminase	APP by APP-ase	APP By acid hydrolysis	ATP	ADP	AMP
R-1	74	18	148	.45	1.15	38	1.72	6.73	4.75	5.03	5.11	5.00	2.32	.37	.13
R-2	45	15	120	.33	1.12	45	2.87	6.13	5.13	5.86	5.87	5.64	2.69	.48	.14
R-3	24	6	44	.33	.85	27	4.16	5.21	4.05	4.53	4.59	4.96	2.06	.41	.17
R-4	60	22	97	.32	.85	38	1.93	6.72	3.80	5.38	5.36	5.08	2.51	.37	.19
R-5	55	12	120	.42	.85	25	3.08	5.61	4.87	5.35	5.46	5.65	2.43	.48	.19
R-6	40	14	30	.36	.89	57	2.33	7.00	3.40	4.22	4.70	4.47	1.88	.43	.16
R-7	42	19	103	.37	1.06	15	2.21	7.27	3.79	5.27	5.56	5.58	2.42	.42	.18
Mean	48.6	15.1	94.6	.37	.97	35.0	2.61	6.38	4.25	5.08	5.24	5.20	2.33	.42	.17
± SE	±6.1	±2.0	±16.1	±.02		±5.3	±.33	±.29	±.25	±.21	±.17	±.16	±.10	±.02	±.01

* APP (labile P of ATP and ADP) was determined by three different methods. The values for APP calculated from the values for ATP and ADP, determined by the Kalckar "deaminase method," are considered to be the most accurate. See section on METHODS for details.

† "Relative amplitude" is contraction amplitude at end of period indicated, divided by maximal amplitude attained at end of initial incubation period.

tions are given in terms of micromols per gram of moist tissue.[5]

It will be noted that APP (high energy phosphate of ATP and ADP), with a mean concentration of 5.26 $\mu M/g$, contributes somewhat more to the total high energy phosphate content than does CP, with a mean of 4.19 $\mu M/g$. The mean concentration of IP, 6.24 $\mu M/g$, is higher than that of either CP or APP. Of the APP high energy phosphate 91.5% is contributed by ATP and 8.5% by ADP on the average. On a molar basis the adenine nucleotide fraction consists of about 78% ATP, 14% ADP and 8% AMP.

In all experiments in which APP was determined with the use of adenylpyrophosphatase or by acid-heat treatment, the results are in rather close agreement with those obtained by the more complex and specific deaminase method. This finding, which applies not only in the case of atria before failure but also in the case of atria in failure and atria after recovery (table 1), indicates that either of these simpler methods gives a fairly reliable value for the APP concentration in cardiac tissue.

Atria in failure. The analytical results on atria in failure are given in the second section of table 1. The contraction amplitude at the time of freezing varied from 18 to 65% of the initial maximal amplitude. Although the average CP concentration is slightly higher in failure than in the control series and the average APP concentration is slightly lower, the difference in neither case is statistically significant ($p > .05$). If the values for the APP and CP concentrations of individual atria are considered with respect to the degree of failure (as indicated by the fall in contraction amplitude), no correlation is found. In addition there is no significant difference between either the mean ATP concentrations or the mean ADP concentrations before and during failure. The reason why the mean AMP value in the failure experiments is significantly lower ($p < .001$) than that in the control experiments is not clear. However, it would appear that the fall in AMP is more dependent on the longer duration of the failure experiments rather than on the development of failure itself since strophanthin does not significantly raise the AMP concentration when it restores the failing atria (table 1, third section).

Atria after restoration from failure with strophanthin. Strophanthin-K (Inland Alkaloid Co.) was the cardiac glycoside used to restore the contractile force of failing atria. When an atrium had reached the desired degree of failure, a 1:1000 aqueous stock stolution of this glycoside was added by micropipette to give a final concentration of about 5×10^{-7} in the muscle chamber. Successive additions of equal or smaller amounts of the drug were then added at intervals of 10 to 20 minutes (fig. 3) until the recording indicated that the "positive frequency effect" (see first section under RESULTS) was overcome. Once this effect was overcome, positive inotropic action was considered to be maximal and the atrium was then frozen for analysis. In all cases the final amplitude attained after treatment with the cardiac glycoside was well above the initial maximal amplitude existing before failure.

The results on atria restored from failure with strophanthin-K are shown in the third section of table 1. No significant differences were found between the concentrations of IP, CP, APP, ATP or ADP in the atria after strophanthin and the respective concentrations of those fractions in control or in failed atria. The mean AMP concentration of atria restored with strophanthin was significantly below that of control atria ($p = .001$), but did not differ significantly from that of failed atria not treated with strophanthin. As noted in the preceding section, this fall in AMP seems to be related to the longer duration of the experiments in which failure was produced.

Atria stimulated with epinephrine and norepinephrine. These sympathomimetic amines were added to atria in the control state (after attainment of initial maximal amplitude and before the onset of a hypodynamic period, as shown in fig. 3). Solutions of commercial *l*-epinephrine hydrochloride (Parke-Davis) and *l*-norepinephrine bitartrate (Winthrop-Sterling) were used. The experiments with epinephrine have been divided into 2 groups: those in which a high final concentration of the drug ($1–10 \times 10^{-6}$) was used, and those in which a low final concentration ($1–2 \times 10^{-7}$) was used (table 2). In the "high epinephrine" group, a maximal positive inotropic

[5] At the outset of the present investigation we intended to express concentrations in micromols per mg protein in each atrium. However, in the first series of experiments carried out, namely those at room temperature (table 4), it was found that the standard errors of the means (in % of the means) were no smaller when concentrations were expressed on the basis of protein (determined by the method of Lowry *et al.*, 1951) than they were when concentrations were expressed on the basis of moist weight. As a result of this finding, we decided to express all concentrations in this work on the basis of moist weight of tissue.

TABLE 2

Effect of agents which increase contractile force on high energy phosphates and adenine nucleotides of guinea pig left atrium at 37°C

Treatment (No. of Expts.)	Mean Rel. Ampl. (Range)	Mean Concn. in μM Phosphate per g Moist Tissue			Mean Concn. of Adenine Nucleotides in μM/g Moist Tissue		
		IP	CP	APP	ATP	ADP	AMP
None (control series) (10)	1	6.24 ±.24	4.19 ±.16	5.26 ±.14	2.41 ±.06	0.43 ±.06	0.23 ±.01
Low epinephrine, 1–2 × 10^{-7} (8)	3.1 (1.6–5.6)	6.15 ±.22	4.12 ±.24	4.94 ±.25	2.21 ±.12	0.52 ±.02	0.21 ±.01
High epinephrine, 1–10 × 10^{-6} (9)	4.0 (1.6–7.8)	7.56* ±.22	3.26** ±.36	4.97 ±.21	2.21 ±.12	0.55 ±.03	0.26 ±.02
Norepinephrine, 1–16 × 10^{-6} (7)	4.7 (2.6–8.0)	6.14 ±.24	3.57** ±.26	5.01 ±.34	2.19 ±.15	0.63 ±.07	0.20 ±.01
High Ca^{++}, 3–5× normal (7)	4.1 (2.5–6.0)	6.80 ±.15	4.14 ±.24	5.01 ±.12	2.30 ±.08	0.41 ±.04	0.22 ±.01
Low K^+, ⅕–⅒ of normal (3)	1.7 (1.2–2.3)	6.94 (6.36–7.40)	3.00 (2.40–3.57)	4.58 (4.18–4.92)	1.94 (1.70–2.18)	0.70 (.55–.79)	0.29 (.23–.33)

Note: Control series is same as in table 1. In all experiments APP concentration was calculated from ATP and ADP concentrations determined by Kalckar deaminase procedure. Relative amplitude is contraction amplitude of atrium at time of freezing after treatment, divided by initial maximal amplitude prior to treatment.

* Difference from control value is highly significant ($p < .01$).

** Difference from control value is significant ($.05 > p > .01$).

effect was achieved in all 9 atria (as judged by the abolition of the "positive frequency effect"), and, in addition, 2 of the atria developed rapid spontaneous contractile activity shortly before they were frozen. In the "low epinephrine" group, the positive inotropic effect was short of maximal, and 2 of the 8 atria in the group showed occasional spontaneous beats prior to freezing. In the case of the atria treated with high concentrations of norepinephrine (1–16 × 10^{-6}), all 8 gave a maximal positive inotropic response, and 3 showed occasional spontaneous beats before freezing.

The mean concentrations of IP, CP, APP, ATP, ADP and AMP in atria treated with the low concentrations of epinephrine did not differ significantly ($p > .05$) from the corresponding mean concentrations in control atria. On the other hand, the atria treated with high concentrations of epinephrine showed a significant 21% increase ($p = .001$) in mean IP concentration above the control level, and a significant 22% decrease ($p = .02$) in mean CP concentration (table 2). Atria treated with high concentrations of norepinephrine also showed a significant decrease (14%, $p = .02$) in mean CP concentration. Despite the decrease in CP, there was no significant change in mean APP, ATP, ADP or AMP in atria subjected to high concentrations of epinephrine or norepinephrine. Incidentally, the decrease in the mean CP concentration cannot be attributed to the spontaneous contractions sometimes induced by high concentrations of these sympathomimetic amines, since the CP values in the atria which exhibited spontaneous beating just prior to freezing were well within the range of values obtained in the other atria in this series.

Atria stimulated with high calcium or low potassium. Krebs bicarbonate solution contains 5.2 mEq of Ca^{++} and 5.6 mEq of K^+ per liter. Increasing the Ca^{++} concentration 3 to 5 times by the appropriate addition of a calcium chloride solution produces in the guinea pig left atrium a positive inotropic effect about equal to that obtained with optimal concentrations of epinephrine or cardiac glycosides, and the "positive frequency effect" is practically abolished. Decreasing the K^+ concentration, by reducing the KCl and KH_2PO_4 in the Krebs solution, to about 1/5 to 1/10 of the usual level also causes a positive inotropic effect; however, the stimulation of contraction amplitude obtained by reducing K^+ is less than that obtained by increasing Ca^{++}. In addition, low K^+, unlike high Ca^{++}, cannot maintain increased contraction amplitude at 37°C for long periods of time, and frequently leads to spontaneous contractile activity.

The results obtained with atria in the presence of high Ca^{++} or low K^+ concentrations are shown in table 2. In all cases changes in the concentrations of these ions in the medium were made after the contraction had reached the initial maximal amplitude in regular Krebs solution. In the experiments with high Ca^{++}, atria were frozen after the "positive frequency effect" had been abolished. In the experiments with low K^+ they were frozen after contraction amplitude had reached a maximal level, and a moderate degree of spontaneous contractile activity had become manifest.

In the atria stimulated with high Ca^{++}, the mean concentrations of IP, CP, APP and adenine nucleotides did not differ significantly ($p > .05$) from the corresponding mean concentrations in the control series. In contrast, in the atria stimulated with low K^+, there was a considerable fall in the high energy phosphate content, especially the CP fraction, for which the mean level was twenty-five% below the mean control level. Since only 3 experiments were carried out with low K^+, statistical comparisons of the results with those in the control series are not warranted. Yet, from these preliminary experiments it would appear that the effect of low K^+ on high energy phosphates rather closely resembles that produced by toxic levels of cardiac glycoside (see below).

Atria poisoned with excess cardiac glycosides. In 4 experiments hypodynamic atria were exposed to sufficiently high concentrations of strophanthin-K ($>2 \times 10^{-6}$) or ouabain ($>7 \times 10^{-7}$) for sufficient periods of time to allow the toxic action of the glycosides to supersede their positive inotropic action. This toxic action in guinea pig atria, as in cat papillary muscles (Lee, 1953a), is manifested by a steady decrease in contraction amplitude following the initial rise in amplitude after addition of the cardiac glycoside, and frequently by the appearance of bursts of spontaneous contractile activity.

Atria frozen after being poisoned with excess cardiac glycoside contained significantly lower high energy phosphate concentrations (table 3). The mean APP level was 77% and the mean CP level only 36.5% of the corresponding levels in the control atria. As would be expected, the drop in high energy phosphate led to a marked increase in the mean IP level (60% above that of the controls). ATP concentration was significantly below the control level, while ADP and AMP concentrations were significantly elevated. However, the total adenine nucleotide concentration (ATP + ADP + AMP) was not significantly different from that found in atria before failure, during failure, or after restoration from failure with strophanthin.

Atria depressed with acetylcholine. To 4 atria which had attained their initial maximal amplitude of contraction acetylcholine was added to give a final concentration of 1 to 7×10^{-7}. In each experiment contraction amplitude fell within 2 minutes after addition to less than 10% of the initial maximal amplitude, and the atrium was then frozen for analysis. The results of these experiments show that the marked depression in contractile amplitude produced by acetylcholine is not associated with any significant change in the content of high energy phosphate (CP and APP) from that in control atria (table 3).

Atria depressed with ryanodine. Ryanodine, a purified alkaloid from the South American plant *Ryania speciosa Vahl,* has been reported to cause marked depression of contractile force in isolated mammalian atria (Furchgott and de Gubareff, 1956c; Hillyard and Procita, 1956). The mechanism of depression is not understood, but it appears to be different from that of other known cardiac depressants.

In the present work ryanodine (kindly supplied by Dr. E. F. Rogers of Merck, Sharp and Dohme) was added to atria after they had attained their initial maximal amplitudes of contraction. In 2 experiments a final concentration of 10^{-6} led to a relatively rapid depression so that when the atria were frozen 24 minutes after addition of ryanodine, their contraction amplitudes were only about 10% of the pre-ryanodine levels. The analytical results on these atria, presented in table 3, show that the concentrations of both CP and APP were within the

TABLE 3

Effect of anoxia and of drugs which decrease contractile force on high energy phosphates and adenine nucleotides of guinea pig left atrium at 37°C

Treatment (No. of Expts.)	Mean Rel. Ampl. (Range)	Mean Concn. in μM Phosphate per g Moist Tissue			Mean Concn. of Adenine Nucleotides in μM/g Moist Tissue		
		IP	CP	APP	ATP	ADP	AMP
None (control series) (10)	1	6.24 ±.24	4.19 ±.16	5.26 ±.14	2.41 ±.06	.43 ±.06	.23 ±.01
Anoxia, 18 min (1)	.07	8.54	1.29	4.98	2.24	.50	.19
Anoxia, 75 min (1)	.04	10.19	0.39	3.24	1.37	.50	.51
Excess cardiac glycoside (4)	.43 (.12–.85)	10.03* ±.24	1.49* ±.38	4.04* ±.34	1.65* ±.13	.73* ±.14	.31* ±.05
Acetylcholine 1–7 × 10^{-7} (4)	.06 (.05–.07)	5.65 ±.44	3.84 ±.28	5.52 ±.22			
Ryanodine, 10^{-6} for 24 min (2)	.10 (.05–.15)	6.45 (5.80–7.10)	4.15 (3.79–4.51)	5.43 (5.39–5.48)			

Note: Control series is same as in table 1. APP was determined by acid hydrolysis in experiments with acetylcholine and ryanodine, and by Kalckar deaminase methods in all other experiments. "Relative amplitude" has same meaning as in table 2. "Poisoning" with excess cardiac glycoside was achieved with concentrations of strophanthin-K exceeding 2 × 10^{-6} or of ouabain exceeding 7 × 10^{-7}.

* Difference from control value is highly significant ($p < .01$).

respective ranges found for these fractions in untreated atria, despite the marked decreases in contraction amplitude. In a third experiment with ryanodine in which an atrium was exposed to this drug for a much longer period, namely 1 hour, before being frozen for analysis, both the CP concentration (2.84 μM/g) and APP concentration (3.66 μM/g) were well below the respective ranges in control atria. It would therefore appear that prolonged exposure to a relatively high concentration of ryanodine may cause some reduction in high energy phosphate of atrial muscle, but that this reduction is not responsible for the initial negative inotropic action of this drug.

Atria subjected to anoxia. If 95% N_2–5% CO_2 is substituted for 95% O_2–5% CO_2 as the gas being bubbled through the Krebs bicarbonate medium in the muscle chamber, the contraction amplitude of the atrium quickly declines, reaching a level of less than 10% of the initial level within 15 to 20 minutes. In 2 experiments atria which had attained their initial maximal amplitudes under O_2-CO_2 were subjected to N_2-CO_2 for 18 minutes and 75 minutes respectively, and then frozen for analysis (table 3). In the shorter anaerobic experiment the APP concentration was within the lower part of the range for APP obtained in the control series, but the CP concentration was only 29% of the control value. In the longer anaerobic experiment, the APP concentration was more markedly reduced, falling to 60% of the mean control value, while CP concentration was almost negligible at 9% of the mean control value. In both experiments IP was markedly elevated as a result of the net breakdown in CP and APP. In the experiment with prolonged anaerobic exposure the concentration of total adenine nucleotides (ATP + ADP + AMP) was considerably lower than the mean control value for total adenine nucleotides.

Atria beating at two different frequencies at room temperature. As already mentioned, electrically driven guinea pig atria show a "positive frequency effect"—that is, an increase in contraction amplitude with increase in frequency over a fairly wide range of frequencies. This effect is more marked at room temperature (26–28°C) than at 37°C (fig. 3), and for that reason it was decided to analyze for high energy phosphate content of atria beating at 2 different frequencies at room temperature instead of 37°C. Each atrium was first allowed to attain its initial maximal amplitude at a frequency of 1 beat per second. It was then driven at various frequencies ranging from 1 per second to 1 per 10 seconds, and the steady state amplitude at each frequency was recorded. Finally the atrium was frozen for analysis while exhibiting a steady state amplitude at a frequency of either 1 per second or 1 per 10 seconds. At either frequency it was plunged into liquid nitrogen about one-half second after the last observed beat.

The results obtained with atria beating at the 2 selected frequencies are given in table 4. The APP values here are based on analysis for extra phosphate liberated by treatment of the extract with adenylpyrophosphatase or by acid-heat hydrolysis. In several experiments APP was also determined by the Kalckar deaminase method, and as in the experiments at 37°C (table 1), there was good agreement between the APP values obtained with all 3 methods. The results of table 4 show that there was no decrease in either CP or APP associated with the markedly reduced amplitude at the lower frequency. Indeed the mean CP concentration at the lower frequency was somewhat higher than that at the higher frequency, though not significantly so on statistical analysis. It may be noted, however, that the mean concentrations of CP in these experiments carried out at room temperature were significantly higher than the mean concentration of CP in those control experiments carried out at 37°C (table 2).

TABLE 4

Effect of frequency of stimulation on contraction amplitude and high energy phosphate of guinea pig atria at room temperature (26° to 28°C)

No. of Expts.	Freq. in Beats per Sec	Relative Amplitude*	Mean Concn. in μM Phosphate per g Moist Tissue		
			IP	CP	APP
10	1.0	1	5.68 ±.15	4.75 ±.18	5.64 ±.16
11	0.1	0.4 (0.1–0.8)	5.27 ±.22	5.25 ±.24	5.68 ±.16

* "Relative amplitude" is contraction amplitude at frequency indicated divided by amplitude at frequency of one beat per second.

Discussion. For *in vitro* studies in which the purpose is to determine the effects of changes in experimental conditions on both contractile force and high energy phosphate compounds of cardiac muscle, the left atrium of the guinea pig has many of the same suitable characteristics as does the cat papillary muscle (Greiner, 1952). Both preparations are thin enough (less than 1 mm) to allow diffusion of oxygen from the surrounding medium to maintain good aerobic conditions in the deeper tissue layers as long as the frequency of stimulation is not too high. Both preparations readily undergo spontaneous "experimental failure" at 37°C, and can be restored from failure with small concentrations of cardiac glycosides. Both preparations are sufficiently small and thin to permit almost instantaneous freezing in liquid nitrogen at any desired point in an experiment. One advantage of the guinea pig atrium over the cat papillary muscle is that its mass is usually about 5 times larger; and this larger mass permits more accurate analyses of the relatively low concentrations of high energy phosphate compounds in the tissue.

Because of both the unusual suitability of the left atrium of the guinea pig for *in vitro* studies, as noted above, and the refinements of the freezing and extraction techniques and microanalytical procedures used in the present work, it is of some interest to compare our mean "control" values for atrial CP, APP and the adenine nucleotides with values reported by previous workers. Our value of 4.19 μM/g for CP is approximately double the highest values previously reported for rabbit and dog atrial muscle (Burns and Cruickshank, 1937; Chang, 1938; Mulder *et al.*, 1956). This discrepancy is not surprising since CP is an extremely labile compound, and will undergo significant breakdown during the preparation of tissue extracts for analysis if due precautions are not taken to prevent this breakdown (Furchgott and de Gubareff, 1956a; Fawaz and Hawa, 1953). On the other hand, our mean control value of 5.26 μM/g for APP, which is much more stable than CP, is rather close to values previously reported for rabbit atria (Davies *et al.*, 1947; Chang, 1938) and for dog atria (Mulder *et al.*, 1956). For freshly excised, normal guinea pig ventricles Harvey (1955) has reported mean values of 3.2 μM/g for CP and 9.5 μM/g for APP. The fact that his value for ventricular CP is lower than our value for atrial CP is somewhat surprising, but may be due to differences in experimental conditions. However, the fact that his APP value is considerably higher than ours is not unexpected in view of the findings of previous investigators that both in rabbit (Chang, 1938; Davies *et al.*, 1947) and in dog (Mulder *et al.*, 1956) the APP concentration is approximately twice as high in ventricles as in atria.

To our knowledge no figures for atrial ATP, ADP and AMP have been previously reported. If our mean control value for the total concentration of these adenine nucleotides, namely 3.07 μM/g, is compared with values obtained for ventricular muscle, it is found to be significantly lower than that of 4.1 μM/g reported by Greiner (1952) for "fresh" cat papillary muscle and that of approximately five μM/g reported by Khairallah and Mommaerts (1953a) for dog ventricle. On the other hand, the percentage contributions of ATP, ADP and AMP to the total mols of adenine nucleotide in our "control" atria (78%, 13% and 8%, respectively) are almost the same as found by Greiner in "fresh" papillary muscles. The fact that Khairallah and Mommaerts (1953b) found the adenine nucleotide fractions of "relaxed" cat ventricle to contain no AMP, and in some experiments no ADP, may be attributed to their markedly different experimental conditions. The report of these latter investigators that a new adenine nucleotide, "nucleotide H," is present in "contracted" ventricle is neither supported nor contradicted by our findings.

Failure. Wollenberger in 1949 reviewed the older literature on the subject of whether failure in cardiac muscle is attributable to a fall in high energy phosphate concentrations. He concluded, largely on the basis of his own extensive work on dog heart-lung preparations, that spontaneous failure was not associated with a decrease in CP or APP (Wollenberger, 1947, 1949). On the other hand, Greiner (1952) reported a significant fall in the APP concentration in "severely hypodynamic" cat papillary muscles in spontaneous failure. It should be noted that Greiner's determination of APP were made with the enzymatic-spectrophotometric method of Kalckar (1947a), which permits the separate analysis of ATP or ADP, whereas Wollenberger's determinations were made with the less specific acid-heat hydrolysis method for labile pyrophosphate.

The results of the present work are in accord with those of Wollenberger. We have found that the isolated guinea pig left atrium undergoes spontaneous failure without any significant decrease in either CP or APP; and like Wollenberger, we have even found a small increase in CP in failure (although not statistically significant in our case). Moreover, our results show that individually neither ATP nor ADP, the two nucleotides which contribute to APP, are significantly reduced in failure. Wollenberger's conclusion that failure is not due to a depletion of APP has been criticized by Greiner (1952), who pointed out that the acid-heat hydrolysis method used by Wollenberger would determine inorganic pyrophosphate as well as adenylpyrophosphate, and by Proctor *et al.* (1955), who pointed out that it would also determine inosyl pyrophosphate. Our results negate this criticism, since in 20 experiments in which APP was determined by both the less specific acid-heat hydrolysis method and by the Kalckar deaminase method (table 1), the mean difference is only 2% in favor of the former method and is not statistically significant. The results of these 20 experiments also indicate that still a third method—that with potato adenylpyrophosphatase—is satisfactory for determining APP. The mean difference for APP concentration by this latter method over the specific Kalckar method was 4.3%. Although small, this difference was significant and probably indicates that the enzyme prepration contained minor amounts of other organic phosphatases besides adenylpyrophosphatase.

It is difficult to explain why Greiner found a significant decrease in ATP (50% below control level) in 4 papillary muscles in "severe" failure (force reduced to 29 to 42% of control level), expecially since he found no decrease in 3 muscles in "moderate" failure (force reduced to 45 to 54%). We have not divided our failures (table 1) into "severe" and "moderate," but if this is done on Greiner's basis of percentage reduction in force, we obtain no significant decreases in ATP in either subdivision. Probably Greiner's determination of adenine nucleotides were less accurate than ours because he used smaller tissue samples and less purified enzymes (see METHODS), but it is unlikely that his analytical errors could accidentally have given him such a large reduction in ATP.[6] In our opinion, at

[6] The accuracy of Greiner's CP determinations may also be questioned since they are based on the difference in phosphate concentrations obtained with the Lowry-Lopez and Fiske-Subbarow procedures. Indeed, it was the unreliability of this method (as well as other previously used "differ-

present, a likely possibility is that in each of the 4 muscles in Greiner's "severely hypodynamic" group, a sizeable fraction of the cardiac cells were injured and therefore had extremely low ATP levels, and thus markedly reduced the average ATP concentration of the whole muscle.

Regardless of whether a suitable explanation can be found of the discrepancy between Greiner's results and ours, our results clearly show that acute spontaneous failure can occur in isolated, functioning cardiac muscle without significant changes in the concentrations of the 3 high energy phosphate compounds, CP, ATP and ADP. Certainly our results do not prove that chronic heart failure in humans or in experimental animals is not associated with decreases in these high energy phosphate compounds, but they definitely leave this interesting possibility open.

Restoration from failure by a cardiac glycoside. In atria which were restored from failure with strophanthin-K, we found ATP, ADP and CP levels which did not differ significantly from those levels found in unfailed control atria or from those in atria in spontaneous failure. Thus, we would agree with Wollenberger (1951) that the positive inotropic action of cardiac glycosides is not attributable to an increase in the concentrations of high energy phosphate compounds in cardiac muscle, but to a more efficient utilization of these compounds in the contractile process. In contrast to our findings on guinea pig atria and those of Wollenberger on the dog heart-lung preparation, Greiner (1952) reported that cat papillary muscles which had been restored from "severe failure" with ouabain had an ATP level significantly higher than that in untreated muscles in "severe" failure. He interpreted his findings to mean that cardiac glycosides restored force of contraction by restoring the ATP level to that existing prior to severe failure. However, in view of our present findings, and our doubts concerning the meaningfulness of Greiner's low ATP values for "severe" failure (see above), we cannot agree with his interpretation.

Drugs and ionic changes which increase contractile strength. Like strophanthin-K, both epinephrine in concentrations of the order of 10^{-7} and substantial increases in Ca^{++} concentration in the Krebs solution were able to increase contractile strength markedly without producing any significant changes in the concentrations of high energy phosphate compounds. On the other hand, both epinephrine and norepinephrine in concentrations of the order of 10^{-6} to 10^{-5}, which are capable of producing a maximal stimulation of contractile strength, led to significant moderate decreases in CP concentration. The question arises as to why these sympathomimetic amines in high concentration caused a decrease in CP, whereas strophanthin-K and excess Ca^{++}, which also produced maximal stimulation of contractile strength, did not do so. A possible answer is to be found in the results of K. S. Lee (1953a, b) in experiments in which he simultaneously measured the effects of drugs on both contractile force and oxygen consumption of cat papillary muscles. Lee found that the increase in force produced by epinephrine or norepinephrine was always accompanied by a simultaneous marked increase in the rate of oxygen consumption. On the other hand, the maximal positive inotropic action of the cardiac glycoside, ouabain, was attained with essentially no increase in rate of oxygen consumption. (For a discussion of the final increase in rate accompanying the development of toxicity, see below.) Excess Ca^{++} also was able to increase force without increasing rate of oxygen consumption appreciably (Lee, personal communication). If in our experiments the rate of oxygen consumption was also markedly stimulated by "high" concentrations of epinephrine and norepinephrine, the deeper cell layers in the atrial preparations may well have become hypoxic because of the much more rapid removal of diffusing oxygen by the outer layers. Since oxygen lack produces a fall in CP (see below), the total CP concentration in atria in the presence of high epinephrine or norepinephrine may have fallen moderately because of a marked lowering of the CP concentration in hypoxic deeper cell layers. On the other hand, if nontoxic levels of cardiac glycoside and excess Ca^{++} give essentially no increase in the rate of oxygen consumption while increasing contractile strength, they would not be expected to cause a decrease in CP. A possible explanation of why our "low" epinephrine concentrations also gave no significant decrease in CP is that these concentrations, although stimulating oxygen consumption, did not do so to the extent of the "high" concentrations, and thus the deeper cell layers in the atria did not suffer from hypoxia.

In contrast to the lack of effect of increases in

ence" methods) for determining CP in cardiac muscle, which led us to the development of the more accurate method used in the present work (Furchgott and de Gubareff, 1956a).

Ca^{++} concentration on high energy phosphates, decreases in K^+ concentration sufficient to cause considerable increases in contractile force did cause an appreciable decrease in CP and a moderate (though possibly not significant) fall in ATP. There has been a certain amount of speculation that cardiac glycosides increase contractile force either by lowering the potassium concentration of cardiac cells (Hajdu and Szent-Györgyi, 1952; Hadju, 1953, 1957) or by increasing the calcium concentration of such cells (Moulin and Wilbrandt, 1955). On the basis of our present work, as well as unpublished results on the similarities of action of cardiac glycosides and excess calcium, we would favor the "calcium hypothesis" to explain the positive inotropic effect of cardiac glycosides. On the other hand, our finding that exposure to very low potassium causes a decrease in high energy phosphates rather similar to the decrease caused by poisoning with excess glycoside (see below) would support the hypothesis that the glycosides produce their cardiotoxic effects by causing an excessive loss of cellular potassium (Hadju, 1953).

Drugs and experimental conditions which decrease contractile strength. Our finding of a marked decrease in CP and a moderate decrease in ATP in atria poisoned with excess cardiac glycoside is similar to that of Wollenberger (1951) in dog ventricles. Harvey (1955) has also reported a decrease in CP and APP of ventricles of guinea pigs treated with digitoxin, although in his case no signs of cardiotoxic effects indicating over-digitalization of the animals were reported. Greiner (1952), too, working with cat papillary muscles, reported a fall in high energy phosphate content following poisoning with ouabain; however, his results differ from ours in that his major decrease was in the ATP fraction, whereas ours was in the CP fraction.[6]

The mechanism by which toxic doses of cardiac glycosides produce a fall in high energy phosphate concentration is not clear. The possibility that such doses lead to an uncoupling of oxidative-phosphorylation is still attractive despite the fact that several workers have not been able to find any uncoupling action of cardiac glycosides (except in combination with dinitrophenol) on mitochondrial suspensions (Herrmann, 1950; Wollenberger, 1951; Grisolia, 1955; Lee, personal communication). Another possibility is that the marked stimulation of oxygen consumption which occurs along with the development of toxic signs (Lee, 1953a) leads to an inadequate oxygen supply in deeper cell layers. Such a situation would be similar to, but presumably more severe than, that proposed in the preceding section to explain the decrease in CP produced by high concentrations of epinephrine and norepinephrine.

That oxygen deprivation leads to marked reduction in high energy phosphates in cardiac muscle has been shown by numerous previous investigators. In our anaerobic experiments, as in those of Greiner (1952) on cat papillary muscle and Chang (1938) on rabbit atria, CP falls very much more than does APP. Indeed in our experiment in which the anerobic exposure was only 18 minutes, ATP and ADP were still within the range for control levels, when CP was less than one-third of the mean control level. Yet, despite the high ATP of the atrium used in this experiment, its contractile amplitude had fallen to less than 10% of the preanoxic level. It is our opinion that the relatively rapid, dramatic depression of contractile strength under anoxia cannot, as Greiner suggested, be attributed to a decrease in ATP, but must be due to other intracellular changes resulting from the oxygen deficit.

That a drug-induced depression of contractile strength can occur with no reduction in either CP or APP was shown by Wollenberger (1947) and by Fawaz and Hawa (1953) in their experiments with pentobarbital and certain other drugs on the dog heart-lung preparation. In the present work 2 additional drugs, namely acetylcholine and ryanodine, have been shown to depress severely the contractile strength of atria without reducing either CP or APP. It has been suggested that the depression of contractility by acetylcholine results from the marked decrease in duration of atrial action potential produced by this drug (Burgen and Terroux, 1953). Such an explanation cannot be applied in the case of the depression by ryanodine, since this drug actually prolongs the duration of the action potential (Sleator and Furchgott, unpublished results). The present results on high energy phosphates would also rule out the possibility that ryanodine acts by interfering with energy metabolism.

Finally, in the present series of experiments we have investigated whether the marked changes in contractile strength due to changes in frequency of contraction are associated with changes in high energy phosphate content. It has been hypothesized that the increase in contractile strength with increase in frequency is due either to a decrease in the steady-state level of cellular potassium (Hadju, 1953) or to an increased steady-state level of cellular calcium (Moulin and Wilbrandt, 1955; Niedergerke, 1956). At the present time we believe our results give more support to the "calcium hypothesis." However, regardless of whether changes in cellular calcium or potassium or both are involved, our present findings clearly show that the changes in contractile strength with changes in frequency cannot be attributed to changes in concentration of high energy phosphates.

SUMMARY

Determinations have been made of the concentrations of adenosine triphosphate, adenosine diphosphate, adenylic acid, creatine phosphate and inorganic phosphate in isolated, electrically driven left atria of guinea pigs under various experimental conditions and in the presence of various drugs which produce changes in contractile strength. It has been shown that values for adenylpyrophosphate concentration (labile phosphate of ATP and ADP) obtained with either the acid-heat hydrolysis method or the potato adenylpyrophosphatase method agree closely with values obtained with the more specific Kalckar deaminase method in which ATP, ADP and AMP are determined individually.

In hypodynamic atria which had undergone spontaneous failure the mean concentrations of the high energy phosphate compounds—ATP, ADP and CP—were not significantly different from the respective mean concentrations in control atria prior to failure, or from those concentrations in atria which had been restored from failure with strophanthin-K.

Decreases in contractile strength resulting from a reduction in frequency of stimulation, addition of acetylcholine or addition of ryanodine were not associated with any significant changes in concentrations of high energy phosphate compounds from the control levels.

Increases in contractile strength resulting from the addition of non-toxic doses of strophanthin-K, of extra $CaCl_2$ or of epinephrine in a final concentration around 10^{-7}, were not associated with any significant changes in concentrations of high energy phosphate compounds from the control levels.

Anoxia produced a marked decrease in both contractile strength and high energy phosphate content, with the fall of CP being much greater than that of ATP. Poisoning with excess glycoside also produced both a decrease in contractile strength and a decrease in CP and ATP. Moderate decreases in these compounds also occurred in atria exposed to a low potassium medium, even though this procedure leads to an increase in contractile strength.

Epinephrine and norepinephrine in concentrations giving maximal stimulation of contractile strength (10^{-6} to 10^{-5}) produced small but significant decreases in CP.

Our findings have been compared with those of previous investigators, and suggestions made to explain certain discrepancies in findings. It is concluded that marked changes in contractile strength of cardiac muscle may be produced by a variety of agents and conditions independently of any changes in the concentrations of high energy phosphate compounds.

REFERENCES

Burgen, A. S. V. and Terroux, K. G.: J. Physiol. **120:** 449, 1953.
Burns, W. and Cruickshank, E.: J. Physiol. **91:** 314, 1937.
Cattell, McK. and Gold, H.: Amer. J. Physiol. **182:** 307, 1955.
Chang, I.: Quart. J. exp. Physiol. **28:** 3, 1938.
Dale, A. S.: J. Physiol. **75:** 1, 1932.
Davies, F., Francis, E. T. B. and Stoner, H. B.: J. Physiol. **106:** 154, 1947.
Fawaz, G. and Hawa, E. S.: Proc. Soc. exp. Biol., N. Y. **84:** 277, 1953.
Furchgott, R. F. and de Gubareff, T.: J. biol. Chem. **223:** 377, 1956a.
Furchgott, R. F. and de Gubareff, T.: This Journal **116:** 21, 1956b.
Furchgott, R. F. and de Gubareff, T.: Fed. Proc. **15:** 425, 1956c.
Furchgott, R. F., de Gubareff, T. and McCaman, M. W.: This Journal **110:** 19, 1954.
Furchgott, R. F. and Sleator, W.: This Journal **110:** 20, 1954.
Greiner, T.: This Journal **105:** 178, 1952.
Grisolia, S.: Biochim. biophys. Acta **18:** 437, 1955.
Hajdu, S.: Amer. J. Physiol. **174:** 371, 1953.
Hajdu, S.: This Journal **120:** 90, 1957.
Hajdu, S. and Szent-Györgyi, A.: Amer. J. Physiol. **168:** 171, 1952.
Harvey, S. C.: Amer. J. Physiol. **183:** 559, 1955.
Herrmann, R.: Arch. int. Pharmacodyn. **81:** 235, 1950.
Hillyard, I. W. and Procita, L.: Fed. Proc. **15:** 438, 1956.
Kalckar, H.: J. biol. Chem. **167:** 445, 1947a.
Kalckar, H.: J. biol. Chem. **167:** 461, 1947b.

KATZUNG, B., ROSIN, H. AND SCHNEIDER, F.: THIS JOURNAL **120:** 324, 1957.

KHAIRALLAH, P. A. AND MOMMAERTS, W. F. H. M.: Circulation Res. **1:** 8, 1953a.

KHAIRALLAH, P. A. AND MOMMAERTS, W. F. H. M Circulation Res. **1:** 12, 1953b.

KREBS, H. A. AND HENSELEIT, K.: Hoppe-Seyl. Z. **210:** 33, 1932.

KRUTA, V.: Arch int. Physiol. **45:** 333, 1937.

LEE, K. S.: THIS JOURNAL **109:** 304, 1953a.

LEE, K. S.: THIS JOURNAL **109:** 313, 1953b.

LEVY, M.: C. R. Lab. Carlsberg, Série chim. **21:** 101, 1936.

LOWRY, O. H., ROSEBROUGH, N. J., FARR, A. L. AND RANDALL, R. J.: J. biol. Chem. **193:** 265, 1951.

MOULIN, M. AND WILBRANDT, W.: Experientia, **11:** 72, 1955.

MULDER, A. G., OMACHI, A. AND REBAR, B. T.: Amer. J. Physiol. **186:** 309, 1956.

NIEDERGERKE, R.: J. Physiol. **134:** 569, 1956.

PROCTOR, C. D., REBAR, J. AND TIGERMAN, B.: Ann. N. Y. Acad. Sci. **62:** 377, 1955.

WOLLENBERGER, A.: Amer. J. Physiol. **150:** 733, 1947.

WOLLENBERGER, A.: Pharmacol. Rev. **1:** 311, 1949.

WOLLENBERGER, A.: THIS JOURNAL **103:** 123, 1951.

8079

ADRENERGIC BLOCKING ACTION OF TETRAZOTIZED DIORTHOANISIDINE

EDWARD J. CAFRUNY, EDWARD F. DOMINO AND LLOYD BECK

Department of Pharmacology, University of Michigan Medical School, Ann Arbor, Michigan

Received for publication May 28, 1958

Diazo and tetrazo salts react with phenols and aromatic amines to form azo dyes. Many of these salts are water-soluble and can couple with various constituents of animal tissues. Reactions between diazo (and tetrazo) compounds and many pressor amines occur *in vitro* at pH 7.4. It was conceivable that similar reactions might take place *in vivo* with resultant chemical inactivation of endogenously released or exogenously administered sympathomimetic amines. Preliminary experiments failed to substantiate this hypothesis but indicated that these substances possessed adrenergic blocking activity.

The bulk of this report deals with the characterization of the adrenergic blocking action of the compound, tetrazotized diorthoanisidine (hereafter referred to as TDA).

METHODS. Forty-six adult mongrel dogs of both sexes were used. All animals were prepared under light pentobarbital anesthesia. A femoral artery and an external jugular vein were isolated and cannulated. A mercury manometer with a lever writing on a smoked paper kymograph was used to record femoral blood pressure. All drugs were dissolved in 0.9% saline and given via the external jugular vein. Blood pressure responses to *l*-epinephrine, *l*-norepinephrine, isoproterenol, histamine and acetylcholine were observed. After 2 or 3 observations on the effects of each compound the *bis*-diazo salt, TDA,[1] was administered intravenously in doses of 2 to 40 mg/kg. In some experiments the diazo compounds, Fast Blue RR[2] and Diazo Red RC,[2] were used in place of TDA. The effects of these compounds on the blood pressure response to autonomic agents were determined at various time intervals. In some experiments effects on the pressor response to bilateral carotid occlusion were also noted. Additional experiments were performed in which the products of reactions between TDA and *l*-epinephrine, *l*-norepinephrine, or isoproterenol were administered intravenously in order to determine whether these coupled products retained pressor or depressor activity. Experiments were also carried out with arterial strips of dog carotid and rabbit aorta prepared in a manner similar to that described by Furchgott (1953). The bath medium (Kreb's-Henseleit solution with a bicarbonate buffer) was oxygenated with 95% O_2 and 5% CO_2. A constant temperature of 37 to 38°C was maintained by warm water circulating through a jacket surrounding the tissue chamber.

RESULTS. Addition of TDA to solutions of epinephrine, norepinephrine, and isoproterenol buffered at pH 7.4 resulted in each case in the rapid development of a pink-orange color. Ten parts of TDA (by weight) were added to one part of each amine in order to favor completeness of reaction. The colored reaction products on standing tended to precipitate. When these reaction products (in a dose of 1 μg of amine/kg) were injected intravenously into anesthetized dogs, typical pressor or depressor responses did not appear. Figure 1 (A, C) shows that epinephrine and isoproterenol so treated are inactivated; figure 1B shows partial inactivation of norepinephrine. In many instances, however, there was no response to norepinephrine-TDA complexes.

Figure 2A shows the typical pressor response to epinephrine given intravenously in a dose of 1 μg/kg. TDA in a dose of 10 mg/kg produced a transient depressor response (figure 2B). Seven minutes later the response to epinephrine was profoundly altered. A slight pressor spike preceded an actual fall in blood pressure. The depressor component increased with time as shown in figure 2C which illustrates the effect 2.5 hours

[1] Purchased from Dajac Laboratories, Leominster, Mass., as "Naphthanil Diazo Blue B," a preparation containing zinc and aluminum sulfate stabilizers. Pure samples were also supplied by Dr. A. C. Bratton, Jr., Parke, Davis & Co., Detroit, Michigan.

[2] Purchased from Dajac Laboratories, Leominster, Mass.

after the administration of TDA. The epinephrine-reversal produced by TDA can be overcome by administration of large doses of epinephrine as shown in figure 2D. In this instance a 5 μg/kg dose of epinephrine resulted in a pressor response. The effects of TDA on the pressor response to norepinephrine are shown in figure 3 (A, C). When the dose of norepinephrine was increased to 5 μg/kg a pressor response almost as great as the initial response to 1 μg/kg was obtained.

The systemic pressor response to bilateral occlusion of the carotid arteries for 60 seconds was not markedly influenced by TDA (figure 3B, E). Spontaneous changes of the same magnitude were often observed in control animals.

Effects of TDA on the depressor responses to isoproterenol and acetylcholine are shown in figure 4. Marked potentiation of the depressor action of isoproterenol can be seen by comparing panels A and C. Potentiation of the depressor action of acetylcholine was also evident in this dog but was not usually observed. On the other hand, the depressor effect of histamine was usually potentiated but not to the same degree as was isoproterenol.

As in the case of other adrenergic blocking agents (Nickerson, 1949), TDA did not block the chronotropic effects of epinephrine.

Isolated arterial strip. Rabbit aortic and dog carotid arterial strips were exposed to TDA in concentrations of 15 to 30 mg/liter for 15 to 60 minutes and subsequently washed twice. Under these circumstances the response to moderate doses of epinephrine or norepinephrine (15 μg/l), which usually produce responses ranging

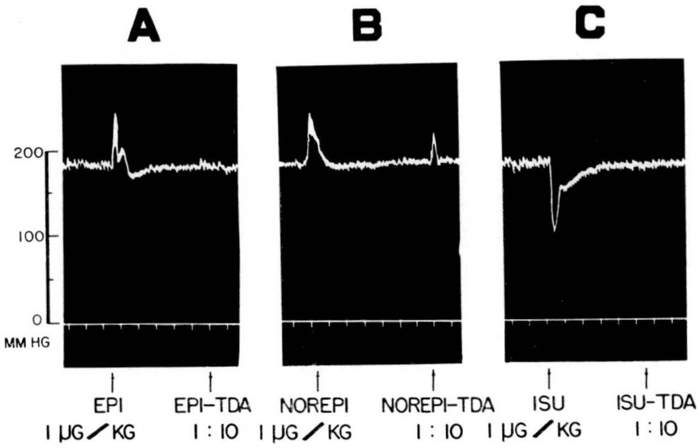

FIG. 1. Femoral arterial blood pressure tracing from a dog lightly anesthetized with pentobarbital. All drugs administered intravenously. Time base in minutes. A. Epinephrine followed by injection of a mixture containing 1 μg of epinephrine and 10 μg of TDA per kg. B. Same as A except norepinephrine was used. C. Same as A except isoproterenol was used.

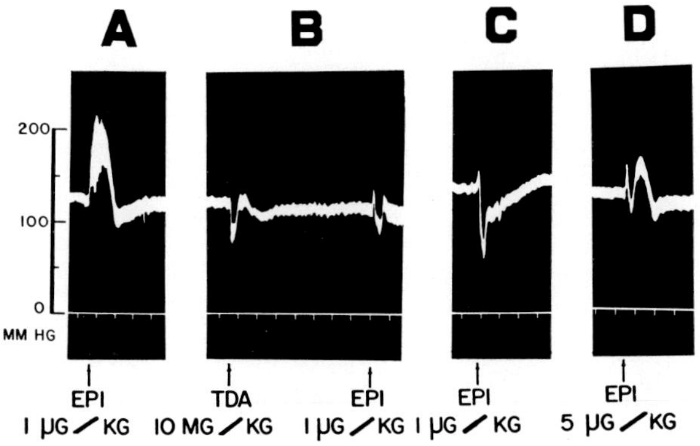

FIG. 2. Femoral arterial blood pressure tracing from a dog lightly anesthetized with pentobarbital. All drugs administered intravenously. Time base in minutes. A. Epinephrine. B. TDA followed by epinephrine. C, D. Epinephrine.

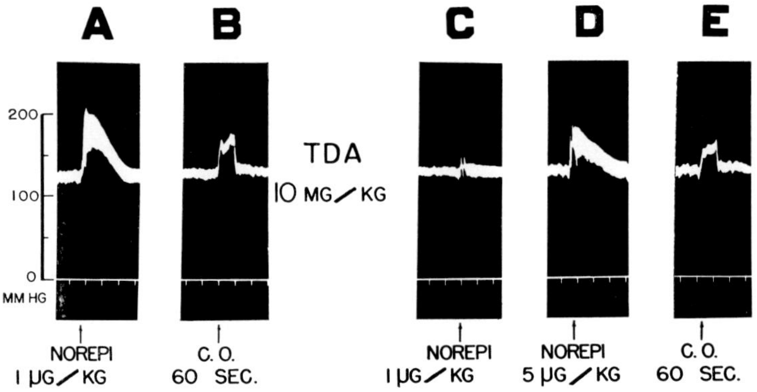

FIG. 3. Femoral arterial blood pressure tracing from a dog lightly anesthetized with pentobarbital. All drugs administered intravenously. Time base in minutes. A. Norepinephrine. B. Responses to bilateral carotid occlusion (CO) for 60 seconds. C, D. Responses to norepinephrine following TDA. E. Response to bilateral carotid occlusion (CO) following TDA.

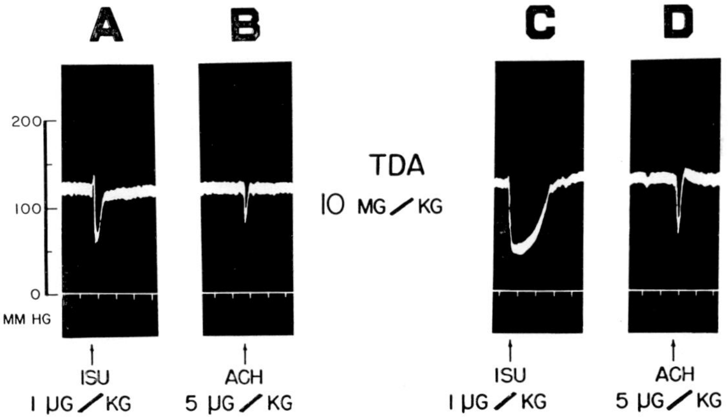

FIG. 4. Femoral arterial blood pressure tracing from a dog lightly anesthetized with pentobarbital. All drugs administered intravenously. Time base in minutes. A. Isoproterenol. B. Acetylcholine. C. Isoproterenol following TDA. D. Acetylcholine following TDA.

from 25 to 75% of maximal contractile height, was reduced to 10 to 25% of the control response. Contractile responses induced by acetylcholine, histamine and 5-hydroxytryptamine of the same order of magnitude as those produced by moderate doses of epinephrine did not appear to be appreciably altered by 15 to 30 mg/l of TDA. When very large doses of epinephrine (up to 100 times maximal contractile dose) were added to the bath the contractile height was increased but never reached that of the control strip. In the dog carotid strip, in which tachyphylaxis to epinephrine does not develop, the same degree of blockade was still present after the large dose of epinephrine had been washed out.

Duration of action. During the course of the investigation it was noted that the adrenergic blockade produced by TDA usually lasted throughout the 4- to 6-hour duration of each experiment.

In 2 experiments in which epinephrine-reversal had occurred, pressor responses were restored within 2 and 5 hours, respectively. Six experiments were conducted in which epinephrine was injected hourly over a 12-hour period. Reversal of the pressor response to epinephrine occurred in all animals. The response returned to control levels in 1 of these but significant adrenergic blockade was still present in the remaining 5.

Related compounds. The diazo salts, Fast Blue RR and Diazo Red RC, in doses of 20 to 40 mg/kg, exhibited less adrenergic blocking activity than TDA. Although responses to these compounds were quite variable, in some instances moderate blockade was observed. The fact that TDA, which contains 2 diazo groups is a more potent adrenergic blocking agent than the compounds containing a single diazo moiety suggests that this activity resides in the diazo linkage. This premise is further supported by the fact that the parent compound of TDA, *o*-dianisidine, was found to have no blocking action.

DISCUSSION. TDA reacts with phenolic sympathomimetic amines to form compounds which have little or no effect on blood pressure. The fact that such amine-TDA complexes do not retain the pressor or depressor action of the parent amine suggested the possibility that TDA might chemically inactivate endogenous sympathomimetic substances but this premise was not substantiated by subsequent experiments. Instead, TDA produced epinephrine reversal, blockade of the pressor response to norepinephrine, and potentiation of the depressor effects of isoproterenol. These results are not compatible with an "inactivation hypothesis" but rather support the conclusion that TDA is an adrenergic blocking agent. In this capacity its action is rapid in onset, being evident in most instances within 5 to 10 minutes and becoming maximal within 30 to 60 minutes. Epinephrine reversal lasts for variable periods ranging from 2 to more than 12 hours. Of interest also is the fact that moderately large doses of epinephrine can overcome the reversal seen with small doses of epinephrine.

Doses of TDA which produced epinephrine reversal did not appear to reduce the pressor response to carotid occlusion or to asphyxia. This demonstrates that TDA can block exogenous epinephrine without apparently affecting sympathetic activity.

In the results it was pointed out that TDA did not greatly modify the depressor response to acetylcholine unless large doses of acetylcholine were given but usually potentiated the depressor response to histamine. In contrast we have observed that phenoxybenzamine (dibenzyline) usually reduces the depressor response to histamine.

The results obtained using arterial strips also indicate that TDA is an adrenergic blocking agent. Preliminary results suggest that the blockade is relatively specific for epinephrine and norepinephrine-induced contraction but additional data are necessary to establish the extent of this specificity.

SUMMARY

The tetrazo compound, tetrazotized diorthoanisidine (TDA), combines with epinephrine, norepinephrine and isoproterenol *in vitro* to produce substances which have little or no effect on blood pressure. Intravenous administration of TDA produces typical adrenergic blockade in the intact anesthetized dog. Adrenergic blockade is also apparent in isolated dog carotid and rabbit aortic strips. The positive chronotropic action of sympathomimetics is not blocked by TDA. The pressor responses to carotid occlusion and asphyxia are not blocked.

It is concluded that the *in vivo* actions of TDA are the result of a relatively specific adrenergic blocking action.

REFERENCES

FURCHGOTT, R. F.: THIS JOURNAL **108**: 129, 1953.
NICKERSON, M.: Pharmacol. Rev. **1**: 27, 1949.

8080

ADRENERGIC BLOCKADE OF THE MAMMALIAN HEART BY A DICHLORO ANALOGUE OF ISOPROTERENOL[1, 2]

NEIL C. MORAN[3] AND MARJORIE E. PERKINS

Department of Pharmacology, Division of Basic Health Sciences, Emory University, Atlanta, Georgia

Received for publication June 23, 1958

Although the cellular receptor mechanisms with which drugs react are poorly understood on the basis of their physico-chemical and morphological properties, the operational classification of receptors is of potential heuristic value. The classification of the adrenergic receptors of mammalian hearts presents a special problem in the pharmacological description of the sympathetic nervous system, a problem implied in the following statement from a current textbook of pharmacology (Goodman and Gilman, 1955): "Dibenamine and dibenzyline [and other adrenergic blocking drugs] effectively prevent the excitatory responses of smooth muscle and exocrine gland cells to adrenergic stimuli; they fail to block inhibitory responses of smooth muscle and also do not prevent the chronotropic and inotropic responses of mammalian cardiac muscle . . ." According to this concept, although the cardiac responses are considered to be excitatory, they, along with the inhibitory responses of other organs, are not consistently inhibited by adrenergic blocking drugs. Because of this seemingly paradoxical situation various schemes of classification of adrenergic receptors have been proposed to explain these differences. Among these is Ahlquist's (1948, 1958) suggestion that there are two types of "adrenotropic" receptors: 1) the *alpha* receptors subserving such excitatory physiological responses as vasoconstriction, contraction of the radial muscle of the iris and arrector pili contraction; and 2) the *beta* receptors involved in such inhibitory responses to sympathetic stimulation as vasodilatation, bronchiolar dilatation and myometrial relaxation. Ahlquist attributes the excitatory responses of cardioacceleration and augmentation of cardiac contractility to the *beta* receptors while he relates myocardial ectopic excitation to *alpha* type receptors. Ahlquist based this schema on the observed relative potencies of several sympathomimetic amines including epinephrine, norepinephrine and isopropylnorepinephrine (isoproterenol).

Since the classification of drug receptors depends, to a large extent, on the use of selective blocking drugs to differentiate one receptor from another, the status of adrenergic cardiac receptors has remained in doubt. Although some investigators (Serin, 1952b; Cotten and Walton, 1951; Cotten, Moran and Stopp, 1957) have observed inhibition of the myocardial stimulant effect of sympathomimetic amines in mammalian hearts by some adrenergic blocking drugs, other workers have not (Nickerson, 1949). Furthermore, the blockade which has been observed is not consistent, requires large doses of the blocking compounds and is not represented in the actions of all members of this class of drugs.

Powell and Slater (1958) have provided an interesting tool for the investigation of this problem. They found that a dichloro analogue of isoproterenol (β-hydroxy-N-isopropyl-3,4-dichlorophenethylamine hydrochloride) blocks the inhibitory, but not the excitatory, effects of sympathomimetic amines. The present report, in addition to confirming part of the observations of Powell and Slater, presents evidence that this compound (Lilly 20522) selectively blocks the positive inotropic and chronotropic effects of adrenergic stimuli. On the basis of the present evidence the hypothesis is proposed that the cardiac adrenergic receptors are functionally homologous to the adrenergic inhibitory receptors of other tissues, or, in Ahlquist's terminology,

[1] A preliminary report of this work was presented before the American Society for Pharmacology and Experimental Therapeutics in Baltimore, September, 1957.

[2] Supported by a grant (H-2953) from the National Heart Institute, U. S. Public Health Service.

[3] The work reported in this paper was performed during the tenure of a Public Health Service Senior Research Fellowship.

the receptors subserving cardioacceleration and augmentation of cardiac contractile force are of the *beta* type.

METHODS. *Experiments with dogs.* Adult mongrel dogs were anesthetized with pentobarbital, 35 mg/kg intravenously. Bilateral mid-cervical vagotomy was performed routinely to eliminate vagally mediated reflex changes in heart rate. With the animals under positive pressure artificial respiration the heart was exposed by a thoracotomy, and a calibrated strain gauge arch (Boniface *et al.*, 1953; Cotten and Bay, 1956) was sutured to the right ventricle for measurement of cardiac contractile force. In several experiments left ventricular contractile force was recorded, and the results obtained were comparable to those obtained with right ventricular force. All experiments in which contractile force was measured were conducted on open-chest dogs maintained with artificial respiration. Arterial blood pressure was measured with a Statham pressure transducer connected to a cannulated femoral artery. Recordings were made on a Sanborn Poly-Viso or a Grass oscillograph. Rectal temperatures of the animals were maintained between 36 to 38°C by the use of heating pads.

All drugs were injected into a cannulated femoral vein and were washed in with 2 to 5 ml of isotonic saline. Injections were rapid unless stated otherwise. In 5 experiments the postganglionic fibers of the cardiac sympathetic nerves were stimulated with a Grass electronic stimulator. Stimulation was maintained for 20-second periods at a frequency of 30/sec, pulse duration of 10 millisec, and voltages producing maximal increases of cardiac contractile force (5 to 10 volts).

Additional details of the experimental procedures will be given in the appropriate sections under RESULTS.

Experiments with isolated rabbit hearts. New Zealand rabbits weighing 2 to 3 kg were killed by a sharp blow to the back of the neck. The hearts were rapidly extirpated and perfused through the aorta by means of an Anderson coronary perfusion apparatus (Anderson and Craver, 1948). The perfusion fluid was of the following composition as grams of anhydrous salts per liter of solution: NaCl, 7.0; KCl, 0.42; $CaCl_2$, 0.24; $MgCl_2$, 0.20; $NaHCO_3$, 2.1; dextrose, 1.8 (Chenoweth and Koelle, 1946). It was maintained at 37.2°C and held at a hydrostatic pressure above the heart of 45 cm of water. The perfusion reservoir was aerated with a 95% oxygen, 5% carbon dioxide mixture. Drugs were injected in single doses above the cannulated aorta in volumes of 0.5 ml or less and were flushed in with 1 ml of perfusing fluid. Since the perfusate was continuously returned to the reservoir bottle, approximately 10 to 20 ml of the perfusate were discarded through a side arm after each injection to prevent recirculation of the drug. Both stimulant and blocking drugs were prevented from recirculating. Contractions of the heart were recorded on a Grass oscillograph with a Grass Model FT .03 Force-Displacement transducer which was connected to the apex of the heart by means of a thread passing around a glass pulley. All drugs were dissolved in the perfusing solution before injection, except for ouabain which was dissolved in 10% ethanol and calcium chloride which was dissolved in water.

Drugs. The following drugs were used: *l*-epinephrine, *l*-norepinephrine (levarterenol) and *dl*-isopropylnorepinephrine (isoproterenol) as the bitartrates prepared in suitable dilutions daily from commercial stock solutions; ephedrine hydrochloride, theophylline hydrochloride and calcium chloride used from stable stock solutions; digoxin and ouabain dissolved in 10% ethanol.

The dichloro analogues of epinephrine, norepinephrine and isopropylnorepinephrine[4] are colorless crystalline compounds readily soluble in water. All were used in the form of racemic mixtures of the hydrochlorides. In all compounds the *meta* and *para* hydroxyl groups of the parent compounds are replaced by chlorine atoms as shown in the following formula:

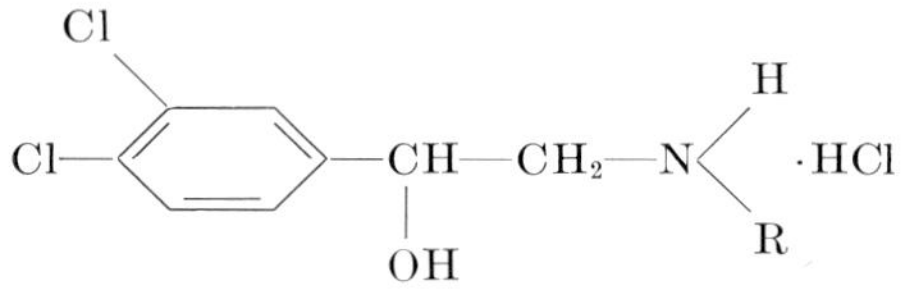

R = H; β-hydroxy-3,4-dichlorophenethylamine hydrochloride (Lilly 28670).[4]

R = CH_3; β-hydroxy-N-methyl-3,4-dichlorophenethylamine hydrochloride (Lilly 28787).[4]

R = —C(CH_3)(CH_3); β-hydroxy-N-isopropyl-3,4-dichlorophenethylamine hydrochloride (Lilly 20522).[4]

The following abbreviations are used: I—isoproterenol; E—epinephrine; NE—norepineph-

[4] The dichloro analogues of epinephrine, norepinephrine and isoproterenol were generously supplied by Dr. Irwin H. Slater of the Lilly Research Laboratories, Indianapolis. Powell and Slater (1958) refer to Lilly Compound 20522 as 1 - (3′,4′ - dichlorophenyl) - 2 - isopropylamino-ethanol. The nomenclature in the present paper has been changed so that 20522, 28678 and 28670 are more closely identified as phenethylamine derivatives.

rine; DCI—dichloroisoproterenol (Lilly 20522); DCE—dichloroepinephrine (Lilly 28787); DCNE—dichloronorepinephrine (Lilly 28670).

RESULTS. *I. Direct effects of DCI on blood pressure, heart rate and ventricular contractile force in dogs.* In vagotomized dogs initial intravenous injections of DCI in doses from 0.25 to 2 mg/kg produced slight to moderate decreases in blood pressure and moderate increases in cardiac contractile force and heart rate. The vasodepressor effect in response to small doses (0.25 to 2 mg/kg) was transient, lasting less than 15 minutes, while the positive inotropic and chronotropic effects persisted for more than 1 hour. Subsequent doses of DCI, whether of the same or greater magnitude than the first dose, depressed contractile force and slowed heart rate. With large doses (4 to 16 mg/kg) the cardiac depression was prolonged, while the depressant action of small doses lasted only 10 to 30 minutes. The depres-

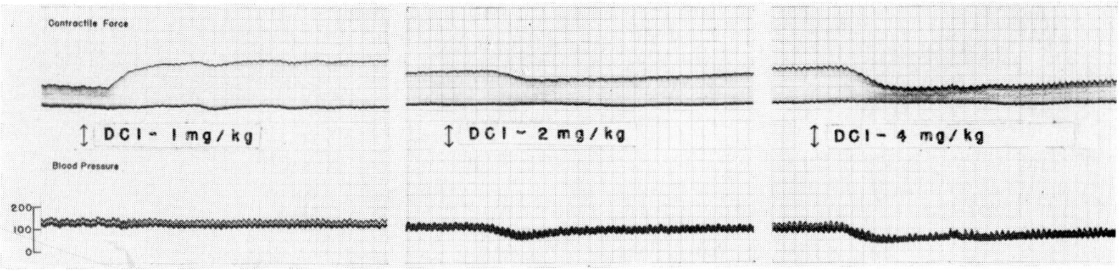

FIG. 1. Effects of a dichloro analogue of isoproterenol (DCI) on right ventricular contractile force and arterial pressure in a vagotomized, anesthetized dog.

At the arrows DCI was injected intravenously in 1, 2 and 4 mg/kg doses. Upper tracing represents contractile force and lower tracing femoral artery blood pressure. Note increased contractile force with first dose and decreased force with subsequent doses. The interval between injections was approximately 20 minutes.

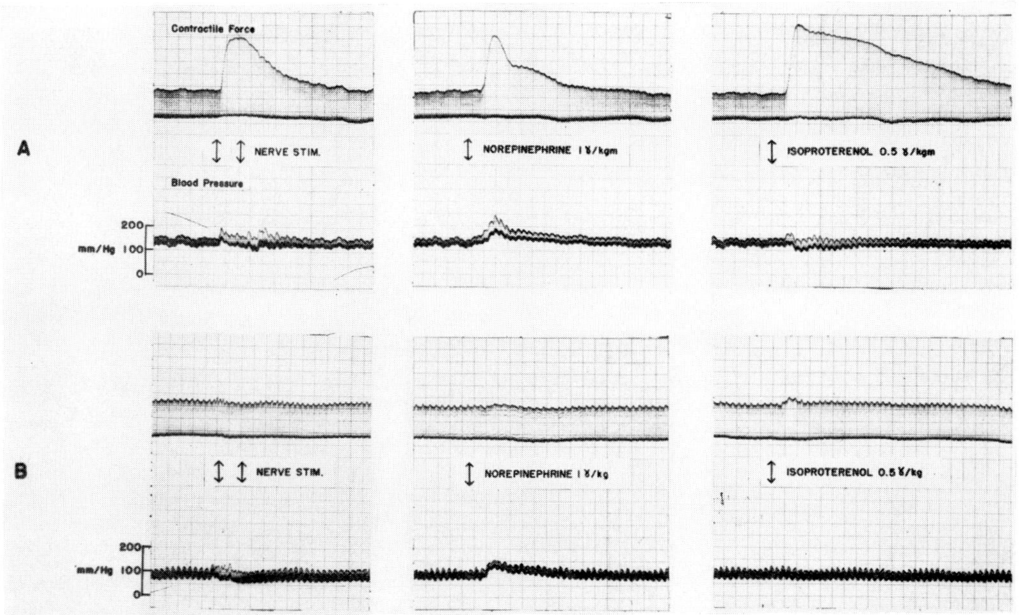

FIG. 2. Blockade of adrenergic augmentation of right ventricular contractile force in a vagotomized, anesthetized dog.

Upper pairs of tracings (A) show responses of heart and blood pressure to electrical stimulation of cardiac sympathetic nerves and to intravenous injections of *l*-norepinephrine (1 μg/kg), and isoproterenol (0.5 μg/kg). Lower set of tracings (B) shows the effect of the same procedures after a cumulative dose of DCI of 7 mg/kg.

sion of contractile force produced by DCI was roughly proportional to the dose. It was not inhibited by atropine in doses of 0.5 to 1 mg/kg intravenously. With repeated administration of DCI the arterial pressure progressively declined over a period of several hours. Figure 1 demonstrates the changes in blood pressure and cardiac contractile force produced by 3 successive doses of DCI in a typical experiment. Large single doses produced profound cardiac depression and reduction of blood pressure often resulting in death of the animal.

II. Blockade of the positive inotropic effect of adrenergic stimuli by DCI in dogs. The increased ventricular contractile force resulting from intravenous injections of small doses of E, NE and I and from electrical stimulation of the cardiac postganglionic sympathetic nerves was partially inhibited by initial doses of DCI as low as 0.25 mg/kg. Progressively greater blockade resulted from progressive increases in the dose of DCI with complete or nearly complete abolition of the responses to adrenergic stimuli occurring with cumulative doses of 7 to 15 mg/kg. In some experiments after cumulative doses of DCI of 3 mg/kg or higher, depression of contractile force was observed in response to the amines and to sympathetic nerve stimulation. Figure 2 demonstrates oscillographic records of a typical experiment showing blockade of the positive inotropic effects of nerve stimulation and of NE and I.

In a group of 9 dogs fixed doses of E, NE and I were injected rapidly before administration of DCI and again after each of successive graded doses of the blocking compound. The doses were as follows: E, 1 μg/kg; NE, 1 μg/kg; and I,

TABLE 1

The effects of dichloroisoproterenol (DCI) on right ventricular contractile force of anesthetized, vagotomized dogs

Mean contractile force in grams ±S.E.

	Before DCI		After DCI—Cumulative Doses of DCI in mg/kg							
			1		3		7		15	
	Control	Change	Control	Change	Control	Change	Control	Change	Control	Change
Epinephrine 1 μg/kg	68.9 ±6.0	90.2 (9) ±10.4	101.5 ±8.6	10.6 (9) ±6.9	88.4 ±7.2	6.6 (9) ±5.4	67.1 ±8.3	6.2 (9) ±7.3	43.6 ±8.5	6.6 (5) ±7.6
5 μg/kg									60.7 ±5.3	−1.9 (5) ±9.1
Norepinephrine 1 μg/kg	70.0 ±5.9	96.4 (9) ±10.6	100.1 ±7.2	21.6 (9) ±9.6	90.6 ±8.9	10.3 (9) ±7.3	79.2 ±9.0	−1.5 (9) ±5.2	64.7 ±7.9	−3.3 (5) ±6.7
5 μg/kg									58.7 ±2.6	12.5 (5) ±8.2
Isoproterenol 0.5 μg/kg	71.5 ±5.3	127.2 (9) ±28.7	100.8 ±7.7	49.1 (9) ±11.5	93.9 ±8.2	23.5 (9) ±6.6	82.9 ±9.4	9.5 (9) ±3.1	71.3 ±8.9	1.3 (5) ±4.4
2.5 μg/kg									58.7 ±3.4	27.7 (5) ±7.6
Cardiac symp. nerve stimulation	50.2 ±5.7	85.1 (5) ±10.9	91.1 ±7.9	19.8 (5) ±4.7	76.6 ±8.4	3.3 (5) ±2.3	58.1 ±11.5	3.3 (5) ±2.1	46 56	0.0 (2) 0.0
DCI			67.5 ±7.8	35.2 (9) ±9.3	96.4 ±8.7	−21.3 (9) ±2.1	91.6 ±9.4	−49.1 (9) ±6.1	95.7 ±16.5	−67.3 (5) ±17.7

Numbers in parentheses refer to number of animals used.
Change refers to maximal change in force.

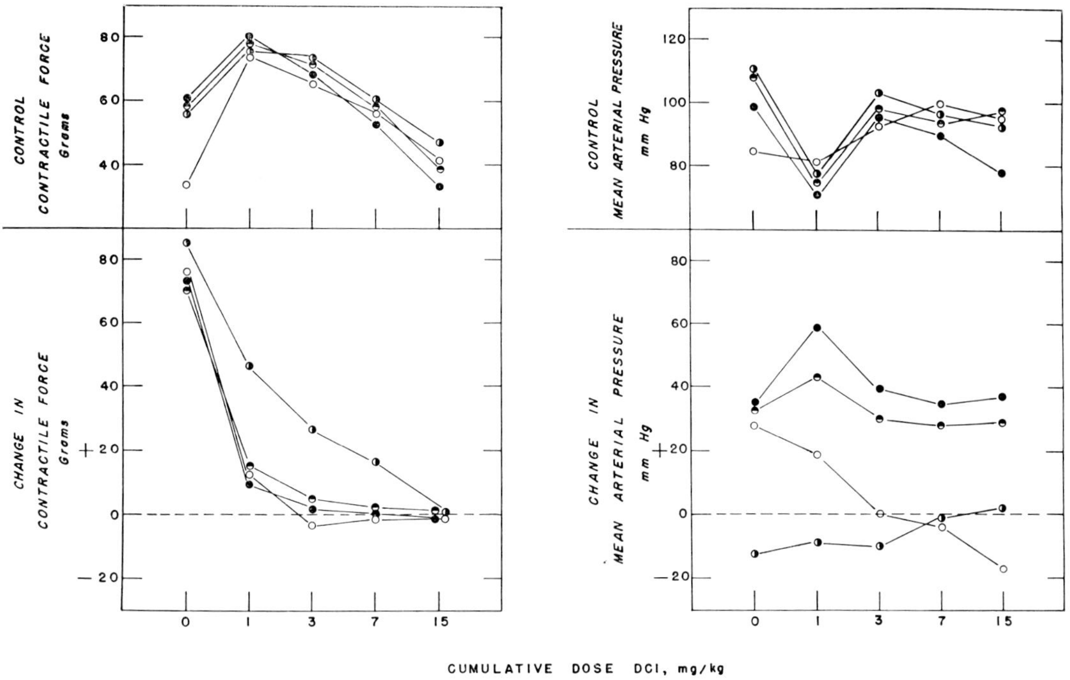

FIG. 3. Graphic demonstration of the blockade by DCI of the cardiac positive inotropic effects of sympathomimetic amines and of cardiac sympathetic nerve stimulation and of the vasodepressor effect of isoproterenol in a typical experiment.

Each point of the upper part of the graphs represents "control" right ventricular contractile force in grams (left graph) and mean arterial pressure in mm Hg (right graph). Each point of the lower parts of the graphs depicts the change in contractile force in grams (left) and the change in mean arterial pressure in mm Hg (right) in response to intravenous injections of epinephrine, 1 μg/kg (●——●); norepinephrine, 1 μg/kg (◓——◓); and isoproterenol, 0.5 μg/kg (◑——◑); and to electrical stimulation of the cardiac sympathetic nerves (○——○). Plotted on the abscissae are cumulative doses of DCI in mg/kg.

0.5 μg/kg; DCI was given in geometrically increasing doses starting with 1 mg/kg. In 5 dogs the cardiac postganglionic sympathetic nerves were stimulated in addition to giving the amines. The maximum change in contractile force in response to E, NE, I and nerve stimulation was measured after each dose and was compared with the corresponding response before administration of DCI. Table 1, which summarizes the results in terms of mean changes in contractile force, shows the progressive blockade of the inotropic responses to adrenergic stimuli. The depression of cardiac contractile force produced by the sympathomimetic amines and by sympathetic nerve stimulation after large doses of DCI is apparent from the extension of the standard errors below zero. Figure 3 graphically depicts the results of 1 experiment. Also shown in Table 1 are the responses to higher doses of the adrenergic agents after blockade of the responses to the smaller doses. A 5-fold increase in the dose of E and NE was not sufficient to overcome the antagonism to any significant extent. A 5-fold increase in dose of I, however, produced an increase in contractile force, but the mean increase was less than one-fourth the magnitude of the mean response to the small dose in the control period before administration of DCI.

Because of the initial stimulation produced by DCI, the responses to the sympathomimetic amines and nerve stimulation after the first dose of DCI started at a higher "control"[5] contractile force than before administration of DCI. However, the fact that the maximum force developed in response to the amines and to nerve stimulation was always less after administration of DCI than before suggests that the blockade was

[5] "Control" as used in this context refers to the stable contractile force, heart rate or blood pressure existing immediately prior to the injection of the test drugs or before nerve stimulation. Changes in these parameters are in respect to the "control" values.

"real." Furthermore, the depression of contractile force by subsequent doses of DCI resulted in a "control" force equal to or less than that obtained in the period before administration of DCI, substantiating the validity of the blockade (see figure 2). Figure 3 demonstrates the relationships between "control" force and the responses to the adrenergic stimuli in a typical experiment.

III. Blockade of the positive chronotropic effects of adrenergic stimuli by DCI in dogs. The cardioacceleration produced by small intravenous doses of I (0.5 μg/kg), E (1 μg/kg) and NE (1 μg/kg) was measured in a group of 5 dogs in which acute cardiac denervation was accomplished by bilateral mid-cervical vagotomy and bilateral excision of the para-vertebral sympathetic chains from the stellate ganglion to the level of T-5 or T-6. Sympathetic denervation was evident by the conspicuous slowing of the heart rate and a moderate decrease in ventricular contractile force. The effects of E, NE and I were tested before DCI administration and after each of 3 geometrically increasing doses of DCI (1, 2 and 4 mg/kg). Because of the small increases in heart rate produced by E and NE and because the tachycardia produced by the initial dose of DCI was not materially reduced by higher doses of DCI, it was not possible to demonstrate blockade of the chronotropic effects of these two amines. However, I was substantially blocked by a cumulative dose of 7 mg/kg of DCI (table 2). More definitive blockade of I was obtained in a group of 5 vagotomized dogs in which the "control" heart rate was essentially the same after administration of 7 mg/kg of DCI as before (table 2).

IV. Interactions between DCI and ephedrine in dogs. Three experiments were performed in which the cardiac stimulant action of intravenous injections of ephedrine (0.1 mg/kg) was blocked by DCI in doses which inhibited the cardiac stimulant effects of E, NE and I.

Because ephedrine resembles DCI in produc-

TABLE 2

A comparison of the effects of dichloroisoproterenol (DCI) on the heart rate responses of dogs to sympathomimetic amines and theophylline

Number and Status of Animals	Drug and Dose	Mean Heart Rate—Beats/Minute ± S.E.						"P" Values for Difference between A and B
		A Without DCI			B After DCI—7 mg/kg			
		Control	Maximum	Change	Control	Maximum	Change	
I One group 5 dogs Vagotomy and cardiac sympathectomy	Epinephrine 1 μg/kg, i.v.	123.0 ±8.9	174.0 ±16.1	51.0 ±7.3	162.0 ±4.3	165.0 ±13.9	3.0 ±1.1	Control < .01* Maximum > .1 Change < .01
	Norepinephrine 1 μg/kg, i.v.	124.0 ±10.8	160.0 ±15.9	36.0 ±7.9	167.0 ±15.1	168.0 ±15.4	1.0 ±1.7	Control < .01* Maximum = .1 Change < .05
	Isoproternol 0.5 μg/kg, i.v.	118.0 ±6.2	214.0 ±13.9	96.0 ±7.0	155.0 ±12.7	164.0 ±13.4	9.0 ±6.0	Control <.001* Maximum < .001 Change < .001
II One group 5 dogs Vagotomy	Isoproterenol 0.5 μg/kg, i.v.	193.6 ±14.6	243.6 ±8.1	50.2 ±6.8	184.6 ±8.3	185.0 ±8.8	0.4 ±0.2	Control = .5* Maximum < .001 Change < .001
III Two groups 5 dogs each.** Vagotomy	Theophylline HCl 10 mg/kg, i.v.	178.0 ±12.3	214.0 ±10.2	36.0 ±3.7	188.2 ±8.1	216.5 ±8.0	28.2 ±2.1	Control > .5 Maximum > .5 Change = .1

* Analyzed by paired "t" test (Walker and Lev, 1953).

** Group IIIB same as Group II.

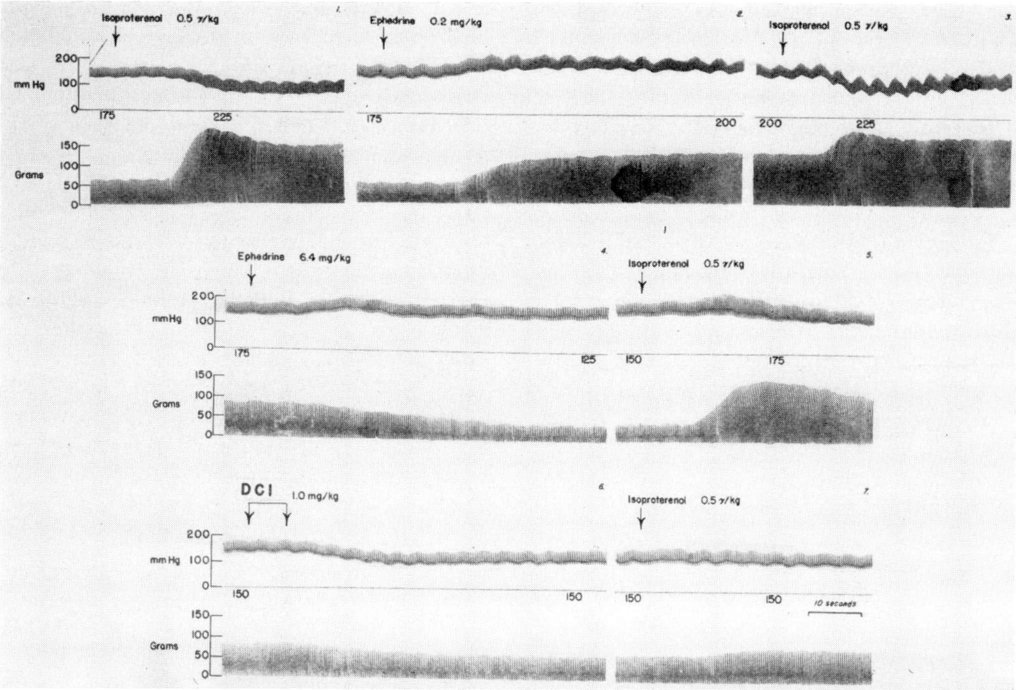

FIG. 4. Lack of cardiac adrenergic blockade by ephedrine in a vagotomized, anesthetized dog. The upper tracing of each pair of oscillograph records represents femoral arterial blood pressure (mm Hg); the lower tracings represent right ventricular contractile force (grams). The numbers above contractile force tracings represent heart rates (beats/min). From left to right the following drugs were injected intravenously at the arrows: First row, isoproterenol, 0.5 μg/kg; ephedrine, 0.2 mg/kg; isoproterenol 2 minutes after the injection of ephedrine. Second row, ephedrine, representing the last of a series of injections of ephedrine given at 0.4, 0.8, 1.6, 3.2 and 6.4 mg/kg doses over a period of 40 minutes; isoproterenol 2 minutes after the last dose of ephedrine. Bottom row, DCI, 1.0 mg/kg, and isoproterenol 2 minutes after DCI. Note lack of cardiac adrenergic blockade of isoproterenol by ephedrine compared to blockade by DCI. Also note cardiac depression produced by DCI after ephedrine. (Compare with response to first dose of DCI in figure 1).

ing a prolonged increase in heart rate and force with initial doses and a depression of the heart with subsequent doses, 4 additional experiments were conducted in which ephedrine was employed in place of DCI with the small standard doses of E, NE and I being given after each dose of ephedrine. Ephedrine was administered in geometrically increasing doses beginning with 0.1 mg/kg. In no experiment did ephedrine block either the positive inotropic or chronotropic effects of E, NE or I, even after the contractile force was profoundly depressed by ephedrine. Figure 4 shows the result of a typical experiment. The initial administration of 1 mg/kg of DCI after the appearance of the cardiac depressant effect of ephedrine invariably caused depression of contractile force and some slowing of heart rate (figure 4) in contrast to the usual stimulation of the heart by this dose alone (see figure 1). DCI, when administered after large doses of ephedrine, blocked the cardiac stimulant actions of E, NE and I (figure 4).

V. Effect of DCI on vasomotor actions of adrenergic stimuli. In all of the experiments cited above femoral artery blood pressure was measured simultaneously with cardiac contractile force and rate. In most experiments the vasopressor effect of E was augmented following administration of DCI, that of NE slightly depressed, and in all experiments the vasodepressor response to I was progressively inhibited by increasing doses of DCI. The vasopressor effect of cardiac sympathetic nerve stimulation was progressively inhibited with increasing doses of DCI. The inhibition of the vasodepressor response to I and of the pressor response to nerve stimulation is significant at the 1% level by paired analysis (Walker and Lev, 1953). The augmentation of the pressor effect of E is significant at the 1% level by paired analysis, but the slight inhibition of the pressor effect of NE is not significant. Table 3 shows the mean changes in blood pressure in response to the 3 amines and to cardiac sympathetic nerve stimulation before and after several doses of DCI. Figure 3 graphically depicts the results of a typical experiment.

VI. Duration of the cardiac adrenergic blockade by DCI in dogs. Duration of action of DCI was estimated in 4 vagotomized dogs in which blood pressure, ventricular contractile force and heart rate were measured. After obtaining control responses to E (1 μg/kg), NE (1 μg/kg) and I (0.5 μg/kg) a single intravenous injection of 1 mg/kg of DCI was given. At periodic intervals thereafter the 3 amines were again administered and the responses measured. The positive inotropic effects of E, NE and I were partially blocked immediately after injection of DCI (by 60 to 90%) after which a gradual recovery ensued. However, in 3 experiments which were maintained for 4 hours complete recovery did not occur within this time. In the other experiment partial blockade persisted for the 2½ hours of the experiment. The duration of the chronotropic blockade was less consistent. Inhibition of the cardioacceleration induced by I persisted for the duration of the experiment in 3 instances (2½ to 4 hours), but in the fourth experiment there was apparent complete recovery within 1 hour. The changes in heart rate in response to E and NE in vagotomized dogs were minimal with the small doses used (in contrast to the changes in dogs with denervated hearts) so that evaluation of the duration of the

TABLE 3

Effects of dichloroisoproterenol (DCI) on blood pressure of anesthetized, vagotomized dogs

Average mean arterial pressure in mm Hg ± S.E.

	Before DCI		After DCI—Cumulative doses of DCI in mg/kg							
	Control	Change	1		3		7		15	
			Control	Change	Control	Change	Control	Change	Control	Change
Epinephrine 1 μg/kg	121.9 ±7.1	54.0 (9) ±5.7	103.8 ±7.9	61.3 (9) ±3.4	91.5 ±6.7	67.5 (9) ±7.0	76.3 ±6.2	62.6 (9) ±8.6	66.4 ±9.3	63.6 (5) ±13.2
5 μg/kg									86.2 ±9.8	85.0 (5) ±12.5
Norepinephrine 1 μg/kg	125.7 ±6.8	59.3 (9) ±7.2	106.2 ±8.1	44.7 (9) ±4.4	92.2 ±7.9	45.8 (9) ±3.9	81.1 ±7.1	45.0 (9) ±5.3	77.8 ±10.4	44.6 (5) ±6.6
5 μg/kg									78.8 ±7.5	73.0 (5) ±14.3
Isoproterenol 0.5 μg/kg	123.0 ±6.5	−16.1 (9) ±5.3	108.0 ±8.4	−11.8 (9) ±2.5	92.5 ±7.6	−8.8 (9) ±3.0	78.7 ±6.5	0.8 (9) ±0.9	79.4 ±9.5	−0.6 (5) ±2.4
2.5 μg/kg									81.4 ±2.4	−3.4 (5) ±1.8
Cardiac symp. nerve stimulation	120.2 ±11.7	35.0 (5) ±5.0	112.8 ±8.8	25.2 (5) ±6.6	96.6 ±7.5	7.2 (5) ±11.8	70.2 ±11.8	10.4 (5) ±9.0	95.0 63.0	−17.0 (2) −5.0
DCI			116.3 ±7.4	−15.6 (9) ±3.6	107.4 ±6.5	−29.3 (9) ±4.5	94.4 ±7.6	−40.4 (9) ±4.9	90.0 ±7.8	−41.0 (5) ±5.9

Numbers in parentheses refer to numbers of animals used.

Change refers to maximal change in mean arterial pressure.

TABLE 4

A comparison of the effects of dichloroisoproterenol (DCI) on the contractile force responses of anesthetized, vagotomized dogs to digoxin, calcium chloride, theophylline and isoproterenol

	Mean Contractile Force in grams ± S.E.						"P" Values for Differences between A and B
	A Without DCI			B After DCI*			
	Control	Maximum	Change	Control	Maximum	Change	
Digoxin 0.15 mg/kg, i.v.	48.4 ±6.8 (6)	66.4 ±6.9	17.9 ±2.1	69.7 ±10.3	98.0 ±15.7	28.3 ±7.2	Control < .01 Maximum > .05 Change > .1
				(7) Separate dogs from Group A			
Calcium chloride 20 mg/kg, i.v.	82.5 77.0 77.0	143.0 143.0 132.0	60.5 66.0 55.0	126.5 93.5 77.0	165.0 154.0 137.5	38.5 60.5 60.5*	
				Same dogs as in Group A			
Theophylline HCl 10 mg/kg, i.v.	65.6 ±10.8 (5)	103.4 ±15.0	37.8 ±7.7	87.7 ±9.9	123.2 ±19.5	35.2 ±10.3	Control > .1 Maximum > .5 Change > .5
				(5) Separate dogs from Group A			
Isoproterenol† 0.5 μg/kg, i.v.	71.5 ±5.3 (9)	198.7 ±26.7	127.2 ±28.6	82.8 ±9.4	92.3 ±11.2	9.5 ±3.1	Control > .1‡ Maximum < .001 Change < .001
				(9) Same dogs as in Group A			

Numbers in parentheses refer to number of dogs used in each group.

* Doses of DCI: digoxin group, 2 dogs 7 mg/kg, 5 dogs 15 mg/kg; calcium group, 2 dogs 7 mg/kg, 1 dog 15 mg/kg; theophylline group, 3 dogs 15 mg/kg, 2 dogs 23 mg/kg; isoproterenol group, 7 mg/kg.

† Data from experiments summarized in table 1.

‡ Analyzed by paired "t" test (Walker and Lev, 1953).

blockade of these 2 drugs was difficult. However, in 1 experiment in which increases of heart rate of 50 to 60 beats/min were obtained with E and I in the control period, the blockade of this response lasted for 4 hours. The duration of the blockade of the vasodepressor action of I by DCI was shorter than that of heart rate and contractile force. In 4 experiments it lasted from 1 hour to less than 3 hours.

VII. Specificity of cardiac adrenergic blockade by DCI. A. Contractile force: In order to determine the specificity of blockade by DCI several cardiac stimulants other than sympathomimetic amines were tested. Digoxin, 0.15 mg/kg, was administered slowly, intravenously, to 7 of the dogs used for the experiments which are summarized in tables 1 and 3 (section II). The glycoside was given after complete blockade of the inotropic responses to sympathomimetic amines had been achieved with DCI (after cumulative doses of DCI of 15 mg/kg in 5 dogs and 7 mg/kg in 2 dogs). The mean maximal change in contractile force induced by digoxin in this group of dogs was compared with the mean maximal change in a second group of 6 vagotomized dogs in which the same dose of digoxin was given alone. The results, summarized in table 4, show that DCI has no significant blocking effect on the positive inotropic action of digoxin.

In 6 experiments in which calcium chloride was given in a dose of 20 mg/kg by rapid intravenous injection there was no evidence of blockade of the positive inotropic action of this compound. Table 4 summarizes the results of 3 experiments, and figure 5 shows the lack of blockade of calcium chloride in a typical experiment.

The changes in contractile force induced by intravenous injections of 10 mg/kg of theophylline were compared before and after administration of 7 mg/kg of DCI in one group of 5 vagotomized dogs. The increase in force was less after administration of DCI than before although the difference was of borderline significance. Evaluation of a possible blockade of theophylline by DCI was also complicated by the fact that the "control" force was higher after DCI than before. On the assumption that tachyphylaxis might account for the apparent reduction in contractile response to theophylline, a second group of 5 dogs was given theophylline in the same dose only after the administration of a cumulative dose of 15 mg/kg or greater of DCI. The theophylline-induced changes in contractile force in this group of dogs were compared with the theophylline effects before administration in the previous group of dogs. As shown in table 4, the "control" forces in the two groups were not significantly different nor did DCI reduce the magnitude of the response to theophylline. Similar results were obtained in isolated rabbit hearts (see section IX and table 5).

B. Heart rate: Specificity of blockade of the chronotropic effects of sympathetic stimuli by DCI is demonstrated in table 2. The cardioacceleration produced by theophylline was not blocked by a cumulative dose of 7 mg/kg of DCI in vagotomized dogs. This was a dose which antagonized the chronotropic action of I. Because of possible tachyphylaxis to theophylline 2 separate groups of dogs were used. Similar specificity was also demonstrated in rabbit hearts (see section IX and table 5). Since both calcium chloride and digoxin produce only slight changes in heart rate in vagotomized dogs it was not possible to use these compounds to demonstrate the specificity of the adrenergic chronotropic blockade by DCI.

VIII. Effects of the dichloro analogue of norepi-

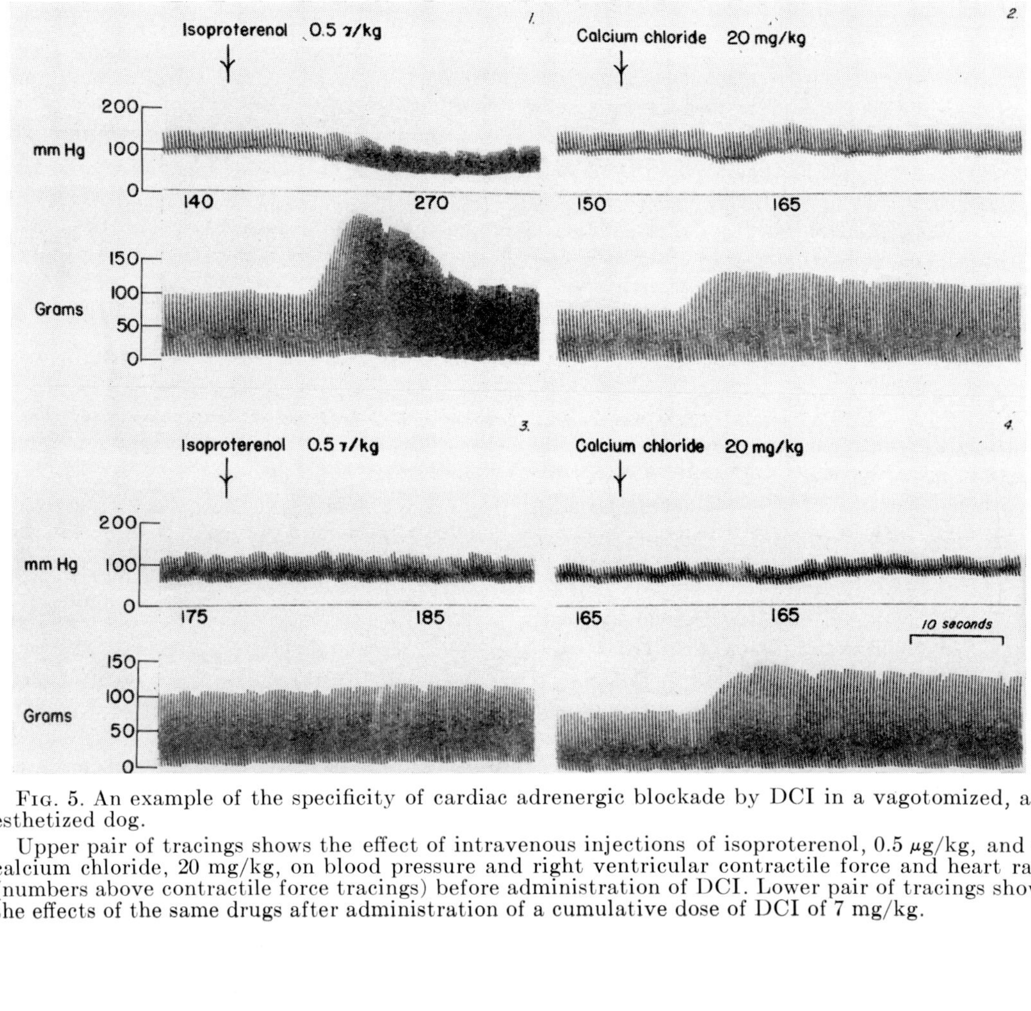

FIG. 5. An example of the specificity of cardiac adrenergic blockade by DCI in a vagotomized, anesthetized dog.

Upper pair of tracings shows the effect of intravenous injections of isoproterenol, 0.5 μg/kg, and of calcium chloride, 20 mg/kg, on blood pressure and right ventricular contractile force and heart rate (numbers above contractile force tracings) before administration of DCI. Lower pair of tracings shows the effects of the same drugs after administration of a cumulative dose of DCI of 7 mg/kg.

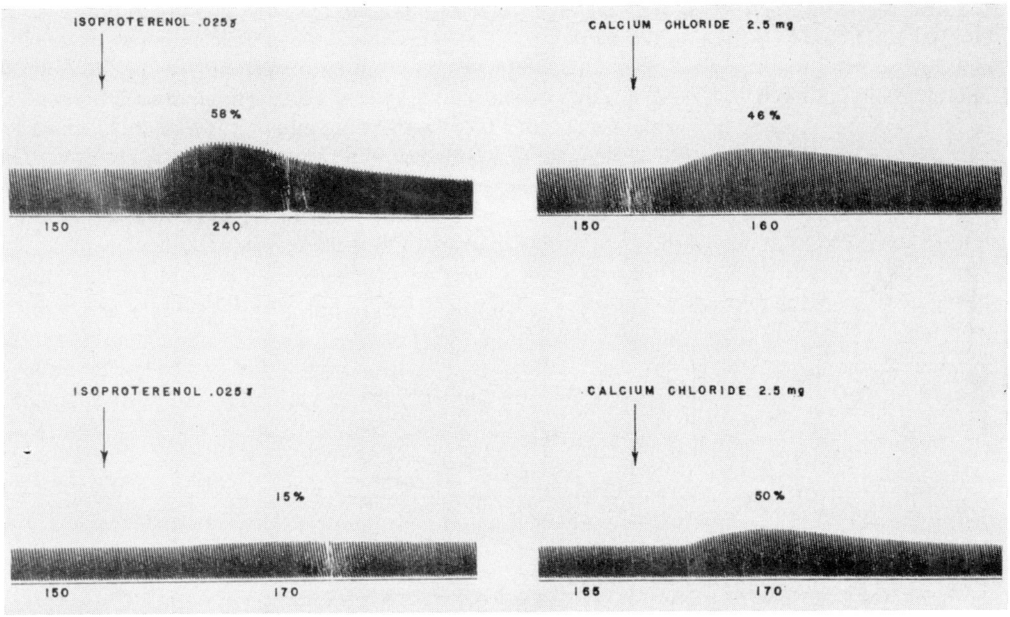

FIG. 6. Selective blockade by DCI of the effects of isoproterenol in an isolated perfused heart of a rabbit.

Upper two tracings represent responses to isoproterenol, 0.025 μg (left), and to calcium chloride, 2.5 mg (right), before administration of DCI. Lower two tracings show responses to same doses of isoproterenol and calcium chloride after administration of 0.65 mg of DCI. Numbers above tracings represent % change in contractile amplitude and numbers under tracings are heart rates, beats/min. Drugs were injected at arrows. Note nearly complete blockade of the inotropic and chronotropic effects of isoproterenol by DCI with no inhibition of the response to calcium.

nephrine (DCNE) in dogs. Two experiments were performed using DCNE. In 1 experiment an initial dose of 1 mg/kg produced a marked, prolonged rise in arterial pressure and only a slight increase in contractile force and heart rate. No blockade of the contractile force effects of E, NE and I was observed after this dose. Larger doses (5 and 10 mg/kg) produced vasopressor responses with marked depression of cardiac contractile force. During the period of cardiac depression the positive inotropic effects of E, NE and I were inhibited, but the blockade persisted for less than 30 minutes. In a second dog an initial injection of 10 mg/kg of DCNE produced a marked rise in blood pressure and profound cardiac depression. Again, blockade of the cardiac effects of E, NE and I was observed only for a short period of time during the phase of cardiac depression. No apparent blockade of the vasodepressor action of I or of the pressor effect of E and NE was noted although evaluation of the latter was difficult because of the high pressure resulting from DCNE.

IX. Experiments on the isolated rabbit heart. In 10 experiments on the continuously reperfused rabbit heart the results obtained were qualitatively similar to those obtained in dogs. Initial doses of DCI of 0.1 mg increased heart rate and contractile activity while subsequent larger doses depressed the heart. Complete blockade of the inotropic and chronotropic effects of E (0.1 μg), NE (0.1 μg) and I (0.025 μg) was obtained by doses of DCI of 0.1 mg and greater. Ten-fold increases in the doses of E, NE and I partially overcame the blockade produced by DCI. As in the experiments with dogs the blockade produced by DCI is specific for sympathomimetic amines. The responses of the heart to calcium chloride (2.5 mg), theophylline (1 mg) and ouabain (0.1 mg) were not depressed by doses of DCI which blocked the amines. Figure 6 shows the blockade of the effects of I in a typical experiment, and table 5 compares the responses to I and theophylline in 2 experiments.

The dichloro analogues of norepinephrine (DCNE) and epinephrine (DCE) produced only depression of contractile activity and heart rate even with low initial doses (0.1 mg). Temporary partial blockade of the effects of E, NE and I were obtained, but the doses required were 2 to 10 times as large as required with DCI. Neither DCNE or DCE inhibited the positive inotropic effects of calcium chloride, theophylline or ouabain.

Discussion. The inhibition of the positive inotropic and chronotropic effects of adrenergic stimuli by the dichloro analogue of isoproterenol appears to represent a specific cardiac adrenergic blockade. The augmentation of cardiac contractile force produced by cardiac glycosides, xanthines and calcium chloride, in both the dog heart *in situ* and in the isolated heart of the rabbit, is unchanged by doses of DCI which block the actions of the amines. Similarly, the positive chronotropic responses of dog and rabbit hearts to adrenergic stimuli are antagonized by doses of DCI which do not alter the chronotropic responses to theophylline. The specificity of this blockade provides a useful pharmacological tool for the differentiation of the cardiac stimulant action of drugs of diverse chemical structure. To our knowledge this represents the first description of specific adrenergic blockade of mammalian hearts with the exception of reports that several conventional adrenergic blocking agents, such as dibenamine, phenoxybenzamine, phentolamine and piperoxan (933F), inhibit the cardiac actions of sympathomimetic amines. However, these agents produce inconsistent cardiac blocking effects. For instance, Serin (1952b) reported that dibenamine and piperoxan inhibit principally the effects of epinephrine and only minimally the effects of norepinephrine on the isolated rat heart. Cotten, Moran and Stopp (1957) observed blockade of the positive inotropic effects of sympathomimetic amines and cardiac sympathetic nerve stimulation in the open-chest dog with phentolamine and phenoxybenzamine. However, only negligible blockade was obtained with azapetine, Hydergine, or piperoxan. The doses of phentolamine and phenoxybenzamine required for complete blockade of the heart varied from 0.5 to 32 mg/kg and 8 to 32 mg/kg, respectively. For the most part, blockade was observed only with doses far in excess of those required to reverse the vasopressor action of epinephrine.

The type of blockade produced by DCI is not known. The fact that in the isolated rabbit heart large doses of the amines are capable of overcoming the blockade suggests an equilibrium type of blockade. However, until appropriate quantitative studies are performed this conclusion must remain tentative. The initial increase in heart rate and force produced by DCI, followed by prolonged blockade of the cardiac responses to adrenergic stimuli, is indicative of a reaction between drug and receptors which results in a primary stimulation of the heart succeeded by blockade, perhaps due to a persistent complex between drug and receptors. Cellular binding of DCI is suggested by the persistence of blockade of the isolated rabbit heart even though DCI was not reperfused through the heart. That the primary stimulation is not essential for blockade, however, is seen in the lack of initial stimulation by DCE and DCNE in the rabbit heart.

TABLE 5

The effects of dichloroisoproterenol (DCI) on the inotropic and chronotropic responses to isoproterenol and theophylline in two rabbit hearts

	Response to Isoproterenol, 0.025 µg				Response to Theophylline*			
	Before DCI		After DCI, 0.6 mg		Before DCI		After DCI, 0.6 mg	
	Control	Change	Control	Change	Control	Change	Control	Change
	heart rate in beats/minute							
5	155	+85	160	0	165	+10	160	+15
6	155	+100	90	+5	130	+55	90	+80
	*Contractile amplitude in mm***							
5	15	+10	13	0	13	+4	13	+3.5
6	16	+12	10	+1	12	+4	11	+4

* Dose of theophylline—1 mg in Expt. 5 and 2 mg in Expt. 6.

** Deflection of galvanometer pen at constant amplification.

It is also apparent that the cardiac adrenergic blockade produced by the dichloro derivatives is not due to either prolonged myocardial stimulation *per se* or to myocardial depression *per se* since ephedrine, which produces both effects on the dog heart, did not block the effects of E, NE and I. However, it seems unlikely that ephedrine is operating through a receptor mechanism which is different from that concerned with the actions of E, NE and I and their analogues since the myocardial stimulant effect of ephedrine is blocked by DCI.

The structural requirements for cardiac adrenergic blocking drugs are poorly defined as yet. On the basis of the present studies chloro (and perhaps other halide?) substitution on the phenyl ring is important in view of the fact that ephedrine, which lacks such substituents, does not have blocking properties. The isopropyl moiety on the nitrogen appears to enhance potency and duration of the blocking action. The importance of the *beta* hydroxy cannot be assessed until dichloro derivatives lacking this group are studied.

With the description of specific cardiac adrenergic blocking compounds a re-evaluation of the classification of adrenergic receptors becomes important. Powell and Slater (1958) found that DCI has relatively weak adrenergic inhibitory properties and virtually no adrenergic excitatory actions. Our observations of moderate vasodepression and absence of vasopressor action confirm these findings. However, DCI possesses excitatory actions on the mammalian heart. Powell and Slater also found that DCI antagonizes the following inhibitory adrenergic actions: the depressor effect of I and E (actions confirmed in our experiments), the inhibitory effect of E on the isolated rabbit intestine, the epinephrine "release" of pilocarpine-induced bronchoconstriction in the dog, and the epinephrine "release" of pilocarpine-induced contraction of isolated tracheal chains of the guinea pig. They found that DCI failed to block the epinephrine-induced relaxation of the rat uterus. The selective blockade of most inhibitory functions and the lack of blockade of vasoconstriction coupled with the present demonstration of blockade by DCI of cardiac positive inotropic and chronotropic effects of adrenergic stimuli support the postulate of Ahlquist (1948) that the adrenotropic inhibitory receptors and the cardiac chronotropic and inotropic adrenergic receptors are functionally identical, *i.e.*, that both are *beta* type receptors. The concept of *alpha* and *beta* receptors represents, therefore, a useful classification of adrenergic receptors. It is suggested that this terminology be extended to the realm of adrenergic blocking drugs, *e.g.*, that blocking drugs be designated according to the receptor for which they have the greatest affinity, as either *alpha* or *beta* adrenergic blocking drugs.

There are many areas in the actions of sympathomimetic amines in which the receptor type remains in doubt. For instance, the arrhythmic action of adrenergic stimuli on the heart has been classified as an *alpha* function by Ahlquist in spite of the fact that other cardiac functions were considered to be subserved by *beta* receptors. Our present evidence concerning the actions of DCI allows neither confirmation nor rejection of this hypothesis. However, preliminary experiments in this laboratory using the technique described by Maling and Moran (1957) indicate that DCI also inhibits the myocardial arrhythmic action of epinephrine and norepinephrine in the dog following coronary artery ligation. Also, recent studies by Moore and Swain (1958) demonstrate that the ventricular fibrillation induced by epinephrine or isoproterenol in dogs following the administration of α-phenyl-α-dimethylaminoethyl propiophenone (Upjohn-0882) can be prevented by DCI but not by phenoxybenzamine.

Other types of adrenergic actions which merit reinvestigation with DCI are the intestinal inhibitory action (which Ahlquist classifies as an *alpha* receptor function) and the metabolic actions for which the receptor status remains in doubt.

An interesting aspect of the present study is the phenomenon of adrenergic cardiac depression in mammalian hearts. All three analogues, DCI, DCE and DCNE, cause conspicuous depression of ventricular contractile force in both the dog and rabbit heart. Also, in many experiments in dogs following the administration of blocking doses of DCI, depression of cardiac contractile force and rate were produced by E, NE and sympathetic nerve stimulation but to a lesser extent with I. Similar depression by sympathomimetic amines in the isolated rabbit heart has not been observed even after complete blockade of the stimulant effects by DCI. Myocardial depression resulting from sympathomimetic amines has been observed by other workers (see Burridge, 1917; Claes, 1924; MacDonald, 1925; Sollmann and Barlow, 1926 and Serin, 1952a). A unique instance of inhibition of the stimulant effect of sympathomimetic amines with appearance of a depressant action is found in the recent experiments of Cotten and Cooper (personal communication) in which ouabain blocks and even reverses the augmented cardiac contractile force produced by epinephrine and norepinephrine in hypothermic but not in normothermic dogs. The evidence from several sources of an adrenergically induced depression of cardiac contractility substantiates the validity of this type of action. The nature of this depression is not clear, except that it does not appear to be cholinergic in that it is not prevented by atropine (our data and that of Cotten and Cooper). It probably is not observed in most experiments with short acting sympathomimetic amines in the absence of a blocking drug because the action is slight compared to the stimulant action (in the case of E, NE and I) and is, therefore, obscured by the latter.

SUMMARY AND CONCLUSIONS

DCI, a dichloro analogue of isoproterenol (β - hydroxy - N - isopropyl - 3,4 - dichloro - phenethylamine hydrochloride; Lilly 20522), selectively blocks the cardiac positive inotropic and chronotropic effects of adrenergic stimuli in dogs with intact circulatory systems and in isolated hearts of rabbits. In dogs complete blockade of the cardiac positive inotropic effects of small doses of epinephrine, norepinephrine and isoproterenol and of supramaximal stimulation of the cardiac sympathetic nerves is obtained with cumulative doses of DCI of 3 mg/kg and greater. Depression of contractile force was frequently observed in response to sympathomimetic amines and to sympathetic nerve stimulation after administration of large doses of DCI. No inhibition of the positive inotropic effects of digoxin, theophylline or calcium chloride was observed. In dogs blockade of the positive chronotropic effects of isoproterenol but not of theophylline was obtained with DCI. In isolated rabbit hearts DCI has qualitatively the same blocking action on the effects of the amines but not on those of calcium, theophylline or ouabain. The dichloro analogues of epinephrine (DCE) and norepinephrine (DCNE) have similar blocking actions to those of DCI but are less potent.

DCI, in both dog and rabbit heart, initially stimulates and with subsequent doses depresses the heart. DCNE has similar effects in the dog, but in the rabbit heart it, like DCE, produces only depression. The cardiac depressant effects are not antagonized by atropine.

Ephedrine, which also produces initial cardiac stimulation and subsequent depression with high doses in the dog, does not inhibit the cardiac stimulant actions of other sympathomimetic amines.

The vasopressor effect of epinephrine in dogs is potentiated by DCI, that of norepinephrine is relatively unchanged, while that of cardiac sympathetic nerve stimulation is blocked, presumably due to the cardiac blockade. The vasodepressor effect of isoproterenol is completely blocked, but not reversed, by DCI in the dog. DCI, on intravenous administration, transiently lowers blood pressure, while DCNE produces a prolonged rise. DCNE does not appear to inhibit the vasopressor actions of epinephrine and norepinephrine or the vasodepressor action of isoproterenol.

On the basis of the selective blockade by DCI of the excitatory effects of adrenergic stimuli on the heart and of their inhibitory effects on other organs (*e.g.*, the vasodepressor effect of isoproterenol) and the lack of blockade of adrenergic vasopressor action, it is concluded that the adrenergic receptors of mammalian hearts are functionally homologous to the adrenergic inhibitory receptors of other tissues. This conclusion agrees with the hypothesis of Ahlquist that the cardiac inotropic and chronotropic sympathetic receptors are of the *beta* type, receptors which subserve inhibitory functions in other organs, in contrast to the *alpha* receptors which subserve sympathetic excitatory responses in all organs except the heart.

REFERENCES

AHLQUIST, R. P.: Amer. J. Physiol. **153:** 586, 1948.
AHLQUIST, R. P.: Chapter 27 in Pharmacology in Medicine, 2nd ed., Drill, V. A., ed., McGraw-Hill Book Company, Inc., New York, 1958.
ANDERSON, F. F. AND CRAVER, B. N.: THIS JOURNAL **93:** 135, 1948.
BONIFACE, K. J., BRODIE, O. J. AND WALTON, R. P.: Proc. Soc. exp. Biol., N. Y. **84:** 263, 1953.
BURRIDGE, W.: Quart. J. Med. **10:** 163, 1917.

CHENOWETH, M. B. AND KOELLE, E. S.: J. Lab. clin. Med. **31:** 600, 1946.
CLAES, E.: J. Physiol. Path. gén. **22:** 322, 1924.
COTTEN, M. DEV. AND WALTON, R. P.: Proc. Soc. exp. Biol., N.Y. **78:** 810, 1951.
COTTEN, M. DEV. AND BAY, E.: Amer. J. Physiol. **187:** 122, 1956.
COTTEN, M. DEV., MORAN, N. C. AND STOPP, P. E.: THIS JOURNAL **121:** 183, 1957.
GOODMAN, L. S. AND GILMAN, A.: The Pharmacological Basis of Therapeutics, 2nd ed., p. 572, The Macmillan Company, New York, 1955.
MACDONALD, A. D.: Quart. J. Exp. Physiol. **15:** 69, 1925.
MALING, H. M. AND MORAN, N. C.: Circulation Res. **4:** 409, 1957.
MOORE, J. I. AND SWAIN, H. H.: Fed. Proc. **17:** 396, 1958.
NICKERSON, M.: Pharmacol. Rev. **1:** 27, 1949.
POWELL, C. E. AND SLATER, I. H.: THIS JOURNAL **122:** 480, 1958.
SERIN, F.: Acta physiol. scand. **26:** 291, 1952a.
SERIN, F.: Acta physiol. scand. **26:** 297, 1952b.
SOLLMANN, T. AND BARLOW, O. W.: THIS JOURNAL **29:** 233, 1926.
WALKER, H. M. AND LEV, J.: Statistical Inference, Henry Holt and Company, New York, 1953.

8081

THE EFFECTS OF SYMPATHOMIMETIC DRUGS ON RENAL VESSELS[1]

D. M. AVIADO, Jr., A. L. WNUCK and E. J. De BEER

Department of Pharmacology, University of Pennsylvania School of Medicine, Philadelphia, Pennsylvania and Wellcome Research Laboratories, Tuckahoe, New York

Received for publication June 6, 1958

The ability of adrenal medullary extracts to constrict renal vessels was first demonstrated by Richards and Plant in 1922, using the perfused dog's kidney. Other investigators using other techniques have subsequently confirmed this local constriction of renal vessels, not only for adrenal extracts but also for synthetic epinephrine and levarterenol (see Discussion for references).

The information on the renal vascular effects of the other sympathomimetic drugs is either incomplete or absent. Only isoproterenol has been injected directly into the renal artery, and its observed effect is a weak vasoconstriction, as compared to that of epinephrine (Spencer, 1956). This fact is surprising because isoproterenol, a depressor amine, can dilate almost all other blood vessels and the kidney vessels appear to be an exception. The intravenous injections of ephedrine and methamphetamine, which are pressor amines, do not reduce renal blood flow (Maxwell *et al.*, 1951; Nickel *et al.*, 1954; Churchill-Davidson *et al.*, 1951). On the other hand the intravenous injections of phenylephrine, hydroxyamphetamine, pholedrine and methoxamine cause a reduction in renal blood flow (Corcoran and Page, 1943; Ranges and Bradley, 1943; Crosley *et al.*, 1951; Mills and Moyer, 1957). These results suggest that the latter drugs can constrict whereas the former ones do not constrict the renal vessels. Confirmation in the form of injections into the renal artery is still lacking. There is no available information regarding the renal effects of any of the other sympathomimetic drugs.

The experiments reported below were undertaken to compare the renal vascular effects of all commercially available sympathomimetic drugs. Compound 45-50 (β-hydroxyl-β-(2,5-diethoxyphenyl)isopropylamine), a new selective pulmonary vasodilator, has been included (Aviado and Schmidt, 1957). The general approach has been to compare the response of renal blood flow to such drugs using the same method as that utilized by Ahlquist and his collaborators (1954), *i.e.*, insertion of a rotameter into the renal artery of anesthetized dogs. The injections of the drug either directly into the cannulated renal artery or intravenously allowed the observation of each of the following actions: 1) local action on renal vessels derived from intraarterial injections; 2) systemic pressor or depressor action derived from intravenous injections, which can passively alter renal blood flow; and 3) the combined outcome on renal blood flow of the local and systemic actions. The various sympathomimetics fall into one of four patterns of renal vascular action, namely: potent renal vasoconstrictor exemplified by levarterenol; weak renal vasoconstrictor exemplified by ephedrine; renal vasodilator exemplified by isoproterenol; no or variable effect on renal vessels exemplified by methamphetamine.

Methods. Mongrel dogs were anesthetized with morphine sulfate (2 mg/kg, s.c.) and chloralose (70 mg/kg, i.v.). The following measurements were routinely recorded on a Sanborn Polyviso: a) aortic blood pressure by a transducer (Statham) from a catheter inserted via one carotid artery, which was integrated electrically; b) blood flow by a Shipley-Wilson rotameter (1951), inserted into the left renal artery and supplied with blood from one femoral artery; and in some experiments, c) urine flow by a catheter in the left ureter connected to a drop recorder. Manuronate (30 mg/kg) was used routinely as the anticoagulant.

A complete list of the sympathomimetic drugs used are listed in fig. 6. Each drug was injected either into the external jugular vein or into the renal artery, distal to the flowmeter. The drug concentrations for intraarterial injection were

[1] This study was aided by a grant to the University of Pennsylvania from the Surgeon General, Department of Defense, under contract no. DA-49-007-MD-200.

selected such that the total volume injected did not exceed 0.2 ml.

RESULTS. *Renal arterial injections on renal blood flow.* The control values of blood flow to the left kidney in 45 dogs, as measured by the Shipley-Wilson rotameter, ranged from 50 to 150 ml/min. Three or more drugs were intentionally injected into the renal artery of the same dog to permit comparison of vascular effects. The occurrence of cross-tachyphylaxis was minimized by altering the sequence of drug injections. Each of the 23 drugs was the first one injected in at least one dog.

The intraarterial injection of levarterenol (0.1 μg total dose) caused an immediate reduction in renal blood flow lasting from 1 to 3 minutes (fig. 1). Since aortic blood pressure remained unchanged, the reduction in flow was interpreted to mean local renal vasoconstriction. The dependability of eliciting vasoconstriction by levarterenol made it possible to check repeatedly the comparative sensitivity of the same preparation to levarterenol and to each of the other sympathomimetic drugs.

A similar reduction in renal blood flow, with no change in aortic blood pressure, resulted from the intraarterial injections of the following drugs with the respective total doses: epinephrine, 0.1 μg; phenylephrine, 1 μg; methoxamine, 10 μg; metaraminol, 10 μg; naphazoline, 10 μg; and compound 45-50, 100 μg. Renal vasoconstriction was also encountered by injections of the following drugs in 1-mg doses: ephedrine, hydroxyamphetamine and phenylpropanolamine (see fig. 2).

Several drugs did not behave like levarterenol when injected into the renal artery. One such drug was isoproterenol which caused either an increase or no change in blood flow when injected in 1 μg total dose (fig. 3). Nylidrin (100 μg), methoxyphenamine and cyclopentamine (each in 1 mg dose) also gave either no response or more usually an increase in blood flow as shown in fig. 4. The duration of renal vasodilatation brought about by such drugs lasted for about 1 minute and was much shorter in duration than the renal vasoconstriction brought about by other drugs (1 to 3 minutes). This difference may

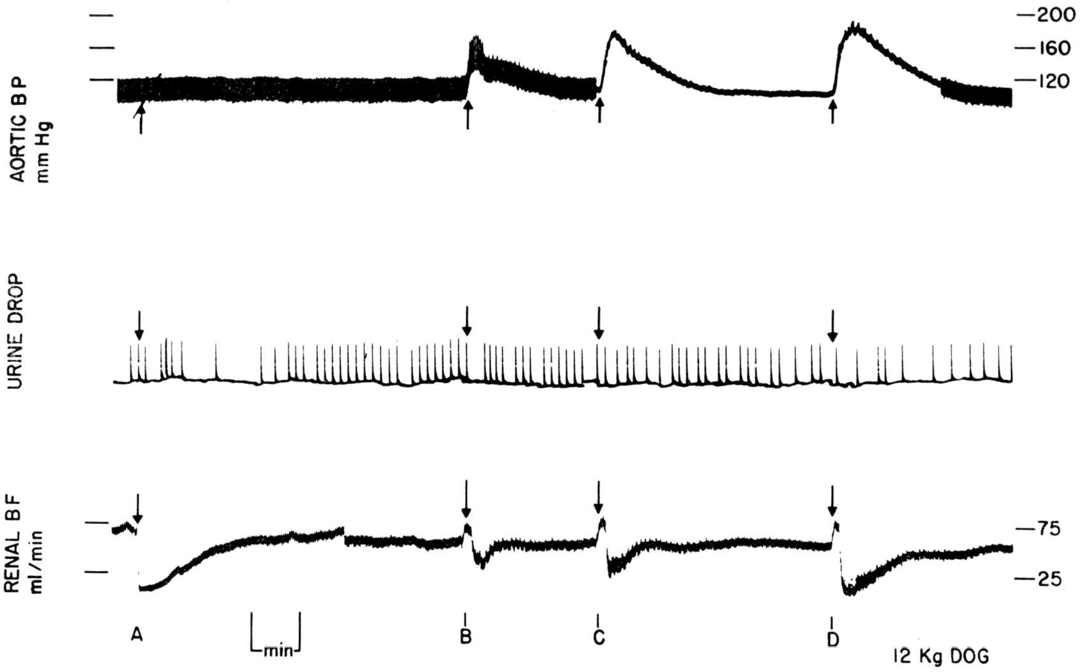

FIG. 1. Levarterenol injections.

A. 0.1 μg total into renal artery causes a reduction in renal blood flow and a delayed anuria. B. Intravenous injection of 1 μg/kg causes an initial increase in flow, coincident with aortic hypertension, and followed by a reduction in flow presumably from local action. C. Intravenous injection of 3 μg/kg. D. Intravenous injection of 6 μg/kg. Blood pressure was electrically integrated during C and D.

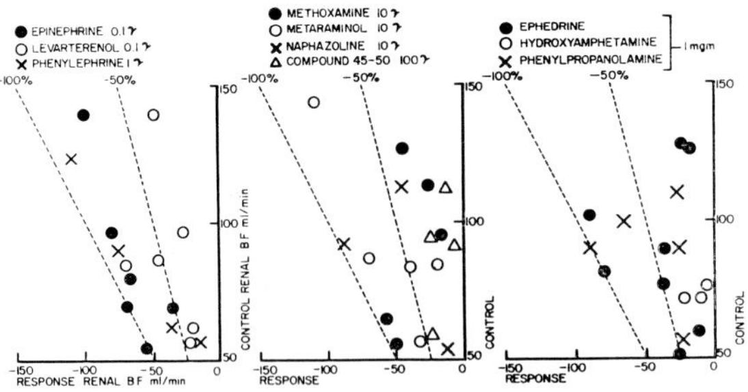

FIG. 2. Effect of injections of drugs (expressed as total dose) into renal artery.

Control flows are on the ordinate and maximal responses are on the abscissa. Diagonal lines represent % changes. Note that all drugs cause a reduction in renal blood flow in doses of 0.1 to 1 μg (left panel), 1 to 100 μg (middle panel) and 1 mg (right panel).

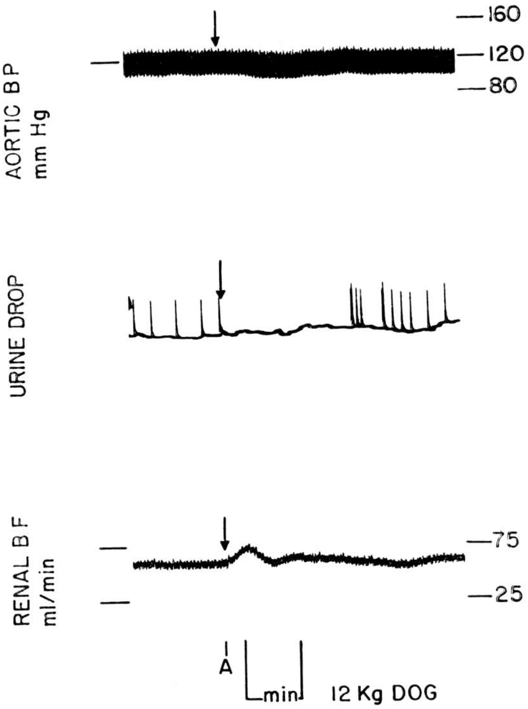

FIG. 3. Isoproterenol injection.

Injection of 1 μg total dose into renal artery causes a rise in renal blood flow and anuria.

be explained in the following manner. The renal vasodilator drug is immediately flushed by the increased blood flow whereas the renal vasoconstrictor drug is temporarily trapped by the reduction in flow.

The remaining sympathomimetic drugs had no or variable effect on renal vessels. This was true for intraarterial injections of 1 mg total dose of

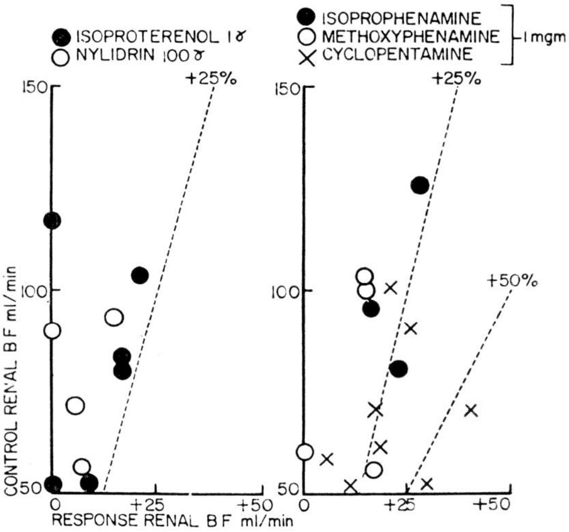

FIG. 4. Effect of injections of drugs (expressed as total dose) into renal artery.

Control flows are on the ordinate and maximal responses are on the abscissa. Diagonal lines represent % changes. Nylidrin and isoproterenol cause either no change or usually a rise in renal blood flow. Isoprophenamine, methoxyphenamine and cyclopentamine usually cause a rise in flow.

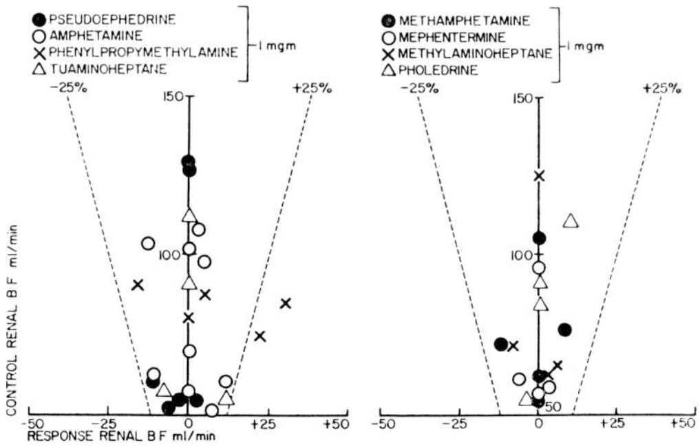

FIG. 5. Effect of injections of drugs (expressed as total dose) into renal artery.

Control flows are on the ordinate and maximal responses are on the abscissa. Diagonal lines represent % changes. All drugs in 1 mg dose cause either no change or a variable effect on flow.

each of the following: methamphetamine, mephentermine, methylaminoheptane, pholedrine, pseudoephedrine, amphetamine, phenylpropylmethylamine and tuaminoheptane (fig. 5). The cause of the variability in response to the same drug encountered even in the same preparation is not known and is under investigation. The fact remains that in the same preparation, this group of drugs give variable response whereas the other drugs (listed above) are either dependable renal vasoconstrictors or vasodilators.

Intravenous injections on aortic blood pressure

and renal blood flow. The immediate effect of isoproterenol (1 to 3 μg/kg) injected intravenously was a simultaneous reduction in aortic blood pressure and renal blood flow. The latter can be explained entirely on the basis of the former. A reduction in renal blood flow, secondary to a systemic depressor action, was also encountered with the intravenous injection of the following drugs: nylidrin, 0.1 mg/kg; isoprophenamine, 1 mg/kg; and methoxyphenamine, 1 mg/kg. Cyclopentamine (1 mg/kg, i.v.), the remaining drug in the group of renal vasodilators, caused a systemic pressor or depressor response, which was accompanied by an increase or decrease in renal blood flow, respectively.

The members of the group of drugs, exemplified by methamphetamine, that have been shown to have no or variable effect on renal vessels, were injected intravenously in doses of 1 mg/kg. The aortic blood pressure and renal blood flow were either increased or decreased simultaneously. The major cause for the alteration in renal blood flow is the rise or fall in aortic blood pressure brought about by the primary effects of these drugs on the heart and other systemic vascular beds.

All of the sympathomimetic drugs with proven local renal vasoconstricting action, exemplified by levaterrenol, consistently caused aortic hypertension when injected intravenously (in doses ranging from 1 to 10 μg/kg). The simultaneous effect on renal blood flow was a biphasic one consisting of an initial increase followed by a decrease (fig. 1). This biphasic action means that renal vasoconstriction brought about by this group of drugs can overshadow the increase in flow accompanying the hypertensive action. Four drugs belonging to this group (ephedrine, phenylpropanolamine, hydroxyamphetamine and compound 45-50), injected intravenously in doses of 1 mg/kg, caused either a biphasic response, or a uniphasic increase in renal blood flow. This is interpreted to mean that the local constricting action of these four drugs may be completely overshadowed by the accompanying primary increase in aortic pressure.

Urine flow responses. The measurements of urine drops by catheterization of the ureter were not completely helpful in understanding the effect of renal blood flow alterations on urine formation. Intraarterial injections of levarterenol and isoproterenol caused a temporary reduction in the number of collected drops of urine although the former caused a decrease in blood flow and the latter an increase (fig. 1 and 3). The fact that an increase in blood flow is

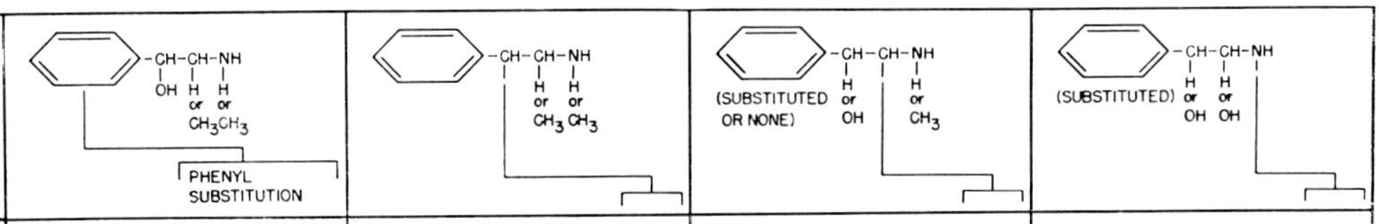

Group	Drug	Phenyl substitution	α	β	N	No.
RENAL VASO-CONSTRICTOR (0.1-10γ)	EPINEPHRINE	3-OH, 4-OH	OH	H	CH_3	(1)
	LEVARTERENOL	3-OH, 4-OH	OH	H	H	(2)
	PHENYLEPHRINE	3-OH	OH	H	CH_3	(3)
	METARAMINOL	3-OH	OH	CH_3	H	(4)
	METHOXAMINE	2-CH_3O, 5-CH_3O	OH	CH_3	H	(5)
	*NAPHAZOLINE	*				(6)
RENAL VASO-CONSTRICTOR (100-1000γ)	COMPOUND 45-50	2-C_2H_5O, 5-C_2H_5O	OH	CH_3	H	(7)
	EPHEDRINE		OH	CH_3	CH_3	(8)
	PHENYLPROPANOLAMINE		OH	CH_3	H	(9)
	HYDROXYAMPHETAMINE	4-OH	H	CH_3	H	(10)
VARIABLE EFFECTS (1000γ)	METHAMPHETAMINE		H	CH_3	CH_3	(11)
	PSEUDOEPHEDRINE		OH	CH_3	CH_3	(12)
	AMPHETAMINE		H	CH_3	H	(13)
	PHOLEDRINE	4-OH	H	CH_3	CH_3	(14)
	*METHYLAMINOHEPTANE	*	H	CH_3	H	(15)
	*TUAMINOHEPTANE	*	H	CH_3	H	(16)
	*MEPHENTERMINE	*	H	$(CH_3)_2$	CH_3	(17)
	PHENYLPROPYMETHYLAMINE		CH_3	H	CH_3	(18)
RENAL VASODILATOR (1-1000γ)	ISOPROTERENOL	3-OH, 4-OH	OH	H	C_3H_7	(19)
	NYLIDRIN	4-OH	OH	CH_3	3 Ph-Pr	(20)
	ISOPROPHENAMINE	2-CL	OH	H	C_3H_7	(21)
	METHOXYPHENAMINE	2-CH_3O	H	CH_3	CH_3	(22)
	*CYCLOPENTAMINE	*	H	CH_3	CH_3	(23)

FIG. 6. Chemical structure of sympathomimetic drugs grouped according to their local renal vascular effects.

The amounts in column 1 represent total doses for renal arterial injections. Drugs indicated by * possess chemical structures different from the basic phenylethylamine structure.

accompanied by a reduction in collected urine suggested the possibility of the injected drug relaxing the pelvis of the ureter. Since it was not possible to segregate actions of the drug on the smooth muscle of the ureter from that secondary to changes in renal blood flow, further interpretation of kidney function by this method was dropped.

Correlation of chemical structure with renal vascular action. The chemical structures of the 23 drugs investigated above are summarized in fig. 6. The following generalizations are apparent: 1) Five of the six drugs with powerful renal vasoconstrictor action are characterized by one or two hydroxy or methoxy substitution in the phenyl ring (lines 1 to 6). 2) Three of the four drugs with weak renal vasoconstrictor action have hydroxy substitution in the β-carbon of the ethyl chain (lines 7 to 10). Two of them have phenyl substitutions which have minor differences from those characterizing the drugs with powerful renal vasconstrictor action. 3) All five of the renal vasodilators are secondary amines (lines 19 to 23). Two of the five have substitutions in the phenyl ring similar to those listed for the renal vasoconstrictors which means that their presence may be nullified by the additional substitution to the amine. d) Seven of the eight drugs with variable renal vascular effects have methyl substitution in the α-carbon of the ethyl chain (lines 11 to 18). Five of them are secondary amines (like the renal vasodilators) and one possesses a substitution in the phenyl ring (like the weak renal vasoconstrictor).

Discussion. The measurement of renal blood flow by means of a rotameter inserted into the renal artery of anesthetized dogs afforded an opportunity to group sympathomimetic drugs into the following four types:

Type A. Sympathomimetic drugs capable of constricting renal vessels when injected into the renal artery and intravenously: levarterenol, epinephrine, phenylephrine, metaraminol, methoxamine and naphazoline. The constriction of renal vessels by levarterenol and epinephrine injected directly into the renal artery reported above confirms similar conclusions obtained by others using perfusion techniques (Richards and Plant, 1922; Gaddum *et al.*, 1949; Page and McCubbin, 1953), rotameter (Ahlquist *et al.*, 1954) and electromagnetic flowmeter (Spencer *et al.*, 1954). That this local action can be elicited by intravenous injection of pressor doses of both amines has been shown by the experiments reported above and also by previously reported measurements of renal blood flow in anesthetized cats (Burn and Hutcheon, 1949), anesthetized dogs (Moyer and Handley, 1952; Berne *et al.*, Marson 1956a, 1956b; Frank *et al.*, 1956), unanesthetized dogs (Corcoran and Page, 1947) and human subjects (Chasis *et al.*, 1938; Corcoran and Page, 1943; Barnett *et al.*, 1950; Smythe *et al.*, 1952; Nickel *et al.*, 1954; King and Baldwin, 1956; Lathem, 1956). Almost all of such studies utilized renal clearance methods with the exception of the experiments using anesthetized animals in which renal arterial flow or venous outflow was measured directly.

The demonstration of renal vasoconstriction by the other drugs belonging to type A is new. It would be desirable to seek confirmation in the intact animal or human subject to prove that renal vasoconstriction can be elicited following the intravenous injection of all of these drugs. So far, such information is available only for phenylephrine (Crosley *et al.*, 1951), and hydroxyamphetamine (Corcoran and Page, 1943).

Type B. Sympathomimetic drugs capable of constricting renal vessels when injected into the renal artery; when the drugs are injected intravenously, renal vasoconstriction is not always encountered: ephedrine, phenylpropanolamine, hydroxyamphetamine and compound 45-50. The local effects of all these drugs on renal vessels are described in the above experiments. When ephedrine is administered intravenously in dogs (Chen and Schmidt, 1930) and human subjects (Maxwell *et al.*, 1951; Nickel *et al.*, 1954), the local constriction of renal vessels is masked by the pressor action so that renal blood flow and urine formation are not reduced. The three other drugs appear to behave similarly but human experiments are essential for completeness. The major difference between drugs belonging to type B and those belonging to type A is the comparative importance of renal vasoconstriction with constriction of other systemic blood vessels and with cardiac stimulation. This is now under investigation and preliminary results indicate that the renal vascular action of ephedrine is less important than its other circulatory actions.

Type C. Sympathomimetic drugs that have no important renal action when injected into the renal artery; when these drugs are injected intravenously, renal blood flow is increased as a result of their systemic pressor effect: methamphetamine, pseudoephedrine, amphetamine, pholedrine, methylaminoheptane, tuaminoheptane, mephentermine and phenylpropylmethylamine. The results of intraarterial injections of these drugs are most surprising because this is the first indication that not all pressor amines can locally constrict renal vessels. This type of action has more than theoretical importance because it may be one of the several considerations in the choice of clinically useful pressor drugs. If renal function may be jeopardized by reduction in renal blood flow, drugs that do not constrict renal vessels (type C) are preferable to drugs that constrict them (types A and B). Confirmation of all these results by human studies are necessary. So far, only methamphetamine has been tried and the results obtained from subjects rendered hypotensive by ganglion blocking drugs show that this drug does not reduce renal blood flow (Churchill-Davidson *et al.*, 1951).

Type D. Sympathomimetic drugs that have a local dilator renal action when injected into the renal artery; when injected intravenously, renal blood flow decreases, secondary to the arterial depressor effect: isoproterenol, nylidrin, isoprophenamine, methoxyphenamine and cyclopentamine. Spencer (1956) reported a weak constrictor action by isoproterenol but this was not encountered in the above experiments because smaller doses were used. The dilator action presently encountered, is interpreted to mean that the renal vessels behave pharmacologically like other systemic vessels in that they can dilate to some sympathomimetic drugs. This renal vasodilator action of isoproterenol is in general agreement with the reduction in calculated renal vascular resistance observed by Corcoran and Page (1947) and by Handley and Huggins (1954) following intravenous injection of isoproterenol in human subjects.

SUMMARY

The effects of sympathomimetic drugs on renal blood flow in anesthetized dogs were investigated by insertion of a rotameter in the renal artery. The drugs can be grouped into four types:

Type A: Sympathomimetic drugs that are capable of constricting renal vessels when injected into the renal artery and intravenously: levarterenol, epinephrine, phenylephrine, metaraminol, methoxamine and naphazoline.

Type B: Drugs that are capable of constricting renal vessels when injected into the renal artery; when these drugs are injected intravenously, renal vasoconstriction is not always encountered: ephedrine, phenylpropanolamine, hydroxyamphetamine and compound 45-50.

Type C: Drugs that have no important renal actions when injected into the renal artery; when these drugs are injected intravenously, renal blood flow is increased as a result of their systemic pressor effect: methamphetamine, pseudoephedrine, amphetamine, pholedrine, methylaminoheptane, tuaminoheptane, mephentermine and phenylpropylmethylamine.

Type D: Drugs that have a local renal dilator action when injected into the renal artery; when injected intravenously, renal blood flow is decreased as a result of their arterial depressor effect: isoproterenol, nylidrin, isoprophenamine, methoxyphenamine and cyclopentamine.

REFERENCES

Ahlquist, R. P., Taylor, J. P., Rawson, C. W., Jr. and Sydow, V. L.: This Journal **110:** 352, 1954.

Aviado, D. M., Jr. and Schmidt, C. F.: This Journal **120:** 512, 1957.

Barnett, A. J., Blacket, R. B., Depoorter, A. E., Sanderson, P. H. and Wilson, G. M.: Clin. Sci. **9:** 151, 1950.

Berne, R. M., Hoffman, W. K., Jr., Kagan, A. and Levy, M. N.: Amer. J. Physiol. **171:** 564, 1952.

Burn, J. H. and Hutcheon, D. E.: Brit. J. Pharmacol. **4:** 373, 1949.

Chasis, H., Ranges, H. A., Goldring, W. and Smith, H. W.: J. clin. Invest. **7:** 683, 1938.

Chen, K. K. and Schmidt, C. F.: Medicine, Baltimore **9:** 1, 1930.

Churchill-Davidson, H. C., Wylie, W. D., Miles, B. E. and de Wardener, H. E.: Lancet **2:** 803, 1951.

Corcoran, A. C. and Page, I. H.: J. exp. Med. **35:** 868, 1943.

Corcoran, A. C., and Page, I. H.: Proc. Soc. exp. Biol., N.Y. **66:** 148, 1947.

Crosley, A. P., Jr., Clark, J. K. and Barker, H. G.: This Journal **101:** 153, 1951.

Frank, E. D., Frank, H. A., Jacob, S., Weizel, H. A. E. Korman, H. and Fine, J.: Amer. J. Physiol. **186:** 74, 1956.

Gaddum, J. H., Peart, W. S. and Vogt, M.: J. Physiol. **108:** 467, 1949.

Handley, C. A. and Huggins, R. A.: Texas Rep. Biol. Med. **12:** 464, 1954.

King, S. E. and Baldwin, D. S.: Amer. J. Med. **20:** 217, 1956.

Lathem, W.: J. clin. Invest. **35:** 1277, 1956.

Marson, F. G. W.: Brit. J. Pharmacol. **11:** 431, 1956a.

MARSON, F. G. W.: Arch. int. Pharmacodyn. **107:** 94, 1956b.

MAXWELL, M. H., MORALES, P. AND CROWDER, C. H., JR.: Proc. Soc. exp. Biol., N.Y. **77:** 539, 1951.

MILLS, L. C. AND MOYER, J. H.: Amer. J. med. Sci. **233:** 409, 1957.

MOYER, J. H. AND HANDLEY, C. A.: Circulation **5:** 91, 1952.

NICKEL, J. F., SMYTHE, C. McC., PAPPER, E. M. AND BRADLEY, S. E.: J. clin. Invest. **33:** 1687, 1954.

PAGE, I. H. AND McCUBBIN, J. W.: Amer. J. Physiol. **173:** 411, 1953.

RANGES, H. A. AND BRADLEY, S. E.: J. clin. Invest. **22:** 687, 1943.

RICHARDS, A. N. AND PLANT, O. H.: Amer. J. Physiol. **59:** 184 and 191, 1922.

SHIPLEY, R. E. AND WILSON, C.: Proc. Soc. exp. Biol., N.Y. **78:** 724, 1951.

SMYTHE, C. McC., NICKEL, J. F. AND BRADLEY, S. E.: J. clin. Invest. **31:** 499, 1952.

SPENCER, M. P.: THIS JOURNAL **116:** 237, 1956.

SPENCER, M. P., DENISON, A. B. AND GREEN, H. D.: Circulation Res. **2:** 537, 1954.

8082

STUDIES ON VERATRUM ALKALOIDS. XXVII. THE NEGATIVE CHRONOTROPIC ACTION OF VERATRAMINE AND RESERPINE IN THE HEART DEPLETED OF CATECHOL AMINES[1, 2]

I. R. INNES[3] AND O. KRAYER

Department of Pharmacology, Harvard Medical School, Boston, Massachusetts

Received for publication June 24, 1958

It has been demonstrated by Paasonen and Krayer (1957, 1958) that the dog heart no longer contains detectable amounts of epinephrine and norepinephrine 2 to 3 days after the animal has been treated with appropriate doses of reserpine. The heart-lung preparation (HLP) of dogs with hearts thus depleted of catechol amines was used to extend the study made by Krayer and Fuentes (1956, 1958) of the heart rate-decreasing action of reserpine.

In the dog HLP veratramine was shown to antagonize the cardioacceleration due to epinephrine (Krayer, 1949), to cardioaccelerator nerve stimulation and norepinephrine (Krayer and van Maanen, 1949) and to ephedrine and other sympathomimetic amines (Krayer, 1950). The site of veratramine action was shown to be at the pacemaker, and the action was attributed to a reduction in sensitivity of the pacemaker to the action of sympathomimetic amines.

Reduction by veratramine of the initial heart rate also was shown by Krayer (1949), Krayer and Ourisson (1954) and Krayer *et al.* (1955) in the HLP and by Kosterlitz *et al.* (1954) in the denervated cat heart. Since this action of veratramine might be explainable in terms of antagonism to such sympathomimetic amines as are found in the vicinity of the pacemaker tissue, it is important to examine the effect of veratramine upon the heart rate in the HLP depleted of epinephrine and norepinephrine by reserpine.

[1] Some of the results of this study were reported at a meeting of the British Physiological Society in Aberdeen, September, 1957 (Innes and Krayer, 1957).

[2] This work was supported by grants from the American Heart Association, the U. S. Public Health Service (H-2205) and the Eugene Higgins Trust.

[3] The investigation was made during the tenure of a Carnegie Trust Grant. Present address: Department of Physiology, University of Aberdeen, Scotland.

METHODS. All experiments reported in this paper were carried out on the HLP of male and female dogs of unselected breed (8 to 13 kg of body weight) to which an intraperitoneal injection of 0.5 mg/kg of reserpine had been administered 3 days and again 2 days prior to the experiment. In order to allow a comparison of the present data obtained on the HLP of reserpine-pretreated dogs with earlier data collected on the HLP of normal dogs, the technique was kept the same as in the earlier studies, and there were comparable conditions of mean arterial blood pressure (approximately 100 mm Hg), systemic output (500 to 700 ml/min) and total blood volume (about 1000 ml). The state of sedation characteristic of treatment with reserpine generally persisted until the time of the experiment, and the dose of sodium pentobarbital giving adequate anesthesia, normally 35 mg/kg, could be reduced to 20–25 mg/kg. Even with this dosage complete inhibition of respiration was occasionally observed. In all experiments the defibrinated blood needed for the HLP was obtained from large normal dogs under ether anesthesia. A mixture of 95% oxygen and 5% carbon dioxide was used for ventilation of the lungs. The temperature of the blood varied from experiment to experiment over the range of 37.4 to 39°C, but temperature changes were not greater than ±0.3°C throughout an individual experiment.

The heart rate was counted every minute from electrocardiographic recordings taken by a Grass ink-writing oscillograph.

Reserpine base[4] was brought into solution by acetic acid and diluted with 5 % glucose solution to give 2 mg/ml. Veratramine base was brought into solution by 0.1 N HCl and adjusted to the required concentration with distilled water or with 5% glucose solution. Ephedrine sulfate was dissolved in 0.9% NaCl solution. All doses mentioned refer to the bases. The drugs were administered by injection into the venous supply tube

[4] Generously supplied by Dr. Norbert Neuss, Eli Lilly and Company, Indianapolis, Ind.

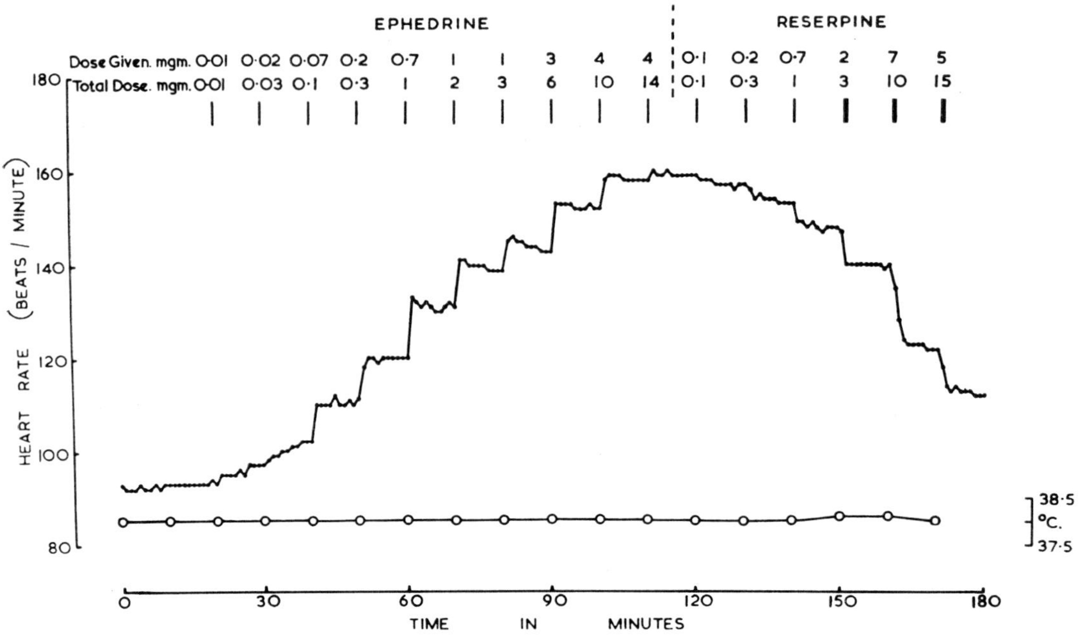

FIG. 1. The cardioaccelerator action of ephedrine and the antiaccelerator action of reserpine in the heart-lung preparation depleted of catechol amines by pretreatment with reserpine.

Dog, male, 10 kg. Reserpine, 0.5 mg/kg injected intraperitoneally 3 days and 2 days before experiment. Heart-lung preparation. Mean arterial pressure, 100 mm Hg. Total blood volume at the beginning was 1050 ml. Systemic output, 600 ml/min. (For further explanation see text.)

close to the heart, each injection extending over 1 minute, or, with large doses of veratramine and reserpine, 2 to 3 minutes.

RESULTS. *The influence of pretreatment with reserpine upon the initial heart rate.* The initial heart rate was taken to be the heart rate immediately prior to injection of the first dose of ephedrine, veratramine or reserpine, usually 30 minutes after the beginning of recording. The mean initial heart rate of 21 experiments was 130.1 ± 20.1 (S.D.) beats/min. In the results of Krayer and Benforado (1955) on the HLP of 330 dogs under similar experimental conditions but without treatment with reserpine the mean initial heart rate was 140.8 ± 15.1 (S.D.). The initial heart rate in the HLP from pretreated dogs was significantly lower by 10.7 ± 3.5 (S.E.) beats/min. ($P < 0.01$).

The influence of pretreatment with reserpine upon the cardioaccelerator action of ephedrine. In 5 experiments increasing doses of ephedrine were injected into the circulating blood at intervals of 10 minutes, a period sufficient to allow conditions of equilibrium to be reached after each dose. The first part of figure 1 shows the course of a typical experiment. The results were compared with those of earlier experiments of a similar nature on the HLP of 14 normal dogs (Krayer and Ourisson, 1954).

In all 5 experiments (see table 1), maximal cardioacceleration was attained only with a dose of 10 mg ephedrine, whereas in the normal dogs the maximal rate was always reached with 2 or 3 mg (see figure 2). Following the most effective dose of ephedrine the rate of the HLP of the reserpine-treated dogs came within the range 160 to 215 beats/min, mean 188.6. This was compared with the corresponding data from normal dogs where the range for the maximal heart rate following ephedrine was 211 to 275 beats/min, mean 240.3. The difference was highly significant, 51.7 ± 9.0 (S.E.) beats ($P < 0.001$). The mean acceleration with the optimal dose of ephedrine was 71.2 ± 16.7 (S.D.) in the present experiments, compared with 105.9 ± 10.3 (S.D.) in the HLP of normal dogs, a difference of 34.7 ± 6.3 (S.E.) ($P < 0.001$).

Following the procedure adopted by Krayer and Ourisson (1954) for the HLP of the normal dog, for each experiment a probit plot of the ac-

TABLE 1

The cardioaccelerator effect of ephedrine and the antagonistic action of reserpine in the heart-lung preparation of the dog pretreated with reserpine

Heart Rate		Maximal Acceleration	Ephedrine ED_{50} dose‡	Reserpine I_{50} dose‡
Initial rate*	Maximal rate after ephedrine†			
beats/min	*beats/min*	*beats/min*	*mg*	*mg*
155	212	57	0.45	1.3
93	159	66	0.55	8
108	166	58	0.9	7
113	210	97	1.7	9
112	190	78	1.4	14

* Temperature range in the 5 experiments: 37.5 to 38.4°C (av. 38°C).

† In all 5 experiments the maximally effective dose of ephedrine was 10 mg and the total dose was 14 mg.

‡ Obtained from probit plots of the individual experiments.

celeration, expressed as a percentage of the total acceleration, was made against the logarithm of the corresponding total cumulate dose of ephedrine. From this the dose of ephedrine causing 50% of the total acceleration (ED_{50}) was estimated for each individual experiment (table 1). In addition a probit plot was made of the mean values of acceleration between 15% and 85%, giving a dose of 0.85 mg for the ED_{50}. A similar probit plot of the data from normal dogs had yielded an ED_{50} value of 0.2 mg ephedrine.

Once the maximal heart rate has been produced by ephedrine, it is normally maintained with little decrease over a period of 2 hours. In the present experiments this effect was not studied since injections of reserpine were made 10 to 15 minutes after the final dose of ephedrine. In 3 experiments, however, the heart rate per minute fell by 5 to 7 beats within this 15-minute period.

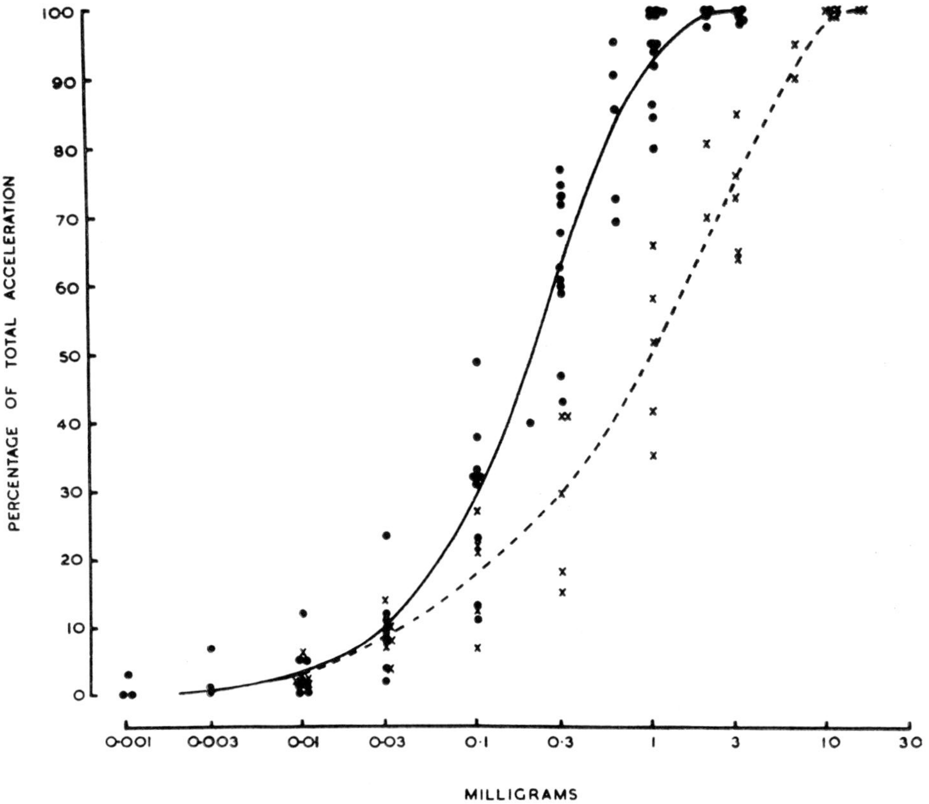

FIG. 2. The cardioaccelerator action of ephedrine in the heart-lung preparation of dogs.
The log dose-response data (●——●) of 14 experiments on the HLP of normal dogs (Krayer and Ourisson, 1954), (× – – ×) of the experiments of table 1 on the HLP of dogs pretreated with reserpine, 0.5 mg/kg intraperitoneally 3 days and 2 days before experiment.

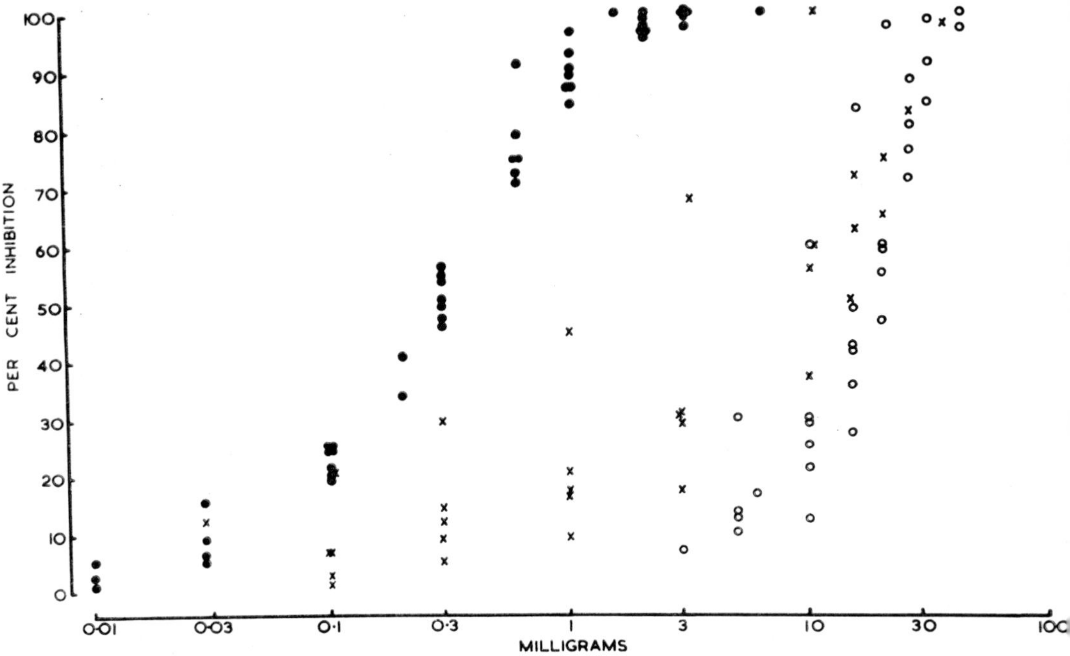

FIG. 3. The antiaccelerator action of reserpine in the heart-lung preparation of dogs injected with 0.5 mg/kg of reserpine 3 days and 2 days prior to experiment.

Comparison with the antiaccelerator action of veratramine and of reserpine in the HLP of normal dogs. Abscissae, dose of antiaccelerator agent in mg. Ordinates, decrease in heart rate expressed as percentage of the maximal cardioacceleration following ephedrine (see text). ×, reserpine on hearts depleted of intrinsic catechol amines; ●, veratramine on normal hearts (from Krayer and Ourisson, 1954); ○, reserpine on normal hearts (from Krayer and Fuentes, 1958).

The rate was maintained in the other two experiments.

The antiaccelerator action of reserpine in the HLP of pretreated dogs. In the experiments of table 1, after ephedrine had caused its maximal cardioacceleration, the antiaccelerator action of reserpine was tested by injecting successive and increasing doses of reserpine at intervals of 10 minutes.

Reduction of the heart rate was observed with 0.1 to 50 mg reserpine. Since the heart rate had already fallen slightly in 3 experiments it was not always possible to assess accurately the antiaccelerator effect of the smaller doses of reserpine, but doses of 0.3 to 1 mg consistently reduced the rate. With further increases in dosage the heart rate was reduced in a series of steps as illustrated in the second part of figure 1, in the same way as in the observations of Krayer and Fuentes (1958) on the HLP of normal dogs.

Three experiments were terminated by failure of the heart muscle after 15 to 25 mg reserpine had been injected. In another experiment A-V rhythm developed after administration of 29 mg. The remaining HLP tolerated a dose of 50 mg reserpine which reduced the heart rate from 204 to 90 beats/min, 22 beats lower than the initial heart rate of the preparation.

The results are plotted in figure 3 where earlier data from normal dogs are included for comparison. The antagonistic effect of veratramine (Krayer and Ourisson, 1954) is shown on the left; of reserpine (Krayer and Fuentes, 1958) on the right. The more moderate doses, especially doses of less than 3 mg of reserpine, exert a greater antagonistic action on the hearts of pretreated than of normal dogs. In the final column of table 1 are entered the doses of reserpine causing 50% inhibition of acceleration (I_{50}), read for each experiment from a probit plot of the values of inhibition between 15% and 80%. The mean I_{50} dose was 6.0 mg of reserpine, estimated from a probit plot of the mean values of percentage inhibition. In the 6 similar experiments on the HLP of normal dogs, Krayer and Fuentes (1958) reported the mean I_{50} dose of reserpine to be 16.5 mg.

The negative chronotropic action of reserpine in the HLP of dogs pretreated with reserpine. When the antiaccelerator action of reserpine was being studied, the heart rate in 2 experiments was finally depressed by large doses of the drug to a level lower than the initial heart rate of the HLP before ephedrine had been injected. This suggested that reserpine exerted a rate-decreasing action in the absence of a cardioaccelerator drug, an action which had already been observed by Paasonen and Krayer (1958) as a slight decrease in rate after a dose of 3 mg of reserpine. Accordingly 3 experiments were carried out where reserpine action was tested after the initial heart rate had been established.

The dose of 3 mg reserpine reduced the rate from 153 to 142, 130 to 126 and 116 to 111, respectively. An additional dose of 7 mg in the second and in the third experiment caused a further reduction to 118 and 103, respectively, and in the third experiment an additional dose of 10 mg (to a total of 20 mg) lowered the rate to 96 beats/min. In order to establish the new rate levels approximately 30 minutes were required after each administration. In the third experiment myocardial failure ensued after a further dose of 3 mg (to a total of 24 mg) had been administered.

The negative chronotropic action of veratramine in the HLP of dogs pretreated with reserpine. Graded responses to increasing doses of veratramine were obtained in 5 experiments. The heart rate decreases caused by total cumulate doses of 0.1, 0.3, 1, 3 and 10 mg of veratramine are presented in table 2. As can be seen, a dose of 0.1 mg was effective in each experiment. While larger doses were increasingly effective in diminishing the heart rate, a dosage of 1 mg in 3 experiments and of 3 mg in one further experiment established characteristic irregularities of rhythm. These irregularities were similar to those caused by veratramine in earlier experiments on the HLP of normal dogs (Krayer *et al.*, 1955) and consisted of periodic faster runs of sinus rate lasting for several beats. As in the earlier experiments, the difference between these faster runs and the slower rate was about 10 to 15 beats/min. The heart rate immediately prior to the appearance of the irregular rhythm showed no consistent level, varying from 75 to 133 beats/min.

The rate-decreasing effect of veratramine developed rapidly and, with doses of 1 mg or more, maximal slowing was reached in 2 to 4 minutes, a time course similar to that found in experiments on the HLP of normal dogs.

TABLE 2

*Negative chronotropic action of veratramine in the heart-lung preparation of the dog pretreated with reserpine**

Initial Heart Rate†	Maximal Decrease in Heart Rate Corresponding to Cumulate Dose of Veratramine				
	0.1 mg	0.3 mg	1 mg	3 mg	10 mg
beats/min	*beats/min*				
162	20	29	27‡	27‡	27‡
152	9	18	32	39	47
111	2	4	8‡	10‡	10‡
119	6	19	44‡	48‡	48‡
141	4	9	25	28‡	28‡

* Reserpine, 0.5 mg/kg, was administered intraperitoneally 72 and again 48 hours prior to setting up the HLP.

† Temperature range in the 5 experiments: 38.4–39°C (av. 38.6°C).

‡ Irregular rhythm established. See text.

The mean decrease in heart rate following veratramine was compared with the mean decrease in heart rate found by Krayer *et al.* (1955) after like doses of veratramine in the HLP of normal dogs. The degree of slowing caused by pretreatment with 0.1 to 3 mg veratramine was not significantly different from that observed in normal dogs. In the earlier experiments the level of the initial heart rate was found to influence the action of veratramine on the heart; the decrease in heart rate was therefore expressed as a percentage of the initial heart rate. No significant difference was observed between the earlier and the present data expressed in this way.

DISCUSSION. Veratramine and reserpine cause slowing in the dog heart depleted of catechol amines by previous treatment with reserpine. Paasonen and Krayer (1958) established that such pretreatment with reserpine reduced the norepinephrine content of the right atrium, normally ranging from 0.89 to 1.62 μg/g, to amounts which were not detectable (less than 0.012 to 0.037 μg/g). The epinephrine content was also low, showing values less than 0.002 to 0.013 μg/g. Veratramine is therefore shown by the present results to exert a rate-decreasing action which is not appreciably altered by exhaustion of the measurable intrinsic catechol amines.

In earlier studies the rate-decreasing action of veratramine was assessed on the basis of its ability to antagonize the cardioacceleration caused by accelerans nerve stimulation, by epinephrine, norepinephrine or ephedrine. Krayer and van Maanen (1949) suggested that possibly this action of veratramine blocked the effect of the responsible sympathomimetic amines upon the pacemaker tissue.

Veratramine was shown to possess a substantial rate-decreasing action in the absence of extrinsic sympathomimetic amines in hearts disconnected from their adrenergic nervous supply in the HLP (Krayer *et al.*, 1955) and in the denervated cat heart (Kosterlitz *et al.*, 1955). Since the presence of sympathomimetic amines at the site of their chronotropic action might, as indicated by Krayer (1950), be partly responsible for maintaining the level of the initial heart rate, it was not then possible to judge whether the negative chronotropic effect could be attributed to antagonism to these amines. Although the possibility cannot be entirely excluded that undetectable but physiologically significant quantities of amines may still be acting at the pacemaker after reserpine pretreatment, the present results indicate, in our opinion, that the rate-decreasing action can be only slightly if at all dependent upon antagonism to sympathomimetic amines. This view gains support from the fact that a difference of only 11 beats/min is found between the initial heart rates of the HLP of pretreated and normal dogs, while the mean heart rate decrease following the optimal dose of veratramine is 32 beats/min.

Were the negative chronotropic action of veratramine caused by interference in the undoubtedly complex mechanism of impulse generation at a more fundamental stage than the receptor site for sympathomimetic amines, the over-all reduction of pacemaker activity could also antagonize the action of these accelerator drugs. Such a reduction in activity might be associated with inhibition of tissue respiration, an effect of veratramine which has been observed by Reiter (1950) on atrial tissue. The possibility of veratramine exhibiting a dual action has already been considered by Innes *et al.* (1956), namely a competitive antagonism as envisaged by Krayer (1950), responsible in part for the observed antiaccelerator action, and an independent negative chronotropic action such as has been reported in the present study.

In the normal HLP where the action of reserpine on the heart rate was studied by Krayer and Fuentes (1958), analysis of the rate-decreasing action was difficult since it is masked by an initial increase in rate which is adequately explained by the assumption that the drug causes the release of the store of catechol amines. The antiaccelerator action was examined after ephedrine had maximally increased the heart rate. This method of analysis necessarily involved antagonism not only to the effect of catechol amines normally present at the pacemaker, maintaining the initial heart rate, but also to the catechol amines released at the heart under the influence of the first dose of reserpine. In the absence of the complication of intrinsic sympathomimetic amines, the greater inhibition of cardioacceleration and the greater sensitivity to smaller doses of reserpine observed in the present investigation are not entirely unexpected. Additional factors, however, vitiate the comparison of these results, since the hearts of dogs treated with reserpine respond less to ephedrine and consequently in these experiments reserpine opposes a smaller degree of cardioacceleration caused by a larger dose of ephedrine.

Reserpine, like veratramine, exerts its rate-decreasing action also in the absence of catechol amines. Large doses of reserpine, in contrast to equivalent rate-decreasing doses of veratramine, greatly impair the force of contraction of the heart, and thus interfere with the maintenance of the HLP. The proper observation of the full extent of the negative chronotropic action is therefore precluded. Perhaps for this reason the irregularities of rhythm characteristic of maximal veratramine action have not been found with reserpine.

Although reserpine exhibits a distinct rate-decreasing action, the evidence does not favor the possibility that this action is responsible for the lower initial heart rate and for its lowered sensitivity to ephedrine. Using reserpine labelled with C^{14}, Sheppard *et al.* (1955) have shown that the heart muscle of rats attains its greatest concentration of reserpine less than 1 hour after injection and that little remains at the end of 6 hours. It therefore appears unlikely that reserpine would remain in the dog heart in sufficient amount to cause substantial effects 2 days after its latest administration. The lower initial rate can best be explained by the assumption that catechol amines near the pacemaker in the HLP of the normal dog exert a cardioaccelerator influence which is removed when the heart is depleted of these amines.

SUMMARY

Experiments were conducted on the heart-lung preparation (HLP) of dogs whose hearts had been depleted of catechol amines by injection of reserpine, 0.5 mg/kg, 3 and 2 days before experiment.

The initial heart rate is significantly lower than in the HLP of normal dogs. The sensitivity to the cardioaccelerator action of ephedrine is reduced. A 3 to 5 times larger dosage of ephedrine is required to obtain the maximal increase in heart rate; and this maximal increase is much less than that found in the HLP of normal dogs.

A definite rate-decreasing action of reserpine, masked in the HLP of normal dogs by the release of catechol amines, is shown in the depleted heart after doses of 3 to 20 mg. Measured against cardioacceleration evoked by ephedrine, the antiaccelerator potency of reserpine is greater in the HLP of reserpine-treated than of normal dogs; the mean I_{50} dose is reduced from 16.5 mg to 6.0 mg.

Veratramine has a negative chronotropic effect on the heart in the HLP depleted of catechol amines. The decrease in rate is not significantly less than in the HLP of normal dogs. The action must be regarded as distinct from an inhibition of the cardioaccelerator action of intrinsic norepinephrine and epinephrine.

ACKNOWLEDGMENTS. It is a pleasure to acknowledge the expert technical assistance given by Miss Brigitte Hofheinz and Mr. Werner Mosimann in the course of this investigation.

REFERENCES

INNES, I. R., KOSTERLITZ, H. W. AND KRAYER, O.: THIS JOURNAL **117:** 317, 1956.
INNES, I. R. AND KRAYER, O.: J. Physiol. **139:** 18P, 1957.
KOSTERLITZ, H. W., KRAYER, O. AND MATALLANA, A.: THIS JOURNAL **113:** 460, 1955.
KRAYER, O.: THIS JOURNAL **96:** 422, 1949.
KRAYER, O.: THIS JOURNAL **98:** 427, 1950.
KRAYER, O., ARORA, R. B. AND MEILMAN, E.: THIS JOURNAL **113:** 446, 1955.
KRAYER, O. AND BENFORADO, J. M.: Pflüg. Arch. ges. Physiol. **260:** 177, 1955.
KRAYER, O. AND FUENTES, J.: Fed. Proc. **15:** 709, 1956.
KRAYER, O. AND FUENTES, J.: THIS JOURNAL **123:** 145, 1958.
KRAYER, O. AND OURISSON, P.: THIS JOURNAL **112:** 341, 1954.
KRAYER, O. AND VAN MAANEN, E. F.: THIS JOURNAL **97:** 301, 1949.
PAASONEN, M. K. AND KRAYER, O.: Fed. Proc. **16:** 326, 1957.
PAASONEN, M. K. AND KRAYER, O.: THIS JOURNAL **123:** 153, 1958.
REITER, M.: THIS JOURNAL **99:** 132, 1950.
SHEPPARD, H., LUCAS, R. C. AND TSIEN, W. H.: Arch. int. Pharmacodyn. **103:** 256, 1955.

8083

CONCENTRATION OF FREE AND CONJUGATED MORPHINE IN BRAIN AND OTHER TISSUES OF TOLERANT AND NONTOLERANT RABBITS[1]

ROBERT SIMINOFF[2] AND PAUL R. SAUNDERS

Department of Pharmacology, School of Medicine, University of Southern California, Los Angeles, California

Received for publication May 29, 1958

Szerb and McCurdy (1956) have shown that the free morphine content of the brains of tolerant rats is significantly less than that of nontolerant animals 1 hour after the administration of a test dose of the drug. These authors used large intravenous doses of morphine, which produced respiratory arrest for more than 1 hour in normal animals and for several minutes in tolerant animals; such doses gave brain concentrations of the drug in the range of the analytical method used (3 μg/g of tissue or greater). No other adequate data are available on brain concentrations of morphine in tolerant as compared to nontolerant animals.

We have investigated this problem in rabbits, using smaller doses of drug so that respiratory arrest did not occur when the test dose was given to nontolerant animals; such a procedure is somewhat more comparable to the manner in which the drug is normally used. Such low doses of morphine required, however, that the sensitivity of existing analytical methods for morphine be increased in our experiments, because of the low concentrations in the brain. We have used a procedure which is in large part a combination of the methods of Fujimoto *et al.* (1954) and of Woods *et al.* (1954), with modifications to permit the determination of as little as 0.2 μg of morphine per g of brain. We have used this method to investigate the concentration of morphine in the brain, blood, liver and kidney of tolerant and nontolerant rabbits.

[1] This investigation was supported (in part) by research grant B-1252 from the National Institute of Neurological Diseases and Blindness, U. S. Public Health Service.

[2] This paper represents a portion of the research conducted by Robert Siminoff in partial fulfillment of requirements for the degree of Doctor of Philosophy in pharmacology.

METHODS. *Evaluation of response to morphine.* The action of morphine upon the rate of respiration was used as a measure of the effect of the drug. Unanesthetized male albino rabbits (average weight 3 kg) were tied to an animal board and the rate of respiration recorded by means of a lever attached to a thread sewn to the skin above the diaphragm. The rate attained a mean steady value of 165 per minute after about 30 minutes, at which point morphine sulfate was administered intraperitoneally and the effect upon the rate determined.

Development and evaluation of tolerance. Rabbits were given 5 mg/kg of morphine intraperitoneally (calculated as free base) daily for approximately 2 weeks. The dose was then increased to 10 mg/kg daily for 2 weeks, and finally to 20 mg/kg daily. Complete tolerance to the respiratory effect of the latter dose eventually occurred; drug administration was continued at this level for at least an additional 2 weeks thereafter (average total period of drug administration was 100 days).

Tissue concentration of morphine in tolerant and nontolerant rabbits. A group of normal rabbits was given 20 mg/kg of morphine intraperitoneally and

TABLE 1

Depression of respiratory rate after administration of morphine (20 mg/kg)

Time after Administration of Drug	% Depression of Respiratory Rate	
	Nontolerant*	Tolerant*
Hr		
0.5	88 (4)	0 (3)
1	93 (4)	0 (3)
2	91 (4)	0 (3)
4	62 (2)	0 (3)
8	15 (1)	0 (2)
24	0 (1)	0 (2)

* Mean values. Number of animals given in parentheses.

TABLE 2

Concentration (μg/g wet wt.) of free and conjugated morphine after intraperitoneal administration (20 mg/kg)*

Tissue			Time after Administration of Drug (Hours)†				
			0.5	1	2	4	8
Brain‡	Free	Tolerant	1.4 ± 0.3 (3)§	1.9 ± 0.1 (3)	0.9 ± 0.1 (3)	0.7(0.6–0.8) (3)	0.35(0.3–0.4) (2)
		Nontolerant	1.5 ± 0.2 (4)	1.8 ± 0.4 (4)	1.1 ± 0.2 (4)	0.9(0.8–1.0) (2)	0.2 (1)
Blood	Free	Tolerant	3.6 ± 0.1	4.1 ± 0.2	2.2 ± 0.1	0.3(0.2–0.4)	0.25(0.2–0.3)
		Nontolerant	3.6 ± 0.4	4.5 ± 0.1	1.8 ± 0.9	0.3(0.2–0.4)	<0.1
	Conj.	Tolerant	0.6 ± 0.2	4.6 ± 0.1	3.3 ± 0.8	0.5(0.4–0.5)	0.25(0.2–0.3)
		Nontolerant	0.3 ± 0.1	4.2 ± 0.2	3.8 ± 0.8	0.5(0.3–0.7)	0.2
Liver	Free	Tolerant	0.5 ± 0.2	4.5 ± 0.2	0.6 ± 0.1	0.4(0.3–0.6)	0.25(0.2–0.3)
		Nontolerant	0.7 ± 0.5	5.2 ± 1.3	0.7 ± 0.3	0.4(0.3–0.5)	<0.1
	Conj.	Tolerant	2.1 ± 0.1	0.9 ± 0.3	1.3 ± 0.1	0.9(0.9)	0.3(0.2–0.4)
		Nontolerant	1.9 ± 0.3	0.5 ± 0.3	1.4 ± 0.3	0.95(0.9–1.0)	0.4
Kidney	Free	Tolerant	17.4 ± 2.6	25.0 ± 1.6	12.0 ± 1.0	0.7(0.5–0.9)	0.5(0.4–0.6)
		Nontolerant	17.8 ± 0.2	25.2 ± 4.2	12.1 ± 2.3	0.6(0.5–0.7)	0.3
	Conj.	Tolerant	44.9 ± 0.3	58.9 ± 3.9	38.7 ± 0.6	12.1(11.9–12.3)	3.8(3.6–4.1)
		Nontolerant	44.0 ± 1.1	60.5 ± 4.2	38.2 ± 0.3	12.4(11.9–13.0)	4.0

* Mean values. Standard deviations are given following the values for 0.5, 1 and 2 hours, and the range for 4 and 8 hours.

† Analyses carried out on 2 tolerant animals and 1 nontolerant animal 24 hours after administration of morphine indicated a concentration of less than 0.1 μg/g in all tissues.

‡ No conjugated morphine detected in brain.

§ Number of animals given in parentheses (same animals used for analyses of blood, liver and kidney).

the degree of depression of respiratory rate determined. The animals were then killed by exsanguination at varied times after administration of the drug and the tissues removed for analysis for free and total morphine (see below). Tolerance was produced in a second group of rabbits as described above, and the test dose (20 mg/kg) was administered 24 hours after the last regular daily dose. The respiratory rate was measured, the animal killed and the tissues analyzed as in the normal rabbits.

Method for determination of free and conjugated morphine. The method used was essentially that of Woods *et al.* (1954), except that extraction was carried out with n-butanol and then chloroform (instead of ethyl acetate), in a manner similar to that of Fujimoto *et al.* (1954); in addition, considerably larger amounts of tissue were used with resultant higher concentrations of morphine in the final solution used for spectrophotometric determination.

Ten g (wet weight) of brain, liver, or kidney was homogenized with 70 ml of 0.5 N HCl in a VirTis Model 23 homogenizer, or 10 ml of blood stirred with the same volume of acid. Forty ml of 15% trichloroacetic acid (w/v) was added, and the mixture stirred and then filtered through Whatman #7 paper. For the determination of total (free plus conjugated) morphine, 5 ml of concentrated HCl was added to a 50-ml aliquot of filtered homogenate and the solution autoclaved for 30 minutes at 15 pounds pressure. To the stirred solution cooled in an ice-bath were added slowly 2 ml of 40% $NaHSO_3$ (w/v), 55 ml of 16 N KOH and 75 ml of n-butanol.[3] For the determination of free morphine, a 50-ml aliquot (not autoclaved) was treated as above with $NaHSO_3$, KOH, and n-butanol except that only 50 ml of 16 N KOH was used. After stirring for 10 minutes, the mixture was placed in a separatory funnel, and the separated n-butanol layer transferred to a second funnel. The extraction was repeated with an additional 75 ml of n-butanol. The combined

[3] n-Butanol and chloroform were analytical reagent grade, passed through a silica gel-alumina column and then distilled.

n-butanol extract was then extracted twice with 75 ml of N H_2SO_4 each time. One drop of 0.25% phenolphthalein was added to the combined acid extracts and 16 N KOH added to a pink color. One g of solid $NaHCO_3$ (which should discharge the pink color) was added, and the neutralized acid solution extracted with 75 ml of 80% chloroform-20% n-butanol mixture[3] while stirring for 10 minutes. The entire contents were poured into a separatory funnel and the solvent layer drained off into a second funnel. The extraction was repeated with an additional 75 ml of mixed solvent. The solvent layers were combined and extracted twice with 10 ml-portions of 0.5 N NaOH, which was poured into a 50-ml glass-stoppered centrifuge tube. One ml of 40% $NaHSO_3$ and 10 ml of 2% *p*-nitrobenzoyl chloride in ethylene dichloride (Woods *et al.*, 1954) were added. The subsequent procedure was as described by Woods *et al.* (1954), except that the final ethylene dichloride solution was shaken with 3.0 ml of N H_2SO_4 instead of 4.0 ml of N HCl. The optical density at 510 mμ was determined in a 1-cm cell with a Beckman model DU spectrophotometer. Duplicate reagent blanks and morphine standards were run each day.

A low tissue blank (compared against the reagent blank) of average optical density 0.003 was obtained for approximately 1.5 g of brain per ml of the final acid solution used for the spectrophotometric determination, as compared to a value of 0.005 to 0.010 for less than 150 mg of tissue per ml of final solution in the method of Woods *et al.* (1954). Experiments in which known amounts of morphine were added to brain samples gave recoveries of $100 \pm 13\%$ (S.D.) at a level of 0.2 μg of morphine per g of tissue. Comparable recoveries were obtained with larger amounts of morphine.

Woods (1957) has recently modified his method in order to determine the small amounts of morphine in brain, and was able to determine 0.5 to 1.0 μg of drug per g of tissue, with a recovery of $70 \pm 10\%$ of added morphine.

RESULTS. Table 1 summarizes the data on the degree of respiratory depression produced by morphine as a function of time after injection. In the normal rabbits the depression was marked within 10 minutes and reached a maximum in about 30 minutes (no further significant change in rate occurred during the following 1.5 hours). The respiratory rate of tolerant rabbits was unaffected by the same dose of the drug.

The morphine concentrations (free and conjugated) of the various tissues are given in table 2. It is clear that there is no appreciable difference in the distribution of morphine in the tolerant and nontolerant rabbit.

DISCUSSION. We have found that the concentration of free morphine in the brain of tolerant rabbits at various times after the administration of a test dose of the drug does not differ from that in nontolerant animals. Szerb and McCurdy (1956) found that the value in tolerant rats given large doses was significantly lower than in nontolerant animals 60 minutes after administration, although there was no appreciable difference 10 and 180 minutes after the drug was given. It is apparent from our results that the phenomenon of tolerance cannot be explained on the basis of an altered distribution in the brains of tolerant animals.

Furthermore, we found no difference in the concentration of free or bound morphine in the liver, kidney, or blood of tolerant as compared with nontolerant rabbits. Woods (1954) came to the same conclusion from his studies with rats and dogs, as did Mellett and Woods (1956) in their work with monkeys.

SUMMARY

Existing methods for the determination of morphine in tissues have been modified to permit the determination of the low concentrations of drug present in the brain after the administration of moderate doses. The method has been applied to a study of the concentration of free morphine in the brain and of free and bound drug in the liver, kidney and blood of tolerant and nontolerant rabbits.

No difference was found in the concentration of morphine in tolerant as compared to nontolerant rabbits, at intervals of ½, 1, 2, 4 and 8 hours after intraperitoneal administration of the drug.

REFERENCES

FUJIMOTO, J. M., WAY, E. L. AND HINE, C. H.: J. Lab. clin. Med. **44:** 627, 1954.
MELLETT, L. B. AND WOODS, L. A.: THIS JOURNAL **116:** 77, 1956.
SZERB, J. C. AND MCCURDY, D. H.: THIS JOURNAL **118:** 446, 1956.
WOODS, L. A., COCHIN, J., FORNEFELD, E. G. AND SEEVERS, M. H.: THIS JOURNAL **111:** 64, 1954.
WOODS, L. A.: THIS JOURNAL **112:** 158, 1954.
WOODS, L. A.: THIS JOURNAL **120:** 58, 1957.

8084

ACUTE PHARMACOLOGICAL STUDIES OF SOME NEW MORPHINE DERIVATIVES[1]

RONALD OKUN AND HENRY W. ELLIOTT

Departments of Pharmacology and Experimental Therapeutics and Anesthesia, University of California Medical Center, San Francisco 22, California

Received for publication June 21, 1958

Modifications of the C-ring of the morphine molecule in the neighborhood of the alcoholic hydroxyl group have resulted in a number of potent analgetics some of which have achieved a degree of clinical acceptance. For example, dihydromorphinone (Dilaudid) and 5-methyldihydromorphinone (Metopon) have enjoyed fairly extensive clinical usage. Related compounds including dihydrodesoxymorphine, 6-methyldihydromorphine and 6-methyl-Δ-6-desoxymorphine, have been potentially useful but have either been difficult to prepare or have shown no real advantages over morphine. Rapoport and coworkers were intrigued by the structure-action relationships of these compounds and noted that all have ring C either reduced or methylated or both and the hydroxyl at C_6 is absent. They succeeded in preparing several new structural variants of this type including morphinone, 6-methylmorphine (Rapoport, Baker and Reist, 1957), 6-methyldihydrodesoxymorphine, 6-methylenedihydrodesoxymorphine and 6-methyl-7-hydroxydihydrodesoxymorphine (Chadha and Rapoport, 1957).

This report presents the results of a study of the analgetic properties, acute toxicity and effects on gastrointestinal motility in mice of these 5 compounds. 6-methylenedihydrodesoxymorphine appeared most promising; therefore it was studied in dogs for analgetic, cardiovascular, respiratory and gastrointestinal effects.

METHODS. The mice used in this study were Swiss strain albinos of both sexes maintained on a standard laboratory diet and weighing 14 to 36 grams.

The names and formulas of the drugs used are shown in figure 1. Henceforth, they will be referred to by the assigned numbers shown in figure 1 (*e.g.*, morphinone = compound #2).

The morphine derivatives were supplied to us as chemically pure free bases which were converted to acetates by the addition of one mole of acetic acid per mole of base. The solutions were stored at 5°C in brown bottles until used. Doses given were calculated as free bases.

"Analgesia" in mice was tested by the method of D'Amour and Smith (1941). The animals were secured in ventilated glass tubes and their protruding tails were blackened with charcoal. Control reaction times to a standard heat stimulus were determined at least 3 times, once every 15 minutes just prior to injection of the drug. Average control time was 5 ± 2 seconds. The reaction to the thermal stimulus was tested in each mouse every 15 minutes after subcutaneous injection of the drug until the reaction time was within 2 standard deviations of the control time and remained there for two separate recordings. A significant degree of "analgesia" was considered to be present when a delay in reaction time of at least 2 standard deviations from the mean of each animal's control reaction time occurred within 30 minutes after injection of the drug. If no reaction occurred within 15 seconds, the stimulus was stopped.

Acute toxicity (within 24 hours) was determined by subcutaneous injection of mice with graded doses of the compounds.

The ED_{50} (analgesia) and LD_{50} for all compounds and morphine were estimated by the method of Litchfield and Wilcoxon (1949). The results were compared to those obtained for morphine under identical conditions. Temporal variations were partly controlled by running morphine controls at random intervals in all studies. At least 25 mice per dose level per compound were used in studying analgesia and toxicity except for the toxicity studies on compound #4 in which 5 mice per dose level were used.

Gastrointestinal motility changes were observed

[1] This investigation was supported in part by research grant B-570 from the Division of Research Grants of the National Institutes of Health, U. S. Public Health Service; the work was carried out during the tenure of a Lederle Medical Faculty Award to H. W. Elliott.

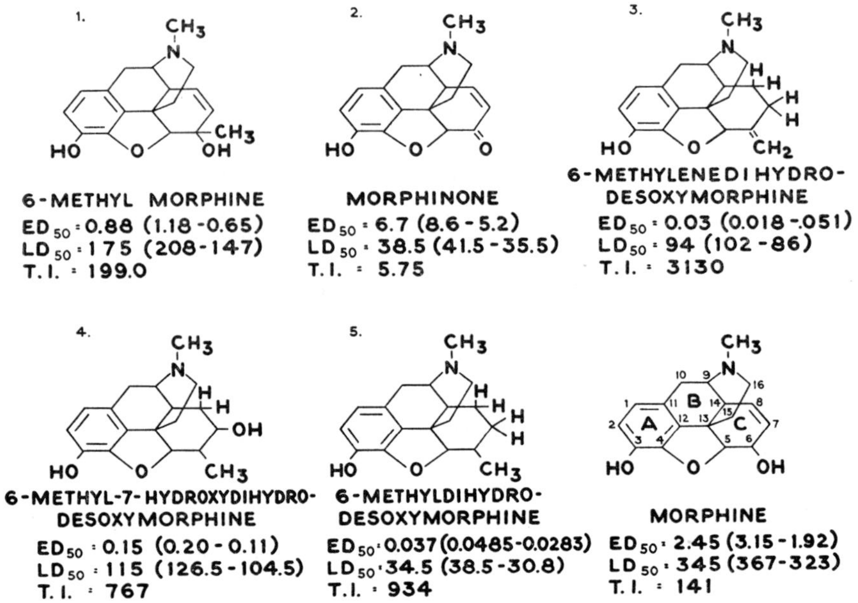

FIG. 1. Structural formulas of the compounds used in these studies with ED_{50} and LD_{50} values for mice in mg/kg.

Ninety-five % confidence limits in parenthesis. T.I. = calculated therapeutic index.

in mice by the method of Van Arsdel and David (1953). The mice were fasted over-night, injected subcutaneously with the ED_{50} (analgesia) dose of a compound and one-half hour later anesthetized briefly with ether. A PE #90 polyethylene catheter was passed into the stomach through which 0.25 ml of a 5% carbon black in 5% gum tragacanth solution was introduced into the stomach. One-half hour after the "meal," the mice were killed with ether, and the stomach and small intestine were removed and suspended with a constant weight for 30 seconds. The distance the front of the meal traveled down the small intestine was measured as well as the length of the small intestine from the pylorus to the ileocecal valve. The percentage of small intestine traversed by the meal was then calculated.

Dogs used in this study were mongrels of both sexes, weighing 7.2 to 16.0 kg, maintained on a standard laboratory diet.

Three dogs were injected subcutaneously with doses of compound #3 of 0.01, 0.015 and 0.02 mg/kg and compared to 3 dogs injected similarly with 4 mg/kg of morphine (sulfate) for changes in behavior, response to footpad and skin pinching, changes in respiratory rate and amplitude, pulse, vomiting, defecation, rectal temperature, pupillary size and response to nalorphine.

Fifteen dogs were anesthetized with sodium pentobarbital intraperitoneally at varying doses (25 to 50 mg/kg). The dogs were then intubated and after a stable basal state was attained, respiratory changes were measured after injection of compound #3 and compared to the preinjection stable state by the method of Gaddum (1941).

Different doses of nalorphine were injected by the same route as compound #3 in all dogs at varying times after injection of the drug, depending on when a new stable state had been reached after drug injection. Two dogs were similarly treated with 6 mg/kg of morphine (sulfate) and nalorphine.

In 4 dogs under sodium pentobarbital anesthesia the left common carotid artery was dissected free and cannulated. The cannula was connected to a strain-gauge transducer (pressure range 0 to 75 cm Hg) and arterial pressure recorded by means of a Grass pen writing polygraph. The terminal ileum was located through a small midline abdominal incision and a #12 mushroom catheter was inserted 8 inches proximally up the ileum. The bowel wall was closed around the stem of the catheter which was connected to a strain-gauge transducer (pressure range 0 to 5 cm Hg) and pressure changes recorded by means of the same pen writing polygraph. The femoral vein was exposed for injection. Basal records of the blood pressure, pulse, pulse pressure and small bowel action were taken. Compound #3 was injected intravenously and continuous records obtained.

Nalorphine was injected intravenously at various times depending on the changes noted and records obtained.

RESULTS. All compounds except morphinone (#2) were more potent analgetics, milligram for milligram, than morphine. In mice 6-methylenedihydrodesoxymorphine (#3) is 82 times as powerful; 6-methyldihydrodesoxymorphine (#5) is 61 times as powerful; 6-methyl-7-hydroxydihydrodesoxymorphine (#4) is 16 times as powerful; 6-methylmorphine (#1) is 2 to 3 times as powerful and morphinone (#2) is less than half as powerful as morphine (figure 1). However, in mice, compound #1 is twice as toxic as morphine, compound #4 is 3 times as toxic, compound #3 is 3 to 4 times as toxic, compound #2 is 9 times as toxic and compound #5 is 10 times as toxic (figure 1).

The resulting Therapeutic Index (T.I.) of each compound and morphine (figure 1) suggests their range of safety. All compounds but compound #2 have greater T.I.'s than morphine; compound #3 has a T.I. of 3130, which is 22 times as great as the T.I. of 141 for morphine.

All 5 compounds produced analgesia after subcutaneous injection within 15 minutes compared to 30 minutes for morphine. Duration of analgesia was proportional to dose. Within the dose range studied, morphine had the longest duration of analgesia (60 to 150 minutes) followed by #2 (90 minutes) > #3 (60 to 90 minutes) > #1 (75 minutes) > #5 (60 to 75 minutes) > #4 (30 to 90 minutes).

Toxicity occurred latest with compound #2 followed by morphine > #1 > #3 > #4 > #5. Approximate time of death ranged from 1 to 10 hours for compound #2 down to 10 to 60 minutes for compound #5. Again signs of toxicity appeared sooner as doses were increased. Toxicity was manifested by convulsions in all cases except with compound #2, which appeared to depress the mice.

Because of the known ability of morphine to inhibit gastrointestinal motility these compounds were tested for this property and the results compared to those obtained with morphine. With the method used, compounds #3 and #5 accelerated, compounds #1 and #4 had little effect on and compound #2 and morphine significantly slowed passage of the standard meal (table 1). Morphine was by far the most potent inhibitor of gastrointestinal motility.

TABLE 1

Gastrointestinal motility studies in mice at ED_{50}

Drug	No. of Mice	% of Small Intestine Traversed by Meal		Comparison to Control
		Mean ± S.E.	Range	
Control	23	54 ± 2.6	37–84	—
#1	12	47 ± 4.0	21–69	no significant slowing
#2	12	40 ± 4.7	21–86	significant slowing (P = >0.01)
#3	12	68 ± 3.1	48–82	significant acceleration (P = <0.01)
#4	12	49 ± 3.2	38–79	no significant slowing
#5	12	63 ± 4.0	41–92	questionable acceleration (P = 0.07)
Morphine	12	25 ± 2.0	12–35	significant slowing (P = <0.01)

Compound #3 appeared to be the most promising analgetic and was further studied in dogs. An average dose of one-half the ED_{50} for mice produced analgesia in dogs as determined by response to toe pad and skin pinching. Compared to morphine at 4 mg/kg (3 dogs), compound #3 in doses of 0.01 to 0.02 mg/kg (3 dogs) had the following effects: equally profound analgesia of shorter duration, lighter sedation, equal degrees of bradycardia, no vomiting, defecation or salivation, less hypothermia and less miosis. The animals given morphine were depressed for 4 to 5 hours whereas the animals given compound #3 recovered in 2 hours. Analgesia after morphine lasted 200 to 260 minutes compared to 40 to 90 minutes after compound #3.

Respiratory changes after 0.015 to 0.02 mg/kg of compound #3 were inconsistent. Whereas the minute volume of 1 dog given 0.015 mg/kg dropped to 30% of control, the minute volume of another dog given 0.03 mg/kg increased to 150%. Similarly, the minute volume of another dog rose to 133% after 0.05 mg/kg but 2 other dogs were little affected by 0.10 and 0.20 mg/kg. Intraperitoneal injection seemed to produce fewer respiratory changes possibly because of absorption into the portal blood supply and detoxification by the liver.

Nalorphine following compound #3 usually

increased minute volume but the results were indefinite due to the inconsistent effects of the small doses of compound #3 on ventilation. Consequently, 4 dogs were given 0.5 to 1.0 mg/kg of compound #3, which consistently decreased the minute volume as shown in table 2. An equal dose of nalorphine consistently increased ventilation immediately, proving that nalorphine can antagonize the respiratory depressant effects of compound #3 (table 2).

TABLE 2

Decrease in minute volume of dogs produced by compound #3 i.v. and its reversal by equal doses of nalorphine given after the ten minute measurement; changes expressed as % of control (100%)

Minutes	Dog			
	1	2	3	4
Dose of #3	0.5 mg/kg	0.5 mg/kg	0.5 mg/kg	1.0 mg/kg
0	100%	100%	100%	100%
5	47%	48%	57%	82%
10	61%	66%	79%	77%
Dose of nalorphine	0.5 mg/kg	0.5 mg/kg	0.5 mg/kg	1.0 mg/kg
1 (after nalorphine)	125%	—	107%	—
5	103%	124%	139%	162%
10	105%	124%	128%	134%

Four dogs were studied for blood pressure, pulse and gastrointestinal changes after intravenous doses of compound #3. Increases in intestinal tone and wave amplitudes were found with doses as small as 0.1 μg/kg (figure 2). These changes lasted only 5 to 10 minutes. Transient bradycardia occurred inconsistently with 1.0 μg/kg (figure 3). Consistently, doses of 25 μg/kg caused bradycardia which lasted 15 to 30 seconds. Doses of 100 μg/kg resulted in a greater pulse pressure with diastolic decrease and slight systolic decrease which lasted for 5 to 30 minutes. Nalorphine did not consistently reverse these changes.

DISCUSSION. The results with mice indicate that saturation of the C-ring of the morphine molecule combined with methylene or methyl substitution at C_6 increases analgetic potency more than toxicity. Thus, 6-methylenedihydrodesoxymorphine, 6-methyl-7-hydroxydihydrodesoxymorphine and 6-methyldihydrodesoxymorphine are 16 to 80 times more potent than morphine and possess therapeutic indices 5 to 22 times as great. On the other hand, 6-methylmorphine with its unsaturated C-ring is only moderately more active than morphine and shows

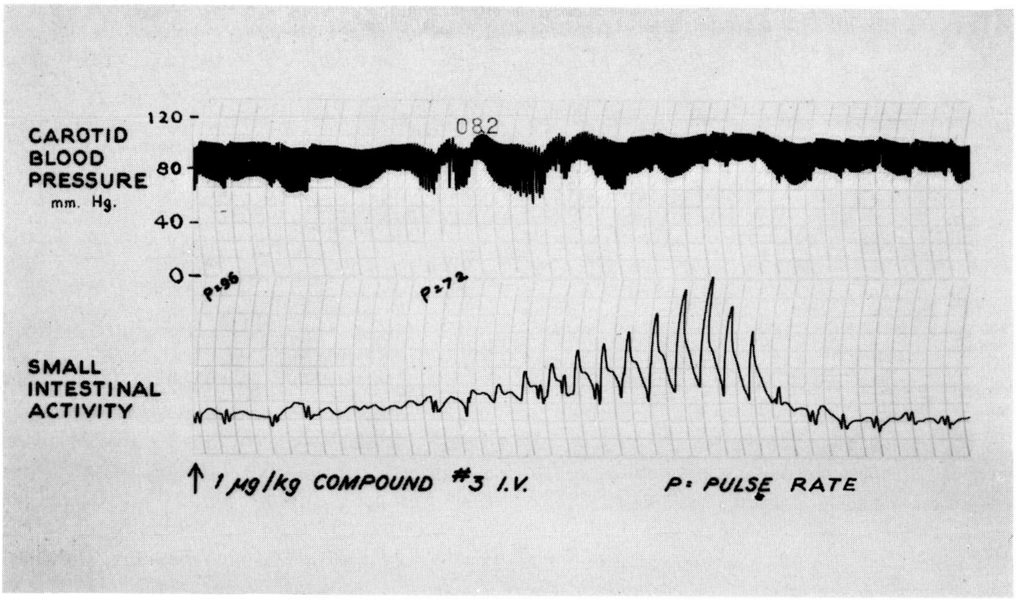

FIG. 2. Changes in blood pressure, pulse rate and ilial motility in a dog due to 1 μg/kg of compound #3. Each division equals 10 seconds.

little improvement in its therapeutic index. Since these compounds are briefer in action than morphine, slightly different indices might result if determined on the basis of dosage necessary to ensure equivalent continuous analgesia.

In addition to their increased potency and safety as compared to morphine, gastrointestinal motility is increased by compounds #3 and #5 and is unaffected by #1 and #4. This is in marked contrast to the slowing produced by morphine and if this proves true for man these compounds will have a distinct advantage over morphine.

Morphinone (#2) behaved quite differently from the methylated compounds. It was less potent and more toxic than morphine and decreased gastrointestinal motility. However, it killed by respiratory depression rather than by convulsions and its high toxicity may be due to inability to self-antagonize its depressant effects. The proportion of depressant and stimulant properties varies among the relatives of morphine and morphinone may be deficient in the latter. Thus, even though the findings do not appear as favorable as with the other compounds, morphinone may be a more specific analgetic.

Preliminary studies in dogs indicate that compound #3 produces analgesia in the 0.01 to 0.02 mg/kg dose range as compared to 1.25 to 2.0 mg/kg for morphine (Amsler, 1921) (Koll and Reffert, 1938). When compared to morphine at 4.0 mg/kg fewer side-effects were noted but the duration of action was much shorter. It was necessary to increase the dose to 0.5 mg/kg to produce consistent respiratory depression as measured by minute volume determinations and in all cases the depression was reversed by nalorphine. This demonstration of antagonism by nalorphine confirms the belief that this new agent has the qualitative if not the quantitative effects of morphine.

Studies of gastrointestinal motility in dogs seem to confirm the findings in mice inasmuch as doses as low as 0.1 μg/kg briefly increased motility. Similar changes in motility have been observed after 50 μg/kg of morphine by Lamid and Meyers (unpublished data) but this has been followed by depression of activity. Further work will be necessary to establish differences between the 2 agents in this regard.

In short, 6-methylenedihydrodesoxymorphine and related compounds show promise as very potent, short-acting narcotic analgetics which may prove to have minimal side-effects in analgetic doses. These properties should make the drugs useful for preanesthetic medication or as constituents of balanced anesthesia. However, if their duration of action is too short in man they will not be useful for control of pain unless the side-effects are truly minimal.

SUMMARY

Five new morphine derivatives were studied in mice with regard to analgesia, acute toxicity and gastrointestinal inhibition. 6-methylmorphine, 6-methylenedihydrodesoxymorphine, 6-methyl-7-hydroxydihydrodesoxymorphine, and 6-methyldihydrodesoxymorphine are more potent and have higher therapeutic indices than morphine. Morphinone is less potent and has a lower therapeutic index. All compounds cause less gastrointestinal motility inhibition in mice.

6 - methylenedihydrodesoxymorphine was studied in dogs with regard to analgesia, sedation, cardiovascular and gastrointestinal changes, hypothermia, miosis, and reversal of actions by nalorphine. The findings suggest it may cause analgesia in doses which have minimal side-effects.

Acknowledgment. The authors wish to thank Dr. F. H. Meyers and Dr. Sofian Lamid for their help with the ileal motility studies and Dr. T. K. Adler for her assistance with the initial screening of the compounds for analgetic activity.

REFERENCES

Amsler, C.: Arch. exp. Path. Pharmak. **90:** 257, 1921.

Chadha, M. S. and Rapoport, H.: J. Amer. chem. Soc. **79:** 5730, 1957.

D'Amour, R. E. and Smith, D. L.: This Journal **72:** 74, 1941.

Gaddum, J. H.: J. Physiol. **99:** 257, 1941.

Koll, W. and Reffert, H.: Arch. exp. Path. Pharmak. **190:** 687, 1938.

Litchfield, J. T. and Wilcoxon, F.: This Journal **96:** 99, 1949.

Rapoport, H., Baker, D. R. and Reist, H. N.: J. org. Chem. **22:** 1489, 1957.

Van Arsdel, W. C. and David, N. A.: Fed. Proc. **12:** 375, 1953.

8085

ANALGESIC POTENCY OF NORMORPHINE IN PATIENTS WITH POSTOPERATIVE PAIN[1]

LOUIS LASAGNA AND THOMAS J. DE KORNFELD

Departments of Medicine (Division of Clinical Pharmacology) and Pharmacology and Experimental Therapeutics, Johns Hopkins University School of Medicine, and the Department of Anesthesiology, Baltimore City Hospitals, Baltimore, Maryland

Received for publication July 21, 1958

Most of the available data on normorphine suggest that this compound is a less potent analgesic than morphine, with potency ratios (normorphine/morphine) variably reported as: $\frac{1}{18}$ (subcutaneously administered, in mice, Eddy *et al.*, 1956), $\frac{1}{10}$ to $\frac{1}{8}$ (in rats; Orahovats and Lehman, 1958), $\frac{1}{7}$ (intraperitoneally administered, in mice; Miller and Anderson, 1954), and $\frac{1}{2}$ (subcutaneously or intramuscularly administered, in dogs; Orahovats and Lehman, 1958). Only the latter authors have reported data in which normorphine is as potent as morphine in producing analgesia, *viz.*, some experiments in which the intravenous route was used in dogs.

Published data for humans have been obtained only in volunteers from a population imprisoned for narcotic offenses (Fraser *et al.*, 1958). These studies indicate that 30 mg (single) doses of normorphine produced less sedation, miosis and vomiting, and less depression of respiration and rectal temperature, than did equal doses of morphine. Repeated doses of normorphine, however, led to marked cumulation of sedative effects, so that under such conditions (*i.e.*, chronic administration) normorphine became a more potent drug than morphine. Normorphine is, like morphine, an addicting drug, since it is capable of suppressing the morphine abstinence syndrome, since an abstinence syndrome is seen after abrupt withdrawal of normorphine, and since nalorphine can precipitate an "abstinence" syndrome when administered to volunteers given repeated doses of normorphine (Fraser *et al.*, 1958).

The present studies were undertaken to measure the clinical analgesic potency of normorphine, utilizing patients suffering from postoperative pain.

METHODS. Patients were selected from the surgical wards of the Baltimore City Hospitals. They ranged in age from 15 to 62, with a mean age of 36 years. Forty females and 29 males constituted the total sample. The types of operations included: hysterectomy, herniorraphy, appendectomy, lobectomy, cholecystectomy, vein stripping, hemorrhoidectomy, thyroidectomy, suprapubic prostatectomy and a variety of orthopedic procedures. Approximately one-quarter of the group required only 1 dose of narcotic postoperatively, another 25% needed 2 doses, about one-third of the patients required 3 or 4 doses, and the remaining 16% needed 5 to 13 doses during the period of observation, *i.e.*, the first 48 hours after surgery.

The patients were selected by one physician (T. De K.), who wrote orders for pain relief, prescribing alternate doses of subcutaneous medication, identified only by code letters. In the first group of patients, 10 mg of morphine[2] were alternated with 10 mg of normorphine. In the second and third groups of patients, 10 mg of morphine were alternated with 20 and 40 mg of normorphine, respectively. In approximately half of the patients in any group the standard (morphine) was administered first, and in the other half of the patients normorphine was given first. Neither patients nor interviewing technicians were aware of the nature of the medications. Medication was administered only on request of the patient for pain relief, and no medication could be given less than 2 hours after the preceding medication. Patients were interviewed prior to injection, and at intervals of ½, 1, 2, 3 and 4 hours after injection. At these interviews, patients were awakened[3]

[1] This investigation was supported in part by a grant (D57-4) awarded by the Committee on Drug Addiction and Narcotics, National Academy of Sciences National Research Council, from funds contributed by a group of interested pharmaceutical manufacturers, and by a grant (B865–C2) from the National Institutes of Health.

[2] Weights of drugs refer to the salts of the two compounds, *i.e.*, morphine sulfate and normorphine hydrochloride.

[3] Of the first 45 interviews where patients had to

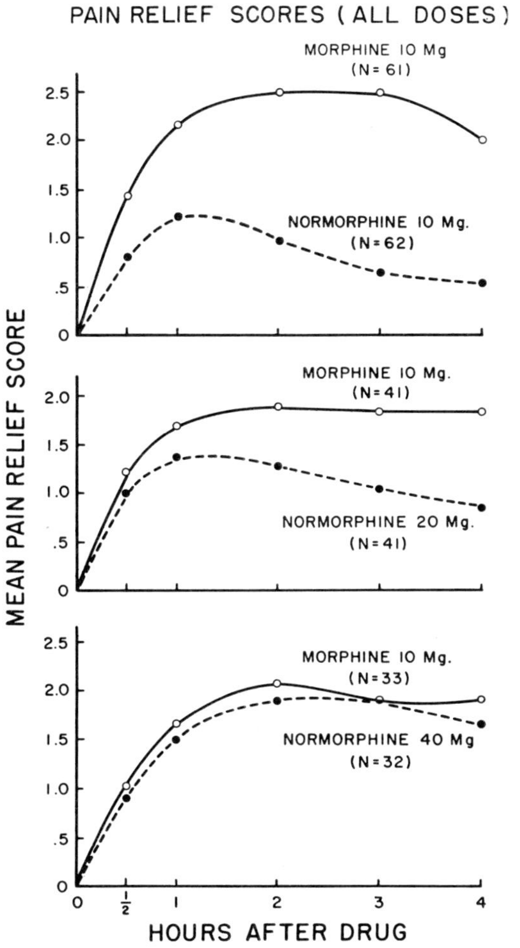

FIG. 1. Mean pain relief scores for all doses administered.

if necessary and asked to categorize their pain as absent, slight, moderate, severe, or very severe. A decrease in pain from predrug level to the next level was counted as a score of +1, a drop of two levels as +2, etc. If no change occurred a score of zero was given, and if pain increased over the predrug level (a relatively rare phenomenon) a negative score was given. If a medication was administered less than 4 hours after a previous medication, scores of zero were automatically counted for whatever interviews were thus ruled out for the earlier drug.

be awakened for questioning after a dose of drug, only one-third of the patients were completely free of pain, and one-fourth of the group had pain that was at least moderately severe. It is thus obvious that any assumption about degree of pain present in a sleeping patient is likely to result in a loss of accuracy. Keats (1956) has reported similar experiences.

RESULTS. The data are presented in a variety of ways:

Mean pain relief scores for all doses administered. (See figure 1.) Here each dose contributes equally to the score, but some patients contribute considerably more than others, since the number of doses administered to a given patient varied from 1 to 13.

Mean "individual" pain relief scores. (See figure 2.) Here each patient contributes equally to the total score, since a mean score is computed at each interview point for each drug for each patient (regardless of how many times drug was given) and then a mean of these average scores is calculated.

Mean pain relief scores for first doses only. (See figure 3.) The purpose of this score is to eliminate possible order effects.

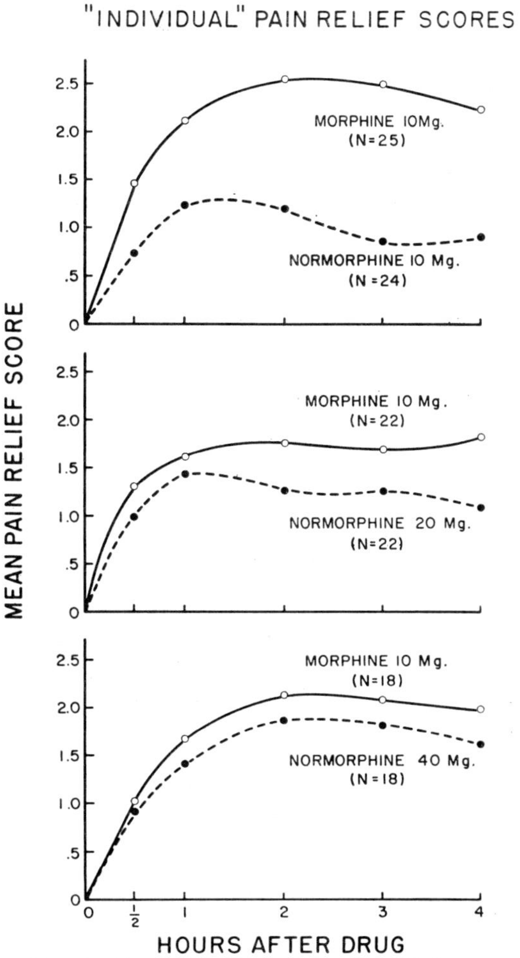

FIG. 2. Mean "individual" pain relief scores. (See text.)

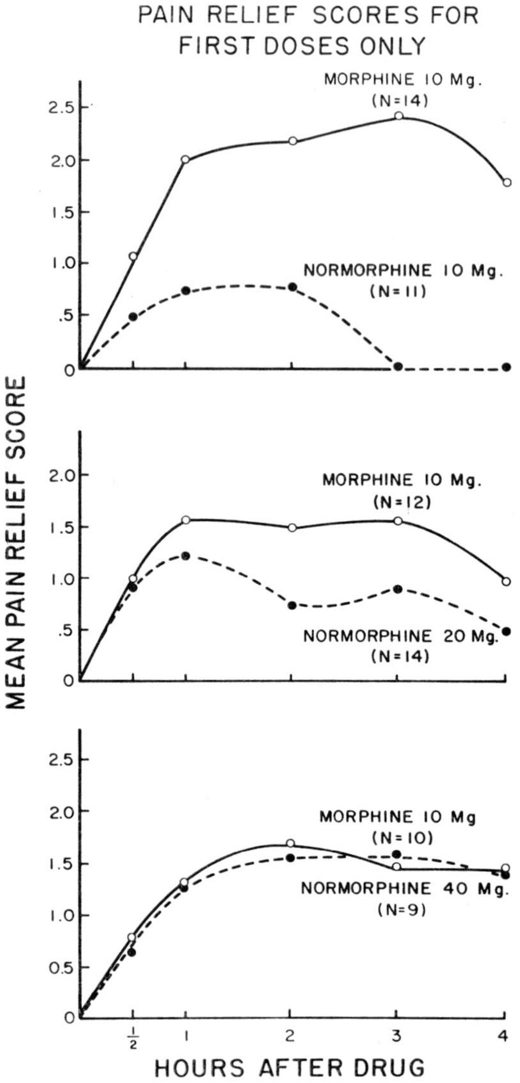

FIG. 3. Mean pain relief scores for first doses only.

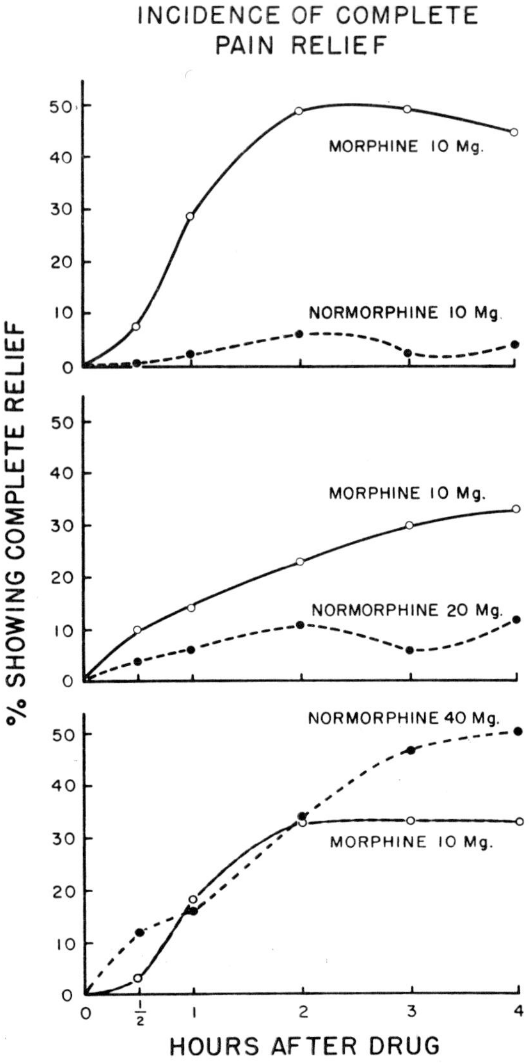

FIG. 4. Incidence of complete pain relief (all doses.)

Incidence of complete pain relief (all doses). (See figure 4.) The percentage of doses providing complete relief at the various time intervals is shown.

Incidence of "successful" doses. An arbitrary definition was established *a priori*, *viz.*, that to qualify as effective a dose had to supply a pain relief score of at least +2 (unless initial pain was described as moderate or slight, when the score had to be +1) within the first hour and maintain this degree of relief for at least another hour. (See table 1.)

Side-effects. No obvious side-effects attributable to medication were volunteered by the subjects or observed by the technicians, but it should be emphasized that the subjects were bed-patients, and that specific inquiries regarding side-effects were not made.

DISCUSSION. *Methodology.* Our basic experimental design and system of data collection combines the features of a number of techniques (Keele; Houde and Wallenstein; Denton and Beecher; Lasagna and Beecher; see Beecher, 1957). Although the sets of data presented in figures 1–4 and table 1 each answer somewhat different questions, it is reassuring to note that

TABLE 1

Incidence of "successful" doses (all doses)*

Group	N†	Drug	% Successful
I	61	Morphine, 10 mg	77
	62	Normorphine, 10 mg	26
II	41	Morphine, 10 mg	54
	41	Normorphine, 20 mg	24
III	33	Morphine, 10 mg	58
	32	Normorphine, 40 mg	53

* See text.

† N = number of doses.

each set leads to similar conclusions, *i.e.*, that 10 mg of morphine was a better analgesic than an equal dose of normorphine, that doubling the dose of normorphine improved the performance of this latter drug compared to the standard dose of morphine, and that 40 mg of normorphine yielded analgesia essentially indistinguishable from that provided by 10 mg of morphine.

The use of all doses employed permits a larger N for statistical analysis, but is at least theoretically susceptible to undue influence by patients requiring large number of doses. The computation of mean scores for each patient avoids such problems, but does not permit the utilization of the added confidence one ought to have in a mean based on a good many replicates in one patient as opposed to a "mean" based on only one dose in another patient. The use of first doses only is quite wasteful of data, but is an important check on possible drug-order interactions, such as might have been suggested by the preliminary data for humans (Fraser *et al.*, 1958). The "complete pain relief" scores are useful primarily because many clinicians find such data of help in extrapolating to clinical usage. Finally, the incidence of "successful doses" represents an arbitrary criterion employed to allow the use of some single figure to encompass such factors as speed of onset, magnitude of effect and duration of pain relief.

Comparison with findings of others. Our data agree with those of Fraser *et al.* (1958) as to the greater potency of morphine when morphine and normorphine are administered parenterally to humans in acute experiments. No evidence of cumulation was seen in our studies, which were not designed to answer the question of the usefulness of normorphine administered repeatedly over a period of days. Indeed, the duration of pain in most postoperative patients is not sufficient to permit such a question to be readily answered. No untoward effects were seen with either drug, but the findings of Fraser *et al.* suggest that 30 mg doses of normorphine are not devoid of depressant effects on respiration, and can produce nausea. It appears unlikely, therefore, that normorphine will offer any advantage over morphine in the treatment of acute pain. Fraser *et al.* have postulated that normorphine may have usefulness in the management of patients with chronic pain. Only controlled studies in such patients can reveal whether the cumulative tendencies of normorphine could represent an advantage or a disadvantage.

Our data also tend to confirm the conclusion of Miller and Anderson (1954) that N-demethylation of morphine to normorphine is probably not a crucial step in the analgesic effect of morphine. The relatively low potency of normorphine could be reconciled with the N-demethylation hypothesis of pain relief only if normorphine were formed at cell receptor sites after the entry of morphine into such sites (Beckett *et al.*, 1956). Since, however, N-demethylation occurs chiefly or exclusively in the liver (Axelrod, 1956), whereas the prime effects of morphine are on the nervous system, this latter explanation seems unlikely.

SUMMARY

A controlled clinical comparison of morphine and normorphine in 60 patients suffering from postoperative pain is reported. Normorphine was found to be approximately one-fourth as active as morphine. It appears unlikely that N-demethylation of morphine is necessary for the analgesic effect of morphine in man.

ACKNOWLEDGMENTS. The authors would like to thank the surgical staff of Baltimore City Hospitals for the opportunity to study their patients, and Mrs. Diane Keyes and Mr. Richard Schillaci for collecting the data.

REFERENCES

AXELROD, J.: THIS JOURNAL **117:** 322, 1956.
BECKETT, A. H., CASY, A. F. AND HARPER, N. J.: J. Pharm., Lond. **8:** 874, 1956.
BEECHER, H. K.: Pharmacol. Rev. **9:** 59, 1957.
EDDY, N. B., HALBACH, H. AND BRAENDEN, O. J.: Bull. World Hlth. Org. **14:** 353, 1956.
FRASER, H. F., WIKLER, A., VAN HORN, G. D., EISENMAN, A. J. AND ISBELL, H.: THIS JOURNAL **122:** 359, 1958.
KEATS, A. S. J. chron. Dis. **4:** 72, 1956.
MILLER, J. W. AND ANDERSON, H. H.: THIS JOURNAL **112:** 191, 1954.
ORAHOVATS, P. D. AND LEHMAN, E. G.: THIS JOURNAL **122:** 58A, 1958.

8086

EFFECTS OF SINGLE DOSES AND CHRONIC ADMINISTRATION OF ETHANOL ON EXPERIMENTAL SEIZURES IN MICE[1, 2]

D. G. McQUARRIE[3] AND E. FINGL

Department of Pharmacology, University of Utah College of Medicine, Salt Lake City, Utah

Received for publication May 22, 1958

The relationship between ethanol and seizures has been the subject of continuing interest and much controversy. As definitively reviewed by Victor and Adams (1953), some of the conflicting opinions can be traced to studies based upon chronic alcoholics, in whom the effects of ethanol *per se* can be separated only with difficulty from the effects of concomitant variables, such as trauma and nutritional deficiencies. Many other contradictory views of the past are now known to have been a consequence of the failure to distinguish between the primary effects of the drug and those secondary to abstinence from the drug after a period of chronic abuse (Kalinowsky, 1942; Victor and Adams, 1953; Isbell *et al.*, 1955).

The laboratory evaluation of the effects of ethanol on the properties of experimental seizures would appear to afford an excellent opportunity to assess the pharmacological effects of the drug without the intrusion of many of the variables inherent in comparable clinical studies. In spite of this possibility, previous studies have been limited almost entirely to the effects of single doses of ethanol on seizure thresholds. Therefore, the present investigation was undertaken to provide a more complete analysis of the effects of ethanol on the properties of experimental seizures. Special attention has been directed to the effects of chronic administration of ethanol and to the effects of abstinence from the drug after abrupt cessation of chronic medication.

METHODS. *General procedures.* Carworth (CF #1) adult male albino mice, weighing 18 to 28 grams at the start of the experiments, were employed as experimental animals. Except during the periods of testing, the animals had free access to water and to Purina laboratory chow. Ethanol was administered in aqueous solution by gavage. Dilutions of ethanol were such that all animals received a constant volume of solution per unit of body weight (0.2 ml/10 g); control animals received an equivalent volume of water. Except as otherwise indicated, all tests were conducted 20 minutes after administration of the drug, the previously determined time of peak anticonvulsant effect for intermediate doses of the drug for both maximal alternating current and minimal low-frequency electroshock seizures.

Experimental seizure techniques. Changes in seizure *threshold* were evaluated by a chemoshock (intravenous pentylenetetrazol [Metrazol]) technique and by two electroshock (alternating current and low-frequency electroshock) procedures. Alterations in maximal seizure *pattern* were assessed by an electroshock (alternating current) method.

Minimal and *maximal* alternating current electroshock seizures were evoked with the apparatus described by Woodbury and Davenport (1952); the stimulus parameters and endpoints employed were those suggested for mice by Swinyard and co-workers (1952). Minimal *low-frequency* electroshock ("psychomotor") seizures were elicited with a Grass S4A stimulator; the stimulus parameters employed were those recommended by Toman and associates (1952), as modified by Brown and co-workers (1953). The endpoint used was at least 7 seconds of persistent seizure activity including jaw movements and "purposeful" foreleg clonus. *Intravenous pentylenetetrazol* seizures were produced by the "timed intravenous infusion" method of Orloff and co-workers (1949), except that continuous intravenous infusion of pentylenetetrazol solution (5 mg/ml; 0.005 ml/sec) was substituted for intermittent intravenous injections at fixed intervals. The endpoint selected was at least 3 seconds of persistent clonic seizure activity. To avoid possible recording errors, the 3-second interval required to establish the seizure

[1] This investigation was supported by a research grant (B-381) from the National Institute of Neurological Diseases and Blindness, National Institutes of Health, U. S. Public Health Service.

[2] A preliminary report of this work appeared in Fed. Proc. **14:** 369, 1955.

[3] Present address: Department of Surgery, University of Minnesota Hospitals, Minneapolis, Minnesota.

endpoint was not subtracted from the total infusion time. It is recognized, however, that such omission results in slight systematic distortion of changes in seizure threshold ratio. Suitability of the modified procedure was evaluated by testing the effects of several representative anticonvulsant agents. Diphenylhydantoin (40 mg/kg, orally) did not change seizure threshold; trimethadione (250 mg/kg, orally) increased seizure threshold 1.56-fold (95% fiducial limits: 1.21 to 2.02). These observations are in satisfactory agreement with those previously reported for the original procedure (Chen *et al.*, 1954).

Standard anticonvulsant and neurotoxicity tests. Preliminary evaluation of the anticonvulsant properties of ethanol was accomplished by several of the standard tests suggested by Swinyard and co-workers (1952) and Brown and associates (1953). The tests employed included: a) maximal electroshock seizure pattern test, b) minimal electroshock seizure threshold test, c) minimal low-frequency electroshock ("psychomotor") seizure threshold test and d) test for minimal neurological deficit. Each of these tests is designed as a quantal-endpoint procedure. Both a 2-times-threshold quantal stimulus and the usual 4-times-threshold challenge were employed for the low-frequency electroshock seizure threshold test. For each test the dose of ethanol required to produce the stated endpoint in 50% of animals (ED50 or TD50) was estimated from the effects of 5 or 6 graded doses of ethanol administered to groups of at least 10 animals each.

Evaluation of the quantitative effects of single doses of ethanol on seizure thresholds. The quantitative effects of ethanol on thresholds for minimal alternating current electroshock, minimal low-frequency electroshock and intravenous pentylenetetrazol convulsions were evaluated by comparison of seizure thresholds of groups of animals which had received graded doses of ethanol. For the two electroshock procedures, groups of 15 to 25 animals were assigned to each dose of the drug. Seizure threshold, defined as the stimulus intensity (milliamperes or volts) required to evoke typical minimal convulsive activity in 50% of animals, was determined indirectly. Electroshock stimuli were varied within groups in "staircase" sequence (Finney, 1952a). For the chemoshock method, groups of 10 animals were assigned to each dose of ethanol, and seizure threshold was determined directly. Threshold determinations in the various dosage groups and by the two procedures being compared simultaneously were interspersed. All results have been expressed as the seizure threshold ratio, threshold for ethanol group/threshold for control group.

Evaluation of the effects of chronic administration of ethanol. Two groups of animals were employed for examining the effects of chronic administration of ethanol on *maximal electroschock seizure pattern* and on *neurotoxicity*. One group of 50 mice received 1800 mg of ethanol/kg, a dose intermediate between the ED50 for abolition of the hind-leg extensor component of maximal seizures and the neurological TD50. A second group of 15 mice received water and served as controls. Ethanol solution or water was administered at 8-hour intervals for a period of 14 days. Following the first dose and after each subsequent morning dose, the mice were examined for neurotoxicity and then for protection from maximal electroshock seizures. The durations of the tonic flexor, tonic extensor and clonic components of the evoked convulsions were measured daily in both groups and compared. After cessation of drug administration, the animals were tested at 24-hour intervals until residual anticonvulsant effects of ethanol were no longer detectable.

The effects of chronic administration of ethanol on *electroshock seizure threshold* were examined by daily determination of thresholds for minimal low-frequency electroshock seizures. Two groups of 40 animals each were employed. One group received 2000 mg of ethanol/kg at 8-hour intervals; the other group received equivalent volumes of water. The dose of ethanol was that which was expected to provide an approximately 2.5-fold increase in threshold for this seizure. The threshold for each group was determined after the first dose of ethanol and on subsequent days following the morning dose. After cessation of ethanol administration, thresholds were determined and compared at intervals of 24 hours or more until the thresholds for the two groups did not differ significantly for two successive determinations.

Statistical evaluation. Median anticonvulsant and neurotoxic doses of ethanol (ED50's and TD50), ratios of these values (protective indices) and their fiducial limits were estimated by the semigraphic method of Litchfield and Wilcoxon (1949). Median effective stimuli for the electroshock threshold determinations, ratios of these values and their fiducial limits were similarly estimated. However, calculations for threshold ratios in the early drug-withdrawal period were also subjected to full probit analysis (Finney, 1952a).

Measured endpoints (intravenous pentylenetetrazol seizure thresholds and durations of the components of maximal electroshock seizures) were evaluated by analysis of variance (Snedecor, 1946). For the chemoshock threshold determinations, lognormal distribution of the individual

TABLE 1

Comparison of anticonvulsant potency (ED50), neurotoxicity (TD50) and protective index (P.I.) of ethanol, trimethadione and phenobarbital by various anticonvulsant tests in mice†*

Drug	Time of Peak Effect	Neurotoxicity	Maximal Electroshock Seizure Pattern Test		Minimal Low-frequency Electroshock Seizure Threshold Test			
					4× threshold		2× threshold	
		TD50	ED50	P.I.	ED50	P.I.	ED50	P.I.
		mg/kg	*mg/kg*		*mg/kg*		*mg/kg*	
Ethanol	20 min	1900 (1670–2160)‡	1630 (1280–2070)	1.2 (0.9–1.5)	3400 (2650–4350)	0.56 (.42–.74)	1330 (1060–1660)	1.4 (1.1–1.8)
Trimethadione	2 hr	760§ (680–850)	740§ (650–850)	1.0 (0.9–1.2)	525 (460–598)	1.4 (1.2–1.7)	282 (236–337)	2.7 (2.2–3.3)
Phenobarbital	3 hr	51§ (43–60)	11.5 (8.4–15.9)	4.4 (3.1–6.4)	27 (22–33)	1.9 (1.4–2.5)	9.6 (7.8–11.7)	5.3 (4.0–7.0)

* P.I. = TD50/ED50.

† Ethanol was administered by gavage in aqueous solution; trimethadione and phenobarbital, by gavage in 10% acacia suspension.

‡ Values in parentheses are 95% fiducial limits.

§ Data reported by Brown, 1953.

pentylenetetrazol tolerances was assumed, and analysis of covariance was employed to eliminate differences between body weights (Finney, 1952b).

Comparison of dose-effect curves for the graded effects of ethanol on the various seizure thresholds was accomplished by application of standard statistical procedures employed for biological assays (Gaddum, 1953).

RESULTS. *Effects of single doses of ethanol.* Modifications of maximal electroshock seizure pattern by single doses of ethanol were similar to those produced by clinically effective antiepileptic agents. With increasing intensity of ethanol effect, tonic extension was progressively shortened and ultimately abolished, tonic flexion was initially prolonged but later decreased and subsequently eliminated, and clonus was lengthened. Also like many anticonvulsant agents, ethanol elevated seizure thresholds.

Median effective and median neurotoxic doses of ethanol, as determined by several representative standard laboratory tests, are compared with those of trimethadione and phenobarbital in table 1. Protective index (P.I.), the ratio of the median neurotoxic dose to the median effective dose, has been calculated for each test. Compared with the clinically effective antiepileptic drugs, ethanol is much less potent as an anticonvulsant agent. Of more importance, however, the protective indices for ethanol are distinctly less favorable than are those for the other two drugs, particularly phenobarbital.

The quantitative effects of single doses of ethanol on thresholds for minimal low-frequency electroshock, minimal alternating current electroshock and intravenous pentylenetetrazol seizures are compared in figures 1 and 2. Seizure threshold ratio (threshold for ethanol group/threshold for control group) is plotted as a function of dose. Thresholds for minimal low-frequency electroshock convulsions and for intravenous pentylenetetrazol seizures (figure 1) were increased in parallel ($P > 0.4$, for deviation from parallelism) by doses of ethanol between 1000 and 4000 mg/kg. The slight displacement ($P < 0.01$) of the two dose-effect curves along the dose axis would have been reduced, but not completely eliminated, if the 3-second interval required to establish the convulsive endpoint for the chemoshock seizure had been subtracted from all observations. In contrast, threshold for minimal alternating current electroshock convulsions (figure 2) was not significantly increased by doses of ethanol which elevated threshold for minimal low-frequency electroshock seizures more than 2.5-fold.[4]

[4] Estimates of the dose of ethanol required to produce a 20% increase in minimal alternating current electroshock seizure threshold (minimal seizure threshold test) have varied from 2400 to more than 4000 mg/kg in experiments on different days. However, in both experiments in which the effects of ethanol on thresholds for the two convulsions have been determined *concurrently*, the effective dose for elevation of minimal alternating current electroshock seizure threshold has exceeded that required to produce a 2.5- to 3-fold increase in minimal low-frequency electroshock seizure threshold.

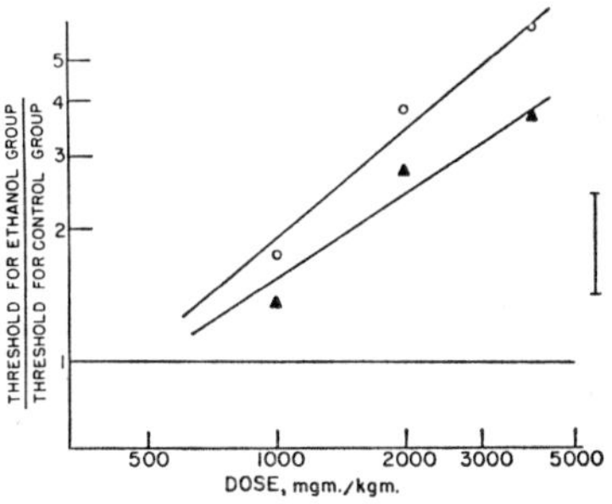

FIG. 1. Effects of single graded doses of ethanol on threshold ratios for minimal low-frequency electroshock (○) and for intravenous pentylenetetrazol (▲) seizures in mice.

Vertical bracket indicates 95% fiducial limits for each threshold ratio. Thresholds for control groups: minimal low-frequency electroshock seizure, 13.4 volts; intravenous pentylenetetrazol seizure, 30.5 mg/kg.

Careful determination of the full time course of the effects of ethanol on seizure threshold revealed a brief period of hypersusceptibility to experimental convulsions (lowering of seizure threshold) after the primary elevation of seizure threshold had waned. Typical observations following a single large dose (4000 mg/kg) of ethanol, as detected by the intravenous pentylenetetrazol threshold procedure, are summarized in figure 3. In other experiments, similar transient lowering of threshold for minimal low-frequency electroshock seizures has also been noted.

Effects of chronic administration of ethanol. Results with regard to modification of maximal electroshock seizure pattern and incidence of minimal neurotoxicity during chronic administration of ethanol (1800 mg/kg, orally, every 8 hours for 14 days) are summarized in figure 4. Percentage protection and percentage neurotoxicity are plotted as a function of time. The initial dose of ethanol abolished the hind-leg extensor component of the maximal seizure in 48% of animals and caused minimal neurotoxicity in 40% of mice. This high incidence of neurotoxicity reflects the poor protective index of ethanol also detected by the standard anticonvulsant tests (table 1). No statistically significant change in percentage protection ($P > 0.3$) or percentage neurotoxicity ($P > 0.9$) occurred during the 14-day period of ethanol administration. All animals in the control group exhibited full maximal seizures during the entire period of the experiment.

During the period of ethanol administration,

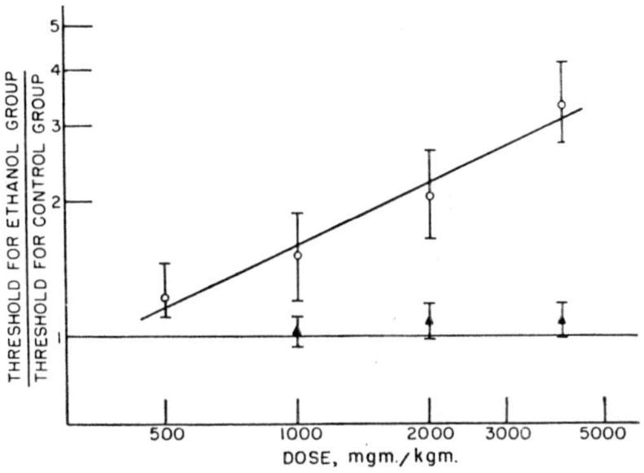

FIG. 2. Effects of single graded doses of ethanol on threshold ratios for minimal low-frequency electroshock (○) and for minimal alternating current electroshock (▲) seizures in mice.

Vertical brackets indicate 95% fiducial limits for each threshold ratio. Thresholds for control groups: minimal low-frequency electroshock seizure, 22.5 volts; minimal alternating current electroshock seizure, 7.6 mA.

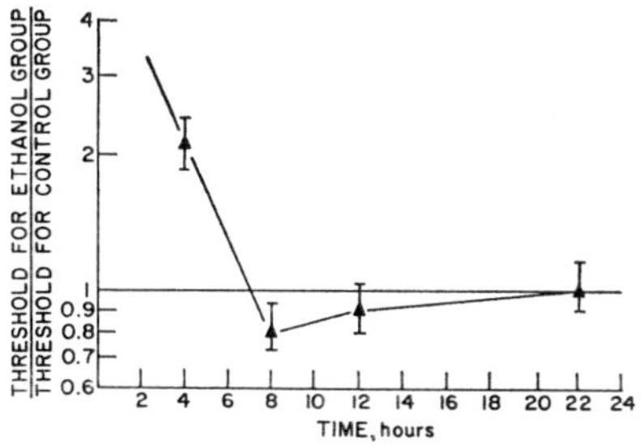

FIG. 3. Time course of effect of a single dose of ethanol (4000 mg/kg, orally) on threshold ratio for intravenous pentylenetetrazol seizures in mice.

Vertical brackets indicate 95% fiducial limits for each threshold ratio. Mean seizure threshold for control groups: 37.8 mg/kg.

durations of the components of the evoked seizures, both in the control and the ethanol-treated animals, showed statistically significant daily variation. None of the three components in the control animals nor the *clonic* component in the drug-treated group varied systematically with time. However, durations of the tonic flexor and tonic extensor components of the ethanol-treated mice which still exhibited the tonic extensor component did show progressive change during the period of medication. The tonic *flexor* component, increased by the initial dose of the drug to 2.8 seconds (control mean: 2.0 seconds), was further lengthened to 3.6 seconds ($P < 0.001$). The tonic *extensor* component, decreased by the first dose of ethanol to 5.1 seconds (control mean:

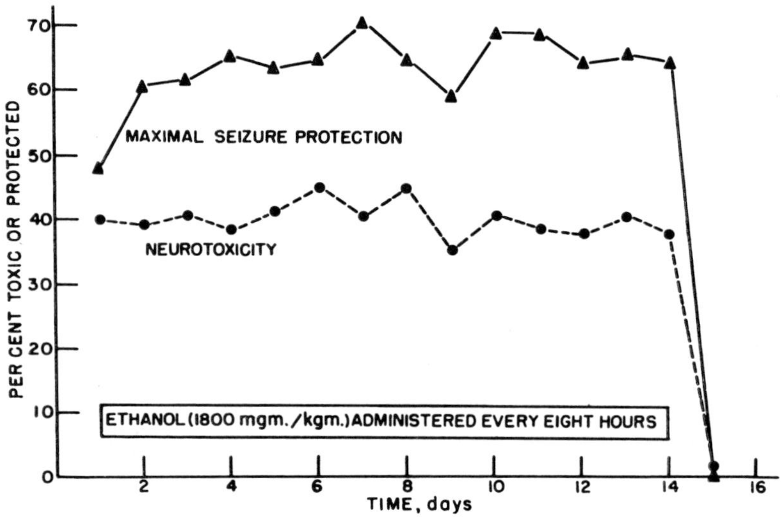

FIG. 4. Effects of chronic administration of ethanol (1800 mg/kg, orally, every 8 hours for 14 days) and of its withdrawal on maximal alternating current electroshock seizure pattern (▲) and on minimal neurotoxicity (●) in mice.

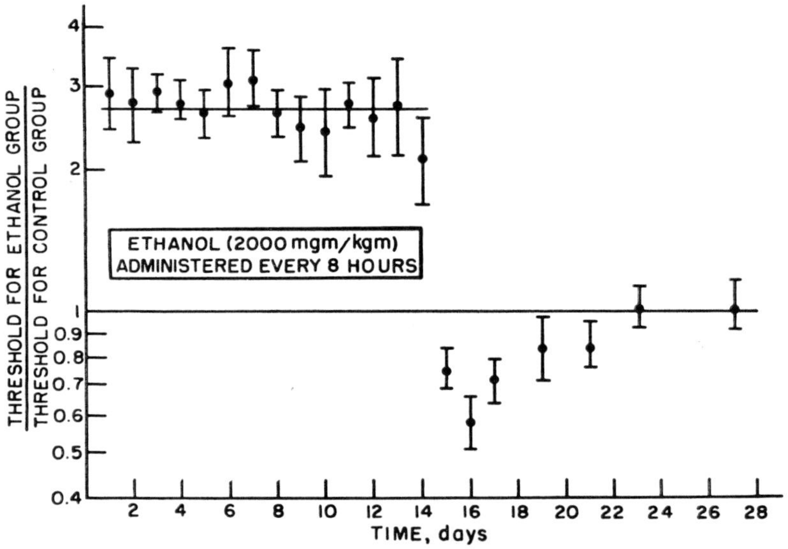

FIG. 5. Effects of chronic administration of ethanol (2000 mg/kg, orally, every 8 hours for 14 days) and of its withdrawal on threshold ratio for minimal low-frequency electroshock seizures in mice.

Vertical brackets indicate 95% fiducial limits for each threshold ratio. Upper solid horizontal line indicates mean seizure threshold ratio during period of drug administration. Mean threshold for control group: 19.2 volts.

10.8 seconds), was further progressively shortened to 3.0 seconds ($P < 0.001$).

Twenty-four hours after cessation of drug administration, all mice previously receiving ethanol exhibited full maximal seizures in response to the routine test, and only one animal manifested evidence of residual neurological deficit. Seven of the 42 post-ethanol animals died in maximal seizure evoked by the test stimulus, whereas only 14 deaths resulted from 417 maximal convulsions during the preceding 14 days ($P < 0.001$).

The effects of chronic administration of ethanol on minimal low-frequency electroshock seizure threshold are summarized in figure 5. Seizure threshold ratio (threshold for ethanol group/

threshold for control group) is plotted as a function of time. Each point represents the ratio derived from observations on 40 ethanol-treated mice compared with 40 control animals. The upper solid horizontal line represents the mean threshold ratio for the 14 days of drug administration. After abrupt cessation of ethanol administration, the drug-elevated threshold returned not only to the control level but declined significantly below that of the control animals. Hyperexcitability was maximal on the second day after medication had been stopped and did not subside until after the seventh day. Parallel hypersusceptibility to both minimal low-frequency electroshock and intravenous pentylenetetrazol seizures has been noted in subsequent experiments. Hyperexcitability following ethanol withdrawal developed more slowly, was slightly greater in magnitude and was distinctly longer in duration than that which occurs after a single dose of the drug.

Throughout the period of chronic ethanol administration and during the period of postethanol hyperexcitability, body weights of the ethanol-treated animals did not differ significantly from those of the control mice.

Discussion. The complex effects of ethanol on the central nervous system are traditionally explained solely on the basis of its primary depressant properties. According to this almost universally accepted view, which was advocated as early as 1883 by Schmeideberg, excitatory manifestations of the drug are attributed to "release" of lower motor centers from cortical or other rostral inhibitory influences. The consequent emphasis on mechanism of action has tended to obscure the fact that ethanol does cause excitatory effects. A major result of the present study is the demonstration that transient hyperexcitability temporally supersedes the primary anticonvulsant effects of single doses of ethanol and that hypersusceptibility to seizures persists for at least several days after abrupt cessation of chronic administration of the drug.

Elevation of threshold for experimental seizures and modification of the pattern of maximal seizures by various aliphatic alcohols have been reported previously (Merritt and Putnam, 1938; Tainter *et al.*, 1943; Driver, 1947; Allan, 1949; Allan and Swinyard, 1949; Schaffarzick, 1950; Schaffarzick and Brown, 1952; Dember *et al.*, 1953; Greenberg and Lester, 1953). The present studies confirm the above findings for ethanol. In these respects, ethanol resembles many of the clinically useful anticonvulsant agents (Toman and Goodman, 1946, 1948; Toman, 1949; and many others). However, the present observations also emphasize that the anticonvulsant properties of ethanol are observed only with doses which approximate or exceed those causing neurological impairment.

The view held by most epileptologists that patients with epilepsy should abstain from alcoholic beverages would appear to be inconsistent with the known depressant and anticonvulsant properties of ethanol. However, as reviewed by Berry (1952), support for this view can be found in several clinical surveys. In response to questionnaires in these studies, 10 to 20% of patients with epilepsy expressed the opinion that ethanol, usually when taken in excessive amounts, did sometimes precipitate their attacks. Exacerbation of their disease was most frequently noted as the primary effects of the drug were waning (Lennox, 1941). The transient hyperexcitability (reduction of seizure threshold) which temporally superseded the initial anticonvulsant effects of ethanol in the present studies (figure 3) is interpreted as the experimental counterpart of these clinical observations.

Similar biphasic effects of single doses of ethanol (and several opiate analgesics) on pain threshold have been observed in man by Mullin and Luckhardt (1934, 1935). Seevers and Pfeiffer (1936), who confirmed these observations for the opiates, suggested that the acute "excitatory" effects might be related to the manifestations of physical dependence observed upon cessation of chronic medication. Indeed, the occurrence of "excitatory" effects after single doses of the opiates constitutes the basis of the so-called "dual action" theory of tolerance and physical dependence (Tatum *et al.*, 1929; Seevers and Woods, 1953; Seevers, 1954). The possibility that the transient hyperexcitability after *single* doses of ethanol might be similarly related to the tolerance and physical dependence which develops to this drug clearly merits further study. Whatever the result, such an analysis might also provide important clues to the neurophysiological factors which determine seizure threshold. However, we have preferred, at least initially, to confine our attention to the hyperexcitability following drug withdrawal after *chronic* administration, a phenomenon more clearly related to that of physical dependence. Even if withdrawal hyperexcitability were proved to be an exaggeration of the transient reduction in seizure threshold observed in acute experiments, the factors which operate during chronic administration to magnify and to prolong the hyperexcitability would appear to be of equal or greater importance.

In the present experiments in mice, cessation of chronic administration of ethanol resulted in hypersusceptibility to seizures, as evidenced by lowering of threshold for minimal low-frequency electroshock convulsions (figure 5) and by an increased incidence of deaths during evoked maximal seizures. This withdrawal hyperexcitability is qualitatively reproducible and has a time course measured in days. In other experiments (McQuarrie and Fingl, unpublished observations, 1958), reduction of threshold for minimal low-frequency electroshock seizures during the withdrawal period has been paralleled by lowering of threshold for intravenous pentylenetetrazol convulsions; withdrawal hyperexcitability has been found to be proportional to the intensity and, to a lesser extent, to the duration of chronic medication; and it has not appeared to be a result of nutritional deficiency. In addition, hypersusceptibility to seizures in mice has also been observed following cessation of chronic administration of chloral hydrate and of phenobarbital, central nervous system depressants which induce abstinence syndromes qualitatively resembling that precipitated by ethanol withdrawal (Kalinowsky, 1942; Isbell *et al.*, 1950, 1955; Wikler *et al.*, 1956; Fraser *et al.*, 1957). For these reasons, it has been concluded that hypersusceptibility to seizures during the withdrawal period represents a manifestation of *physical dependence* which develops during the period of chronic ethanol administration. Should this tentative conclusion survive further test, these studies could be readily extended to an analysis of the mechanisms underlying the development of physical dependence. It is also possible that the occurrence of withdrawal hyperexcitability after cessation of chronic administration of other central nervous system depressants might constitute presumptive evidence that the abstinence syndromes induced by such drugs will be characterized by convulsions. In addition, the general experimental design utilized in the present study also appears applicable for evaluation of the physical dependence liability of other classes of pharmacological agents.

Because of the key significance of *tolerance* in various theories of physical dependence (Seevers and Woods, 1953; Wikler, 1953; Seevers, 1954), unequivocal demonstration of the occurrence or absence of tolerance to the anticonvulsant effects of ethanol in the present study would be of interest. Unfortunately, an experimental design other than that used in this phase of the study is required to provide this information. In addition, a final conclusion must also await the direct comparison of the effects of the drug with blood or, preferably, brain ethanol concentrations.

The various procedures employed for detecting changes in seizure threshold require brief consideration. The justifiable prejudice of the authors for methods which demonstrate graded intensities of effects, in preference to those which merely detect arbitrary "all-or-none" endpoints, is amply supported by the results of the present study. It is likely that both the hyperexcitability after single doses of the drug and that which occurs upon abrupt ethanol withdrawal after chronic medication would have escaped detection if only quantal-endpoint procedures had been employed. The significant quantitative variability of the anticonvulsant effects of ethanol, apparent by comparison of the data summarized in figures 1 and 2 and table 1, also merits brief comment. These differences can be attributed, at least in part, to the simple, but frequently overlooked, fact that neither ED50's, threshold ratios, nor similar derived data possess inherent stability with time. As expressed by Finney (1952a), standard errors, fiducial limits or other measures of precision must not be accepted as an indication of the variation to be encountered in *any* repetition of an experiment. Rather, measures of precision calculated from internal evidence of one experiment relate only to repetition under *identical* conditions.

SUMMARY

The effects of single doses and chronic administration of ethanol on the properties of experimental seizures were investigated in mice.

Anticonvulsant effects of ethanol were observed only with doses of the drug which approached or exceeded those causing general central nervous system depression.

Transient lowering of seizure threshold temporally superseded the primary anticonvulsant effects of single doses of the drug. The possible significance of this hyperexcitability with regard to the usual recommendation that patients with epilepsy abstain from alcohol is discussed.

Hypersusceptibility to seizures, as evidenced by lowering of seizure threshold, persisted for at least several days after abrupt cessation of chronic administration of ethanol. It has been tentatively concluded that this withdrawal hyperexcitability represents an easily measured manifestation of physical dependence which develops during chronic administration of ethanol.

ACKNOWLEDGMENTS. The authors wish to express their appreciation to Dr. Louis S. Goodman for proposing this series of experiments and for his valuable advice and criticism throughout the course of this study. The assistance of Dr. William C. Brown in the preliminary phases of this investigation is also gratefully acknowledged.

REFERENCES

ALLAN, F. D.: M. S. Thesis, University of Utah, 1949.

ALLAN, F. D. AND SWINYARD, C. A.: Anat. Rec. **103:** 419, 1949.

BERRY, R. G.: Epilepsia, third series **1:** 21, 1952.

BROWN, W. C.: Epilepsia, third series **2:** 127, 1953.

BROWN, W. C., SCHIFFMAN, D. O., SWINYARD, E. A. AND GOODMAN, L. S.: THIS JOURNAL **107:** 273, 1953.

CHEN, G., BOHNER, BARBARA AND ENSOR, C. R.: Proc. Soc. exp. Biol., N. Y. **87:** 334, 1954.

DEMBER, W. N., ELLEN, P. AND KRISTOFFERSON, A. B.: Quart. J. Stud. Alc. **14:** 390, 1953.

DRIVER, R. L.: Proc. Soc. exp. Biol., N. Y. **64:** 248, 1947.

FINNEY, D. J.: Probit Analysis. A Statistical Treatment of the Sigmoid Response Curve, Cambridge University Press, Cambridge, 1952a.

FINNEY, D. J.: Statistical Method in Biological Assay, Hafner Publishing Co., New York, 1952b.

FRASER, H. F., WIKLER, A., ISBELL, H. AND JOHNSON, N. K.: Quart. J. Stud. Alc. **18:** 541, 1957.

GADDUM, J. H.: Pharmacol. Rev. **5:** 87, 1953.

GREENBERG, L. A. AND LESTER, D.: Quart. J. Stud. Alc. **14:** 385, 1953.

ISBELL, H., ALTSCHUL, S., KORNETSKY, C. H., EISENMAN, A. J., FLANARY, H. G. AND FRASER, H. F.: Arch. Neurol. Psychiat., Chicago **64:** 1, 1950.

ISBELL, H., FRASER, H. F., WIKLER, A., BELLEVILLE, R. E. AND EISENMAN, ANNA J.: Quart. J. Stud. Alc. **16:** 1, 1955.

KALINOWSKY, L. B.: Arch. Neurol. Psychiat., Chicago **48:** 946, 1942.

LENNOX, W. G.: Quart. J. Stud. Alc. **2:** 1, 1941.

LITCHFIELD, J. T., JR. AND WILCOXON, F.: THIS JOURNAL **96:** 99, 1949.

MERRITT, H. H. AND PUTNAM, T. J.: Arch. Neurol. Psychiat., Chicago **39:** 1003, 1938.

MULLIN, F. J. AND LUCKHARDT, A. B.: Amer. J. Physiol. **109:** 77, 1934.

MULLIN, F. J. AND LUCKHARDT, A. B.: Amer. J. Physiol. **113:** 100, 1935.

ORLOFF, M. J., WILLIAMS, H. L. AND PFEIFFER, C. C.: Proc. Soc. exp. Biol., N. Y. **70:** 254, 1949.

SCHAFFARZICK, R. W.: Proc. Soc. exp. Biol., N. Y. **74:** 211, 1950.

SCHAFFARZICK, R. W. AND BROWN, BEVERLY J.: Science **116:** 663, 1952.

SEEVERS, M. H.: Fed. Proc. **13:** 672, 1954.

SEEVERS, M. H. AND PFEIFFER, C. C.: THIS JOURNAL **56:** 166, 1936.

SEEVERS, M. H. AND WOODS, L. A.: Amer. J. Med. **14:** 546, 1953.

SNEDECOR, G. W.: Statistical Methods Applied to Experiments in Agriculture and Biology, Iowa State College Press, Ames, Iowa, 1946.

SWINYARD, E. A., BROWN, W. C. AND GOODMAN, L. S.: THIS JOURNAL **106:** 319, 1952.

TAINTER, M. L., TAINTER, E. G., LAWRENCE, W. S., NEURU, E. N., LACKEY, R. W., LUDUENA, F. P., KIRTLAND, H. B., JR. AND GONZALEZ, R. I.: THIS JOURNAL **79:** 42, 1943.

TATUM, A. L., SEEVERS, M. H. AND COLLINS, K. H.: THIS JOURNAL **36:** 447, 1929.

TOMAN, J. E. P.: Electroenceph. clin. Neurophysiol. **1:** 33, 1949.

TOMAN, J. E. P., EVERETT, G. M. AND RICHARDS, R. K.: Texas Rep. Biol. Med. **10:** 96, 1952.

TOMAN, J. E. P. AND GOODMAN, L. S.: Proc. Ass. Res. nerv. Dis. **26:** 141, 1946.

TOMAN, J. E. P. AND GOODMAN, L. S.: Physiol. Rev. **28:** 409, 1948.

VICTOR, M. AND ADAMS, R. D.: Proc. Ass. Res. nerv. Dis. **32:** 526, 1953.

WIKLER, A.: Opiate Addiction. Psychological and Neurophysiological Aspects in Relation to Clinical Problems, Charles C Thomas, Publisher, Springfield, Ill., 1953.

WIKLER, A., PESCOR, F. T., FRASER, H. F. AND ISBELL, H.: Amer. J. Psychiat. **113:** 106, 1956.

WOODBURY, L. A. AND DAVENPORT, VIRGINIA D.: Arch. int. Pharmacodyn. **92:** 97, 1952.

8087

BIOCHEMICAL ALTERATIONS OF LIVER FUNCTION BY THE HALOGENATED HYDROCARBONS.[1, 2] I. *IN VITRO* AND *IN VIVO* CHANGES AND THEIR MODIFICATION BY ETHYLENEDIAMINE TETRAACETATE

DEANE N. CALVERT AND THEODORE M. BRODY

Department of Pharmacology, University of Michigan Medical School, Ann Arbor

Received for publication July 17, 1958

Recently, considerable interest has been shown in attempting to solve the problem of the mechanism of toxicity of carbon tetrachloride at the cellular level. In general, two approaches have been used; the administration of the drug to the animal and the examination of liver mitochondrial functions after a suitable interval and the *in vitro* treatment of the mitochondria after isolation from normal liver. Christie and Judah (1954) found a reduction in the activity of the diphosphopyridine nucleotide (DPN) linked dehydrogenases after administration of the drug to the animal. A similar reduction was seen after *in vitro* addition of carbon tetrachloride to the isolated mitochondria. Addition of DPN to the reaction mixture was found to partially restore the activity of the mitochondrial dehydrogenases. They were unable to find a decrease in phosphorylation coupled to oxidation 20 hours after administration of the compound to the animal. Dianzani (1954) however, showed that there was an uncoupling of oxidative phosphorylation and no change in the hydrolysis of adenosine triphosphate (ATP) by mitochondria from treated animals (See also Dianzani, 1955, 1955a). Recknagel and Anthony (1957) have reported an activation of a magnesium-dependent adenosine triphosphatase (ATP-ase) after both *in vivo* and *in vitro* treatment with carbon tetrachloride. Bridgers *et al.* (1957) were able to demonstrate a loss of beta-hydroxybutyrate dehydrogenase activity after *in vitro* treatment. The addition of DPN restored oxidation but not phosphorylation and ethylenediamine tetraacetate (Versene)[3] exerted a protective effect in this system.

The present investigation confirms the loss of DPN-linked dehydrogenase activity of liver mitochondria treated with carbon tetrachloride *in vivo* and *in vitro*, the disruption of oxidative phosphorylation and the activation of a magnesium ATP-ase. Intensive study with Versene had been undertaken and the protective effects shown to extend to oxidative phosphorylation and the activation of the ATP-ase. Other criteria of liver damage have been examined and found to be altered by carbon tetrachloride and in general protected by Versene administra tion or treatment. Concomitant histological studies have failed to reveal a correlation between carbon tetrachloride-induced fatty liver and the metabolic changes observed in liver mitochondria.

METHODS. *In vitro studies.* Liver homogenates were prepared by the method of Potter and Elvehjem (1936) and mitochondria isolated according to the procedures described by Hogeboom, Schneider and Palade (1948). Carbon tetrachloride was added to the suspending medium (0.25 M sucrose) to give a final concentration of 1.45×10^{-2} M. The use of this mixture for the initial homogenization and for the wash of the isolated mitochondria represented *in vitro* treatment. In the Versene and 8-hydroxyquinoline experiments these agents were added to the suspending medium containing the carbon tetrachloride in amounts to give a final concentration of 3×10^{-3} M. After isolation from the wash the mitochondria were resuspended in cold 0.25 M sucrose to a volume equivalent to the wet weight of tissue used. Contents of the reaction mixtures and specific experimental conditions are given in the appropriate tables.

Oxygen consumption was determined by conventional manometric techniques and oxidative phosphorylation studies performed as described by Brody and Bain (1951).

In vivo studies. Albino rats of both sexes and weighing approximately 200 g were used through-

[1] Supported by USPHS Grant RG 4759.

[2] Preliminary studies were reported in Fed. Proc. **18:** 356, 1958.

[3] Versene is the registered trade mark of the Dow Chemical Company for the salts of ethylenediamine tetraacetic acid.

TABLE 1

*The effect of the in vitro addition of CCl_4 upon the oxidative activity of the DPN-linked dehydrogenases of rat liver mitochondria and the prevention of these effects by Versene**

Treatment	µAt O_2 Uptake Per Hour							
	PA & MA†		α-Keto glutarate		Citrate		Glutamate	
	—	DPN	—	DPN	—	DPN	—	DPN
Untreated control	11.5	12.7	9.9	12.0	10.0	12.4	15.0	18.0
CCl_4	0.91	9.40	1.65	8.15	0.78	15.9	0.48	6.96
CCl_4 + Versene	5.70	10.2	13.2	25.0	8.45	17.0	12.1	22.0

Vessel contents: 2.5×10^{-2} M K Phosphate buffer, pH 7.4; 1.00×10^{-2} M glycylglycine buffer; 1.5×10^{-2} M KCl; 1.2×10^{-2} M $MgCl_2$; 1.0×10^{-5} M Cytochrome c; 2.8×10^{-3} M K ATP; 30 units of yeast hexokinase; 3.3×10^{-2} M Glucose; 0.4 ml of the rat liver mitochondrial suspension. The final volume was 2.0 ml. 0.2 ml 2N KOH was placed in the center well, the gas phase was air and the temperature 30°C. Substrate concentrations were 0.01 M except for citrate which was in a final concentration of 0.05 M. The "sparking" concentration of malate was 5×10^{-4} M. DPN when added was 1×10^{-3} M (final concentration).

* Disodium salt of ethylenediamine tetraacetate.

† Pyruvate and malate.

out the course of the investigation. Carbon tetrachloride was mixed with an equal volume of peanut oil and 0.5 ml of the mixture per 100 g body weight was administered by stomach tube. The rats were fasted until sacrificed. Disodium Versene in aqueous solution was given in a dose of 400 mg/kg by intraperitoneal injection at the time of the carbon tetrachloride administration. A dose of 200 mg/kg of 8-hydroxyquinoline was given in a similar manner. Choline chloride was administered by stomach tube in a dose of 1.25 g/kg simultaneously with carbon tetrachloride administration. In some experiments this dose was repeated 10 to 12 hours later. Mitochondria were isolated from the livers of treated animals and oxygen consumption and oxidative phosphorylation determined as described above.

ATP-ase determination. Mitochondrial ATP-ase was determined by a modification of the method of Schneider (1948). The reaction mixture used is indicated in the appropriate table. Inorganic phosphate released was determined by the method of Fiske and Subbarow (1925).

Glutamic-oxaloacetic transaminase. The glutamic-oxaloacetic transaminase (GOT) activity in the serum of treated animals was determined by the method of Steinberg, Baldwin and Ostrow (1956). Spectrophotometric determinations were carried out in a Beckman Spectrophotometer Model DU, using quartz cells with a 1 cm light path.

Cation determinations. The supernatant fluid which was obtained after the first mitochondrial sedimentation was made to a suitable dilution with distilled water and sodium and potassium concentration determined using the Beckman Flame Photometer, Model 4100.

Materials. Dipotassium adenosine triphosphate (ATP), diphosphopyridine nucleotide (DPN) and hexokinase were obtained from Pabst Laboratories. Cytochrome c, glycylglycine, alpha-ketoglutarate and malic dehydrogenase were from Sigma Chemical Company. Glutamic acid, aspartic acid and citric acid were products of Nutritional Biochemical Corporation; succinic acid and carbon tetrachloride were Mallinckrodt Analytical Reagents. Choline chloride and 8-hydroxyquinoline sulfate were obtained from Eastman Kodak Company. The tetrasodium, disodium and magnesium-disodium salts of ethylenediamine tetraacetic acid were products of Dow Chemical Company. Reduced DPN was prepared from DPN as described by Umbreit *et al.* (1957). All other materials were reagent grade.

RESULTS. *A. Alteration of Mitochondrial Activity.* 1. Oxidation of DPN-linked enzymes: The effect of *in vitro* treatment with carbon tetrachloride on DPN-linked dehydrogenase activity of mitochondria from normal rat liver is shown in a typical experiment (table 1). There were no marked differences in the action upon the various dehydrogenases. Table 1 illustrates the ability of DPN to partially restore the oxidative functions of treated mitochondria. Ordinarily, freshly prepared normal rat liver mitochondria do not exhibit such a DPN requirement. The addition of Versene (final concentration 0.003M) to the homogenization medium simultaneous with the carbon tetrachloride addition protected against the loss of dehydrogenase activity. While the results of Versene treatment were somewhat variable, in 25 experiments 17 showed good protection while in 8 minimal protective effects were observed. Only in a few experiments was Versene able to restore the oxygen consumption to untreated control values.

Results very similar to those obtained by *in vitro* treatment with carbon tetrachloride were seen after *in vivo* experiments (table 2). In a limited number of experiments it was observed that the β-hydroxybutyrate dehydrogenase activity was somewhat more sensitive while α-ketoglutarate dehydrogenase seemed resistant to carbon tetrachloride treatment. Our experiments also confirmed previous observations that a very definite time factor is operative in the biochemical changes following carbon tetrachloride administration. With our drug dosage we were rarely able to detect oxidative changes if the animals were sacrificed before 20 hours post-treatment. Histological examination of the livers, however, showed that morphological alterations occurred some time before 20 hours had elapsed. It was not unusual to see these changes as early as 5 hours after drug administration.

TABLE 2

Oxidative activity of liver DPN-linked dehydrogenases following administration of CCl_4 and following the simultaneous administration of CCl_4 and disodium versene in the intact animal

Treatment	μAt O_2 Uptake per 25 Minutes							
	PA & MA		α-Keto glutarate		Citrate		Glutamate	
	—	DPN	—	DPN	—	DPN	—	DPN
Untreated control....	11.3	12.70	19.00	24.40	19.8	17.60	19.8	24.0
CCl_4........	0.56	4.75	2.94	3.96	0.57	4.80	0.82	4.50
CCl_4 + Versene...	5.15	7.00	8.40	9.95	6.25	7.00	11.8	13.0

Conditions same as Table 1.

tion. The intraperitoneal administration of Versene (400 mg/kg) simultaneous with the carbon tetrachloride administration and the measurement of mitochondrial dehydrogenase activities after 20 hours revealed the protective action of Versene (table 2). Once again the results of these studies were somewhat variable but 13 of 15 experiments were similar to the one depicted in the table. During the course of our studies it was also observed, in confirmation of Cameron and Karunaratne (1936), that young rats were remarkably resistant to the effects of carbon tetrachloride. Nitrogen determinations were performed on mitochondria from treated and control animals and a reduction of about 20% was observed in the treated group. The dehydrogenase activities listed in the table are not corrected for mitochondrial nitrogen.

2. Oxidative Phosphorylation: A sensitive indicator of integrated mitochondrial function is the measurement of oxidative phosphorylation. Table 3 shows the marked inhibition of this process in a typical experiment. It was shown previously (table 1) that DPN addition partially restores the oxidative activity of treated mitochondria. It is apparent, however, that such addition has no beneficial effect on coupled phosphorylation. The data above on succinoxidase activity is interesting primarily because

TABLE 3

Inhibition of oxidative phosphorylation following in vitro treatment with CCl_4 and protection with Versene

Treatment	Glutamate			PA & MA			Succinate		
	μAt O_2* uptake	μmol Pi†	P:O‡	μAt O_2 uptake	μmol Pi	P:O	μAt O_2 uptake	μmol Pi	P:O
CCl_4..................	0	0	0	0	0	0	10.15	0	0
CCl_4 + DPN..........	6.30	0	0	1.94	0	0	—	—	—
CCl_4 + Versene.......	6.50	9.60	1.40	1.90	3.00	1.58	11.50	15.2	1.45
CCl_4 + Versene + DPN............	8.50	16.00	1.88	2.93	4.00	1.37	—	—	—
Untreated.............	7.50	19.2	2.56	3.87	10.0	2.62	9.00	15.0	1.65
Untreated + DPN....	9.00	24.00	2.68	4.33	9.6	2.22	—	—	—

Vessel contents: 2.5×10^{-2} M K Phosphate buffer pH 7.4; 1.00×10^{-2} M glycylglycine buffer pH 7.4; 1.6×10^{-2} M KCl; 1.25×10^{-2} $MgCl_2$; 2.8×10^{-3} M K-ATP; 1.0×10^{-5} M Cytochrome c; 30 units yeast hexokinase; 3.3×10^{-2} M glucose; drug treatment as indicated under methods; rat liver mitochondria equivalent to 400 mg tissue wet weight, and 1.5×10^{-2} M NaF. DPN 1×10^{-3} M final concentration. Total volume 1.9 ml. The sidearm contained 0.1 ml 75% trichloroacetic acid and the center well 0.2 ml 2N KOH. The temperature was 30°C and the gas phase air. Incubation time 10 minutes.

* Microatoms oxygen uptake.

† Micromoles inorganic phosphate uptake.

‡ Ratio of micromoles phosphate uptake to microatoms oxygen uptake.

TABLE 4

Inhibition of liver mitochondrial oxidative phosphorylation following in vivo administration of CCl_4 and the partial protection with concomitant Versene administration

Treatment	Glutamate			Pyruvate & malate			Succinate		
	μAt O_2 uptake	μmol Pi	P:O	μAt O_2 uptake	μmol Pi	P:O	μAt O_2 uptake	μmol Pi	P:O
CCl_4	0	0	0	0	0	0	7.70	6.90	0.89
CCl_4 + DPN	1.35	0	0	0.50	0	0	—	—	—
CCl_4 + Versene	4.55	5.6	1.23	1.03	1.24	1.20	8.10	11.8	1.45
CCl_4 + DPN + Versene	5.62	9.6	1.71	2.00	3.60	1.80	—	—	—
Untreated	7.50	19.2	2.56	5.50	13.30	2.42	9.75	14.4	1.48
Untreated + DPN	9.00	24.0	2.68	5.20	12.30	2.36	—	—	—

Experimental conditions the same as table 3. Incubation time 10 minutes.

TABLE 5

Activation of a mitochondrial ATP-ase by in vitro and in vivo CCl_4 treatment and protection by Versene

Time	5′	10′	15′
	μmol Pi liberated		
In vitro			
Untreated control	0.16	0.20	0.32
CCl_4	0.72	1.44	1.68
CCl_4 + Versene	0.12	0.40	0.60
In vivo			
Untreated control	0.00	0.16	0.28
CCl_4	0.48	0.84	1.32
CCl_4 + Versene	0.08	0.36	0.56

Tube contents: 1.25×10^{-2} M glycylglycine buffer pH 7.4; 5×10^{-3} M $MgCl_2$; 2.5×10^{-2} M KCl; 2.5×10^{-3} M ATP; for the *in vitro* study mitochondria equivalent to 25 mg tissue wet weight and for the *in vivo* and control experiments mitochondria equivalent to 50 mg tissue wet weight; 0.5 ml of 75% trichloroacetic acid was used to stop the reaction. Versene treatment *in vitro* and *in vivo* as indicated under methods.

succinate oxidation is not DPN-linked and carbon tetrachloride fails to depress the activity of this enzyme. Moreover, Versene treatment (the simultaneous addition of Versene and carbon tetrachloride to the homogenate) results in essentially the complete return of phosphorylation coupled with succinate oxidation. In contrast, when using pyruvate or glutamate (or other DPN-linked carboxylic acids) as substrate, Versene treatment effects only a partial restoration of phosphorylation. With succinoxidase, P:O ratios are approximately 1.5, a value which is the same as the untreated control ratio and consistent with the theoretical P:O ratio of 2.0. With the DPN-linked dehydrogenase the best ratios obtained with Versene-carbon tetrachloride treated mitochondria were in the range of 1.5 to 2.0, with the untreated control value being 2.6 to 3.0. From the above it would appear that Versene protects two coupled phosphorylations but not the third.

A depression of oxidative phosphorylation was also observed in mitochondria from carbon tetrachloride-treated animals. Similar data has also been obtained by Dianzani (1954). In these experiments there was considerable variability from animal to animal and the degree of inhibition could not be predicted. In experiments in which the oxidation was not as severely depressed as that in table 4 some residual phosphorylative activity was retained. This was most commonly observed in measuring phosphorylation during succinate oxidation where P:O ratios were usually depressed about 50% and only rarely was oxidative phosphorylation completely inhibited. The data also indicated that like *in vitro* experiments Versene *in vivo* restored completely the phosphorylation associated with succinate oxidation but was incapable of protecting the full complement of coupled phosphorylation associated with the DPN-linked dehydrogenases. In several experiments, 3×10^{-3} M Versene was added to the homogenate prepared from livers of carbon tetrachloride-treated animals. No protection of oxidation or coupled phosphorylation was observed in mitochondria isolated under these conditions.

3. Hydrolysis of ATP: From the observations of Recknagel and Anthony (1957) that a mag-

TABLE 6

Oxidation of choline following in vitro treatment with CCl_4 and effect of chelating agents

Exp.	Treatment	μAt O_2 Uptake per Hour				
		Pyruvate + Malate	Choline concentrations			
			1×10^{-3} M	1×10^{-2} M	5×10^{-2} M	1×10^{-1} M
1	CCl_4	0.51	5.8	15.2	—	16.0
	CCl_4 + Versene	18.3	3.1	5.7	—	7.3
2	CCl_4	0.72	5.8	18.4	—	18.4
	CCl_4 + 8-OH Q	0.48	3.1	16.7	—	15.7
3	CCl_4	0.00	5.5	11.2	15.1	—
	None	13.8	4.3	5.7	6.6	—
4	Versene	10.5	—	3.9	—	4.7
	None	12.30	—	4.4	—	6.7

Experimental conditions the same as table 1, except 1.0μmol DPN was added to each flask containing choline.

nesium-dependent ATP-ase is activated by carbon tetrachloride and indications from our data that Versene could protect against the inhibition of oxidative phosphorylation produced by this agent, ATP-ase studies were pursued. The data presented in table 5 confirm the activation of a mitochondrial ATP-ase and demonstrate that Versene is effective in reducing this hydrolysis of ATP by carbon tetrachloride both *in vivo* and *in vitro*. While *in vitro* treatment seems to produce a greater splitting of ATP than is observed *in vivo*, this difference may merely be a function of the drug concentration at the site of action. Negligible ATP-ase activation was obtained if magnesium was omitted from the reaction mixture and fluoride did not influence the rate of hydrolysis in the complete system. The ATP-ase determinations were usually run at the same time and with the same enzyme preparations as were used for the oxidative phosphorylation studies. The ability of Versene to protect against oxidative and phosphorylative changes in treated mitochondria parallels its protective action against the magnesium ATP-ase.

4. Stimulation of choline oxidation: It has been demonstrated that under suitable conditions the mitochondrion may exhibit a permeability barrier for choline (Williams, 1955). From our earlier studies with DPN addition, there appeared to be an increase in mitochondrial permeability with carbon tetrachloride treatment. The choline oxidase system, which is known to be associated with the mitochondrion (Kensler and Langemann, 1951), was investigated using the previously described carbon tetrachloride regime. From table 6 it is apparent that exposure to carbon tetrachloride does indeed allow the oxidation of choline to proceed at a greatly accelerated rate. Pyruvic oxidase activity was run concomitantly to indicate the degree of inhibition of the DPN-linked dehydrogenases. Versene in these experiments also exerted a protective effect upon the mitochondria. It will be noted that the rate of choline oxidation by Versene-carbon tetrachloride treated mitochondria was quite similar to rates of the untreated control. Versene *per se* when added to the suspending medium for the isolation of normal liver mitochondria had no effect on the rate of choline oxidation. The chelating agent, 8-hydroxyquinoline, did not possess the protective property on mitochondrial permeability exhibited by Versene.

B. Other criteria of cellular damage. 1. Changes in ion content: It is well known that concentration gradients exist for ions in cells and even in cell particulates. Since it had been demonstrated that permeability of mitochondria is altered by carbon tetrachloride, it seemed likely that normal ionic gradients within cells might be sensitive to these permeability changes. Since the sodium and potassium content of the surrounding intracellular environment is considerably lower than that found in the mitochondria (MacFarlane and Spencer, 1953), it was felt that ionic changes would more readily be reflected in the supernatant fluid. The supernatant is not a natural fluid but a mixture of intracellular and extracellular fluids in 0.25 M sucrose. Examination of table 7 shows that after *in vivo* treatment with carbon tetrachloride, the sodium content of the supernatant

TABLE 7

Cation concentrations (mEq/l) following in vivo treatment with CCl_4 and Versene

Treatment	Supernatant Fluid			Plasma		
	No. of animals	Na+*	K+	No. of animals	Na+	K+
Untreated control	9	68.2 (57.2–77.5)	71.9 (63.6–84.0)	8	158	7.1
Versene	2	57.0†	70.0	2	154	6.6
CCl_4	6	107.2 (91.0–130)	33.8 (19.5–46.7)	8	150	7.3
CCl_4 + Versene	4	86.0 (82.0–94.0)	40.4 (33.8–54.5)	8	152	7.4

* Mean and range.
† Mean of indicated no. of animals.

TABLE 8

Serum glutamic-oxaloacetic transaminase time study following carbon tetrachloride and Versene treatment

Treatment	Change in OD/min/ 0.1 ml	Change in GOT Activity*	No. of Animals
Untreated control	0.011	1	10
CCl_4 (5 hr)	0.057	5.2	3
CCl_4 + Versene (5 hr)	0.060	5.4	2
CCl_4 (10 hr)	0.100	9.1	2
CCl_4 + Versene (10 hr)	0.150	13.6	2
CCl_4 (15 hr)	0.140	12.7	2
CCl_4 + Versene (15 hr)	0.140	12.7	2
CCl_4 (20 hr)	0.600	54.5‡	11
CCl_4 + Versene (20 hr)	0.220	20.0	16
CCl_4 (30 hr)	0.150	13.6	2
CCl_4 + Versene (30 hr)	0.270	24.6	2

* The change in activity is expressed as a multiple of the untreated serum value where the untreated control value equals 1.
‡ Significantly different from Versene-treated at a level of $p = <0.01$.

fluid is increased while the potassium content is decreased. Versene alone has no appreciable effect on ion content. After carbon tetrachloride and Versene administration the sodium content of the supernatant fluid is decreased toward normal but little change is observed in the potassium concentration. Simultaneous plasma measurements indicate no alteration of cation concentration in the plasma.

When sodium and potassium concentrations were determined in the supernatant fluid after *in vitro* carbon tetrachloride treatment no deviation from control values was observed.

2. Serum glutamic-oxaloacetic transaminase activity: Increases in serum GOT have been reported in man following exposure to carbon tetrachloride (Wroblewski *et al.*, 1956). Block and Cornish (1958) exposed rats to carbon tetrachloride vapor and found the greatest increase in serum GOT occurred after 24 hours. In the present study changes in GOT were determined after carbon tetrachloride administration and after simultaneous Versene treatment. In table 8, it will be noted that marked changes in enzyme activity occurred over a period of 5 to 30 hours in the carbon tetrachloride treated animals, rising to a maximum after 20 hours and then regressing. Versene and carbon tetrachloride treated animals also showed a rise in GOT activity but at no time did the values approach those of the carbon tetrachloride animals at 20 hours post-treatment.

3. Microscopic studies: The histological examination of livers from untreated controls, carbon tetrachloride-treated animals and Versene-carbon tetrachloride treated animals was also undertaken to attempt to correlate these with the metabolic alterations observed. Marked fatty infiltration and some necrosis, particularly surrounding the central veins was observed in varying degrees in the carbon tetrachloride treated animals. After 5 to 10 hours the changes were minimal but definite, and were most marked from 20 to 44 hours. Versene administration together with carbon tetrachloride did not seem to alter the liver pathology. In several instances it appeared that Versene actually had a deleterious effect when administered with carbon tetrachloride. Versene, when given to untreated controls did not affect the normal histology of the liver. A detailed study of these findings will be presented elsewhere.

C. Attempts to protect against metabolic changes with other agents. 1. Choline: Choline is probably the most popular and most widely studied of the lipotropic agents. In a recent study Christie and Judah (1954) reported that the coincident oral administration of choline chloride prevented the enzymatic changes observed with carbon tetrachloride alone. In ten animals pretreated in the manner described by the above workers we have been unable to verify their findings. In some experiments, the depression of functional activity produced by carbon tetrachloride seems to be increased by choline. A two-fold increase in choline dosage was also ineffective. A typical experiment is shown in table 9.

2. Other chelators: Since we had obtained significant protection with Versene, studies were undertaken to determine whether other chelating agents might not also exhibit this property. We had shown that 8-hydroxyquinoline which has about the same chelating potential as Versene was unable to prevent choline oxidase stimulation. *In vivo* studies also indicated that 8-hydroxyquinoline was ineffective in protecting against oxidative and phosphorylative changes induced by carbon tetrachloride (table 10). It should be pointed out, however, that the dose of 8-hydroxyquinoline was only one-half that of Versene administered. Larger amounts could not be used because of the toxicity of the compound *per se.*

TABLE 9

Failure of administration of choline to reverse the effects of CCl_4 on liver function

Treatment	μAt O_2 Uptake per 20 Minutes				ATP-ase as % control*
	Pyruvate	α-Keto glutarate	Citrate	Succinate	
Control	11.2	15.3	15.8	18.4	100
CCl_4	2.80	4.30	0.70	11.40	370
CCl_4 + Choline	0.50	0.50	0.20	16.1	640

Conditions the same as table 1 and table 5.
* 15 minute incubation.

If the beneficial effects exerted by Versene were the result of its ability to bind magnesium ion, then a compound like magnesium-disodium ethylenediamine tetraacetate ($Mg\text{-}Na_2$ Versene) which would not bind magnesium and perhaps would even increase the magnesium concentration within the cell, should be ineffective. Such was found to be the case when the magnesium-disodium Versene was administered with carbon tetrachloride. Equimolar doses or concentrations of $Mg\text{-}Na_2$ Versene did not protect either *in vivo* (table 10) or *in vitro.*

Discussion. *In vitro* and *in vivo* experiments carried out in our laboratory indicate that carbon tetrachloride increases the permeability of the mitochondrion with a subsequent loss of DPN. The evidence presented shows that addition of DPN is able to restore toward normal the oxidative activity of the DPN-linked dehydrogenases. However, it is also apparent that replacement of this co-factor is only partially effective in the restoration of oxidative function. Nor is phosphorylative activity enhanced with coenzyme addition. These findings might indicate that there may be further co-factors released by the action of carbon tetrachloride or that the binding site of exogenous DPN differs from that of the endogenous coenzyme and is thus less effective functionally (Hunter *et al.*, 1958). Generally, the activation of the magnesium-dependent ATP-ase parallels the decrease in DPN-linked dehydrogenase activity. The data do not permit any

TABLE 10

The inability of $MgNa_2$ Versene and of 8-OH quinoline to exert protective effects upon the function of the liver of rats treated with CCl_4

Treatment	Glutamate*			Succinate*			ATP-ase† % Normal	GOT OD Change per Minute per 0.1 ml
	μAt O_2 uptake	μmol Pi	P:O	μAt O_2 uptake	μmol Pi	P:O		
Untreated	8.85	21.6	2.44	8.10	16.0	1.98	100	0.008
CCl_4	0.74	0	0	9.50	4.6	0.69	233	0.58
CCl_4 + Na_2 Vers	8.10	14.40	1.78	8.86	15.8	1.79	143	0.14
CCl_4 + $MgNa_2$ Vers	0	0	0	9.80	8.80	0.90	245	0.62
CCl_4 + 8-OH Q	0	0	0	4.95	4.00	0.81	287	—

* Incubation time 10 minutes. Conditions the same as for tables 1 and 5.
† Incubation time 15 minutes.

speculation as to which of these phenomena is primary and which is secondary, or whether they might occur simultaneously.

The increase in the oxidation of choline by carbon tetrachloride treated liver mitochondria also suggests an increase in the permeability of the mitochondrial membrane since choline is a charged molecule passing animal barriers with difficulty. The step-wise increase in choline oxidation by untreated mitochondria which occurs as the concentration is increased is probably an indication of the difficulty this molecule has in permeating the mitochondrion. The absence of any marked difference in the activity of choline oxidase in the carbon tetrachloride-poisoned mitochondrion after a concentration greater than 10^{-2} M choline has been attained may mean that the now freely-diffusible substrate has saturated the enzyme. Richter (1951) has also reported increased choline oxidase activity in livers of carbon tetrachloride-treated rats.

Alterations of activity observed with *in vivo* treatment which may be manifestations of gross cellular damage rather than specific mitochondrial effects are the increased serum GOT activity and the changes in cation concentration. The increase in GOT activity in the serum of carbon tetrachloride treated animals is doubtless an indication of a loss of enzyme from the cell into its external environment. Block and Cornish (1958) suggest that this is the case. It should be noted that only when GOT values were increased by some 50-fold was there any decrease in functional activity as we have measured it.

The cation changes seen in the supernatant fluid appear to be a more a reflection of cellular rather than mitochondrial damage. Such changes do not occur with *in vitro* carbon tetrachloride treatment. Since sodium ion is in higher concentration in the extracellular fluid and potassium high in the intracellular compartment we are probably measuring changes due to an equilibration of the two cations from their higher to their lower concentration spaces. Since *in vitro* treatment does not alter the ion concentrations in the supernatant fluid it seems unlikely that the changes seen with *in vivo* administration of carbon tetrachloride result from shifts in mitochondrial ion concentrations. It is more likely that the integrity of the cellular membrane has been disrupted allowing the free diffusion of ions. Still another possibility is the inhibition of an active ion transport mechanism, or alternatively, both of these phenomena may be operative. One can still not rule out the explanation that a yet unstudied cation may be primarily affected and that the changes seen in sodium and potassium concentrations may merely be a reflection of the earlier effect. Further study is indicated in this area.

Our studies intimate that there may be two mechanisms by which Versene is exerting its protective effects. The ability to partially prevent the loss of oxidative activity in mitochondria from carbon tetrachloride-treated animals and from *in vitro* treated mitochondria seems to suggest an effect upon the membrane of these organelles. While this would seem to be unrelated to the chelating properties of Versene, it is well documented that calcium ion will cause a disruption of mitochondrial integrity (Slater and Cleland, 1952, 1953; Lindberg and Ernster, 1954). Raaflaub (1953, 1953a, 1955) has discussed the relationship between mitochondrial swelling and energy-rich phosphate bond compounds and has suggested that one of the functions of ATP may be to bind calcium ion and thus prevent the permeability effects. If such is the case then Versene may be acting to bind both magnesium and calcium, the former ion directly and thus inhibiting the activation of a magnesium ATP-ase the latter indirectly by maintenance of ATP concentrations which in turn bind calcium ion. Or, one may speculate that some complex of calcium ion and ATP forms the structural unit of the mitochondrial membrane and mitochondrial integrity is dependent upon the maintenance of this structure. Indeed, carbon tetrachloride treatment does increase calcium content of rat liver mitochondria (Thiers and Reynolds, 1958).

Undoubtedly, the inhibition of oxidative phosphorylation and its protection by Versene is related to the chelating properties of this compound. The effects on oxidative phosphorylation parallel the activation of the magnesium ATP-ase in the absence and presence of Versene. It would appear therefore from these studies and from those utilizing other chelating agents that protection is afforded by the binding of magnesium ion.

The failure of Versene to protect the phosphorylation between DPN and flavoprotein deserves further comment. The observations of Myers and Slater (1957) lend credence to the possibility that a separate ATP-ase exists for each individual phosphorylation. One may speculate that the DPN-flavoprotein ATP-ase may be a non-metal activated one and thus resistant to the protective effects of chelators. Another explanation might be that the DPN-flavoprotein phosphorylation is uniquely dependent upon the integrity of the mitochondrial structure and early modifications of structure by carbon tetrachloride cannot be reversed by the addition of Versene.

We do not believe that the protection against the increase in choline oxidation by Versene is related to its chelating properties. Our only evidence to support this contention, however, is the negative data obtained with 8-hydroxyquinoline (table 6).

No explanation is offered for the failure of choline to alter the enzymatic changes induced by carbon tetrachloride.

A facet of the present study which must be emphasized is that fatty infiltration of the liver was not indicative of loss of mitochondrial function as we have measured it. In many instances there is very definite fatty infiltration of the liver at a time when no functional change occurs. For example, within 5 hours after carbon tetrachloride administration marked fatty infiltration is seen, yet it is difficult to observe functional alterations in mitochondria before 20 hours post-treatment. Moreover, the animals treated with Versene show excessive fatty degeneration when the metabolic processes under study are essentially intact. Recknagel *et al.* (1958) also have presented evidence indicating that fatty infiltration cannot be correlated with mitochondrial injury.

SUMMARY

In vitro treatment of liver mitochondria with carbon tetrachloride results in a depression of DPN-linked dehydrogenase activity. The addition of DPN partially restores oxidation. Oxidative phosphorylation is inhibited, but this effect is probably the result of a magnesium ATP-ase activation. The oxidation of choline is enhanced. These changes can be blocked by the concomitant addition of Versene.

The same general pattern in oxidation and phosphorylation is observed with the oral administration of carbon tetrachloride. In addition changes are seen in tissue sodium and potassium concentrations and in serum glutamic-oxaloacetic transaminase activity. All effects are modified by Versene administered simultaneously.

Choline administration failed to protect against the metabolic changes induced by carbon tetrachloride.

There did not appear to be any correlation between metabolic alterations and histologic findings.

The possible mechanisms by which Versene protects are discussed.

ACKNOWLEDGMENT. The authors wish to acknowledge the technical assistance of Mrs. Annette Hulett and thank the Upjohn Company for donating most of the animals used in this study.

REFERENCES

BLOCK, W. D. AND CORNISH, H. H.: Proc. Soc. exp. Biol., N. Y. **97:** 178, 1958.
BRIDGERS, W. F., ABELE, D. AND HUNTER, F. E., JR.: Fed. Proc. **16:** 158, 1957.
BRODY, T. M. AND BAIN, J. A.: Proc. Soc. exp. Biol., N. Y. **77:** 50, 1951.
CAMERON, G. R. AND KARUNARATNE, W. A. E.: J. Path. Bact. **42:** 1, 1936.
CHRISTIE, G. S. AND JUDAH, J. D.: Proc. roy. Soc. **B142:** 241, 1954.
DIANZANI, M. U.: Biochim. biophys. Acta **14:** 514, 1954.
DIANZANI, M. U. AND VITI, J.: Biochem. J. **59:** 141, 1955.
DIANZANI, M. U.: Biochim. biophys. Acta **17:** 391, 1955a.
FISKE, C. H. AND SUBBAROW, Y.: J. biol. Chem. **66:** 375, 1925.
HOGEBOOM, G. H., SCHNEIDER, W. C. AND PALLADE, G. E.: J. biol. Chem. **172:** 619, 1948.
HUNTER, F. E., JR., SHUTZ, B., MALISON, R. AND ATCHISON, A.: Fed. Proc. **17:** 247, 1958.
KENSLER, C. J. AND LANGEMANN, H.: J. biol. Chem. **192:** 551, 1951.
LINDBERG, O. AND ERNSTER, L.: Nature **173:** 1038, 1954.
MACFARLANE, M. G. AND SPENCER, H. G.: Biochem. J. **54:** 569, 1953.
MYERS, D. K. AND SLATER, E. C.: Biochem. J. **67:** 558, 1957.
POTTER, V. R. AND ELVEHJEM, C. A.: J. biol. Chem. **114:** 495, 1936.
RAAFLAUB, J.: Helv. chim. acta **38:** 27, 1955.
RAAFLAUB, J.: Helv. physiol. acta **11:** 142, 1953.
RAAFLAUB, J.: Helv. physiol. acta **11:** 157, 1953a.
RECKNAGEL, R. O. AND ANTHONY, D. D.: Fed. Proc. **16:** 105, 1957.
RECKNAGEL, R. O., STADLER, J. AND LITTERIA, M.: Fed. Proc. **17:** 129, 1958.
RICHTER, M.: THIS JOURNAL **102:** 94, 1951.
SCHNEIDER, W. C.: J. biol. Chem. **165:** 585, 1948.
SLATER, E. C. AND CLELAND, K. W.: Nature **170:** 118, 1952.
SLATER, E. C. AND CLELAND, K. W.: Biochem. J. **55:** 566, 1953.
STEINBERG, D., BALDWIN, O. AND OSTROW, B. H.: J. Lab. clin. Med. **48:** 44, 1956.
THIERS, R. E. AND REYNOLDS, E. S.: Fed. Proc. **17:** 537, 1958.
UMBREIT, W. W., BURRIS, R. H. AND STAUFFER, J. F.: Manometric Techniques, Burgess Publishing Co., Minneapolis, 1957.
WILLIAMS, G. R.: Fed. Proc. **14:** 304, 1955.
WROBLEWSKI, F., JERVIS, G. AND LADUE, J.: Ann. intern. Med. **45:** 782, 1956.

8088

DEGRADATION OF MESCALINE BY AMINE OXIDASES

E. ALBERT ZELLER, JAMES BARSKY, ELAINE R. BERMAN, MARSHALL S. CHERKAS AND JAMES R. FOUTS

Department of Biochemistry, Northwestern University, Medical School, Chicago, Illinois

Received for publication July 7, 1958

Various mammals are able to convert mescaline into 3,4,5-trimethoxyphenylacetic acid and excrete it in this form (Slotta and Mueller, 1936). Since this acid is devoid of the specific biologic activity of mescaline the metabolic steps involved in this conversion are factors in the system controlling the psychopharmacologic effects of mescaline. The search for enzymes catalyzing the formation of 3,4,5-trimethoxyphenylacetic acid originated with the classical investigation by the Bernheims, who demonstrated that rabbit liver preparations effectively inactivate mescaline by oxidative deamination (Bernheim and Bernheim, 1938). Surprisingly, the mescaline-oxidizing enzyme differed markedly from monoamine oxidase (MO). This observation was confirmed subsequently in several laboratories (Blaschko, 1944; Steensholt, 1947; Werle and von Pechmann, 1949).

In the course of our studies on the reactive surface of amine oxidases some of the structural requirements for substrates of diamine oxidase (DO) were defined: a primary aliphatic amino group (residue A), and a nucleophilic residue (residue B), *viz.*, a second amino group or a methoxy-residue, form suitable combinations for binding the substrate to the enzymic surface (Zeller *et al.*, 1956). Since mescaline fulfilled these conditions, the question arose as to whether this amine is a substrate of DO. Preliminary results indicated that the characteristics of DO and "mescaline oxidase" in rabbit liver were similar (Zeller, 1956; Zeller *et al.*, 1957); however, further evidence disclosed that in some other species DO is not the sole system for the oxidation of mescaline.

MATERIALS AND METHODS. Tissues of the common laboratory animals were obtained from normal adults of both sexes which had been maintained on standard diets. Cattle, sheep and hog organs were procured directly from the processing plants. Human tissues were received at autopsy generally within 12 hours post mortem.

Liver slices were prepared according to the procedure of Deutsch (1936) (See also Cohen, 1957). To produce homogenates, the tissues were forced through an Altmann hand press or an hydraulically operated press (Witter *et al.*, 1953); the macerated pulp was then homogenized with an appropriate medium in a glass vessel cooled by an ice bath, using a motor-driven glass or teflon pestle. For assay as such, homogenates were suspended 1:10 (w/v) in M/15 phosphate buffer pH 7.2 (Sorensen). When required, dialysis was carried out in a continuous flow system in the cold.

Fractionation of tissues for the isolation of intracellular components by differential centrifugation in 0.88 M sucrose was performed according to the method of Hogeboom *et al.* (1948) with the refinements of Cotzias and Dole (1951). In the experiments where 0.25 M sucrose was employed as the homogenization medium (Schneider, 1948), the resultant supernatant after sedimentation of the mitochondria was separated into microsoma and soluble cytoplasmic fractions by spinning at 12,600 centrifugal units ("unit" = $1/1000 \times g \times$ minutes) in the Spinco ultracentrifuge (preparative model L). The various fractions were suspended or diluted with phosphate buffer for enzymic assay.

Solubilization of mitochondrial MO was accomplished by two methods: (a) Mitochondrial suspensions in 0.25 M sucrose were subjected to sonic oscillation (9 kilocycles sonic vibrator, type R 22-3, Raytheon, Waltham, Mass.) for 30 minutes in the presence of 10 to 20 mg of desoxycholic acid per ml (Barsky *et al.*, 1953). The preparation was maintained at 10° by means of a water-cooler jacket. Intact mitochondria were removed by sedimentation at 400 centrifugal units. On further ultracentrifugation for 6000 units, 40% of the MO activity (hog liver) appeared in the precipitate and 60% remained in the supernatant. (b) Washed mitochondria isolated from 0.88 M sucrose homogenates were suspended in M/15 phosphate buffer with 2 "Cutscum" (isooctylphenoxypolyethoxyethanol, Fisher Scientific) (Cotzias *et al.*, 1954) and gently shaken at intermittent periods during several hours in the cold. The lysed mitochondria were then spun for 26,000 centrifugal units in the ultracentrifuge. The supernatant which was reddish-brown in color was perfectly clear, and contained approximately 70% of the MO activity of the original mitochondria (beef liver). This soluble MO preparation was stable for at least 1 week when stored in the cold; after several weeks the solution activity declined to about 60% of the initial activity in 2 months.

Purified DO was prepared from fresh hog kidney cortex by differential heating, precipitation with acetone and ammonium sulfate and by elution from aluminum hydroxide gel (cγ). The detailed description of the procedure will be presented in a following paper.

Cadaverine dihydrochloride, histamine dihydrochloride, mescaline hydrochloride, isonicotinhydrazine (Rimifon, INH, isoniazid), 1-isonicotinyl-2-isopropyl hydrazine phosphate (Marsilid, IIH, iproniazid), obtained from F. Hoffmann-La-Roche, Inc., Basel, Switzerland and Nutley, N.J., and choline-*p*-tolyl ether, hydrobromide obtained from Professors W. A. Bain and B. G. Brown, Leeds, England, were used without further purification. These compounds were received as gifts for which we express our deep gratitude. The remainder of the substrates and inhibitors were purchased from commercial sources. All free bases were converted into hydrochlorides or sulfates.

Standard assays of MO activity were carried out with the enzyme suspended in phosphate buffer in the main well of the vessel (1.6 ml); the sidearm contained buffered tyramine (0.4 ml M/20) or other amines to yield a final substrate concentration of 0.01 M. The inner well of the vessel held a strip of pleated filter paper soaked with 10% NaOH (0.1 ml) to absorb any liberated CO_2. In order to simplify conditions for the evaluation of inhibitors, cyanide and semicarbazide were not included routinely to block secondary oxidations. Instead, the reactions were permitted to run to completion (2 hours), and the extent of oxidation was derived then from the O:N ratio (microatoms of oxygen consumed:micromoles of ammonia liberated). Inhibitors were added to the main vessel to allow an adequate interval (15 minutes) for preincubation with the enzyme before tipping in the substrate from the sidearm to initiate the reaction (Zeller *et al.*, 1955). Enzyme and reagent blanks were carried through in the same manner. The Q_{ox}, calculated from the initial portion of the curve of oxygen consumption, was defined as the number of microatoms of oxygen consumed per hour, per gram of fresh tissue or its equivalent (*e.g.*, mitochondria derived from 1 g of fresh tissue). Standard assays for DO activity were performed similarly except for the use of cadaverine as the substrate. DO reactions were followed over periods ranging up to 15 hours. In such experiments a bacteriostatic agent was generally required; when permissible n-octanol was used for this purpose, otherwise, a mixed penicillin-dihydrostreptomycin suspension (Abbott; final concentration 1:3000) was added to the system.

Ammonia liberated in the course of deamination reactions was determined by the technique of microdiffusion and microanalysis in Conway-units (Conway, 1957). The inner well of the units contained boric acid-indicator solution which permitted a direct titration with 0.01 N HCl upon completion of the diffusion process. The vessels were generally allowed to stand overnight before titration. Since the ammonia value here represents only a single point in the reaction, it cannot in itself serve as a direct measure of the rate of the reaction. Initial lag periods as indicated by oxygen consumption in certain inhibition reactions may frequently be overcome, and over the entire incubation period as much total oxygen will be taken up and ammonia liberated as in the control system. The ammonia value, however, is a sensitive measure of the extent of the reaction and, when coupled with oxygen data to give O:N ratios, provides an index of the oxygen uptake beyond the primary MO reaction. The Q_{am} values found in the tables, therefore, represent the average production of ammonia in micromoles per hour of incubation, and per gram of fresh tissue, with no regard to initial reaction velocities.

RESULTS. *Degradation of mescaline and other amines by rabbit liver preparations.* Mescaline was gradually oxidized in the presence of rabbit liver slices (Q_{ox} = 10) and homogenates (Q_{ox} = 21, Q_{am} = 19, average of 4 determination). On cell fractionation, 23% of the activity of the homogenate was found in the fraction labelled nuclear, 29% in the mitochondria, 43% in the microsomes and 8% in the supernatant. In addition to mescaline the mitochondrial preparations attacked other amines which are typical substrates of both MO and DO (table 1). However, the inhibitor pattern for mescaline degradation is clearly characteristic of DO. Rabbit liver DO seemingly is more sensitive to iproniazid inhibition than the classical hog kidney DO (Zeller *et al.*, 1952; Fouts *et al.*, 1957, fig. 2). In addition to semicarbazide (10^{-3}M), aminoguanidine and isoniazid (10^{-4}M) blocked the oxidation of mescaline efficiently, while the MO-inhibitor choline-*p*-tolyl ether (10^{-3}M) was without influence.

To exclude the possibility that the inhibitors acted on systems involved in the transfer of the reaction components into the mitochondria rather than on the reactive surface of DO, the experiments were repeated with solubilized mitochondria. The results were essentially the same as those for whole mitochondria (table 2).

Since the microsomal fraction exhibited substantial mescaline-degrading activity, some alternative mechanism as described by Brodie (1956) for the inactivation of foreign or non-

TABLE 1

Degradation of amines by rabbit liver mitochondria

Standard assays, each vessel contained mitochondria equivalent to 0.2–0.4 g of liver.

Substrate	Q_{ox}	Inhibition*		
		10^{-3} M Semicarbazide	10^{-4} M Iproniazid	Sat. octanol
		%	%	%
n-Butylamine	26 ± 11.5 (5)†	0	75	100
n-Amylamine	67 ± 16.4 (9)	0	76	71
Tyramine	79 ± 27 (5)	0	78	100
Mescaline	4.7 ± 1.5 (9)	100	100	0
Histamine	2.1 ± 1.6 (7)	100	100	6‡
Cadaverine	2	100	100	25

* Calculated from initial oxygen uptake.
† Number of determinations given in parenthesis.
‡ Activation instead of inhibition.

TABLE 2

Action of amine oxidase inhibitors on the degradation of mescaline by solubilized rabbit liver mitochondria

Standard assays, each vessel contained mitochondria equivalent to 0.2 g of liver.*

Inhibitor	Enzyme Affected	Inhibition	
		Oxygen consumption	Ammonia liberation
		%	%
10^{-3} M Semicarbazide	DO	83	91
10^{-5} M Thiocarbohydrazide	DO	54	68
10^{-4} M Aminoguanidine	DO	89	95
10^{-4} M Isoniazid	DO	77	87
10^{-3} M Iproniazid	MO + DO	94	94
Saturated n-octanol	MO	20	2

* Q_{ox}-values for tyramine, mescaline and histamine were 29.5, 4.6 and 0.9, respectively. Mescaline: Q_{am} = 1.8, O/N = 2.4.

TABLE 3

Action of amine oxidase inhibitors on the degradation of amines by rabbit liver microsomes

Standard assays, each vessel contained microsomes equivalent to 0.2 g of liver.

Substrates	Q_{ox}	Inhibition			
		10^{-4} M Aminoguanidine		8 mM Octanol	
		Oxygen consumption	Ammonia liberation	Oxygen consumption	Ammonia liberation
		%	%	%	%
Tyramine	71	0	18	96	70
Mescaline	4.9	100	100	0	0
Histamine	2.7	100	100	0	10

physiological compounds by microsomal systems, was considered. Examination of this particulate fraction with inhibitors (table 3) reaffirmed the indications that a DO-like enzyme is concerned with the oxidative deamination of mescaline by microsomes of rabbit liver.

Degradation of mescaline by purified hog kidney diamine oxidase. The results just reported speak for DO as the agent responsible for the degradation of mescaline by rabbit liver. If this is the case, purified DO should be expected to attack mescaline. To test this point, the effect of partially purified DO from hog kidney on mescaline was investigated. The enzyme preparation was shown previously to be free of MO and yet was able to attack tyramine (Fouts *et al.*, 1957). Mescaline was oxidized by purified DO at a rate similar to that for tyramine. The resistance of this enzyme toward octanol and its sensitivity toward aminoguanidine exclude MO entirely and point to DO as the catalyzing entity (table 4).

Aminoguanidine, apparently, is not as efficient an inhibitor of mescaline oxidation, as it is for the degradation of cadaverine by DO (Schuler, 1952). This quantitative difference may be due to the fact that cadaverine, after undergoing oxidative deamination, becomes an aminoaldehyde which quickly forms an intramolecular Schiff's base (Mann and Smithies, 1955; Hasse and Maisack, 1957; Cavallini *et al.*, 1957). Obviously, this reaction is excluded when a monoamine is oxidized by DO. In this instance, the aldehyde isolated by Fouts *et al.* (1957) could condense with aminoguanidine and eliminate it as an inhibitor. A simi-

TABLE 4

Degradation of mescaline by purified hog kidney diamine oxidase

Standard assay for DO, 12.5 units of DO per vessel; enzyme concentration 2800 units per g of nitrogen.

Inhibitor	Q_{ox}	Oxygen uptake	Ammonia liberation
		µat	*µmol*
—	0.7	4.2	1.4
10^{-3} M Aminoguanidine	0	0	0.4
2.5 × 10^{-4} M Iproniazid	0.1	1.4	0.4
Saturated n-octanol	0.7	4.2	1.4

TABLE 5

Degradation of mescaline and other amines by sheep plasma

Standard assay with 0.2 g of lyophilized plasma in a total volume of 2 ml per manometric vessel.

Substrates	Inhibitors	Q_{ox}	$\frac{O}{N}$	Inhibition	
				Oxygen consumption	Ammonia liberation
				%	%
Mescaline	—	35	4.1	—	—
	Sat. octanol	25	3.2	29	0
	10^{-3} M semicarbazide	0	—	100	100
Spermine	—	140	1.8	—	—
	Sat. octanol	64	1.5	54	11
	10^{-3} M semicarbazide	0	—	100	100
Tyramine	—	28	3.4	—	—
	10^{-3} M semicarbazide	0	—	100	100

lar interaction between the reaction product of DO and cyanide has been analyzed previously (Zeller, 1940); cyanide reacts with the aldehyde even more rapidly than this group forms a Schiff's base with the second amino residue of the substrate molecule.

Oxidation of mescaline in the presence of sheep plasma. Tabor *et al.* (1954) investigated a purified spermine oxidase of beef plasma which attacks spermine, 1,10-decamethylene diamine, tyramine, mescaline and other monoamines. The ratio of oxidation velocities of spermine to mescaline was 10. In sheep plasma, we found a similar enzyme with a velocity ratio of 4. Since the Q-value with mescaline indicated good activity, it was readily possible to study the nature of the enzyme responsible for the oxidation of this amine (table 5). The oxidative deamination of spermine, tyramine and mescaline displayed the same inhibitor pattern as the beef plasma enzyme and as diamine oxidases in general. The partial inhibition by octanol is due to blocking of the oxidation steps following the amine oxidase reaction as indicated by the O:N ratios.

Degradation of mescaline by hog tissue preparations. While little doubt remains that in rabbit liver, hog kidney cortex and sheep plasma DO-like enzymes are able to attack mescaline, experiments carried out with hog kidney particulates suggested the existence of mescaline-oxidizing enzymes other than DO. Hog kidney cortex homogenate was fractionated in 0.88 M sucrose solution and the occurrence of the two amine oxidases in the various cellular fractions was determined (table 6). It was observed that the mescaline-inactivating enzyme displays a distribution similar to that of semicarbazide-insensitive MO, and different in topography when compared with the semicarbazide-sensitive DO. When the mitochondria were partially solubilized by sonic oscillation (without desoxycholic acid) and spun down at 400 centrifugal units, the supernatant fluid did not contain tyramine- or mescaline-degrading entities, although some DO was present. In the centrifugate DO was absent, and the ratio of tyramine- to mescaline-oxidizing velocities was observed to be 5.2, which is close to the ratios observed for the intact mitochondria (6.4). Finally, the mescaline-destroying enzyme

TABLE 6

Degradation of amines by hog kidney cortex fractions

Standard assay except that the vessels contained a total amount of mitochondria equivalent to 0.32 g of cortex (tyr.) and 0.64 g of cortex (cad., mesc.), respectively. Total volume for experiments with the supernatant fraction was 4.0 ml containing the equivalent of 1.62 g of cortex. Activity as percentage of Q-values of homogenate.

	Tyramine	Cadaverine	Mescaline
	%	%	%
Supernatant fluid (microsomes and cytoplasm)	14	51	17
Precipitate (mitochondria)	62	11	69

TABLE 7

Degradation of amines by hog liver mitochondria

Standard assay, in each vessel the equivalent of 0.25 g of liver was present. With tyramine, Q_{ox} = 169 and Q_{am} = 32.

Inhibitors	Inhibition*			
	Tyramine		Mescaline	
	Oxygen consumption	Ammonia liberation	Oxygen consumption	Ammonia liberation
	%	%	%	%
0.001 M Semicarbazide	2	0	7	7
0.008 M Octanol	74	73	100	100

* Initial rate of oxygen consumption and final ammonia liberation.

in hog kidney was completely blocked by 2.5 × 10^{-4}M iproniazid. Thus it seems likely that in hog kidney mitochondria mescaline is oxidized predominantly by a MO-like enzyme. If this conclusion is correct, hog liver which is rich in MO (homogenates Q_{ox} = 242), but poor in DO (Zeller *et al.*, 1939) should attack mescaline fairly well. The experimental evidence secured with mitochondria confirmed this assumption and made it clear that the inhibitor pattern of the mescaline degradation was that of MO (table 7).

Occurrence of mescaline-oxidizing enzymes in various species. Since organs from only a few species have been investigated with reference to their mescaline-degrading ability, various tissue preparations from two ornithologic and seven mammalian species were examined to establish the distribution of mescaline-oxidizing enzymes and the extent of their action (table 8). When adequate incubation periods were allowed in order to overcome the lag period which was frequently encountered, a measurable degradation could be observed with nearly all of the lung, kidney and liver preparations tested; however, no systematic relationship could be detected from the ratios of tyramine:mescaline oxidation rates in the various preparations. Predictably, tissues of the rabbit were considerably more active than the tissues of other species which are known to be less resistant to mescaline intoxication *in vivo*. Rabbit lung homogenate proved to be the most potent preparation (Q_{ox} = 35); it was followed by liver, pancreas, kidney and spleen homogenates. Rat, dog and human lung homogenates also displayed activities superior to other tissues in these species. Rat intestinal mucosa was inactive. Rabbit brain homogenate showed no sign of attacking mescaline, while only a trace of activity was noted with human brain (gray matter). According to the preceding

TABLE 8

Mescaline oxidation by tissue preparations of various species

	Q_{ox}	Q_{am}	O:N	No.*	Hrs†
Chicken					
Liver homogenate	+	0		2	3
Liver mitochondria	+	0		2	3
Pigeon					
Liver homogenate	+	+		2	3
Liver mitochondria	0	0		2	3
Rabbit					
Liver homogenate	21	18.6	1.6	4	2
Lung homogenate	35.7	21.7	2.7	5	3
Kidney homogenate	10	6	1.6	2	3
Pancreas homogenate	13.6	1.6	4.2	2	3
Spleen homogenate	4.6	1.4	1.7	2	3
Mouse					
Liver homogenate	+	1.4		2	3
Liver mitochondria	3.6	1.2	2.9	1	2
Lung homogenate	+	1.7		2	3
Rat					
Liver homogenate	‡	2.3		2	3
Lung homogenate	4.8	3.4	1.9	2	3
Kidney homogenate	‡	+		1	3
Dog					
Liver homogenate	+	0.6		2	4
Lung homogenate	5.1	1.3	3.7	2	4
Kidney homogenate	+	+		2	4
Hog					
Liver homogenate	9.8	3.7	2.0	2	6
Lung homogenate	3.7	3.7	2.7	1	4
Beef					
Liver mitochondria	7.2	2.5	2.2	2	3
Lung homogenate	4.6	3.5	2.3	4	3–10
Kidney homogenate	5.9	3.5	2.2	2	6
Human					
Liver homogenate	+	1.0		3	4
Lung homogenate	6.2	0.7	2.0	2	4
Kidney homogenate	1.5	0.8	1.6	2	4
Brain homogenate	‡	+		2	4
Placenta homogenate	3	0.4	8	2	3

* Number of individual determinations.

† Period of incubation.

‡ Mescaline depresses endogenous respiration of tissue preparation.

sections either MO or DO, or prototypes of both groups of enzymes may be responsible for the inactivation of mescaline. Thus, for the present, the question of which group a given mescaline-oxidizing enzyme belongs to must be determined experimentally. In addition to the examples presented above, the enzyme of mouse liver mitochondria displayed an inhibitor pattern typical for MO, comparable to that given for hog liver mitochondria.

Discussion. The many enzymes which catalyze the oxidative deamination of various amines can be separated into two distinct groups; the representatives of one group of the amine oxidases are insensitive toward 1 mM of semicarbazide, while those of the second group are generally blocked by this reagent (Zeller, 1938; Werle, 1940). In contrast to the former, the latter group of homologous enzymes seems to contain a carbonyl residue (aldehyde?) in its reactive site. This carbonyl residue probably takes an active part in the degradation of the substrates, perhaps by forming a Schiff's base (Zeller, 1938b, Goryachenkova, 1956) with amino group A of diamines (Zeller *et al.*, 1956). The semicarbazide-sensitive enzymes, called diamine oxidases, comprise the histaminase-diamine oxidase of hog kidney (Best, 1929; McHenry and Gavin, 1932, 1935; Zeller, 1938a, 1942, 1951), mescaline oxidase of rabbit liver (Bernheim and Bernheim, 1938), spermine oxidase of beef plasma (Tabor *et al.*, 1954) and benzylamine oxidase of horse plasma (Bergeret and Blaschko, 1957).

The available evidence suggests that the last 3 enzymes belong to a subdivision of DO, tentatively called DO-I, as opposed to DO-II, which includes the hog kidney enzyme. Mescaline is readily oxidized by at least 2 representatives of DO-I. In contrast, the degradation of this amine by hog kidney DO is achieved with more difficulty, requiring the use of a partially purified enzyme and long incubation periods to demonstrate the oxidation.

Mescaline oxidase of rabbit liver was characterized by its cyanide-sensitivity (Bernheim and Bernheim, 1938; Steensholt, 1947), and by its resistance toward octanol (Blaschko, 1944). These properties served as the criteria for the separation of mescaline oxidase from monoamine oxidase. They are, however, typical for DO, and thus in agreement with the results and conclusions presented in this paper.

It is interesting to note that with the introduction of an increasing number of methoxy residues into phenylethylamine the substrate is diverted from MO to a typical DO-type of enzyme (Alles and Heegaard, 1943; Steensholt, 1947). The nucleophilic methoxy residues display a tendency to interact with MO residues in such a way that the hydrogen-donating moiety of the substrate cannot adequately approach the hydrogen-accepting moiety of the enzyme. The reverse seems to be true for DO, which suggests that here the methoxy residues are located in the right position to facilitate proper attachment of the molecule to the enzymic surface. Other cases have been found in which one amino group of a DO substrate can be replaced successfully by a methoxy residue (Zeller *et al.*, 1958).

The experiments carried out with hog tissue preparations indicate that some classical semicarbazide-resistant monoamine oxidases are able to attack mescaline. It is, therefore, concluded that the electrophilic residues are situated on the active site in a manner that does not prevent the proper orientation of the mescaline molecule. Apparently, then, two different enzymes are present in hog tissues which are capable of destroying mescaline. In the rabbit, however, only the DO-like enzyme seems to be responsible for the rapid inactivation of mescaline, since, on blocking DO in liver preparations with cyanide, no appreciable oxidation was observed (Alles and Heegaard, 1943).

The inactivation of mescaline *in vivo*, therefore, may follow different pathways; either through MO, or DO, or both. This conclusion may be of interest to the pharmacologist for two different reasons: (a) Potentiation of the effects of mescaline in a manner similar to the potentiation of serotonin by iproniazid requires that either MO be blocked by iproniazid, benzylhydrazine, etc., or DO be inhibited by semicarbazide, aminoguanidine, etc. (b) It has been shown recently that epinephrine is methylated prior to degradation by MO (Armstrong *et al.*, 1956; Axelrod, 1957; Resnick *et al.*, 1958). It would be of interest to determine whether the acquired methoxy group in epinephrine increases the affinity of this compound for some amine oxidases.

The data presented here do not exclude the possibility that enzymes other than MO and DO are involved in the metabolism of mescaline. Axelrod (1955) has described a TPN-requiring system in rabbit liver microsomes which catalyzes the deamination of amphetamine. Iproniazid at a 10^{-4} M concentration is without effect on "amphetamine oxidase" while rabbit liver MO and DO are virtually inactivated at this level. Thus it seems unlikely that this system is concerned to any substantial extent with the degradation of mescaline. The high oxygen:nitrogen ratios encountered in many instances indicate that the immediate product of oxidative deamination—3,4,5-trimethoxyphenylacetaldehyde—more readily undergoes further oxidation to form the corresponding acid than the products of other substrates. A major involvement in further oxidations of microsomal enzymes which oxidize aromatic ethers seems to be doubtful due to differences in substrate specificity, cellular localization and cofactor requirements. In addition, mescaline is a rather poor substrate of the microsomal system in rabbit liver with a Q-value corresponding to less than one (Axelrod, 1956). The products of the oxidative deamination of mescaline, however, have not been tested.

SUMMARY

The oxidative deamination of mescaline by various tissue preparations from 9 vertebrate species was investigated. The mescaline oxidase of rabbit liver was found to be present in the mitochondrial and microsomal fractions of the cell. The inhibitor pattern for the rabbit liver enzyme resembled that characterizing a typical diamine oxidase (DO). Similar results were obtained for the oxidation of mescaline by a partially purified hog kidney DO (histaminase) and for sheep plasma spermine oxidase. These 3 enzymes are classified as belonging to the group of semicarbazide-sensitive diamine oxidases. The experimental evidence for the degradation of mescaline by particulate preparations from hog kidney and liver, and mouse liver, implicates the action of a semicarbazide-resistant monoamine oxidase in these species.

Acknowledgments. This work was supported by research grants from the National Institute of Health, United States Public Health Service (grant No. E-1413 (C5)), from the Lilly Research Laboratories, Indianapolis, Indiana and from the Multiple Sclerosis Foundation of America, Chicago, Illinois, Dr. Lewis J. Pollock, Responsible Investigator.

REFERENCES

Alles, G. A. and Heegaard, E. V.: J. biol. Chem. **147:** 487, 1943.
Armstrong, M. D., Shaw, K. N. F. and Wall, E.: J. biol. Chem. **218:** 293, 1956.
Axelrod, J.: J. biol. Chem. **214:** 753, 1955.
Axelrod, J.: Biochem. J. **63:** 634, 1956.
Axelrod, J.: Science **126:** 400, 1957.
Barsky, J., Berman, E. R. and Zeller, E. A.: Abstr., Communications, XIX Internat. Physiol. Congress, p. 191, Montreal, 1953.
Bergeret, B. and Blaschko, H.: Brit. J. Pharmacol. **12:** 513, 1957.
Bernheim, F. and Bernheim, M. L. C.: J. biol. Chem. **123:** 317, 1938.
Best, C. H.: J. Physiol. **67:** 256, 1929.
Blaschko, H.: J. Physiol. **103:** 13P, 1944.
Brodie, B. B.: J. Pharm., Lond. **8:** 1, 1956.
Cavallini, D., DeMarco, C. and Mondovi, B.: Biochim. biophys. Acta **24:** 353, 1957.
Cohen, P. P.: in Manometric Techniques, Umbreit, W. W., Burris, R. H. and Stauffer, J. F., editors, p. 135, Burgess Publishing Co., Mineapolis, 1957.
Conway, E. J.: Microdiffusion Analysis and Volumetric Error, Crosby, Lockwood and Son, London, 1957.
Cotzias, G. C. and Dole, V. P.: Proc. Soc. exp. Biol., N. Y. **78:** 157, 1951.
Cotzias, G. C., Serlin, I. and Greenough, J. J.: Science **120:** 144 (1954).
Deutsch, W.: J. Physiol. **87:** 56 P, 1936.
Fouts, J. R., Blanksma, L. A., Carbon, J. A. and Zeller, E. A.: J. biol. Chem. **225:** 1025, 1957.
Goryachenkova, E. V.: Biochemistry (Leningr.) **21:** 323, 1956.
Hasse, K. and Maisack, H.: Biochem. Z. **328:** 429, 1957.
Hogeboom, G. H., Schneider, W. C. and Palade, G. E.: J. biol. Chem. **172:** 619, 1948.
Mann, P. J. G. and Smithies, W.: Biochem. J. **61:** 89, 1955.
McHenry, E. W. and Gavin, G.: Biochem. J. **26:** 1365, 1932.
McHenry, E. W. and Gavin, G.: Biochem. J. **29:** 622, 1935.
Resnick, O., Wolfe, J. M., Freeman, H. and Elmadjian, F.: Science **127:** 1116, 1958.
Schneider, W. C.: J. biol. Chem. **176:** 259, 1948.
Schuler, W.: Experientia, **8:** 230, 1952.
Slotta, K. H. and Mueller, J.: Hoppe-Seyl. Z. **238:** 14, 1936.
Steensholt, G.: Acta physiol. scand. **14:** 356, 1947.
Tabor, C. W., Tabor, H. and Rosenthal, S. M.: J. biol. Chem. **208:** 645, 1954.
Werle, E.: Biochem. Z. **304:** 201, 1940.
Werle, E. and von Pechmann, E.: Z. Vitam.-Horm.- u. Fermentforsch. **2:** 433, 1949.
Witter, R. F., Pories, W. J. and Cottone, M. A.: Proc. Soc. exp. Biol., N. Y. **84:** 674, 1953.
Zeller, E. A.: Helvet. chim. acta **21:** 880, 1938a.
Zeller, E. A.: Helvet. chim. acta **21:** 1645, 1938b.
Zeller, E. A.: Helvet. chim. acta **23:** 1418, 1940.
Zeller, E. A.: Advanc. Enzymol. **2:** 93, 1942.
Zeller, E. A.: in The Enzymes: Chemistry and Mechanism of Action, Summer, J. B. and Myr-

BÄCK, K., editors, Vol. 11, p. 536, Academic Press, Inc., New York, 1951.
ZELLER, E. A.: in Ciba Foundation Symposium on Histamine, p. 258, Little, Brown and Co., Boston, 1956.
ZELLER, E. A., BARBATO, L. M., BARSKY, J., BLANKSMA, L. A. AND LAZANAS, J. C.: Fed. Proc. **17**: 342, 1958.
ZELLER, E. A., BARSKY, J. AND BERMAN, E. R.: J. biol. Chem. **214**: 267, 1955.
ZELLER, E. A., BARSKY, J., BLANKSMA, L. A. AND LAZANAS, J. C.: Fed. Proc. **16**: 276, 1957.
ZELLER, E. A., BARSKY, J., FOUTS, J. R., KIRCHHEIMER, W. F. AND VAN ORDEN, L. S.: Experientia **8**: 349, 1952.
ZELLER, E. A., BIRKHÄUSER, H., MISLIN, H. AND WENK, M.: Helvet. chim. acta **22**: 1381, 1939.
ZELLER, E. A., FOUTS, J. R., CARBON, J. A., LAZANAS, J. C. AND VOEGTLI, W.: Helvet. chim. acta **39**: 1632, 1956.

8089

THE COMPARATIVE DISTRIBUTION OF C^{14}-LABELED 2-DIMETHYLAMINOETHANOL AND CHOLINE IN THE MOUSE[1, 2]

D. P. GROTH, J. A. BAIN AND C. C. PFEIFFER

Departments of Pharmacology and Biochemistry, Division of Basic Health Sciences, Emory University, Atlanta, Georgia

Received for publication July 28, 1958

The chronic administration of 2-dimethylaminoethanol (DMAE) to mice and rats has revealed the stimulant action of DMAE upon the central nervous system (Pfeiffer *et al.*, 1957). Similar administration of choline does not produce stimulation. Since DMAE has been shown to be a precursor of choline in liver (Artom and Crowder, 1949), it appeared likely that the tertiary amine DMAE could serve more effectively as a precursor of central nervous system acetylcholine than choline. A series of tracer studies to provide background information for this possibility was therefore undertaken.

METHODS. DMAE-1,2 C^{14}, choline-methyl-C^{14} and choline-1,2 C^{14} having a specific activity of 1 mc per m*M* were employed as tracers.[3] The radiochemical purity of these preparations was determined by chromatography on Whatman #1 filter paper. The DMAE-1,2 C^{14} was chromatographed with a 95% MeOH-5% HCl solvent system and revealed one component upon radioautography. The choline preparations, after chromatography according to Tolbert *et al.* (1953), revealed that considerable radiation self-decomposition had occurred. However, after elution of the papers in the region corresponding to choline and rechromatography with an 80% n-propanol-10% HCOOH-10% H_2O (PFH) solvent system, both the choline-methyl-C^{14} and the choline-1,2 C^{14} preparations showed the presence of only one radioactive component. These purified preparations were used shortly after chromatography and were stored in H_2O solution at $-10°C$ to prevent self-decomposition.

Animals used in these experiments were Taconic-Swiss female mice, 23–25 g, fed *ad lib.* prior to the experiments, but starved throughout the experimental periods. Drinking water, however, was supplied continuously.

From 1 to 3 μc of each tracer, together with the indicated amount of nonradioactive diluent in a final volume of 0.1 ml per mouse were injected intraperitoneally. Thereafter each mouse was housed in a metabolism cage which allowed the continuous collection of respiratory carbon dioxide and urine separate from feces. At each point after injection the mice were sacrificed by decapitation. The whole brain and liver were quickly removed and homogenized in cold 1 *M* Perchloric Acid (PCA). The suspension was centrifuged at 10,000 *g* for 15 minutes, and the pellet was washed twice with cold 1 *M* PCA. The combined PCA supernates were adjusted to pH 7.0 with 5 *N* KOH and centrifuged to remove the precipitated $KClO_4$. The pellet was extracted with cold 95% EtOH and then twice with boiling 3:1 95% EtOH:ether to extract the lipids. The residue (protein fraction), the lipids and the acid PCA soluble material were plated on sintered glass discs and radioactivity was measured with a thin window flow counter[4] by counting for a sufficiently long time to allow for a 5% statistical accuracy with correction for self-absorption. The respiratory carbon dioxide samples were precipitated as $BaCO_3$ on paper discs and radioactivity was measured as described above.

The radioactivity present in each tissue fraction was then characterized further as described below. Aliquots of the lipid (after removal of the alcohol-ether) and of the acid-soluble fractions were added to 1 mg of nonradioactive choline in water solu-

[1] This investigation was supported in part by research grants No. M-875 from the National Institute of Mental Health and No. B-660 from the National Institute of Neurological Diseases and Blindness, Public Health Service, and by a grant from the Geschickter Fund for Medical Research, Washington, D.C.

[2] A preliminary report has been presented to the Society (Groth, Bain and Pfeiffer, 1958).

[3] The first two compounds were obtained from the Volk Radiochemical Co., Chicago, Ill., upon allocation from the Atomic Energy Commission. The third compound was obtained from Tracerlab, Inc., Waltham, Mass.

[4] Nuclear-Chicago, Model D-47.

tion. $Ba(OH)_2$ was added to saturation, and the mixture was autoclaved for 6 hours. The mixture was cooled and centrifuged. After adjustment of the supernate to pH 9 to 10, excess 2% methanolic ammonium reineckate was added, and the mixture was allowed to stand in the cold for at least 3 hours. The precipitated reineckates were centrifuged, washed twice with cold n-propanol, and then dissolved in a small volume of 5 *N* HCl by heating for 15 minutes at 100°C. These isolated carrier choline samples were then chromatographed on Whatman #1 paper using as solvent the PFH system described above. Location of the choline upon the papers was made by spraying with dipicrylamine (0.2% dipicrylamine in 50% water-acetone). The choline was eluted from the papers with water, and the specific activity determined to within 10% statistical accuracy as described above, using as assay the colorimetric procedure of Kushner (1956). Many of the samples were rechromatographed using a 40% n-butanol–10% EtOH–50% H_2O system. The specific activity of none of the samples changed significantly upon this rechromatography.

The protein fractions were in some cases hydrolyzed in 6 *N* HCl to the constituent amino acids, and methionine was isolated by two-dimensional paper chromatography using 40% n-butanol–10% acetic acid–50% H_2O in the first direction and 1:1 BuOH-benzyl alcohol (saturated with water in an atmosphere of Et_2NH) in the second direction. The specific activity of the isolated methionine samples was determined to within 10% statistical accuracy as described above, using as assay the colorimetric ninhydrin procedure of Troll and Cannan (1953).

Results. All data presented in the figures and tables represent the average of 2 to 4 mice for each determination. For purposes of comparison, the data in the figures and in table 1 have been calculated as % of the administered dose of radioactivity found per gram tissue. In tables 2 and 3, the data have been calculated as % of the administered dose of radioactivity and as the % of the radioactivity in each fraction accounted for by either choline or methionine.

Figure 1 illustrates the excretion of isotope from DMAE and choline in the respiratory carbon dioxide. Label from choline-methyl-C^{14} or choline-1,2 C^{14} appeared in the carbon dioxide at a rate which is approximately 7 times that obtained when DMAE-1,2 C^{14} was injected. The rate of excretion of label from all 3 tracers reached a peak at approximately 30 minutes to 1 hour after injection and then fell rapidly, that of DMAE falling to a constant rate after 3 hours. This low rate of excretion of label was then maintained for the entire 24-hour period. The rate of label excretion from choline continued to fall until it reached zero after 24 hours when choline-methyl-C^{14} was used, and approached zero with choline-1,2 C^{14} at 24 hours. The 24-hour urinary excretion of label from equivalent

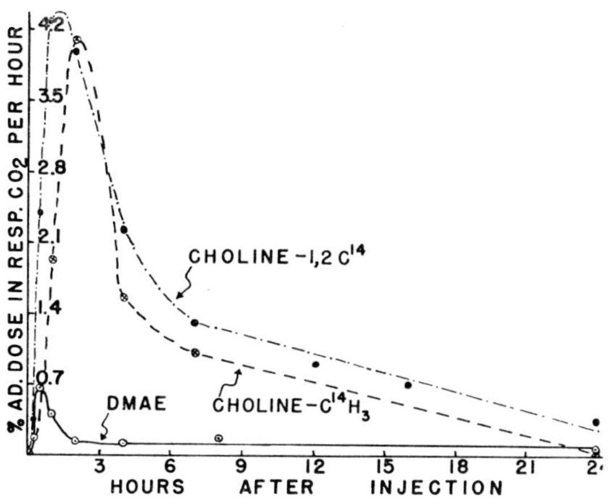

Fig. 1. A comparsion of the rates of excretion of radioactivity from DMAE-1,2 C^{14}, choline-methyl-C^{14}, and choline-1,2 C^{14} in the respiratory carbon dioxide of mice.

The total recovery of radioactivity in the carbon dioxide, expressed as % of the administered dose of radioactivity, is presented at selected time intervals from 15 min to 24 hr after intraperitoneal injection. Each point on the curves in this figure, in the succeeding figures and in the tables represents the numerical average of 2 to 4 mice.

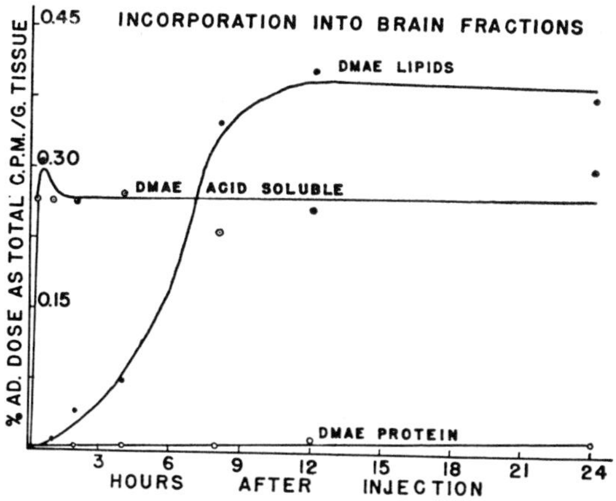

Fig. 2. Recovery of radioactivity from DMAE-1,2 C^{14} in various brain fractions.

Recovered radioactivity is expressed as % of the administered dose of radioactivity found per g wet weight of brain.

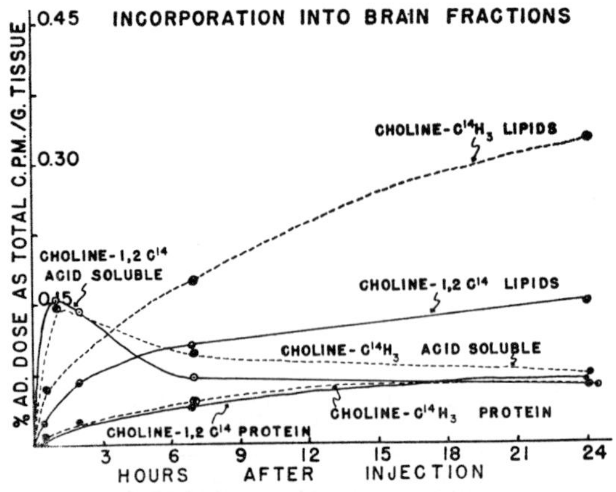

Fig. 3. Recovery of radioactivity from choline-methyl-C^{14} and choline-1,2 C^{14} in various brain fractions.

Recovered radioactivity is expressed as % of the administered dose of radioactivity found per g wet weight of brain.

0.1 mg/kg doses of choline-methyl-C^{14}, choline-1,2 C^{14} and DMAE-1,2 C^{14} was 36, 20 and 12%, respectively.

The time course distribution of DMAE in various brain fractions is presented in figure 2. The amount of radioactivity from DMAE appearing in the acid-soluble attained a constant level at about 30 minutes and was then retained over the 24-hour period. In the lipids, radioactivity became incorporated more slowly than in the acid-soluble, although after 7 hours, the total amount of radioactivity became greater in the lipid fraction. Only a negligible amount of radioactivity was incorporated into the protein fraction. There was no apparent relationship, from the product-precursor point of view, between the acid-soluble and lipid incorporated radioactivities, indicating that DMAE equilibrated slowly with acid-soluble choline. Further evidence on this point will be presented below.

Significant differences in the incorporation into brain of DMAE and choline were obtained as is illustrated by a comparison of figure 2 with figure 3. Choline-methyl-C^{14} or choline-1,2 C^{14} was incorporated into the acid-soluble at only 50% of the rate of DMAE incorporation. In addition, radioactivity from choline was progressively lost from the acid-solubles. Although the brain lipids became more quickly labeled when choline was administered, DMAE was over-all more effective.

Radioactivity from choline was incorporated at much higher rate into the protein fraction of brain than radioactivity from DMAE.

There was little difference between the rate of incorporation of either choline-methyl-C^{14} or choline-1,2 C^{14} into the brain fractions (figure 3), except that the label of choline-$C^{14}H_3$ was about twice as effective a precursor of brain lipids as was that of choline-1,2 C^{14}.

Figure 4 presents the relationship between the acid-soluble incorporated radioactivity from DMAE and radioactivity incorporated into the lipid fraction of liver. Similar results have been reported by Artom (1952). It is to be noted that the level of incorporation into liver is approxi-

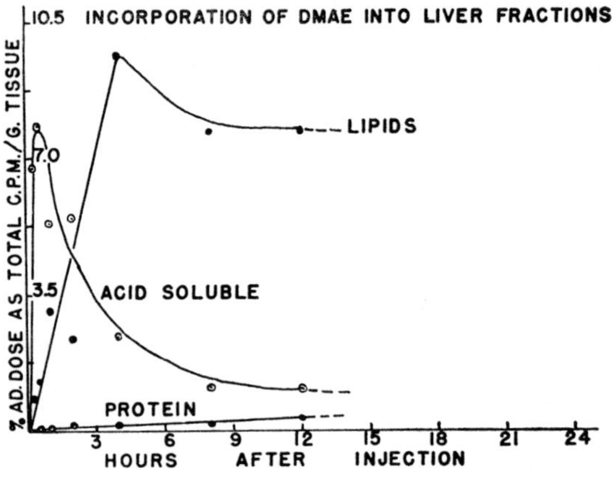

Fig. 4. Recovery of radioactivity from DMAE-1,2 C^{14} in various liver fractions.

Recovered radioactivity is expressed as % of the administered dose of radioactivity found per g wet weight of liver.

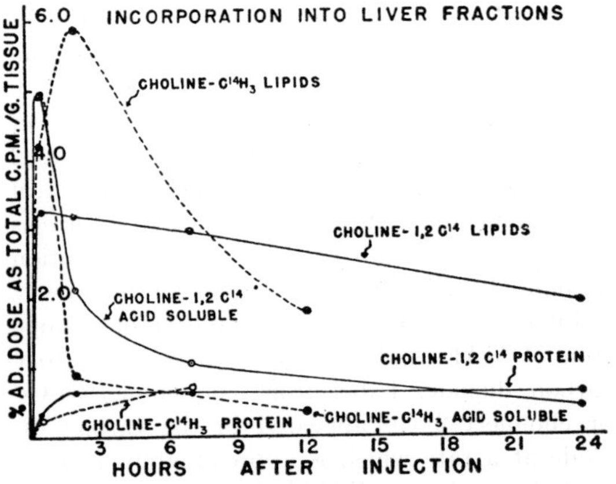

Fig. 5. Recovery of radioactivity from choline-methyl-C^{14} and choline-1,2 C^{14} in various liver fractions. Recovered radioactivity is expressed as % of the administered dose of radioactivity found per g wet weight of liver.

TABLE 1

Effect of dose upon incorporation in brain fractions

Time after Injection	Dose	Total C.P.M. as % of the Administered Dose	
		Acid-soluble	Lipids
	mg/kg		
DMAE administration			
30 min	0.1	0.26	0.02
	150	0.33	0.10
7 hr	0.1	0.29	0.33
	150	0.27	0.29
Choline administration			
30 min	0.1	0.15	0.02
	0.1	0.15*	0.06*
	150	0.14	0.01
	150	0.13*	0.05*
7 hr	0.1	0.08	0.10
	0.1	0.10*	0.18*
	150	0.06	0.06
	150	0.09*	0.23*

* Starred numerals—Choline-methyl-C^{14}; other numerals—Choline-1,2 C^{14}.

mately 30 times that of brain on a weight basis. This may be in part due to the semipermeability characteristics of the hematoencephalic barrier (Mayer and Bain, 1956), and in part due to the known higher metabolic activity of liver.

Similar results were obtained with labeled choline as illustrated in figure 5. Again choline-methyl-C^{14} was at first more effective in labeling the lipid fraction of liver than choline-1,2 C^{14} although eventually this relationship was reversed. Choline was about twice as effective in labeling liver protein as DMAE.

Results comparable to those described above were obtained with the administration of DMAE and choline at levels between a "tracer" (0.1 mg/kg) dose and dosages as high as 150 mg/kg (table 1). With intermediate doses the same relationships resulted. The only consistently significant effect of increasing the dose of either DMAE or choline was to decrease the rate of appearance of label in the respiratory carbon dioxide.

Table 2 presents data on the rate of equilibration of the tracers with total brain acid-soluble and lipid choline as determined by the carrier technique. These experiments represent a preliminary attempt to evaluate the relative efficacy of conversion of both DMAE and choline into precursors of pharmacological agents present in the acid-soluble and lipid fraction of brain. The results are presented to indicate what percentage of the total radioactivity in a fraction is accounted for by choline and choline-containing compounds. It is evident that choline-methyl-C^{14} and choline-1,2 C^{14} are more effective immediate precursors of acid-soluble and lipid choline than is DMAE.

Only a small proportion of the radioactivity incorporated into the protein fraction of both liver and brain could be accounted for by incorporation into methionine (table 3). It appears that transmethylation or other small carbon fragment transfer mechanisms are not important factors in the total incorporation process considered in these experiments.

Discussion. DMAE apparently serves as a precursor of choline but is not formed as a product of choline demethylation. Dubnoff (1949a, b), Muntz (1950) and Pilgeram (1953) have demonstrated that choline is first oxidized to betaine and the product of betaine demethylation is dimethyl glycine. Dubnoff showed that no methionine was formed when choline and homocysteine were incubated with the livers of the rabbit, guinea pig, or chick which contain little or no choline dehydrogenase. Muntz employed rat liver homogenates which were incubated with homocysteine and N^{15}-labeled choline. A high concentration of N^{15} was found in dimethyl glycine, whereas none was found in DMAE. Artom and Crowder (1950) also failed to find any radioactivity in DMAE when liver slices were incubated with C^{14} methyl-labeled choline with DMAE added as carrier.

In further studies, Artom and Crowder (1949) found that after the administration of a large dose of DMAE to rats, detectable quantities could be found in the lipids as well as in the aqueous extracts of muscle and liver. In contrast, after single large doses of choline, no DMAE could be detected in the tissues. Artom and Crowder were unable to extract DMAE from the phospholipid of rat tissue under various conditions such as dietary restriction of methyl donors. Levine and Chargaff (1951) also failed to detect DMAE in a paper chromatographic analysis of the nitrogenous components of phospholipids. Artom (1952) concluded that

TABLE 2

Recovery of administered radioactivity in brain fractions as choline

Time after injection	Acid-Soluble				Lipids			
	Total C.P.M. as % of the administered dose		% of acid-soluble C.P.M. as choline		Total C.P.M. as % of the administered dose		% of lipid C.P.M. as choline	
DMAE administration								
15 min	0.0092		3.5		—		—	
30 min	0.0046		1.5		—		—	
1 hr	0.0013		0.5		—		—	
2 hr	0.0027		1.1		—		—	
4 hr	0.0086		3.2		0.0103		14.3	
8 hr	0.0108		4.7		0.0443		13.1	
12 hr	0.0380		14.9		0.0571		14.1	
Choline administration								
30 min	0.0233	(0.0507)*	15.4	(33.0)*	0.0106	(—)	45.9	(—)
2 hr	0.0176	(—)	12.3	(—)	0.0219	(—)	32.7	(—)
7 hr	0.0541	(0.0152)	69.3	(15.4)	0.0576	(0.1770)	55.4	(100.0)
24 hr	0.0160	(—)	24.6	(—)	0.0686	(—)	45.4	(—)

* Numerals in parentheses—Choline-methyl-C^{14}; other numerals—Choline-1,2 C^{14}.

under physiological conditions, DMAE is formed in tissues but is probably methylated to choline very rapidly. Du Vigneaud *et al.* (1946) found 43% of the deuterium-labeled methyl groups of DMAE in liver choline at 3 weeks after administration to rats. It appeared that DMAE was slowly converted to choline.

Although in the studies reported here the importance of DMAE as a precursor of central nervous system acetylcholine is still obscure, the significant differences observed in the metabolism of DMAE as compared to choline have stimulated interest in this laboratory to ascertain an explanation of the physiological effects of DMAE administration. The remarkable retention of DMAE by the brain and the somewhat higher DMAE uptake by the brain as compared to choline uptake and retention perhaps are sufficient to account for these effects. In addition, the correlation between this retention by the brain and the slow rate of metabolism and excretion of DMAE in the respiratory carbon dioxide and urine would indicate that an administered dose of DMAE has potentially a much longer duration of action than an equivalent dose of choline. Although choline serves as a more immediate precursor of central nervous system choline, within 12 to 24 hours DMAE becomes a comparable and perhaps a more effective intracellular precursor.

These observations would tend to clarify the observations of Pfeiffer and Jenney (1957) who found that DMAE is effective as a central nervous system stimulant when administered chronically but not acutely.

TABLE 3

Recovery of administered radioactivity as methionine in liver and brain protein

Time after Injection	Total C.P.M. as % of the Administered Dose	% of Protein C.P.M. as Methionine
DMAE administration		
Liver 4 to 12 hr	0	0
Brain 4 to 12 hr	0	0
Choline-1,2 C^{14} administration		
Liver 7 to 24 hr	0	0
Brain 7 to 24 hr	0	0
Choline-methyl-C^{14} administration		
Liver 7 hr	0.042	6.0
Brain 7 hr	0.00032	0.64

SUMMARY

The time course distribution of radioactivity from dimethylaminoethanol-1,2 C^{14}, choline-methyl-C^{14} and choline-1,2 C^{14} in the acid-soluble, lipid, and protein fractions of mouse brain and liver was determined following the intraperitoneal injection of from 0.1 to 150 mg/kg of the labeled compounds. Incorporated radioactivity into choline and choline derivatives of the acid-soluble and lipid extracts was determined by carrier technique. Incorporation of radioactivity into protein methionine was also followed. Dimethylaminoethanol was incorporated and retained by the brain to a greater extent than choline, although choline was a more effective immediate precursor of acid-soluble and lipid choline. Label from choline appeared in the respiratory carbon dioxide and was excreted in the urine at a higher rate than the label from dimethylaminoethanol. The relative efficacy of dimethylaminoethanol and choline as precursors of brain acid-soluble and lipid choline and the implication of the results obtained to the pharmacological properties of dimethylaminoethanol was discussed.

Acknowledgment. Acknowledgment is made to Miss Jane Beck and Miss Mary Alice Ratchford for their excellent technical assistance.

REFERENCES

Artom, C.: Phosphorus Metabolism **2:** 203, Johns Hopkins Press, Baltimore, 1952.

Artom, C. and Crowder, M.: Fed. Proc. **8:** 180, 1949.

Artom, C. and Crowder, M.: Arch. Biochem. **29:** 227, 1950.

Dubnoff, J. W.: Arch. Biochem. **22:** 474, 1949a.

Dubnoff, J. W.: Arch. Biochem. **24:** 251, 1949b.

du Vigneaud, V., Chandler, J. P., Simmonds, S., Moyer, A. W. and Cohn, M.: J. biol. Chem.: **164:** 603, 1946.

Groth, D. P., Bain, J. A. and Pfeiffer, C. C.: This Journal **122:** 28A, 1958.

Kushner, D. J.: Biochim. biophys. Acta **20:** 554, 1956.

Levine, C. and Chargaff, E.: J. biol. Chem. **192:** 465, 481, 1951.

Mayer, S. E. and Bain, J. A.: This Journal **118:** 17, 1956.

Muntz, J. A.: J. biol. Chem. **182:** 489, 1950.

Pfeiffer, C. C., Jenney, E. H., Gallagher, W., Smith, R. P., Bevan, W. Jr., Killam, K. F., Killam, E. K. and Blackmore, W.: Science **126:** 610, 1957.

Pilgeram, L. O., Gal, E. M., Sassenrath, E. H. and Greenberg, D. M.: J. biol. Chem. **204:** 367, 1953.

Tolbert, B. M., Adams, P. T., Bennett, E. L., Hughes, A. M., Kirk, M. R., Lemmon, R. M., Noller, R. M., Ostwald, R. and Calvin, M.: J. Amer. chem Soc. **75:** 1867, 1953

Troll, W. and Cannan, R. K.: J. biol. Chem. **200** 803, 1953.

8090

METABOLIC FATE OF LEVO-3-HYDROXY-N-ALLYLMORPHINAN (LEVALLORPHAN)[1, 2]

G. J. MANNERING AND L. S. SCHANKER[3]

Department of Pharmacology and Toxicology, The University of Wisconsin, Service Memorial Institutes, Madison 6, Wisconsin

Received for publication July 16, 1958

Levallorphan (fig. 1), the N-allyl analogue of *l*-3-hydroxy-N-methylmorphinan (Dromoran), has received considerable attention in the recent literature because of its potent antagonistic effect against the pharmacologic actions of morphine-type analgesics. However, little is known about its metabolic disposition. The present study was undertaken in an attempt to determine the metabolic fate of levallorphan in the rat and several other laboratory animals.

METHODS. *In vitro metabolism.* Albino rats (Holtzman strain) of both sexes, weighing 160 to 220 g, were employed. Approximately 500 mg of liver slices from these animals, prepared by free-hand slicing with a razor blade, were suspended in 10 ml of calcium-free Krebs-Ringer phosphate solution, pH 7.4 (Field, 1948) containing 1.0 mg of levallorphan tartrate.[4] The mixture was incubated under oxygen at 38°C in a Dubnoff metabolic shaker for 3 hours (120 oscillations per minute). Several of the beakers containing the above mixture were placed in a boiling water bath for 10 minutes to inactivate the tissue prior to incubation. These preparations served as controls. The same procedures were followed in studying the metabolism of levallorphan by liver slices from the mouse, guinea pig, rabbit and dog.

In vivo metabolism. The rats used had the same specifications as those described previously. Levallorphan tartrate was injected subcutaneously (250 mg per kg), the animals were housed in individual metabolism cages, and urine was collected for 24 hours. During this period water was supplied, but food was withheld to reduce contamination of the urine. As controls, non-injected rats were placed in metabolism cages and their urine was collected in containers to which the drug had been added in amounts equal to the injected doses. Except for drug dosage, the procedure described for the rat was also employed when other species were studied. Mice, guinea pigs, rabbits and dogs received 150, 40, 5 and 10 mg per kg of levallorphan tartrate respectively.

Fractionation. Tissue preparations and urine were processed in the following manner. One volume of concentrated HCl was added to 9 volumes of the specimen and the mixture was autoclaved under 15 lbs of pressure to hydrolyze conjugates which might have formed. The acid-autoclaved preparations were filtered and the filtrates were shaken with equal volumes of chloroform. The chloroform phase, which contained no apparent metabolites, was discarded. The aqueous phase was adjusted to pH 11 to 12 with NaOH and extracted twice by shaking with equal volumes of chloroform. The combined chloroform extracts were filtered and evaporated to dryness. The resulting residue was dissolved in a small volume of ethanol, spotted multiply on paper and chromatographed. The strongly alkaline aqueous phase was adjusted to pH 8 to 8.5 by acidifying with HCl and then adding solid $NaHCO_3$ in excess. The resulting solution was extracted twice with equal volume of 10% ethanol in chloroform and the combined, filtered ethanol-chloroform extracts were evaporated to dryness. The residue was dissolved in ethanol and chromatographed on paper.

Chromatography. Chromatographic procedures described previously (Mannering *et al.*, 1954) were

[1] Abstracts of part of this work have been published: Fed. Proc. **14:** 365, 1955; THIS JOURNAL **119:** 164, 1957. Material in this investigation appeared in a thesis by L. S. Schanker in partial fulfillment of the requirements for the degree of Doctor of Philosophy in the Department of Pharmacology and Toxicology, University of Wisconsin, Madison, Wisconsin, 1955.

[2] Supported in part by the Research Committee of the Graduate School from funds supplied by the Wisconsin Alumni Research Foundation and by Hoffmann-LaRoche Inc., Nutley, New Jersey.

[3] Present address: The Laboratory of Chemical Pharmacology, National Heart Institute, National Institutes of Health, Public Health Service, U. S. Department of Health, Education and Welfare, Bethesda, Maryland.

[4] Levallorphan tartrate and all other morphinan derivatives were generously supplied by Hoffmann-LaRoche Inc., Nutley, New Jersey.

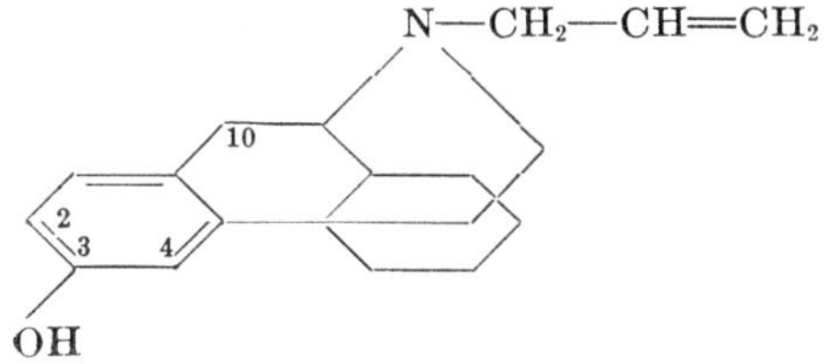

FIG. 1.

employed. Ascending chromatograms were developed with an isoamyl alcohol-acetic acid-water solvent. Levallorphan and its metabolites were located on the paper by spraying with potassium iodoplatinate reagent.

Isolation of crystalline metabolites. The spots representing levallorphan or its metabolites were cut from the paper, wetted with concentrated NH_4OH, and shaken with hot chloroform. The chloroform extract was decanted into a sublimation flask and the chloroform was removed by evaporation in a boiling water bath. Crystalline materials were obtained by sublimation under reduced pressure using a modification of the apparatus described by Gettler *et al.* (1950).

All melting points (uncorrected) were obtained with a Fisher-Johns micromelting point apparatus. Ultraviolet absorption measurements were made with a Beckman Spectrophotometer Model DU. Infrared absorption spectra were obtained with a Baird infrared spectrophotometer employing the potassium bromide pellet technique.

RESULTS. *In vitro studies.* Paper chromatography of chloroform and chloroform-ethanol extracts of mixtures obtained by incubating rat liver slices with levallorphan, and subsequent spraying of the chromatograms with potassium iodoplatinate reagent revealed 3 alkaloids, presumably the parent compound and 2 of its metabolites.

Chromatography of the chloroform extract obtained at pH 8 to 8.5 yielded a prominent spot in the R_f value range of 0.33 to 0.39. No such spot was observed when heat inactivated liver was incubated with the drug. The combined spots from 21 experiments were extracted from the paper and the resulting residue was sublimed. About 2 mg of crystalline material was collected between 165 and 185°C at a pressure of about 0.03 mm of mercury. The crystals melted with decomposition at 235–240°C. When chromatographed, the material gave a single spot with the expected R_f value. The crystalline material was designated Metabolite I.

When the material extracted at pH 11 to 12 was chromatographed, large spots were obtained in the R_f value range of 0.53 to 0.70. The uneven color density of this diffuse spot suggested the presence of more than one compound. Accordingly, an extract of this spot was chromatographed on phosphate-buffered paper (pH 7.0) using isoamyl alcohol saturated with water as the developing solvent (Mannering *et al.*, 1954). This procedure resolved the diffuse spot from the previous chromatogram into two well-defined spots. The R_f value (0.82–0.88) of the larger upper spot corresponded with that obtained with authentic levallorphan. The residues obtained by extracting several of these spots were combined and sublimed. The crystalline sublimate obtained at 120–140°C (0.04 mm of mercury) was identified as levallorphan base (m.p. of sublimate, 180–182°C; m.p. of authentic levallorphan base, 180–182°C; mixed m.p., 180–182°C). The smaller lower spot had an R_f value in the range of 0.55 to 0.65. The material represented by this spot was designated Metabolite II. It was not present in sufficient quantity to permit its isolation in crystalline form. Extracts of heat inactivated liver incubated with levallorphan yielded only the parent compound.

When rat liver slices were incubated with levallorphan in an atmosphere of nitrogen, only unchanged drug was detected. Homogenized liver incubated under oxygen in either the medium described previously or with the re-enforced medium of Pardee and Potter (1949), failed to yield metabolites. Of four tissues studied, liver, brain, kidney, and muscle (diaphragm), only liver effected the formation of either Metabolite I or II.

In vivo studies. The paper chromatograms from the *in vivo* and *in vitro* experiments were strikingly similar.[5] Employing the same isolation procedures described in the *in vitro* experiments, totals of about 55 mg of apparent Metabolite I and about 7 mg of apparent Metabolite II were obtained from pooled rat urine. The physical and chemical properties of Metabolites I and II were determined using these crystalline samples. Unaltered levallorphan was identified by its melting point.

The melting point of apparent Metabolite I

[5] In addition to the spots observed in the *in vitro* studies, a small spot was consistently observed immediately above the area occupied by Metabolite I. No attempt was made to isolate this metabolite in crystalline form.

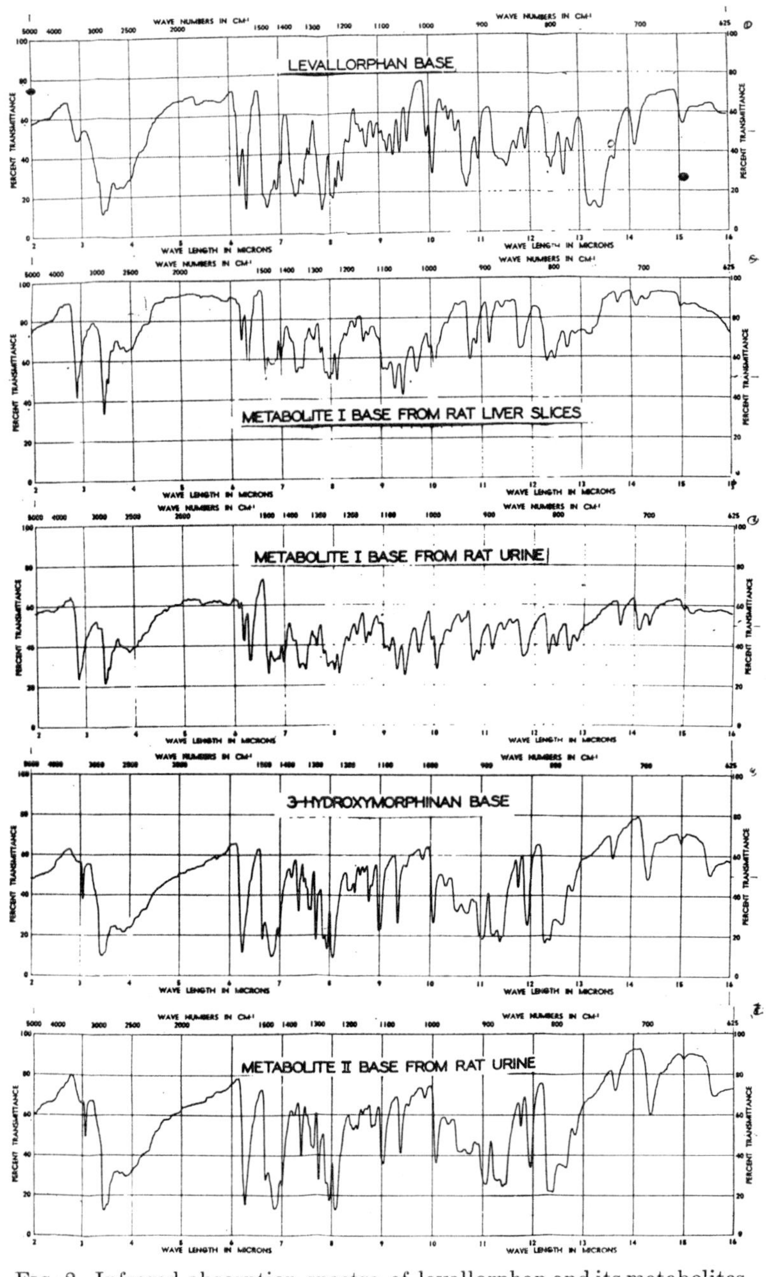

FIG. 2. Infrared absorption spectra of levallorphan and its metabolites.

from urine (237–243°C) compared favorably with that of Metabolite I from liver slices (235–240°C). A mixture of the two materials gave a single spot in each of the two chromatographic systems described previously. Infrared absorption spectra further confirm their identity (fig. 2).

To rule out the possibility that the huge doses of levallorphan tartrate (250 mg per kg) administered in these studies might precipitate an "emergency" metabolism of the alkaloid quite different from that which would occur when more reasonable amounts of the drug were injected, doses of 10 and 70 mg per kg were administered to a number of rats. No qualitative differences were noted in the metabolic fate of the drug at the 3 dose levels.

Some physical and chemical properties of Metabolite I. The ultraviolet absorption spectra of Metabolite I and of levallorphan in both alkaline and acid solutions are qualitatively similar, thus indicating that the parent compound has undergone no drastic structural alteration in the formation of this metabolite. Both levallorphan and Metabolite I bases dissolved in 0.2 N NaOH solution exhibited maxima at 240 and 300 mμ. Dissolved in 0.2 N H_2SO_4 solution, both compounds showed a single maximum at 280 mμ. The infrared absorption spectra of Metabolite I and levallorphan are shown in fig. 2.

From duplicate carbon, hydrogen and nitrogen analyses of Metabolite I (C, 75.24 and 74.77; H, 8.50 and 8.11; N, 4.64 and 4.52; and O, by difference, 11.62 and 12.60%), the empirical formula $C_{19}H_{25}NO_2$ was derived. Thus, in forming Metabolite I, levallorphan has gained an oxygen atom. From chemical considerations one might expect the unsaturated *beta* carbon of the allyl side chain to suffer metabolic oxidation. Accordingly, Metabolite I was compared with *l*-3-hydroxy-N-(2-hydroxypropyl)morphinan, *l*-3-hydroxy-N-acetonylmorphinan and *l*-3-hydroxy-N-(3-hydroxypropyl)morphinan. Melting point and chromatographic data showed none of these compounds to be Metabolite I. The possibility of oxidation of the side chain in the 1-position was not investigated.

Metabolite I gave a positive Folin-Ciocalteu reaction, indicating the presence of a phenolic hydroxyl group, presumably the intact 3-hydroxyl group.

The possibility that hydroxylation might have occurred at the 2- or 4-positions was eliminated when Metabolite I failed to react positively to the catechol reaction described by Azouz *et al.* (1953). 2,3-Dihydroxy-N-methylmorphinan and 3,4-dihydroxy-N-methylmorphinan gave positive catechol tests.

Rapoport and Masamune (1955) have shown that certain morphine-type compounds are hydroxylated in the 10-position when they are subjected to controlled chromic acid oxidation, and Häfliger *et al.* (1956) demonstrated that oxidation of the 10-position of 3-methoxy-N-methylmorphinan can be accomplished photochemically and with chromic acid. The possibility is thus presented that Metabolite I might result from a similar oxidation occurring biologically. Comparison of ultraviolet absorption data shows that this is not the case. In ethanolic solution 3-methoxy-10-keto-N-methylmorphinan shows absorption maxima at 233 and 288 mμ, and 3-methoxy-10-hydroxy-N-methylmorphinan yields maxima at 230, 278 and 285 mμ (Häfliger *et al.*, 1956). In acid solution (0.2 N H_2SO_4) levallorphan, Metabolite I and 3-methoxy- N-methylmorphinan showed absorption peaks at 280 mμ only, while 3-methoxy-10-hydroxy-N-methylmorphinan gave maxima at 230 and 280 mμ.

To test for the presence of terminal unsaturation in the N-alkyl chain of Metabolite I, permanganate-periodic acid oxidation as described by Lemieux and von Rudloff (1955) was employed. In this test the first stage of the oxidation of the terminal methylene group produces the glycol and ketol. Subsequent periodate oxidation of these substances yields formaldehyde. The overall conversion to formaldehyde is not quantitative. Each of the following morphinan compounds was oxidized for 7.5, 15, and 30 minutes: *l*-3-hydroxymorphinan hydrobromide, *l*-3-hydroxy-N-methylmorphinan hydrochloride (Dromoran), *l*-3-hydroxy-N-allylmorphinan hydrobromide (levallorphan), *l*-3-hydroxy-N-acetonylmorphinan hydrobromide, *l*-3-hydroxy-N-(2 hydroxypropyl)morphinan hydrobromide, *l*-3-hydroxy-N-propylmorphinan hydrobromide, *l*-3-hydroxy-N-(3-hydroxypropyl) morphinan hydrobromide and Metabolite I hydrochloride. Only levallorphan, Metabolite I and Dromoran yielded formaldehyde. The highest conversions of levallorphan and Metabolite I to formaldehyde (42 and 37%, respectively on a molar equivalency basis) occurred at the 7.5 minute interval of oxidation, with the amounts of formaldehyde recovered decreasing as oxidation was prolonged. Considerably less formaldehyde was obtained from Dromoran and this increased with time (8.8, 9.7 and 12.3% conversion at 7.5, 15 and 30 minutes, respectively). Formaldehyde presumably derives from the N-methyl group of Dromoran. No formaldehyde was formed from Metabolite I when oxidation was performed with periodate alone. It would thus appear that in the transformation of levallorphan to Metabolite I, the alkyl side chain remains unsaturated.

Metabolite I does not appear to be an amine oxide. Morphine-N-oxide derivatives are reduced to their parent compounds when refluxed with sodium bisulfite solution (Kelentey *et al.*, 1957). Two milligrams of Metabolite I was treated with bisulfite in the prescribed manner. The reaction mixture was subjected to the procedure previously described for the isolation of levallorphan and its metabolites from urine with the exception that the mixture was not acid-autoclaved. The chromatograms yielded spots indicative of Metabolite I only, and the crystalline material isolated from these spots gave the melting point of authentic Metabolite I. Treatment of levallorphan with hydrogen peroxide, as described by Freund and Speyer (1910) for the synthesis of morphine-N-oxide from morphine, failed to yield anything chromatographically suggestive of Metabolite I.

At this time Metabolite I remains unidentified. Current efforts are directed toward accumulation of enough of the compound to permit more thorough characterization.

Identification of Metabolite II as 3-hydroxymorphinan. The melting point and chromatographic behavior of Metabolite II led to its comparison with 3-hydroxymorphinan.

Metabolite II melted with decomposition at 235–240°C. The crystalline sublimate of authentic *l*-3-hydroxymorphinan base prepared from its hydrobromide melted at 245–250°C. About 0.5 mg of Metabolite II was mixed with a drop of HBr. Water and excess acid were removed by heating at 90°C *in vacuo*. Metabolite II hydrobromide prepared in this manner melted at 218–220°C. A mixture of authentic *l*-3-hydroxymorphinan hydrobromide (m.p., 220–222°C) and Metabolite II hydrobromide melted at 219–221°C.

Two mg of Metabolite II was subjected to an eight plate countercurrent distribution. The immiscible solvent pair consisted of equal volumes (10 ml) of 0.5 M borate buffer, pH 8.8, and chloroform, each phase saturated with respect to the other. After distribution had been effected, each tube was analyzed for Metabolite II in the following manner. A 5.0 ml aliquot from each aqueous phase was added to 1.0 ml of 2 N NaOH solution and the optical density was determined at 240 mμ. A 5.0 ml aliquot of each chloroform phase was evaporated to dryness, the residue was dissolved in 5.0 ml of 0.2 N NaOH solution and the optical density was observed at 240 mμ. The distribution ratio for *l*-3-hydroxymorphinan was 0.961. A theoretical distribution curve was constructed as described by Way and Bennett (1951) and compared with the experimental curve obtained for Metabolite II. The curves were superimposable.

The infrared absorption spectra of *l*-3-hydroxymorphinan and Metabolite II (fig. 2) further confirm their identity.

Excretion of levallorphan and its metabolites by the rat. Quantitative studies. Five female rats, weighing about 250 g each, were placed in individual metabolism cages without food and their urines were collected for a 24 hour "control" period. The animals were then removed from the cages and allowed to eat for two hours. Each rat then received a subcutaneous injection of 250 mg per kg of levallorphan tartrate, following which, it was returned to its cage where urine was collected for a 24-hour "experimental" period. A second 24-hour urine collection was obtained from two of the rats.

Quantitative analyses of urinary levellorphan and its metabolites was accomplished through application of differential solvent extraction, paper chromatography of these extracts, removal of the resulting alkaloid spots from the paper, and analysis of the extracts from paper. The extent of metabolic conjugation of each of the alkaloids was determined by comparing hydrolyzed and nonhydrolyzed portions of urine. Each 24-hour urine sample was made acid (litmus) with HCl, filtered and diluted to 100 ml. Five ml of concentrated HCl was added to 50 ml of the diluted urine and this half of the sample was autoclaved for 30 minutes under 15 lbs of pressure. Autoclaved and nonautoclaved portions of the urine were processed in the same manner. A sample was diluted to 60 ml and then divided into equal portions which were transferred to 250 ml centrifuge bottles. The pH of one aliquot was adjusted to about 8.3 by adding $NaHCO_3$. The pH of the other aliquot was adjusted to about 11.5 with Na_2CO_3. One hundred and fifty ml of 10% ethanol in chloroform was added to each bottle and the mixtures were shaken mechanically for 15 minutes. The mixtures were centrifuged and then transferred to separatory funnels from which the chloroform-ethanol phase was withdrawn and filtered. The chloroform-ethanol extraction was repeated. The combined extracts were evaporated to dryness in 30-ml conical centrifuge tubes placed in a boiling water bath. Preliminary trials, where known quantities (50 to 150 μg) of levallorphan, 3-hydroxymorphinan, or Metabolite I were added to "control" rat urine, showed that the extraction procedure permitted 100 ± 5% recovery of each of the alkaloids. No destruction of levallorphan or its metabolites resulted from acid hydrolysis.

The individual alkaloids contained in the final extraction residues were separated by paper chromatography. The pH 8.3 extraction residues from the autoclaved and nonautoclaved urine aliquots were chromatographed using the isoamyl alcohol-acetic acid-water solvent as described previously. These chromatograms revealed well-defined Metabolite I spots and partially fused spots of levallorphan and 3-hydroxymorphinan. Corresponding extracts from "control" urines were chromatographed on the same sheet of paper. The pH 11.5 extraction residues from the autoclaved and nonautoclaved urine aliquots were chromatographed on pH 7.0 buffered paper as described previously. These chromatograms yielded well-defined levallorphan and 3-hydroxymorphinan (Metabolite II) spots. Residues from extracts of "control" urine were chromatographed on the same paper.

The Metabolite I spot from the chromatographed pH 8.3 residue was cut from the paper and placed in a small test tube. The spot was wetted with concentrated NH_4OH and covered with chloroform. The chloroform was boiled carefully for a few seconds and transferred to a clean test tube. This extraction was repeated twice and the pooled chloroform solutions were evaporated to dryness. Levallorphan and 3-hydroxymorphinan spots were cut from the buffered paper and extracted in the same manner. Residues representing possible interfering substances found in normal urine were obtained by extracting areas of paper from chromatographed "control" urine extracts corresponding to the areas occupied by the levallorphan, Metabolite I and 3-hydroxymorphinan spots. In order to determine the thoroughness of extraction of these three alkaloids from the paper, 50, 100 and 150 μg quantities of each were chromatographed and extracted in the described manner. Recovery of the compounds was consistently 90 ± 2%, and this was not improved by increasing the number of extractions. Accordingly, a correction factor of 1.1 was employed in making calculations.

The final residues were taken up in measured volumes of chloroform and suitable aliquots were

TABLE 1

Twenty-four hour urinary excretion of levallorphan, Metabolite I and Metabolite II (3-hydroxymorphinan) by five rats following the subcutaneous injection of 250 mg per kg of levallorphan tartrate

	Recovery (% of Administered Dose)		
	Free	Conjugated	Total
Levallorphan....	1.4 (1.2–1.9)	3.3 (1.9–4.3)	4.7 (3.1–5.6)
Metabolite I....	3.5 (3.3–3.9)	2.8 (1.9–3.2)	6.3 (5.2–7.1)
Metabolite II (3-hydroxymorphinan).......	trace	1.0 (0.8–1.3)	1.0 (0.8–1.3)
Total........	4.9	7.1	12.0

analyzed for their alkaloid content employing methyl orange according to the method of Brodie and Udenfriend (1945). The optical density of each sample was measured and the concentrations of levallorphan, 3-hydroxymorphinan and Metabolite I were determined by comparison with standard curves prepared concurrently. The optical densities of all "control" samples were negligible (< 0.005). The results are summarized in table 1. It is seen that the combined urinary excretion of levallorphan and its recognizable metabolites during the first 24 hours after administration of the drug amounts to only 12% of the injected dose. The urines of the 2 animals which were studied for a second 24-hour period yielded only traces of the three compounds.

The poor recovery of levallorphan and its metabolites from urine suggested the possibility that a major portion of the drug might be excreted in the feces. Accordingly, the previous experiment was repeated, and this time feces were collected for analysis. Three 240-g female rats were used in this study. The experimental conditions of the previous experiment were followed except that feces were collected throughout both the 24-hour "control" period and the 48-hour "experimental" period. Feces were analyzed in the same manner as that described for urine. No attempt was made to distinguish between conjugated and free forms of levallorphan and its metabolites in either the feces or in the second 24-hour urine collection. The results are summarized in table 2. Almost all of the total 48-hour recovery of levallorphan and its metabolites was found in the urine excreted during the first 24 hours following administration of the drug.

TABLE 2

Forty-eight hour urinary and fecal excretion of levallorphan, Metabolite I and Metabolite II (3-hydroxymorphinan) by three rats following the subcutaneous injection of 250 mg per kg of levallorphan tartrate

	Recovery (% of Administered Dose)					
	Urine				Feces	Urine and feces
	1st 24 hr			2nd 24 hr	48 hr	48 hr
	free	conjugated	total	total	total	total
Levallorphan	1.3 (1.1–1.6)	3.8 (3.4–4.0)	5.1	0.3 (0.2–0.4)	0.2 (0.1–0.2)	5.6
Metabolite I	3.6 (3.5–3.7)	3.3 (3.2–3.3)	6.9	0.4 (0.4–0.4)	0.6 (0.5–0.8)	7.9
Metabolite II (3-hydroxymorphinan)	0.3 (0.2–0.3)	1.2 (1.0–1.3)	1.5	0.1	0.3	1.9
Total	5.2	8.3	13.5	0.8	1.1	15.4

Fecal excretion accounted for only a small fraction of the alkaloids recovered. The combined recovery of unaltered drug, Metabolite I and 3-hydroxymorphinan leaves about 85% of the administered drug unaccounted for.

Metabolism of levallorphan by liver slices from rats. Quantitative studies. Liver slices (500 mg) from female rats were incubated as described previously with 1.0 mg of levallorphan tartrate for periods of 0, 1, 2 and 3 hours. Slices incubated without drug served as controls. Duplicate incubation mixtures were combined and quantitative analyses of levallorphan and its metabolites were performed as described in the *in vivo* experiments. The results are presented graphically in fig. 3. After three hours of incubation only 18.4% of the original levallorphan could be accounted for in the recovery of unmetabolized drug and its metabolites, a figure comparing favorably with the recoveries observed in the *in vivo* experiments. Most of the drug disappeared during the first hour of incubation and the major metabolic end product(s) of levallorphan remained undetected. This would suggest that either some highly polar metabolite of levallorphan had been formed, thus escaping solvent extraction, or that some drastic molecular alteration, such as ring cleavage, had occurred, the resulting metabolite escaping detection either because of failure to extract into chloroform or to react with idoplatinate reagent.

Metabolism of levallorphan by species other than the rat. The *in vitro* and *in vivo* metabolism of levallorphan by the mouse, guinea pig, rabbit and dog were studied as described under METHODS. Metabolites were identified by their behavior in the two chromatographic systems.

Liver slices from all species, with the exception of the rabbit, yielded chromatographic spots with R_f values of Metabolite II (3-hydroxymorphinan). Only mouse and rabbit liver extracts showed indications of the formation of Metabolite I, and in the case of the rabbit, the chromatographic behavior of the metabolite was slightly different from that of authentic Metabolite I. When the extracted residue from chromatographic spots obtained from the rabbit was mixed with authentic Metabolite I and chromatographed using the isoamyl alcohol-acetic acid-water system, two partially merged spots were observed. It would thus appear that rabbit liver produces a metabolite of levallorphan which is neither Metabolite 1 nor 3-hydroxymorphinan.

In the *in vivo* studies, 16 mice of both sexes, three guinea pigs (one male and two females), 2 female dogs, and 2 female rabbits were employed. Chromatographic results indicated that Metabolite II (3-hydroxymorphinan) was excreted in the urines of all four species. Only the mouse appeared to form Metabolite I. In the case of the rabbit a spot was observed with the approximate R_f value of Metabolite I which behaved much like that obtained from rabbit liver slices. The urine from several rabbits which had been injected with levallorphan tartrate was processed in an attempt to isolate the metabolite in crystalline form. About 2 mg of a glassy sublimate was obtained which crystallized on standing.

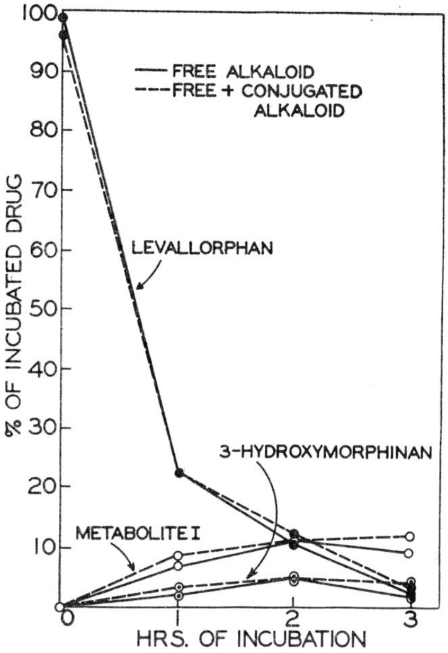

FIG. 3. *In vitro* metabolism of levallorphan tartrate (1.0 mg in 10 ml of incubation mixture containing 500 mg of rat liver slices). The curves represent the average results obtained from three rats.

This material melted over a wide temperature range (100°–110°C), suggesting that more than one compound was present. Fractional sublimation and paper chromatography also provided evidence that the crystalline material was a mixture. Thus, it would seem that the rabbit forms a third metabolite (Metabolite III). The possibility that it also forms Metabolite I has not been eliminated.

The results obtained with liver slices parallel those found in the *in vivo* studies with the exception that 3-hydroxymorphinan was found in rabbit urine but was not detected in *in vitro* experiments with rabbit liver slices. The demonstration of 3-hydroxymorphinan as a metabolic product of levallorphan in the dog is at variance with the findings of Brossi *et al.* (1955), who detected only unchanged levallorphan in the urine of dogs receiving 20 mg per kg of the drug. The amount of 3-hydroxymorphinan excreted by the dog is small in comparison with that produced by other species, and differences in the extraction procedures employed by the two laboratories could account for the discrepancy of results.

SUMMARY

The metabolic fate of levallorphan was studied in the rat, mouse, guinea pig, rabbit and dog as well as in surviving liver slices from these species.

In both *in vivo* and *in vitro* studies the formation of two metabolites of levallorphan was demonstrated. These were designated Metabolite I and Metabolite II. Crystalline Metabolite I was isolated from rat urine and from rat liver incubation mixtures. Some chemical and physical properties of this metabolite are described but its structure remains unknown. Crystalline Metabolite II, isolated from rat urine, was identified as 3-hydroxymorphinan.

Quantitative aspects of the metabolic fate of levallorphan in the rat were studied. Urine collected during the first 24 hours after a single subcutaneous injection of levallorphan tartrate (250 mg per kg) was found to contain levallorphan, Metabolite I and 3-hydroxymorphinan in the following equivalent percentages of injected drug: 5.1, 6.9 and 1.5, respectively. Levallorphan and its metabolites were found to be excreted during this period largely in conjugated form (levallorphan, 75, Metabolite I, 48, and 3-hydroxymorphinan, 80% conjugated). About 1% of the administered drug was recovered as parent compound and metabolites during the second 24-hour urine collection. Only a trace (about 1%) of levallorphan and its metabolites was found in the feces collected during the 48 hours following injection. Thus, the combined recovery of unaltered drug, Metabolite I and 3-hydroxymorphinan in the excreta leaves about 85% of the administered drug unaccounted for.

When incubated with rat liver slices, levallorphan disappears rapidly. After 3 hours of incubation only about 18% of the drug was recovered as levallorphan, Metabolite I and 3-hydroxymorphinan (3.0, 12.0 and 3.4%, respectively). Most of the drug disappears during the first hour of incubation.

Evidence is presented to show that all of the species studied form 3-hydroxymorphinan. The guinea pig and the dog do not appear to form Metabolite I. Chromatographic data indicate that Metabolite I is produced by the mouse. In addition to 3-hydroxymorphinan, the rabbit makes a metabolite which differs from Metabolite I in its chromatographic behavior.

REFERENCES

Azouz, W. M., Parke, D. V. and Williams, R. T.: Biochem. J. **55**: 146, 1953.

Brodie, B. B. and Udenfriend, S.: J. biol. Chem. **158**: 705, 1945.

Brossi, A., Häfliger, O. and Schnider, O.: Arzneim.-Forsch. **5**: 62, 1955.

Field, J.: in Methods in Medical Research, **1**: 298, The Year Book Publishers, Inc., Chicago, 1948.

Freund, M. and Speyer, E.: Ber. dtsch. chem. Ges. **43**: 3310, 1910.

Gettler, A. O., Umberger, C. J. and Goldbaum, L. R.: Analyt. Chem. **22**: 600, 1950.

Häfliger, O., Brossi, A., Chopard-dit-Jean, L. H., Walter, M. and Schnider, O.: Helv. chim. acta **39**: 2053, 1956.

Kelentey, B., Stenszky, E., Czollner, F., Szlávik, L. and Mészáros, Z.: Arzneim.-Forsch. **10**: 594, 1957.

Lemieux, R. V. and von Rudloff, E.: Canad. J. Chem. **33**: 1710, 1955.

Mannering, G. J., Dixon, A. C., Carroll, N. V. and Cope, O. B.: J. Lab. clin. Med. **44**: 292, 1954.

Pardee, A. B. and Potter, V. R.: J. biol. Chem. **181**: 739, 1949.

Rapoport, H. and Masamune, S.: J. Amer. chem. Soc. **77**: 6359, 1955.

Way, E. L. and Bennett, B. M.: J. biol. Chem. **192**:335, 1951.

8091

URINARY 17-KETOSTEROID EXCRETION DURING A CYCLE OF ADDICTION TO MORPHINE[1]

ANNA J. EISENMAN, H. F. FRASER, JEWELL SLOAN AND HARRIS ISBELL

U. S. Department of Health, Education, and Welfare, Public Health Service, National Institute of Mental Health, Addiction Research Center, Lexington, Kentucky

Received for publication July 21, 1958

There is evidence that the cortico-adrenal and gonadal functions are altered during addiction to morphine and following withdrawal of the drug. During addiction sexual drives are reduced, whereas spontaneous excitation appears on withdrawal. Fraser and Isbell (1953) used blood eosinophil counts as a measure of adrenal-cortical function. They found that: (1) when morphine was withdrawn, eosinophils fell to values near zero at the time of maximal symptoms of abstinence, (2) administration of morphine during acute withdrawal promptly relieved abstinence and concurrently the eosinophil counts returned to normal. Cortisone or ACTH administered during withdrawal failed to alleviate the distress of abstinence; in fact, both tended to aggravate and to hasten the appearance of symptoms. No biochemical-endocrinological data during a cycle of morphine addiction have been reported for human subjects. We, therefore, decided to make such a study using 17-ketosteroid excretion as the index of adrenal and gonadal function. The investigation was carried out in two parts: Experiment 1 was a study of 17-ketosteroid (hereafter referred to as 17-KS) excretion in a cycle of morphine addiction. In experiment 2, the response of the adrenal cortex and gonads to exogenous hormonal stimulation was measured during a cycle of addiction. Thyroid function was assessed by measuring the butanol-extractable iodine in blood serum.

METHODS. *Experiment 1*. Healthy male prisoners who had been addicts but who were abstinent from all drugs volunteered to serve as subjects for the experiment. All patients were housed in a special ward devoted to clinical research. The general conditions, precautions taken and the clinical observations made have been described previously by Fraser and Isbell (1953). Single injections of morphine were given to 7 subjects. Nine men were studied, 4 of them twice, throughout cycles of addiction comprising these periods: (1) preaddiction or control (19 to 45 days); (2) addiction (35 to 144 days); (3) withdrawal (usually the first 4 days); and (4) recovery (beginning at the 14th day after withdrawal and lasting from 24 to 60 days). Addiction was started with 10 mg of morphine sulfate administered subcutaneously 4 times daily and the amount of morphine was gradually increased to the stabilizing dosage of about 240 mg daily over a period of 15 to 17 days. In some subjects this initial "stabilizing" dosage was increased after a period of time. During withdrawal, subjects A_1, B_1, C_1, and D received no medication. Subjects E_1, E_2, F, G, H, and I received small doses of morphine sulfate (ranging from 7 to 16 mg on the second day, to half that amount on the third day of abstinence). Subjects A_2, B_2, and C_2 received 90 mg of morphine sulfate on the third day of withdrawal. Urine was collected continuously and aliquots of collections for 24, 48 or 72 hours were analyzed for 17-KS and creatinine.

It was necessary to combine and adapt several published methods for urinary 17-KS in order to ensure the flexibility necessary to span the extreme ranges of 17-KS encountered during addiction and withdrawal. The extraction method used was that of Drekter *et al.* (1952). The color development of the extracts was according to Holtorff and Koch's (1940) modification of the Zimmerman reaction, using varying aliquots according to steroid concentrations. Readings in the Evelyn colorimeter were made at two wave lengths, as recommended by Callow *et al.* (1938). Urinary creatinine excretions were determined by the method of Peters (1942). Blood eosinophil counts were made by the method of Randolph (1949) at the following times: during preaddiction and addiction, one count at 9 a.m. 3 times weekly; one week prior to withdrawal and on the first 3 or 4 days of withdrawal, counts were made daily at 9 a.m., 1 p.m., 5 p.m., and 9 p.m. daily.

[1] Preliminary reports have been made from this laboratory; Eisenman, A. J. *et al.*, Fed. Proc. **12:** 200, 1953; **13:** 203, 1954.

TABLE 1

Effects of a cycle of morphine addiction on the daily excretion of urinary 17-ketosteroids

Subject	Days Addicted	Preaddiction	Addiction	Third Day of Withdrawal	Recovery
A1	70	10.0 ± 0.34* (16)†	4.8 ± 0.28 (27)	16.4	14.5 ± 1.38 (7)
A2	143	11.2 ± 0.43 (29)	5.4 ± 0.21 (87)	22.2	12.7 ± 1.39 (14)
B1	58	5.5 ± 0.37 (16)	2.3 ± 0.171 (25)	12.9	5.9 ± 0.58 (6)
B2	144	5.2 ± 0.26 (32)	4.2 ± 0.14 (91)	6.2	5.2 ± 0.44 (15)
C1	63	20.8 ± 0.84 (16)	8.6 ± 0.43 (26)	15.2	17.9 ± 1.2 (8)
C2	101	20.2 ± 0.8 (27)	8.2 ± 0.38 (59)	13.6	19.8 ± 0.89 (14)
D	35	5.4 ± 0.36 (16)	3.2 ± 0.24 (15)	11.5	6.2 ± 0.37 (14)
E1	75	17.7 ± 0.82 (14)	6.5 ± 0.59 (28)	25.1	19.3 ± 0.61 (22)
E2	62	20.2 ± 1.1 (9)	5.7 ± 0.36 (21)	17.3	18.8 ± 0.71 (13)
F	97	13.6 ± 0.57 (14)	5.3 ± 0.26 (33)	17.7	13.8 ± 0.41 (29)
G	62	9.2 ± 0.30 (9)	3.9 ± 0.36 (21)	22.7	7.4 ± 0.47 (12)
H	69	8.4 ± 0.35 (10)	3.3 ± 0.26 (25)	18.4	9.4 ± 0.8 (11)
I	69	17.4 ± 0.79 (10)	6.1 ± 0.42 (23)	21.0	16.2 ± 0.8 (13)
Averages.....		12.7	5.2	16.9‡	12.9

* Figures represent mean of all measurements expressed as mg/24 hours ± standard error of mean, except in column for withdrawal in which figures represent excretion for that man for that day only. All preaddiction and recovery means are significantly higher than their respective addiction means at 1% level, except recovery mean on subject B_2 which is significantly higher than the addiction mean at the 5% level.

† Numbers in parenthesis represent number of observations.

‡ This average is significantly different (t-test for paired observations) from average of preaddiction means at 5% level, and from average of addiction mean at 1% level.

Experiment 2. Three of the subjects employed in experiment 1, A_2, B_2, and C_2, also served as subjects in experiment 2. Their respective ages were 43, 51 and 30 years. The reactivity of the adrenal cortex and the gonads was evaluated during the preaddiction, addiction and recovery phases by periodically administering ACTH and chorionic gonadotropin according to the schedule described below. The men were addicted to morphine in accordance with the schedule for experiment 1. By the 15th to the 17th day they had attained a daily dosage of 240 mg of morphine sulfate. This level was maintained for 80 days, then the dosage was raised to 360 mg and was maintained at this level for 48 days in 2 of the subjects, and for 6 days in the 3rd subject. Abrupt withdrawal of morphine followed for 48 hours. The recovery period of subject C_2 lasted for 35 days. The other 2 subjects obtained some unauthorized barbiturate during this time, vitiating some of the values obtained. Therefore, 3 months later they were studied during a 25-day drug-free period which was used as the "recovery" or postaddiction phase. During each phase, 10 IU of ACTH in 1 l of saline were administered by intravenous drip over an 8-hour period, and 1000 IU of chorionic gonadotropin were administered intramuscularly once daily for 4 or 5 consecutive days. Tests with ACTH and gonadotropin were separated by intervals of not less than 5 days. Corresponding placebo administrations of one liter of saline intravenously and saline intramuscular injections were also made from time to time. Smaller doses of ACTH of 5 and 2½ IU of ACTH were used during some of the phases. In addition to the analyses made in the first experiment, blood was drawn at intervals for serum butanol extractable iodine determinations.[2]

RESULTS. *Experiment 1. Single doses.* Single subcutaneous injections of morphine sulfate were given to 4 subjects in a series of ascending doses three to five days apart. A dose of 45 mg caused a decrease in 17-KS excretion of from 34 to 55 per cent on the day following administration. The 60-mg dose had less effect, and the 75-mg dose caused less change than the 60-mg dose. Single injections of 40 mg in 3 other subjects were associated with 12 to 48% decreases. Creatinine values for each man did not vary significantly,

[2] Serum iodines were done by Dr. Evelyn Man, Yale University School of Medicine, by her method for butanol-extractable iodine (Man and Kydd, 1951) which is equivalent to precipitable iodine.

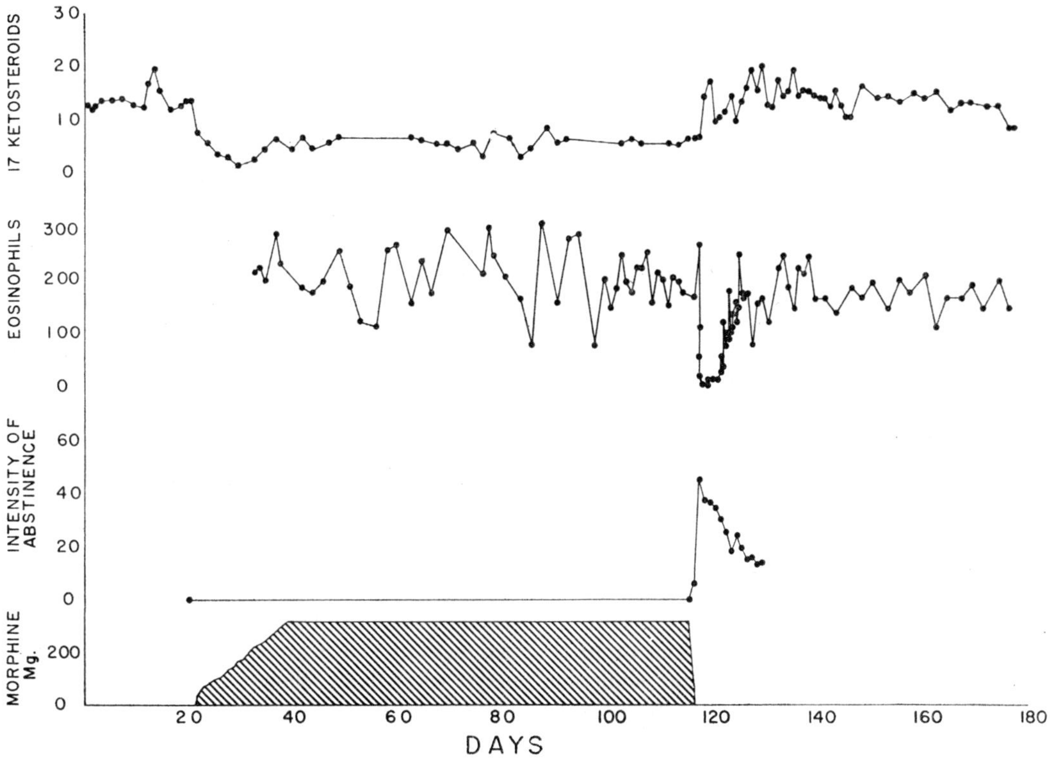

FIG. 1. Record of a typical subject (F, table 1). Urinary 17-KS in a cycle of addiction and their relation to eosinophil counts and intensity of abstinence.

showing that the urine collections were satisfactory.

Addiction Cycle. During preaddiction the average values for 17-KS among the subjects ranged from 5 to 21 mg for 24 hours. Each man showed day-to-day variations but there was an average characteristic value for each subject (table 1). During addiction, 17-KS excretion was decreased on the average to less than 50% of its preaddiction level (table 1). In 11 of the 13 tests there was no definite evidence of tolerance to this depressing effect of morphine on 17-KS excretion. In 2 subjects (A_2 and B_2) when addiction was extended for 143 days, partial tolerance developed since during the first month of morphine administration to A_2 the average excretion of 17-KS for 14 consecutive days was 3.0 ± 0.42[3] mg, and for B_2, 3.2 ± 0.26 mg as compared with 6.2 ± 0.39 mg and 4.8 ± 0.32 mg respectively for 14 consecutive days during the last month of addiction. There were no significant changes in the eosinophil counts during addiction (figure 1).

[3] Plus or minus the standard error of the mean.

Abrupt withdrawal was followed by a striking rise in 17-KS excretion, usually on the second or third day. The values presented in table 1 are for the third day. Subjects A_2, B_2, and C_2 had received 90 mg of morphine sulfate on the third day of withdrawal. This probably caused the 17-KS values for that day to be decreased. B_2 and C_2 showed higher excretion on the second than on the third day, and their levels on the third day are lower than they were during experiment 1. E_2 also had a higher level of excretion on the second day. These rises in 17-KS excretion corresponded in time to a sharp depression of the eosinophil count to zero or near-zero values. Both effects coincided with the time of maximal severity of symptoms of abstinence (figure 1).

In most cases the excretion of 17-KS returned to normal about the fifth day of withdrawal. By that time eosinophil counts had risen to preaddiction levels. The data during the recovery period in table 1 are taken from the 14th day onward after discontinuation of morphine in order to rule out possible residual effects of abstinence. In most subjects the average excretion of 17-KS

TABLE 2

Effect of 10 IU of ACTH on the daily urinary excretion of 17-ketosteroids

	Subject A2				Subject B2				Subject C2			
	ACTH		Increase		ACTH		Increase		ACTH		Increase	
	Before	After			Before	After			Before	After		
	mg	*mg*	*mg*	%	*mg*	*mg*	*mg*	%	*mg*	*mg*	*mg*	%
Preaddiction	12.2	16.9	4.7	39	6.1	11.3	5.2	85	22.9	42.0	19.1	83
	11.5	18.0	6.5	57	6.1	12.0	5.9	97	18.1	33.0	14.9	82
Addiction	3.3	6.6	3.3	100	3.6	7.6	4.0	111	8.8	11.0	2.2	25
	6.4	8.8	2.4	38	4.3	8.9	4.6	107	10.2	17.1	6.9	68
	6.5	10.1	3.6	55	4.5	13.5	9.0	200	8.1	12.8	4.7	58
	8.3	7.6	−0.7	−8	4.6	9.2	4.6	100				
	6.5	9.6	3.1	48								
Recovery	11.6	16.2	4.6	40	4.3	9.1	4.8	112	20.9	37.1	16.2	78

The figures under "Before ACTH" are the averages of the daily excretion of 17-KS for 4–5 days prior to the day on which ACTH was given.

during the recovery phase agreed within 2 mg with the preaddiction average, and the overall averages were very similar.

Experiment 2. Of 21 administrations of 10 IU of ACTH before, during, and after addiction, variously distributed among the 3 subjects, only one failed to cause a distinct increase in 17-ketosteroid excretion (table 2). This aberration cannot be explained since adrenal response as measured by fall to zero or near-zero of eosinophil counts occurred here as well as after other infusions of ACTH. After ACTH the increased excretion of 17-KS, expressed as the increase above the average excretion level for the 4- or 5-day period preceding the test, was usually less during addiction. If expressed as percentage change from the preinfusion level, the increases during addiction and drug-free periods were of the same order of magnitude. The response to ACTH stimulation may have been retarded during addiction, since in two of the three cases the maximal decrease in eosinophils was delayed about two hours. Ten IU of ACTH given to the 3 subjects on the fourth day of gonadotropin stimulation hastened but did not elevate the response to gonadotropin. During the addiction and withdrawal phases, 2 of the subjects received smaller amounts of ACTH (5 and 2½ units). Responses to the latter doses were within the range of those observed with the 10-unit doses, showing that the preparation of ACTH used was extremely potent.

Gonadotropin. The effects of 1000 IU of chorionic gonadotropin given intramuscularly once daily for 5 days on the urinary 17-KS during the various phases of the addiction cycle are illustrated in table 3. The values in the table are the averages of 17-KS excretion during periods of 5 days selected as follows: preinjection, the five days immediately preceding hormone injection; postinjection, the third, fourth and fifth day of the course of gonadotropin, and the 2 days after the last injection. Increases in excretion seldom appeared before the third day of administration of gonadotropin. This delay in response was also noted by Landau *et al.*, (1950), using roughly comparable doses on normal men. During addiction the maximal response was often delayed until after the injections were completed. During preaddiction and recovery phases, small milligram increments and percentage rises in 17-KS excretion usually followed the injection of the hormone, although 2 negative responses were observed. In terms of milligram increments, the excretion of 17-KS was higher in the addiction phase than during the drug-free periods, and the percentage rises were much higher during addiction. Maximal response tended to be delayed during addiction. In the tests where 10 units of ACTH was infused on the fourth day of the gonadotropin course, the maximal rise in 17-KS occurred on that day, but the increase was no greater than would be expected from one hormone alone. Administration of gonadotropin was without effect on the eosinophil counts. Responses to placebos simulating the administration of ACTH or gonadotropin were uniformly negative.

Thyroid. No changes in the butanol-extractable

iodine content of serum occurred throughout the cycle of addiction. Variations greater than 1 μg % were noted rarely.

DISCUSSION. *Single Doses.* There have been no reports of experiments dealing with the effects of single doses of morphine on excretion of 17-KS in human subjects. In this investigation single injections of from 45 to 75 mg of morphine subcutaneously always caused a decrease in 17-KS excretion ranging from 12 to 58%. Single large doses in the rat (George and Way, 1955; Briggs and Munson, 1955) caused a fall in adrenal ascorbic acid; i.e., adrenal-cortical stimulation. A fraction of our observed decrease could be due to gonadal effects, since in other experiments which will be published later single large doses of morphine (from 60 to 80 mg), either once or on 3 consecutive days, caused erratic responses in the excretion of urinary 17-KS, indicating that adrenal-cortical stimulation can occur in man after morphine. This might be a nonspecific reaction to the stress of the large doses used. The consistent adrenal-cortical stimulation obtained by George and Way (1955) and by Briggs and Munson (1955) may have been caused by differences in stress responses to the relatively massive doses of the drug used, and in the case of the former authors, by the handling of the rats. At the less unreasonable dose of 1/15 of the LD_{50} of morphine, no adrenal-cortical stimulation occurred after morphine in rats studied by George and Way (1955).

Addiction. In our experiments a marked decrease in 17-KS excretion always occurred during addiction. The results suggest that addiction causes hypofunction of the adrenal, the testes or both. There have been no experiments on man with which to compare these results. Rats have been subjected to short courses of morphine. Tanabe and Cafruny (1958) started with a daily dose of 20 mg/kg and increased it to 190 mg/kg in 21 days. Injections were made twice daily. During this experiment young rats failed to gain weight and mature rats lost weight, indicating that the procedure was stressful. Adrenal weights at the end of the addiction were about 200% those of control animals. Neither of these effects occurred in hypophysectomized rats. Barraclough and Sawyer (1955) observed suppression of ovulation in rats receiving morphine for 5 or more days. Briggs and Munson (1955) observed that in unanesthetized rats morphine stimulated the adrenal cortex. In animals anesthetized with barbiturates, the adrenal response to histamine was blocked by morphine. In rats made "tolerant" to morphine by 5 daily i.p. injections, 20 mg/kg of histamine did not cause depletion of ascorbic acid from the adrenals. Briggs and Munson (1955) interpreted their data as meaning that when tolerance was obtained, an initial stimulant effect of morphine on the pituitary-adrenal system no longer obscured a depressant effect on this system. Except for the initial stimulating effects of morphine on adrenals of unanesthetized rats, Briggs and Munson's observations on tolerant rats are consistent with our findings

TABLE 3

Effect of chorionic gonadotropin on the daily urinary excretion of 17-ketosteroids

	Subject A_1				Subject B_2				Subject C_2			
	Gonadotropin		Increase		Gonadotropin		Increase		Gonadotropin		Increase	
	Before	After			Before	After			Before	After		
	mg	*mg*	*mg*	%	*mg*	*mg*	*mg*	%	*mg*	*mg*	*mg*	%
Preaddiction	11.9	13.2	1.3	11	5.5	4.9	−0.6	−11	22.2	24.3	2.1	9
Addiction	2.8	5.9	3.1	111	2.8	5.2	2.4	86	5.7	12.5	6.8	119
	4.8	9.7	4.9	102	4.2	5.2	1.0	24	9.8	16.9	7.1	72
	4.3	8.3	4.0	93	2.9	7.6	4.7	162				
Recovery	10.2	10.8	0.6	6	4.9	4.5	−0.4	−8	18.1	22.9	4.8	27
	8.8	10.4	1.6	18	3.7	4.3	0.6	16				

Dosage of gonadotropin was 1000 international units intramuscularly daily for 5 days.

Figures under "Before" are averages of excretion during 5-day control period immediately preceding the first day of injection.

Levels after gonadotropin are averages of the values on the 3rd, 4th, and 5th day of injections and the 1st and 2nd day after last injection.

on human subjects. Both Briggs and Munson (1955) and Tanabe and Cafruny (1958) used doses of morphine which were relatively large and the time of addiction was relatively short as compared with those used in man. In the investigations herein reported, depression of 17-KS excretion began on the first day of chronic drug administration and persisted throughout a long addiction. No tolerance developed during addiction periods of less than 100 days and complete tolerance was not reached in 130 days.

Withdrawal. In these experiments abrupt withdrawal of morphine was followed by increases in excretion of 17-KS of 66 to 480% above addiction levels. In most cases excretion of 17-KS on the third day of withdrawal exceeded the preaddiction levels. The peak 17-KS excretion coincided with the lowest level of blood eosinophils and the most severe symptoms of withdrawal. These findings might suggest that increased activity of the adrenals and/or the gonads might be partly responsible for symptoms of abstinence. However, the effects induced by large amounts of adrenal or gonadal hormones do not resemble the phenomena observed during abstinence. Moreover, Tanabe and Cafruny (1958) observed that withdrawal symptoms were the same in hypophysectomized and intact rats. It therefore seems that abstinence symptoms are not due to increased production of 17-KS. The gonads may possibly contribute to the increased excretion of 17-KS during withdrawal, since spontaneous sexual excitation commonly occurs at this time.

ACTH and Gonadotropin. Although adrenal and gonadal functions are suppressed during addiction, the target organs were very responsive to specific exogenous hormonal stimulation during addiction. The chief difference noted was a tendency to delayed response during addiction; the eosinophil minimum may be delayed by about 2 hours, and peak response to the chronic administration of gonadotropin may be postponed for several days. Briggs and Munson (1955) also found that morphine did not interfere with the response to ACTH in hypophysectomized rats. The adrenal cortex was still sensitive to ACTH, although morphine prevented secretion of ACTH by the pituitary in response to stressful stimuli.

Taken together the evidence indicates that morphine does not act directly upon the adrenal cortex or the testes, since these organs respond to appropriate hormonal stimuli even when their functions are suppressed. The actions of morphine probably occur at the level of the anterior pituitary and may be mediated through effects on hypothalamic centers which control pituitary activity (George and Way, 1955; Briggs and Munson, 1955) or on central nervous system structures which affect the hypothalamus such as the reticular formation (Sawyer *et al.* 1955).

These experiments suggest that gonadal and adrenal functions are suppressed during addiction and enhanced during withdrawal. They leave undetermined the relative role of the adrenal cortex and the testes, and the question as to whether low rates of 17-KS excretion during addiction are due to decreased production or increased destruction of the steroids. Further experiments, which will be reported later and in which plasma levels and urinary excretion of 17-hydroxycorticoids will be determined, will attempt to answer some of the questions.

SUMMARY

Single doses of 45 or more mg of morphine sulfate administered to human male subjects were followed by decreased excretion of 17-KS.

Addiction to morphine, lasting from 35 to 144 days, caused a significant fall in the excretion of 17-KS. Evidence of partial tolerance to the depressant effect of morphine on urinary 17-KS appeared during periods of addiction lasting 143 days.

A striking rise in urinary 17-KS, with levels usually exceeding those of the predrug period, occurred on the second to fourth day of withdrawal. The maximal increase coincided with the most severe symptoms of abstinence and the greatest drop in eosinophil counts.

During recovery, urinary 17-KS returned to preaddiction levels.

Administration of ACTH (10 IU) resulted in a striking rise in 17-KS excretion and a fall in eosinophil counts during control, addiction, and recovery periods. Similar responses to 5 and 2½ units occurred.

Administration of 5000 units of chorionic gonadotropin over a 5-day period caused enhanced excretion of 17-KS which was greater during addiction than during control and recovery periods.

During addiction there was some evidence of delay in the response to hormonal stimulation.

The maximal fall in eosinophil counts was sometimes retarded for about 2 hours after ACTH infusion. The maximal response to gonadotropin was usually postponed for 2 or more days. ACTH and gonadotropin administered in combination did not have additive effects on excretion of urinary 17-KS.

A cycle of morphine addiction did not affect the content of butanol-extractable iodine in blood serum.

REFERENCES

BARRACLOUGH, C. A. AND SAWYER, C. H.: Endocrinology **57:** 329, 1955.
BRIGGS, F. N. AND MUNSON, P. L.: Endocrinology **57:** 205, 1955.
CALLOW, N. H., CALLOW, R. R. AND EMMONS, C. W.: Biochem. J. **7:** 32, 1938.
DREKTER, I. J., HEISLER, A., SCISM, G. R., STERN, S., PEARSON, S. AND MCGAVAK, T. H.: J. clin. Endocrinol. **12:** 55, 1952.
FRASER, H. F. AND ISBELL, H.: Ann. intern. Med. **38:** 234, 1953.
GEORGE, R. AND WAY, E. L.: Brit. J. Pharmacol. **10:** 260, 1955.
HOLTORFF, A. F. AND KOCH, F. C.: J. biol. Chem. **135:** 377, 1940.
LANDAU, R. L., KNOWLTON, K., LUGIBIHI, K., BRANDT, M. AND KENYON, A. T.: J. clin. Invest. **29:** 619, 1950.
MAN, EVELYN B. AND KYDD, DAVID M.: J. clin. Invest. **30:** 531, 1951.
PETERS, J. H.: J. biol. Chem. **146:** 179, 1942.
RANDOLPH, T. G.: J. Lab. clin. Med. **34:** 1696, 1949.
SAWYER, C. H., CRITCHLOW, B. V. AND BARRACLOUGH, C. A.: Endocrinology **57:** 345, 1955.
TANABE, T. AND CAFRUNY, E. J.: THIS JOURNAL **122:** 148, 1958.

8092

ENHANCEMENT OF SODIUM SALICYLATE ABSORPTION BY MEPHENESIN[1]

JULIUS J. CARR, GEORGE J. MOURATOFF[2] AND ROBERT C. BATTERMAN

Department of Medicine and Arthritis Services of New York Medical College, Metropolitan Medical Center, Flower and Fifth Avenue Hospitals, Metropolitan Hospital, and Bird S. Coler Memorial Hospital and Home, New York, N. Y.

Received for publication June 16, 1958

Factors which influence the absorption of salicylates from the gastrointestinal tract of man have been under investigation in our laboratory for many years. Since in our experience (Batterman, 1958) antacids or buffers have not been satisfactory, we have sought other means of enhancing absorption of salicylate. Hanske (1951) demonstrated the effectiveness of sodium salicylate in increasing the solubility of 3-ortho-toloxy-1,2-propanediol (mephenesin) from approximately 1 g to 10 g per 100 ml of water. Although the original concept of this report was to increase the solubility of mephenesin, there was no indication that the reverse situation might also apply. In view of this chemical observation, it was thought advisable to study the influence of mephenesin and sodium salicylate upon the absorption of each from the gastrointestinal tract in man. Preliminary studies revealed that although the simultaneous administration of mephenesin and sodium salicylate did not increase mephenesin absorption over the administration of mephenesin alone, there was a marked increase in blood salicylate level. The following studies were then performed to delineate this effect in greater detail.

METHODS. In order to evaluate properly the effect of mephenesin upon the absorption of salicylate, it was necessary to establish statistically reliable reference curves of plasma salicylate levels at selected intervals following usually employed therapeutic doses of sodium salicylate or of aspirin. Such data are not available in the literature. Corresponding curves following administration of mephenesin with salicylate could then be obtained by the same procedure.

Of the two methods available for determining curves of absorption, namely, 1) utilization of individual subjects for all selected intervals after ingestion and 2) establishment of a composite picture by using as many subjects as possible, with each subject contributing one to three blood samples until for each interval a sufficiently large number of values is attained, we chose the latter. We believe that the second approach is more practical and has fewer shortcomings. The difficulty in obtaining 10 blood samples from each subject in a 6-hour period, as would be required for the complete curve of blood levels, would impose obvious limitations on this procedure. On the other hand, a composite curve of absorption, obtained from many subjects, permits a more reliable application of this information to the population at large. Furthermore, the determination of one or more points of the curve on different days tends to eliminate bias due to possible minor variations in technique or to other variable factors which might enter into the final results.

None of the subjects had any gastrointestinal disease, liver, kidney or cardiac dysfunction, which might have affected salicylate absorption or excretion. Salicylate was withheld from all subjects for at least 48 hours prior to the start of the test period. Each subject was brought to a fasting basal state and a control blood sample was taken. To establish the standard curves, 38 subjects received 500 mg of sodium salicylate and 49 subjects received 600 mg of aspirin. Forty-six additional subjects received a combination of 500 mg sodium salicylate and 500 mg mephenesin given in the same capsule.[3] Following administration of the medication, one to three blood samples were drawn from each patient at random time intervals of 5, 7½, 10, 30, 60, 120, 180, 240 and 360 minutes. Each composite curve of absorption included a minimum of 10 subjects for each inter-

[1] Presented before the American Society for Pharmacology and Experimental Therapeutics, April 14, 1958.

[2] Fellow in Medicine, Department of Hospitals, N.Y.C.

[3] Crookes-Barnes Laboratories, Inc., Mountain View, N. J. generously supplied the medication known as Mephosal and other aid for this investigation.

val. Determination of the influence of mephenesin (500 mg) upon aspirin (600 mg) absorption was performed in 9 subjects and was limited to 2 specific time intervals.

Analytical procedure. Free and total salicylate in plasma were determined by the modification described below of the method of Brodie, Udenfriend and Coburn (1944). This modification provides a desirable increase in sensitivity when small oral doses, i.e. 500 or 600 mg of sodium salicylate or aspirin are given. We have determined the following partition coefficients at 25°C for salicylic acid:

$$k_1 \text{ for } \frac{\text{ethylene dichloride}}{1.2 \text{ N HCl}} = 7.2,$$

$$k_2 \text{ for } \frac{\text{ferric nitrate reagent}}{\text{ethylene dichloride}} = 17.1.$$

These values are in excellent agreement with levels of ferric-salicylate complex which are observed when known quantities of salicylic acid are carried through the complete procedure.

Two ml of blood plasma, salicylic acid standard (2 ml = 0.10 mg) and distilled water are acidified separately in 60-ml glass-stoppered bottles with 3 ml of 2 N HCl. Each mixture is shaken for 10 minutes with 15 ml of ethylene dichloride. The mixture is then transferred to a suitable sturdy test tube, the contents are centrifuged and the upper phase containing water and precipitated protein is removed by aspiration. Ten ml of the clear ethylene dichloride extract are shaken for 10 minutes in a second bottle with 3 ml of a freshly prepared diluted ferric nitrate reagent (a forty-fold dilution of Brodie's reagent, 1% $Fe(NO_3)_3$ in 0.07 N HNO_3). The absorbance of the clear, centrifuged aqueous phase, in a suitable cuvette (Coleman no. 6-310B) is measured against the reagent blank at 540 mμ.

$$\text{Mg salicylic acid per 100 ml} = \frac{A_a}{A_s} \times 5$$

For the determination of plasma total salicylate, a loosely stoppered bottle containing acidified plasma (2 ml plasma, 3 ml 2 N HCl) is kept partially immersed in a boiling water bath for one hour. The cooled hydrolyzed contents are then treated according to the above procedure for free salicylate. Aside from effecting hydrolysis of acetylsalicylic acid, this procedure does not influence the determination of salicylate. Determination of levels in 98 samples of plasma from subjects given sodium salicylate showed an average difference of but 0.05 mg % salicylate between hydrolyzed and unhydrolyzed specimens.

The volume of acidified plasma was increased from 2.5 to 5.0 ml in order to avoid troublesome emulsions which frequently formed when the more concentrated plasma-HCl mixture was shaken with ethylene dichloride after hydrolysis. Increase in volume of acidified plasma and decrease in volume of ethylene dichloride resulted in an insignificant decrease in extraction of salicylic acid, i.e. from 99% to 96%. The concentration of salicylate in the final extract is 3.1 times that

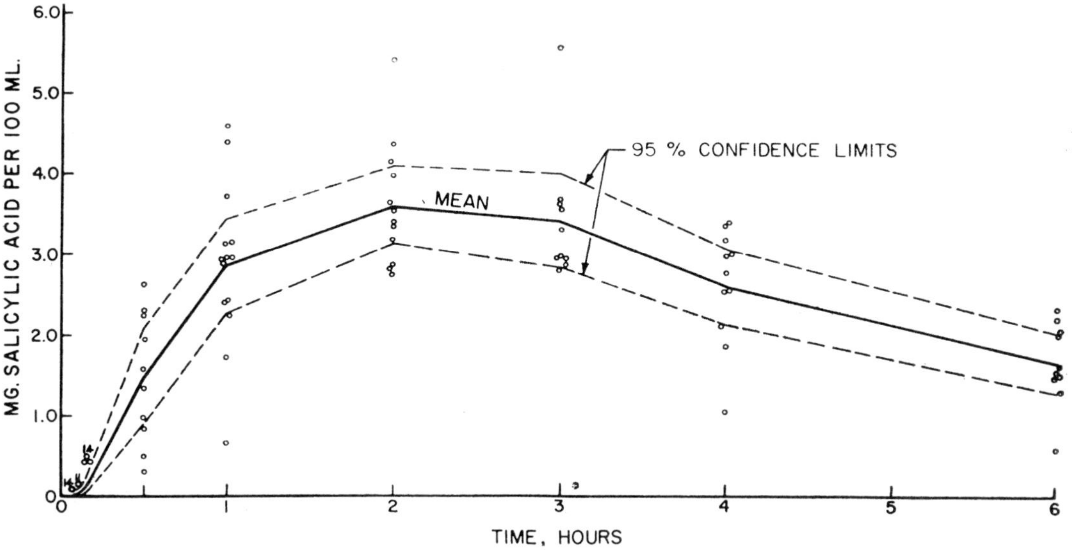

FIG. 1. Composite curve of plasma salicylate levels following administration orally of 0.5 g sodium salicylate to 38 subjects. Ten or more determinations were performed at each time interval.

which is obtained by the original procedure from equal plasma concentrations. Allowing for a 50% decrease in light path, owing to the smaller volume of final extract, the sensitivity of the present modification is 50% greater than that of the original procedure.

The feasibility of determining salicylate in the presence of mephenesin is supported by the following observations. 1) Six determinations of plasma salicylate following oral administration of 1 g mephenesin gave apparent salicylate levels averaging slightly below 0.1 mg %. With the usual dose of 0.5 g mephenesin this interference is, therefore, negligible. 2) Addition of mephenesin did not alter the recovery of salicylate from plasma.

TABLE 1

Mean plasma salicylate levels, mg per 100 ml, following administration orally of 0.5 g sodium salicylate with and without 0.5 g mephenesin and 0.6 g of aspirin alone. Standard deviation of each mean follows in parentheses

Time	Sodium Salicylate	Salicylate-Mephenesin	Aspirin
min			
5	0.02 (0.01)	0.25 (0.11)	0.22 (0.06)
7.5	0.06 (0.02)	1.16 (0.24)	0.38 (0.11)
10	0.16 (0.05)	1.92 (0.24)	0.87 (0.19)
30	1.46 (0.26)	4.67 (0.31)	3.40 (0.30)
60	2.86 (0.27)	4.62 (0.17)	4.27 (0.31)
120	3.61 (0.22)	4.01 (0.18)	4.56 (0.38)
180	3.42 (0.26)	3.65 (0.20)	3.71 (0.32)
240	2.60 (0.22)	3.22 (0.21)	4.06 (0.35)
360	1.66 (0.16)	2.62 (0.17)	3.43 (0.45)

RESULTS. The absorption of 0.5 gm of sodium salicylate administered alone by the oral route is shown in fig. 1. Individual plasma levels for each interval, the composite curve drawn through the mean levels at each period and upper and lower limits of 95% confidence levels are illustrated. The mean plasma salicylate levels and their standard deviations are seen in table 1. It will be noted that salicylate appears in the blood in very small but significant amounts in 5 minutes, reaches a peak at 2 hours and decreases by about 50% in the next four hours. Each salicylate value reported in this paper has been corrected by subtraction of a very small plasma "salicylate" value obtained as control for each subject immediately before administration of drug. The following values, in mg salicylic acid per 100 ml, were obtained from 201 control samples: mean 0.073, sample standard deviation of mean ($S/\sqrt{n}$) 0.004, sample standard deviation (S) 0.051. Utilizing these values, we decided to reject data obtained from a few subjects with control

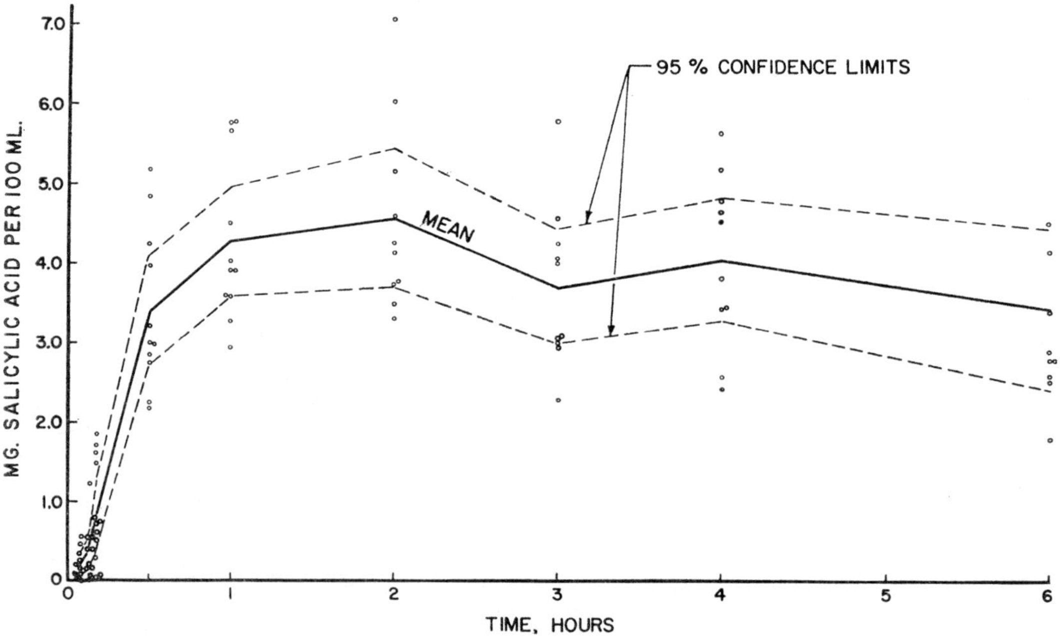

FIG. 2. Plasma total salicylate levels following administration orally of 0.6 g aspirin to 49 subjects. Ten or more values were measured at each time interval.

levels above 0.21 mg per 100 ml. The probability that a level above 0.21 mg would be observed without prior salicylate therapy is less than .001.

Fig. 2 and table 1 present similar data for 0.6 g of aspirin. Significant plasma total salicylate levels appear in 5 minutes, reach a peak at 2 hours and decrease by 25% in the next 4 hours.

Fig. 3 and table 1 illustrate the results obtained with the combination of 0.5 g each of mephenesin and sodium salicylate. It is quite evident that mephenesin influences markedly the absorption of sodium salicylate. This is already apparent at 7½ minutes, when a significant increase occurs over salicylate given alone. Not only does the attainment of a peak effect at 30 minutes as compared with 2 hours reflect the

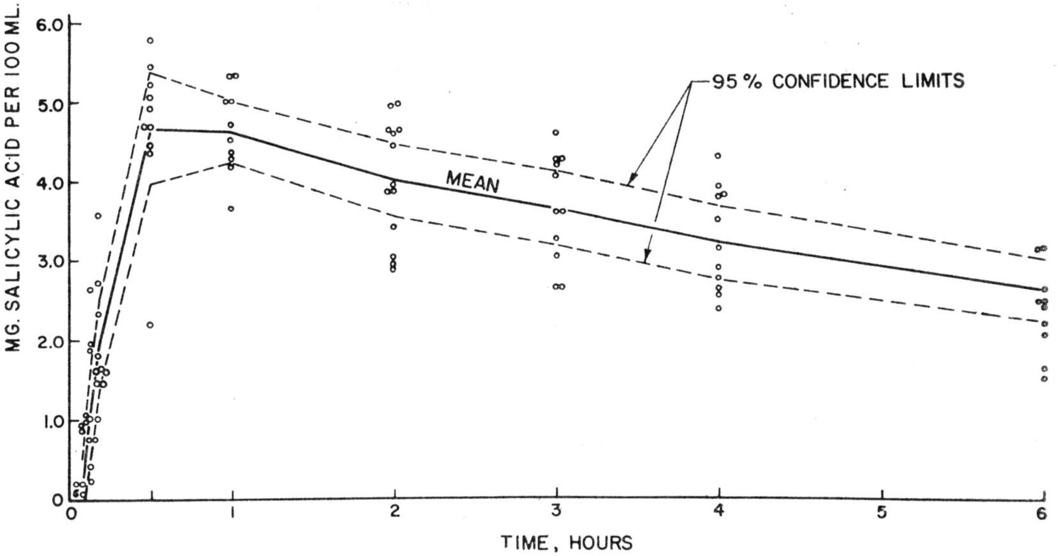

FIG. 3. Plasma salicylate levels following administration orally of 0.5 g sodium salicylate and 0.5 g mephenesin (in the same capsule) to 46 subjects. Ten or more values were measured at each time interval.

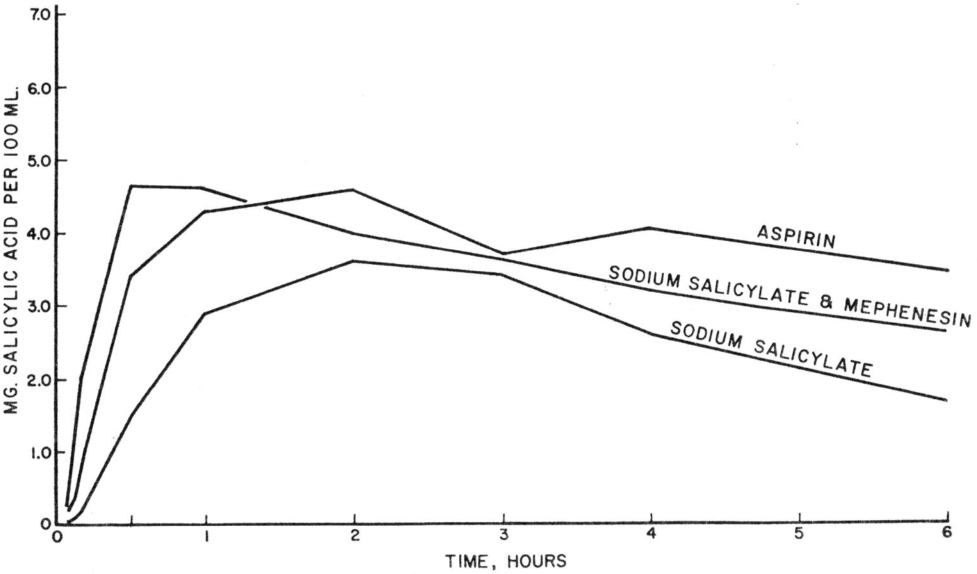

FIG. 4. Comparison of mean plasma salicylate levels. Curves are superimposed from preceding figures.

enhanced rate of absorption, but in addition the peak level of plasma salicylate is considerably higher than that achieved at the peak of salicylate alone. The slope of the steepest portion of the ascending limb of the mephenesin-salicylate curve (17.0 mg per 100 ml per hour) is 4 times that of the corresponding portion of the sodium salicylate curve (4.2 mg per 100 ml per hour).

Fig. 4 presents the mean curve for all three preparations. The differences in levels and the influence of mephenesin upon sodium salicylate absorption (table 2) are upheld by definitive statistical analysis (Cochran and Cox, 1957; Snedecor, 1956).

Contrary to the results obtained with sodium salicylate, the absorption of aspirin was not affected by simultaneous administration of mephenesin. Total salicylate levels at 30 and 60 minutes after administration of 0.5 g mephenesin and 0.6 g aspirin were essentially the same as corresponding points on the standard curve for aspirin alone.

The amount of mephenesin required to increase sodium salicylate absorption was studied in 2 additional groups of 10 subjects each. Administration of 100 or 250 mg of mephenesin with 0.5 g of sodium salicylate, followed by determination of plasma salicylate levels at 30 and 60 minutes, revealed that similar results were achieved with 100, 250 or 500 mg of mephenesin.

Comparative absorption curves following small therapeutic doses of sodium salicylate or of aspirin are not readily available. Smith *et al.* (1946), using 2 g doses, reported more rapid absorption of sodium salicylate than of aspirin. Lolli and Smith (1946) administered 0.6 g aspirin to 2 patients and obtained plasma levels which were essentially similar to those reported in this paper. Our levels are also in good agreement with those reported by Carlo *et al.* (1955) following administration of 0.6 g aspirin to 10 subjects.

TABLE 2

Statistical analysis of significance of differences between mean plasma levels. Comparison of sodium salicylate-mephenesin combination vs a) sodium salicylate and b) aspirin

	Sodium Salicylate + Mephenesin vs Sodium Salicylate				Sodium Salicylate + Mephenesin vs Aspirin			
Time	Difference	t	Limit of significance*	Significance	Difference	t	Limit of significance*	Significance
min	*mg%*				*mg%*			
5	0.23	2.12	2.26	−	0.03	0.27	2.26	−
7.5	1.10	4.59	2.26	+	0.78	2.96	2.26	+
10	1.76	7.27	2.26	+	1.05	3.51	2.24	+
30	3.22	7.99	2.26	+	1.27	2.94	2.25	+
60	1.76	5.51	2.19	+	0.35	1.00	2.24	−
120	0.40	1.31	2.19	−	−0.55	1.27	2.24	−
180	0.23	0.71	2.25	−	−0.06	0.16	2.26	−
240	0.62	2.07	2.23	−	−0.84	2.08	2.25	−
360	0.96	4.04	2.26	+	−0.80	1.67	2.26	−

* Figures represent the t value which would be required to make the difference significant at P = 0.05.

DISCUSSION. There remain several questions, some of which can be answered in full while others require further investigation. The first question that comes to mind is: does the more rapid attainment of higher blood levels with the salicylate-mephenesin combination reflect a more effective clinical preparation? Recently completed studies (Batterman *et al.*, 1958) demonstrate that this is so. We cannot at this time point out the specific mechanism by which mephenesin influences sodium salicylate absorption, nor can we explain why aspirin absorption is unaffected while sodium salicylate absorption is increased markedly. Whether other salicylates can be affected remains to be seen. Elucidation of the mechanism of enhancement may be facilitated by studies in progress with other agents used in place of mephenesin.

SUMMARY AND CONCLUSIONS

The simultaneous administration orally of sodium salicylate and mephenesin results in a marked increase of salicylate absorption from the gastrointestinal tract of man.

In 38 subjects, the composite curve of absorption of sodium salicylate alone reveals that absorption begins at 5 minutes, and reaches a peak at 2 hours.

The combination of sodium salicylate-mephenesin, studied in 46 additional subjects, is rapidly absorbed so that a marked increase is noted at 7½ minutes and peak absorption occurs at 30 minutes.

Mephenesin does not influence the absorption of acetylsalicylic acid.

Statistical analysis reveals that the more rapid and greater salicylate blood levels attained with the combination of sodium salicylate-mephenesin are significant when compared with sodium salicylate alone or acetylsalicylic acid.

REFERENCES

BATTERMAN, R. C.: New Engl. J. Med. **258:** 213, 1958.

Batterman, R. C., Carr, J. and Mouratoff: J. Amer. Geriatric Soc., in press.
Brodie, B. B., Udenfriend, S. and Coburn, A. S.: This Journal **80:** 114, 1944.
Carlo, P. E., Cambosos, N. M., Feeney, G. C. and Smith, P. K.: J. Amer. pharm. Ass. **44:** 396, 1955.
Cochran, W. G. and Cox, G. M.: Experimental Designs, 2nd ed., John Wiley and Sons, Inc., New York, 1957.
Lolli, G. and Smith, R.: New Engl. J. Med. **253:** 80, 1946.
Nachf, H. M. (Hanske, W., inventor): Chem. Abst. **45:** 1736, 1951.
Smith, P. K., Gleason, H. L., Stoll, C. G. and Ogorzalek, S.: This Journal **87:** 237, 1946.
Snedecor, G. W.: Statistical Methods, 5th ed., pp. 85–101, Iowa State College Press, Ames, Iowa, 1956.

8093

DIURETIC EFFECTS OF FORMOGUANAMINE AND OTHER S-TRIAZINES

C. M. KAGAWA AND C. G. VAN ARMAN

Division of Biological Research, G. D. Searle and Co., Chicago

Received for publication July 9, 1958

Water metabolism is strongly affected by triazines. Lipschitz and Hadidian (1944) showed in diuretic tests in rats that formoguanamine (2,4-diamino-*s*-triazine) and melamine (2,4,6-triamino-*s*-triazine) were 347 and 77 times as potent as urea on a molar basis. Qualitatively, a similar ranking was found in dogs (Lipschitz and Stokey, 1945). Since these early observations, the diuretic action of formoguanamine has been confirmed in other studies with dogs (Freire, 1948; Turchetti, 1950) and in man (Ludwig, 1946; Freire, 1947; Lipschitz and Stokey, 1948).

Summarized in the present report are the diuretic effects of formoguanamine and twenty-seven other *s*-triazines synthesized by Dr. Viktor Papesch of our Chemistry Division. In general, our results in rats and dogs confirm and extend the basic information available in earlier and recent publications (LeSher and Shideman, 1956; Kuhn, 1957; Shapiro *et al.*, 1957) concerning this class of compounds.

METHODS. *Rat.* Diuretic activity was determined by a modified method (Van Arman, 1954) of Lipschitz *et al.* (1943). Male rats deprived of food and water overnight were dosed orally with 25 ml 0.85% saline/kg body weight. Compounds were given to groups of 16 rats either dissolved in the solution or as a fine suspension. Another group received an oral dose of 960 mg urea/kg as a standard of comparison. After treatment, the animals were placed in metabolism cages for collection of a 5-hour sample of urine. The volume for each group was recorded, and the samples analyzed for sodium content. Results were expressed as T/U, in which T is the effect with the compound and U, that with urea treatment. A T/U response of 0.81 for urine volume and 0.72 for sodium excretion with 16 animals represents activity at a 95% level of confidence. The minimal active dose for a compound was obtained by interpolation to these activity limits, using a log scale for the dosage coordinate. In this test, amisometradine (Rolicton) is active at approximately 10 mg/kg for the two responses; acetazolamide (Diamox) is active at 1.7 and 0.9 mg/kg for volume and sodium, respectively. A saline load with no drug gives a T/U response of 0.3 to 0.4.

Dog. Activity in this species was determined by a previously described method (Van Arman, 1954). Female mongrel dogs weighing 10 to 20 kg were given a standard meal and allowed water *ad libitum* overnight. At 9 A.M. the following day, each animal was catheterized to remove all urine from its bladder, and was then placed in a metabolism cage for a 5-hour collection of control urine. Total volume was recorded, and the sample analyzed for sodium. Similar procedures were done the next day except that a drug was given orally in a gelatin capsule before the collection of urine. Results were expressed as (T − C)/kg body weight, in which T and C represent 5-hour responses with and without treatment, respectively. Compounds were rated active ($P < 0.05$) in a 3-dog assay if (T − C)/kg was equal to or greater than 3.1 ml for volume and 0.64 mmol for sodium. Standard diuretics, such as meralluride sodium, acetazolamide and Rolicton, are all effective in this method.

Urinary sodium and potassium were determined with the Beckman flame photometer. Chloride was analyzed by the method of Van Slyke and Hiller (Hawk, Oser and Summerson, 1947).

RESULTS. Formoguanamine (SC-1430) caused water and sodium diuresis at a dose of about 3.5 mg/kg (table 1). Activity disappeared when various groups were placed at position 6 in the molecule (category I). Varying degrees of activity were found with substitutions in the amino radicals at 2 and 4. Potency was reduced to approximately half with acetylamino groups, unaltered with propionylamino and absent with benzoylamino (category II). Introduction of acetylamino and N-acetyl-*p*-chloroanilino groups at 2 and 4 caused a potent diuretic action (SC-5692). This compound had about nine times the activity of formoguanamine by comparison of minimal active doses.

TABLE 1

Diuretic effects of various s-triazines after oral administration in rats

Triazine		Substituents in Structure 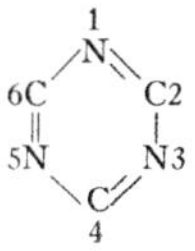			Minimal Active Dose, mg/kg	
Category	SC-number	2	4	6	Volume	Sodium
I	1430 (formoguanamine)	NH_2	NH_2	H	3.4	3.5
	1465	NH_2	NH_2	SH	Inact.	Inact.
	1491	NH_2	NH_2	Cl	Inact.	Inact.
	1544	NH_2	NH_2	OCH_3	Inact.	Inact.
	1546	NH_2	NH_2	$OCH_2CH_2N(CH_3)_2$	Inact.	Inact.
	6106	NH_2	NH_2	$CH_2N^+(CH_3)_3Cl^-$	Inact.	Inact.
II	1568	$NHCOCH_3$	$NHCOCH_3$	H	6.6	9.3
	1962	$NHCOCH_2CH_3$	$NHCOCH_2CH_3$	H	3.6	4.4
	1932	NHCO 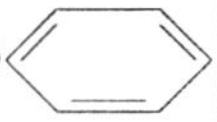	NHCO 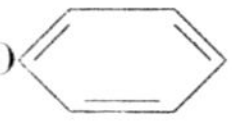	H	Inact.	Inact.
	5692	$NHCOCH_3$	$N(COCH_3)$ 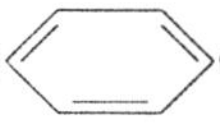 Cl	H	0.3	0.5
III	5871	NH_2	NH 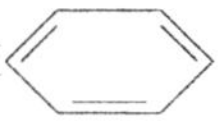	H	0.7	0.9
	5586	NH_2	NH 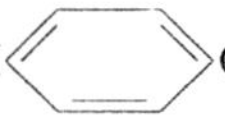 Cl	H	0.4	0.4
	6854	NH_2	NH 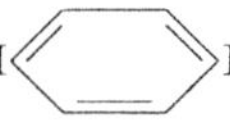 F	H	0.4	0.5
IV	5783	NH_2	NH  Cl Cl	H	Inact.	Inact.
	5862	NH_2	NH 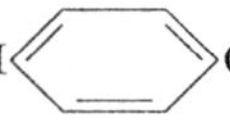 Cl	$COOC_2H_5$	Inact.	Inact.
	5918	NH_2	NH  Cl	$CH_2N(CH_3)_2$	Inact.	Inact.
V	6030	NH_2	NH  $CONH_2$	H	7.4	Inact.
	6566	NH_2	NH 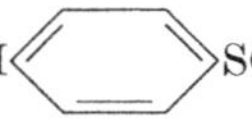 SO_2NH_2	H	8.2	10.7

TABLE 1—*Continued*

Triazine		Substituents in Structure 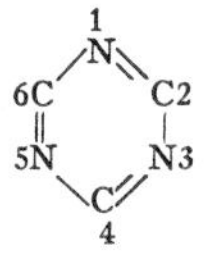			Minimal Active Dose, mg/kg	
Category	SC-number	2	4	6	Volume	Sodium
VI	5953	NH_2	NH  $COCH_3$	H	Inact.	Inact.
	6039	NH_2	NH 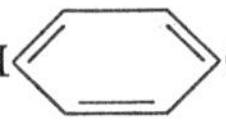 CN	H	Inact.	Inact.
	6384	NH_2	NH 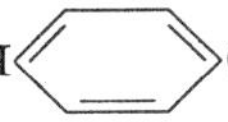 $COOC_2H_5$	H	Inact.	Inact.
	6473	NH_2	NH 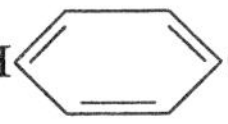 $CONHNH_2$	H	Inact.	Inact.
VII	6044	NH_2	NH 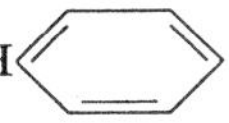	$COOC_2H_5$	Inact.	Inact.
VIII	1537	OCH_2CH_3	OCH_2CH_3	OCH_2CH_3	Inact.	Inact.
	1551	OH	OH	CH_3	Inact.	Inact.
	1647	$NHCOCH_3$	$NHCOCH_3$	NH_2	Inact.	Inact.
	6090	NH_2	NH 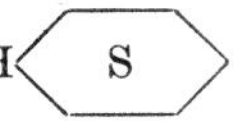	Cl	Inact.	Inact.
	7475	OH	OH	COOH	Inact.	Inact.

Inact. = inactive at a dose of 24 mg/kg.

Several other derivatives of formoguanamine also showed profound activity. A phenyl substituent in the 4-amino group gave SC-5871 (2-amino-4-anilino-*s*-triazine) which was four to five times as active as formoguanamine in water and sodium diuresis. SC-5586 (2-amino-4-*p*-chloroanilino-*s*-triazine) showed a nine-fold increase in activity, and the fluoro-counterpart, SC-6854, was also approximately as active. Additional changes led to loss of activity (cf. category III and IV). Some loss of potency occurred when para-substitutions in the phenyl ring of SC-5871 consisted of carbamido and sulfonamido radicals (category V). Interestingly enough, diuresis of water only, and not of sodium, occurred with the carbamido derivative (SC-6030). Substitutions in para-position with acetyl, cyano, carbethoxy, and hydrazinocarbonyl groups removed all activity (category VI), as did modification at position 6 (SC-6044). Other inactive *s*-triazines are listed in category VIII.

Dose-response curves for formoguanamine and SC-5586 are shown in fig. 1 (water excretion) and fig. 2 (sodium excretion). The large difference in potency between the compounds can be seen by comparing the doses required for an equal T/U response of 0.81 for water and 0.72 for sodium. Increasing effects were seen in a relatively narrow range of small doses, and at higher levels there was a plateau in response. Most of the responses on volume fell either within or below the confidence limits for total excretion of the load; this fact suggests that the compound was not able to deplete body water to values less than normal. The effects on sodium with SC-5586 are somewhat different. Fig. 2 demonstrates a number of ob-

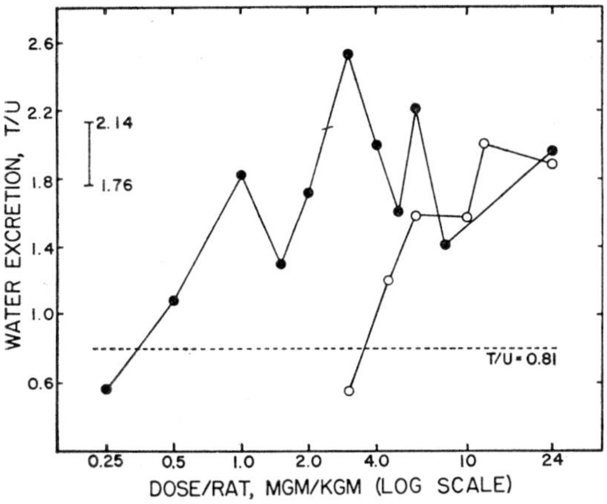

FIG. 1. Water excretion with various doses of SC-5586 (-●-) and formoguanamine (-O-) in rats. Range of T/U (1.76 to 2.14) describes the 95% confidence limits for total excretion of the administered load.

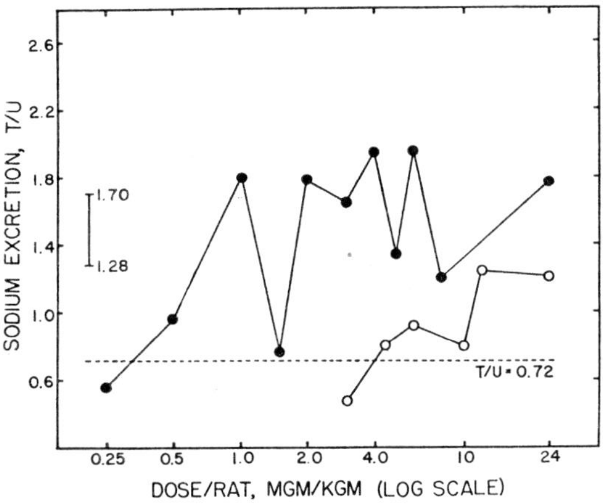

FIG. 2. Sodium excretion with various doses of SC-5586 (-●-) and formoguanamine (-O-) in rats. Range of T/U values (1.28 to 1.70) describes the 95% confidence limits for total excretion of the load.

servations greater than T/U = 1.70, the upper 95% confidence limit for total excretion.

The effects of the compounds in 5-hour tests in dogs are shown in table 2. Formoguanamine caused water diuresis, but sodium excretion remained unaffected (cf. legend, table 2). A similar lack of sodium effect, with water diuresis, can be seen with other triazines. SC-5692, a potent diuretic in the rat, was inactive in both water and sodium excretion. While some activity was demonstrable with 2-amino-4-anilino-*s*-triazine (SC-5871) and its para-halo modifications (SC-5586 and SC-6854), their relative activities did not correspond to those in rats. The effects of 2-amino-4-*p*-chloroanilino-*s*-triazine (SC-5586) given intravenously in 5-hour tests were also determined. Significant three-fold increments in the excretion of water, sodium and chloride occurred, but potassium excretion was unaffected (table 3).

DISCUSSION. Two interesting facts have become apparent. First, a loss of potency occurs when various groups are placed in position 6 of formoguanamine, SC-1568, SC-5871 and SC-5586. Lipschitz and Hadidian (1944) also found that substitution at 6 caused a loss of activity. These observations contrast with those of Ettel and Nosek (1952), who reported activity with a series of related triazines. A second fact can be seen with modifications of SC-5871: the para-chloro and -fluoro analogs possess potent diuretic

TABLE 2

Diuretic effects of triazines after oral administration in dogs (three dogs/treatment)

Treatment*		Mean (T − C) / kg		Remarks
SC-number	Dose	Urine vol	Sodium	
	mg/kg	*ml*	*mmol*	
1430 (formoguanamine)	10	5.85	0.02	
	20	9.64	0.12	Crystalluria (1 dog)
1568	12	1.37	0.12	
	24	7.36	0.11	Crystalluria (3 dogs)
5586	10	1.49	0.33	
	25	3.51	−0.07	
5871	12	4.04	0.52	Bloody urine (1 dog)
	24	5.15	0.57	Emesis (1 dog)
6030	25	4.33	0.23	Emesis (1/4 dogs)
6854	6	−3.68	−0.12	
	12	3.56	0.56	

* SC-1962 and -5692 were inactive at 12 mg/kg dose.

Meralluride sodium in a 0.37 ml total dose intramuscularly showed (T − C)/kg values of 6.08 ml and 1.29 mmol; acetazolamide, 2.5 mg/kg orally, gave values of 6.70 ml and 1.67 mmol; amisometradine, 25 mg/kg orally, gave 4.03 ml and 0.72 mmol.

TABLE 3

Water and electrolyte effects of 2-amino-4-p-chloroanilino-s-triazine after intravenous administration in dogs

Urinary Measurement	Mean ± Standard Error	
	Control	Treatment*
Volume, ml	38 ± 5	122 ± 20†
Sodium, mmol	4.71 ± 0.88	14.75 ± 3.91†
Potassium, mmol	2.15 ± 0.51	2.90 ± 0.32
Chloride, mmol	4.13 ± 0.54	14.84 ± 4.90†

* Dose of 3 mg/0.26 ml propylene glycol/kg body weight was injected into cephalic vein in 13 dogs; the solvent alone was not effective in producing changes in the measurements.

† $P < 0.05$, using student's "t" test (Fisher, 1946).

action. A small amount of activity was retained with carbamido and sulfonamido groups, but not with others. Clauder and Bulcsu (1951) observed reduction of activity with substitutions of methyl, dimethylamino, methoxy and ethoxy radicals; this fact suggests, as verified by the recent studies of Shapiro *et al.* (1957) that only specific para-modifications confer strong activity.

The triazines appear to increase diuretic effects only within a narrow range of doses. Lipschitz and Hadidian (1944) observed with formoguanamine a plateau of water excretion which was limited to the load administered. Our results with formoguanamine, SC-5586 and other *s*-triazines, agree with this observation. It does appear, however, that in some instances sodium loss in excess of the load occurs with certain triazines (fig. 2).

In dogs, the effects of the triazines have been disappointing. It appears that the structure-activity relationships found in the rat are not manifest in this species. None of the triazines which were more potent than formoguanamine in rats were so effective in dogs. Limited studies with one of the triazines make us believe that poor absorption from the gastrointestinal tract may explain the lack of response in dogs. Thus, intravenous administration of a small amount of SC-5586 caused a strong diuresis not only of water but also of sodium. In contrast, by oral administration, water diuresis was more strongly stimulated than sodium excretion. In our particular assay, standard diuretics consistently show sodium loss with an approximately equal degree of water diuresis (table 2). These facts show that the triazines may produce separable effects on water and on sodium excretion depending upon special conditions of treatment.

Occasional side effects found with triazine administration in dogs were crystalluria and emesis (table 2). Crystalluria (Lipschitz and Stokey, 1945; Asper, 1948; Newman *et al.*, 1948), anuria (Freire, 1947, 1948; Mach and Dubois, 1948), and the poor excretion of sodium (Newman *et al.*, 1948; Turchetti, 1950) have all been discussed as reasons for not trying such compounds in man. For certain triazines, however, there are recent reports suggesting a sufficient margin of safety between diuresis and side effects for trials in man (Lueg and Hess, 1955; Henchel, 1956; Moyer *et al.*, 1957; Miller and Ford, 1958).

SUMMARY

The oral diuretic properties of formoguanamine and other *s*-triazines were studied in rats and dogs. By a comparison of minimal active doses, four compounds were found to be more active than formoguanamine in rats. Potency was increased four to five times in 2-amino-4-anilino-*s*-triazine. Its derivatives, 2-amino-4-*p*-chloroanilino-*s*-triazine, 2-amino-4-*p*-fluoroanilino-*s*-triazine, and 2-acetylamino-4-N-acetyl-*p*-chloroanilino-*s*-triazine, were approximately nine times as potent as formoguanamine. Substitutions at position 6 in active compounds caused a loss of activity. Compounds found active in the rat were then studied in dogs. Water diuresis was more strongly stimulated than sodium excretion with relatively large oral doses. The structure-activity relationships found in the rat were not manifest in dogs. Intravenously, a small dose of 2-amino-4-*p*-chloroanilino-*s*-triazine was strongly effective in causing water and sodium diuresis; poor absorption thus appears to be an important factor for the response in dogs.

Acknowledgments. The authors acknowledge with gratitude the technical assistance of Miss Elizabeth D. Griffin, Mrs. Ronald Hoffman and Mrs. Edwin N. Thomas, and that of Dr. Raymond Knauff who conducted the analyses for urinary sodium, potassium and chloride.

REFERENCES

Asper, S. P., Jr.: In reference to Newman *et al.* (see below).

Clauder, O. and Bulcsu, G.: Mag. chem. Fólyt. **57:** 68, 1951.

ETTEL, V. AND NOSEK, J.: Chem. Listy **46:** 289, 1952.
FISHER, R. A.: Statistical Methods for Research Workers, 10th ed., Hafner Publishing Co., New York, 1946.
FREIRE, S. A.: Arquiv. biol. **31:** 141, 1947.
FREIRE, S. A.: Rev. bras. Biol. **8:** 1, 1948.
HAWK, P. B., OSER, B. L., AND SUMMERSON, W. H.: Practical Physiological Chemistry, 12th ed., The Blakiston Co., Philadelphia, 1947.
HENCHEL, G.: Münch. med. Wschr. **23:** 822, 1956.
KUHN, G.: Klin. Wschr. **35:** 346, 1957.
LESHER, D. A. AND SHIDEMAN, F. E.: THIS JOURNAL **116:** 38, 1956.
LIPSCHITZ, W. L., HADIDIAN, Z. AND KERPCZAR, A.: THIS JOURNAL **79:** 97, 1943.
LIPSCHITZ, W. L. AND HADIDIAN, A.: THIS JOURNAL **81:** 84, 1944.
LIPSCHITZ, W. L. AND STOKEY, E.: THIS JOURNAL **83:** 235, 1945.
LIPSCHITZ, W. L. AND STOKEY, E.: THIS JOURNAL **92:** 131, 1948.
LUDWIG, H.: Schweiz. med. Wschr. **76:** 822, 1946.
LUEG, W. AND HESS, A.: Med. Klinik **50:** 2113, 1955.
MACH, R. S. AND DUBOIS, J. P.: Praxis **37:** 317, 1948.
MILLER, D. V. AND FORD, R. V.: Amer. J. med. Sci. **236:** 32, 1958.
MOYER, J. H., FORD, R. HANDLEY, C., PEVEY, K. AND SEIBERT, R.: Antibiotic Med. clin. Therapy **4:** 685, 1957.
NEWMAN, E. V., FRANKLIN, J. AND GENEST, J.: Johns Hopk. Hosp. Bull. **82:** 409, 1948.
SHAPIRO, S. L., PARRINO, V. A., GEIGER, K., KOBRIN, S. AND FREEDMAN, L.: J. Amer. chem. Soc. **79:** 5064, 1957.
TURCHETTI, A.: Rif. med. **64:** 405, 1950.
VAN ARMAN, C. G.: THIS JOURNAL **111:** 285, 1954.

8094

THE ACTION OF RAUWOLFIA ALKALOIDS ON THE HEART RATE AND ON THE FUNCTIONAL REFRACTORY PERIOD OF ATRIO-VENTRICULAR TRANSMISSION IN THE HEART-LUNG PREPARATION OF THE DOG[1, 2]

I. R. INNES,[3] O. KRAYER AND D. R. WAUD[4]

Department of Pharmacology, Harvard Medical School, Boston, Massachusetts

Received for publication July 7, 1958

Reserpine has been shown to cause a reduction in the catechol amine content of brain, peripheral sympathetic nervous tissues, adrenal medulla, heart and artery walls (Holzbauer and Vogt, 1956; Muscholl and Vogt, 1958; Carlsson and Hillarp, 1956; Bertler *et al.*, 1956; Carlsson *et al.*, 1957; Krayer and Paasonen, 1957; Paasonen and Krayer, 1957, 1958; Burn and Rand, 1958). Plummer *et al.* (1954) and Krayer and Fuentes (1956, 1958) found that reserpine caused cardioacceleration in the heart-lung preparation of the dog (HLP). The transient increase in heart rate was ascribed by Paasonen and Krayer (1958) to the action of sympathomimetic amines, especially norepinephrine (NE),[5] released from the heart by reserpine during the early period of its action. This view was supported by the observation that no cardioacceleration was caused by reserpine in the HLP of dogs whose hearts had been depleted of NE by treatment with reserpine 2 and 3 days earlier. In such preparations Innes and Krayer (1958) showed that reserpine caused a marked slowing of the heart.

A similar decrease in heart rate followed the action of veratramine on the HLP of normal dogs (Krayer *et al.*, 1955) and of reserpine-treated dogs (Innes and Krayer, 1958). In view of the similarity between veratramine and reserpine in their action on the heart rate, a comparison of other cardiac actions of these alkaloids became of importance.

It was found by Krayer *et al.* (1951) that veratramine, in doses which cause slowing of the heart, had no influence upon the time of propagation of an impulse from atrium to ventricle (A-V propagation time). In the same study, veratramine had no effect upon the minimal interval between two ventricular impulses propagated from the atrium, *i.e.*, the functional refractory period of A-V transmission as defined by Rosenblueth *et al.* (1949). It was the purpose of the present work to examine the effect of reserpine and other rauwolfia alkaloids upon these intervals.

Moreover, Krayer *et al.* (1951) showed that a continuous infusion of epinephrine caused a shortening of the functional refractory period of A-V transmission and of A-V propagation time. It was therefore possible, by measurement of these intervals in the HLP of the normal dog, to strengthen the view that release of NE may account for the rate-increasing action of reserpine.

Since various types of rauwolfia alkaloids are now available and are well characterized (Bein, 1956), it seemed important to carry out a comparative study of the action of alkaloids of the different types on the HLP of normal and reserpine-pretreated dogs, with the aim of finding out whether there are quantitative differences between the reserpine-type alkaloids raunescine, isoraunescine, deserpidine (canescine, recanescine), reserpine[6] and rescinnamine and what qualitative differences exist between these and

[1] Some of the results of this investigation were reported at a meeting of the Physiological Society in Aberdeen, September, 1957 (Innes and Krayer, 1957).

[2] This work was supported by grants from the American Heart Association, the Eugene Higgins Trust and the U. S. Public Health Service (H-2205).

[3] The investigation was made during the tenure of a Carnegie Trust Grant. Present address: Department of Physiology, University of Aberdeen, Scotland.

[4] Life Insurance Medical Research Fellow.

[5] The expressions "NE depletion" and "release or liberation of NE" will subsequently be used to denote depletion or release of the stores of intrinsic sympathomimetic catechol amines. While the evidence shows norepinephrine to be the substance prominently involved it does not completely exclude the involvement of other catechol amines such as epinephrine.

[6] Reserpine was generously supplied by Dr. Norbert Neuss, Eli Lilly and Co., Indianapolis, Ind.

the alkaloids of the other types, *i.e.*, ajmaline; serpentine; aricine and reserpinine; α-yohimbine.[7]

METHODS. Thirty-six experiments were carried out on the HLP of the dog. In 5 experiments, in order to deplete the heart of catechol amines, the dogs were given 0.5 mg/kg of reserpine by intraperitoneal injection 3 days and 2 days before the experiment. The general conditions of the preparation, as in earlier studies, were maintained as nearly uniform as possible; mean arterial pressure was approximately 100 mm Hg, total blood volume about 1000 ml and systemic output about 600 ml/min. The temperature of the blood varied from experiment to experiment within the range 37.5 to 39°C, but temperature changes within an individual experiment were seldom as great as ±0.2°C. The lungs were ventilated with a mixture of 95% oxygen and 5% carbon dioxide. To reduce interference with the right atrium, the right atrial pressure was recorded by means of a cannula inserted through the inferior vena cava.

When the A-V propagation time and the functional refractory period of A-V transmission were to be measured the technique described by Krayer *et al.* (1951) was used. Two pairs of stimulating electrodes were attached to the tip of the right atrial appendix (auricle). For selected periods during the experiment the heart was driven at a constant rate by stimuli applied through one pair of electrodes. The driving rate varied in different experiments from 150 to 220 beats/min. The rate selected was dependent upon the initial heart rate of the HLP and the maximal heart rate to be expected after administration of the alkaloids. Since alkaloids with a reserpine-type action caused an increase in heart rate, a driving rate of higher frequency was required. With other alkaloids, or in experiments on the HLP previously depleted of catechol amines, lower frequencies were used. While the driving rate has some influence on the functional refractory period of A-V transmission, this did not affect the results since the same driving rate was used throughout an individual experiment and comparisons were made within experiments. A Grass rectangular wave stimulator was used to supply the driving stimuli which were of 0.5 msec duration and of double the voltage of the threshold stimulus. After a steady state had been reached at the selected heart rate, a second Grass stimulator delivered a single test stimulus via the second pair of electrodes at a variable interval after the driving stimulus every 3 seconds, or about every eleventh driving stimulus. During each period of recording, this interval ranged from the maximum possible for the selected heart rate to the point where the test stimulus no longer evoked a response.

The characteristics of the test stimulus were usually identical with those of the driving stimuli, but occasionally the voltage, double the threshold value, was greater owing to small differences in threshold intensity. Atrial and ventricular electrograms were recorded simultaneously on a Grass ink-writing oscillograph by means of two pairs of recording electrodes, one attached to the right atrial and the other to the right ventricular epicardium. The intervals between the responses of the atrium to the driving stimulus and to the succeeding test stimulus were plotted against the intervals between the corresponding ventricular responses. The minimum interval between ventricular responses thus recorded gives the functional refractory period of A-V transmission.

A-V propagation time was taken as the delay between atrial and ventricular responses, measured after steady state conditions had been reached at the selected heart rate and before test stimuli were applied. As pointed out by Krayer *et al.* (1951), the time of propagation includes that of transmission across varying masses of heterogeneous tissues and measurements are therefore comparable only within individual experiments.

Solutions of the rauwolfia alkaloids were prepared by dissolving the individual alkaloid in glacial acetic acid and diluting with distilled water to yield concentrations of 2 mg/ml of 1% acetic acid. Such solutions of reserpine were shown by Krayer and Fuentes (1958) to cause no detectable changes of blood pH. When large volumes had to be administered it was advisable that solutions should be isotonic to prevent lung edema. Since the alkaloids were almost insoluble in 0.9% sodium chloride solution, a 5% solution of glucose was used as diluent. Aricine dissolved only momentarily in glacial acetic acid and the procedure described yielded a fine suspension of this alkaloid. Since a suitable solvent was not found, this suspension was used. All doses refer to the bases. The drugs were administered by injection into the venous supply tube close to the heart, each injection extending over 1 minute, or, when large volumes were administered, over 2 to 4 minutes.

The general course of an experiment is illustrated in figure 1. One or more control recordings for measurement of the functional refractory period of A-V transmission were made during the control period. The rauwolfia alkaloid to be tested was then injected, generally in a dose of 3 mg. The subsequent conduct of the experiment was dependent upon the observed heart rate. In all cases

[7] The alkaloids, with the exception of reserpine, were generously donated by S. B. Penick & Co., New York, N. Y.

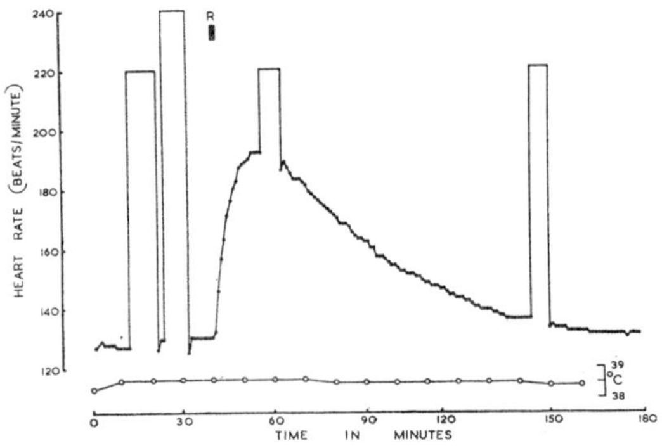

FIG. 1. The effect of raunescine on the heart rate.

Dog. Female. 11.2 kg. Heart-lung preparation (May 14, 1957). Abscissae: time in minutes. Ordinates: for full circles, heart rate, beats/min; for open circles, temperature, °C. The vertical lines indicating sudden increases and decreases in heart rate represent the beginning and end of periods where the heart was driven electrically by rectangular pulses of 5 V and 0.5 msec at a rate indicated by the corresponding horizontal line. At R, raunescine 3 mg was injected.

a further recording was made between 15 and 30 minutes after injection. In experiments where cardioacceleration occurred, the recording was made during the period of maximal heart rate. Additional recordings were made as the heart rate returned towards the initial level. In experiments where cardioacceleration was absent the recording was generally followed by injection of larger doses of the alkaloid; a recording was made 15 minutes after each dose.

RESULTS. 1. *The influence of rauwolfia alkaloids on the heart rate of the dog HLP.* a. The cardio-accelerator effects of raunescine, isoraunescine, deserpidine, reserpine and rescinnamine: The action of raunescine, isoraunescine, deserpidine and rescinnamine on the heart rate of the dog HLP resembled that of reserpine. The data from 18 experiments are shown in table 1. Comparable increases in heart rate were caused by equal doses (3 mg) of raunescine, deserpidine, reserpine and rescinnamine. The time course of the action, illustrated in figure 1, was also similar. The maxi-

TABLE 1

The effect of reserpine-type rauwolfia alkaloids on the heart rate, A-V propagation time and functional refractory period of A-V transmission in the dog heart-lung preparation

Drug	Dose	Time to Maximal Heart Rate	Heart Rate: Initial	Heart Rate: Maximal	Heart Rate: Maximal increase	Heart Rate: Final†	Frequency of Driving Stimuli	A-V Propagation Time (msec): During control period	A-V Propagation Time (msec): During maximal acceleration	A-V Propagation Time (msec): At end of decrease in heart rate	Functional Refractory Period of A-V Transmission (msec): During control period	Functional Refractory Period of A-V Transmission (msec): During maximal acceleration	Functional Refractory Period of A-V Transmission (msec): At end of decrease in heart rate
	mg	*min*	*beats/min*		*beats/min*	*beats/min*	*stimuli/min*						
Raunescine	3	10	142	203	61	166	220	133	76	110	215	190	225
Raunescine	3	12	164	210	46	174	220	155	83	121	273	212	250
Raunescine	3	12	145	189	44	145	220	165	114	149	217	187	225
Raunescine	3	12	137	189	52	155	200	144	115	134	220	182	225
Raunescine	3	11	152	194	44	152	200	112	80	130	227	200	264
Isoraunescine	10*	45	120	139	19		220	157	122		214	200	
Isoraunescine	10	32	113	128	15	117	175	160	152	225	280	255	240
Rescinnamine	3	13	166	204	38	160	220	170	104	212	257	208	272
Rescinnamine	3	18	155	198	43	160	220	117	90	114	207	178	208
Deserpidine	3	12	162	212	50	170	220	102	75	94	217	184	207
Deserpidine	3	13	157	220	63	168	240	110	97	102	192	167	195
Reserpine	3	13	130	192	62	131	220	160	107	125	217	175	215
Reserpine	3	13	152	191	39	140	220	139	117	134	215	174	209
Reserpine	0.03*	26	152	162	10		200	150	134		209	189	
Reserpine	0.03*	45	150	162	12		200	120	112		232	216	
Reserpine	0.03*	60	140	160	20		200	162	127		244	236	
Reserpine	0.01*	22	143	150	7		200	130	127		206	202	
Reserpine	0.01*		177	179	2		220	132	115		219	209	

* In these experiments the initial dose was followed by one or more larger doses of the alkaloid.
† See text.

mal cardioacceleration was reached within 10 to 18 minutes of injection. The duration of the maximal effect could not be precisely measured, since the heart was electrically stimulated to beat at an increased rate over this period, but on no occasion was the maximal rate maintained longer than 13 minutes. Thereafter the heart rate gradually became less to reach a constant rate, sometimes slightly faster than before administration of the alkaloids, within 80 to 140 minutes of injection. The action of isoraunescine was less marked. The increase of heart rate caused by 10 mg of isoraunescine was only a little greater than the increase following 30 μg of reserpine. The time course of isoraunescine action was extended; the maximal rate was reached only after 32 to 45 minutes and in one experiment was maintained for 60 minutes. The action of 30 μg of reserpine followed a similarly extended time course, in accordance with the earlier observations of Krayer and Fuentes (1958).

b. The negative chronotropic action of ajmaline, serpentine, aricine, reserpinine and α-yohimbine: A decrease in heart rate followed the injection of ajmaline (3 to 9 mg), serpentine (3 to 9 mg), aricine (3 to 30 mg), reserpinine (3 to 45 mg) or α-yohimbine (3 to 30 mg). The results are given in table 2.

Ajmaline caused a moderate decrease in heart rate in doses up to 6 mg. When the dose was increased to 9 mg by a final dose of 3 mg, atrial fibrillation occurred within 3 minutes of injection in one experiment and after 20 minutes in the other. Aricine and α-yohimbine caused only a slight decrease in heart rate. In one experiment, not included in table 2, atrio-ventricular nodal rhythm appeared after 10 mg of α-yohimbine had been injected. The decrease in heart rate due to reserpinine, small with a dose of 3 mg, became marked when the dose was increased to 30 to 45 mg. No disturbances of cardiac rhythm followed these large doses of reserpinine.

Serpentine in a dose of 3 mg possessed a powerful negative chronotropic action (figure 2). Irregularities of rhythm occurred in each experiment with a dose of 6 mg. In one experiment the rhythm was already occasionally irregular after administration of 3 mg. The irregularities consisted of periods of alternating faster and slower rhythm lasting for several beats and were similar to the disturbances of rhythm caused in the HLP by veratramine (Krayer *et al.*, 1955).

c. The negative chronotropic action of raunescine, deserpidine, reserpine and rescinnamine on the HLP of dogs pretreated with reserpine: Since the cardioaccelerator effect of reserpine was attributed to the release of NE from the heart

TABLE 2

The effect of various rauwolfia alkaloids on the heart rate, A-V propagation time and functional refractory period of A-V transmission in the dog heart-lung preparation

Drug	Maximal Dose Used	Initial Heart Rate	Decrease in Heart Rate *beats/min*		Frequency of Driving Stimuli	A-V Propagation Time *msec*			Functional Refractory Period of A-V Transmission *msec*		
			Due to 3 mg	Due to maximal dose		During control period	After 3 mg	After maximal dose	During control period	After 3 mg	After maximal dose
	mg	*beats/min*			*stimuli/min*						
Ajmaline	6*	126	5	15	150	125	144	175	235	252	325
Ajmaline	6*	147	12	24	150	139	154	184	250	277	345
Aricine	6	133	3	7	160	120	122	122	244	257	260
Aricine	30	140	0	2	170	120	122	124	236	240	248
Reserpinine	30	160	1	17	175	124	124	132	236	252	270
Reserpinine	30	151	5	31	170	97	103	117	235	245	270
Reserpinine	45	148	4	35							
Serpentine	3*	181	48								
Serpentine	3*	132	28		150	144	175		205	252	
Serpentine	6*	125	32	47	150	129	182	304	257	307	329
α-Yohimbine	6	160	3	6	180	122	115	205	225	229	287
α-Yohimbine	30	140	0	9	170	142	135	180	226	234	317

The temperature range in this series of experiments was 37.9–38.8°C (av. 38.3°C).

* Larger doses caused disturbances of heart rhythm.

(Paasonen and Krayer, 1958), 5 experiments were carried out on hearts already depleted of NE by previous treatment with reserpine. The results are shown in table 3. Instead of cardioacceleration a definite decrease in heart rate occurred. Subsequently, epinephrine was introduced into the circulating blood as a constant infusion of 0.2 to 1 μg/min. In each case the ability of the heart to respond to epinephrine was indicated by a substantial increase in heart rate.

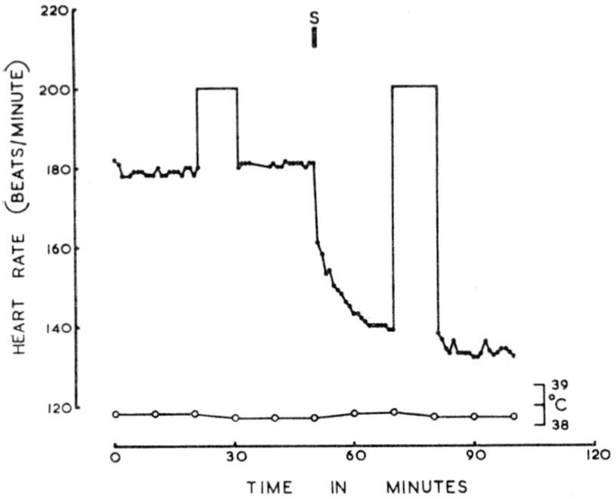

FIG. 2. The effect of serpentine on the heart rate. Dog. Female. 9.7 kg. Heart-lung preparation (June 10, 1957). Abscissae: time in minutes. Ordinates: for full circles, heart rate, beats/min; for open circles, temperature, °C. The vertical lines indicating sudden increases and decreases in heart rate represent the beginning and end of periods where the heart was driven electrically by rectangular pulses of 5 V and 0.5 msec at a rate indicated by the corresponding horizontal line. At S, serpentine 3 mg was injected.

2. *The influence of rauwolfia alkaloids on the A-V propagation time and the functional refractory period of A-V transmission in the HLP of the dog.* a. The action of raunescine, isoraunescine, deserpidine, reserpine and rescinnamine: During the control period, when the atrial interval was progressively shortened, the corresponding ventricular interval was also shortened. This shortening was not normally continued throughout the whole range of atrial intervals. In 27 out of 29 experiments a limit was reached, varying from experiment to experiment, beyond which further shortening of the ventricular interval did not occur. After this point, continued shortening of the atrial interval was generally accompanied by an increase in the ventricular interval (20 experiments). In 7 experiments further shortening of the atrial interval was followed by a constant ventricular interval throughout the remaining range of atrial intervals. In the remaining 2 experiments only, shortening of the ventricular interval continued throughout the entire range of progressively shortened atrial intervals. These observations agree with the findings of Krayer *et al.* (1951).

Under the influence of the alkaloids which caused an increase in heart rate characteristic changes occurred, best observed in the recording made 15 to 30 minutes after injection, during the period of maximal cardioacceleration. With progressive shortening of the atrial interval, the ventricular interval continued to shorten beyond the limiting point found during the control period. The minimum ventricular interval, *i.e.*,

TABLE 3

The effect of reserpine-type rauwolfia alkaloids on the heart rate, A-V propagation time and functional refractory period of A-V transmission in the dog heart-lung preparation previously depleted of catechol amines

Drug	Maximal Dose Used	Initial Heart Rate	Decrease in Heart Rate *beats/min*		Frequency of Driving Stimuli	A-V Propagation Time *msec*			Functional Refractory Period of A-V Transmission *msec*		
			Due to 3 mg	Due to maximal dose		During control period	After 3 mg	After maximal dose	During control period	After 3 mg	After maximal dose
	mg	*beats/min*			*stimuli/min*						
Reserpine	10	130	4	12	150	122	144	192	240	255	324
Reserpine	20	116	5	21	150	140	150	249	234	264	375
Raunescine	20	125	4	24	150	110	112	127	249	252	310
Rescinnamine	10	122	7	13	150	117	125	134	250	265	305
Deserpidine	3	146	14		175	129	135		250	259	

The temperature range in this series of experiments was 37.5–38.8°C (av. 38.2°C).

the functional refractory period, as represented by the lowered point of inflexion of the curve, was therefore shortened.

In the experiment of figure 3, raunescine (3 mg) shortened the functional refractory period of A-V transmission from 227 to 200 msec. At the same time the A-V propagation time was shortened from 112 to 80 msec. The characteristic shortening of functional refractory period and of A-V propagation time due to raunescine, isoraunescine, deserpidine, reserpine and rescinnamine is shown in table 1. These changes are similar in every respect to those found by Krayer *et al.* (1951) during constant infusion of epinephrine into the blood of the HLP.

In experiments with reserpine, doses as small as 10 to 30 μg were effective in causing the typical alterations in functional refractory period and A-V propagation time. The sensitivity of the heart to reserpine in respect to shortening of these intervals and increase of heart rate appeared to be of the same order.

The facilitating action of the alkaloids on A-V transmission, like their cardioaccelerator action, was only transient. Between 70 and 160 minutes after injection of the drug, the effect became less pronounced than during the first 30 minutes and in many cases it finally disappeared. The duration of the functional refractory period generally returned to the value during the control period, and frequently exceeded it. The A-V propagation time also became prolonged, and the value found during the control period was usually approached and sometimes exceeded. The maximal lengthening of the functional refractory period and of A-V propagation time coincided with the return to the initial heart rate or the establishment of a constant heart rate. In the experiment of figure 3 already referred to, the functional refractory period lengthened to 240 msec at 75 minutes after injection of raunescine and to 264 msec at 120 minutes, when the heart rate had decreased to the initial rate of 152 beats/min. At the same times the A-V propagation time increased to 109 msec and 130 msec.

At the end of the 5 experiments with raunescine the hearts were removed, 85 to 150 minutes after injection of the alkaloid, and assays of norepinephrine and epinephrine content were made by Dr. M. K. Paasonen. The mean concentrations (μg/g ± standard deviation) were as follows: right atrium, norepinephrine 0.045 ±

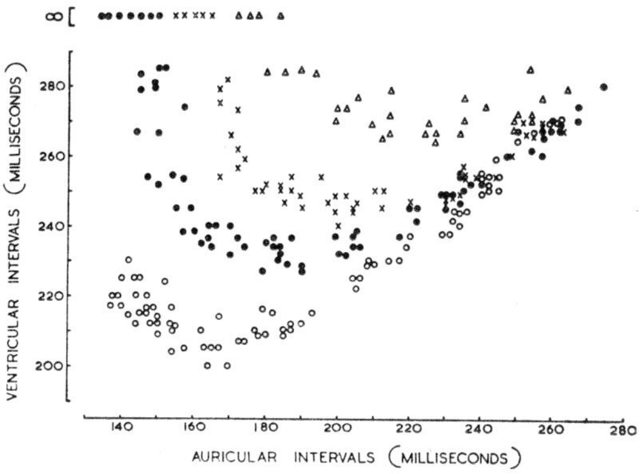

Fig. 3. The action of raunescine on the functional refractory period of A-V transmission.
Dog. Male. 11.5 kg. Heart-lung preparation (May 17, 1957). Driving stimuli: 5 V, 0.5 msec, 200/min; test stimuli: 5 V, 0.5 msec. Abscissae: auricular (*read:* atrial) interval in msec. Ordinates: ventricular interval in msec. Full circles: control observations. Open circles, crosses, triangles: 15 min, 75 min and 120 min, respectively, after raunescine 3 mg. At ∞ are shown the atrial intervals between impulses of which the second failed to be propagated to the ventricle.

0.051, epinephrine 0.017 ± 0.018; left ventricle, norepinephrine 0.014 ± 0.022, epinephrine 0.009 ± 0.007. The corresponding normal values (Paasonen and Krayer, 1958, table 1) are: right atrium, norepinephrine 1.20 ± 0.299, epinephrine 0.043 ± 0.043; left ventricle, norepinephrine 0.38 ± 0.146, epinephrine 0.022 ± 0.021.

The effects on A-V conduction of raunescine, deserpidine, reserpine and rescinnamine were examined in the HLP which had been depleted of NE by previous treatment with reserpine (table 3). In these experiments the alkaloids, in doses which caused the transient shortening of the A-V propagation time and functional refractory period in the HLP of normal dogs, instead caused lengthening of both these time intervals. Prolongation of the functional refractory period (figure 4) and of the A-V propagation time was especially striking in experiments where the dose was increased to 10 to 20 mg. At the end of experiments of this type the effect of a constant infusion of epinephrine (0.1 to 1 μg/min) was tested. The typical action of shortening A-V propagation time and functional refractory period was observed in each case.

b. The action of ajmaline, serpentine, aricine, reserpinine and *alpha*-yohimbine: In experiments with the alkaloids which lacked a cardioaccelerator action, shortening of the functional refrac-

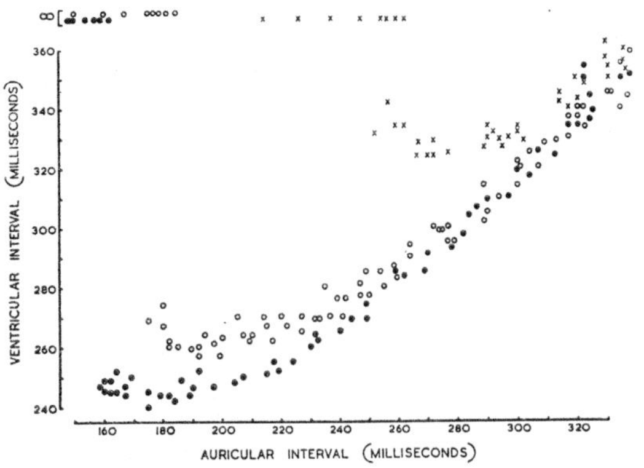

FIG. 4. The action of reserpine on the functional refractory period of A-V transmission in the heart depleted of catechol amines.

Dog. Male. 10 kg. Intraperitoneal injection of reserpine 0.5 mg/kg, 3 days and 2 days before experiment. Heart-lung preparation (May 16, 1957). Driving stimuli: 5 V, 0.5 msec, 150/min; test stimuli: 5 V, 0.5 msec. Abscissae: auricular (*read:* atrial) interval in msec. Ordinates: ventricular interval in msec. Full circles: control observations. Open circles, crosses: after reserpine 3 mg and 10 mg respectively. At ∞ are shown the atrial intervals between impulses of which the second failed to be propagated to the ventricle.

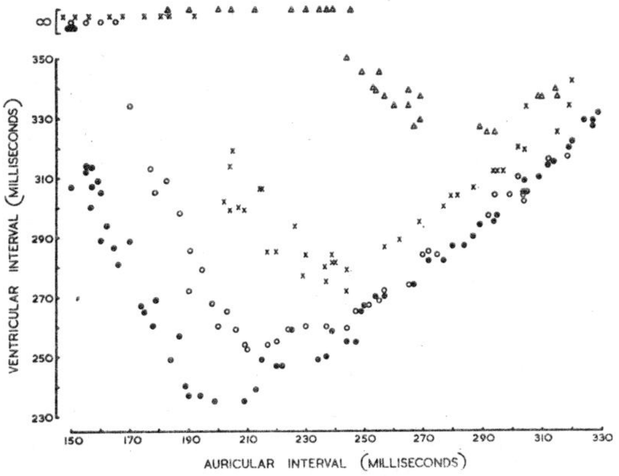

FIG. 5. The action of ajmaline on the functional refractory period of A-V transmission.

Dog. Male. 12 kg. Heart-lung preparation (June 5, 1957). Driving stimuli: 5 V, 0.5 msec, 150/min; test stimuli: 5 V, 0.5 msec. Abscissae: auricular (*read:* atrial) interval in msec. Ordinates: ventricular interval in msec. Full circles: control observations. Open circles, crosses, triangles: after ajmaline 3 mg, 6 mg and 9 mg, respectively. At ∞ are shown the atrial intervals between impulses of which the second failed to be propagated to the ventricle.

tory period and of A-V propagation time did not occur (table 2). When these alkaloids were given in a dose of 3 mg the functional refractory period was prolonged. The degree of prolongation varied with the alkaloid used. The effect of aricine and α-yohimbine was slight, while the effect of serpentine was striking. The A-V propagation time was generally lengthened also, only to a small degree by aricine and reserpinine, but markedly by serpentine. In the two experiments with α-yohimbine, this dose caused a slight shortening of A-V propagation time.

With larger doses prolongation of the functional refractory period (figure 5) and of A-V propagation time became more pronounced. Aricine (6 to 30 mg) caused only a moderate lengthening, while reserpinine (10 to 30 mg) was more effective. Ajmaline (3 to 9 mg) caused a great prolongation of both time intervals. *Alpha*-yohimbine was of particular interest since doses of 6 to 30 mg caused the functional refractory period and A-V propagation time to be greatly prolonged, while this action was accompanied by only a small decrease in the heart rate. Increase in the dose of serpentine to 6 mg in one experiment caused increased lengthening of both time intervals, already greatly prolonged by 3 mg. After the dose was increased to 9 mg in this experiment and to 6 mg in another, the heart could not be driven at the selected rate; the atrium failed to respond to the driving stimuli. Consequently further measurement of the time intervals was precluded.

DISCUSSION. All the rauwolfia alkaloids used in this investigation cause a decrease in heart rate and a lengthening of the functional refractory period of A-V transmission and of A-V propagation time. Ajmaline, serpentine, aricine, reserpinine and α-yohimbine show these effects on the HLP without interference by other actions. On the other hand, raunescine, isoraunescine, deserpidine, reserpine and rescinnamine have a biphasic action in that initially they cause an opposite, but transient, effect. The actions of this latter group may be adequately explained by the assumption, already made by Krayer and Fuentes (1956, 1958) to account for the cardioaccelerator action of reserpine, that these alkaloids cause liberation of the intrinsic cardiac NE. The released NE would then exert its well-known cardioaccelerator action and at the same time facilitate A-V transmission, an action known to be possessed by epinephrine (Krayer *et al.*, 1951) and by norepinephrine (Krayer and Waud, unpublished observations). In this way the ability of the alkaloids to decrease the heart rate and retard A-V transmission would be concealed until NE was no longer released in sufficient amount to antagonize its specific action.

Strongly in favor of the view presented is the time course of the increase in heart rate and of the facilitation of A-V transmission which would be caused by an infusion of epinephrine or norepinephrine, first in rapidly rising amounts and later in diminishing quantities. Furthermore, at the end of experiments on the dog HLP with reserpine or raunescine, the norepinephrine and epinephrine content of the heart was found to be markedly reduced.

In the later stages of the experiments raunescine, isoraunescine, deserpidine, reserpine and rescinnamine decrease the heart rate and retard A-V transmission. Moreover, these actions are present throughout the whole course of the experiments in preparations where release of NE has been made impossible by previous depletion. Additional support is given by the fact that, after the alkaloid has substantially reduced the heart rate and markedly retarded A-V transmission in such experiments, epinephrine is capable not only of abolishing this action but also of substituting its own characteristic effect.

Further evidence suggesting the release of sympathomimetic amines from tissues of intact animals is provided by manifestations of epinephrine-like activity which occur only during the early period of the action of reserpine, rescinnamine and deserpidine. A short-lived hyperglycemia occurs in rabbits given reserpine (Kuschke and Frantz, 1955) and in cats after reserpine and rescinnamine (Kroneberg, 1956). Everett *et al.* (1957) report pilo-erection in rats and mice during the first 30 minutes after giving reserpine. Reserpine causes a transient contraction of the denervated nictitating membrane in cats and dogs and a rise in blood pressure in dogs (Maxwell *et al.*, 1957), while deserpidine causes a brief rise in the blood pressure of cats and dogs (Schneider *et al.*, 1955). More direct evidence of the release of catechol amines comes from a rise in the plasma concentration of epinephrine following the administration of reserpine to rabbits (Muscholl and Vogt, 1957).

It is certain, therefore, that the rauwolfia alkaloids examined here can be divided into 2 pharmacological groups which are differentiated by the presence or absence of the ability to release intrinsic sympathomimetic amines from the heart and, in all probability, other tissues. The specific action characteristic of both groups is their depressing action on the heart rate and on A-V transmission.

Comparing the potency of the alkaloids in respect to their epinephrine-like action, no clear difference emerges between the effects of 3 mg doses of raunescine, deserpidine, reserpine and rescinnamine in causing cardioacceleration or facilitation of A-V transmission. Isoraunescine alone shows a clear difference in potency, being less active than the other 4 alkaloids in this group.

The results of the catechol amine assay at the end of experiments with raunescine give some indication that this alkaloid may be more active in depleting the heart of norepinephrine and epinephrine than reserpine, since the figures are much lower than those found by Paasonen and Krayer (1958) for reserpine, and also that the depleting action may proceed faster. The conditions, however, are not strictly comparable, since in the experiments with raunescine, but not reserpine in the earlier study, the heart was driven at a rapid rate for several periods.

The action of decreasing the heart rate, which is shown for all the alkaloids of the present study, agrees well with earlier observations of bradycardia due to serpentine (Kadatz, 1955) and, 20 hours after administration, deserpidine and rescinnamine (Cronheim *et al.*, 1954, 1955). Plummer *et al.* (1954) have shown bradycardia following reserpine in large doses or after repeated administration in chronic experiments. The present experiments emphasize the direct action upon the pacemaker of the heart.

From the present results serpentine is clearly the most effective of the alkaloids in decreasing the heart rate and prolonging the functional refractory period of A-V transmission and the A-V propagation time. Except for aricine, whose solubility is very low, all the alkaloids are capable of causing a definite lengthening of A-V propagation time and a more striking prolongation of the functional refractory period when large doses are given. This is equally true for the reserpine-type alkaloids when release of NE is precluded.

In the dog heart, depleted of NE by previous treatment of the animal with reserpine, both veratramine and reserpine have been shown to decrease the heart rate (Innes and Krayer, 1958). This similarity between the effects of veratramine and reserpine does not extend to their actions on A-V transmission. The failure of veratramine, in doses which have a striking effect on the heart rate, to influence A-V transmission, shown by Krayer *et al.* (1951), is in contrast to the action of reserpine and the other rauwolfia alkaloids in lengthening the functional refractory period of A-V transmission and prolonging the A-V propagation time. However, the effect of equal doses of veratramine, rather than of equivalent rate-decreasing doses, remains to be explored.

SUMMARY

The heart-lung preparation of the dog was used in an examination of the action of 10 rauwolfia alkaloids on the heart rate, the functional refractory period of atrio-ventricular transmission and the A-V propagation time.

Two distinct pharmacological groups were found. One group, consisting of ajmaline, serpentine, aricine, reserpinine and α-yohimbine, caused a decrease in heart rate accompanied by prolongation of the functional refractory period of A-V transmission and of the A-V propagation time.

The second group consists of the reserpine-type alkaloids—raunescine, isoraunescine, deserpidine, reserpine and rescinnamine. In the early period of their action the heart rate was increased and the functional refractory period and A-V propagation time were shortened. After 90 to 150 minutes, using a dose equivalent in effect to 3 mg reserpine, the heart rate fell while the functional refractory period and the A-V propagation time returned towards their original duration and were frequently further prolonged.

Raunescine, deserpidine, reserpine and rescinnamine lacked this transient cardioaccelerator action and facilitating action on A-V transmission in experiments where the HLP was depleted of intrinsic sympathomimetic amines by previous treatment of the experimental animal with reserpine. Instead, slowing of the heart and prolongation of the functional refractory period and of A-V propagation time occurred under these conditions.

Both groups of rauwolfia alkaloids possess a depressant action on heart rate and A-V transmission. The transient cardioacceleration and facilitation of A-V transmission found with the reserpine-type group is explained by release from the heart of sympathomimetic amines, especially norepinephrine, which are known to cause these effects. The depressant action of the reserpine-type alkaloids is thus concealed until the release of sympathomimetic amines is no longer sufficient to counteract it.

The retarding action of the rauwolfia alkaloids on A-V transmission distinguishes their action from that of veratramine which also decreases the heart rate, but in equivalent rate-decreasing doses is known to have no effect on A-V transmission.

ACKNOWLEDGMENTS. The authors gratefully acknowledge the expert technical assistance given to them in the course of this investigation by Mr. Werner Mosimann, Miss Brigitte Hofheinz, Miss Margaret Young and Mrs. Shirley Ruane. The authors are also indebted to Dr. M. K. Paasonen, who carried out estimations of the catechol amine content of the heart in 5 experiments.

REFERENCES

BEIN, H. J.: Pharmacol. Rev. **8:** 435, 1956.

BERTLER, Å., CARLSSON, A. AND ROSENGREN, E.: Naturwissenschaften **43:** 521, 1956.

BURN, J. H. AND RAND, M. J.: Brit med. J. I (5076): 903, 1958.

CARLSSON, A. AND HILLARP, N.-Å.: K. Fysiogr. Sällsk. Lund Förh. **26:** 90, 1956.

CARLSSON, A., ROSENGREN, E., BERTLER, Å. AND NILSSON, J.: in Psychotropic Drugs, ed. by S. Garattini and V. Ghetti, Elsevier Publ. Co., Amsterdam, 1957, p. 363.

CRONHEIM, G., BROWN, W., CAWTHORNE, J., TOEKES, I. M. AND UNGARI, J.: Proc. Soc. exp. Biol., N. Y. **86:** 120, 1954.

CRONHEIM, G., ORCUTT, J. A. AND TOEKES, I. M.: Proc. Soc. exp. Biol., N. Y. **89:** 21, 1955.

EVERETT, G. M., TOMAN, J. E. P. AND SMITH, A. H., JR.: Fed. Proc. **16:** 295, 1957.

HOLZBAUER, M. AND VOGT, M.: J. Neurochem. **1:** 8, 1956.

INNES, I. R. AND KRAYER, O.: J. Physiol. **139:** 18P, 1957.

INNES, I. R. AND KRAYER, O.: THIS JOURNAL **124:** 245, 1958.

KADATZ, R.: Arzneim.-Forsch. **5:** 715, 1955.

KRAYER, O., ARORA, R. B. AND MEILMAN, E.: THIS JOURNAL **113:** 446, 1955.

KRAYER, O. AND FUENTES, J.: Fed. Proc. **15:** 709, 1956.

KRAYER, O. AND FUENTES, J.: THIS JOURNAL **123:** 145, 1958.

KRAYER, O., MANDOKI, J. J. AND MENDEZ, C.: THIS JOURNAL **103:** 412, 1951.

KRAYER, O. AND PAASONEN, M. K.: Acta physiol. scand. **42:** Suppl. 145, 88, 1957.

KRONEBERG, G.: Arzneim.-Forsch. **6:** 579, 1956.

KUSCHKE, H. J. AND FRANTZ, J.: Arch. exp. Path. Pharmak. **224:** 269, 1955.

MAXWELL, R. A., ROSS, S. D., PLUMMER, A. J. AND SIGG, E. B.: THIS JOURNAL **119:** 69, 1957.

MUSCHOLL, E. AND VOGT, M.: Brit. J. Pharmacol. **12:** 532, 1957.

MUSCHOLL, E. AND VOGT, M.: J. Physiol. **141:** 132, 1958.

PAASONEN, M. K. AND KRAYER, O.: Fed. Proc. **16:** 326, 1957.

PAASONEN, M. K. AND KRAYER, O.: THIS JOURNAL **123:** 153, 1958.

PLUMMER, A. J., EARL, A., SCHNEIDER, J. A., TRAPOLD, J. AND BARRETT, W.: Ann. N. Y. Acad. Sci. **59:** 8, 1954.

ROSENBLUETH, A., ALANIS, J. AND MANDOKI, J. J.: J. cell. comp. Physiol. **33:** 405, 1949.

SCHNEIDER, J. A., PLUMMER, A. J., EARL, A. E., BARRETT, W. E., RINEHART, R. AND DIBBLE, R. C.: THIS JOURNAL **114:** 10, 1955.

8095

THE DUAL NATURE OF THE ACTION OF SUCCINYLCHOLINE ON RESPIRATION IN CROSS-CIRCULATED DOGS[1, 2]

M. H. HARMEL, B. D. KING[3] AND FREDERICK F. KAO

Departments of Anesthesiology and Physiology, State University of New York, Downstate Medical Center, Brooklyn, New York

Received for publication June 25, 1958

The peripheral myoneural blocking action of succinylcholine has been well demonstrated. The manner in which this muscle relaxant may affect respiration has suggested that sites other than the myoneural junction also may be affected. Indeed, evidence has been advanced from time to time that all the muscle relaxants may have an action on central mechanisms (Fegler, 1940; Frey *et al.*, 1952; Ellis *et al.*, 1952; McCawley, 1949; McIntyre *et al.*, 1951; Salama and Wright, 1950; Krivoy *et al.*, 1951; Pick and Unna, 1945; Everett, 1948; Harvey, 1940). Brodie in 1811 was the first to suggest that curare might act centrally. However, modern interest has proceeded largely from clinical observations regarding unanticipated responses to muscle relaxants in patients under anesthesia (Dripps, 1953). Whether succinylcholine has a central effect on respiratory activity is still a matter of dispute. Paton and Zaimis (1951) in studying the effect of this drug on the amplitude of action potentials, recorded from the phrenic nerve, and Haber *et al.* (1957) using microelectrodes implanted in the respiratory center, concluded from their recordings that there is no central action of succinylcholine. On the other hand, Frey (1952), Frey *et al.* (1952) and Ellis *et al.* (1952), studying action potentials again recorded from the phrenic nerve have concluded that there is a central effect of succinylcholine. While phrenic nerve action potentials and the potentials recorded by microelectrodes in the respiratory center may yield significant information concerning the rhythmicity of the respiratory center, these methods cannot give quantitative data on ventilation. For the study of drug action on the totality of respiratory activity, it is essential to measure quantitatively the effects of drugs on ventilation. Wherever the action of a drug on respiration may be at a central or peripheral locus the peripheral actions of such a drug can readily mask its central effects. It is therefore essential in studies of possible central actions of drugs like succinylcholine, to devise a method whereby ventilatory activity can be measured and central effects are separable from peripheral actions.

This may be accomplished by employing various cross-circulation devices and the well-known isolated-head technique. In such preparations simultaneous observation of peripheral actions of the drug can be observed in the donor animal and central effects in the recipient, since only the neural connections remain between the respiratory center and the recipient's respiratory muscles with no drug reaching the myoneural junctions of the recipient animal from the donor. Accordingly, a modification of Heymans and Heymans (1926) technique of cross-circulation to the isolated head, in which ventilation can be quantitatively measured in both donor and recipient dogs, has been employed in an effort to determine whether succinylcholine has an action on central mechanisms governing respiration.

METHODS. *Preparation of the animals and operations.* Intact animals: Initial experiments were carried out in intact animals to determine dose-response curves for succinylcholine. For this purpose 4 mongrel dogs (2 males and 2 females) weighing 10 to 16 kg were anesthetized with pentobarbital sodium, 30 mg/kg, i.v. A tracheal cannula was inserted and connected to a Benedict-Roth metabolimeter. The carotid arteries and femoral veins were exposed for the injection of succinyl-

[1] This investigation was supported in part by a grant (B-458) from the National Institute of Neurological Diseases and Blindness, National Institutes of Health, Bethesda, Md.

[2] Presented in a preliminary form in the Proceedings of the Conference on Myoneural Junction, sponsored by Columbia University, Department of Anesthesiology, and Burroughs Wellcome and Co. (U. S. A.), New York City, November 4–5, 1955.

[3] Present address: E. J. Meyer Memorial Hospital, Buffalo, New York.

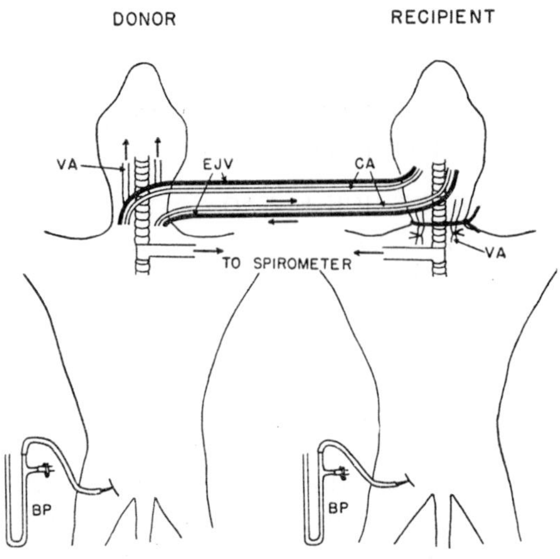

FIG. 1. The experimental scheme: VA—Vertebral artery; EJV—External jugular vein; CA—Carotid artery; BP—Hg manometer.

choline. In order to maintain respiration comparable to that of normal anesthetized dogs (VE_{O_2} = 3.1; Kao *et al.*, 1955)[4] additional small doses of pentobarbital sodium were given whenever necessary.

Cross-circulation (fig. 1): For the cross-circulation studies dogs of similar size (10 to 16 kg) were selected. Anesthesia was obtained with pentobarbital sodium, 30 mg/kg, i.v. The common carotid arteries and the external jugular veins of both dogs were exposed and prepared for cannulation. In the recipient dog both vertebral arteries were ligated. The neck muscles were tied in bundles but the vagi and phrenic nerves were left intact. Prior to the establishment of the vascular anastomosis both dogs were heparinized (0.5 mg/kg). Cross-circulation was established by anastomosing the common carotid arteries of the donor dog to those of the recipient and by anastomosing the external jugular veins of the two dogs. Siliconized glass cannulae with tygon tubing connections, selected to fit the lumen of the anastomosed vessels, were used. Special caution was exercised to avoid blood loss and air embolism. All incisions were made with an electric cautery to assure maximum hemostasis. Tracheal cannulae were inserted in both dogs and connected to separate Benedict-Roth metabolimeters to provide for a continuous recording of tidal volume, O_2 uptake and respiratory rate. (Ventilation was then expressed as BTPS[5] and oxygen uptake as STPD[6]). The femoral arteries were used for the measurement of mean arterial blood pressure. The femoral veins were cannulated for the injection of drugs. For maintenance of hydration during the course of the experiment a continuous drip of 5% glucose in water was employed. In recipient dogs 1, 2 and 3, bilateral denervation of the carotid sinus was carried out. In the studies for dose-response in the intact animals, the carotid artery and femoral veins were exposed and used for injection. Injection of drugs in the cross-circulated animals was made into the carotid artery leading to the recipient's head, in the femoral vein of the recipient dog and the femoral vein of the donor dog. All the biometric analyses were carried out by methods according to Snedecor (1946). Since steady states were not obtained in these experiments, conventional use of liters per minute to express the magnitude of the ventilatory response would be misleading, inasmuch as comparable volume changes may occur over differing periods of time. By converting volume per minute to unit areas of increment or decrement a more satisfactory description of the magnitude of change is thus afforded.

The transient ventilatory changes before and after the administration of succinylcholine were plotted as functions of time. Identical coordinates were employed for all available experimental data. The increment or decrement in ventilatory response thus plotted in graphs was then measured by means of a planimeter and expressed in cm^2. The unit of such a measurement equals $L^3/T \times T = L^3$ = ventilation in liters; where L = length, T = time, and L^3 = volume. Thus, it is possible to use the unit (Δ A) as the absolute amount of volume of ventilatory exchange independent of time, where each cm^2 equals one liter of ventilation.

Initial experiments were conducted to evaluate the adequacy of circulatory isolation of the recipient's head from its body with the nerves intact, and the integrity of the respiratory center in the recipient animal after the establishment of cross-circulation.

The adequacy of circulatory isolation of the recipient's head from its body with the nerves intact. *Alpha*-lobeline: *Alpha*-lobeline (0.01 g) was injected via the femoral vein into the body of the donor and into the body of the recipient. The ventilatory response of both dogs was then recorded simultaneously. These data are presented in table 1. When *alpha*-lobeline was injected into the recipient's body via the femoral

[4] VE_{O_2} (ventilatory equivalent for oxygen) = $\dfrac{\text{total ventilation in l/min BTPS}}{\text{oxygen consumption in 100 ml/min STPD}}$

[5] BTPS = Body temperature, ambient barometric pressure, saturated.

[6] STPD = Standard temperature (0°C or 273 Absolute) and pressure (760 mm Hg) perfectly dry.

vein the ventilation in the recipient dog increased whereas that in the donor remained unchanged. The increase in ventilation in the recipient can be attributed to the stimulation of the peripheral chemoreceptors exclusive of the carotids. However, when *alpha*-lobeline was injected into the donor's body, the ventilation of both animals increased significantly. While the increase in ventilation in the donor is of considerable magnitude, that in the recipient though significant is small. The latter probably reflects the central effect alone, whereas in the donor we were observing the summation of the peripheral and central action of *alpha*-lobeline. The response of the blood pressure paralleled that of ventilation, *i.e.*, when *alpha*-lobeline was injected into the donor there was a significant rise in blood pressure in *both* dogs. When *alpha*-lobeline was injected into the recipient's body, the rise in blood pressure was limited to the recipient. These responses indicated that circulatory isolation of the recipient's head from its body adequate for the purposes of this study had been achieved, and that the respiratory center was physiologically active.

Inhalation of 5% CO_2-95% O_2 mixture: This mixture was also employed to test the completeness of separation of the circulation of the recipient's head from its body. The data thus obtained are presented in table 2. As can be seen in the table, when the recipient's body was given this mixture to breathe, the variations seen in the donor during this time were only a few ml (3.557 to 3.605 liters per minute). This increment of 0.049 is statistically insignificant ($P > 0.5$) and indicates that significant physiologic cross-circulation between the recipient's body and its head has been prevented. Otherwise the blood from the recipient's body with high CO_2 concentration could be expected to exert some stimulatory effect on the donor dog and the recipient. When the donor was given the same gas mixture to breathe, the ventilation of both donor and the recipient increased significantly. The ventilatory response of the recipient when the donor was breathing CO_2 is presented in the second column of table 2. This increase went from an average of 2.93 to 10.49 l/min BTPS. The average increment of 7.56 l/min at the peak is highly significant ($P < 0.01$). This finding also demonstrates that the sensitivity of the chemoreceptors to CO_2 in the recipient's head and neck was adequate.

Rebreathing: Rebreathing, in addition to providing higher concentration of CO_2 in the inspired air, also produces oxygen lack, as an additional stimulus to augment respiratory activity. As is shown in figure 2, during such an experimental procedure the ventilation of the recipient dog increased significantly ($P < 0.01$) whereas that of the donor dog remained unchanged ($P > 0.50$).

TABLE 1

Ventilatory response of the cross-circulated dog to alpha-lobeline (0.01 g, i.v.)

Expt. No.	Site of Injection	Ventilation L/min BTPS			
		Donor dog		Recipient dog	
		Control	*Alpha*-lobeline	Control	*Alpha*-lobeline
1	Recipient's body	2.88	3.08	2.81	10.95
2	Recipient's body	1.34	1.31	4.66	7.82
3	Donor's body	2.16	6.75	5.45	6.03
4	Donor's body	3.28	6.65	3.23	3.88

TABLE 2

Ventilatory response of the donor and recipient dog when its counterpart was given 5% CO_2 – 95% O_2 to breathe

Expt. No.	Recipient Given 5% CO_2-95% O_2		Donor Given 5% CO_2-95% O_2	
	Donor control	Donor after 5% CO_2–95% O_2	Recipient control	Recipient after 5% CO_2–95% O_2
	ventilation l/min BTPS		*ventilation l/min BTPS*	
1	1.11	1.02	5.09	27.15
2	3.14	3.24	3.06	9.15
3	5.41	5.07	2.63	8.92
4	2.76	3.26	1.93	3.62
5	4.27	4.37	1.92	3.62
6	5.65	4.67	—	—
Mean	3.557	3.605	2.926	10.492

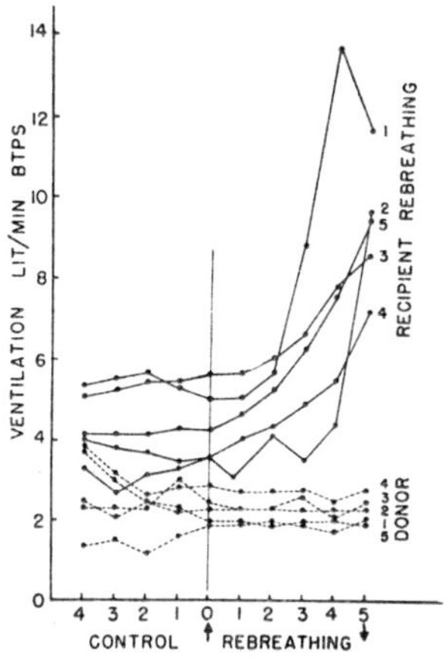

FIG. 2. Ventilatory response in donor and recipient dogs when recipient was subjected to rebreathing.

Evans Blue dye: Limited experiments employing T-1824 were carried out. Dye was injected into the donor dog and plasma dye concentrations were then assayed in both dogs using a Beckman

TABLE 3

Effect of succinylcholine on 4 intact dogs under pentobarbital (28 determinations)

Dosage	Route	ΔA*	Average Duration of Effect
mg/kg			*min*
0.0985	IA	31.84	13.2
0.0985	IV	35.07	12.7

ΔA (IA − IV) = −3.23; $t = 0.558$; $P > 0.50$
Duration (IA − IV) = 0.50; $t = 0.403$; $P > 0.50$

IA—Intracarotid.
IV—Via femoral vein.
* ΔA—average magnitude of the decrement in ventilation.

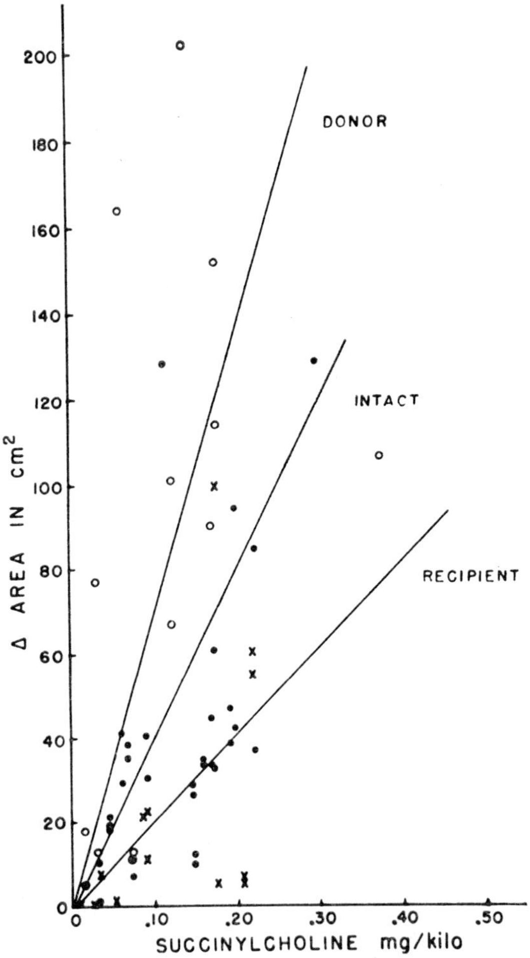

FIG. 3. Relationship between dose of succinylcholine and inhibition of ventilation (Δ Area cm²; see text) in donor, intact and recipient dogs.

spectrophotometer (model D) at a wave length of 620 Å. No dye was detected in the plasma sample of the uninjected dog within a 5-minute period. However, in 10 minutes a trace of dye could be detected in the plasma of the uninjected dog. This evidence would tend to support the view that the effects observed within 10 minutes were significant but after this time drugs may diffuse across the barriers imposed.

The integrity of the respiratory system after cross-circulation. The respiratory responses elicited by *alpha*-lobeline, 5% CO_2-95% O_2 and by rebreathing imposed upon the donor indicate that the central respiratory mechanisms of the donor and recipient heads were intact and functioning at a relatively normal level. Comparing the VE_{O_2} of both dogs after cross-circulation likewise supports this assumption. The ventilatory equivalent of normal unanesthetized dogs has been found to be 3.1 at rest and during muscular activity (Kao *et al.*, 1955). In our studies after cross-circulation, it was found that the VE_{O_2} of the donor averaged 2.56 whereas that of the recipient averaged 3.43. These values are not significantly different from the values obtained in dogs given pentobarbital sodium or chloralose (Kao *et al.*, 1955). In addition, electrically induced exercise caused a normal response in both dogs after cross-circulation had been established (Kao, 1956).

RESULTS. *A. The central respiratory action of succinylcholine in the intact animal.* The complete data on 33 injections of succinylcholine in 4 intact dogs (expressed in mg/kg of body weight) are presented in table 3. Succinylcholine (0.033 to 0.294 mg/kg in 1 ml of solution) was given to dogs through either the femoral vein or carotid artery. The data show no difference in either the duration ($P > 0.50$) or magnitude (ΔA) ($P > 0.50$) of the respiratory depression produced by intravenous or intraarterial injection of succinylcholine. Figure 3 shows the relationship between ventilation (ΔA) and dosage of succinylcholine in intact dogs. A regression line (zero order approximation) was fitted to the data and it has the following equation:

Vent. (ΔA) = 394.27 (±96) mg/kg − 1.77, with $r = 0.67$. The slope of the line and the correlation coefficient are both significant.

The data obtained from intact dogs indicates that the route of injection of succinylcholine has no significantly different effect on ventilation in the intact anesthetized dog. The quantitative expression of ventilation as a function of dosage of succinylcholine provides a means for comparison in cross-circulated dogs.

TABLE 4

The ventilatory responses of cross-circulated dogs after the administration of succinylcholine

Expt. No.	Test	Route of Adm.	Succinyl	Donor			Recipient			
				Wt.	Dose	Vent. (ΔA)	Wt.	Dose	Vent. (ΔA)	
			mg	*kg*	*mg/kg*		*kg*	*mg/kg*		
1	1	D's body	0.50	13.6	0.0344	−19.85	12.7	0.0393		−3.75
	2	D's body	0.50		0.0344	−75.50		0.0393		−8.90
(CSD)	3	D's body	1.00		0.0688	−0.60		0.0786		−5.25
	4	D's body	1.00		0.0688	−52.50		0.0786		−1.20
	5	D's body	2.00		0.1308	pump		0.1572		−9.20
	6	D's body	5.00		0.3444	pump		0.3931		−114.00
	7	D's body	0.50		0.0344	−131.60		0.0393		−6.40
2	8	R's head	1.00	13.6	0.0695	−90.15	11.4	0.0877	+40.50	−21.20
(CSD)	9	R's head	2.00		0.1389	−202.75		0.1754	+0.30	−99.35
	10	R's body	1.00		0.0695	no change		0.0877		−172.20
	11	D's body	10.00		0.6950	died		0.8770	+0.60	−78.95
3	12	R's head	1.00	12.7	0.0741	−11.00	10.9	0.0917	+0.40	−11.55
	13	R's head	1.00		0.0741	−12.40		0.0917	+2.00	−22.10
(CSD)	14	R's head	5.00		0.3710	−107.85		0.4580	+0.50	died
4	15	R's head	2.00	15.9	0.1207	−67.65	9.6	0.2080	+5.55	−5.45
	16	R's head	2.00		0.1207	−101.30		0.2080	+1.50	−6.35
	17	R's head	0.50		0.0302	−77.40		0.0521	+0.20	−1.00
	18	R's head	0.25		0.0151	−18.55		0.0260	+15.80	no dpr.
	19	R's head	1.00		0.0603	−164.25		0.0104	+38.50	−0.55
5	20	R's head	2.00	10.9	0.1734	−152.20	9.1	0.2198	+5.90	−60.25
	21	R's head	2.00		0.1734	−114.30		0.2198	+50.00	−55.30
6	22	R's head	0.20	12.3	0.0153	−5.25	11.4	0.0176	+0.30	−4.25
	23	R's head	0.40		0.0306	−13.10		0.0352	+1.20	−7.50
	24	R's head	2.00		0.1531	pump		0.1761	+50.00	−5.55
	25	R's body	2.00		0.1531	no change		0.1761	—	−92.15

R—Recipient.
D—Donor.
−—Decrease of ventilation.
+—Increase in ventilation.
ΔA—cm^2.
CSD—Carotid sinus denervation (recipient only).

Cross-circulated dogs. In table 4 the data on the njection of succinylcholine into 6 pairs of dogs is presented. The tissue mass or capacity of the donor isolated head compartment was calculated by adding 7% of the recipient's body weight (the approximate weight of the recipient's head, which then represents the tissue mass or capacity of the donor). Fifteen injections via the carotid artery to the recipient's head, 2 injections into the recipient's body and 8 injections into the donor dog's femoral vein were carried out. The effective dose for each injection in mg/kg was calculated and the ventilation computed as (ΔA). In the first 3 pairs of animals the carotid sinus was denervated bilaterally in the recipient dog.

Carotid artery leading to the recipient dog's head: Succinylcholine (0.010 to 0.458 mg/kg) was injected directly into the tygon tubing leading via the recipient's carotid artery to its brain. A definite stimulating action of the drug was observed to take place in 4 to 10 seconds. ($N = 15$, mean increment in cm^2 (ΔA) $= 11.5$, $P < 0.05$). Within 45 to 75 seconds depression of ventilation occurred in the recipient. As can be seen in table 4 respiratory depression was present in the donor as well as in the recipient dog. The magnitude of respiratory depression is consistently greater in the donor animal under these circumstances. Denervation of the carotid sinus did not alter this response.

Body of recipient via the femoral vein: In 2

experiments succinylcholine was injected into the recipient's body alone (test No. 10 and 25 in table 4). In each of these instances there was a profound depression of respiration that was limited to the recipient, there being no measurable change in the donor.

Body of donor via femoral vein: When succinylcholine was given to the donor via its femoral vein (0.015 to 0.695 mg/kg) depression of ventilation occurred in the donor. Two experiments (No. 5 and 6) required artificial respiration for the donor animal. Death from anoxia followed the injection of 0.695 mg/kg in donor No. 2 (test No. 11).

In all of the experiments in which succinylcholine was given to the donor, depression of respiration also occurred in the recipient and as is seen in table 4 there was a marked difference in the magnitude of ventilatory depression between donor and recipient.

HCl and succinic acid, adjusted to the same pH (4.5) and volume (1.0 ml) as succinylcholine, were also given via the carotid artery leading to the recipient's brain. Neither of these drugs produced a measurable response.

It seems reasonable to conclude that the increase in ventilation occurring within 4 to 10 seconds in the recipient dog following the administration of succinylcholine is due to a specific action of succinylcholine and not to its pH. This stimulatory response likewise is too immediate to be related to respiratory depression in the donor dog and a consequent CO_2 excess or anoxic stimulus.

The relationship between decrease in ventilation in the recipient dog following the intracarotid injection of succinylcholine and the dosage of succinylcholine in the recipient dog may be quantitated as follows: Vent. $(\Delta A) = 159.88$ (± 78.93) mg/kg $+ 2.96$ with $r = 0.51$. The quantitative relationship for the donor is: Vent. $(\Delta A) = 485.98$ (± 150.62) mg/kg $+ 30.58$ with $r = 0.67$.

In both cases the r's and the slopes of the lines are significant. It is pertinent to point out that the slope in the recipient dog is significantly lower than that in control dogs (slope = 394.47). The slope (485.98) of the line fitted to the data obtained in the donor dogs is not significantly different from that of the control dogs (394.27).

Discussion. The present investigation has demonstrated that circulatory isolation of the head and brain from its body adequate for the present study can be achieved by the method described. The results with *alpha*-lobeline, CO_2, rebreathing, etc. indicate that in addition to effective isolation, the respiratory center of the recipient dog continued to function with normal responsiveness and permitted quantitative measurement of ventilation. In all instances when *alpha*-lobeline, CO_2 or succinylcholine was administered to the recipient body or it was subjected to anoxia, the response was limited to the recipient, which would constitute strong evidence against an anastomotic leak from recipient body to recipient head and the donor. If sufficient leak were to be ascribed to the anterior spinal artery of the recipient to cause the effects observed it would seem that the donor should have also been affected.

On the other hand, leak from the donor to the recipient body via vertebral venous plexus, etc. cannot be absolutely excluded. While the fact that leak can occur is clear from the data obtained with Evans Blue dye; it should be noted that such leak became apparent as a trace and then only after a period of 10 minutes. Indeed, the effects of succinylcholine became manifest in less than a minute. An examination of our data (fig. 3), judging from the slopes of the lines fitted to the data of the intact and recipient dogs, respectively (slope 394.27 and 159.88), indicates that respiratory depression of the magnitude observed in the recipient would require a leak of succinylcholine of at least 40% of the total drug. Under the circumstances this seems unlikely. In the experiments of Irwin and Wells (1957) in which complete vascular isolation of the head was achieved by the method of Nowak and Samaan (1935), these authors concluded that succinylcholine did not "affect breathing by action on central mechanisms." Although in Irwin and Wells' experiments the responsiveness of the respiratory center to CO_2 and thiopental appeared to be adequate, we feel that the extensive surgical procedure may well have impaired its reactivity. This may be best appreciated by comparing the measured response to CO_2 inhalation in their experiments and in the present study. It cannot be denied that after a period of 10 minutes, the effects observed can be ascribed to leak. Even this appears somewhat insignificant in view of the length of action and known rapid hydrolysis of succinylcholine.

It is to be noticed that when succinylcholine was given to the donor dog, while there was depression in the donor there was also depression of ventilation in the recipient. On the other hand, when the injections were made into the carotid artery leading to the recipient's brain, stimulation of respiration was always evoked in the recipient. This may be explained by the relatively high initial dosage of drug to which the brain was subjected in the latter in contrast to the relative dilution and dosage of succinylcholine in the former. The dose range of succinylcholine employed in the study was well within the range which the experiments in the control animals indicated were effective in producing ventilatory depression. It was considered that a minimal rather than a maximal effective dose as desirable, in the event that leak from recipient's head to body might possibly occur. That the responses observed were elicited with small doses of the drug becomes therefore even more significant.

In unpublished observations by the authors in five patients in whom radical dissection of the neck was being performed, 20 to 30 mg of succinylcholine was injected into the internal carotid artery. There was no observable or measurable stimulation of respiration. Respiratory depression supervened promptly and could not be differentiated essentially from the effect of the drug injected intravenously. It was shown that these results in man are comparable to the control dog experiments.

Succinylcholine may be said to have a biphasic action on central mechanisms controlling respiration. This is characterized by an initial, almost immediate but brief stimulation of ventilation which is then followed by a more prolonged period of depression. Both of these components are readily masked by the peripheral myoneural blocking action of this drug. However, in a suitable cross-circulation preparation the action of succinylcholine on the central mechanisms is revealed.

SUMMARY

A total of 25 experiments in 6 pairs of cross-circulated dogs has shown that succinylcholine injected into the donor's femoral vein results in depression of ventilation in both donor and recipient; that succinylcholine injected into the recipient's femoral vein depresses ventilation in the recipient's body only; that succinylcholine injected into the carotid artery leading to the recipient's brain causes first an increase, then a decrease of ventilation in the recipient and decrease in ventilation in the donor.

Additional experiments in 4 intact nembutalized dogs established dose-response curves and showed that similar depression of ventilation occurs when succinylcholine is injected either i.v. or via the intracarotid route.

The validity of the experimental procedure and the mode of action of succinylcholine were briefly discussed.

REFERENCES

Brodie, B. C.: Phil. Trans. **101:** 178, 1811.
Dripps, R. D.: Ann. Surg. **137:** 145, 1953.
Ellis, C. H., Morgan, W. V. and deBeer, E. J.: This Journal **106:** 3, 1952.
Everett, G. M.: This Journal **92:** 236, 1948.
Fegler, G.: C. R. Soc. Biol., Paris **134:** 193, 1940.
Frey, R.: Anaesthesist, Berl. **1:** 10, 1952.
Frey, R., Göpfert, H. and Raule, W.: Anaesthesist, Berl. **1:** 33, 1952.
Haber, E., Kohn, K. W., Ngai, S. H., Holaday, D. A. and Wang, S. C.: Amer. J. Physiol. **19:** 350, 1957.
Harvey, A. M.: Johns Hopk. Hosp. Bull. **66:** 52, 1940.
Heymans, J. F. and Heymans, C.: Arch. int. Pharmacodyn. **32:** 9, 1926.
Irwin, R. L. and Wells, J. B.: This Journal **119:** 329, 1957.
Kao, F. F.: Amer. J. Physiol. **185:** 145, 1956.
Kao, F. F., Schlig, B. B. and Brooks, C. Mc.: J. appl. Physiol. **7:** 397, 1955.
Krivoy, W. A., Hart, E. R. and Marrazzi, A. S.: Abstracts of the Fall Meetings, American Society for Pharmacology and Experimental Therapeutics, Omaha, Nebraska, p. 48, 1951.
McCawley, E. L.: This Journal **97:** 129, 1949.
McIntyre, A. R., Bennett, A. L. and Hamilton, C.: Ann. N. Y. Acad. Sci. **54:** 301, 1951.
Nowak, S. J. G. and Samaan, A.: Arch. int. Pharmacodyn. **51:** 206, 1935.
Paton, W. D. M. and Zaimis, E. J.: J. Physiol. **112:** 311, 1951.
Pick, E. P. and Unna, K.: J. Pharmacol. **83:** 59, 1945.
Salama, S. and Wright, S.: Brit. J. Pharmacol. **5:** 49, 1950.
Snedecor, G. W.: Statistical Methods, Iowa State College Press, Ames, Iowa, 1946.

THRESHOLD DOSE AND TIME COURSE OF NOREPINEPHRINE DEPLETION OF THE MAMMALIAN HEART BY RESERPINE[1,2]

DOUGLAS R. WAUD[3], SRI R. KOTTEGODA[4] AND OTTO KRAYER

Department of Pharmacology, Harvard Medical School, Boston, Massachusetts

Received for publication July 28, 1958

Previous work in this laboratory (Krayer and Fuentes, 1956, 1958) has demonstrated that reserpine causes an increase in heart rate in the heart-lung preparation of the dog (HLP) and that this can be explained by a release of intrinsic sympathomimetic amines, especially norepinephrine (NE)[5] from the heart. Further studies (Innes *et al.*, 1958) showed that reserpine causes changes in conduction compatible with a release of NE, and Paasonen and Krayer (1957, 1958) found that the action of reserpine leads to a decrease in the NE content of the heart in the HLP.

Paasonen and Krayer also observed, in the dog and in the rat, as Carlsson *et al.* (1957) had found in the rabbit, that reserpine depletes the heart *in situ* of NE. Moreover, they demonstrated that pretreatment of a dog with reserpine prevents the heart rate-increasing effect of reserpine in the HLP subsequently prepared from such an animal. Since this pretreatment effect can be produced by a wide dosage range and is long lasting, quantitative data on the dose-response relationship, on the time course, and on cumulative action have been collected and are presented in this communication.

[1] This work was supported in part by grants from the U. S. Public Health Service, H-2205; the Life Insurance Medical Research Fund; the American Heart Association; and the Eugene Higgins Trust.

[2] A preliminary report of this work was given at the meetings of the American Society for Pharmacology and Experimental Therapeutics in Ann Arbor, Michigan, August, 1958.

[3] Life Insurance Medical Research Fellow, 1957–1959.

[4] Rockefeller Fellow.

[5] Paasonen and Krayer (1958) have demonstrated that a loss of norepinephrine accounts for most of the decrease in cardiac content of sympathomimetic amines. In the present paper "decrease in content of sympathomimetic amines" will be written "decrease in NE." There is no implication that other amines, for example, epinephrine, may not take part in the phenomenon.

METHODS. Forty-four experiments on the HLP were made in a manner already described (Krayer, 1931; Paasonen and Krayer, 1958). The dogs used for the preparation had previously been treated with reserpine according to various dose schedules. Reserpine was administered intraperitoneally, except in one experiment in which the intravenous route was chosen. Sodium pentobarbital (35 mg/kg i.p.) served as anesthetic agent. Normal bleeder dogs were anesthetized with ether. Defibrinated blood was used. Right atrial pressure was measured from a cannula in the inferior vena cava so as to leave the right atrium undisturbed for future assay.

The blood supply and arterial resistance were adjusted to give a systemic output of 659 $\pm$ 78[6] ml/min and a mean arterial pressure of 97.5 $\pm$ 5.7 mm Hg. The right atrial pressure was 30.6 $\pm$ 9.3 mm water. The inflow level (Krayer, 1931) averaged 121.4 $\pm$ 15.7 mm above the right atrium. The temperature ranged from 37.5–39.0° C, with not more than 0.7° C variation in any single experiment and less than 0.3° C shift in 42 of the 44 experiments.

Control conditions were observed for about 30 minutes to establish the initial rate (Krayer, 1950) after which a challenging dose of 3 mg reserpine was administered in 3 minutes into the inflow tubing close to the heart. This dose of reserpine was used because Krayer and Fuentes (1958) have demonstrated that it produces the maximum increase in heart rate. The estimated blood volume of the 44 experiments was 1097 $\pm$ 121 ml. Thirty minutes after the injection of reserpine, as a rule, the right atrium and tip of left ventricle were removed for assay. An occasional experiment was followed throughout the entire time course of the reserpine effect, *i.e.*, about 2 hours (see figure 1).

In the present series of experiments special attention was given to the effect of the challenging dose of reserpine upon right atrial pressure, because close inspection of earlier data indicated a consistent relationship between the effective-

[6] Mean $\pm$ standard deviation.

ness of the challenging dose and decrease in right atrial pressure. The experimental procedure is illustrated in the experiment of figure 1.

Biological assay was used for the estimation of the NE content of the myocardium. The procedure used was essentially that described by Paasonen and Krayer (1958). Right atrial samples (weighing 1.6–3.6 g) were taken so as to include the auricular appendage and most of the anterolateral aspect of the atrium excluding fat. Ventricular samples (weighing 4.3–7.5 g) were taken from the apex of the left ventricle as this permitted fairly uniform sampling.

Samples were weighed and ground with 5% trichloroacetic acid and sand, filtered and adsorbed onto aluminum hydroxide generated *in statu nascendi* at pH 8.6. The alumina was then separated by centrifugation and washed twice with saline. The NE was eluted at pH 3, an ethanol-acetone mixture was added and the mixture refrigerated overnight. It was then filtered and concentrated *in vacuo* to 2 to 4 ml. The pH was adjusted to 5 immediately before bioassay. Recovery was about 80% but variable enough that correction for it did not reduce the variance significantly.

Assay was performed only on the cat blood pressure since Paasonen and Krayer (1958) have already demonstrated that the change in sympathomimetic amine level is largely or wholly due to a decrease in norepinephrine content. Spinal preparations of the cat were made under ether anesthesia. The animals were given mepyramine maleate 8 mg/kg s.c., atropine sulfate 2 mg/kg s.c. and cocaine hydrochloride 3 mg/kg i.m. Injections were made into the femoral vein. The NE equivalents (Euler, 1956) are expressed in μg/g wet tissue uncorrected for recovery.

It was assumed that assays of heart muscle made 30 minutes after a challenging dose of reserpine would be a satisfactory measure of the NE content at the time of challenge since Paasonen and Krayer (1958) were unable to show a change in level until 2 hours after the administration of reserpine to the HLP.

All doses of drugs refer to the base unless otherwise stated. The reserpine used was a lyophilized preparation containing 2 mg ascorbic acid and 12 mg lactose per mg reserpine. A corresponding placebo preparation was inactive.[7]

Results. 1. *Threshold dose for depletion.* Krayer and Fuentes (1958) suggested and Paasonen and Krayer (1958) supported the concept that inability of a dose of reserpine to produce an increase in the heart rate in the HLP can be due to prior depletion of the NE stores of the heart. Therefore, absence of a heart rate-increasing effect of the challenging dose of 3 mg reserpine is presumptive evidence that these stores are depleted.

Upon this basis it can be seen from the data assembled in table 1 that the single dose of 0.1 mg/kg reserpine, given to a dog 24 hours prior to setting up the HLP, consistently depletes the heart, 0.03 mg/kg possibly has some effect, and 0.01 mg/kg is without effect. The dose of 0.1 mg/kg does not lead to obvious toxic effects such as diarrhea, weight loss, and rhinorrhea and appears to be the minimum single safe dose to produce depletion of the NE stores of the dog heart. Depletion can be achieved with doses smaller than 0.1 mg/kg provided they are administered repeatedly.

The absence of a rate-increasing effect of reserpine, as Krayer and Fuentes (1958) have al-

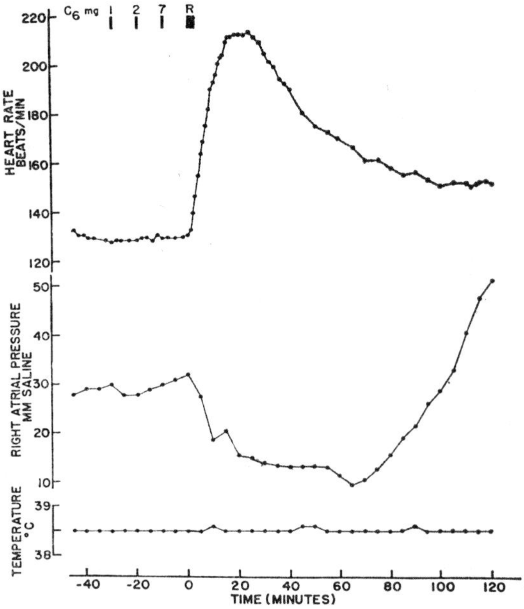

Fig. 1. Lack of influence of hexamethonium upon the rate-increasing effect of reserpine on the HLP.

Dog, 8.9 kg, blood volume about 1120 ml, arterial pressure 99 mm Hg, systemic output 550 ml/min. Upper curve, heart rate as ordinate plotted against time as abscissa. Middle curve, right atrial pressure as ordinate against the same abscissa. Bottom curve, temperature against time. Hexamethonium injections are indicated by the symbol C_6. Injection of 3 mg reserpine (R) at time zero.

[7] Reserpine ('Serpasil' Phosphate) and the placebo preparation without the alkaloid were generously supplied by Dr. A. J. Plummer, Ciba Pharmaceutical Products Inc., Summit, N. J.

TABLE 1

Heart rate-increasing effect of 3 mg reserpine in the HLP of dogs pretreated with reserpine

Pretreatment Schedule		Heart Rate		Increase in Heart Rate, beats/min**
Dose/day*	No. of doses†	Initial beats/min	Maximal beats/min	
mg/kg				
0.01	1	108	148	40
0.03	1	138	156	18
0.1	1	121	122	1
0.1	1	114	117	3
0.1	1	124	128	4
0.1‡	1	114	114	0
0.003	2	163	216	53
0.01‡	2	159	160	1
0.03‡	2	130	132	2
0.1‡	2	118	117	−1
0.001	10	132	172	47
0.003	10	134	137	3
0.003	10	125	135	10§
0.003‡	10	108	107	−1

* Given intraperitoneally.

** The heart rate increase caused by 3 mg reserpine in the HLP of 11 normal dogs (Krayer and Fuentes, 1958) was 57.3 ± 13.5 (S. D.) beats/min.

† The preparation of the HLP from the pretreated dogs was timed so that the challenging dose could be given exactly 24 hours after the last pretreatment dose.

‡ In these experiments a continuous infusion of 3 μg/min of norepinephrine were given 30 min after the administration of the challenging dose of reserpine.

§ This figure is probably too high because the challenging dose was given on a rising baseline of initial rate.

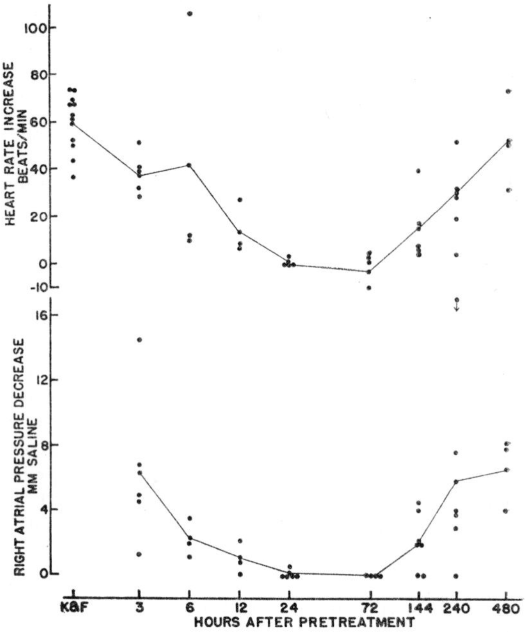

FIG. 2. Time course of depletion of norepinephrine in the heart of the dog by reserpine. Thirty-four heart-lung preparations (HLP). The HLP was challenged with 3 mg reserpine. Dogs pretreated with a single dose of 0.1 mg/kg reserpine intraperitoneally. Full circles each represent individual values except those joined by the solid line which are the means. The upper curve presents the course of the increase in heart rate due to the challenging dose as ordinate plotted against the time elapsed since pretreatment of the dog as abscissa. Heart rate responses obtained by Krayer and Fuentes (1958) in HLP of normal dogs are given at the left for comparison. The lower curve shows the course of the decrease in right atrial pressure following the challenge as ordinate against the same abscissa. (The circle with arrow belongs to the lower curve.)

ready noted, is not due to the inability of the effector organ to respond to NE. In five of the experiments of table 1, in which there was no heart rate increase within thirty minutes following the challenging dose of 3 mg reserpine, an infusion of 3 μg/min norepinephrine was then given. In no case did there appear to be a diminished response of the heart to this substance since we obtained an increase in the heart rate of 48.4 ± 14.3[6] beats/min.

2. *Time course.* Pretreatment of dogs with a single dose of 0.1 mg/kg reserpine was carried out 3, 6, 12, 24, 72, 144, 240, and 480 hours prior to challenging the heart in the HLP. The influence of pretreatment according to these schedules upon the change in heart rate and right atrial pressure, caused by the challenging dose of 3 mg reserpine, is given in figure 2. The values for increase in heart rate in the HLP of normal dogs obtained by Krayer and Fuentes (1958) are used for comparison.

Three hours after pretreatment, the heart rate increase caused by the challenging dose is identical to that found in the HLP of normal dogs. (Use of an intravenous pretreatment dose, in one animal 3 hours prior to setting up the HLP, produced results within the range of those obtained by the usual intraperitoneal route. The rate of absorption from the peritoneal cavity, therefore, does not appear to be a limiting factor in determining the time course of depletion.) By 12 hours the curve appears to be falling. The lowest values are reached between 24 and 72 hours. Thereafter, a gradual and slow return to control values is observed, with normal values being obtained from most of the hearts by the tenth and from all by the twentieth day. The curve for right atrial pressure decrease (a measure of positive inotropic effect) follows a similar course.

Because effects were studied at 7 points on the time axis, the number of estimations at each point could not be very large without greatly increasing the number of experiments on the HLP. To offset the influence upon the calculation of the small sample sizes at each point, the values obtained for change in heart rate and change in right atrial pressure at the 3-hour and 480-hour periods (*i.e.*, when depletion has not yet started or has worn off) have been grouped together and compared to those of the combined 24-hour and 72-hour samples (*i.e.*, when depletion appears maximal). The differences for both heart rate increase and right atrial pressure decrease are present at the 99.99% probability level[8] when treated in this manner.

It can be seen from figure 3 that the curves for NE content of atria and ventricles follow similar though not so clear-cut courses. The variability of the results, when a method of biological assay is used at or near its threshold sensitivity, probably accounts for the greater spread. Nevertheless, statistical treatment similar to that for the changes of heart rate and right atrial pressure yields a difference at the 98% level.

3. *Effect of reserpine pretreatment upon the initial heart rate.* Since it is possible that a background level of norepinephrine plays a role in the maintenance of the resting heart rate even in an isolated preparation such as the HLP (Krayer, 1950; Krayer and Fuentes, 1958) the initial rates in our preparations were studied. They follow a time course (figure 4) similar to that already described for heart rate increase, decrease of right atrial pressure and levels of NE. Statistical treatment similar to that used for these other measurements demonstrates that

[8] Two-tailed probability test; for example, see Wilks (1949).

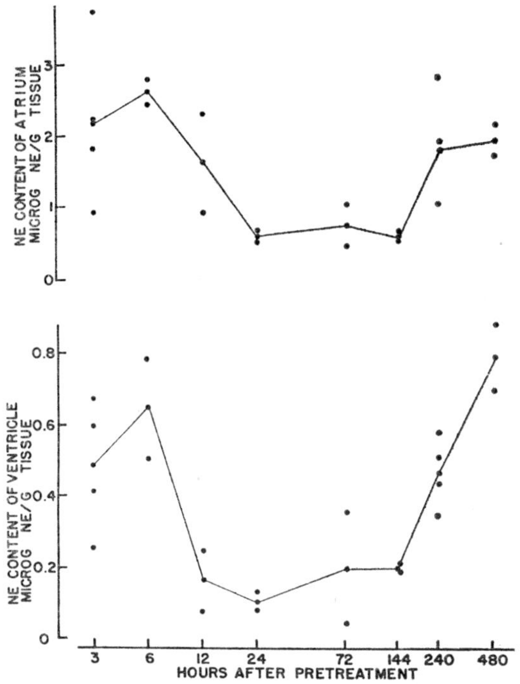

FIG. 3. The time course of the effect of reserpine upon the NE content of the heart.

(Twenty of the 34 HLP experiments of fig. 2.) Dogs pretreated with a single dose of 0.1 mg/kg intraperitoneally. Full circles represent individual values except those joined by the solid line which represent the means. Upper curve shows atrial content of NE plotted as ordinate against the same time abscissa as in fig. 2. Lower curve shows ventricular content of NE plotted against the same abscissa.

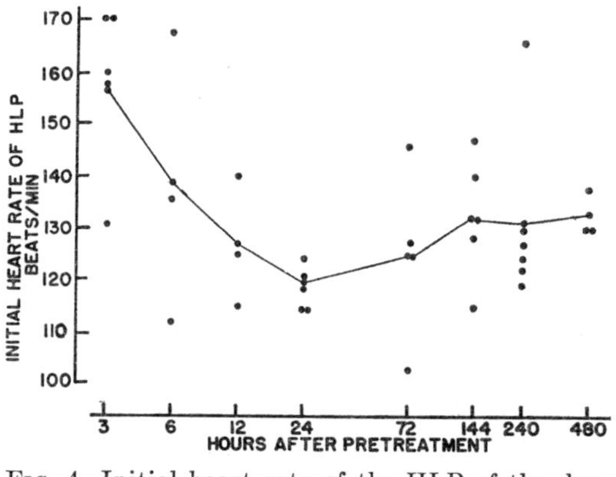

FIG. 4. Initial heart rate of the HLP of the dog.

Dogs pretreated with 0.1 mg/kg of reserpine intraperitoneally. Same 34 HLP as in fig. 2. Ordinate is the initial heart rate measured just before the reserpine challenging dose (about 20–30 min after beginning). Abscissa is the same as in fig. 2.

initial heart rates 24 to 72 hours after pretreatment (121.6 ± 11.8) are lower than those after 3 and 480 hours (148.2 ± 17.8) at the 99% probability level. The mean temperature in both instances was 38.6 (range 38–39)°C. The initial heart rate, when the depletion is presumably maximal, can also be demonstrated (at the 99% probability level) to be lower than the value (141.7 ± 12.8 beats/min) given by Krayer and Benforado (1955) for the HLP of 213 normal dogs at a mean temperature of 38.3 (range 38–39)°C.

4. *The cumulative action of reserpine.* The time course of the cardiac effects of the single pretreatment dose of 0.1 mg/kg reserpine is characteristic of pharmacological agents with marked cumulative action. It was to be expected therefore that much smaller doses than 0.1 mg/kg, if administered repeatedly, would have the ability to deplete the heart of NE. This is borne out by the data assembled in table 1. The dose of 10 μg/kg given on two successive days and the dose of 3 μg/kg given on 10 successive days are fully as active as the single dose of 0.1 mg/kg; they, likewise, lead to a heart depleted of NE 24 hours after the last administration.

5. *Lack of influence of hexamethonium on release of NE.* The release of intrinsic sympathomimetic amines by reserpine might be nicotinic in nature, *e.g.*, due to stimulation of sympathetic ganglion cells or chromaffin tissue in the heart itself (Hoffmann *et al.*, 1945). In order to exclude this possibility, 10 mg hexamethonium, a dose known to block the effect of nicotinic agents upon ganglion cells (Kottegoda, 1953), was administered to the HLP prepared from normal dogs (3 experiments). The challenging dose of 3 mg reserpine (see figure 1) resulted in the usual rise in heart rate and fall in right atrial pressure. Hexamethonium, therefore, does not prevent the release of NE.

DISCUSSION. Carlsson *et al.* (1957) reported complete depletion of NE in the heart of the rabbit 3 hours after 5 mg/kg reserpine given intravenously. In the rat heart Paasonen and Krayer (1958) found 90% depletion of NE 2 hours after 5 mg/kg reserpine administered intraperitoneally. In our experiments in the dog with a pretreatment dose of 0.1 mg/kg i.p., depletion of NE required 12 to 24 hours to become complete. Whether this slow development of the full effect is due to species difference or to the lower dosage we used, or both, cannot be stated with certainty at present. The fact that, in the HLP of the dog, depletion occurs in about 3 hours after a dose of 3 mg reserpine (Paasonen and Krayer, 1958) indicates that the size of the dose probably is of importance. That even such large doses as 3 mg in the HLP of the dog or 5 mg/kg in the intact rabbit or rat do not cause the developmet of the full effect earlier than 2 to 3 hours is a peculiar feature of the mechanism of action of reserpine upon the heart for which there is at present no adequate explanation.

Despite the difference in dosage, our experiments in the dog agree with those of Carlsson *et al.* (1957) in the rabbit, and of Paasonen and Krayer (1958) in the rat in regard to the duration of action. In all 3 instances 2 to 3 weeks were required for the effects of reserpine upon NE depletion to wear off completely. Whatever the nature of the lesion reserpine produces, it appears to be difficult to repair. The slow reversibility of the reserpine effect possibly is not linked to a long lasting retention of the alkaloid at the site of action, since, according to the experiments of Sheppard *et al.* (1955) with C^{14}-labelled reserpine, the heart muscle of the rat shows the greatest intensity of radioactivity less than one hour after intravenous injection, and little remains at the end of six hours. However, recognizing that the radioactive labelling in a methoxy group of the acid moiety of the ester alkaloid reserpine is not a reliable indicator of the location of the as yet unknown parts of the molecule upon which its action depends, Sheppard *et al.* (1958) carried out experiments in the guinea pig with randomly labelled (H^3) reserpine. They found a similar time course of the intensity of radioactivity in brain and liver.

More adequate information on the fate of reserpine in the mammalian organism is needed also to explain the cumulative action of the alkaloid. This may well be due to what, in their studies on cardiac glycosides, Bauer and Fromherz (1933) called "cumulation of effect rather than cumulation of substance," *i.e.*, a progressively increasing change of the function of a tissue or organ by repeated administration of a substance in doses and at intervals not leading to a progressive increase of its concentration at the site of action.

In previous work from this laboratory (Paasonen and Krayer, 1958; Innes *et al.*, 1958) in which NE release from the HLP by reserpine was studied, pretreatment of some of the dogs with reserpine to cause NE depletion was carried out by doses of 0.5 mg/kg once a day on two successive days and the HLP was prepared 48 hours after the second dose. In the dog, this dosage leads to very severe side effects such as lassitude, weakness, running nose, diarrhea, decreased food intake, weight loss, and occasionally death. Even higher doses have been used in the rabbit (*e.g.*, Brodie *et al.*, 1957; Carlsson *et al.*, 1957; Burn and Rand, 1958) and in the rat (Paasonen and Krayer, 1958). All these doses are well above the therapeutic range in man, so it was questionable whether the phenomenon of NE depletion might be of importance clinically.

The results presented on the threshold pretreatment dose of reserpine and on cumulative action in the dog indicate that 3 μg/kg given once per day on 10 successive days can deplete the heart of NE. This dose corresponds to about 0.2 mg in a 70 kg man and is well within the clinically useful range. Assuming no species difference in sensitivity, it might be expected to put the human heart *in situ* into a poor position, *e.g.*, to cope with increased work loads, or with the effects of general anesthesia upon the circulatory system. Indeed, Coakley *et al.* (1956) reported difficulties with patients on reserpine therapy undergoing general anesthetic procedures. In view of our observations, it would probably be advisable to postpone any elective surgery until a patient on reserpine therapy has had time to replenish his cardiac stores of NE (*i.e.*, 2–3 weeks). Canary *et al.* (1957) found improvement in the symptoms and signs of thyrotoxicosis under reserpine treatment using 0.75 to 4 mg/day orally or 7.5 to 15 mg/day i.m. Those doses are well above the threshold we have described. It is of interest to note that "the pulse slowed . . . showing maximal effect in twenty-four to seventy-two hours," a time course in remarkable agreement with our experimental observation.

In this connection it should be borne in mind that depletion of NE may be caused by the clinical use of reserpine in systems other than the circulation leading to possible disturbance of their functions, and that, in general, sites of action of reserpine outside the central nervous system may be much more important than previously recognized.

The initial heart rate of the HLP of dogs pretreated with reserpine is lower than the initial heart rate of the HLP of normal dogs even if, as in the present experiments, a single pretreatment dose of 0.1 mg/kg is used. This further strengthens earlier suggestions by Krayer (1950), Krayer and Fuentes (1958) and Innes and Krayer (1958) that norepinephrine is involved in maintaining the initial rate of the HLP. It is impossible that the slowing could be due to the primary rate-decreasing effect of reserpine since this requires a dose of at least 3 mg for its demonstration in the NE-depleted HLP (Paasonen and Krayer, 1958; Innes *et al.*, 1958), far above our pretreatment dose of 0.1 mg/kg.

The absence of the phenomenon of release of NE in the HLP of the dog with its characteristic influence upon heart rate and right atrial pressure appears to be a reliable indicator that depletion of the NE stores of the heart has occurred. It is more sensitive than the direct biological method of assaying the cardiac tissue for its content of intrinsic sympathomimetic amines. It would seem possible therefore to use this NE-depleting action of reserpine as a pharmacological tool. Indeed, if a substance is considered to act by a mechanism involving endogenous norepinephrine and epinephrine, an alteration in its effect should be observable in the depleted system or organ of the animal. It is of importance in this connection that, with a single dose of 0.1 mg/kg i.p., or with repeated administrations of considerably smaller doses, depletion of the NE stores of the heart can be obtained in the dog without apparent disturbing side effects.

SUMMARY

The heart rate-increasing effect of a challenging dose of 3 mg reserpine given to the heart-lung preparation of the dog is a reliable measure of the cardiac content of intrinsic sympathomimetic catechol amines, especially norepinephrine. There is a close correlation between increase in heart rate decrease in right atrial pressure and content of norepinephrine in the heart. Hexamethonium does not prevent the release of norepinephrine from the heart in the heart-lung preparation. Reserpine in a single dose of 100 μg/kg given i.p. in the dog depletes the heart of norepinephrine in 24 hours without causing any apparent side effect. After 6 days some accumulation becomes detectable, by 10 to 20 days normal stores of norepinephrine are again found. In depleting the heart of norepinephrine reserpine has a marked cumulative action. In the dog a dose of 10 μg/kg given i.p. once a day on 2 successive days and a dose of 3 μg/kg given once a day on 10 successive days lead to a heart depleted of norepinephrine 24 hours after the last dose.

The dose of 3 μg/kg is within the therapeutically useful range and depletion of norepinephrine stores in the circulatory system, and possibly in other systems of the human organism, may be of clinical importance, for example, in general anesthesia.

If the mechanism of action of a substance is considered to involve the release of intrinsic norepinephrine, depletion by reserpine might serve as a pharmacological tool to ascertain this involvement.

ACKNOWLEDGMENT. The authors take pleasure in acknowledging the careful technical assistance given by Mr. Stefan Winkler throughout the course of this investigation.

REFERENCES

BAUER, H. AND FROMHERZ, K.: Klin. Wschr. **12:** 973, 1933.
BRODIE, B. B., OLIN, J. S., KUNTZMAN, R. G. AND SHORE, P. A.: Science **125:** 1293, 1957.
BURN, J. H. AND RAND, M. J.: Brit. med. J. I. (5076): 903, 1958.
CANARY, J. J., SCHAAF, M., DUFFY, B. J., JR. AND RYLE, L. H.: New Engl. J. Med. **257:** 435, 1957.
CARLSSON, A., ROSENGREN, E., BERTLER, Å. AND NILSSON, J.: in Psychotropic Drugs, Elsevier Publ. Co., Amsterdam, 1957, p. 363.
COAKLEY, C. S., ALPERT, S. AND BOLING, J. S.: J. Amer. med. Ass. **161:** 1143, 1956.
EULER U. S. v.: Noradrenaline, C. C. Thomas Publishers, Springfield, Ill., 1956.
HOFFMANN, F., HOFFMANN, E. J., MIDDLETON, S. AND TALESNIK, J.: Amer. J. Physiol. **144:** 189, 1945.
INNES, I., KRAYER, O. AND WAUD, D. R. THIS JOURNAL **124:** 324, 1958.
KOTTEGODA, S. R.: Brit. J. Pharmacol. **8:** 83, 1953.
KRAYER, O.: Arch. exp. Path. Pharmak. **162:** 1, 1931.
KRAYER, O.: THIS JOURNAL **98:** 427, 1950.
KRAYER, O. AND BENFORADO, J. M.: Pflüg. Arch. ges. Physiol. **260:** 177, 1955.
KRAYER, O. AND FUENTES, J.: Fed. Proc. **15:** 709, 1956.
KRAYER, O. AND FUENTES, J.: THIS JOURNAL **123:** 145, 1958.
PAASONEN, M. AND KRAYER, O.: Fed. Proc. **16:** 326, 1957.
PAASONEN, M. AND KRAYER, O.: THIS JOURNAL **123:** 153, 1958.
SHEPPARD, H., LUCAS, R. C. AND TSIEN, W. H.: Arch. int. Pharmacodyn. **103:** 256, 1955.
SHEPPARD, H., TSIEN, W. H., PLUMMER, A. V., PEETS, E. A., GILETTI, B. U. AND SHULERT, A. R.: Proc. Soc. exp. Biol., N. Y. **97:** 717, 1958.
WILKS, S. S.: Elementary Statistical Analysis, Princeton University Press, Princeton, N. J., 1949, p. 213.

8097

COMPARATIVE PHARMACOLOGY OF CHLORPHENIRAMINE (CHLOR-TRIMETON) AND ITS OPTICAL ISOMERS

FRANKLIN E. ROTH AND WILLIAM M. GOVIER

Department of Pharmacology, Scientific Research Division, Schering Corporation, Bloomfield, New Jersey

Received for publication July 28, 1958

The successful resolution of racemic chlorpheniramine maleate (*dl*-CTM) into its *d*- and *l*-isomers[1] has permitted us to compare the antihistaminic potency and toxicity of the 3 compounds. For convenience, we have designated the isomers as *dl*-, *d*-, or *l*- on the basis of optical rotation without regard to their true spatial configuration. These studies present the evidence that the antihistaminic activity of *dl*-CTM exists predominantly in the *d*-isomer[2]. A detailed analysis of the pharmacology of *dl*-CTM has been reported by Labelle and Tislow (1955).

METHODS. *In vitro, guinea pig intestinal strip.* Standard Magnus-type assays were performed on ileal segments to estimate the effective dose of test compound (average of at least 6 trials) required to produce a 50% inhibition (ED_{50}) of muscle spasm induced with histamine (0.2 μg/ml of bath solution).

In vivo oral antihistamine activity in the guinea pig. 1) Protection against intravenous histamine lethality: Protective dose 50 (PD_{50}) values with confidence limits (Litchfield and Wilcoxon, 1949) were determined for the 3 compounds according to a method described elsewhere (Labelle and Tislow, 1955). 2) Protection against aerosolized histamine lethality: Comparative PD_{50} values also were determined by an aerosol method as described by Roth *et al.* (1957).

General pharmacodynamics in the anesthetized dog. A series of 15 dogs were anesthetized with sodium pentobarbital (35 mg/kg), and arranged for kymographic recording of blood pressure and tidal air volume. The test antihistamines were injected intravenously, and their effects on these parameters were recorded. The action of the drugs in modifying the blood pressure response to histamine (0.5–4.0 μg/kg), acetylcholine (5 μg/kg), epinephrine (2 μg/kg), and DMPP (1,1-dimethyl-4-phenyl piperazinium iodide) (10 μg/kg) also was investigated.

Central nervous system side effects in the mouse and cat. Preliminary oral studies in these species were performed according to the method of Irwin *et al.* (1958) in attempts to define the direction and degree of the central action of the 3 compounds.

Acute toxicity by various routes in the guinea pig, mouse and rat. Comparative LD_{50} values with confidence limits (Litchfield and Wilcoxon, 1949) were obtained in these species. The oral LD_{50}'s of the compounds in the guinea pig were utilized for the determination of therapeutic indices. Only *d*-CTM and *dl*-CTM were evaluated in the mouse and rat.

Oral subacute toxicity in the rat and monkey. The *d*- or *dl*-CTM was administered by stomach tube to 4 groups of Charles River rats, each group consisting of 8 males plus 8 females. The dose regimen was 5 and 10 mg/kg/day, 5 days/week for 6 weeks. The dose of 10 mg/kg is approximately 50 times the recommended daily dose in man (6 mg/70 kg, b.i.d.). The vehicle alone (1% tragacanth) was administered to 24 control animals. The same compounds also were given to 3 groups of Rhesus monkeys (Macaca Mulatta, 1 male plus 1 female/group) in a dose schedule of 20 mg/kg/day, 5 days/week for 7 weeks. This dose is approximately one hundred times the recommended daily dose in man. The third group served as controls, receiving the vehicle only (distilled water). In both studies the drug-treated and control animals were compared in reference to the following data: General appearance, body weight, organ weight, complete hemograms, gross pathology at necropsy and histological evaluation of tissue sections. In addition, blood chemistry determinations (urea-nitrogen, creatinine and glucose) and liver function tests were carried out in the monkeys.

The maleate salts of the 3 drugs were utilized in the above procedures, but the data reported are expressed in terms of the free bases in all tests except the subacute toxicity studies.

[1] We are indebted to Dr. L. Walter of the Medicinal Chemistry Dept. for this achievement.

[2] This isomer is designated as Polaramine (brand of *d*-chlorpheniramine) by Schering Corp. It was determined to be 95% pure by solubility analysis.

TABLE 1

In vivo oral antihistamine activity of dl-, d-, and l-chlorpheniramine (CTM) in the guinea pig

Drug*	No. of Animals	PD₅₀† Against		Relative Potency (*dl* = 1.0)
		Hist., i. v.	Hist. aerosol	
		mg/kg	*mg/kg*	
dl-CTM	30	0.13 (0.11–0.16)		1.0
	54		0.18 (0.13–0.24)	1.0
d-CTM	30	0.056 (0.033–0.085)		2.32
	30	0.053 (0.035–0.080)		2.45
	54		0.10 (0.07–0.13)	1.8
l-CTM	30	5.4 (4.0–7.2)		0.024
	30	5.0 (4.5–5.9)		0.026

* Drugs administered 1 hr before histamine challenge.
† With (confidence limits), $p < 0.05$.

TABLE 2

Oral LD_{50}, therapeutic index (TI) and relative safety of dl-, d-, and l-chlorpheniramine (CTM) in the guinea pig

Drug	No. of Animals	LD_{50}*	TI = LD_{50}/PD_{50}†	lative Safety
		mg/kg		
d-CTM	32	169 (141–203)	3380	100
dl-CTM	54	186 (166–207)	1430	42
l-CTM	32	124 (101–151)	25	0.7

* With (confidence limits), $p < 0.05$.
† Against intravenous histamine (table 1).

TABLE 3

Acute toxicity of dl- and d-chlorpheniramine in the mouse and rat

Species	No. of Animals/Drug	Route	LD_{50}*	
			d-CTM	*dl*-CTM
			mg/kg	
Rat	40	p.o.	188 (140–252)	118 (95–148)
	40	i.p.	84 (66–107)	89 (73–108)
Mouse	40	p.o.	133 (109–162)	121 (102–143)
	40	i.p.	82 (70–97)	73 (60–68)
	40	i.v.	20 (14–28)	20 (14–29)

* With (confidence limits), $p < 0.05$.

RESULTS. *In vitro, intestine.* It was apparent that the *d*-isomer was approximately twice as potent as the racemic compound since the ED_{50}'s for *d*- and *dl*-CTM were 0.8 μg/l and 1.7 μg/l, respectively. The ED_{50} of *l*-CTM was 190 μg/l, or approximately one-one hundredth the potency of *dl*-CTM.

In vivo oral antihistamine activity. Preliminary experiments revealed that the potency of *d*-CTM was of the order of 2 to 3 times that of *dl*-CTM in protecting guinea pigs from fatal asphyxial collapse following the intravenous injection of histamine (1.1 mg/kg) one hour after drug administration. Further detailed assays, employing logarithmically-spaced doses of drug, demonstrated that *d*-CTM was at least 2 times the potency of *dl*-CTM; whereas, *l*-CTM was one-fiftieth the potency of *dl*-CTM and one-one hundredth that of *d*-CTM (table 1). When the histamine challenge was delivered by aerosol, 1 hour after drug administration, *d*-CTM had slightly less than 2 times the potency of *dl*-CTM in protecting 50% of the animals against death (table 1). Untreated control animals which had received histamine intravenously or by aerosol never survived for longer than 5 to 6 minutes.

General pharmacodynamics in the dog. It is known to be difficult to clearly distinguish antihistaminic potency when employing the hypotensive response to intravenous histamine in the anesthetized dog. However, it was generally observed that *d*-CTM (0.5–4.0 mg/kg i.v.) produced a slightly greater effect than did the same doses of *dl*-CTM. At lower doses (0.05–0.10 mg/kg) this difference was less evident. The *d*-isomer produced other effects typical of that observed with the *dl*-compound, *e.g.*, moderate, prolonged hypertension at doses above 0.10 mg/kg if administered slowly; transient hypotension at doses above 1.0 mg/kg varying in degree depending upon the rate of injection; increase in respiratory rate with a depression of tidal air volume at doses of 1.0 mg/kg and higher; potentiation of the pressor responses to epinephrine and DMPP; and slight anticholinergic action at 8.0 mg/kg. Whereas, the *d*- or *dl*-CTM demonstrated potent blockade of histamine hypotension at 0.05 mg/kg, the *l*-isomer had only weak action at 4.0 mg/kg. It also seemed apparent that *l*-CTM elicited a more precipitous and marked hypotension at the higher doses than was observed with the other compounds.

Central nervous system. Preliminary oral studies in the mouse and cat with the 3 compounds (0.05–12.0 mg/kg) revealed a general pattern of central stimulation. Attempts to demonstrate clear-cut potency differences or detect signs of sedative action were not successful.

Acute toxicity. The acute, oral LD_{50} and PD_{50} values obtained in the guinea pig were utilized to approximate the therapeutic indices and relative safety of the 3 drugs (table 2). The LD_{50} of the *d*-isomer was not significantly different ($p > 0.05$) from that found for *dl*-CTM. However, the relatively weak antihistamine, *l*-CTM was significantly ($p < 0.05$) more toxic than the *d*- or *dl*-compounds. The LD_{50} values of the *d*- and *dl*-CTM, by various routes of administration in the mouse and rat were generally comparable (table 3). The evidence of toxic activity in the species tested was typical of that observed for most antihistaminic drugs. The general pattern of central nervous stimulation was characterized by signs of irritability at lower doses, and then the development of tremors, mydriasis, and finally convulsions at higher doses.

Subacute toxicity. The data compiled from the 6 and 7 week oral study in the rat and monkey, respectively, did not reveal any unusual changes in appearance, behavior, organ weights, hemograms, function tests, or tissue sections, which could be distinguished from observations obtained from control animals or attributed to the administration of *d*- or *dl*-CTM. There was observed, however, an unexplained tendency of male rats in both drug-treated groups to demonstrate a greater gain in body weight (20–30%) than was recorded for control male rats.

DISCUSSION. The antihistaminic activity and toxicity of *d*-CTM in the intact guinea pig have demonstrated that this isomer is approximately twice as potent but no more toxic than the standard *dl*-CTM. It is well known that the central nervous activity of certain antihistamines is predominantly stimulatory in the animal but generally tends to produce sedation in man. Although this difference in species response is not necessarily related, our data suggest that either the *d*- or *l*-isomers could possibly produce clinical side effects similar to those observed with *dl*-CTM. However, it also would seem probable that a reduction in clinical dosage allowable with the use of the more potent *d*-CTM would result in a lesser degree of such side effects. Preliminary clinical observations have confirmed the greater potency of the *d*-isomer, and there is positive evidence of a lessened degree of sedative-like side effects at effective doses. More detailed and extensive studies are in process at this time.

Recently, "*dl*-bromtrimeton" was resolved into its *d*- and *l*-isomers, and initial studies have indicated that the predominant antihistaminic activity of this compound also is in the *d*-isomer.

SUMMARY

In vitro antihistamine studies on guinea pig gut have demonstrated that *d*-chlorpheniramine was approximately twice as potent as the racemic compound. The *l*-isomer had only about one-one hundredth the potency of *dl*-chlorpheniramine.

The oral protective action of the *d*-isomer against death induced by intravenous or aerosolized histamine in guinea pigs revealed an average potency of 1.8–2.4 times that observed for the racemic compound.

The general pharmacodynamics of the *d*-isomer in the anesthetized dog were similar to those of the *dl*-compound.

The central nervous system effect of all 3 drugs in mice and cats was manifested as general stimulation of approximately the same degree.

The acute toxicity of the *d*-isomer in guinea pigs, rats and mice was no greater than that of the *dl*-compound.

Oral subacute studies in the rat and monkey did not reveal any abnormalities which could be attributed to administration of either *d*- or *dl*-chlorpheniramine.

REFERENCES

IRWIN, S., SLABOK, M., DEBIASE, P. AND GOVIER, W.M.: Arch. int. Pharmacodyn. (in press, 1958).

LABELLE, A. AND TISLOW, R.: THIS JOURNAL **113:** 72, 1955.

LITCHFIELD, J. T. AND WILCOXON, F.: THIS JOURNAL **96:** 99, 1949.

ROTH, F. E., WINBURY, M. M. AND GOVIER, W. M.: THIS JOURNAL **121:** 487, 1957.

8098

ANALYSIS OF THE RELATIONSHIP BETWEEN DRUG-INDUCED CONVULSIONS AND MORTALITY IN RATS

BARUCH BLUM AND SHELEMYAHU ZACKS

With the technical assistance of Hanoch Otmy

Department of Experimental Biology, The Weizmann Institute of Science, Rehovoth, and The Technion, Israel Institute of Technology, Haifa, Israel

Received for publication July 9, 1958

Death may follow convulsions (Penfield and Jasper, 1954) though such a result is usually attributable to secondary effects, *e.g.*, to anoxia, anoxemia, exhaustion of the respiratory apparatus or a break in the circulatory system at some "locus of minor resistance."

The observation that with some drugs, almost all convulsing animals die (Berger, 1953), may merely indicate that their convulsant $dose_{50}$ (CD_{50}) is very close to their LD_{50}. Primary convulsive death could, nevertheless, be envisaged with certain specific drugs. These possibilities were investigated experimentally in the present study.

The drugs chosen were 1-n-butylamino-3-*p*-tuluidino-2-propanol (compound W-181), an experimental mephenesin antagonist; the antihistaminic phenindamine (Thephorin), the classic convulsant strychnine; and the analeptic drugs caffeine, pentylenetetrazol (Metrazol) and nicotine.[1]

METHODS. The experiments were conducted with mature male albino rats 120 days old, thus ensuring that the animals used were at their optimal strength in bearing the strain of the convulsions. They were derived from our own breeding colony, and maintained under highly favorable conditions of diet, temperature, etc. Randomization of the animals was performed according to Tables of Random Numbers. Fifteen to 30 animals were usually used at each dose. Duplicate experiments which showed an insignificant difference between the observed proportions were pooled together.

The drugs were freshly prepared in isotonic solution for each experiment and were injected intraperitoneally. Compound W-181, the only one that was not readily soluble in saline, was first dissolved in 3 ml of 50% ethanol and then diluted with saline to 100 ml. (The amount of alcohol at such low concentrations was shown to have no apparent effects on the results.)

Each of the drugs was administered at a dose range suitable for the evaluation of the functional relationship between the fraction convulsion and fraction mortality versus dose.

Assuming that the frequencies of convulsions and of mortality at any dose were binomially distributed,[2] a "normit"[3] transformation of the obtained frequencies was used for determining the regression lines of the above variables. These linear regression lines of the normits versus the logarithms of doses for the 5 drugs were then fitted according to the "method of minimum normit chi-square."[4] Different weights were given to

[1] Compound W-181 was kindly supplied by Wallace Laboratories, New Brunswick, N.J., Thephorin by Hoffmann-La Roche, Inc., Nutley, N.J.

[2] This assumption is common in bioassay analysis. It means that the probability of convulsion or of mortality at each dose is constant, and that the samples of animals are random.

[3] "Normit percentage" is a function of the percentage frequency. It is mathematically defined as the inverse of the normal distribution function at that point which equals the given percentage of the observed frequency:

$$P = \frac{100}{\sqrt{2\pi}} \int_{-\infty}^{N(P)} e^{-\frac{1}{2}t^2}\, dt \ (\%),$$

where N(P) denotes the normit % and P denotes percentage. Values of N(P) equivalent to experimental percentage frequencies can be obtained from tables of normit functions (Berkson, 1955).

[4] The "minimum normit chi-square" estimates of the parameters α & β of a regression line are those values of α & β which minimize the equation:

$$X = \sum_{i=1}^{k} n_i\, w_i\, (y_i - \alpha - \beta x_i)^2$$

where n_i are the number of animals at each dosage x_i; y_i are the normit values corresponding to x_i; w_i are the normit weights.

Berkson (1955) had shown that these "minimum normit chi-square" estimates of the regression coefficients α & β are more efficient estimates when samples are small, than the "maximum likelihood" estimates given by Finney (1947).

different points of the regression lines, according to the number of animals used at the corresponding doses and the "normit" value (Berkson, 1955).[5] Estimates of the correlations between convulsions and mortality at different doses were then computed, using the estimated values of the dosage convulsions and dosage-mortality regression lines, and thus the correlation functions of dosage were obtained for each of the drugs. In this way the correlations are expressed as functions of dosage. The mathematical derivation of the formulae of these functions is summarized under the following four points.

1. In the derivation of the function of the correlation of death with convulsions we have assumed that convulsions always precede death. This was true for all the drugs chosen for analysis. If this condition was not fulfilled by a drug the latter was excluded from our analysis for reasons to be stated in the discussion. The probability of death occurring without convulsions is therefore zero, and the correlation is never negative. This can be represented schematically as follows:

convulsions {C} → death {D}

dose ↗ ↘ (to convulsions {C} and to no convulsions {$\bar{C}$}); no convulsions ↘ no death

no convulsions {$\bar{C}$} → no death {$\bar{D}$}

2. In cases where the probability of convulsion P{C} = 1, or where the probability of death P{D} = 0, we have a situation where convulsions and death are independent of each other.

At doses where the P{C} in the sample is significantly smaller than unity and the P{D} is significantly larger than zero, the correlation value between convulsions and mortality is regarded significantly larger than zero, and there is dependence between convulsions and death. On the other hand, when the P{D} does not differ significantly from the P{C}, the correlation was regarded as equal to unity. Since the comparison of P{C} and P{D} could be done by comparing the proportion of convulsions to proportion of mortality, the problem of comparing correlation values is reduced to that of comparing linear regression values.

3. In measuring the dependence of convulsions and death we used the following equation for the correlation coefficient between convulsions and death (Yule and Kendall, 1950):

$$\text{(i)} \qquad R = \frac{P\{C \cap D\} - P\{C\}P\{D\}}{+\sqrt{P\{C\}P\{C\}P\{D\}P\{D\}}}$$

Since P{C ∩ D} = P{D} we obtain:

$$\text{(ii)} \qquad R = +\sqrt{\frac{P\{D\}\,[1 - P\{C\}]}{P\{C\}\,[1 - P\{D\}]}}$$

The probabilities P{C} and P{D} could be estimated for every dose by means of the dosage-response regression lines. The estimates of P{D} and P{C} for each dose, Z, is given by $\Phi(\hat{\alpha}_D + \hat{\beta}_D \log Z)$ and $\Phi(\hat{\alpha}_C + \hat{\beta}_C \log Z)$ where $\Phi(X) = \frac{1}{\sqrt{2\pi}} \int_{-\infty}^{x} e^{-\frac{1}{2}t^2}\,dt$ is the N (0,1) distribution function $\alpha_D;\beta_D$; α_C,β_C are the corresponding intercepts and slopes of the Normit to log-dose linear regression lines (Finney, 1947). We then obtain:

(iii) R(Z)

$$= +\sqrt{\frac{\Phi(\hat{\alpha}_D + \hat{\beta}_D \log Z)\,[1 - \Phi(\hat{\alpha}_C + \hat{\beta}_C \log Z)]}{\Phi(\hat{\alpha}_C + \hat{\beta}_C \log Z)\,[1 - \Phi(\hat{\alpha}_D + \hat{\beta}_D \log Z)]}}$$

as the *correlation function of convulsions with death versus dose.*

4. Three main types of correlation functions are possible, corresponding to the three types of possible relationships between the dosage-convulsions and the dosage-mortality regression lines: 1) Whenever the two regression lines intersect at the lower end of the "dosage range," the probability of convulsions grows more rapidly than that of mortality; hence the correlation between convulsions and mortality decreases monotonically towards zero. 2) Whenever the two regression lines intersect at the upper end of the "dosage range," the probability of death, which is practically zero at the lower end of the dose range, grows more rapidly than that of the convulsions, and the correlation between convulsions and mortality rises monotonically towards absolute dependence, *i.e.*, towards a coefficient of correlation of unity. 3) The third and last possibility is that the regression lines would be parallel to one another. In such a case, if there is also an overlapping of the dosage ranges of convulsions and mortality the correlation first increases monotonically up to a maximum and then decreases also monotonically. By substituting

$$Z = CD_{50}$$

$$= \exp. \frac{-\alpha_c}{\beta} \text{ in the correlation function (III),}$$

and

$$Z = LD_{50} = \exp. \frac{-\alpha_d}{\beta}$$

[5] For the same number of animals, the weights of points with normit values close to zero are greater than the weights of points with larger absolute normit values.

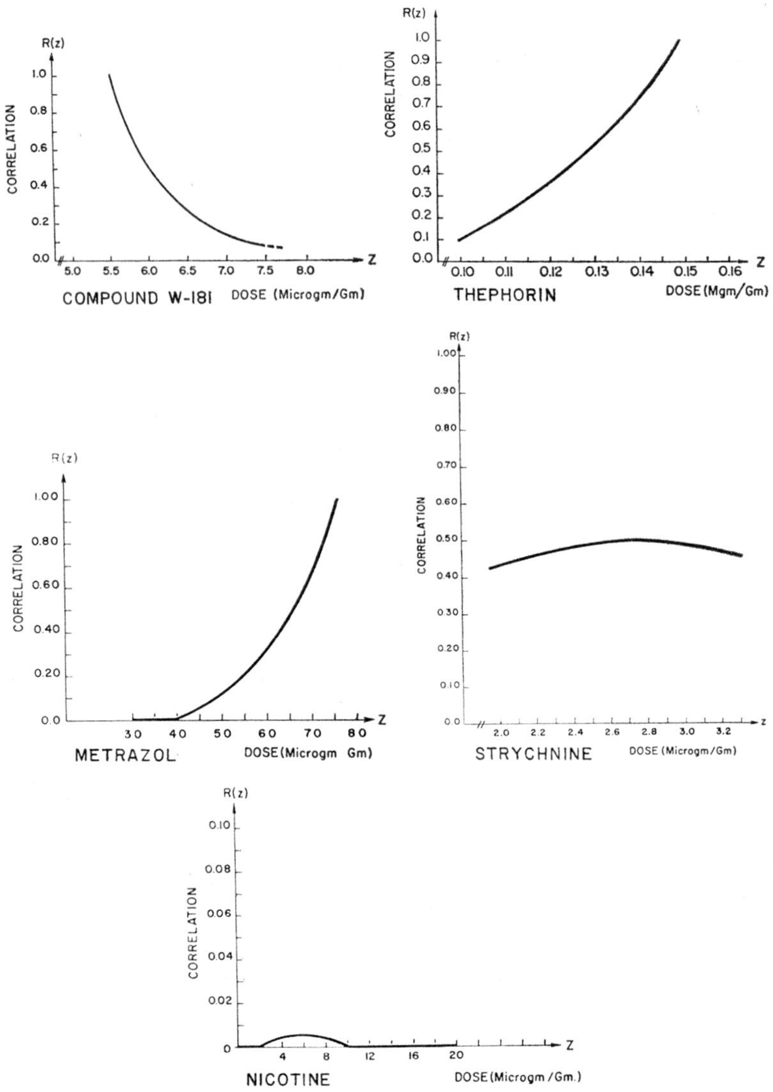

FIG. 1. The coefficient of correlation of convulsions (Z) vs. mortality (R (Z)) in relation to dosage for five convulsant drugs.

it is found that the correlation value at CD_{50} and LD_{50} are equal. Hence the maximum point R(Z) of such a function must be interposed between the CD_{50} and the LD_{50}.

However, it is also possible that the parallel regression lines would not have a significant overlap of dose ranges, and that the distance between their CD_{50} and LD_{50} would be so large that the convulsions and mortality are practically independent of one another. In a case such as this, almost all the correlation values would be zero. The general conditions under which zero correlation can occur have already been stated above.

RESULTS. The drugs studied (W-181, Thephorin, strychnine, Metrazol and nicotine) gave evidence of three entirely different types of correlation functions (fig. 1). These differences are evident also from the various relative positions of their dosage-convulsions and dosage-mortality regression lines (fig. 2). Examining these figures one can see that in one type, given by W-181, the regression lines are very close to another at the lower end of the dose range, departing rapidly as the dose is increased (fig. 2). The corresponding correlation function was an exponential which

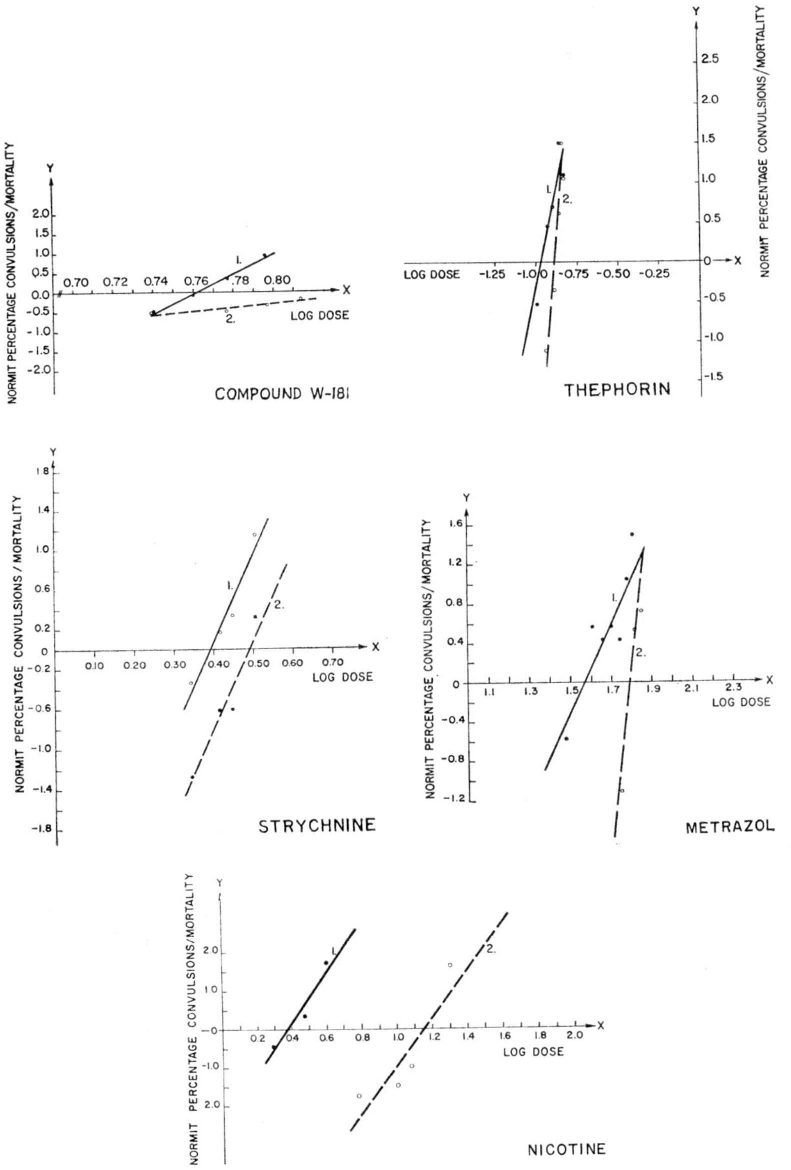

FIG. 2. Log dose (X) in relation to normit percentage (Y) for five convulsant drugs. 1 = convulsions; 2 = mortality.

decreased monotonically[6] (fig. 1). On the other hand, Thephorin and Metrazol gave regression lines which converged at the upper end of the dose ranges (fig. 2). The correlation function of Thephorin was a monotonically increasing exponential (fig. 1), and that of Metrazol showed zero correlation for the lower part of the dose range and a correlation function similar to that of Thephorin for the rest of the dose range. Strychnine and nicotine gave two parallel regression lines (fig. 2) and the resulting correlation function had a maximum point located between the CD_{50} and the LD_{50}, with very mild changes on both sides of this maximum point (fig. 1). The correla-

[6] A monotonically decreasing function is a function which decreases when the values of the argument increase, and *vice versa*; *e.g.*, for every x_1 and x_2, if $x_1 > x_2$ then $f(x_1) \leqslant f(x_2)$.
A monotonically increasing function is a function which increases when the values of the argument increase, and *vice versa*; *e.g.*, for every x_1 and x_2, if $x_1 > x_2$ then $f(x_1) \geqslant f(x_2)$.

TABLE 1

Dosage-convulsions and dosage-mortality, normit to log-dose, regression lines

Drugs	Regression Lines*		Standard Error of Intercept		Standard Error of Slope		CD_{50}	LD_{50}
	Dosage-convulsions	Dosage-mortality	Dosage-convulsions	Dosage-mortality	Dosage-convulsions	Dosage-mortality		
W-181	Y = −19.79 + 25.93 log Z†	Y = −4.38 + 5.10 log Z	±1.623	±1.354	±2.115	±1.716	5.792 μg/g	7.220 μg/g
Thephorin	Y = 9.37 + 9.61 log Z	Y = 20.59 + 23.11 log Z	±2.757	±4.261	±3.012	±4.799	0.106 mg/g	0.129 mg/g
Strychnine	Y = −3.48 + 8.87 log Z	Y = −4.35 + 8.87 log Z	±0.960	±1.062	±2.285	±2.427	2.471 μg/g	3.093 μg/g
Metrazol	Y = −7.28 + 4.64 log Z	Y = −32.15 + 17.88 log Z	±2.945	±9.048	±1.748	±5.009	37.26 μg/g	62.83 μg/g
Nicotine	Y = −2.37 + 6.28 log Z	Y = −7.29 + 6.28 log Z	±0.684	±1.310	±1.612	±1.235	2.39 μg/g	14.56 μg/g

* The variance for all the regression lines is not significant.
† Z denotes dose.

tion values for nicotine were zero or very close to zero throughout the dose range.

The coefficients of the various regression lines and other relevant information about these data are given in table 1. The raw material from which these relationships were derived is presented in table 2, and more details on the mathematical derivations of these relationships are given under METHODS.

The variances of the deviations in all the regression lines were not significantly different from unity, which shows that the data were homogeneous (Finney, 1947). One point on the regression line of dosage-mortality of W-181 deviated considerably from the regression value, however, because of its very small weight relative to those of the other four points which showed high homogeneity, but the variance about that regression line is not significant.

DISCUSSION. Death does not usually follow epileptic convulsions in man, even when these are severe (Penfield and Jasper, 1954; Goodman and Gilman, 1955). The situation is different with drug-induced convulsions, with which the danger of fatal outcome is widely recognized clinically, especially in children (Judge and Dumars, 1953; McGavack, Weissberg and Boyd, 1948; Herlitz and Lindberg, 1952; Goodman and Gilman, 1955; Holt, Hagerman and Whitehead, 1948). The special danger in children, with most convulsant drugs, is apparently attributable to the weakness of their respiratory muscles which predisposes them to respiratory paralysis from the strain of the convulsions.

Experimentally, a number of otherwise useful drugs (*e.g.*, Thephorin) may produce convulsions, some of which terminate fatally, even with relatively low doses. This makes the problem of accurate evaluation and of pharmacodynamic studies of the interrelationship between drug convulsions versus the mortality which may follow, and of dosage, important from a practical standpoint.

In the present study, we were interested in the causal relationship between drug convulsions and lethality. We have therefore included in it only drugs with which death occurred always after convulsions have taken place. If death also occurred without preceding convulsions, as was the case with caffeine, we have excluded it from our analysis.

It is rather noteworthy that our studies revealed experimentally most of the theoretically possible types of relationships between the correlation of convulsion rate to mortality rate and dosage, *i.e.*, ascending relationships, a descending one, and correlations with a maximum point which changes, however, very little.

TABLE 2

Frequencies of convulsion and death at various doses of five tested drugs

Drugs	Doses	Number of Animals	Number of Convulsed Animals	Number of Animals Convulsed and Died
	μg/g			
W-181	5.5	10	3	3
	5.75	10	5	1
	6.00	22	14	7
	6.25	22	18	8
	6.50	21	17	9
	mg/g			
Thephorin	0.100	10	3	0
	0.115	25	17	3
	0.125	25	19	9
	0.135	15	14	11
	0.145	15	15	14
	0.150	15	13	13
	μg/g			
Strychnine	2.2	30	11	3
	2.6	30	17	8
	2.8	30	19	8
	3.2	24	21	15
	μg/g			
Metrazol	30	7	2	0
	40	7	5	0
	45	15	10	0
	50	7	5	0
	55	15	10	2
	60	7	6	0
	65	15	14	11
	70	22	22	17
	μg/g			
Nicotine	2	24	8	0
	3	14	9	0
	4	24	23	0
	6	24	24	1
	10	14	14	1
	12	24	24	4
	20	20	20	19

The occurrence of convulsions associated with action on certain parts of the brain is known to be accompanied, for instance in epilepsy, by the paralysis of the normal functions of these particular parts (Penfield and Jasper, 1954). If we assume a similar phenomenon in the case of drug-induced convulsions, one can see why the indirect or the direct involvement of vital systems in the convulsive action may lead to death.

Our analysis of correlation between convulsions and mortality in the case of Thephorin suggests that the occurrence of convulsions with this drug plays an important, although not a sole, role in the production of lethality. In the first place, there is a close proximity between the convulsive and the lethal dose ranges. However, the correlation seems to be a secondary rather than a primary one, *i.e.*, the lethality seems to be an indirect result of postconvulsive depression or exhaustion of the organism. At the lower end of the dose range convulsions occur without production of lethality. Only when the dose is increased until the lethal range is reached, does lethality begin to increase rapidly at even a faster rate than the convulsions.

Metrazol behaves similarly, but only at high doses, and it does not show a close proximity between the convulsive and lethal dose ranges. At the lower doses it has zero correlation over a large portion of its dosage range. Nicotine also showed zero correlations practically for its entire dosage range. These two latter drugs apparently can cause convulsions which are not detrimental to vital functions. It is also possible that the respiratory stimulating action of these drugs affords a protection against the depression of respiration which their convulsant action produces.

If our results with all the other drugs studied agreed with the above interpretations, it could be said that there is no basic difference between drug-induced convulsions and epileptic convulsions with respect to the correlation between the convulsion rate and mortality rate. In both, with increased convulsive action the chances for a secondary implication of vital systems may be increased in such a way that fatality may occur, although with drugs ancillary harmful effects may also contribute to this event. However, our results with W-181, strychnine, and also to some extent with nicotine, do not allow such a conclusion. With W-181 mortality began to occur practically at the same dose range as the convulsions and the correlation function obtained was one which continuously descended from a maximum value towards zero. With strychnine we obtained a relatively constant positive correlation which, however, possessed a maximum point on both sides of which it descended. Although nicotine showed practically a zero correlation for the entire dose range, at those dose regions where small correlation values were obtained, it behaved functionally in a way similar to that of strychnine. These results indicate interrelationships entirely different from those of the drugs previously discussed.

It seems to us that when vital systems are affected in a relatively direct manner a high rate of lethality may result even at the beginning of the convulsive dose range. When in such a case the dose is increased, other parts indirectly related to vital systems also become involved, but then the correlation of convulsions and death becomes less. A mechanism such as this could, we think, account for our results with W-181.

Although in general agreement with the accepted pharmacodynamics, our results with strychnine and with nicotine are more difficult to interpret biologically. Both these drugs are ubiquitous in their action in the CNS, and nicotine, furthermore, has wide-ranging peripheral actions which could influence our results. It is not surprising that strychnine, the dangerously potent ubiquitous CNS convulsant drug with strong spinal specificity of action, gave a correlation between convulsions and mortality which changed but little with dosage. Death from strychnine is thought to occur as a result of medullary depression (Goodman and Gilman, 1955) consequential to convulsive action. When mortality occurs with this drug, it is apparently directly associated with the occurrence of convulsions throughout the dose range, with an optimum dosage for such correlation lying between the CD_{50} and the LD_{50}. For the mathematical discussion of this optimum point see METHODS.

SUMMARY

The changes that occur in the correlation between drug-induced convulsions and mortality with dosage were studied in adult rats for several convulsant drugs.

Three types of positive correlations and also zero correlations were found. The correlation in the case of W-181 decreased monotonically and exponentially; with Thephorin it increased exponentially and monotonically, and similarly with high doses of Metrazol, whereas with lower doses of this drug, a zero correlation was manifested. Strychnine gave a correlation which changed very little with dose, but a maximum correlation was given by a dose lying between the CD_{50} and the LD_{50}, on both sides of which the correlation decreased monotonically, although very little. Nicotine gave a zero correlation for practically the entire "dosage range."

It was suggested that with drugs eliciting a positive correlation between convulsions and death, two types of action may be involved, one implicating more or less directly, and the other indirectly, vital systems. In one, mortality occurs as a result of the convulsions, and in the other, secondarily to them (W-181 and Thephorin, respectively). Although with most drugs this correlation changes with dosage, it is possible for it to stay relatively constant (as with strychnine).

With some drugs at least, at a certain wide dose range the correlation may be zero (nicotine, Metrazol), apparently because they can cause convulsions without implicating vital functions in a deleterious manner.

ACKNOWLEDGMENT. The authors wish to express their sincere thanks to Prof. I. Berenblum for criticism and correction of this manuscript, to J. Shalom for supply of animals and to P. Kardosh for preparing the diagrams.

REFERENCES

BERGER, F. M.: THIS JOURNAL **107:** 250, 1953.

BERKSON, J.: J. Amer. statist. Ass. **50:** 529, 1955.

FINNEY, D. J.: Probit Analysis, The University Press, Cambridge, 1947.

GOODMAN, L. S. AND GILMAN, A.: The Pharmacological Basis of Therapeutics, 2nd ed., The Macmillan Co., N.Y., 1955.

HERLITZ, G. AND LINDBERG, G.: Nord. med. **47:** 871, 1952.

HOLT, D. E., HAGERMAN, D. D. AND WHITEHEAD, R. W.: J. Allergy **19:** 384, 1948.

JUDGE, D. J. AND DUMARS, K. W.: Amer. J. Dis. Child. **85:** 545, 1953.

MCGAVACK, T. H., WEISSBERG, J. AND BOYD, L. J.: J. Lab. clin. Med. **33:** 595, 1948.

PENFIELD, W. AND JASPER, H.: Epilepsy and the Functional Anatomy of the Human Brain, Little, Brown & Co., Boston, 1954.

YULE, G. U. AND KENDALL, M. G.: Introduction to the Theory of Statistics, 14th ed., Charles Griffin and Co. Ltd., London, 1950.

ABSORPTION
acetylsalicylic acid 8092
gastrointestinal tract 8092
mephenesin influence 8092
sodium salicylate 8092
ACETAZOLAMIDE
anticonvulsant potency 8071
maximal electroshock seizure 8071
ACETYLCHOLINE
atropine inhibition 8069 8070
heart contractile force 8078
high energy phosphates 8078
intestinal motility 8067
intraarterial injection 8067 8069 8070
mammalian striated muscle 8069
mesenteric reflexes 8067
myotonic goat muscle 8070
reflex apnea 8067
supersensitivity 8070
ACETYLSALICYLIC ACID
gastrointestinal absorption 8092
mephenesin 8092
plasma salicylate levels 8092
ACTH
abstinence response 8091
human subjects 8091
morphine addiction 8091
urinary 17-ketosteroid elevation 8091
ADENINE NUCLEOTIDES
heart contractile force 8078
heart muscle content 8078
isolated guinea pig atrium 8078
ADRENALECTOMY
blood pressure 8054
cardiac arrhythmia 8054
cigarette smoke 8054
denervated nictitating membrane 8068
Su-4029 8068
ADRENERGIC BLOCKADE
dibenamine 8068
dichloroisoproterenol 8080
isoproterenol vasodepressor effect 8080
phentolamine 8068
positive chronotropic effects 8080
positive inotropic effects 8080
Su-4029 antagonism 8068
sympathomimetic amines 8080
ADRENERGIC BLOCKING AGENTS
dichloroisoproterenol 8080
mammalian heart 8080
tetrazotized diorthoanisidine (TDA) 8079
AJMALINE
atrial fibrillation 8094
A-V transmission 8094
bradycardia 8094
functional refractory period 8094
heart-lung preparation 8094
ALCOHOL
abrupt cessation 8086
abstinence effects 8086
anticonvulsant properties 8086
anticonvulsant tests 8086
chronic administration 8086
CNS depression 8086
hyperexcitability 8086
MES patterns 8086
neurotoxicity 8086
physical dependence 8086
protective index 8086
seizure thresholds 8086
ALCOHOL, ALLYL
action mechanism 8064
blood concentration 8064
hemoconcentration 8064
hypotension 8064
metabolism 8064
microquantitation method 8064
oxygen uptake 8064
pharmacodynamics 8064
plasma histamine 8064
tissue slices 8064
tissue swelling 8064
toxicity 8064
ALPHA-LOBELINE
cross-circulation 8095
ventilatory response 8095
ALPHAPRODINE
intestinal motility 8073
levallorphan antagonism 8073
ALSEROXYLON
antiarrhythmic effect 8057
atrial flutter 8057
auricular fibrillation 8057
quinidine-like activity 8057
ventricular tachycardia 8057
AMINE OXIDASE
hog kidney cortex 8088
mescaline degradation 8088

rabbit liver microsomes 8088
rabbit liver mitochondria 8088
sheep plasma 8088
2-AMINO-4-p-CHLOROANILINO-s-TRIAZINE
diuretic effects 8093
electrolyte excretion 8093
intravenous administration 8093
water excretion 8093
AMMONIUM CHLORIDE
anticonvulsant augmenting effect 8071
maximal electroshock seizure 8071
ANALGESIC-ANTAGONISTS
analgesics 8073
intestinal motility 8073
ANALGESICS
antagonistic drugs 8060
antagonists 8073
denervated intestinal loops 8073
human subjects 8085
innervated intestinal loops 8073
intestinal loop tone 8073
intestinal motility 8073
intestinal segments 8073
morphine 8085
new morphine derivatives 8084
normorphine 8085
postoperative pain 8085
sedative potency 8073
testing method 8060
tremorine 8060
ANAPHYLAXIS
acetylcholine response 8062
antibody-containing cells 8062
histamine response 8062
nonsensitized guinea pigs 8062
nonspecific antigen 8062
organ responses *in vitro* 8062
sensitized guinea pigs 8062
specific antigen 8062
ANOXIA
heart contractile force 8078
heart muscle 8078
high energy phosphate 8078
isolated guinea pig atria 8078
ANTIARRHYTHMICS
ataraxic agents 8057
quinidine-like activity 8057
ANTIBIOTICS
biological disposition 8052
streptovaricin 8052
ANTICHOLINESTERASES
atropine block 8070
atropine inhibition 8069
DFP 8069 8070
enzymatic production 8077
eserine 8069 8070
intraarterial injection 8069 8070
mammalian striated muscle 8069
myotonia congenita 8070
organic thiophosphate conversion 8077
sarin 8069
skeletal muscle 8070
ANTICONVULSANTS
alcohol 8086
carbonic anhydrase inhibitors 8071
diphenylhydantoin 8071 8072 8086
initial seizure severity 8072
maximal electroshock seizure 8071
mephobarbital 8072
MES test 8072
mesantoin 8072
paramethadione 8072
phenacemide 8072
phenobarbital 8072
recovery time 8072
seizure duration 8072
trimethadione 8072 8086
ANTIHISTAMINICS
chlorpheniramine 8097
comparative study 8097
optical isomers 8097
ARTERIES, RENAL
renal blood flow 8081
sympathomimetic drug injections 8081
ATARAXIC AGENTS
antiarrhythmic effect 8057
quinidine-like activity 8057
ATROPINE
acetylcholine response 8069
dibromopyruvic acid 8059
DMPP vascular responses 8053
extraocular muscle 8069
goat skeletal muscle 8070
intraarterial injection 8069 8070

mammalian striated muscle 8069
myotonia congenita 8070
nerve stimulation 8069
neuromuscular transmission 8069
relaxation time 8070
TMA vascular responses 8053
AUTONOMIC BLOCKING AGENTS
DMPP vascular actions 8053
TMA vascular actions 8053
AUTONOMIC NERVOUS SYSTEM
DMPP 8053
ganglionic stimulation 8053
peripheral stimulation 8053
TMA 8053

BENACTYZINE
antiarrhythmic effect 8057
antiveratrinic activity 8057
atrial flutter 8057
auricular fibrillation 8057
quinidine-like activity 8057
toxicity 8057
ventricular tachycardia 8057
BENZOTRIAZINE DITHIOPHOSPHORIC ACID (GUTHION)
anticholinesterase formation 8077
enzymatic oxidation 8077
methylcholanthrene pretreatment 8077
rat liver microsomes 8077
toxicity 8077
BIOASSAY
minimum error table 8063
parallel line 8063
percent potency estimate 8063
precision level 8063
BISHYDROXYCOUMARIN
hemorrhagic necrosis 8075
menadione treatment 8075
myocardial damage 8075
vitamin E treatment 8075
vitamin K_1 treatment 8075
BLOOD FLOW
atropine pretreatment 8053
cardiac output fractionation 8074
DMPP 8053
estrogens 8074
femoral artery 8053
hexamethonium pretreatment 8053
intestine 8074
intraarterial injection 8081
isotope tracer technique 8074
kidney 8074
ovariectomized rats 8074
phentolamine pretreatment 8053
renal vascular bed 8081
sympathomimetic amines 8081
TMA 8053
uterus 8074
BLOOD PRESSURE
acetylcholine depressor response 8079
acetylcholine response 8097
adrenalectomy 8054
allyl alcohol hypotension 8064
atropine pretreatment 8053
azapetine pretreatment 8053
biphasic response 8053
cardiac sympathetic nerve stimulation 8080
carotid occlusion 8079
chlorpheniramine optical isomers 8097
cigarette smoke 8054
dibromopyruvic acid 8059
dichloroisoproterenol 8080
DMPP 8053 8097
epinephrine response 8059 8097
hexamethonium influence 8059
hexamethonium pretreatment 8053
histamine depressor response 8079
histamine response 8097
intraarterial veratridine 8067
levarterenol response 8059
mecamylamine influence 8059
new morphine derivatives 8084
norethandrolone 8058
phentolamine pretreatment 8053
pressor response 8054
renal blood flow 8081
sympathomimetic amines 8079 8080 8081
TDA adrenergic blockade 8079
TMA 8053
BRAIN
choline retention 8089
DMAE retention 8089
iproniazid administration 8076
iproniazid concentration 8076

isonicotinic acid concentration 8076
morphine concentration 8083
morphine tolerance 8083
tracer studies 8089
BRAIN STEM
chlorpromazine 8061
evoked potentials 8061
latency 8061
medial reticular formation 8061
pentobarbital 8061
recovery cycle 8061
sciatic nerve stimulation 8061
1-n-BUTYLAMINO-3-p-TOLUIDINO-2-PROPANOL (W-181)
convulsion dosage 8098
correlation values 8098
mortality dosage 8098

CALCIUM
dichloroisoproterenol 8080
heart contractile force 8078
high energy phosphates 8078
isolated rabbit heart 8080
ventricular contractile force 8080
CARBON DIOXIDE
CO_2 5%-O_2 95% inhalation 8095
cross-circulation 8095
ventilatory response 8095
CARBON TETRACHLORIDE
choline oxidation *in vitro* 8087
DPN 8087
DPN-linked dehydrogenases 8087
enzymatic changes 8087
8-hydroxyquinoline 8087
inhibitory action 8087
liver function 8087
liver mitochondria 8087
magnesium ATP-ase activation 8087
magnesium-disodium versene 8087
oxidative activity 8087
oxidative phosphorylation 8087
serum GOT activity 8087
tissue cation concentrations 8087
versene protective action 8087
CARBONIC ANHYDRASE
anticonvulsant inhibitors 8071
brain inhibitor concentration 8071
plasma inhibitor concentration 8071
CARDIAC GLYCOSIDES
digitoxin 8066
heart contractile force 8078
high energy phosphates 8078
intracellular distribution 8066
CARDIOVASCULAR SYSTEM
acetylcholine 8067
alpha receptor substance 8068
blood pressure 8054
8059
cardiac oxygen utilization 8054
cigarette smoke 8054
dibromopyruvic acid 8059
l-epinephrine 8067
heart rate 8059
hemodynamic changes 8054
intraarterial injection 8067
mesenteric reflexes 8067
6-methylenedihydro-desoxymorphine 8084
norethandrolone 8058
progesterone 8058
pulse pressure 8059
Su-4029 8068
TEA pretreatment 8054
testosterone 8058
veratridine 8067
CATECHOL AMINES
cardiac depletion 8082
ephedrine cardioaccelerator action 8082
heart-lung preparation 8082
reserpine antiaccelerator action 8082
reserpine pretreatment 8082
veratramine 8082
CENTRAL NERVOUS SYSTEM
atropine 8059
chlorpheniramine optical isomers 8097
EEG activation 8059
levorphanol depression 8050
mephenesin 8059
patellar reflex 8059
stimulant effects 8097
CHELATING AGENTS
carbon tetrachloride 8087
enzymatic changes 8087
liver function 8087
CHLORISONDAMINE
ganglionic blockade 8068
Su-4029 pressor response 8068

CHLORPHENIRAMINE
aerosolized histamine 8097
comparative pharmacology 8097
intravenous histamine 8097
optical isomers 8097
oral antihistamine activity 8097
oral toxicity 8097
therapeutic index 8097
CHLORPROMAZINE
evoked potentials 8061
midbrain reticular formation 8061
recovery cycle 8061
sciatic nerve stimulation 8061
CHOLINE
carbon tetrachloride 8087
chelating agents 8087
liver function 8087
oxidase stimulation 8087
oxidation *in vitro* 8087
CHOLINE-1,2 C^{14}
comparative distribution 8089
dimethylaminoethanol-1,2 C^{14} 8089
radioactivity recovery 8089
CHOLINE-METHYL-C^{14}
comparative distribution 8089
dimethylaminoethanol-1,2 C^{14} 8089
radioactivity recovery 8089
CIGARETTE SMOKE
cardiac oxygen utilization 8054
hemodynamic changes 8054
CONVULSIONS
alcohol 8086
anticonvulsants 8072
dosage changes 8098
drug-induced 8098
MES test 8072
mortality correlation 8098
postictal recovery time 8072
seizure patterns 8086
seizure thresholds 8086
tonic-clonic seizures 8072
vital functions 8098
CORONARY BLOOD FLOW
cigarette smoke 8054
CROSS-CIRCULATION
succinylcholine 8095
ventilatory response 8095
CYANIDE
intraarterial injection 8067
mesenteric reflexes 8067
DIBENAMINE
epinephrine pressor response 8068
dl-norepinephrine pressor response 8068
Su-4029 8068
DIBROMOPYRUVIC ACID
action sites 8059
analgesia 8059
atropine 8059
blood pressure 8059
cardiovascular system 8059
central actions 8059
cholinergic effects 8059
ECG 8059
EEG 8059
EMG 8059
mephenesin antagonism 8059
nerve muscle preparation 8059
patellar reflex 8059
peripheral actions 8059
smooth muscle 8059
toxicity 8059
DICHLOROISOPROTERENOL (DCI)
blood pressure 8080
cardiac adrenergic blockade 8080
cardiac sympathetic nerve stimulation 8080
heart rate 8080
isolated rabbit heart 8080
sympathomimetic amines 8080
ventricular contractile force 8080
DIETHYLSTILBESTROL
enzyme activity 8077
rat liver microsomes 8077
thiophosphate oxidation 8077
DIGITOXIN
binding distribution *in vitro* 8066
blood levels 8066
intracellular distribution *in vivo* 8066
metabolites 8066
radioactive 8065
radioisotopic tracers 8066
serum protein binding 8065
subcellular localization 8066
tissue slices 8066
DIGOXIN
dichloroisoproterenol 8080
positive inotropic effect 8080
DIHYDROCODEINE
intestinal motility 8073
levallorphan antagonism 8073

DIMETHYLAMINOETHANOL-1,2 C^{14}
brain fractions 8089
choline precursor 8089
choline-1,2 C^{14} 8089
choline-methyl-C^{14} 8089
comparative tissue distribution 8089
liver fractions 8089
protein methionine 8089
radioactivity recovery 8089
respiratory carbon dioxide 8089
urinary excretion 8089
1,1-DIMETHYL-4-PHENYLPIPERAZINIUM (DMPP)
atropine pretreatment 8053
autonomic ganglionic stimulation 8053
comparative study 8053
hexamethonium pretreatment 8053
hind limb denervation 8053
local vasodilatation 8053
peripheral localization 8053
phentolamine pretreatment 8053
TMA 8053
vascular actions 8053
DIPHENYLHYDANTOIN
ammonium chloride pretreatment 8071
anticonvulsant action 8071
hyponatremia 8071
maximal electroshock seizure 8071
repeated oral administration 8071
reserpine pretreatment 8071
sodium chloride pretreatment 8071
DIURETICS
formoguanamine 8093
related s-triazines 8093

ELECTROCARDIOGRAM
cigarette smoke 8054
norethandrolone 8058
ELECTROMYOGRAM
atropine inhibition 8070
myotonic goat muscle 8070
ELECTROSHOCK
alcohol 8086
anticonvulsants 8072
carbonic anhydrase inhibitors 8071
diphenylhydantoin 8071
maximal electroshock seizures 8071
maximal seizure pattern 8072
MES patterns 8086
recovery time 8072
seizure threshold 8086
ENZYMES
allyl alcohol 8064
amine oxidases 8088
anticholinesterase formation 8077
ATP-ase activation 8087
carbon tetrachloride 8087
chelating agents 8087
DPN-linked dehydrogenases 8087
liver dehydrogenases 8064
liver microsomal system 8077
liver microsomes 8051
liver mitochondria 8087
mescaline degradation 8088
oxidative activity 8087
oxidative phosphorylation 8087
papaverine metabolism 8051
serum GOT activity 8087
thiophosphate oxidation 8077
tissue preparations 8088
tissue slices 8064
EOSINOPENIA
human subjects 8091
morphine abstinence 8091
EPHEDRINE
cardiac catechol amine depletion 8082
cardioaccelerator action 8082
dichloroisoproterenol 8080
heart-lung preparation 8082
reserpine antagonism 8082
reserpine pretreatment 8082
sympathomimetic amines 8080
ventricular contractile force 8080
l-EPINEPHRINE
dichloro analogue (DCE) 8080
dichloroisoproterenol 8080
epinephrine-reversal 8079
heart contractile force 8078
high energy phosphates 8078
intraarterial injection 8067
mesenteric reflexes 8067
TDA adrenergic blockade 8079
vasopressor effect 8080
ventricular contractile force 8080
ESTROGENS
ethinyl estradiol 8074

intestinal blood flow 8074
isotope tracer technique 8074
ovariectomized rats 8074
renal blood flow 8074
"specific tissue activities" 8074
uterine blood flow 8074

ETHIONINE
liver thiophosphate-oxidizing enzyme 8077
methylcholanthrene response 8077
thiophosphate susceptibility 8077

ETHYLENEDIAMINE TETRAACETATE
ATP-ase activation 8087
carbon tetrachloride 8087
DPN-linked dehydrogenases 8087
liver mitochondrial function 8087
oxidative activity 8087
oxidative phosphorylation 8087
protective action 8087
serum GOT activity 8087
tissue cation concentrations 8087

FORMOGUANAMINE
diuretic effects 8093
related s-triazines 8093
sodium excretion 8093
water excretion 8093

GONADOTROPIN, CHORIONIC
abstinence response 8091
human subjects 8091
morphine addiction 8091
urinary 17-ketosteroid elevation 8091

HEART
adrenal denervation 8054
adrenalectomy 8054
adrenergic receptors 8080
arrhythmia 8054
atropine pretreatment 8054
cardiac output 8054
cardiac work 8054
catechol amine depletion 8082
cigarette smoke 8054
coronary A-V oxygen difference 8054
coronary blood flow 8054
dichloroisoproterenol 8080
dynamics 8054
ECG 8054
ectopic ventricular systoles 8054
negative chronotropic effects 8082
nicotine 8054
nodal rhythm 8054
norethandrolone 8058
oxygen utilization 8054
piperoxan pretreatment 8054
rate 8054 8058
reserpine 8082
sinus bradycardia 8054
specific adrenergic blockade 8080
sympathetic nerve stimulation 8080
sympathomimetic amines 8080
"tobacco angina pectoris" 8054
vagotomy 8054
ventricular contractile force 8080
veratramine 8082

HEART ARRHYTHMIA
antiarrhythmic effects 8057
ataraxic agents 8057
auricular flutter 8058
coronary ligation 8058
norethandrolone reversion 8058
procaine amide 8058
progesterone reversion 8058
quinidine 8057
refractory period 8057
testosterone reversion 8058
ventricular origin 8058

HEART, ISOLATED
catechol amine depletion 8082
contractile force 8058 8059
DCI adrenergic blockade 8080
dibromopyruvic acid 8059
ephedrine cardioaccelerator action 8082
heart-lung preparation 8082 8094
norethandrolone 8058
perfused rabbit heart 8080
progesterone 8058
rate 8058 8059 8094
rauwolfia alkaloids 8094
reserpine antiaccelerator action 8082

reserpine pretreatment 8082
rhythm 8058
8059
sympathomimetic amines 8080
testosterone 8058
HEART MUSCLE
adenine nucleotides 8078
anoxia 8078
ATP concentration 8055
calcium concentration 8055
cardiac depressants 8078
cardiac stimulants 8078
contractile force 8078
contraction 8055
dicumarol-induced lesions 8075
ethylenediaminetetraacetic acid (EDTA) 8055
glycerinated myocardial fibers 8055
hemorrhagic necrosis 8075
high energy phosphates 8078
ionic strength 8055
isolated guinea pig atria 8078
menadione treatment 8075
pH 8055
potassium ion 8055
sodium ion 8055
spontaneous failure 8078
stimulation frequency 8078
tension generation 8055
vitamin K_1 treatment 8075
HEART RATE
cardiac catechol amine depletion 8082
cardiac norepinephrine depletion 8096
dichloroisoproterenol 8080
ephedrine accelerator action 8082
heart-lung preparation 8082
8094 8096
hexamethonium influence 8096
rauwolfia alkaloids 8094
reserpine acceleration 8096
reserpine antiaccelerator potency 8082
reserpine pretreatment 8082
sympathomimetic amines 8080
theophylline 8080
HEXAHYDRO-1-AZEPINEPROPIONAMIDOXIME (SU-4029)
action mechanisms 8068
adrenalectomy 8068
alpha receptor substance 8068
amphetamine pressor response 8068
blocking effects 8068
cardiovascular system 8068
chlorisondamine 8068
C-O pressor response 8068
denervated nictitating membrane 8068
dibenamine 8068
epinephrine pressor response 8068
iproniazid pretreatment 8068
isopropylarterenol depressor action 8068
dl-norepinephrine pressor response 8068
phentolamine 8068
pressor action 8068
sympathomimetic pressor amines 8068
tyramine pressor response 8068
HEXAMETHONIUM
allyl alcohol 8064
DMPP vascular responses 8053
oxygen uptake 8064
protective action 8064
tissue slices 8064
TMA vascular responses 8053
HYDROCARBONS, HALOGENATED
chelating agents 8087
enzymatic changes 8087
liver function 8087
1-3-HYDROXY-N-ALLYLMORPHINAN (LEVALLORPHAN)
metabolic fate 8090

ILEUM
antigen reactions *in vitro* 8062
sensitized guinea pigs 8062
INTESTINAL MOTILITY
acetylcholine 8067
analgesic-antagonists 8073
analgesics 8073
atropine 8073
barium response 8073
chlorpheniramine optical isomers 8097
DMPP 8073
hexamethonium 8073
histamine response 8073
histamine spasm 8097

"intestinal bio-dialysate" 8073
intraarterial injection 8067
mesenteric reflexes 8067
methacholine response 8073
new morphine derivatives 8084
reflex inhibition 8067
serotonin response 8073
splanchnic nerve section 8067
vagotomy 8067
veratridine 8067

INTESTINE
blood flow 8074
estrogens 8074
isotope tracer technique 8074
ovariectomized rats 8074

IPRONIAZID
action mechanism 8076
isonicotinic acid formation 8076
metabolism 8076
monoamine oxidase activity 8076
plasma levels 8076
rat tissue distribution 8076

ISONICOTINIC ACID
iproniazid metabolite 8076
plasma levels 8076
tissue distribution 8076

ISOPROTERENOL
depressor potentiation 8079
depressor response 8068
dichloro analogue (DCI) 8080
dichloroisoproterenol 8080
intraarterial injection 8067
intravenous injection 8081
isolated rabbit heart 8080
mesenteric reflexes 8067
renal artery injection 8081
renal blood flow 8081
renal vasodilator action 8081
Su-4029 augmentation 8068
TDA adrenergic blockade 8079
vasodepressor effect 8080
ventricular contractile force 8080

17-KETOSTEROID
abstinence response 8091
ACTH effect 8091
eosinophil count 8091
gonadotropin effect 8091
human subjects 8091
morphine addiction 8091
urinary excretion 8091

KIDNEY
allyl alcohol 8064
blood flow 8074
diamine oxidase 8088
estrogens 8074
intraarterial injection 8081
isotope tracer technique 8074
local action 8081
mescaline degradation 8088
ovariectomized rats 8074
oxygen uptake 8064
sympathomimetic amines 8081
tissue preparations 8088
tissue slices 8064
vasomotor responses 8081

LEVALLORPHAN
chromatographic fractionation 8090
conjugation 8090
3-hydroxymorphinan formation 8090
infrared absorption spectra 8090
intestinal motility 8073
levorphan 8073
metabolic disposition 8090
metabolism *in vitro* 8090
metabolites 8090
tissue slices 8090
urinary excretion 8090

LEVARTERENOL
blood pressure 8080
8081
dichloro analogue (DCNE) 8080
dichloroisoproterenol
blockade 8080
heart contractile force 8078
high energy phosphates 8078
renal artery injection 8081
renal blood flow 8081
renal vasoconstrictor action 8081
TDA adrenergic blockade 8079
ventricular contractile force 8080

LEVORPHAN
intestinal motility 8073
levallorphan antagonism 8073

LEVORPHANOL
biological disposition 8050
CNS depression 8050
$C^{14}O_2$ elimination 8050
conjugation 8050
distribution 8050
estimation 8050

excretion 8050
$N-C^{14}$ methyl 8050
plasma levels 8050
synthesis 8050
LIVER
age influence 8077
allyl alcohol 8064
amine degradation 8088
carcinogenic hydrocarbons 8077
castrated animals 8077
diamine oxidase 8088
enzyme activity 8077
enzyme synthesis 8077
guthion toxicity 8077
hexamethonium protection 8064
hormone-treated animals 8077
iproniazid administration 8076
iproniazid concentration 8076
isonicotinic acid concentration 8076
MAO inhibition 8076
mescaline oxidase 8088
microsomal enzyme system 8051
microsomal fractions 8088
mitochondrial fractions 8088
oxygen uptake 8064
papaverine metabolism 8051
partial hepatectomy 8077
phenoxybenzamine protection 8064
protein-free diet 8077
rat liver microsomes 8077
thiophosphate-oxidizing enzyme 8077
tissue preparations 8088
tissue slices 8064
water content 8064
LIVER DAMAGE
allyl alcohol 8064
LIVER FUNCTION
carbon tetrachloride inhibition 8087
choline oxidation 8087
DPN 8087
DPN-linked dehydrogenases 8087
fatty infiltration 8087
8-hydroxyquinoline 8087
magnesium-disodium versene 8087
mitochondria 8087
oxidative activity 8087
oxidative phosphorylation 8087
versene treatment 8087
MENADIONE
dicumarol-induced myocarditis 8075
protective action 8075
MEPHENESIN
sodium salicylate absorption 8092
MEPROBAMATE
antiarrhythmic effect 8057
antiveratrinic activity 8057
toxicity 8057
ventricular tachycardia 8057
MESCALINE
amine oxidases 8088
inhibitor pattern 8088
oxidative deamination 8088
tissue preparations 8088
vertebrate species 8088
METHAZOLAMIDE
absorption 8071
ammonium chloride pretreatment 8071
anticonvulsant action 8071
carbonic anhydrase inhibitor 8071
maximal electroshock seizure 8071
repeated oral administration 8071
reserpine pretreatment 8071
seizure spread 8071
seizure threshold 8071
sodium chloride pretreatment 8071
3-METHYLCHOLANTHRENE
ethione pretreatment 8077
liver thiophosphate-oxidizing enzyme 8077
protein-free diet 8077
thiophosphate susceptibility 8077
6-METHYLDIHYDRODESOXYMORPHINE
acute toxicity 8084
analgesia 8084
G-I motility 8084
6-METHYLENEDIHYDRODESOXYMORPHINE
acute toxicity 8084
analgesia 8084
cardiovascular effect 8084
G-I motility 8084
hypothermia 8084
miosis 8084
nalorphine reversal 8084
sedation 8084
6-METHYL-7-HYDROXYDIHYDRO-DESOXYMORPHINE
acute toxicity 8084
analgesia 8084

G-I motility 8084
6-METHYLMORPHINE
acute toxicity 8084
analgesia 8084
G-I motility 8084
MONOAMINE OXIDASE
iproniazid 8076
iproniazid metabolism 8076
persistent inhibition 8076
MORPHINE
acute toxicity 8084
analytical method 8083
blood pressure 8084
brain concentration 8083
conjugation 8083
human subjects 8085
intestinal motility 8073
8084
nalorphine antagonism 8073
new derivatives 8084
normorphine comparison 8085
pharmacological studies 8084
postoperative pain 8085
respiratory minute volume 8084
respiratory rate 8083
tissue distribution 8083
tolerance 8083
MORPHINE ADDICTION
abstinence response 8091
ACTH effect 8091
eosinophil count 8091
gonadotropin effect 8091
human subjects 8091
urinary 17-ketosteroid depression 8091
MORPHINONE
acute toxicity 8084
analgesia 8084
G-I motility 8084
MUSCLE, SKELETAL
acetylcholine 8070
acetylcholine response 8069
action potentials 8070
antagonism 8059
anticholinesterase potentiation 8070
anticholinesterases 8069
atropine 8059
atropine block 8069
atropine inhibition 8070
cholinergic responses 8069
cholinesterase levels 8070
CO_2-bicarbonate medium 8056
denervation 8059
dibromopyruvic acid 8059
EMG 8059
intraarterial injection 8069
8070
isolated rat diaphragm 8056
mephenesin 8059
myotonic goat muscle 8070
nerve stimulation 8069
8070
resting potential 8056
temperature 8056
MUSCLE, SMOOTH
acetylcholine 8059
atropine antagonism 8059
dibromopyruvic acid 8059
intestinal motility 8059
isolated rabbit ileum 8059
neostigmine 8059

NALORPHINE
antagonistic action 8084
intestinal motility 8073
6-methylenedihydro-desoxymorphine 8084
morphine 8073
NEPHRECTOMY
streptovaricin elimination 8052
NEUROMUSCULAR JUNCTION
acetylcholine response 8069
atropine inhibition 8069
intraarterial injection 8069
NICOTINE
cardiac arrhythmia 8054
cardiac dynamics 8054
cardiac oxygen utilization 8054
convulsion dosage 8098
correlation values 8098
ECG 8054
intestinal motility 8067
intraarterial injection 8067
mesenteric reflexes 8067
mortality dosage 8098
reflex apnea 8067
NICTITATING MEMBRANE
acute denervation 8068
adrenalectomy 8068
chronic denervation 8068

phentolamine 8068
Su-4029 8068
NOREPINEPHRINE
cardiac depletion 8096
reserpine 8096
dl-NOREPINEPHRINE
dibenamine blockade 8068
phentolamine blockade 8068
pressor action 8068
Su-4029 8068
NORETHANDROLONE
blood pressure 8058
cardiovascular effects 8058
ECG 8058
eurhythmic potency 8058
NORMORPHINE
analgesic potency 8085
human subjects 8085
morphine comparison 8085
postoperative pain 8085

OUABAIN
dichloroisoproterenol 8080
isolated rabbit heart 8080
positive inotropic effect 8080
OXYGEN CONSUMPTION
allyl alcohol 8064
tissue slices 8064
OXYGEN CONSUMPTION, CARDIAC
cardiovascular hemodynamics 8054
cigarette smoke 8054
ECG 8054
nicotine 8054

PAPAVERINE
absorption 8051
enzymatic transformation 8051
estimation 8051
excretion 8051
glucuronide conjugation 8051
human subjects 8051
mammalian species 8051
metabolic fate 8051
phenolic metabolites 8051
physiological disposition 8051
plasma levels 8051
tissue distribution 8051
PENTOBARBITAL
evoked potentials 8061
midbrain reticular formation 8061
recovery cycle 8061
sciatic nerve stimulation 8061
PENTYLENETETRAZOL
alcohol 8086
convulsion dosage 8098
correlation values 8098
mortality dosage 8098
seizure threshold 8086
PHENOBARBITAL
alcohol comparison 8086
anticonvulsant potency 8086
anticonvulsant tests 8086
neurotoxicity 8086
protective index 8086
PHENOXYBENZAMINE
allyl alcohol 8064
oxygen uptake 8064
protective action 8064
tissue slices 8064
PHENTOLAMINE
DMPP vascular responses 8053
epinephrine pressor response 8068
dl-norepinephrine pressor response 8068
Su-4029 antagonism 8068
TMA vascular responses 8053
PHOSPHATES, ENERGY-RICH
heart contractile force 8078
heart muscle content 8078
isolated guinea pig atria 8078
PLASMA
amine oxidase 8088
gastrointestinal absorption 8092
iproniazid administration 8076
iproniazid concentration 8076
isonicotinic acid concentrations 8076
mephenesin influence 8092
mescaline degradation 8088
salicylate levels 8092
POTASSIUM
heart contractile force 8078
high energy phosphates 8078
PROCAINE AMIDE
cardiac arrhythmia 8058
coronary occlusion 8058
norethandrolone 8058
PROGESTERONE
cardiovascular effects 8058
enzyme activity 8077
rat liver microsomes 8077

thiophosphate oxidation 8077
PROTEIN, DIETARY
3-methylcholanthrene 8077
protein-free diet 8077
thiophosphate-oxidizing enzyme synthesis 8077
PROTEIN, SERUM
component composition 8065
digitoxin binding 8065
lipid content globulin 8065
salt fractionation 8065
serum albumin 8065
zone electrophoresis 8065

QUINIDINE
antiarrhythmic effect 8057
ataraxic agents 8057
atrial flutter 8057
auricular fibrillation 8057
ventricular tachycardia 8057

RAUNESCINE
A-V transmission 8094
functional refractory period 8094
heart rate 8094
heart-lung preparation 8094
reserpine pretreatment 8094
RAUWOLFIA ALKALOIDS
A-V propagation time 8094
A-V transmission 8094
bradycardia 8094
cardiac catechol-amine depletion 8094
functional refractory period 8094
heart rate 8094
heart-lung preparation 8094
pharmacological groups 8094
reserpine pretreatment 8094
reserpine-type 8094
REFLEXES
dibromopyruvic acid 8059
patellar 8059
REFLEXES, MESENTERIC
acetylcholine 8067
afferent pathway 8067
apnea 8067
l-epinephrine 8067
intestinal motility 8067
intraarterial injection 8067
isoproterenol 8067
mesenteric traction 8067
nicotine 8067
splanchnic nerve section 8067
vagotomy 8067
veratridine 8067
REFRACTORY PERIOD
antiarrhythmic agents 8057
ataraxic agents 8057
A-V propagation time 8094
A-V transmission 8094
cardiac arrhythmia 8057
heart-lung preparation 8094
quinidine 8057
rauwolfia alkaloids 8094
RESERPINE
antagonistic action 8071
antiaccelerator action 8082
antiarrhythmic effect 8057
atrial flutter 8057
auricular fibrillation 8057
A-V transmission 8094
cardiac catechol depletion 8082
cardioaccelerator action 8096
cumulative action 8096
diphenylhydantoin anticonvulsant action 8071
functional refractory period 8094
heart rate 8094
heart-lung preparation 8082 8094 8096
mammalian heart 8096
methazolamide anticonvulsant effect 8071
negative chronotropic action 8082
norepinephrine depletion 8096
quinidine-like activity 8057
reserpine pretreatment 8082 8094 8096
right atrial pressure 8096
ventricular tachycardia 8057
RESPIRATION
acetylcholine 8067
allyl alcohol depression 8064
alpha-lobeline 8095
carotid sinus denervation 8095
central mechanisms 8095
chlorpheniramine optical isomers 8097
CO_2-O_2 inhalation 8095
cross-circulation 8095

intraarterial injection 8067
mesenteric reflexes 8067
minute volume 8084
morphine administration 8083
morphine tolerance 8083
new morphine derivatives 8084
nicotine 8067
rate changes 8083
rebreathing response 8095
reflex apnea 8067
splanchnic nerve section 8067
succinylcholine 8095
tidal air volume 8097
ventilatory depression 8095
veratridine 8067

RYANODINE
heart contractile force 8078
high energy phosphates 8078

SALICYLATE, SODIUM
gastrointestinal absorption 8092
mephenesin influence 8092
plasma concentration 8092
statistical analysis 8092

SALIVARY GLANDS
dibromopyruvic acid 8059

SEDATIVE AGENTS
6-methylenedihydro-desoxymorphine 8084

SEMINAL VESICLES
antigen reactions *in vitro* 8062
sensitized guinea pigs 8062

SERPENTINE
bradycardia 8094
cardiac arrhythmia 8094
heart-lung preparation 8094

SHOCK
allyl alcohol intoxication 8064

STATISTICAL ANALYSIS
dosage changes 8098
drug-induced convulsions 8098
mephenesin-salicylate absorption 8092
mortality correlation 8098
plasma salicylate levels 8092

STATISTICAL EVALUATION
minimum error table 8063
parallel line bioassay 8063
percent potency estimate 8063
precision level 8063

STREPTOVARICIN
absorption 8052
biliary excretion 8052
biological disposition 8052
diffusion rate 8052
enzymatic destruction 8052
nephrectomy 8052
renal excretion 8052
serum levels 8052
tissue distribution 8052

STROPHANTHIN-K
heart contractile force 8078
high energy phosphates 8078
isolated guinea pig atria 8078
spontaneous heart failure 8078

STRYCHNINE
convulsion dosage 8098
correlation values 8098
mortality dosage 8098

SUCCINYLCHOLINE
cross-circulation 8095
femoral vein injection 8095
intracarotid injection 8095
ventilatory depression 8095

SYMPATHETIC NERVOUS SYSTEM
cardiac nerve stimulation 8080
dichloroisoproterenol blockade 8080

SYMPATHOMIMETIC AMINES
amine-TDA complexes 8079
cardiac stimulant action 8080
chemical specificity 8081
dichloroisoproterenol blockade 8080
heart contractile force 8078
heart rate 8080
high energy phosphates 8078
pressor response 8068
renal artery injection 8081
renal blood flow 8081
renal vasomotor responses 8081
Su-4029 8068
systemic depressor effects 8081
systemic pressor effects 8081
TDA adrenergic blockade 8079
urine flow responses 8081

TEMPERATURE
CO_2-bicarbonate medium 8056
diaphragm muscle fibers 8056

resting potential 8056
TESTOSTERONE
cardiovascular effects 8058
enzyme activity 8077
rat liver microsomes 8077
thiophosphate oxidation 8077
TETRAETHYLAMMONIUM
cardiovascular hemodynamics 8054
cigarette smoke 8054
TETRAMETHYLAMMONIUM
atropine pretreatment 8053
autonomic ganglionic stimulation 8053
cholinergic effector stimulation 8053
comparative study 8053
DMPP 8053
hexamethonium pretreatment 8053
hind limb denervation 8053
local vasodilatation 8053
phentolamine pretreatment 8053
vascular actions 8053
TETRAZOTIZED DIORTHOANISIDINE (TDA)
acetylcholine 8079
adrenergic blocking action 8079
asphyxial pressor response 8079
blood pressure 8079
C-O pressor response 8079
epinephrine-reversal 8079
histamine 8079
5-hydroxytryptamine 8079
isolated arterial strips 8079
related compounds 8079
sympathomimetic amines 8079
THEOPHYLLINE
dichloroisoproterenol 8080
heart rate 8080
isolated rabbit heart 8080
positive inotropic effect 8080
THEPHORIN
convulsion dosàge 8098
correlation values 8098
mortality dosage 8098
THIOPHOSPHATES, ORGANIC
anticholinesterase formation 8077
cholinesterase inhibition 8077
enzymatic oxidation 8077
guthion susceptibility 8077
rat liver microsomes 8077
SKF 525A 8077
susceptibility 8077
TRANSMISSION, NEUROMUSCULAR
atropine block 8069
intraarterial injection 8069
mammalian striated muscle 8069
TREMORINE
analgesic effect 8060
antagonistic drugs 8060
atropine antagonism 8060
hyoscine antagonism 8060
morphine comparison 8060
nalorphine 8060
testing method 8060
_s_-TRIAZINES
chemical specificity 8093
crystalluria 8093
diuretic effects 8093
formoguanamine 8093
oral administration 8093
side effects 8093
TRIMETHADIONE
alcohol comparison 8086
anticonvulsant potency 8086
anticonvulsant tests 8086
neurotoxicity 8086
protective index 8086
TYRAMINE
pressor response 8068
Su-4029 antagonism 8068

UTERUS
antigen reactions _in vitro_ 8062
blood flow 8074
estrogens 8074
isotope tracer technique 8074
ovariectomized rats 8074
sensitized guinea pigs 8062

VAS DEFERENS
antigen reactions _in vitro_ 8062
sensitized guinea pigs 8062
VASOCONSTRICTION
atropine influence 8053
DMPP 8053
femoral arterial blood flow 8053
hexamethonium influence 8053
VASODILATATION, LOCAL
acetylcholine 8053
atropine pretreatment 8053

denervated leg 8053
DMPP 8053
hexamethonium pretreatment 8053
histamine 8053
intraarterial injection 8053
nitroglycerine 8053
phentolamine pretreatment 8053
TMA 8053

VASOMOTOR RESPONSES
blood pressure 8053
DMPP 8053
femoral blood flow 8053
renal artery injection 8081
renal blood flow 8081
renal vascular bed 8081
sympathomimetic amines 8081
TMA 8053

VERATRAMINE
cardiac catechol amine depletion 8082
heart-lung preparation 8082
negative chronotropic action 8082
reserpine pretreatment 8082

VERATRIDINE
blood pressure 8067
heart rate 8067
intestinal motility 8067
intraarterial injection 8067
mesenteric reflexes 8067
reflex apnea 8067

VERATRINE RESPONSE
antiveratrinic activity 8057
benactyzine pretreatment 8057
meprobamate 8057

VERATRUM ALKALOIDS
cardiac action 8082
cardiac catechol amine content 8082

VITAMIN K, DEFICIENCY
dicumarol-induced 8075
hemorrhagic necrosis 8075
myocardial damage 8075
prevention 8075

VITAMIN K_1
dicumarol-induced myocarditis 8075
protective action 8075

Abdulian D H 8059
Andersen K S 8050
Arora R B 8057
Aviado D M Jr 8081
Axelrod J 8051

Bain J A 8089
Barsky J 8088
Batterman R C 8092
Beck L 8079
Berman E R 8088
Blum B 8098
Briggs F N 8055
Brody T M 8087
Busch H 8059

Cafruny E J 8079
Calvert D N 8087
Carr J J 8092
Chen G 8060
Cherkas M S 8088
Creese R 8056

Daniel A I 8068
de Beer E J 8081
de Gubareff T 8078
De Kornfeld T J 8085
DeMaar E W J 8061
Dessau F I 8075
Domino E F 8079
Drill V A 8058
DuBois K P 8077

Eisenman A J 8091
Elliott H W 8084

Fingl E 8086
Fouts J R 8088
Fraser H F 8091
Furchgott R F 8078

Govier W M 8097
Gray G W 8073
Gray W D 8071
Groth D P 8089

Harmel M H 8095
Hendrie K H 8063
Hess S 8076
Hine C H 8064

Innes I R
8082 8094
Inscoe J K 8051
Isbell H 8091

Kagawa C M 8093
Kalman S M 8074
Kao F F 8095
Katsh S 8062
Kien G A 8054
King B D 8095
King W M 8051
Klein S 8075
Kodama J K 8064
Kottegoda S R 8096
Krayer O
8082 8094 8096

Lasagna L 8085
Lasker N 8054
Lipchuck L
8071 8075

McQuarrie D G 8086
Mannering G J 8090
Martin W R
8059 8061
Maxwell R A 8068
Mellett L B 8050
Moran N C 8080
Mouratoff G J 8092
Murphy S D 8077

O'Grady J 8075
Okita G T
8065 8066
Okun R 8084
Osterberg A C 8071

Perkins M E 8080
Pfeiffer C C 8089
Plummer A J 8068
Povalski H 8068

Rauh C E 8071
Redfield B G 8076
Riker W K 8067
Roth F E 8097

Saunders P R 8083
Schanker L S 8090
Schneider F 8068
Scholes N W 8056
Sheps M C 8063
Sherrod T R 8054
Shofer R 8051
Siminoff R 8083
Sjoerdsma A 8051
Sloan J 8091
Spratt J L
8065 8066
Stoufer R M 8070
Swinyard E A 8072

Taylor D B 8056
Tedeschi D H 8072
Tsalikis J 8075
tum-Suden C
8069 8070

Udenfriend S 8076
Unna K R
8059 8061

Van Arman C G
8058 8093

Wagner J G 8052
Wallach D P 8052
Waud D R
8094 8096
Weissbach H 8076
Winbury M M 8053
Wnuck A L 8081
Woods L A 8050

Zacks S 8098
Zeller E A 8088